DOMESDAY BOOK

Essex

History from the Sources

DOMESDAY BOOK

A Survey of the Counties of England

LIBER DE WINTONIA

Compiled by direction of

KING WILLIAM I

Winchester
1086

DOMESDAY BOOK

general editor

JOHN MORRIS

32

Essex

edited by

Alexander Rumble

from a draft translation prepared by
Judy Plaister and Veronica Sankaran

PHILLIMORE
Chichester
1983

1983
Published by
PHILLIMORE & CO. LTD.
London and Chichester
Head Office: Shopwyke Hall,
Chichester, Sussex, England

ISBN 0 85033 483 7 (case)
ISBN 0 85033 484 5 (limp)

Printed in Great Britain by
Titus Wilson & Son Ltd.,
Kendal

ESSEX

Introduction

The Domesday Survey of Essex

Notes
Appendix
Index of Persons
Index of Places
Maps
Systems of Reference
Technical Terms

History from the Sources
General Editor: John Morris

The series aims to publish history
written directly from the sources
for all interested readers, both
specialists and others. The first
priority is to publish important
texts which should be widely
available, but are not.

DOMESDAY BOOK

The contents, with the folio on which each county begins, are:

Supplementary volume (35) BOLDON BOOK

Domesday Book is termed *Liber de Wintonia* (The Book of Winchester) in column 332c

INTRODUCTION

The Domesday Survey

In 1066 Duke William of Normandy conquered England. He was crowned King, and most of the lands of the English nobility were soon granted to his followers. Domesday Book was compiled 20 years later. The Saxon Chronicle records that in 1085

> at Gloucester at midwinter ... the King had deep speech with his counsellors ... and sent men all over England to each shire ... to find out ... what or how much each landholder held ... in land and livestock, and what it was worth ... The returns were brought to him.[1]

William was thorough. One of his Counsellors reports that he also sent a second set of Commissioners 'to shires they did not know, where they were themselves unknown, to check their predecessors' survey, and report culprits to the King.'[2]

The information was collected at Winchester, corrected, abridged, chiefly by omission of livestock and the 1066 population, and fair-copied by one writer into a single volume, now known as Domesday Book Volume I, or DB. The task of abridgement and codification was not complete by the time work stopped at the death of King William. The remaining material, the commissioners' circuit returns for Norfolk, Suffolk and Essex, which there had not been time to reduce, was left unabridged, copied by several writers, in a second volume, smaller than the first, usually now referred to as Domesday Book Volume II or Little Domesday Book or LDB, which states that 'the Survey was made in 1086'. The surveys of Durham and Northumberland, and of several towns, including London, were not transcribed, and most of Cumberland and Westmorland, not yet in England, was not surveyed. The whole undertaking was completed at speed, in less than 12 months, though the fair-copying of the main volume may have taken a little longer. Both volumes are now preserved at the Public Record Office. Some versions of regional returns also survive. One of them, from Ely Abbey,[3] copies out the Commissioners' brief. They were to ask

> The name of the place. Who held it, before 1066, and now?
> How many *hides*?[4] How many ploughs, both those in lordship and the men's?
> How many villagers, cottagers and slaves, how many free men and Freemen?[5]
> How much woodland, meadow and pasture? How many mills and fishponds?
> How much has been added or taken away? What the total value was and is?
> How much each free man or Freeman had or has? All threefold, before 1066,
>   when King William gave it, and now; and if more can be had than at present.

The Ely volume also describes the procedure. The Commissioners took evidence on oath 'from the Sheriff; from all the barons and their Frenchmen; and from the whole Hundred, the priests, the reeves and six villagers from each village'. It also names four Frenchmen and four Englishmen from each Hundred, who were sworn to verify the detail.

---

[1]Before he left England for the last time, late in 1086. [2]Robert Losinga, Bishop of Hereford 1079-1095 (see *E.H.R.* 22, 1907, 74). [3]*Inquisitio Eliensis*, first paragraph. [4]A land unit, reckoned as 120 acres. [5]*Quot Sochemani.*

The King wanted to know what he had, and who held it. The Commissioners therefore listed lands in dispute, for Domesday Book was not only a tax-assessment. To the King's grandson, Bishop Henry of Winchester, its purpose was that every 'man should know his right and not usurp another's'; and because it was the final authoritative register of rightful possession 'the natives called it Domesday Book, by analogy from the Day of Judgement'; that was why it was carefully arranged by Counties, and by landholders within Counties, 'numbered consecutively ... for easy reference'.[6]

Domesday Book describes Old English society under new management, in minute statistical detail. Foreign lords had taken over, but little else had yet changed. The chief landholders and those who held from them are named, and the rest of the population was counted. Most of them lived in villages, whose houses might be clustered together, or dispersed among their fields. Villages were grouped in administrative districts called Hundreds, which formed regions within Shires, or Counties, which survive today with minor boundary changes; the recent deformation of some ancient county identities is here disregarded, as are various short-lived modern changes. The local assemblies, though overshadowed by lords great and small, gave men a voice, which the Commissioners heeded. Very many holdings were described by the Norman term *manerium* (manor), greatly varied in size and structure, from tiny farmsteads to vast holdings; and many lords exercised their own jurisdiction and other rights, termed *soca*, whose meaning still eludes exact definition.

The Survey was unmatched in Europe for many centuries, the product of a sophisticated and experienced English administration, fully exploited by the Conqueror's commanding energy. But its unique assemblage of facts and figures has been hard to study, because the text has not been easily available, and abounds in technicalities. Investigation has therefore been chiefly confined to specialists; many questions cannot be tackled adequately without a cheap text and uniform translation available to a wider range of students, including local historians.

Previous Editions

The text has been printed once, in 1783, in an edition by Abraham Farley, probably of 1250 copies, at Government expense, said to have been £38,000; its preparation took 16 years. It was set in a specially designed type, here reproduced photographically, which was destroyed by fire in 1808. In 1811 and 1816 the Records Commissioners added an introduction, indices, and associated texts, edited by Sir Henry Ellis; and in 1861-1863 the Ordnance Survey issued zincograph facsimiles of the whole. Texts of individual counties have appeared since 1673, separate translations in the Victoria County Histories and elsewhere.

[6]*Dialogus de Scaccario* 1,16.

This Edition

Farley's text is used, because of its excellence, and because any worthy alternative would prove astronomically expensive. His text has been checked against the facsimile, and discrepancies observed have been verified against the manuscript, by the kindness of Miss Daphne Gifford of the Public Record Office. Farley's few errors are indicated in the notes.

The editor is responsible for the translation and lay-out. It aims at what the compiler would have written if his language had been modern English; though no translation can be exact, for even a simple word like 'free' nowadays means freedom from different restrictions. Bishop Henry emphasized that his grandfather preferred 'ordinary words'; the nearest ordinary modern English is therefore chosen whenever possible. Words that are now obsolete, or have changed their meaning, are avoided, but measurements have to be transliterated, since their extent is often unknown or arguable, and varied regionally. The terse inventory form of the original has been retained, as have the ambiguities of the Latin.

Modern English commands two main devices unknown to 11th century Latin, standardised punctuation and paragraphs; in the Latin, *ibi* ('there are') often does duty for a modern full stop, *et* ('and') for a comma or semi-colon. The entries normally answer the Commissioners' questions, arranged in five main groups, (i) the place and its holder, its hides, ploughs and lordship; (ii) people; (iii) resources; (iv) value; and (v) additional notes. The groups are usually given as separate paragraphs.

In both volumes of the MS, chapters were numbered 'for easy reference'. In the larger volume, sections within chapters are commonly marked, usually by initial capitals, often edged in red. In LDB (representing an earlier stage of the Inquiry's codification) sections are at first usually introduced by a paragraph mark, while red edging is reserved for chapter and Hundred headings; further on, however, the system of paragraphing the text becomes more haphazard and it is thus not always followed in the present translation. Owing to the less tabulated nature of the entries in LDB for Norfolk and Suffolk it is not possible to maintain throughout the translation of these two counties the sub-paragraphing that the late John Morris employed in the translation of other counties in the series. Maps, indices and an explanation of technical terms are also given. Later, it is hoped to publish analytical and explanatory volumes, and associated texts.

The editor is deeply indebted to the advice of many scholars, too numerous to name, and especially to the Public Record Office, and to the publisher's patience. The draft translations are the work of a team; they have been co-ordinated and corrected by the editor, and each has been checked by several people. It is therefore hoped that mistakes may be fewer than in versions published by single fallible individuals. But it would be Utopian to hope that the translation is altogether free from error; the editor would like to be informed of mistakes observed.

The maps are the work of Jim Hardy.

The preparation of this volume has been greatly assisted by a generous grant from the Leverhulme Trust Fund.

This support, originally given to the late Dr. J. R. Morris, has been kindly extended to his successors. At the time of Dr. Morris's death in June 1977, he had completed volumes 2, 3, 11, 12, 19, 23, 24. He had more or less finished the preparation of volumes 13, 14, 20, 28. These and subsequent volumes in the series were brought out under the supervision of John Dodgson and Alison Hawkins, who have endeavoured to follow, as far as possible, the editorial principles established by John Morris.

Conventions

★ refers to note on discrepancy between MS and Farley text

[ ]   enclose words omitted in the MS   ( ) enclose editorial explanation

1 a

1 . W. rex angloȝ

★ Sca Trinitas de cantorbia.

Eps Londonienfis.

Feudū ejdē epifcōpi.

V Canonici Sci Pauli.

★ VI Abbia de uueftmonaſtio.

VII Eps Dunelmenfis.

VIII. Canonici de Waltham

IX Abbia de . . . ingis.

X . Abbia de eli.

XI Abbia sci Edmundi.

XII Canonici Sci Martini. *Londoniensis*

XIII Abbia de bello.

XIIII. Scs Waleric.

★ XV Abbia S. Trinitatis de *cadomo.*

XVI Abbia S. Stephani de eod.

XVII Abbia Sci Audoeni.

XVIII Eps baiocenfis.

★ Eps herefordenfis.

Comes Euftachius.

Comes Alan.

XXII.. W de uuarena.

Ricard fili comitis . G.

★ Suen de Exfeffa.

XXV Eudo dapifer

. XX . Roǧ de otburuiſt.

XX Hugo de montfort.

XX Hamo dapifer.

Henric de ferrarijs.

XXX Goisfrid de magnauiſt.

XXX Comes de Ou.

XXX Rob greno.

XXX Rad baignard.

XXX Ranulf piperell.

XXX Albie de uer

XXX Petr ualonienfis.

XXX Ranulf fr ilgeri

XXX Tihell brito.

XXX Roǧ de ramis.

XL Johs fili Walerami.

. XLI. Rob fili corbucionis. ★

XLII. Galt diacon.

XLIII Roǧ bigot.

XLIIII Rob malet.

XLV .. W . de Scohies.

XLVI Roǧ pictauenfis.

XLVII Hugo de gurnai.

ESSEX

.I EXSESSA. Terræ Regis. Hundret de berdeſtapla.

Benflet tenuit Harold tēpore regis Edduuardi pro uno mane
rio 7 ᵱ . viii . hidis . M̊ cuſtodit hoc maneriū Ranulſ fr̄ ilgeri in
manu regis . Tc̄ . xii . uillani . m̊ . xxi . Sēp . vi . bor . Tc̄ . iii . ſerui . 7 m̊ . iii .
Tc̄ . iii . carrucæ in dn̄io : m̊ . ii . Tc̄ . xi . carruce hominū m̊ . v̇ . 7 xxx .
acræ ſiluæ . Paſtura . cxxx . ouibӡ Dimidiū molendinū . Tc̄ apᵽtiatū
ē . viii . liƀ . m̊ reddit . xii . ſ; tam̄ non ē apᵽtiatū n . viii . liƀ . In hoc
manerio erat tc̄ tēporis quidā liƀ homo de dimidia hiđ . qui m̊ effect ē
un de uillanis : 7 ē in ſupiori cōpoto . De hoc manerio data fuit cuidā
ecclæ de alio manerio : dimidia hida . tēpr̄e regis . E . Poſtquā auꝶ hoc
maneriū uenit in dn̄io regis : ablata fuit de eccƚa . 7 jac& iterū ī manerio ;
In toto hoc hundret ħt rex . xviii . liƀos ħoes tenentes . dimidiam
hidā 7 xlviiii . acras . 7 paſturā . xx . ouibӡ Apᵽtiatū ē . x . ſol .
In dn̄io ſuᵽdic̄ti manerij . ē . i . runcin . 7 . i . aſin . 7 . xxx . porci . lxx . oues .

T̸ Dimidium Hundret de Witham.

Witham tenuit Harold tēpr̄ reḡ . E . ᵱ . i . man̄ . 7 . ᵱ . v . hidis .
m̊ cuſtodit hoc man̄ . Petrus uicecomes in manu regis . Tc̄ . ii . car̄ . in
dn̄io . m̊ . iii . Tc̄ . xxi . uiƚƚi . m̊ . xv . tc̄ . ix . bor . m̊ . x . Tc̄ . vi . ſer̄ . m̊
. ix . Tc̄ . xxiii . ſochemani . 7 m̊ ſimiliꝺ . Tc̄ . xviii . car̄ hominū : M̊ . vii .
7 hec ᵱdicio fuit tēpr̄ ſueani . 7 baignardi uicecomitū . 7 p mortem
beſtiarū . Silua . cl . porc̄ . xxx . ac̄ . ᵽti . Paſtura quæ tc̄ reddebat
vi . den̄ . m̊ . xiiii . Sēp . i . molinū . Ᵽdic̄ti ſochem̄ . tenent . ii . hiđ . 7 . i .
uirḡ . hn̄tes . ii . car̄ . Tc̄ inꞇ totū uaƚ . x . liƀ . m̊ . xx . ſed uicecome˙

inꞇ ſuas conſuetudines 7 placita de dimidio hundret . recipit inde
xxxiiii . liƀ . 7 . iiii . liƀ de gerſuma . In dn̄io huj manerij receᵽ Petrus
. iiii . 7 . xxiiii . animalia . 7 . cxxxvi . por . 7 . ci . oues . Totū m̊ ſimiliꞇ ;

ESSEX

LANDS OF THE KING

Hundred of BARSTABLE

1   Harold held BENFLEET before 1066 as one manor, for 8 hides.
Now Ranulf brother of Ilger has charge of this manor, in the
King's hand.
>   Then 12 villagers, now 21; always 6 smallholders. Then 3 slaves,
>   now 3.
>   Then 3 ploughs in lordship, now 2. Then 11 men's ploughs,
>   now 5.
>   Woodland, 30 acres; pasture for 130 sheep; ½ mill.
Then it was assessed at £8; now it pays £12, but however it is
only assessed at £8.
>   In this manor there was at that time a free man with ½ hide,
who has now been made one of the villagers; he is in the above
reckoning.
>   ½ hide of this manor was given before 1066 to a church of
another manor; but after this manor came into the King's lordship,
it was taken from the church, and again lies in the (lands of the)
manor.
>   In the whole of this Hundred the King has 18 free men, who
hold ½ hide and 49 acres and pasture for 20 sheep. Assessment 10s.
>   In the lordship of the above manor 1 cob, 1 ass, 30 pigs, 70
sheep.

Half-Hundred of WITHAM

2   Harold held WITHAM before 1066 as 1 manor, for 5 hides. Now
Peter the Sheriff has charge of this manor, in the King's hand.
Then 2 ploughs in lordship, now 3.
>   Then 21 villagers, now 15; then 9 smallholders, now 10;
>   then 6 slaves, now 9; then 23 Freemen, now the same.
>   Then 18 men's ploughs, now 7; this loss was in the time of
>   Sheriffs Swein and Baynard, and through the cattle plague.
>   Woodland, 150 pigs; meadow, 30 acres; pasture which then
>   paid 6d, now 14d; always 1 mill.
The aforesaid Freemen, who have 2 ploughs, hold 2 hides and
1 virgate. Then, in total, value £10; now £20, but the Sheriff
receives from it £34 between his customary dues and the pleas of
the Half-Hundred, and £4 in gifts.
>   In the lordship of this manor Peter acquired 4 ... , 24 cattle,
136 pigs and 101 sheep; now, wholly the same.

In hoc manerio adjacebant tepr̄.r.e.xxxiiii.libi hōes.q̄ tc̄ reddebant.x.
fol.de confuetudine.7.xi.d̄; Ex ilł ten& Ilbod.ii.de xlv.ac̄.7 uał
.vi.foł.& reddt̄ manerio fuam confuetudinē. Tedric pointel.viii.
de dimidia hid.7.xxii.ac̄.7.dim.reddentes confuet.7.uał.xx.fol.
Ranulf piperelł.x.de.ii.hid.7.xlv.ac̄.non reddentes confuetudiñ.
7 uał. xv.foł. Witł filī grofse.v.de.i.hid.7 xv.ac̄.uñ tantū redd
eonfuet.7 uał.iii.lib.7.xiii.fol. Rad baignard.vi.de dimid.hid
7.xxxv.ac̄.uñ redd confuetud.7 uał.xx.fol. Hamo dapifer.i.
de dim hid.7 uał.xx.fol. Gofcelm Loremari ht̄ tr̄a uni 7 ñ redd
confuetudinē.fcilic&.i.hid.qua calūpniant monachi sc̄æ Adeldrede.
de eli.7 hundret teftatur eis de dimidia parte & de alia parte nicĥ
fciunt. Tc̄.uał.c.fol.m̄.lx.7 q̄do Gofcelm rec̄.c.fol. Int̄ totū uał
t.r.e.xiiii.lib.ii.fol.min m̄.xii.lib.7.ix.fol.
Dimidiū Hund de herlaua. Hadfeldā ten Harold.t.r.e.
p̄.i.man.7.p̄.xx.hid. Tc̄.li.uillani.m̄.lx. Tc̄.xix.bor.m̄.xxx.
Tc̄.xx.fer.m̄.xxii. Tc̄.ix.car̄ in dñio.m̄.viii.7.iii.runc̄.7.xl.
animalia.7 clxxxxv.por.7.cc.ou.vii.min. Tc̄.xl.car̄.hou
m̄.xxxi.7.dim. hec p̄dicio tepr̄ ōmiū uicecomitū fuit 7 p̄ mortem
beftiarū. Silu.ꝺcccc.porc̄.cxx.ac̄.p̄ti. Paftura que reddit.ix.multones

2 b

in manerio.7 xli.ac̄.de aratura. Ad ecclam huj̄ manerij p̄tinebat
.i.hid 7.xxx.ac̄.q̄d Suen̄ inde abftulit poftquā p̄didit uicecomitatū.
& hec tr̄a reddebat confuetudinē huic manerio. P̄tinebat & iā huic man̄
.i.foc̄.de dim hid.t.r.e.q.G.de magna uilla inde abftulit.huic tr̄e
adjac&.i.uilł.de.i.ac̄.quā ten& Comes.E.7 uał.iiii.d̄. Et.xxx.ac̄
q̄s tenuit.i.fab̄.t.r.e. q̄ p̄pt̄ Latrociniū int̄fect fuit 7 p̄pofit reḡ addi
dit illā tr̄a huic manerio; Et.xl.ac̄ filuæ q̄s ten̄ p̄pofit reḡ.E.7 Ofmund̄
angeuin de faifiuit p̄pofitū regis 7 maneriū & de tr̄a 7 de filua.m̄.ten&
Rob gernon. Dim hid quā ten.i.foc̄.t.r.e. Hoc &iā ten&.R.gernon.

2 a, b

In this manor before 1066 belonged 34 free men who then paid 10s as a customary due, and 11d. Ilbod holds 2 of them with 45 acres, value 6s; they pay their customary due to the manor. Theodoric Pointel (holds) 8, with ½ hide and 22½ acres, who pay the customary due; value 20s. Ranulf Peverel (holds) 10, with 2 hides and 45 acres, who do not pay the customary due; value 15s. William son of Gross (holds) 5, with 1 hide and 15 acres, 1 only pays the customary due; value £3 13s. Ralph Baynard (holds) 6, with ½ hide and 35 acres, 1 pays the customary due; value 20s. Hamo the Steward (holds) 1, with ½ hide, and he pays the customary due; value 20s. Jocelyn Lorimer has the land of one and does not pay the customary due, namely 1 hide which the monks of St. Etheldreda of Ely claim; the Hundred testifies for them for half [of it], but they know nothing of the other part; value then 100s, now 60s; when Jocelyn acquired it, 100s. In total, value before 1066 £14 less 2s; now £12 9s.

Half-Hundred of HARLOW

3 Harold held HATFIELD (Broad Oak) before 1066 as 1 manor, for 20 hides.

> Then 51 villagers, now 60; then 19 smallholders, now 30; then 20 slaves, now 22.
> Then 9 ploughs in lordship, now 8.
> 3 cobs, 40 cattle, 195 pigs and 200 sheep less 7.
> Then 40 men's ploughs, now 31½; this loss was in the time of all of the sheriffs and through the cattle plague.
> Woodland, 800 pigs; meadow, 120 acres; pasture which pays 9 wethers in the manor; 41 acres of ploughland.   2 b

To the church of this manor belonged 1 hide and 30 acres, which Swein took away after he lost the Sheriffdom; this land paid the customary due to this manor.

Before 1066, there also belonged to this manor 1 Freeman with ½ hide, whom G(eoffrey) de Mandeville took away; attached to this land is 1 villager with 1 acre which Count E(ustace) holds, value 4d.

Also 30 acres which a smith, who was put to death on account of robbery, held before 1066, and the King's reeve added that land to this manor; also 40 acres of woodland which King Edward's reeve held; of which land and woodland Osmund of Anjou dispossessed the King's reeve and the manor. Robert Gernon now holds it.

½ hide which 1 Freeman held before 1066; Robert Gernon also holds this.

Pr̃ hoc adjacebant huic manerio . t̃ . r̃ . ẽ . III . bereuuitæ . Herefort . 7
Emuuella . 7 Hodeſduna . jacentes in Herefort ſira . quas ten& m̃ . Rad
de Limeſeio . Et . I . ſoc̃ . de . xxx . ac̃ . ſẽp ꝑtinens huic manerio . 7 tc̃ . ꝏ̃ .
ual . xxxvi . lib̃ . m̃ . lx . ſ; uicecomes inde recipit . lxxx . lib̃ . 7 . c . ſot
de gerſuma . Et . III . berewitæ ual tc̃ . xII . lib̃ . 7 . tr̃a ſochemanoꝛ ꞩ
xlv . ſol . Silu . xl . porc̃ . Poſtea recupauim̃ dimid hid . quã tenuit
. I . ſoc̃ haroldi . t̃ . r̃ . ẽ . m̃ eã ten& Rad de marcei . ad feudũ hamonis
tc̃ ual . x . ſot . m̃ . vii .

⌐Hundret de beuentreu . , Haueringas tenuit Harold
t̃ . r̃ . e . p̃ . I . mañ . 7 . p̃ . x . hid̃ . Tc̃ xlI . uilt . m̃ . xl . Sẽp . xlI . bor .
7 vi . ſer̃ . 7 . II . car̃ in dñio . Tc̃ . xlI . car̃ hom̃ . m̃ . xl . Silu . ꝺ . porc̃ .
. c . ac̃ . p̃ti . m̃ . I . mot . 7 . II . runc̃ . 7 . x . anim̃ . 7 clx . por . 7 . cc . 7
lxix . ou . Huic manerio adjacebant . IIII . libi hõẽs . de . IIII . hid̃ . t̃ . r̃ . ẽ .

3 a

reddentes conſuetudinẽ . M̊ ten& Rob̃ fili̊ corbutionis . III . hid̃ . 7 hug̃
de monteforti . qr̊tã hid̃ . 7 ñ reddider̃ conſuetudinẽ ex q̃ eas habuer̃ . Et
adhuc idẽ Rob̃ . ten& . IIII · hid̃ . 7 . dim̃ . q̊s tenebat . I . lib̃ hõ ad hoc mañ
t̃ . r̃ . ẽ . Attinebat &iam . I . ſoc̃ . de . xxx . ac̃ . reddens conſuetudinẽ .
7 m̃ ten& Johs fili̊ galerami . & hoc mañ t̃ . r̃ . ẽ . ual . xxxvi . lib̃ . M̊ . xl .
& Petr̃ uic̃ inde recip̃ . lxxx . lib̃ de . cenſu . 7 . x . lib de gerſuma .
Huic maner̃ ptinent . xx . ac̃ . jacentes in Lochetuna q̊s tenuit . t̃ . r̃ . ẽ .
p̄poſit haroldi . m̃ ten& p̄poſit regis . 7 ual . xl . đ .

⌐Hund̃ de dommawa . In Scelda . III . ſoc̃ . de . xxxv . ac̃ . 7 . ual
. III . ſot . 7 . x . đ .

⌐Hund̃ de Witbriċteſherna . In Leſſenduna tenuit Aluuin̊
lib̃ hõ t̃ . r̃ . ẽ . dim̃ hid̃ . 7 . xxx . ac̃ . Poſt eã inuaſit Tedric̊ point̃el .
7 . nẽ ħt rex . Sẽp . dim̃ car̃ . 7 . ual . xv . ſot . De ead̃ tr̃a . ten& . I . uilt
. xxx . ac̃ . ad Eſtolleiã . 7 . ual . v . ſot . 7 . ali̊ uilt . xv . ac̃ . 7 . ual . III . ſot .
Et . III . hões tenent . dim̃ . hid̃ . 7 x . ac̃ . 7 . dim̃ . car̃ . Tc̃ . ual . viii . ſot
m̃ . v . ſot . 7 . IIII . đ .

Apart from this, 3 outliers were attached to this manor before 1066, HERTFORD, AMWELL and HODDESDON, which lie in Hertfordshire, (and) which Ralph of Limésy now holds.

Also 1 freeman with 30 acres who always belonged to this manor.

Value of the manor then £36; now £60, but the Sheriff receives £80 from it, and 100s in gifts. Also the value then of the 3 outliers £12, the Freemen's land 45s. Woodland, 40 pigs.

Later on we recovered ½ hide which 1 Freeman of Harold's held before 1066; now Ralph of Marcy holds it in Hamo's Holding.

Value then 10s; now 7[s].

Hundred of BECONTREE

4   Harold held HAVERING (atte-Bower) before 1066 as 1 manor, for 10 hides.

Then 41 villagers, now 40. Always 41 smallholders; 6 slaves; 2 ploughs in lordship. Then 41 men's ploughs, now 40. Woodland, 500 pigs; meadow, 100 acres; now 1 mill.

2 cobs, 10 cattle, 160 pigs and 269 sheep.

Attached to this manor before 1066 were 4 free men with 4 hides who paid the customary due. Now Robert son of Corbucion holds 3 hides and Hugh de Montfort the fourth hide, and they have not paid the customary due since they have had them. And besides, Robert also holds 4½ hides which 1 free man held in this manor before 1066.   3 a

Also associated was 1 Freeman with 30 acres who paid the customary due; John son of Waleran now holds him.

Value of this manor before 1066 £36; now [£] 40; Peter the Sheriff receives from it £80 in dues and £10 in gifts.

To this manor belong 20 acres which lie in Loughton (and) which Harold's reeve held before 1066; now the King's reeve holds them. Value 40d.

Hundred of DUNMOW

5   In SHELLOW (Bowells) 3 Freemen with 35 acres. Value 3s 10d.

Hundred of 'WIBERTSHERNE'

6   In LATCHINGDON Alwin, a free man, held ½ hide and 30 acres before 1066. Later Theodoric Pointel annexed it. Now the King has it. Always ½ plough.

Value 15s.

Of this land, 1 villager holds 30 acres at 'STUDLY', value 5s; another villager (holds) 15 acres, value 3s. Also 3 men hold ½ hide and 10 acres and ½ plough; value then 8s; now 5s 4d.

⌐In Lacenduna . ɪ . liƀ hō Leuuiṅ . xxx . aċ . ṫ . ŕ . ė
tċ dim̃ . car̃ . m̃ . n̄ . Tċ . uał . vɪɪɪ . soł . m̃ . v . 7 . ɪɪɪɪ . đ . In Eađ . vɪɪɪ . liƀi
hōes ṫ . ŕ . ė . m̃ . ɪɪɪɪ . de . ʟɪɪ . aċ . Tċ . uał . vɪɪɪ . soł . m̃ ɪɪɪɪ . soł 7 . ɪɪɪɪ . đ .
In Rodingis ten& Golſtaṅ ſoċ reḡ Wiłłi . ɪ . hiđ . 7 n̄q̣ inde ſeruitiū
ł confueł . reddidit . & idō dedit uade . In q̊ hida . ē . ɪ . caŕ in dn̄io
7 . ɪ . bor . 7 ɪɪɪ . ſeṙ . Silu̇ . x . por . x . aċ . p̃ti . Tċ uał . xx . ſoł . m̃ . xxx.

⌐Hunđ de Odelesforda   Ceſtrefořdā tenuit Comes Edgar̃ . ṫ . ŕ . ė
.p . ɪ . ꝏ̃ . 7 . ꝑ . x . hiđ . m̃ picoṫ uicecomes in manu regis . Sēp . ɪɪɪɪ . caŕ ɪ̈ dn̄io.
Tċ . xvɪɪɪ . caŕ hom̃ . P 7 m̃ . xɪɪɪɪ . Sēp . xxɪɪɪɪ . uiłłi . 7 . xɪɪɪ . bor . 7 . vɪ . ſeṙ.
Silu̇ . ꝏ̃ . porċ . xv . aċ p̃ti . ſēp . ɪɪ . moł . Jac& huic manerio . ɪ . hiđ . 7 . đ
que ē in cantebruge ſira . ſēp . vɪɪ . uiłł . 7 . ɪɪɪ . bor . 7 . moł . 7 . ɪɪɪ . caŕ
hom̃ . hoc totū uał . tċ xxɪɪɪɪ . liƀ P 7 m̃ . xxx . In dn̄io huj manerii . ɪɪ . ř.
sƭ . 7 vɪɪ . aṅ . 7 . ʟxɪ . por . 7 . ʟxxxɪ . ou̇ . 7 ʟxxxvɪɪ . capræ . Huic maṅ
adjacebat . ṫ . ŕ . ė . ɪ . hiđ . 7 . dim̃ . qđ ten& harduiṅ de ſcalarijs . ſ; hunđ
neſċ q̃m̃ . Dim̃ hiđ . erat de dn̄io in q̊ manebat . ɪ . hō . 7 . Aliā hidā teneᵃ
bat . ɪ . ſoċ . q̇ reddebat ſocā in manerio reḡ   Et picoṫ ten& dim̃ hiđ
q̇ ten . ɪ . ſoċ . ṫ . ŕ . ė . In his duabₔ hiđ . ɪɪ . caŕ . 7 uał . xʟ . ſoł.
⌐Becangrā teṅ Horolf . ṫ . ŕ . ė . M taſceliṅ p̃br in elemoſina regis.
.p . ɪ . hiđ . ſēp . ɪ . caŕ . 7 . ɪɪ . bor . 7 . ɪɪ . ſeṙ . Silu̇ . xʟ . por . v . aċ . p̃ti . 7 . ɪ . moł.
tċ 7 p̃ uał . xx . ſoł . m̃ . xxx.

7   In LATCHINGDON 1 free man, Leofwin, (held) 30 acres before 1066.
Then ½ plough, now none.
Value then 8s; now 5[s] 4d.
   In the same (Latchingdon) 8 free men before 1066, now 4,
with 52 acres.
Value then 8s; now 4s 4d.

8   In (White) RODING Goldstan, a Freeman of King William's, holds
1 hide; he has never paid service or the customary due for it, and
hence he has given a pledge. In this hide, 1 plough in lordship;
   1 smallholder; 3 slaves.
   Woodland, 10 pigs; meadow, 10 acres.
Value then 20s; now 30[s].

Hundred of UTTLESFORD   3 b
9   Earl 'Edgar' held (Great) CHESTERFORD before 1066 as 1 manor,
for 10 hides. Now Picot the Sheriff (holds it), in the King's hand.
Always 4 ploughs in lordship. Then 18 men's ploughs; later and
now 14.
   Always 24 villagers; 13 smallholders; 6 slaves.
   Woodland, 1000 pigs; meadow, 15 acres; always 2 mills.
(In the lands of) this manor lie 1½ hides which are in Cambridge-
shire.
   Always 7 villagers; 3 smallholders; a mill; 3 men's ploughs.
Value of the whole then £24; later and now [£] 30.
   In the lordship of this manor are 2 cobs, 7 cattle, 61 pigs,
      81 sheep and 87 goats.
   Attached to this manor before 1066 were 1½ hides which
Hardwin of Scales holds, but the Hundred does not know how; ½
hide was of lordship (land) in which 1 man dwelt; 1 Freeman who
paid suit in the King's manor held the other hide. Also Picot holds
½ hide which 1 Freeman held before 1066. In these 2 hides, 2
ploughs.
Value 40s.

10   Horwulf held BIRCHANGER before 1066. Now Tascelin the priest
(holds it) in the King's alms, for 1 hide. Always 1 plough;
   2 smallholders; 2 slaves.
   Woodland, 40 pigs; meadow, 5 acres; 1 mill.
Value then and later 20s; now 30[s].

Celdefordã tenuit Comes Algar t̃.r̃.ẽ.p̃.i.man̄.7.v.hid̃.7.xxx.ac̃.
poſt ea tenuit regina.M̊ Otto aurifab̃ ad censũ in manu reg̃.Sẽp.iii.
car̃ in dn̄io.Tc̃.vi.car̃.hom̃.P̃ 7 m̃.v.Tc̃ 7 p̃.xiii.uitt.m̃.xii.sẽp.vi,
bor.Tc̃.xii.ſer.p̃ 7 m̃.viii.Silũ.c.por.xx.ac̃.p̃tj.i.mol̃.Tc̃ ual̃
xii.lib̃.Poſt 7 m̃.xxii.In dn̄io.iiii.runc̃.Tc̃ lxv.an̄.m̃.lvi.
7.lii.ou.7.cxviii.por.m̃.lxxx.7.xl.cap̃.De hoc manerio deſt
.xxx.ac̃ ſiluæ q̃s regina dedit.Ricardo filio comitis giſlebti.Huic
man̄ jacebat dim̄ hid de ſoca t̃.r̃.ẽ.q ten& Galt̃ fili guibtj.

4 a

Phincinghefeldã ten̄ Idẽ Algar̃.t̃.r̃.ẽ.7 poſt regina M̊ idẽ.Otto ad
censũ p̃.ii.hid̃.7.dim̄.sẽp.iii.car̃ in dn̄io.7.v.car̃.hom̃.7.x.uitt.7.ix.bor.
Tc̃.vi.ſer.P̃.iiii.m̃.ii.Silũ.lx.por.xvi.ac̃.p̃ti.7.i.mol̃.7.xxv.
an̄.7.ii.runc̃.Tc̃.lxiii.por.m̃.lxi.7.c.ou.Tc̃.ual̃.ix.lib̃.P̃ 7 m̃.⸗
xviii.

Weſtrefeldã ten̄ Idẽ Algar̃ t̃.r̃.ẽ.p̃.m̃.7.p̃.ii.hid̃.xv.ac̃:m̃ Picot̃
p̃ totidẽ in manu regis.Tc̃.iiii.car̃.in dn̄io.P̃.ii.m̃.iii.Tc̃ 7 p̃.xv.car̃
hominũ.m̃.x.Tc̃ 7 p̃ xxiiii.uitt.m̃.xxviii.Tc̃.vii.por.P̃.xv.M̊
xxiiii.Tc̃.vii.ſer.P̃.xiiii.M̊.vii.Tc̃ ſilũ.ɒccc.por.P̃ 7 m̃.ɒ.7
xxiiii.ac̃.p̃ti.Tc̃.7 p̃.i.mol̃.m̃.ii.Tc̃.xvii.an̄.m̃.x.7.c.ou.Tc̃.
.c.por.m̃.xl.Tc̃.lxi.cap̃.m̃.xl.Huic man̄ jacebant.t̃.r̃.ẽ.vi.ſoc̃.m̃
viii.tenentes.i.hid̃.7.xiiii.ac̃.sẽp.ii.car̃.7.i.bor.7.v.ac̃.p̃ti.Tc̃
ual̃.xx.lib̃.P̃ 7 m̃.xxviii.Huic man̄.adjac̃.t̃.r̃.ẽ.xxx.ac̃.træ.q̃s
ten̄.i.prb̃.in elemoſina 7 reddebat ſoca.7 viii.ac̃ 7 dim̄ p̃tinentes ad
aliã ecclam.has.ii.t̃ras ten& Giſlebt̃ fili garini.|Adp̃tinebant ad
huc huic.m̃.vii.ac̃.7.d.q̃s m̃ ten& comes Alam.Et.xlv.ac̃.
de dn̄io q̃s ten& Suen ad feudũ Ricardi.f.comitis.g.7 ual̃.viii.ſol̃.

11   Earl Algar held SHALFORD before 1066 as 1 manor, for 5 hides and 30 acres. Later on the Queen held it. Now Otto the Goldsmith (holds it) as dues in the King's hand. Always 3 ploughs in lordship. Then 6 men's ploughs, later and now 5.

> Then and later 13 villagers, now 12; always 6 smallholders.
> Then 12 slaves, later and now 8.
> Woodland, 100 pigs; meadow, 20 acres; 1 mill.

Value then £12; later and now [£] 22.

> In lordship 4 cobs; then 65 cattle, now 56; 52 sheep; then 118 pigs, now 80; 40 goats.

From this manor, 30 acres of woodland are missing which the Queen gave to Richard son of Count Gilbert.

(In the lands of) this manor lay ½ hide with jurisdiction before 1066, which Walter son of Gilbert holds.

12   (Earl) Algar also held FINCHINGFIELD before 1066. Later the Queen   4 a (held it). Now Otto (the Goldsmith) also (holds it) as dues, for 2½ hides. Always 3 ploughs in lordship; 5 men's ploughs;

> 10 villagers; 9 smallholders. Then 6 slaves, later 4, now 2.
> Woodland, 60 pigs; meadow, 16 acres; 1 mill.
> 25 cattle; 2 cobs; then 63 pigs, now 61; 100 sheep.

Value then £9; later and now [£] 18.

13   (Earl) Algar also held WETHERSFIELD before 1066 as a manor, for 2 hides less 15 acres. Now Picot (holds it) in the King's hand for as much. Then 4 ploughs in lordship, later 2, now 3. Then and later 15 men's ploughs, now 10.

> Then and later 24 villagers, now 28; then 7 pigs, later 15, now 24; then 7 slaves, later 14, now 7.
> Woodland, then 800 pigs, later and now 500; meadow, 24 acres; then and later 1 mill, now 2.
> Then 17 cattle, now 10; 100 sheep; then 100 pigs, now 40; then 61 goats, now 40.

Attached to this manor before 1066 were 6 Freemen, now 8, who hold 1 hide and 14 acres. Always 2 ploughs; 1 smallholder.

> Meadow, 5 acres.

Value then £20; later and now [£] 28.

Attached to this manor before 1066 were 30 acres of land which 1 priest held as alms and paid suit; and 8½ acres belonging to another church; these 2 lands Gilbert son of Warin holds. Value 10s.

There belonged to this manor 7½ acres, which Count Alan now holds.

Also 45 acres of the lordship which Swein holds as a holding of Richard son of Count G(ilbert). Value 8s.

In Ifto hund hĩ rex . xviii . foc̷ . tenent̷ . xxvi . ac̷ . 7 . dim̷ . 7 n̄qua
reddider confuetudinẽ p̃t feruiciũ regis.

⌐ Hund de Witbric̷̃efherna . Benflet ten̷ Leuard̷ lib̷ hõ . t̷ . r̷ . e
P̷ tedric̷ pointel . p̷ . i . hid̷ . Sẽp . i . bor . Tc̃ . i . car̷ . m̃ nulla . Paftura
xl . ouib̵ Tc̃ . i . pifcina . m̃ nulla . 7 . ual̷ . xx . fol̷ .

4 b

⌐ Steplam ten̷ Aluric̷ lib̷ hõ . t̷ . r̷ . e̷ . p̷ . i . hid̷ . Tc̃ . i . bor . m̃ null̷ . Tc̃
. i . car̷ . m̃ . dim̷ . Tc̃ . ual̷ . xx . fol̷ . m̃ . xvi . In Vluuinefcherha̅ . iiii . lib̷i
hõẽs . de . i . hid̷ . vi . ac̷ . min̷ . t̷ . r̷ . e̷ . M n̄ ft̷ ; Tc̃ ual̷ . xx . fol̷ . m̃ . x . hanc
trā calumpniat̷ . Tedric̷ pointel p̷ efcangio . Franci hõẽs tenent . li .
ac̷ . 7 . n̄ ft̷ in firma reg̃ . Tc̃ ual̷ . viii . fol̷ . m̃ . v . hanc trā ten& famul̷
reg̃ 7 n̄ reddit geldũ . In Melduna . ii . lib̷i hõẽs de . x . ac̷ . Ex iħ . hĩ
Ranulf̷ piperell̷ . v . ac̷ . 7 . hugo de monte forti . v . ac̷ . Tc̃ . ual̷ . x . d̷ .
m̃ . xii . Duo lib̷i hõẽs . ten̷ . t̷ . r̷ . e̷ . vi . ac̷ . 7 . jacuer̷ in hund reg̃ 7 n̄c
hĩ baignard̷ .

⌐ In Hund de Rochesfort ten& fẽp Grim̷ p̷pofit . x . ac̷ . 7 . ual̷ . xvi . d̷ .
⌐ Hund de Laffendene . Stanewegā ten̷ harold̷ . t̷ . r̷ . e̷ p̷ . i . c̃ .
7 . p̷ . v . hid̷ . 7 . dim̷ . M hĩ rex p̷ totidẽ . Tc̃ . xii . uiħ . P̷ 7 . m̃ . ix . tc̃ . vi .
bor . p̷ 7 m̃ . ix . Sẽp . vi . fer̷ . 7 . iiii . car̷ in dñio . Tc̃ . xiii . car̷ hom . P̷ 7 m̃
. ii . 7 . dim̷ . fẽp . i . mol̷ . Silu . c . porc̷ . xii . ac̷ . p̷ti . 7 . xx . an̷ . 7 lix . por .
7 . cclx . ou̷ . 7 . xi . runc̷ . Eft &iã . i . bereuuita de . ii . hid̷ . 7 . dim̷
7 . xiii . ac̷ . que uocat̷ . Legra 7 jac& in ifto manerio Sẽp . vii . uiħ .
7 . ii . bor . 7 . iiii . fer̷ . 7 . ii . car̷ . in dñio . Tc̃ . ii . car̷ . hom P̷ . 7 m̃ . i . 7 . d̷ .

13a In this Hundred the King has 18 Freemen who hold 26½ acres and they have never paid the customary due apart from the King's service.

Hundred of 'WIBERTSHERNE'

14 Leofhard, a free man, held BENFLEET before 1066; later Theodoric Pointel (held it) for 1 hide.
   Always 1 smallholder.
   Then 1 plough, now none.
   Pasture for 40 sheep; then 1 fishery, now none.
   Value 20s.

15 Aelfric, a free man, held STEEPLE before 1066, for 1 hide.   4 b
   Then 1 smallholder, now none.
   Then 1 plough, now ½.
   Value then 20s; now 16[s].

16 In *ULUUINESCHERHAM*, 4 free men with 1 hide less 6 acres before 1066. Now they are not there.
   Value then 20s; now 10[s].
   Theodoric Pointel claims this land by exchange.

16a (Certain) freemen hold 51 acres and are not in the King's revenue.
   Value then 8s; now 5[s].
   A servant of the King holds this land and does not pay tax.

17 In MALDON 2 free men with 10 acres; of these, Ranulf Peverel has 5 acres and Hugh de Montfort 5 acres.
   Value then 10d; now 12[d].

17a 2 free men held 6 acres before 1066 and lay in the King's Hundred; now Baynard has them.

In the Hundred of ROCHFORD
18 Grim the reeve has always held 10 acres.
   Value 16d.

Hundred of LEXDEN
19 Harold held STANWAY before 1066 as 1 manor, for 5½ hides. Now the King has it for as much.
   Then 12 villagers, later and now 9; then 6 smallholders, later and now 9.
   Always 6 slaves; 3 ploughs in lordship. Then 13 men's ploughs, later and now 2½.
   Always 1 mill. Woodland, 100 pigs; meadow, 12 acres.
   20 cattle, 59 pigs, 260 sheep and 11 cobs.
   There is also 1 outlier of 2½ hides and 13 acres which is called LAYER and lies in (the lands of) this manor.
   Always 7 villagers; 2 smallholders; 4 slaves;
   2 ploughs in lordship. Then 2 men's ploughs, later and now 1½.

Adhuc ptin& . I . berewita que uocať Leſſendena . de . IIII . hiđ . Tc.
VI . uiłł . P̃ 7 . m̃ . V . Tc . X . bor . p̃ 7 m̃ . XII . Tc . IIII . ſeř . P̃ 7 m̃ . V . ſẽp
. II . cař . in dñio . Tc . IIII . cař hom p̃ 7 m̃ . III . Silu . c . porc . XVIII.
ac . p̃ti . m̃ . II . moł Et . XVI . ſoc . de . II . hiđ . 7 . XXXVI . ac . ſẽp . II . cař
7 . dim . Tc uał totũ . XXII . liƀ . M̃ petř inde recip̃ . XXXIII . liƀ . 7

5 a

. III . liƀ de g̃ſuma . De hoc manerio tulit Reimunđ girald . I . uiłł . de dim
hiđ . 7 reddebat conſuetudinẽ . Sẽp ibi ẽ dim . cař . 7 uał . X . ſoł . hanc tr̃a
tenuit Normann 7 reddidit conſueť . Sed Raimunđ . abſtulit . 7 . Rog
ſimiliť . Et Rog piĉtau . accep̃ . I . uiłłm tenentẽ . I . ac . Et Ingelric
abſtulit . I . feminã briĉteuã tenentẽ . XVIII . ac . & reddebat unoq̃q̃
anno huiç maneř . XXXII . nõmos.
Hunđ de angre . Vlfelmeſtunã tenuit Herold . p̃ man̄ . 7 . p̃ . III.
hiđ . 7 . XL . ac . M̃ . Rex . W . Sẽp . IIII . uiłł . tc . II . bor . m̃ . VI . Tc . inť hões
. I . cař . 7 m̃ ſimiliť . Silu . LX . poc . IIII . ac . p̃ti . Tc . uał . XX . ſoł . m̃ . XL.
Quidã hõ liƀe tenuit . XX . ac . t . r . e . tc . dim . cař . m̃ . nicħ . 7 . uał
. III . Iſte ſẽp fuit dñic ſed m̃ ẽ in manu uicecomitis ad firmã regis.
Hunđ de cesfeworda . Phingheriã ħt rex . q̃ ten Herold . t . r . e
ſẽp . I . cař . in dñio . 7 VI . uiłł . 7 . VIII . bor ħnt . II . cař . ĩ dñio . XXIIII . anim
Silu . ⅗ . porc . III . ac p̃ti . Tc . uał . IIII . liƀ . m̃ . XIIII . In Wochenduna
ħt . Rex . I . ſoc . de . XXV . ac . tc . uał . XXXII . đ . m̃ . LII.

Besides, there belongs 1 outlier which is called LEXDEN, of 4 hides.
Then 6 villagers, later and now 5; then 10 smallholders, later and now 12; then 4 slaves, later and now 5.
Always 2 ploughs in lordship. Then 4 men's ploughs, later and now 3.
Woodland, 100 pigs; meadow, 18 acres; now 2 mills.
Also 16 Freemen with 2 hides and 36 acres. Always 2½ ploughs.
Value of the whole, then £22. Now Peter receives from it £33, and £3 in gifts.

From this manor Raymond Gerald took 1 villager with ½ a hide and he paid a customary due. Always ½ plough there. Value 10s.
Norman held this land and paid a customary due; but Raymond took it away and Roger likewise.
Also Roger of Poitou took 1 villager who held 1 acre.
Also Engelric took away 1 woman, Bricteva, who held 18 acres and paid 32 pennies each year to this manor.

Hundred of ONGAR

20 Harold held WOOLSTON (Hall) as a manor, for 3 hides and 40 acres. Now King William (holds it).
Always 4 villagers. Then 2 smallholders, now 6.
Then among the men 1 plough, now the same.
Woodland, 60 pigs; meadow, 4 acres.
Value then 20s; now 40[s].
A man held 20 acres freely before 1066. Then ½ plough, now nothing.
Value 3[s].
He was always in lordship but is now in the Sheriff's hand in the King's revenue.

Hundred of CHAFFORD

21 The King has FINGRITH (Hall), which Harold held before 1066.
Always 1 plough in lordship;
6 villagers and 8 smallholders have 2 ploughs.
In lordship 24 cattle. Woodland, 1000 pigs; meadow, 3 acres.
Value then £4; now [£] 14.

[Hundred of CHAFFORD]
21a In OCKENDON the King has 1 Freeman with 25 acres.
Value then 32d; now 52[d].

⌐Gingā ten̄ Friebt t̄.r.e.p.m̄.7 p.iii.hid.7 .dim̄.sep.vi.uill.
7.iii.bor. T̄c.ii.ser. m̄.i.sep.ii.car in dn̄io.7.i.car hōu.iiii.ac
p̄ti.7 lxxxviii.por.App̄.in Phingheriā. ⌐Ciltendis ten̄.Her.P regina M uicec de
Surreia.p.i.hid.7.d̄.T̄c.iii.uill.m̄.v.T̄c.iii.bor.M.iiii.i.ser.T̄c.i.c.idio.m̄.i.7.d̄. T̄c.ii c.hōu.
⌐Hund̄ de Celmeresfort. Writelam ten̄ Herold9 p man̄.

⌐p̄7 m̄.i. ſilu'.c.por.paſt'.lx.ou'.t̄c.iii.liḃ.m̄.iiii.

7 p xvi.hid̄.t̄.r.e.M̄.rex.W.p.xiiii. hid. T̄c.c.uill.iii.min
Poſt 7 m̄ lxxiii.T̄c.xxxvi.bor.P̄ 7 m̄.lx.T̄c.xxiiii.ser.p̄ 7 m̄

⌐xviii.

5 b

T̄c.xii.car in dn̄io.P̄ 7 m̄.ix. T̄c int̄ hōes.lxiiii.car.P̄ 7 m̄ xlv.
t̄c.ſilu.M d.por.m̄.M cc.lxxx.ac̄.p̄ti. T̄c.i.mol.m̄.ii.sep.ix.run.
7.v.pulli.7 xl.an.7.cccxviii.ou.7.clxxii.poc̄.T̄c reddidit
hoc meneriū.x.noc̄tes de firma.7.x.liḃ.m̄ reddit.c.liḃ.ad pond.
7.c.ſol.de gerſuma. Ingelric̄ poccupauit.it.hid.de t̄ra p̄poſiti
haroldi reddentis omn̄e conſuet̄ huic manerio.ſcil.xii. liḃ. poſtq̄
rex uenit in angliā; & m̄ ten& comes.E.ido qd̄ anteceſſor ej inde
fuit ſaiſit.7 in t̄pr haroldi fuit.i.porcari reddens conſuet̄ huic
manerio ſedens.ſup.i.uirḡ t̄ræ.7.xv.ac̄.ſ; Roḃ grino pq̄ rex uenit
accepit eum de manerio.& ſec̄ foriſtariū de ſilua reḡ.7.i.hid dedit
Harold cuidā p̄o ſuo.ſ; hundret neſcit ſi dedit liḃæ i in elemoſina.
quā m̄ ten&.R.ep̄c Herefordenſis.7 dim̄ hid quā liḃe tenuit.i.ſoc.
reddens ſoca in manerio.7 cū t̄ra ſua poſſ& ire q̄uell&.hunc Comes.E.
adjunxit ſue t̄ræ. In hoc man̄ ſep.jacent.ii.ſoc.de dim̄.hid.7.x.ac̄.
lintes ſep.dim̄.car.iiii.ac̄.p̄ti.App̄tiatū ē in Sup̄dic̄tis.c.liḃ.

[Hundred of CHELMSFORD]

22 Fridebert held MARGARETTING before 1066 as a manor, for 3½ hides.

Always 6 villagers; 3 smallholders. Then 2 slaves, now 1.
Always 2 ploughs in lordship; 1 men's plough.
Meadow, 4 acres. 88 pigs.
It is assessed in Fingrith (Hall).

[Hundred of CHAFFORD]

23 Harold held CHILDERDITCH. Later the Queen (held it). Now the Sheriff of Surrey (holds it) for 1½ hides.

Then 3 villagers, now 5; then 3 smallholders, now 4; 1 slave.
Then 1 plough in lordship, now 1½. Then 2 men's ploughs, later and now 1.
Woodland, 100 pigs; pasture, 60 sheep.
[Value] then £3; now [£] 4.

Hundred of CHELMSFORD

24 Harold held WRITTLE before 1066 as a manor, for 16 hides. Now King William (holds it) for 14 hides.

Then 100 villagers less 3, later and now 73; then 36 smallholders, later and now 60; then 24 slaves, later and now 18.
Then 12 ploughs in lordship, later and now 9. Then among 5 b the men 64 ploughs, later and now 45.
Woodland, then 1500 pigs, now 1200; meadow, 80 acres; then 1 mill, now 2.
Always 9 cobs, 5 foals, 40 cattle, 318 sheep and 172 pigs.
Then this manor paid 10 nights' provisions and £10; now it pays £100 by weight and 100s in gifts.
After the King came to England, Engelric misappropriated 2 hides of the land of Harold's reeve who paid all customary dues to this manor, namely £12; now Count E(ustace) holds it, since his predecessor was in possession of it.
In Harold's time there was 1 pigman who paid a customary due to this manor (and) who resided on 1 virgate of land and 15 acres, but, after the King came, Robert Gernon took him from the manor and made him a Forester of the King's woodland.
Harold gave 1 hide to a priest of his, but the Hundred does not know if he gave it free or in alms; now R(obert) Bishop of Hereford holds it.
Also ½ hide which 1 Freeman held freely, who paid suit in the manor although he could go whither he would with his land; Count Eustace added this man to his land.
In this manor, there have always been 2 Freemen with ½ hide and 10 acres who have always had ½ plough.
Meadow, 4 acres.
It is assessed in the above £100.

In Wiritela . ten& Idē eṗc . ii . hid̆ . 7 xx . ac̄ . q̇rū . i . fuit t̄ . r̄ . e . in eccł̄a
& alia in feudo reḡ . Sēp . iii . uiłt . 7 . i . pƀr . Tc̄ . ii . bor . m̄ . viii . Tc̄ . ii . feŕ .
Sēp . i . caŕ in dn̄io . 7 . ii . caŕ . hom̄ . Silu . c . por . viii . ac̄ . ṗti . 7 . uał . ʟ . foł .

⌐ Dimidiū Hund̆ de melduna . In Malduna h̄t rex . i . domū . 7 . paśt
ad . c . ou̇ . 7 . i . foċ de . xʟix . ac̄ . hn̄s . i . bor . 7 . t̄ . r̄ . e . i . caŕ . m̄ . dim̄ . Tc̄ uał
x . foł . m̄ . v . In Ead h̄t rex . cʟxxx . domos q̇s tenent burgenſes . 7 .
. xviii . manſuras uaſtatas . q̇ʒ . xv . tenent . dim̄ . hid̆ . 7 . xxi . ac̄ . 7 alij

hōes n̄ tenent ampli q̇ domos fuas in burgo . 7 in̄t eos h̄nt . xii . runc .
7 . cxʟ . an̄ . 7 . ciii . por . 7 . cccxxxvi . ou̇ . De halla reḡ sēp exeunt . vi .
foł . 7 . viii . d̆ . 7 de tr̄a Sueni . iiii . foł . 7 de . ii . domibʒ Eudonis . daṗ . xvi . d̆
q̇s n̄ habuit rex ṗq̇ uenit in hanc tr̄a . De ṗdicto fochemano habuit . Ra .
piperełł . confuet̄ . in uno q̇q̇ anno ṗ . iii . foł . ſ; in tēṗr̄ . r̄ . e . n̄ habuit ej
antec̄ n̄ tantū m̄ c̄m̄doem . 7 tēṗr̄ . r̄ . e . totū fimul reddidit . xiii . liƀ .
7 . ii . foł . 7 q̇do petr̄ rec̄ . xxiiii . liƀ . m̄ . xvi . liƀ ad pond̆ .

⌐ . H . de Tendering & . Brictriceſciā ten̄ . Herold̆ ,p . m̄ . 7 . ,p . x . hid̆ . ★
m̄ . r . W . Sēp . xxiiii . uiłt . Tc̄ . x . bor . ṗ . xi . m̄ . xvi . 7 . x . bor . n̄ tenentes
tr̄a . Tc̄ . iiii . feŕ . m̄ . v . Tc̄ . iii . caŕ . in dn̄io . Ṗ 7 m̄ . ii . Tc̄ . xvi . caŕ . homin̄
poſt . 7 m̄ . xi . filu . c . por . m̄ . i . moł . Paſt . ꝺc . ouibʒ sēp . xvi . an̄ . 7 . v . ŕ .
7 . cʟxvi . ou̇ . 7 ʟxii . por . Tc̄ in̄t brictriceſciā 7 hercheſteda reddideŕ
. ii . noc̄t . de firma . 7 q̇n̄ . ,p . rec̄ . xxv . liƀ . m̄ . xxii . liƀ . S; iſta bereuuit ★
jac& in Sudfolc . In dn̄io . iiii . an̄ . 7 . v . porc .

⌐ Lalefordā ten̄ Har̄ . ,p . i . m̄ . 7 . ,p . x . hid̆ . m̄ . rex W . ,p totid̄e . Sēp . xv .
uiłt . 7 xxiiii . bor . Tc̄ . vii . feŕ . m̄ . vi . sēp . iiii . caŕ in dn̄io . Tc̄ . in̄t hōes
xx . caŕ . 7 q̇do baignard̄ . tenuit . xvi . caŕ . ſ; q̇n̄ . Ṗ . rec̄ . ix . 7 m̄ fimiliŕ ★

In Writtle the Bishop also holds 2 hides and 20 acres of which 1 (hide) was in the (lands of the) Church before 1066 and the other was in the King's Holding.
Always 3 villagers; 1 priest. Then 2 smallholders, now 8; then 2 slaves.
Always 1 plough in lordship; 2 men's ploughs.
Woodland, 100 pigs; meadow, 8 acres.
Value 50s.

Half-Hundred of MALDON

25 In MALDON the King has 1 house and pasture for 100 sheep.
1 Freeman with 49 acres who has 1 smallholder. Before 1066, 1 plough; now ½.
Value then 10s; now 5[s].
In the same (Maldon) the King has 180 houses which burgesses hold and 18 derelict dwellings; 15 of them hold ½ hide and 21 acres, and the other men do not hold more than their houses in the Borough; between them they have 12 cobs, 140 cattle, 103 pigs and 336 sheep. 6 a
From the King's hall have always come 6s 8d, and from Swein's land 4s; and from 2 of Eudo the Steward's houses 16d, which the King has not had since he came to this land.
From the aforesaid Freeman, Ranulf Peverel had a customary due each year for 3s; but before 1066 his predecessor had nothing except for patronage.
Before 1066 the whole together paid £13 2s; when Peter acquired it £24; now £16 by weight.

Hundred of TENDRING

26 Harold held BRIGHTLINGSEA as a manor, for 10 hides. Now King William (holds it).
Always 24 villagers. Then 10 smallholders, later 11, now 16; and 10 smallholders who do not hold land; then 4 slaves, now 5.
Then 3 ploughs in lordship, later and now 2. Then 16 men's ploughs, later and now 11.
Woodland, 100 pigs; now 1 mill; pasture for 600 sheep.
Always 16 cattle, 5 cobs, 166 sheep and 62 pigs.
Then Brightlingsea and Harkstead between them paid 2 nights' provisions; when P(eter) acquired (them) £25; now £22. However, the outlier lies in Suffolk.
In lordship 4 cattle and 5 pigs.

27 Harold held LAWFORD as 1 manor, for 10 hides. Now King William (holds it) for as much.
Always 15 villagers; 24 smallholders. Then 7 slaves, now 6.
Always 4 ploughs in lordship. Then among the men 20 ploughs; when Baynard held (it), 16 ploughs; but when Peter acquired (it), 9, and now the same.

Silua . xv . por . xii . aƈ . p̄ti . tē . i . moł . m̄ . ii . past . ccc . ou . m̄ . i . ſalina.
Tē reddidit . ii . noct de firma . 7 qn̄ baign . ten . xiiii . liɓ . m̄ . xi.
Huic manerio jacuer . xvii . ſoƈ . t . r . e . de . i . hid . reddentes omnē conſu.
7 p̄q̄ rex uenit in hanc t̄r̄a . 7 Bain . fuit uicecomes: occupauit iſt̄a t̄r̄a
Tedriƈ Pointel 7 qn̄ ē̄a acceꝑ manebant in ē̄a . xvii . ſoƈ . hntes . ix . car.

6 b

m̄ ſt in manu reḡ . 7 . xiii . h̄oes tenent hanc t̄r̄a . hntes . iiii . car . Silu
xv . por . ii . aƈ 7 đ . p̄ti . Tē . uał . iiii . liɓ 7 . qn̄ tedriƈ pointel ten . iiii . liɓ
m̄ . xl . ſoł . In dn̄io iſti manerij . receꝑ Petr . xxi . an . 7 . iiii . runƈ.
7 . xlv . porƈ . 7 . cc . ou . x . min . Huic manerio . ꝑtinebat . t . r . e
. i . bereuuita . de . iiii . hid . q̄m inuaſit Engelriƈ . idē ten& comes . E.
Ptinebant adhuc . xxi . ſoƈ . tenentes . i . hid . 7 . ii . uirg . 7 . v . aƈ . q̄s ħt
Roḡ de ramis ꝓ eſcangio: ut dicit . 7 inde uocat libator̄e ſuanu.
Et . iiii . ſoƈ . fuer t . r . e in iſto manerio omnē conſuet reddentes.
q̄s Ricard fili comitis giſleɓti inuaſit tēp̄r illo q̄ Suen erat uicecomes.
tenentes dim̄ . hid . 7 . xv . aƈ . que m̄ ſt in manu reḡ idō qđ nułł fuit
ex parte ej q̄ dixiſſ⁊ q̄m eos habuerit . Sēp . i . car . 7 tēp̄r . r . e . uał.
. xiii . ſoł . 7 hucuſq̣ habuit . R . iſt̄u cenſū . Waleram . inuaſit . i . ſoƈ.
de . xxx . aƈ . tē . i . car . m̄ . nułł . 7 uał . x . ſoł . 7 iſt̄u cenſu uſq̣ huc habuit
Wał . Hageɓt ten& xxx . aƈ q̄s ten . i . ſoƈ 7 . inde reuocat libator̄e
Suanū . Tē . i . car . m̄ . dim . Tē uał . v . ſoł . 7 . iiii . đ . m̄ . xxxii . đ.
Comes . E . ten& . i . hid . 7 . dim . 7 . xlv . aƈ . qđ inuaſit Engelriƈ . 7 . iłł̄a
t̄r̄a tenebant . viii . ſoƈ . Eꝑc baioƈ ten& dim̄ hid . qua ten& Rad
fili turoldi ſub ipſo . Ranulf fr Ilgeri . ten& . xv . aƈ . Hugo de
monfort . xxx . aƈ . Rad baignart dim̄ hid . 7 . xxxv . aƈ . Eudo daꝑ
xxxvii . aƈ . 7 . dim . Roḡ h̄o eꝑi Londonienſis: . i . hid . 7 . xxx . aƈ.
Wałt diacon . v . aƈ . Tota hec t̄r̄a reddebat conſuetudinē omnē ſuꝑ
diƈto manerio . t . r . e.

Woodland, 15 pigs; meadow, 12 acres; then 1 mill, now 2;
pasture, 300 sheep; now 1 salt-house.
Then it paid 2 nights' provisions; when Baynard held (it) £14;
now [£] 11.
Attached to this manor before 1066 were 17 Freemen with 1
hide, who paid all customary dues; after the King came to this
land and Baynard was Sheriff, Theodoric Pointel appropriated
this land; when he acquired it, 17 Freemen dwelt there who had
9 ploughs, now they are in the King's hand. 13 men who have 4   6 b
ploughs hold this land.
Woodland, 15 pigs; meadow, 2½ acres.
Value then £4; when Theodoric Pointel held (it) £4; now 40s.
In this manor's lordship Peter acquired 21 cattle, 4 cobs,
45 pigs and 200 sheep less 10.
There belonged to this manor before 1066 1 outlier with 4
hides, which Engelric annexed. Count E(ustace) holds it.
There also belonged 21 Freemen, who held 1 hide, 2 virgates
and 5 acres, whom Roger of Raismes has by exchange, as he states,
and calls Swein as deliverer of them.
Also there were 4 Freemen in this manor before 1066 who
paid all customary dues, whom Richard son of Count Gilbert
annexed in the time when Swein was Sheriff, (and) who held ½
hide and 15 acres which are now in the King's hand, with the
result that there was no one who might state on his behalf how
he should hold them.
Always 1 plough.
Value before 1066, 13s and up to now R(ichard) has had these
dues.
Waleran annexed 1 Freeman with 30 acres. Then 1 plough,
now none. Value 10s and up to now Waleran has had these dues.
Hagebert holds 30 acres which 1 Freeman held and recalls
Swein as its deliverer.
Then 1 plough, now ½.
Value then 5s 4d; now 32d.
Count E(ustace) holds 1½ hides and 45 acres, which Engelric
annexed; 8 Freemen held that land. The Bishop of Bayeux holds
½ hide which Ralph son of Thorold holds under him. Ranulf
brother of Ilger holds 15 acres; Hugh de Montfort 30 acres; Ralph
Baynard ½ hide and 35 acres; Eudo the Steward 37½ acres;
Roger, a man of the Bishop of London, 1 hide and 30 acres;
Walter the deacon 5 acres.
The whole of this land paid all customary dues to the above
manor before 1066.

⌐ Hund de Odelesfort .   Neuport ten̄ . Harold . t . r . e . p man̄.

7 . p . viii . hid . 7 d . m̄ rex . W . Tc̄ . xviii . uilt . P . xv . m̄ xxvi . Tc̄.

viii . bor . p . vi . M . xiii . Tc̄ . iiii . ser . p 7 m̄ . ii . Tc̄ . ii . car in dn̄io . p

7 . m̄ . i . Tc̄ . 7 p̄ in̄t hōcs . viii . car̄ . m̄ . x . Silu̅ . c . por . xxiiii . ac̄ . p̄ti.

Sēp . ii . mol . 7 . x . an̄ . 7 . i . r̄ . lxxix . porc̄ . cii . ou̅ . Tc̄ reddebat

firmā de duab̄z noctib̄z Est adhuc . i . bereuuita que jac& in Cante

bruge fira 7 uocat̄ . Scelfort . de . iii . hid . 7 . xlvi . ac̄ . Sēp . viii . uilt.

7 . v . bor . 7 . i . car̄ . in dn̄io . 7 . ii . car̄ . hom̄ . 7 xv . ac̄ . p̄ti . Tc̄ . i . runc̄

m̄ . n̄ . sēp . x . an̄ . tc̄ . lxxx . porc̄ . m̄ . l . Tc̄ . lxxx . ou̅ . m̄ . lxxxvii.

Tc̄ . xiii . capræ . m̄ . xxiiii .   Hec berewita ⌐ e in sup̄dicta firma . t . r . e

m̄ u̅ reddit . xxv . lib . 7 . xvi . sol . Rob̄ grino ten& . ii . soc̄ . de . ii . hid

7 . dim̄ . p̄tinentes huic manerio . 7 reddentes omn̄ē consuetudin̄ē

q̄s accepit cū Suen̄ ess& uicecomes . & hund̄ nescit q̄ m̄ eos habuerit

q̄a neq̄ breue neq̄ legat̄ uenit ex parte regis in hund̄ qd rex sibi

dediss& illā tr̄a . Quidā cleric̄ comitis . E . inuaserat xlii . ac̄ . 7 teneb̄

illas ad feudū comitis . e . s̄ hund̄ eas testat̄ ad neuport . 7 . ita m̄ ht̄

rex . Cleric̄ u̅ judicat̄ ē esse in misc̄dia regis . 7 de om̄i cessu suo . 7

de corpore suo . In illa tr̄a erat . tc̄ . i . car̄ . m̄ nulla . i . ac̄ p̄ti . Silu̅

vi . por . 7 . ual . vi . sol.

⌐ Richelingā ten̄ . Har . p m̄ . 7 p̄ . viii . hid . m̄ . rex . W . p totid̄ē

Tc̄ . xiii . uilt . p . xvi . m̄ . xx .   Tc̄ 7 p̄ . vi . bor . m̄ . x . sēp . iiii . ser.

7 . ii . car̄ . in dn̄io . Tc̄ 7 p̄ . viii . car̄ . hom̄ . m̄ . x . Silu̅ . xxx . porc̄.

7 . iii . ac̄ . p̄ti . Tc̄ . ual . viii . lib . m̄ . xii . lib . 7 . xvi . sol . in dn̄io . vii . an̄ . 7

⌐   (lxx . ou̅.

Hundred of UTTLESFORD

28 Harold held NEWPORT before 1066 as a manor, for 8½ hides. Now King William (holds it).
    Then 18 villagers, later 15, now 26; then 8 smallholders, later 6, now 13; then 4 slaves, later and now 2.
    Then 2 ploughs in lordship, later and now 1. Then and later among the men 8 ploughs, now 10.
    Woodland, 100 pigs; meadow, 24 acres; always 2 mills.
    10 cattle, 1 cob, 79 pigs, 102 sheep.
Then it paid (a revenue of) 2 nights' provisions.
    There is besides 1 outlier which lies in Cambridgeshire and is called SHELFORD, with 3 hides and 46 acres.
    Always 8 villagers; 5 smallholders; 1 plough in lordship; 2 men's ploughs.
    Meadow, 15 acres. Then 1 cob, now none; always 10 cattle. Then 80 pigs, now 50; then 80 sheep, now 87; then 13 goats, now 24.
    This outlier was in the above-mentioned revenue before 1066, but now it pays £25 16s. Robert Gernon holds 2 Freemen with 2½ hides who belong to this manor and who pay all customary dues, whom he received when Swein was Sheriff. The Hundred does not know how he should have them, because neither a writ nor a Commissioner came on the King's behalf to the Hundred (to say) that the King had given himself that land.
    A cleric of Count E(ustace) had annexed 42 acres and held them in Count E(ustace)'s Holding, but the Hundred testifies that they (belong) to Newport, so the King now has them; the cleric is judged to be in the King's mercy regarding both all his property and his body.
In that land was then 1 plough, now none.
    Meadow, 1 acre; woodland, 6 pigs.
    Value 6s.

29 Harold held RICKLING as a manor, for 8 hides. Now King William (holds it) for as much.
    Then 13 villagers, later 16, now 20; then and later 6 smallholders, now 10. Always 4 slaves; 2 ploughs in lordship.
    Then and later 8 men's ploughs; now 10.
    Woodland, 30 pigs; meadow, 3 acres.

Value then £8; now £12 16s.
    In lordship 7 cattle and 70 sheep.

/Dimidium Hund de Froſſcewella.

Sanfort tenuit Edeua poſt. Rad comes . m̅ . Godric dapifer in
manu regis . ꝑ . m̅ . 7 ꝑ . vii . hid . 7 . xxx . ac̅ . Tc̅ . xxvi . uiłł . ꝑ . xiii .
m̅ . xvi . Tc̅ . ix . bor . P̅ . vi . m̅ . v . sep . iiii . feɍ . 7 . ii . car̅ . in d̅nio . Tc̅
in̅t h̅oes . xxii . car̅ . ꝑ . xv . m̅ . xiiii . Silu̅ . cl . por . xxx . ac̅ . p̅ti .
sep . i . moł . Tc̅ . uał . xx . lib̅ . P̅ . xxvi . m̅ . xxx .

/Hundret de Tureſtapla .   Wiłł rex . h̅t . iiii . ſalinas in iſto
hund . q̊s cuſtodit uicecomes . 7 . iii . h̅oes . de . x . ac̅ . 7 . uał . xx . ɗ .

8 a

/Terræ Sc̅æ Trinitatis de cantorberia ad uictu monacoꝝ   . II .
Hund de Witham   In Cogheſſala tenuit Sc̅a trinitas . iii . uirg
træ . t̅ . r̅ . e̅ . 7 m̅ . ſimilit̅ . Sep . ii . car̅ . Tc̅ . i . bor . m̅ . viii . Tc̅ . iii . feɍ . m̅ . i .
viii . ac̅ . p̅ti . i . moł . 7 . uał . lx . ſoł . In d̅nio . iiii . r̅ . iii . an̅ . xx . ou̅ . vii . por
/Bochinges ten& sep . S̅ . T̅ . ꝑ . m̅ . 7 ꝑ . iiii . hid . 7 . ɗ . 7 . ii . car̅ . i̅ d̅nio .
Tc̅ . xxxv . car̅ . hom̅ . m̅ . xxix . Tc̅ . xix . uiłł . m̅ . xviii . tc̅ . xxv .
bor . m̅ . xliiii . Tc̅ . iiii . ſeɍ . m̅ . ii . Silu̅ . ccc . por . Paſt . lx . ouib̅ꝫ . xxii .
ac̅ . p̅ti . 7 . i . moł . 7 vi . an̅ . 7 . c . ou̅ . 7 . liiii . por . Huic manerio sep
ptinent . ii . hid . in mereſai . 7 . i . car in d̅nio . 7 . i . car hom̅ . 7 . ii . uiłł .
. 7 . i . bor . paſtura . l . ou̅ . Tc̅ in̅t totu̅ uał . xxiiii . lib̅ . m̅ . xxviii .
/Stieſteda̅ . tenuit sc̅a . t̅ . ꝑ . m̅ . 7 . ꝑ dim̅ . hid̅ .   Tc̅ . iiii . car̅ . in d̅nio . m̅
. iii . Tc̅ . v . car̅ . hom̅ . m̅ . vi . Tc̅ . viii . uiłł . m̅ . xiii . Tc̅ . xi . bor m̅ xxv .
tc̅ . vi . ſeɍ . m̅ . iiii . Silu̅ . bccc . por . xxvii . ac̅ . p̅ti . 7 . i . moł . 7 . iii . r̅ .
7 . xl . an̅ . 7 . cxx . ou̅ . lxxvii . por . Tc̅ uał . x . lib̅ . m̅ . xv .

Half-Hundred of FRESHWELL
30 Edeva held (Great) SAMPFORD; later Earl Ralph (held it). Now
Godric the Steward (holds it) in the King's hand as a manor,
for 7 hides and 30 acres.
     Then 26 villagers, later 13, now 16; then 9 smallholders,
     later 6, now 5. Always 4 slaves; 2 ploughs in lordship.
     Then among the men 22 ploughs, later 15, now 14.
     Woodland, 150 pigs; meadow, 30 acres; always 1 mill.
     Value then £20; later [£] 26; now [£] 30.

Hundred of THURSTABLE
31 King William holds 4 salt-houses in the Hundred, which the
Sheriff has charge of.
     3 men with 10 acres.
     Value 20d.

2   LANDS OF HOLY TRINITY, CANTERBURY,   8 a
         FOR THE MONKS' SUPPLIES

Hundred of WITHAM
1 In (Little) COGGESHALL, Holy Trinity held 3 virgates of land
before 1066; now the same. Always 2 ploughs.
     Then 1 smallholder, now 8; then 3 slaves, now 1.
     Meadow, 8 acres; 1 mill.
     Value 60s.
     In lordship 4 cobs, 3 cattle, 20 sheep, 7 pigs.

[Hundred of HINCKFORD]
2 Holy Trinity has always held BOCKING as a manor, for 4½ hides.
2 ploughs in lordship. Then 35 men's ploughs, now 29.
     Then 19 villagers, now 18; then 25 smallholders, now 44;
     then 4 slaves, now 2.
     Woodland, 300 pigs; pasture for 60 sheep; meadow, 22 acres;
     1 mill. 6 cattle, 100 sheep and 54 pigs.
     To this manor have always belonged 2 hides in (West) MERSEA.
     1 plough in lordship. 1 men's plough.
     2 villagers; 1 smallholder.
     Pasture, 50 sheep.
     In total, value then £24; now [£] 28.

3 Holy Trinity held STISTED as a manor, for ½ hide. Then 4 ploughs
in lordship, now 3. Then 5 men's ploughs, now 6.
     Then 8 villagers, now 13; then 11 smallholders, now 25;
     then 6 slaves, now 4.
     Woodland, 800 pigs; meadow, 27 acres; 1 mill. 3 cobs, 40
     cattle, 120 sheep, 77 pigs.
     Value then £10; now [£] 15.

⌐Hund̄ de Witbricteſherna. Lalinge ten̄ . ſc̄a . T̄ . p̄ m̄ . 7 . p̄.

xiiii . hid̄ . T̄c . xiiii . uilł . m̄ . xxi . T̄c . xvi . bor̄ . T̄c . iii . ſer̄ . m̄ . iiii.

T̄c . ii . car̄ . in dn̄io . m̄ . iii . T̄c . xvii . car̄ . 7 . dim̄ . hom̄ . m̄ . xvi . 7 . đ.

ſēp . i . moł . Silu̅ . đccc . por . 7 . iii . r̄ . 7 . i . muł . 7 xvi . an̄ . 7 . lx . por . 7 . cci

ou̅ . 7 . xviii . cap̄ . T̄c . vał . xii . lib̄ . m̄ . xvi.

⌐Lachenduna ten̄ . S̄ . T̄ . p̄ . m̄ . 7 . ii . hid̄ . 7 . i . car̄ . in dn̄io . m̄ . ii . uiłłi . 7 .

. i . ſer̄ . Paſtura . xxx . ouib₂ . 7 . vi . an̄ . 7 . lx . ou̅ . 7 . xvi . por . T̄c . vał

xx . ſoł . m̄ . xxv.

⌐Niwelant . ten̄ . S̄ . T̄ . p̄ . m̄ . 7 . iii . hid̄ . T̄c . i . uiłł . m̄ . iii . ſēp . ii . ſer̄;

8 b

t̄c . ii . car̄ . m̄ . i . T̄c . xxiiii . ou̅ . 7 . m̄ ſimilit̄ . T̄c vał . xx . ſoł . M̄ . xl.

⌐Hund̄ de Rochefort . Mildentuna̅ ten̄ . S̄ . T̄ . p̄ m̄ . 7 . ii . hid̄.

Sēp . viii . uiłł . T̄c . xiii . bor . m̄ . xv . ſēp . i . ſer̄ . 7 . ii . car̄ in dn̄io . 7 . vi .

car̄ . hom̄ . Silu̅ . lx . por . 7 . viii . an̄ . 7 . ii . r̄ . 7 . xxv . por . 7 . cxxiiii.

ou̅ . T̄c . vał . c . ſoł . m̄ . viii . lib̄.

⌐Sudcerca̅ . ten̄ . S̄ . T̄ . p̄ m̄ . 7 . p̄ . iiii . hid̄ . ſēp . xiiii . uiłł . 7 . v . bor.

T̄c . ii . ſer̄ . m̄ . i . ſēp . ii . car̄ . in dn̄io . 7 . vi . car̄ . hom̄ . paſt . cc . ouib;

Silua . xl . por . 7 . ii . piſc̄ . 7 . iiii . runč . 7 . viii . an̄ . 7 . xiii . por . 7 . cl.

ou̅ . 7 . xvi . cap̄ . T̄c . vał . c . ſoł . m̄ . vii . lib̄.

⌐Stanbruge tenuit Sc̄a t̄ . p̄ . m̄ . 7 . i . hid̄ . t̄ . r̄ . e . M Rad̄ baignar̄.

de ecclia . ſēp . i . car̄ . in dn̄io . T̄c . iii . bor . m̄ . vii . 7 . i . ac . p̄ti . Paſt.

cc . ouib; . 7 . iiii . an̄ . 7 . x . por . 7 . lviii . ou̅ . T̄c . vał . xxx . ſoł . m̄ . xl.

9 a

Hundred of 'WIBERTSHERNE'
Holy Trinity holds
4   LAWLING as a manor, for 14 hides.
Then 14 villagers, now 21; then 16 smallholders, now 20;
then 3 slaves, now 4. Then 2 ploughs in lordship, now 3.
Then 17½ men's ploughs, now 16½.
Always 1 mill. Woodland, 800 pigs. 3 cobs, 1 mule, 16 cattle,
60 pigs, 200 sheep and 18 goats.
Value then £12; now [£] 16.

5   LATCHINGDON as a manor, 2 hides. 1 plough in lordship.
Now 2 villagers; 1 slave.
Pasture for 30 sheep. 6 cattle, 60 sheep and 16 pigs.
Value then 20s; now 25[s].

6   ST. LAWRENCE as a manor, 3 hides.
Then 1 villager, now 3; always 2 slaves. Then 2 ploughs, now 1.   8 b
Then 24 sheep, now the same.
Value then 20s; now 40[s].

Hundred of ROCHFORD
7   MILTON as a manor, 2 hides.
Always 8 villagers. Then 13 smallholders, now 15. Always
1 slave; 2 ploughs in lordship; 6 men's ploughs.
Woodland, 60 pigs. 8 cattle, 2 cobs, 25 pigs and 124 sheep.
Value then 100s; now £8.

8   SOUTHCHURCH as a manor, for 4 hides.
Always 14 villagers; 5 smallholders. Then 2 slaves, now 1.
Always 2 ploughs in lordship; 6 men's ploughs.
Pasture for 200 sheep; woodland, 40 pigs; 2 fisheries.
4 cobs, 8 cattle, 13 pigs, 150 sheep and 16 goats.
Value then 100s; now £7.

9   Holy Trinity held (Little) STAMBRIDGE as a manor; 1 hide before
1066. Now Ralph Baynard (holds it) from the Church. Always 1
plough in lordship.
Then 3 smallholders, now 7.
Meadow, 1 acre; pasture for 200 sheep. 4 cattle, 10 pigs and
58 sheep.
Value then 30s; now 40[s].

[3] *The Bishop of London*   9 a
[4] *The same Bishop's Holding*
[5] *The Canons of St. Paul's, London*
[6] *St. Peter, Westminster*
[7] *The Bishop of Durham*
[8] *The Canons of Waltham Holy Cross*

.III. ⸗ Terra epi Londonienſis. Hund de berdeſtapla. Legendunā

ten& epc quā tenuit Alftred quedā femina . t . r . e . p . 1 . man . 7 . 1x . hid.

Tc . 11 . car . in dnio . m . 111 . Tc . v11 . car hom . m . v1 . Tc . v111 . uilt . m . 111.

m . x1111 . bor . Sep . v1 . fer . Silu . c . por . Paſt . c . ou . Tc ual . 1x . lib . m . x.

f; epc inderecip . x1111 . lib . De hoc manerio tenent Rad . 7 Witt . de

epo . 111 . hid . 7 . Lxxx . ac . 7 . 1 . car in dnio . 7 . 11 . hom . 7 ual . c . fot . in

eod ptio . In dnio recep . Epc . c . ou . 111 . min . 7 . x . por.

⸗ Orſedā ten& Eps . quā tenuit Witt epc t . r . e . p . man . 7 x111 . hid.

f& comes Euſtachi . 1 . ex illis ten& que n e de fuis . c . manſionib; . Sep

. 11 . car in dnio . Tc . xxx1111 . car hom . M . xx11 . Tc . xxx1111 . uitt . m

. xx11 . Tc . v1 . bor . m . xxxv1 . Tc . 1111 . fer . m . 11 . Silu . M . 7 v1 . anim.

7 . cxv . ou . 7 . xL . porc . Tc . ual . xxxv . lib . m . xxv111 . De hoc eodē

manerio tenent . Tidbald . Anſchetill . Witt . Giflebt . 1111 . hid . 7 . d.

7 . xL . ac . 7 v1 . car . 7 ual . v111 . lib in eod ptio.

⸗ Rameſdanā ten& Witt . de epo . p . m . 7 . 111 . hid . Sep . 1 . car in dnio.

7 . dim . car . hom . Tc . v1 . bor . m . v111 . 7 . 1 . fer . Silu . c . por . m . 1 . mot.

Tc ual . Lx . fot . m . xL.

⸗ Hundret de Withā. In Slamondeſheia ten& Rog de epo

xv . ac . 7 . ual . xxx . d.

⸗ Hund de beuentrev . Weneſtedā tenuit Scs paul . iii . Rad

fili brieu depo . p . 1 . man . 7 . 1 . hid . Tc . 1 . car . in dnio . m . 1 . 7 . dim.

Sep . 11 . car . hom . 7 . 111 . uilt . Tc . v11 . bor . m . v111 . tc . 11 . fer . m null.

Silu . ccc . por . m . 1 . mot . sep . 1 . falina . 7 ual . xL . fot.

Hundred of BARSTABLE
1 The Bishop holds LAINDON which Aelfthryth, a woman, held
   before 1066 as a manor; 9 hides. Then 2 ploughs in lordship,
   now 3. Then 7 men's ploughs, now 6.
       Then 8 villagers, now 3; now 14 smallholders; always 6 slaves.
       Woodland, 100 pigs; pasture, 100 sheep.
       Value then £9; now [£] 10, but the Bishop receives from it £14.
       Of this manor, Ralph and William hold 3 hides and 80 acres
   from the Bishop. 1 plough in lordship. 2 men's ploughs.
   Value 100s in the same assessment.
       In lordship the Bishop acquired 100 sheep less 3 and 10 pigs.

2 The Bishop holds ORSETT which Bishop William held before 1066,
   as a manor; 13 hides. But Count Eustace holds 1 of these, which
   is not (part) of his 100 manors. Always 2 ploughs in lordship.
   Then 34 men's ploughs, now 22.
       Then 34 villagers, now 22; then 6 smallholders, now 36;
           then 4 slaves, now 2.
       Woodland, 1000 [pigs]. 6 cattle, 115 sheep and 40 pigs.
       Value then £35, now [£] 28.
       Of this same manor, Tidbald, Ansketel, William (and) Gilbert
   hold 4½ hides and 40 acres. 6 ploughs.
   Value £8 in the same assessment.

3 William holds RAMSDEN (Belhus) from the Bishop as a manor; 3
   hides. Always 1 plough in lordship; ½ men's plough.
       Then 6 smallholders, now 8; 1 slave.
       Woodland, 100 pigs; now 1 mill.
   Value 60s; now 40[s].

Hundred of WITHAM
4 Roger holds 15 acres from the Bishop in SLAMPSEYS.
   Value 30d.

Hundred of BECONTREE
5 St. Paul's held WANSTED. Now Ralph son of Brian (holds it) from
   the Bishop as 1 manor; 1 hide. Then 1 plough in lordship, now 1½.
   Always 2 men's ploughs;
       3 villagers. Then 7 smallholders, now 8; then 2 slaves, now none.
       Woodland, 300 pigs; now 1 mill; always 1 salt-house.
   Value 40s.

⟨Hund de Wenſiſtreu. Legrã tenueꝛ.ıı.lıɓı hões.t.r.e

m̃.Roḡ de eꝑo.p.ııı.hıd.Sēp.ı.caꝛ 7.d̃.ın dñıo.7.ıı.caꝛ homınu̅.

tē.v.uıłłı.m̃.ıııı.Tē.ıııı.bord.m̃.vı.Tē.ııı.ſeꝛ.m̃.ıııı.Sılua.

cʟ.por.7.ıı.ac.p̃tı.tē uał ʟxx.ſoł.m̃.ıııı.lıɓ.

⟨Legrã ten& Id̃e.R.de eꝑo.qd tenuıt.ı.lıɓa fem.t.r.e.p.ııı.hıd.

Sēp.ıı caꝛruc.ın dñıo.m̃.d̃.caꝛ hom.M un uıllan.Tē.Un.

bor.m̃.ıııı.Tē.ııı.ſeꝛ.m̃.ıııı.Sılu.cʟ.por.m̃.ı.moł.sēp.ı.ſalına.

tē uał ʟxx.ſoł.m̃.ıııı.lıɓ.Hec duo manerıa deratıocınauıt Weꝑc

ad op ecclæ ſuæ poſt mortē reḡ.E.juſſu reḡ.Wıłłı.

⟨Hund de hıdınghafort. Raınes ten̄.W.eꝑc.t.r.e.p.ıııı.

hıd.7.xxx ac.Sēp.ıı.caꝛ.ın dñıo.Tē.v.caꝛ hom.m̃.ıııı.Tē

xvı.uıłł.m̃.x.Tē.ıx.bor.m̃.vııı.Tē.ıııı.ſeꝛ.m̃.ııı.Sılua.cc.por

xvı.ac.p̃tı.m̃.ı.moł.7.x.an.xʟv.ou.xxıııı.por.huıc manerıo

addıte ſꝫ.xv.ac.t.r.Wıłłı.q̃s tenuıt.ı.lıɓ hõ.t.r.e.ſıc hund teſtaꝛ.

Tūc uał.x.lıɓ.m̃.xıııı.In hoc maneꝛ ten& Roḡ de eꝑo.ııı.uırḡ.

7.ı.caꝛ.7.ıı.ſeꝛ.7 uał.ʟ.ſoł.

⟨Hund de Wıtbrıctefherna In Sudmunſtrã.xxx.hıd.q̃s tenent

epē ın dñıo
~~xıııı.mılıtes de eꝑo.~~ 7 t.r.e.xxıı.uıłł.m̃.xı.Tē.xxııı.bor.m̃.xxv.

Sēp.v.ſeꝛ.7.ııı.caꝛ ın dñıo.Tē.xvııı.caꝛ hom.m̃.xı.Paſt.ꝏ.ou.

tē uał.xxıııı.lıɓ.m̃.xvı.In hoc manerıo erant.t.r.e.xv.lıɓı

hões tenentes.xvııı.hıd.7.xxx.ac.m̃ ſꝫ xıııı.hões q̃ tenent eas

de eꝑo.Tē.ıııı.bor.m̃.xvı.Tē.ıııı.ſeꝛ.m̃.vııı.Tē.xıı.caꝛ.m̃.vıı.

Hundred of WINSTREE

6   2 free men held LAYER (Marney) before 1066. Now Roger (holds it) from the Bishop, for 3 hides. Always 1½ ploughs in lordship; 2 men's ploughs.

> Then 5 villagers, now 4; then 4 smallholders, now 6; then 3 slaves, now 4.
> Woodland, 150 pigs; meadow, 2 acres.

Value then 70s; now £4.

7   Roger also holds from the Bishop LAYER (Marney), which 1 free woman held before 1066, for 3 hides. Always 2 ploughs in lordship. Now ½ men's plough.

> Now 1 villager; then 1 smallholder, now 4; then 3 slaves, now 4.
> Woodland, 150 pigs; now 1 mill; always 1 salt-house.

Value then 70s; now £4.

> Bishop W(illiam) adjudged these 2 manors to the use of his Church after the death of King Edward, by King William's command.

Hundred of HINCKFORD

8   Bishop W(illiam) held RAYNE before 1066, for 4 hides and 30 acres. Always 2 ploughs in lordship. Then 5 men's ploughs, now 4.

> Then 16 villagers, now 10; then 9 smallholders, now 8; then 4 slaves, now 3.
> Woodland, 200 pigs; meadow, 16 acres; now 1 mill.
> 10 cattle, 45 sheep, 24 pigs.

To this manor were added 15 acres after 1066, which 1 free man held before 1066; so the Hundred testifies.

Value then £10; now [£] 14.

> In this manor, Roger holds from the Bishop 3 virgates. 1 plough. 2 slaves.

Value 50s.

Hundred of 'WIBERTSHERNE'

9   In SOUTHMINSTER 30 hides which the Bishop holds in lordship.

> Before 1066, 22 villagers, now 11; then 23 smallholders, now 25. Always 5 slaves; 3 ploughs in lordship. Then 18 men's ploughs, now 11.
> Pasture, 1000 sheep.

Value then £24; now [£] 16.

> In this manor were 15 free men before 1066 who held 18 hides and 30 acres. Now there are 14 men who hold them from the Bishop.
> Then 4 smallholders, now 16; then 4 slaves, now 8. Then 12 ploughs, now 7.

paſtura . ccc . oǔ . Tc̄ ual . xii . liƀ . m̄ . viii . In dn̄io huǰ manerij . sꝶ
xi . an̄ . 7 . ɒcc . oǔ . iiii . min̄ . 7 . xx . por . Hanc tr̄a tulit Gnut rex . ſ;

Wiƚƚ eꝑc recupauit t̄ . r . Wiƚƚi . ⌐ Copeford̄a ten& eꝑc in dn̄io . ꝑ . i . hid̄ . 7
dim̄ . 7 . xviii . ac̄ . Tc̄ . xvi . bor . m̄ . xiiii . Tc̄ . v . ſer . m̄ . iii . Sēp . ii . car̄ in
dn̄io . Tc̄ . vii . car̄ . hom̄ . m̄ . v . Silu . c . porc̄ . xvi . ac̄ . prat̄ . 7 . vi . an̄ . 7 . xii .
por . 7 . xxxvii . oǔ . Sēp ual . viii . liƀ . Huic manerio ꝓtinebant . t̄ . r̄ . e̅ .
. xii . ſoc̄ . m̄ . x . tenentes . i . hid̄ . 7 . ii . ac̄ . 7 . dim̄ . 7 n̄ potⱥnt recede ſicuti hund̄
teſtat̄ . Tc̄ . int̄ eos . ii . car̄ . m̄ . i . 7 d̄ . Apꝑtiatū e̅ in ſupiori ꝓtio . De hac
tr̄a ten& Roḡ de eꝑo . xxv . ac̄ . 7 . d̄ . car̄ 7 . ual . xv . ſoƚ . In hoc maner̄ .
fuere . xvii . ac̄ . q̃s ten Eꝑc . t̄ . r̄ . e̅ . ſed m̄ ten& Roƀ ḡnon de dono reḡ .
Adhuc ten& . Roƀ . ɪ . uirḡ tr̄æ quā tenuit eꝑc̄ . & q̃dā liƀ h̄o tenuit illā
ita qd̄ poſſ& ire q̃ uell& ſ; ſoca remanebat in manerio .
⌐ Hund de Ceffeorda . Wareleiā tenuit Guert . ꝑ m̄ . 7 . iiii . hid̄ .
xv . ac̄ . min̄ . m̄ Humfrid de eꝑo . sēp . v . uiƚƚ . 7 . ii . bor . m̄ . ii . ſer . Tc̄ . iii .
car̄ in dn̄io . m̄ . ii . sēp . iii . car̄ hom̄ Silua . ɒcc . por . paſt . c . oǔ . tc̄ 7 ꝑ
ual . vi . liƀ . m̄ . vii . de hoc manerio ten& taſcelin ꝓr . xv . ac̄ . hoꝯ man .
dedit Wiƚƚ rex Wiƚƚo eꝑo ꝑq̃ mare tranſiuit . q̃ in antiq̃ tēꝓ fuit de
eccƚa ſc̄i pauli .
⌐ Celmeresfort tenuit Wiƚƚ eꝑc t̄ . r̄ . e̅ . m̄ eꝑc in dn̄io . ꝑ . m̄ . 7 viii . hid̄ .
tc̄ . v . uiƚƚ . m̄ . iiii . Tc̄ . ii . car̄ . in dn̄io . m̄ . iii . Tc̄ . int̄ h̄oes . v . car̄ . m̄ . i .
ſilu . ccc . porc̄ . xxx . ac̄ . ꝓti . sēp . i . moƚ . 7 . ii . an̄ . 7 . xxvii . por . 7 . c . oǔ .
7 . ual . viii . liƀ .

Pasture, 300 sheep.
Value then £12; now [£] 8.
In the lordship of this manor are 11 cattle, 700 sheep less 4
and 20 pigs.
King Canute took this land; but Bishop William recovered it   10 b
after 1066.

[Hundred of LEXDEN]
10 The Bishop holds COPFORD in lordship, for 1½ hides and 18 acres.
Then 16 smallholders, now 14; then 5 slaves, now 3. Always
2 ploughs in lordship. Then 7 men's ploughs, now 5.
Woodland, 100 pigs; meadow, 16 acres. 6 cattle, 12 pigs
and 37 sheep.
Value always £8.
To this manor belonged 12 Freemen before 1066; now 10,
who hold 1 hide and 2½ acres and they cannot withdraw; so the
Hundred testifies. Then among them 2 ploughs, now 1½.
It is assessed in the above assessment.
Of this land, Roger holds from the Bishop 25 acres. ½ plough.
Value 15s.
In this manor were 17 acres which the Bishop held before
1066, but now Robert Gernon holds (them) by the King's gift.
Robert also holds 1 virgate of land which the Bishop held, and a
free man held it on condition that he could go whither he would,
but the jurisdiction stayed in the manor.

Hundred of CHAFFORD
11 Gyrth held (Little) WARLEY as a manor; 4 hides less 15 acres. Now
Humphrey (holds it) from the Bishop.
Always 5 villagers; 2 smallholders. Now 2 slaves. Then 3
ploughs in lordship, now 2. Always 3 men's ploughs.
Woodland, 700 pigs; pasture, 100 sheep.
Value then and later £6; now [£] 7.
Of this manor, Tascelin the priest holds 15 acres.
King William, after he crossed the sea, gave this manor to
Bishop William because in former times it was (in the lands) of
St. Paul's Church.

[Hundred of CHELMSFORD]
12 Bishop William held CHELMSFORD before 1066. Now the Bishop
(holds it) in lordship as a manor; 8 hides.
Then 5 villagers, now 4. Then 2 ploughs in lordship, now 3.
Then among the men 5 ploughs, now 1.
Woodland, 300 pigs; meadow, 30 acres; always 1 mill.
2 cattle, 27 pigs and 100 sheep.
Value £8.

↲Hund de Tureſtapla. Wicham ten& epc̄ in dn̄io qđ tenuit
Will epc̄ . t̄ . r . e . p̄ . m̄ . 7 . iii . hid̄ . Tc̄ . vii . uiłł . m̄ . v . tc̄ . i . bor . m̄ . iiii . Sēp
. iiii . ſer . 7 . ii . car in dn̄io . Tc̄ . iiii . car hom̄ . m̄ . ii . 7 . dim̄ . ſilu . xxx . por.
xxxi . ac̄ . p̄ti . Sēp . i . moł . 7 . vi . an̄ . 7 . l . ou . x . por . xx . cap̄ . 7 uał . vi . lib̄.

11 a

In ead . i . lib̄ hō de . v . ac̄ . 7 uał . xii . đ.
↲Hund de tenderinga . Cice . ten& epc̄ in dn̄io . p̄ . m̄ . 7 . vii.
hid̄ . 7 . t̄ . r . e . xviii . uiłł . m̄ . ix . sēp . v . bor . tc̄ . iii . car in dn̄io . m̄ . i . ac̄ it̄   ★
hōes . ix . car . m̄ . v . iiii . ac̄ . p̄ti . paſtura . cc . ouib; 7 . vi . an̄ . cl . ou 7 xvi . 7
xxx . porc̄ . Tc̄ uał . xviii . lib̄ . m̄ . xii.
↲Clachintuna sēp in epopatu fuit . p̄ m̄ . 7 . xx . hid̄ . Tc̄ . l . uiłł . m̄ . xlv.
Tc̄ . xx . bor . m̄ . l . Tc̄ . xiii . ſer . m̄ . vii . Tc̄ . iiii . car . in dn̄io . m̄ . iii . tc̄ . int̄
hōes . l . car . m̄ . xx . Silu . cccc . porc̄ . xx . ac̄ . p̄ti sēp . i . piſc̄ . m̄ . i . molin.
paſt . c . ou . 7 . i . runc̄ . 7 . vii . an̄ . 7 . xxx . por . 7 . xli . ou . Tc̄ . uał . xl . lib̄ . m̄
xxvi . De hoc eod̄ manerio . tenent . v . milites . iiii . hid̄ . 7 . vi . car̄ . 7
. ii . uiłł . 7 . xlv . bor . 7 . iii . ſer . hntes . iii . car̄ . 7 uał . viii . lib̄ . 7 . ii . ſoł . in eod̄
p̄tio . ↲ In Coleceſtra ħt epc̄ . xiiii . domos . 7 . iiii . ac̄ . n̄ reddentes conſuet.
p̄t Scotū : n epo In Ead̄ ten& hugo de epo . ii . hid̄ . 7 . i . ac̄ . 7 reddit 9ſuet . Sēp . ii . car̄
in dn̄io . 7 . i . car hom̄ . 7 . ii . uiłł . 7 . xi . bor . 7 . i . ſer . vi . ac̄ 7 . đ . p̄t . M . i . moł . Tc̄ 7 p̄ uał . xl . ſoł . m̄ . l.

Hundred of THURSTABLE

13 The Bishop holds in lordship WICKHAM (Bishops), which Bishop
William held before 1066 as a manor; 3 hides.
Then 7 villagers, now 5; then 1 smallholder, now 4.
Always 4 slaves; 2 ploughs in lordship. Then 4 men's
ploughs, now 2½.
Woodland, 30 pigs; meadow, 31 acres; always 1 mill.
6 cattle, 50 sheep, 10 pigs and 20 goats.
Value £6.
In the same (Wickham) 1 free man with 5 acres.   11 a
Value 12d.

Hundred of TENDRING

14 The Bishop holds in lordship ST.OSYTH as a manor; 7 hides.
Before 1066, 18 villagers, now 9; always 5 smallholders.
Then 3 ploughs in lordship, now ... Then among the men
9 ploughs, now 5.
Meadow, 4 acres; pasture for 200 sheep. 6 cattle, 150 sheep
and 16, and 30 pigs.
Value then £18; now [£] 12.

15 CLACTON was always in the (lands of the) Bishopric as a manor;
20 hides.
Then 50 villagers, now 45; then 20 smallholders, now 50;
then 13 slaves, now 7. Then 4 ploughs in lordship, now 3.
Then among the men 50 ploughs, now 20.
Woodland, 400 pigs; meadow, 20 acres; always 1 fishery;
now 1 mill; pasture, 100 sheep. 1 cob, 7 cattle, 30 pigs
and 41 sheep.
Value then £40; now [£] 26.
Of this same manor, 5 men-at-arms hold 4 hides. 6 ploughs.
2 villagers, 45 smallholders and 3 slaves who have 3 ploughs.
Value £8 2s in the same assessment.

In COLCHESTER

16 The Bishop has 14 houses and 4 acres which, apart from the levy,
pay customary dues only to the Bishop.
In the same (Colchester) Hugh holds from the Bishop 2 hides
and 1 acre and pays a customary due. Always 2 ploughs in
lordship; 1 men's plough;
2 villagers; 11 smallholders; 1 slave.
Meadow, 6½ acres; now 1 mill.
Value then and later 40s; now 50[s].

Hund de Ceffeorda. Wocheduna tenuit Aluric . t . r . e .

p . m . 7 . iii . hid . 7 . xl . ac . M ten& Hugo de epo . Tc . vi . uill . m . viii.

Tc . v . bor . m . xv . Tc . vi . fer . m . iiii . Sep . iii . car . in dnio . 7 . iiii . car

hom . Silu . b . por . xx . ac . pti . 7 . iiii . pulli . cxliiii . ou . xx . animal

Tc 7 p ual . iiii . lib . m . vi.

Toteham ten& Will fili brien de epo . qd tenuit Eduuolt p m.

7 . dim hid . 7 . xxx . ac . m . i . uill . Sep . vi . bor . 7 . ii . fer . 7 . i . car . in dnio.

Silu lx . por . iiii . ac pti . 7 . i . pifcator . past . xl . ou . 7 . i . falina . m . iiii.

an . 7 . iiii . por . lx . ou . Sep . ual . xxx . fot.

11 b

Toteham ten& Will balt de epo . qd tenuit . Aluric . p . m . 7 . dim hid

7 xxx . ac . m . iii . bor . sep . i . car . 7 . i . fal . 7 . ii . ac . pti . Silu . xxx . por . Sep.

ual . xxx . fot.

Elesforda tenuit Eduuold . p . m . 7 . ii . hid . træ . m Humfrid de epo.

sep . ii . uill . Tc . ii . bor . m . vi . tc . iii . fer . m . ii . tc . ii . car . in dnio m nulla.

Sep . i . car . hom . Tc ual . xl . fot . m . xx.

Tenderinge ten& Rog de epo . qd tenuit Aluuard p . i . hid . 7 . xlv . ac.

t . r . e . sep . v . bor . Tc . iiii . fer . m . iii . Sep . ii . car in dnio . 7 . iii . ac . pti . past.

. l . ouib; Tc . iii . runc . m . iiii . m . iii . an . Tc . vi . por . m . xvi . Tc xxxvi.

ou . m lxvi . Sep ual . xxx . fot.

Hundret de berdeftapla . Turrucca ten& Anfchetill de epo

q tenuit Vluuin lib ho fub rege . E . p . i . m . 7 . ii . hid . 7 . ii . ac . Sep . ii . car

in dnio . Tc . i . bor . m . vi . Tc . vi . fer . m . i . Silu . l . por . Past . l . ou . Tc . i . pifcin

Hundred of CHAFFORD

1   Aelfric held CRANHAM before 1066 as a manor; 3 hides and 40
acres. Now Hugh holds it from the Bishop.
>Then 6 villagers, now 8; then 5 smallholders, now 15; then 6
>slaves, now 4. Always 3 ploughs in lordship; 4 men's ploughs.
>Woodland, 500 pigs; meadow, 20 acres. 4 foals, 144 sheep,
>20 cattle.

Value then and later £4; now [£] 6.

[Hundred of THURSTABLE]

2   William son of Brian holds TOTHAM from the Bishop, which
Edwold held as a manor; ½ hide and 30 acres.
>Now 1 villager. Always 6 smallholders; 2 slaves; 1 plough
>in lordship.
>Woodland, 60 pigs; meadow, 4 acres; 1 fisherman; pasture, 40
>sheep; 1 salt-house. Now 4 cattle, 4 pigs, 60 sheep.

Value always 30s.

3   William Bold holds TOTHAM from the Bishop, which Aelfric held   11 b
as a manor; ½ hide and 30 acres.
>Now 3 smallholders. Always 1 plough.
>1 salt-house; meadow, 2 acres; woodland, 30 pigs.

Value always 30s.

[Hundred of TENDRING]

4   Edwold held ALRESFORD as a manor; 2 hides of land. Now
Humphrey (holds it) from the Bishop.
>Always 2 villagers. Then 2 smallholders, now 6; then 3 slaves,
>now 2. Then 2 ploughs in lordship, now none. Always 1
>men's plough.

Value then 40s; now 20[s].

5   Roger holds TENDRING from the Bishop, which Alfward held for 1
hide and 45 acres before 1066.
>Always 5 smallholders. Then 4 slaves, now 3. Always 2 ploughs
>in lordship.
>Meadow, 3 acres; pasture for 50 sheep. Then 3 cobs, now 4;
>now 3 cattle; then 6 pigs, now 16; then 36 sheep, now 66.

Value always 30s.

Hundred of BARSTABLE

6   Ansketel holds (Little) THURROCK from the Bishop which Wulfwin,
a free man, held under King Edward as 1 manor; 2 hides and
2 acres. Always 2 ploughs in lordship.
>Then 1 smallholder, now 6; then 6 slaves, now 1.
>Woodland, 50 pigs; pasture, 50 sheep; then 1 fishery,

m̄ . n̄ . Tc̄ . iiii . an̄ . m̄ . v . m̄ . ii . runc̄ 7 . ii . pulli . Tc̄ . xii . por . m̄ xvi . Tc̄
lxxx . ou . m̄ . cxx . 7 viii . Sep . ual . xxx . fol . 7 . iiii . đ.

⌐ Wellā tenent . Rađ . 7 Torold de epo qđ tenuit Idē Vluuin . t . r . e . p . m̄.
7 . p . i . hid . 7 . xxx . ac̄ . Sep . i . car̄ . Tc̄ . i . uilt . m̄ . n̄ . Sep . ii . bor . Silu . xl . por.
7 ual . xx . fol.

⌐ Burgheſtedā ten& Galt de epo . q tenuit . Goduin . t . r . e . p . m̄ . 7 p
. iii . hid . Sep . ii . car in dn̄io . 7 . i . car̄ hom̄ . 7 . ii . uilt . Tc̄ . i . bor . m̄ . vi . Tc̄
. iiii . fer . m̄ . i . Silu . lx . por . 7 aliæ . xxx . ac̄ . calūpniant de tepr̄ . r . e.
m̄ . ii . pulli . 7 . iiii . an̄ . Tc̄ . v . por . m̄ . xxiiii . Tc̄ . l . ou . m̄ lxxxviii.
7 . xliiii . cap . Tc̄ ual lx . fol . m̄ . l.

⌐ Currincham ten& Wilt . de epo qđ tenuit Sigar lib hō . p . i . m̄ . 7 . iiii.

12 a

hid . 7 . x . ac̄ . M . iii . hid . 7 . đ . 7 . x . ac̄ . dimidia hida ē inde ablata quā ten&
epc baioc̄ . Tc̄ . iii . car in dīo . M . ii . 7 dim̄ . Sep . iiii . car̄ . hom̄ . Tc̄ . iii . uilt . m̄ . ii.
Tc̄ . vii . bor . m̄ . xxv . Tc̄ . v . fer . m̄ . iii . Silu . ccc . por . Paſt . cccc . ou . Sep . i . mol.
Tc̄ . ii . runc̄ ; m̄ n̄ . Tc̄ . iii . an̄ . m̄ . vi . Tc̄ . viii . por . m̄ . x . Tc̄ . cccc . ou . m̄ . ꝺ.
7 xxi . cap . Tc̄ ual . vii . lib . m̄ . vii . 7 vi . fol.

⌐ Hornindunā ten& . Idē de epo . q ten Goduin lib hō . p . i . m̄ . 7 . i . hid
7 . dim̄ . Sep . i . car̄ . in dn̄io . 7 . iiii . bor . 7 . i . fer . Silu . x . por . viii pars . i . pifc̄.
Sep ual . xx . fol . De hoc manerio ablata ē dim̄ hid . q ten& epc baiocenfis.

⌐ Celde uuellā ten& Hugolin de epo . qđ ten Aluric teign reḡ . E . p . m̄.
7 . ii . hid . Sep . ii . car̄ . in dn̄io . 7 . i . car̄ 7 đ . hom̄ . Tc̄ . i . pbr̄ . 7 iii . bor . m̄ . i.
pbr̄ . 7 vii . bor . Sep . iiii . fer . paſt . c . ouib; . Tc̄ . i . pifc̄ . m̄ . n̄ . ii . runc̄ . x.
an̄ . lxxxi . ou . Tc̄ 7 p ual ; xl . fol . m̄ . xxx.

now none.
>Then 4 cattle, now 5; now 2 cobs and 2 foals; then 12 pigs, now 16; then 80 sheep, now 128.
Value always 30s 4d.

7 Ralph and Thorold hold WELL (Farm) from the Bishop, which Wulfwin also held before 1066 as a manor, for 1 hide and 30 acres. Always 1 plough.
>Then 1 villager, now none; always 2 smallholders.
>Woodland, 40 pigs.
Value 20s.

8 Walter holds (Little) BURSTEAD from the Bishop, which Godwin held before 1066 as a manor, for 3 hides. Always 2 ploughs in lordship; 1 men's plough.
>2 villagers. Then 1 smallholder, now 6; then 4 slaves, now 1.
>Woodland, 60 pigs; another 30 acres are claimed, from before 1066. Now 2 foals and 4 cattle; then 5 pigs, now 24; then 50 sheep, now 88; 44 goats.
Value then 60s; now 50[s].

9 William holds CORRINGHAM from the Bishop which Sigar, a free man, held as 1 manor; 4 hides and 10 acres. Now 3½ hides and 10 acres. ½ hide, which the Bishop of Bayeux holds, was taken from it. Then 3 ploughs in lordship, now 2½. Always 4 men's ploughs.
>Then 3 villagers, now 2; then 7 smallholders, now 25; then 5 slaves, now 3.
>Woodland, 300 pigs; pasture, 400 sheep; always 1 mill. Then 2 cobs, now none; then 3 cattle, now 6; then 8 pigs, now 10; then 400 sheep, now 500; 21 goats.
Value then £7; now [£] 7 6s.

12 a

10 He also holds HORNDON (-on-the-Hill) from the Bishop which Godwin, a free man, held as 1 manor; 1½ hides. Always 1 plough in lordship;
>4 smallholders; 1 slave.
>Woodland, 10 pigs; the eighth part of 1 fishery.
Value always 20s.
>From this manor, ½ hide has been taken away which the Bishop of Bayeux holds.

11 Hugolin holds CHADWELL from the Bishop which Aelfric, a thane of King Edward's, held as a manor; 2 hides.
Always 2 ploughs in lordship; 1½ men's ploughs.
>Then 1 priest and 3 smallholders, now 1 priest and 7 smallholders; always 4 slaves.
>Pasture for 100 sheep; then 1 fishery, now none. 2 cobs, 10 cattle, 81 sheep.
Value then and later 40s; now 30[s].

⟨ Ramefdanā ten& Wiłł de epo qđ tenuit Godric⁹ . ꝓ . ɪ . m̄ . 7 . ɪ . hid . 7 x.
ac . Sēp . ɪ . car in dn̄io . 7 . ɪɪɪɪ . bor . Silu⁷ . xxv . por; . vɪɪɪ . por . ʟ . ou . xɪɪ . caꝑ.
vał . xx . foł.

⟨ Leiendunā ten& Rađ de epo . qđ tenuit Vlmar⁹ . ꝓ . m̄ . 7 . dim . hid . t . r . e
Tc̄ . ɪ . fer . m̄ . n̄ . 7 uał . vɪ . foł.

⟨ Hund de Witham . Bracteđā ten& Hugolin⁹ de epo . q ten . Aluric⁹
lib hō . ꝓ . m̄ . 7 . ꝓ . ɪ . hid . Sēp . ɪɪ . car in dn̄io . Tc̄ . ɪɪ . car hom̄ . m̄ nulla .
Tc̄ . ɪɪɪɪ . uiłł . m̄ nułł . Tc̄ . ɪɪɪ . bor . m̄ . vɪɪɪ . 7 . ɪ . pbr . Tc̄ . ɪɪɪɪ . fer . m̄ . ɪɪ . Silu⁷
xʟ . por . ɪ . moł . ɪ . runc . ɪɪɪɪ . an . xɪɪɪ . por . cxxx . ou . Sēp . uał . ʟx . foł.

⟨ Hobruge . ten& . Rađ . fiłi brien . q tenuit Aluuin⁹ lib hō . ꝓ . ɪ . m̄ .
7 . dim hid; Sēp . ɪ . car in dn̄io . 7 . ɪ . car hom̄ . 7 . ɪ . uiłł . 7 . x . bor . Tc̄ . ɪɪ . fer
. m̄ nułł . Silu⁹ . c . por . xɪɪ . ac ꝑti . xvɪ . an . c . ou . xx . caꝑ . xɪɪɪɪ . porc⁷ .

⌐ 7 uał . xʟ . foł.

12 b

⟨ Dimidium Hund de herlaua . In Halinghebia ten⁷ Edeua . xxx . ac⁷ .
t . r . e . Sēp . dim . car⁷ . 7 . ɪɪ . ac ꝑti . 7 uał . v . foł.

⟨ Hund de Witbrictefherna . Vleham ten& hugo de epo qđ ten⁷
Goder lib hō . t . r . e . ꝓ . m̄ . 7 . ꝓ . ɪɪ . hid . 7 . xx . ac . Tc̄ . ɪɪɪ . uiłł . m̄ nułł . Tc̄
. ɪɪɪ . bor . m̄ . ɪ . Tc̄ . ɪɪɪɪ . fer . m̄ . ɪɪ . Sēp . ɪɪ . car in dn̄io . Tc̄ . ɪ . car hom̄ . m̄ nułł
paſt . xxx . ou . ɪɪɪ . runc . cxʟ . ou . Tc̄ 7 ꝑ uał . ʟx . foł . m̄ . xʟ.

⟨ Mildemet ten& Rađ fiłi brien de epo qđ tenuit Aluuin⁹ lib hō t . r . e
ꝓ . m̄ . 7 dim . hid . 7 . xɪɪɪɪ . ac . Tc̄ . ɪɪ . uiłł . m̄ . nułł . Sēp . ɪɪɪ . bor . Tc̄ . ɪ . fer . m̄ . ɪɪ.
Sēp . ɪ . car⁷ . Silu⁹ . xx . por . vɪɪɪ . ac ꝑti . vał . xx . foł.

12 William holds RAMSDEN (Belhus) from the Bishop, which Godric
held as 1 manor; 1 hide and 10 acres. Always 1 plough in lordship;
4 smallholders.
Woodland, 25 pigs. 8 pigs, 50 sheep, 12 goats.
Value 20s.

13 Ralph holds LAINDON from the Bishop, which Wulfmer held as a
manor; ½ hide before 1066.
Then 1 slave, now none.
Value 6s.

Hundred of WITHAM

14 Hugolin holds (Little) BRAXTED from the Bishop which Aelfric, a
free man, held as a manor, for 1 hide. Always 2 ploughs in
lordship. Then 2 men's ploughs; now none.
Then 4 villagers, now none; then 3 smallholders, now 8,
and 1 priest; then 4 slaves, now 2.
Woodland, 40 pigs; 1 mill. 1 cob, 4 cattle, 13 pigs, 130 sheep.
Value always 60s.

15 Ralph son of Brian holds HOWBRIDGE which Alwin, a free man,
held as 1 manor; ½ hide. Always 1 plough in lordship; 1 men's
plough;
1 villager; 10 smallholders. Then 2 slaves, now none.
Woodland, 100 pigs; meadow, 12 acres. 16 cattle, 100 sheep,
20 goats, 14 pigs.
Value 40s.

Half-Hundred of HARLOW   12 b
16 Edeva held 30 acres in HALLINGBURY before 1066. Always ½ plough.
Meadow, 2 acres.
Value 5s.

Hundred of 'WIBERTSHERNE'

17 Hugh holds ULEHAM ('s Farm) from the Bishop which Godhere, a
free man, held before 1066 as a manor, for 2 hides and 20 acres.
Then 3 villagers, now none; then 3 smallholders, now 1;
then 4 slaves, now 2. Always 2 ploughs in lordship. Then
1 men's plough, now none.
Pasture, 30 sheep. 3 cobs, 140 sheep.
Value then and later 60s; now 40[s].

18 Ralph son of Brian holds BASSETTS from the Bishop which Alwin,
a free man, held before 1066 as a manor; ½ hide and 14 acres.
Then 2 villagers, now none; always 3 smallholders. Then 1
slave, now 2. Always 1 plough.
Woodland, 20 pigs; meadow, 8 acres.
Value 20s.

⁝TERRA CANONICOꝝ S̃CI PAVLI IN EXSESSA.

Hund de bdeſtapla . Leam . tenuit Edeua . libē . t̕ . r̕ . e̕ . p̕ . m̕ . 7
dimĩ hid . 7 . xxx . ac̕ . Tc̃ . 11 . car̕ in dñio . 7 . 11 . car̕ hom̕ . m̃ nulla . Tc̃ . 11 . uilt̕
m̃ . vi . Tc̃ . vi . bor . m̃ . v . tc̃ . 11 . ſer̕ . m̃ . 111 . Silu̕ . xxv . por . Paſt̕ . c . ouib; 1 . an̕ .
. 1 . porc̕ . vii . ou̕ . Tc̃ . ual̕ . xl . ſol̕ . m̃ . xx . hec tr̃a calũpniata ē ad op̕ regiS .

⁝Hund de Waltham . Cinghefort tenuit Sc̃s paul̕ . t̕ . r̕ . e̕ . p̕ . 1 . m̕ .
7 .p . vi . hid̕ . Sep̕ . 11 . car̕ in dñio . Tc̃ . 111 . car̕ hom̕ . m̃ . 1111 . Tc̃ . vii . uilt̕ .
m̃ . viii . Tc̃ . 111 . bor m̃ . vi . ſep̕ . 1111 . ſer̕ . Silu̕ . ᴅ . por . l . ac̕ . p̃ti . 7 . 11 . piſc̕ .
. ix . an̕ . 11 . runc̕ . xxvii . por . c . ou̕ . Tc̃ ual̕ . 1111 . lib̕ . m̃ . c . ſol̕ . De hoc ma
nerio abſtulit petr̕ de ualonijs . 1 . hid̕ . 7 . viii . ac̕ . p̃ti . que p̃tinebant
manerio . t̕ . r̕ . e̕ . 7 ſiluā ad . l . por . Val̕ . x . ſol̕ . De eod̕ manerio tulit
Goisfrid de magna uilla . x . ac̕ . p̃ti .

⁝Hund de hidingaſorda . Belcham ten̕ . Sc̃s paul̕ . t̕ . r̕ . e̕ . p̕ . m̕ . 7 . v . hid .

Sep̕ . 11 . car̕ in dñio . 7 . xii . car̕ hom̕ . xxiiii . uilt̕ . x . bor . v . ſer̕ . Silu̕ . lx . po̕
xxx . ac̕ . p̃ti . ix . an̕ . 11 . runc̕ . xl . por . c . ou̕ . v . cap̕ . Sep̕ . ual̕ . xvi . lib̕ .
⁝Wicham . ten̕ . S . P . t̕ . r̕ . e̕ . p̕ . m̕ . 7 . 111 . hid . 1 . uirḡ min̕ . Tc̃ . 1 . car̕ i dïo
m̃ . 11 . Tc̃ . 1111 . car̕ hom̕ . m̃ . 111 . Tc̃ . vi . uilt̕ . m̃ . v . Tc̃ . 1111 . bor . m̃ . x . Tc̃ . 1 .
ſer̕ . m̃ . 111 . Silu̕ . cc . porc̕ . x . ac̕ . p̃ti . 11 . runc̕ . 1111 . an̕ . xxiii . por . l . ou̕ .
xxiiii . cap̕ . 11 . uaſa apũ . Tc̃ ual̕ . xl . ſol̕ . m̃ . 1111 . lib̕ .

LAND OF THE CANONS OF ST. PAUL'S IN ESSEX

Hundred of BARSTABLE

1 Edeva held LEE (Chapel) freely before 1066 as a manor; ½ hide and 30 acres. Then 2 ploughs in lordship and 2 men's ploughs, now none.

> Then 2 villagers, now 6; then 6 smallholders, now 5; then 2 slaves, now 3.
> Woodland, 25 pigs; pasture for 100 sheep. 1 (head of) cattle, 1 pig, 7 sheep.
> Value then 40s; now 20[s].
> This land was claimed for the King's use.

Hundred of WALTHAM

2 St. Paul's held CHINGFORD before 1066 as 1 manor, for 6 hides. Always 2 ploughs in lordship. Then 3 men's ploughs, now 4.

> Then 7 villagers, now 8; then 3 smallholders, now 6; always 4 slaves.
> Woodland, 500 pigs; meadow, 50 acres; 2 fisheries. 9 cattle, 2 cobs, 27 pigs, 100 sheep.
> Value then £4; now 100s.
> From this manor, Peter of Valognes took away 1 hide and 8 acres of meadow which belonged to the manor before 1066, and woodland for 50 pigs. Value 10s.
> From the same manor, Geoffrey de Mandeville took 10 acres of meadow.

Hundred of HINCKFORD

3 St. Paul's held BELCHAMP (St. Paul's) before 1066 as a manor; 5 hides. Always 2 ploughs in lordship; 12 men's ploughs; 13 a
> 24 villagers; 10 smallholders; 5 slaves.
> Woodland, 60 pigs; meadow, 30 acres. 9 cattle, 2 cobs, 40 pigs, 100 sheep, 5 goats.
> Value always £16.

4 St. Paul's held WICKHAM (St. Paul's) before 1066 as a manor; 3 hides less 1 virgate. Then 1 plough in lordship, now 2. Then 4 men's ploughs, now 3.

> Then 6 villagers, now 5; then 4 smallholders, now 10; then 1 slave, now 3.
> Woodland, 200 pigs; meadow, 10 acres. 2 cobs, 4 cattle, 23 pigs, 50 sheep, 24 goats, 2 beehives.
> Value then 40s; now £4.

Hund de Witbricteſherna Tillingham teñ.S.P. p̄ m̄.7 xx.hid.
7.vi.ac̄.Sēp.xx.uiłł.7.viii.bor 7.iiii.ſer.Tc̄.iii.car̄.in dñio.m̄.iiii.
Sēp.x.car̄.hom̄.Paſt.cccc.ou.m̄.i.mol.7.i.piſc̄.xv.añ.xxx.por.
cccxl.ou.Pt̄ hanc tr̄a datæ fuer̄ eccłæ.x.ac̄.quæ jacent huic man.
Tc̄ totū uał.x.liƀ m̄.xv.

Hund de Angra Nortunã tenuit Godid.quedã femina.t.r.e
p.dim̄.hid.m̄.S.P.Sēp.ı.car̄.7.ıı.bor.Siłu.xl.por.iiii.ac̄.p̄ti.ı.r.v.añ.
uał.xx.ſoł.Hanc tr̄a dedit Godid ſc̄o paulo p̄q rex uenit in anglĩa
ſ; non oſteñdt̄ breuē neq̃ conceſſum regis.

Naſeſtocã tenuer̄.ıı.liƀi hōes.Houard.7 Vlſi.p.ıı.mañ.7 p.v.hid
.xx.ac̄.min̄.m̄.ħt ſc̄s pauł p totidē꞉ p̄q rex uenit in hanc tr̄a.7
dict̄ ſe habuiſſe ex dono reḡ.Sēp.xii.uiłł.7.xi.bor Tc̄.iiii.ſer̄.m̄.ıı.
ſēp.iiii.car̄ in dñio.7.iiii.car̄ hom̄.Siłu.ɒc.por.xliiii.ac̄.p̄ti.Sēp
xiii.añ.ıı.runc̄.cxvi.ou.xxiiii.por.xxiiii.cap̄.iiii.uaſa apum.
Sēp.uał.x.liƀ.

Aliam neſſetocham.tenuit Turſtiñ ruſſ p.m̄.7.p.ı.hid.7.xl.ac̄.
m̄ ſc̄s pauł inuaſit.7.ē cū alia tr̄a.7 teñ& p tantundē.Tc̄.ı.boi.
m̄.ıı.Sēp.ıı.car̄ Siłu.c.por.Sēp.uał.xxx.ſoł.In ead uiłł

13 b

tenuerunt.vıı.liƀi hōes.ıı.hid.q̃s teñ& Sc̄s pauł ſimilit̄.7.m̄ in iſta
tr̄a.xii.hōes.M.ııı.bor.Sēp.iiii.car̄.Siłu.ccx.por.vıı.ac̄.p̄ti.Sēp uał
xl.ſoł.In Naſſeſtoca teñ&.ı.p̄br̄.dim̄.hid.7.xx.ac̄.ſ; hund fert
teſtimoniū qd ē ſc̄i pauli.Sēp.ıı.bor.Tc̄.ı.car̄.m̄.dim̄.Sēp uał.x.ſoł.
m̄ ē in manu reḡ

13 a, b

Hundred of 'WIBERTSHERNE'

5 St. Paul's holds TILLINGHAM as a manor; 20 hides and 6 acres.
Always 20 villagers; 8 smallholders; 4 slaves. Then 3 ploughs
in lordship, now 4. Always 10 men's ploughs.
Pasture, 400 sheep; now 1 mill; 1 fishery. 15 cattle, 30 pigs,
340 sheep.
Apart from this land, 10 acres which lie in (the lands of) this
manor were given to the Church.
Total value then £10; now [£] 15.

Hundred of ONGAR

6 Godith, a woman, held NORTON (Mandeville) before 1066, for ½
hide. Now St. Paul's (holds it). Always 1 plough;
2 smallholders.
Woodland, 40 pigs; meadow, 4 acres. 1 cob, 5 cattle.
Value 20s.
Godith gave this land to St. Paul's after the King came to
England; but (St. Paul's) shows neither a writ nor the King's assent.

7 2 free men, Howard and Wulfsi, held NAVESTOCK as 2 manors, for
5 hides less 20 acres. Now St. Paul's has it for as much, after the
King came to this land. They state they had it by the King's gift.
Always 12 villagers; 11 smallholders. Then 4 slaves, now 2.
Always 4 ploughs in lordship; 4 men's ploughs.
Woodland, 600 pigs; meadow, 44 acres. Always 13 cattle,
2 cobs, 116 sheep, 24 pigs, 24 goats, 4 beehives.
Value always £10.

8 Thurstan the Red held the other NAVESTOCK as a manor, for 1
hide and 40 acres. Now St. Paul's has annexed it and it is with
the other land and it holds it for as much.
Then 1 smallholder, now 2. Always 2 ploughs.
Woodland, 100 pigs.
Value always 30s.
In the same village 7 free men held 2 hides, which St. Paul's   13 b
holds likewise.
Now in this land 12 men; now 3 smallholders. Always 4 ploughs.
Woodland, 210 pigs; meadow, 7 acres.
Value always 40s.
In Navestock 1 priest holds ½ hide and 20 acres; but the
Hundred bears witness that it is of St. Paul's.
Always 2 smallholders. Then 1 plough, now ½.
Value always 10s.
Now it is in the King's hand.

╓Hund de . Celmeresforda . Runewellā ten& sēp . sēs paul⁹ . ꝑ.
. viii . hid . Sēp . viii . uiłł ꞉ 7 . viii . bor . Tē . ii . fer . ḿ . i . Tē . iii . car 7 . dim
in dñio꞉ 7 ḿ fimiliꞇ . Tē . inꞇ hões . ii . car . 7 . dim . Silu . cc . por . ii . runc.
. i . an . viii . por . c . ou . Sēp uał . viii . liḃ.

╓Hund de Tureſtapla . Tidwolditunā ten& sēp . sēs . P . ꝑ
viii . hid . 7 . ꝑ . i . man . f; Rad baignard ten& dimid . hid 7 hundret
nefcit q̇m̄ eā habuerit ; Sēp . xvi . uiłł . 7 . iiii . bor . 7 . iiii . fer . Tē . ii . ca
in dñio . ḿ . i . 7 . đ . Tē . viii . car hom . ḿ . iii . Silu . lx . por . xxx . ac ꝑti.
paſt . clx . ou . sēp . i . moł . 7 . i . fał . i . runc . viii . an . xii . por . cl . ou . iii.
uafa apū . Sēp . uał . viii . liḃ.

╓Hund de tendringa . Ǣlduluefnasā ten& sēp sēs paul⁹ . ꝑ . man
7 . ꝑ xxvii . hid . Tē lxxxvi . uiłł . ḿ lxiii . Tē . xl . bor . ḿ . l . Sēp . vi . ⁻fer. 7
vi . car in dñio . Tē inꞇ hões . lx . car . ḿ . xxx . Silu . ccc . por . ix . ac
ꝑti . ḿ . ii . moł Tē . iii . fał . ḿ . ii . Paſt . ccc . ou . xxii . an . xxx . porc.
. cc . ou . iiii . uafa apū . Tē uał . xxvi . liḃ . ḿ . xxx . 7 . i . marc argenti.

╓Hund de Rochefort . Berlingā ten& sēp . Sēs paul⁹ . ꝑ . i . man . 7 . ꝑ
. ii . hid . 7 . diṁ . xv . ac min . Tē . ii . uiłł . ḿ . n̄ . Tē . v . bor . ḿ . ix . Sēp . i.
fer . 7 . i . car in dñio . 7 . ii . car hom . Paſt . xl . ou . ii . runc . ii . an . iiii.
por . clx . ou . Tē uał . iiii . liḃ . 7 . x . foł . ḿ . vi . liḃ . In Ead tenuit . i . liḃ hō

14 a
diṁ hid . 7 . x . ac . t . r . e . ḿ sēs . P . Sēp . i . car . 7 uał . xx . foł . hanc tr̄a occu
pauer̄ canonici p̄q rex uenit in angliā ;

Hundred of CHELMSFORD

9 St. Paul's has always held RUNWELL for 8 hides.
Always 8 villagers; 8 smallholders. Then 2 slaves, now 1.
Then 3½ ploughs in lordship, now the same. Then among the men 2½ ploughs.
Woodland, 200 pigs. 2 cobs, 1 (head of) cattle, 8 pigs, 100 sheep.
Value always £8.

Hundred of THURSTABLE

10 St. Paul's has always held HEYBRIDGE for 8 hides, as 1 manor; but Ralph Baynard holds ½ hide and the Hundred does not know how he should have it.
Always 16 villagers; 4 smallholders; 4 slaves. Then 2 ploughs in lordship, now 1½. Then 8 men's ploughs, now 3.
Woodland, 60 pigs; meadow, 30 acres; pasture, 160 sheep; always 1 mill; 1 salt-house. 1 cob, 8 cattle, 12 pigs, 150 sheep, 3 beehives.
Value always £8.

Hundred of TENDRING

11 St. Paul's has always held THE NAZE as a manor, for 27 hides.
Then 86 villagers, now 63; then 40 smallholders, now 50.
Always 6 slaves; 6 ploughs in lordship. Then among the men 60 ploughs, now 30.
Woodland, 300 pigs; meadow, 9 acres; now 2 mills; then 3 salt-houses, now 2; pasture, 300 sheep. 22 cattle, 30 pigs, 200 sheep, 4 beehives.
Value then £26; now [£] 30 and 1 mark of silver.

Hundred of ROCHFORD

12 St. Paul's has always held BARLING as 1 manor, for 2½ hides less 15 acres.
Then 2 villagers, now none; then 5 smallholders, now 9.
Always 1 slave; 1 plough in lordship; 2 men's ploughs.
Pasture, 40 sheep. 2 cobs, 2 cattle, 4 pigs, 160 sheep.
Value then £4 10s; now £6.
In the same (Barling) 1 free man held ½ hide and 10 acres   14 a
before 1066. Now St. Paul's (holds it). Always 1 plough.
Value 20s.
The Canons appropriated this land after the King came to England.

ᛏ Terra sči petri de Weſtmonaſterio . Hund de bdeſtapla .

In Benflet ħt Sčs Petrus. vii . hiđ . 7 . xxx . ač . que jacebant in eccła ſčæ
mariæ t . r̄ . e . ſ; rex . W . dedit eccłam cū t̄ra ſčo petro . de Weſtmonaſterio
jn q̄ t̄ra ſt . ii . car̄ . in dñio . 7 . v . car̄ hom ; ſep . xv . uiłt . Tč . vii . bor̄ . m̄
xii . Paſtur . cc . ou . m̄ . dim . mot . Tč uał . iiii . lib̄ . m̄ . vi . Octauā hiđ de
ead eccła ſčæ mariæ . dedit Ingelric ſčo martino . 7 adhuc ibi ē ut conſu
lat̄ teſtat̄ ſine juſſu regis . ᛁ In Phantuna . iiii . hiđ . 7 xxx . ač . Sep . i .
car̄ in dñio . Tč . iiii . car̄ hom . M̄ . i . Tč . vi . uiłt . m̄ . i . tč . iiii . ſer̄ . Tč . i . bor̄
m̄ . ix . 7 in ead uiłt poſt adhuc fieri . ii . car̄ in dñio ; xxx . ač ſilue uaſtæ .
. ii . runč . xxx . ou . Tč uał . lx . ſot . m̄ . vi . lib̄ . ᛁ In Bura ħt . S . P . l . ač . q̄s
ten& . i . anglic de eo . ſep . i . uiłt . 7 . uał . l . đ .

ᛁ Phantunā tenuit Aleſtan ſtric . t . r̄ . e . p . m̄ . 7 . i . hiđ . Tč . i . car̄ . m̄ . ñ .
Sep . i . bor̄ . Tč . 7 p̄ uał . xx . ſot . m̄ . x . hec t̄ra calūpniata ē ad op̄ reg
qd p falsū breuē uenerit ad eccłam . In dñio . ii . runč . xxx . ou ;

ᛁ Hund de Witham . In Chelleuedana . t . r̄ . e . v . hiđ . q̄s ten&
ſčs pet̄ . Sep . ii . car̄ . in dñio . Tč . viii . car̄ . hom . m̄ . iiii . Tč . xx . uiłt
m̄ . xviii . Tč . iii . bor̄ . m̄ . vii . Sep . iii . ſer̄ . Silu . l . porč . 7 . xxv . ač p̄ti .
. i . mot . Tč . uał . c . ſot . m̄ . viii . lib̄ . 7 abbas ħt inde . xii . lib̄ ; In dñio ꝛ
. ii . runč . vi . an̄ . xxxv . por . xxxv . ou .

LAND OF ST. PETER'S, WESTMINSTER

Hundred of BARSTABLE

1 In (South) BENFLEET, St. Peter's has 7 hides and 30 acres, which
  lay in (the lands of) St. Mary's Church before 1066; but King
  William gave the church with the land to St. Peter's, Westminster,
  on which land there are 2 ploughs in lordship and 5 men's ploughs.
    Always 15 villagers. Then 7 smallholders, now 12.
    Pasture, 200 sheep; now ½ mill. 50 sheep, 3 pigs.
  Value then £4; now [£] 6.
    Engelric gave the eighth hide of the same Church of St. Mary
  to St. Martin's, and it is still there, as the County testifies,
  without the King's command.

2 In FANTON (Hall), 4 hides and 30 acres. Always 1 plough in
  lordship. Then 4 men's ploughs, now 1.
    Then 6 villagers, now 1; then 4 slaves; then 1 smallholder, now 9.
    In the same village, 2 ploughs in lordship still possible.
    30 acres of waste woodland. 2 cobs, 30 sheep.
  Value then 60s; now £6.

3 In BOWERS (Gifford) St. Peter's has 50 acres, which 1 Englishman
  holds from it.
    Always 1 villager.
  Value 50d.

4 Alstan Stric held FANTON (Hall) before 1066 as a manor; 1 hide.
  Then 1 plough, now none.
    Always 1 smallholder.
  Value then and later 20s; now 10[s].
    This land was claimed for the King's use because it had come
  to the Church by a false writ.
    In lordship 2 cobs, 30 sheep.

Hundred of WITHAM

5 In KELVEDON before 1066, 5 hides, which St. Peter's holds.
  Always 2 ploughs in lordship. Then 8 men's ploughs, now 4.
    Then 20 villagers, now 18; then 3 smallholders, now 7;
      always 3 slaves.
    Woodland, 50 pigs; meadow, 25 acres; 1 mill.
  Value then 100s; now £8. The Abbot has from it £12.
    In lordship 2 cobs, 6 cattle, 35 pigs, 35 sheep.

⊬Hund de Beuentreu. Hame.tenuit Sĉs Petr .t .ŕ .é .p̣ .m̂.

7 .ıı .hid .Sẽp .ı .caŕ .Tĉ .ııı .bor .m̂ .v .Silu .vııı .por .Tĉ ual .xx .fol .M̂
lx . ⌐ In Leituna ten& . Rađ baignard.de abb̃e .ı .hid .qua tenuit
Tofti .t .ŕ .é .Tĉ .ı .caŕ .m̂ .dim̂ .m̂ .v .bor .xx .aĉ p̃ti .ı .mol .Tĉ .ual .
xxx .fol .m̂ .xl.

⊬Hund de Lexendena. Pheringas.tenuit Ḥarold .t .ŕ .é .p̣.

.ıııı .hid .7 .xxx .aĉ .M̂ ten& .Ṣ .Ṗ. Tĉ .xxxıııı .uilt .m̂ .xxvıı.
Tĉ .x .bor .m̂ .xxıııı .Sẽp .xı .fer .7 .ıııı .caŕ .in dñio .Tĉ .xv .carŕ.
hom̂ .m̂ .x .Silu .ᴆ .porĉ .xx .aĉ p̃ti .ııı .mol .7 xıı .fochemani
q̃ n̄ pofant recede manentes in duab₂ hid .7 .dim̂ .p̃t ifta fup̃dic̃ta
trã .Sẽp fub ipfis .vı .bor .7 .ıı .caŕ .7 .dim̂ .Silu .xx .por .xıı .aĉ p̃ti.
7 .ıı .dom̂ in cole caftro .que jacent huic manerio; Iɲ dñio .v .runĉ.
xvı .aɲ .lx .por .lxxxıııı .ou .Tĉ ual .xxıı .liƀ .7 .x .fol .M̂ , xxxıııı.
liƀ .7 .x .fol. Roḡ de ramis ten& lxxxv aĉ .de abb̃e .7 reɗdit uno
q̃q; anno .p fuo feruitio ad abb̃m꞉ .x .fol. Malger hõ archiep̃i inuafit
fup regẽ .ı .liƀm hõem q̃ erat de manerio fĉi petri .t .ŕ .é .tenentem
dimiđ uirḡ .7 nĉ ĉ in manu reḡ ; Sẽp .dim̂ .caŕ .7 .ual .v .fol.

⊬Hund de Angra. Keluendunã tenuit Ailriĉ .t .ŕ .é .p̣ .m̂.

7 .ıı .hiđ .m̂ .Ṣ .Ṗ .Sẽp .ı .uilt .Tĉ .v .bor .m̂ .x .Sẽp .ıı .fer .7 .ıı .caŕ i dñio.
7 .ı .caŕ .hom̂ .Silu .cc .por .xvı .aĉ .p̃ti .m̂ .ı .mol .Tĉ .ual .xl .fol,
m̂ .lx. Hic fup̃dic̃t Ailriĉ abiit in nauale p̃liũ cont Willm regẽ
7 qn̄ rediit cecidit in infirmitate .tĉ dedit sĉo petro iftud maneriũ
fed nulli hominũ ex comitatu fcit hoc n̄ uɲ .7 huc ufq₂ tenuit
sĉs p̃etŕ tali m̂ in hoc mañ .7 neq₂ breuẽ neq; famulũ reḡ ex parte

ħabuerunt poftquã rex uenit in iftã trã.

Hundred of BECONTREE

6   St. Peter's held (East) HAM before 1066 as a manor; 2 hides.
   Always 1 plough.
       Then 3 smallholders, now 5.
       Woodland, 8 pigs.
   Value then 20s; now 60[s].

7   In LEYTON Ralph Baynard holds from the Abbot 1 hide, which
   Tosti held before 1066. Then 1 plough, now ½.
       Now 5 smallholders.
       Meadow, 20 acres; 1 mill.
   Value then 30s; now 40[s].

Hundred of LEXDEN

8   Harold held FEERING before 1066, for 4 hides and 30 acres.
   Now St. Peter's holds (it).
       Then 34 villagers, now 27; then 10 smallholders, now 24.
           Always 11 slaves; 4 ploughs in lordship. Then 15 men's
           ploughs, now 10.
       Woodland, 500 pigs; meadow, 20 acres; 3 mills.
       12 Freemen who could not withdraw (and) who live on 2½
   hides apart from the above-mentioned land. Under these, always
   6 smallholders; 2½ ploughs.
       Woodland, 20 pigs; meadow, 12 acres; 2 houses in Colchester
           which lie in (the lands of) this manor.
       In lordship 5 cobs, 16 cattle, 60 pigs, 84 sheep.
   Value then £22 10s; now £34 10s.
       Roger of Raismes holds 85 acres from the Abbot and pays 10s
   every year for his service to the Abbot. Mauger, a man of the
   Archbishop, annexed 1 free man in the King's despite, who was
   of the manor of St. Peter's before 1066 (and) who held ½ virgate.
   Now he is in the King's hand. Always ½ plough.
   Value 5s.

Hundred of ONGAR

9   Alric held KELVEDON (Hatch) before 1066 as a manor; 2 hides.
   Now St. Peter's (holds it).
       Always 1 villager. Then 5 smallholders, now 10.
           Always 2 slaves; 2 ploughs in lordship; 1 men's plough.
       Woodland, 200 pigs; meadow, 16 acres; now 1 mill.
   Value then 40s; now 60[s].
       This above-mentioned Alric went away to a naval battle against
   King William and when he returned he fell ill; then he gave this
   manor to St. Peter's but only one man from the County knows
   this. St. Peter's has held this manor in this way up to now and
   they have had neither a writ nor a servant of the King on (his)
   behalf after the King came to this land.   15 a

⌐ In Wochenduna ten& Will camerari de abbe.ı.hid.7.ı.car.in dnio.
7.ı.car hom.ıııı.uill.val.xl.fol.

⌐ Hund de Ceffeorda Wochenduna ten Harold.p.m.7.ıı.hid.
xl.ac.min.t.r.e.m ten& S.P.Tc.vıı.uill.m.vıı.Tc.v.bor.m.vııı.
Sep.ıııı.fer.7.ıı.car.in dnio.Tc.vı.car.hom.m.ıııı.Silu.ccc.por.
.ı.runc.vı.an.xxx.por.cx.ou.Tc ual.ıııı.lib.m.x. hec tra eft
p efcangio pq rex transfretauit.

⌐ Wemtuna ten& .sep.S.P.p.m.7.ıı.hid.7.dim.Tc.ııı.uill.m.ıı.
Tc.ııı.bor.m.ı.Tc.ıı.fer.m.null.Tc.ı.car in dnio.m.dim.Tc.ı.
car.hom.m.dim.ı.runc.ı.uac.ıııı.por.lx.ou.Tc ual.xl.fol.m
lx.Vn lib ho mifit in sco petro.dim.hid.f; Rob inuefiat ho Rob
grenonis.pocupauit.7 reddit p annu.xx.d.

⌐ Geddefduna ten.S.P.p.ı.hid.Sep.ı.uill.7.ı.bor.Tc.dim.car.m
.ı.Sep.ual.xx.fol.

⌐ Hund de Celmeresfort. Molefham ten& Sep scs Petr.
p.v.hid.xxx.ac.min.Tc.vııı.uill.m.ııı.Tc.ıııı.bor.m.xxı.
M.ıı.fer.Sep.ııı.car.in dnio.7.ıııı.car.hom.Silu.cccc.por.
xxx.ac.pti.ı.mol.ı.runc.ıı.uac.xxxvı.por.c.ou.Tc ual
.ıx.lib.m.xıı.

⌐ Hund de Rochefort. Pachefham ten& scs P.p.m.7.p
.ı.hid.7.dim.Tc.ıı.bor.m.xı.Tc.ıııı.fer.Tc.ıı.car in dnio.m.ı.
Sep.ı.car hom.paft.xx.ou.ı.runc.ıııı.an.c.ou.Tc ual.
.ıııı.lib m.vı. Hanc tra dedit.ı.teign.ecclæ.qn iuit ad bellu i Eurewic·⌐
                                        ⌐ cu haroldo.

15 a

[Hundred of CHAFFORD]

10 In (North) OCKENDON, William the Chamberlain holds 1 hide from the Abbot. 1 plough in lordship. 1 men's plough.
    4 villagers.
    Value 40s.

Hundred of CHAFFORD

11 Harold held (North) OCKENDON as a manor; 2 hides less 40 acres before 1066. Now St. Peter's holds (it).
    Then 8 villagers, now 7; then 5 smallholders, now 8.
    Always 4 slaves; 2 ploughs in lordship. Then 6 men's ploughs, now 4.
    Woodland, 300 pigs. 1 cob, 6 cattle, 30 pigs, 110 sheep.
    Value then £4; now [£] 10.
    This land was (acquired) by exchange after the King crossed the sea.

12 St. Peter's has always held WENNINGTON as a manor; 2½ hides.
    Then 3 villagers, now 2; then 3 smallholders, now 1; then 2 slaves, now none. Then 1 plough in lordship, now ½.
    Then 1 men's plough, now ½.
    1 cob, 1 cow, 4 pigs, 60 sheep.
    Value then 40s; now 60[s].
    A free man disposed of ½ hide to St. Peter's, but Robert the Perverted, a man of Robert Gernon's, misappropriated (it) and pays 20d a year.

13 St. Peter's holds GEDDESDUNA for 1 hide.
    Always 1 villager; 1 smallholder. Then ½ plough, now 1.
    Value always 20s.

Hundred of CHELMSFORD

14 St. Peter's has always held MOULSHAM (Lodge) for 5 hides less 30 acres.
    Then 8 villagers, now 3; then 4 smallholders, now 21; now 2 slaves. Always 3 ploughs in lordship; 4 men's ploughs.
    Woodland, 400 pigs; meadow, 30 acres; 1 mill. 1 cob, 2 cows, 36 pigs, 100 sheep.
    Value then £9; now [£] 12.

Hundred of ROCHFORD

15 St. Peter's holds PAGLESHAM as a manor, for 1½ hides.
    Then 2 smallholders, now 11; then 4 slaves. Then 2 ploughs in lordship, now 1. Always 1 men's plough.
    Pasture, 20 sheep. 1 cob, 4 cattle, 100 sheep.
    Value then £4; now [£] 6.
    1 thane gave this land to the Church when he went to battle in York(shire) with Harold.

.VII. TERRÆ EPI DVNeLmenSiS In EXSESSA.

Dimidium Hundret de Walthā. Walham tenuit Harold t.r.e.

pro uno Man.7.XL.hid.Sep.LXXX.uill.7.XXIIII.bor.Tc.VI.fer.m̄ VII.

Tc.VII.car in dnio.m̄.VI.Sep.XXXVII.car hom.Silu.II.7 cc.por.

LXXX.ac.pti.II.runc.XX.an.LXXX.ou.XII.cap.XL.por. Paſtura

ē ibi que ual.XVIII.ſol.Tc.I.mol.m̄.III. v.piſcinæ.7 tc.XX.cenſarij.

m̄.XXXVI.7.I.car poſ in manerio.reſtaurari.Huic Man adjacent.

.II.ſoc.tenentes.VI.hid.t.r.e.m̄.v.7 medietatē ſextæ hid hr Sca crux.

7 altam partē tulit Will de War.7.IIII.ſoc de.II.hid.7 dim uirg.

7.adhuc ptinebat.huic man.I.hid.XV.ac.min q̄m inde tulit

idē Will. Et Ranulf fr ilgeri.XXX.ac.træ.7.IIII.pti.

Oms illi ſoc q̄ ibi m̄ sē hnt.VII.hid.7.XV.ac.7 habebant.t.r.e.in

eoʒ dnio.IIII.car.m̄.IIII.7.đ.7 ſep.I.uill.Tc.VI.bor.m̄.VIII.Tc.II.

fer.m̄ null.Silu.CLXXX.por.XVI.ac.7.dim.pti.7.IIII.ac.paſturæ.

De hoc toto.7 de manerio habebat Har.t.r.e.XXXVI.lib.7 hoes epi

apptiant.LXIII.lib.7.v.ſol.7.IIII.đ.M u ut alij hoes de hund teſtant.

ual.c.lib.7 Londoniæ.sē.XII.dom ptinentes Manerio.quæ reddt

XX.ſol.7 una.porta q̄m rex dedit ſuo antecessori epi.que &ia reddt

XX.ſol.

.VIII. TERRÆ Canonicoʒ sce Crucis de Waltham Hundret de

Walthā. Epingam.ten& sep.sca crux.p.m̄.7.II.hid.7.XV.ac; Sep

.I.car 7.dim in dnio.7.II.bor.7.II.fer.Silu.L.por.III.ac.pti.X.an.

.I.runc.XX.por.XX.ou.VIII.cap.7 ual.XV.ſol.

Naſingā sep ten& Sca crux.p.v.hid.Tc.I.car in dnio.m̄.I.7 dim.Tc.I.

car hom.m̄.I.7.đ.Sep.v.uill.m̄.II.bor.Tc.II.fer.m̄ null.Silu.L.por.

.XIII.ac.pti.dim piſc.I.r.IIII.an.X.por.Tc.ual.XL.ſol.m̄ LX.

7   LANDS OF THE BISHOP OF DURHAM IN ESSEX

Half-Hundred of WALTHAM

1   Harold held WALTHAM (Holy Cross) before 1066 as one manor; 40 hides.

Always 80 villagers; 24 smallholders. Then 6 slaves, now 7.
Then 7 ploughs in lordship, now 6. Always 37 men's ploughs.
Woodland, 202 pigs; meadow, 80 acres. 2 cobs, 20 cattle, 80 sheep, 12 goats, 40 pigs. Pasture is there which is worth 18s; then 1 mill, now 3; 5 fisheries; then 20 tributaries, now 36; 1 plough can be restored in the manor.

To this manor belong 2 Freemen who held 6 hides before 1066, now 5. Holy Cross has half of the sixth hide. William of Warenne took the other part. 4 Freemen with 2 hides and ½ virgate.
1 hide less 15 acres still belongs to this manor, which the same William took from it. Ranulf brother of Ilger (holds) 30 acres of land and 4 (acres) of pasture.

All the Freemen who are there now have 7 hides and 15 acres. Before 1066 they had in their lordship 4 ploughs; now 4½.

Always 1 villager. Then 6 smallholders, now 8; then 2 slaves, now none.

Woodland, 182 pigs; meadow, 16½ acres; pasture, 4 acres.
From the whole of this and from the manor, Harold had £36 before 1066. The Bishop's men are assessed at £63 5s 4d. But now, as the other men of the Hundred testify, value £100.

In London there are 12 houses which belong to the manor (and) which pay 20s, and a gate which the King gave to the Bishop's predecessor and which also pays 20s.

8   LANDS OF THE CANONS OF WALTHAM HOLY CROSS

Hundred of WALTHAM

1   Holy Cross has always held EPPING as a manor; 2 hides and 15 acres. Always 1½ ploughs in lordship;

2 smallholders; 2 slaves.
Woodland, 50 pigs; meadow, 3 acres. 10 cattle, 1 cob, 20 pigs,
20 sheep, 8 goats.
Value 15s.

2   Holy Cross has always held NAZEING for 5 hides. Then 1 plough in lordship, now 1½. Then 1 men's plough, now 1½.

Always 5 villagers. Now 2 smallholders; then 2 slaves, now none.
Woodland, 50 pigs; meadow, 13 acres; ½ fishery. 1 cob, 4 cattle, 10 pigs, 15 sheep.
Value then 40s; now 60[s].

⌐ Hundret de beuentreu . Wdefort ten& sēp sēa crux . t . r . e.
.v.hid . Sēp . ɪɪ . car . in dnio . Tc . xɪɪɪ . car hom . m̄ . vɪɪ . Sēp . xɪɪɪ . uilt . Silu . ɒ . porc
Tc . ɪɪɪɪ . bor . m̄ . vɪɪ . Tc . ɪɪɪɪ . ser . m̄ nult . Tc . ɪ . an̄ , m̄ . vɪ . c . ou . ʟ . por.   xxvɪ . ac' p̄ti
xʟ . cap̄ . Sēp uat . c . sot.   tc . ɪ . mot . m̄ . n̄;

⌐ Lochintunā ten& sēp . sēa crux . ꝑ . m̄ 7 . ɪɪɪɪ . hid . 7 . xx . ac . Tc . ɪɪ . car
in dnio . m̄ . ɪ . Sēp . ɪ . car hom . 7 . ɪɪ . uilt . Tc . ɪɪ . bor . m̄ . v . Silu . c . por . v . ac . p̄t.
. ɪ . car pot restaurari . v . an̄ . v . ou . 7 uat . xʟ . sot.

⌐ Lochintunā ten& Sca cr̄ . ꝑ . m̄ 7 . ɪɪ . hid . 7 . dim̄ . Sēp . ɪ . car in dnio.
tc . ɪɪ . bor . m̄ . ɪɪɪɪ . Silu . xʟ . por . ɪɪɪɪ . ac . p̄ti . ɪx . an̄ . x . por . xx . ou . vat . xx . sot.

⌐ Hund de Angra . Passefeldā ten& sēp . S . cr̄ . ꝑ . m̄ . 7 . ꝑ . ɪɪ . hid . xxx.
ac . min . Tc . vɪ . uilt . m̄ . v . m̄ . ɪɪɪɪ . bor . Tc . vɪɪ . ser . m̄ . ɪɪɪ . Tc . ɪɪ . car ī dnio
m̄ . ɪɪɪ . Tc . ɪɪɪ . car . hom . m̄ . ɪɪ . Silu . ɒcc . porc . vɪɪɪ . ac . p̄ti . Tc . ɪɪɪ . an̄.
m̄ . vɪ . Tc . xx . por . m̄ . xxx . ʟ . ou . Tc . xvɪ . cap̄ . m̄ . xxxvɪ . M̄ . ɪ . runc.
Sēp uat . vɪ . lib.

⌐ Aluertunā ten& sēp . S . cr̄ . ꝑ . m̄ . 7 . ɪɪɪɪ . hid . 7 . dim̄ . 7 . x . ac . Tc . vɪɪ.
uilt . m̄ . ɪx . Tc . ɪɪ . bor . m̄ . vɪ . Tc . v . ser . m̄ . ɪɪɪ . Sēp . ɪɪ . car in dnio . Tc
. ɪɪɪ . car hom . m̄ . ɪɪ . Silu . cccc . por . xv . ac . p̄ti . ɪɪ . an̄ . vɪɪɪ . ou . x . por
xv . cap̄ . Sēp uat . ɪɪɪɪ . lib.

⌐ Tippedanā ten& sēp tc . cr̄ . ꝑ . m̄ . 7 . ɪɪɪ . hid . 7 . xʟ . ac . Sēp . ɪɪɪɪ . uilt . 7
vɪɪ . bor . Tc . ɪɪɪɪ . ser . m̄ nult . Tc . ɪɪ . car . in dnio . m̄ . ɪ . tc . ɪɪ . car hom m̄ . ɪ.

Hundred of BECONTREE

3 Holy Cross has always held WOODFORD, 5 hides before 1066.
Always 2 ploughs in lordship. Then 13 men's ploughs, now 7.
Always 13 villagers. Then 4 smallholders, now 7; then 4
slaves, now none.
Woodland, 500 pigs; meadow, 26 acres; then 1 mill, now none.
Then 1 (head of) cattle, now 6; 100 sheep, 50 pigs, 40 goats.
Value always 100s.

4 Holy Cross has always held LOUGHTON as a manor; 4 hides and 20
acres. Then 2 ploughs in lordship, now 1. Always 1 men's plough;
2 villagers. Then 2 smallholders, now 5.
Woodland, 100 pigs; meadow, 5 acres; 1 plough could be
restored. 5 cattle, 5 sheep.
Value 40s.

5 Holy Cross holds LOUGHTON as a manor; 2½ hides. Always 1
plough in lordship.
Then 2 smallholders, now 4.
Woodland, 40 pigs; meadow, 4 acres. 9 cattle, 10 pigs, 20 sheep.
Value 20s.

Hundred of ONGAR

6 Holy Cross has always held PASLOW (Hall) as a manor, for 2 hides
less 30 acres.
Then 6 villagers, now 5; now 4 smallholders; then 7 slaves,
now 3. Then 2 ploughs in lordship, now 3. Then 3 men's
ploughs, now 2.
Woodland, 700 pigs; meadow, 8 acres. Then 3 cattle, now 6;
then 20 pigs, now 30; 50 sheep; then 16 goats, now 36;
now 1 cob.
Value always £6.

7 Holy Cross has always held ALDERTON (Hall) as a manor; 4½ hides
and 10 acres.
Then 7 villagers, now 9; then 2 smallholders, now 6; then 5
slaves, now 3. Always 2 ploughs in lordship. Then 3 men's
ploughs, now 2.
Woodland, 400 pigs; meadow, 15 acres. 2 cattle, 8 sheep,
10 pigs, 15 goats.
Value always £4.

8 Holy Cross has always held DEBDEN (Green) as a manor; 3 hides
and 40 acres.
Always 4 villagers; 7 smallholders. Then 4 slaves, now none.
Then 2 ploughs in lordship, now 1. Then 2 men's ploughs,
now 1.

Silu̇ . ccc . por . vi . aċ . p̃ti . ii . aṅ . viii ..por . ix . oủ . Sẽp ual . xl . ſol . ⌈ Q̇dam
liƀ ħõ tenuit . xl . aċ . qu̇e inuaſit eccła . p̄q rex uenit in hanc t̃rã . 7 ten&
adhuc . Tẽ . i . car̃ . m̂ nulla . 7 q̄n recep̃ dim̂ . iiii . aċ . p̃ti . Tẽ ual . vi . ſol 7 . viii .
đ . m̂ . v . ſol . 7 . iiii . đ.

⌐Hunđ de Ceſſeorda. Welda ten& ſẽp . ſċ . cr̃ . p uno maner̃ . 7 . t̃ . r̃ . e
p . ii . hiđ . m̂ . p . i . 7 dim . Goiſfrid de magna uilla ħt aliã dim . ſ; hunđ
neſcit q̇re habeat . 7 . G . dicit ſe habė p eſcangio . Sẽp . x . uilł . 7 . vi . bor .
7 . iii . ſer̃ . 7 . ii . car̃ in dñio . Tẽ . vi . car̃ hom̂ . m̂ . iiii . Silu̇ . cc . por . i . aċ 7 . đ .
p̃ti . m̂ . iiii . aṅ . Tẽ . x . por . m̂ . xxv . Tẽ xxv . oủ . m̂ . lxv . 7 Val vi . liƀ
In ħo manerio jacuit . i . ſoċ . q̇ tenuit . i . carr̃ . t̃ræ . ſ; m̂ ħt Rob̄ ḡnon .
ex dono reḡ ut ipſe diċ.

⌐Vpmonſtrã ten& ſċ . c̃ . p . ii . hiđ . 7 . dim . 7 . xl . aċ . Tẽ . viii . uilł . m̂ vi .
Tẽ . ii . bor . m̂ . iiii . Tẽ . iiii . ſer̃ . m̂ . iii . Sẽp . ii . car̃ in dñio . 7 . iiii . car̃ ħoũ
Silu̇ . ccc . por . vi . aċ p̃ti . ii . aṅ . Tẽ . xx . oủ . m̂ . l . Tẽ . xi . por . m̂ xxx .
Sẽp ual . iiii . liƀ . huic manerio jac& . i . ſoċ . de . xxx . aċ . 7 dim̂ . car̃ .
7 ual . xx . đ.

⌐Walcfarã ten& ſẽp ecła . p . iiii . hiđ . xl . aċ min . Tẽ . iiii . bor . m̂ . x .
Tẽ . vi . ſer̃ . m̂ . iii . Sẽp . ii . car̃ in dñio . 7 . i . car̃ . hom Silu̇ . xxx . por .
xviii . aċ p̃ti . M̂ . i . rum̂c . Sẽp . v . aṅ . v . por . xl . oủ . ii . uaſa ap̄u .
Val . xl . ſol.

Woodland, 300 pigs; meadow, 6 acres. 2 cattle, 8 pigs, 9 sheep. 16 b
Value always 40s.

A free man held 40 acres, which the Church annexed after the King came to this land and still holds. Then 1 plough, now none; when acquired, ½.

Meadow, 4 acres.

Value then 6s 8d; now 5s 4d.

Hundred of CHAFFORD

9 Holy Cross has always held (South) WEALD as one manor; before 1066, for 2 hides, now for 1½. Geoffrey de Mandeville has the other ½ (hide); but the Hundred does not know why he has it. Geoffrey states he had it by exchange.

Always 10 villagers; 6 smallholders; 3 slaves; 2 ploughs in lordship. Then 6 men's ploughs, now 4.

Woodland, 200 pigs; meadow, 1½ acres. Now 4 cattle; then 10 pigs, now 25; then 25 sheep, now 65.

Value £6.

In this manor belongs 1 Freeman who held 1 carucate of land; but now Robert Gernon has it by the King's gift, as he himself states.

10 Holy Cross holds UPMINSTER for 2½ hides and 40 acres.

Then 8 villagers, now 6; then 2 smallholders, now 4; then 4 slaves, now 3. Always 2 ploughs in lordship; 4 men's ploughs.

Woodland, 300 pigs; meadow, 6 acres. 2 cattle; then 20 sheep, now 50; then 11 pigs, now 30.

Value always £4.

To this manor belongs 1 Freeman with 30 acres and ½ plough.

Value 20d.

[Hundred of CHELMSFORD]

11 The Church has always held WALTER (Hall) for 4 hides less 40 acres.

Then 4 smallholders, now 10; then 6 slaves, now 3. Always 2 ploughs in lordship; 1 men's plough.

Woodland, 30 pigs; meadow, 18 acres. Now 1 cob; always 5 cattle, 5 pigs, 40 sheep, 2 beehives.

Value 40s.

SCA . MARIA De berchinges. In Exfeffa.

SCA Aldreda de eli.

SCS ETmund

SCS Martin Londonie.

SCS Martin de bello.

SCS Walerie.

SCA TrinitaS Decadomo.

SCS Stephan de cadomo.

SCS Audoen.

EPS Baiocenfis.

.IX. TERRA SCE MARIE DE BERCHINGIS.

Hund de berdeftapla . Mucinga . ten& Sca maria .p . vii . hid; 7 . xxx . ac.
inde abftulit Turold de Roueceftra . 7 jacent ad feudu epi baiocenfis.
7 t . r . e . i . car in dnio . m . ii . Sep . ix . car uiltis . 7 . xii . uiłł . Tc . xiiii . bor . m
xxv . Tc . iiii . fer . m . null . Silu . ccc . por . Paftura . ccc . ou . xl . ac . pti.
M . i . mot . i . Pifcina . x . an . ii . runc . xviii . por . ccl . ou . Sep ual . x . lib.
Bulgeuen . ten& S . co) . p . vii . hid . Tc . i . car in dnio m . ii . Tc . vii . car hou
m . x . Tc . x . uiłł . m . xvi . Tc . v . bor . m . xvi . iii . fer . Silu . b . porc . viii . an.
xv . por . i . runc . lxxx . ou . Tc ual . viii . lib . m . x . De hac tra tulit Rauen
gari . xxiiii . ac . In Fantuna . xl . ac . tre ten& . i . uiłłs . fep . dim . car . 7 ual
xl . d . De Supdicto manerio fcilic& de Muchinga . ten& Wiłł . dim . hid
7 . xxx . ac . 7 . iii . bor . 7 . ual . xviii . fot in fupdicto ptio ejde manerii.

[9] *St. Mary, Barking. In Essex*
[10] *St. Etheldreda, Ely*
[11] *St. Edmund*
[12] *St. Martin, London*
[13] *St. Martin, Battle*
[14] *St. Valéry*
[15] *Holy Trinity, Caen*
[16] *St. Stephen, Caen*
[17] *St. Ouen*
[18] *The Bishop of Bayeux*

LAND OF ST. MARY'S, BARKING

Hundred of BARSTABLE

1   St. Mary's holds MUCKING for 7 hides. Thorold of Rochester took
    30 acres away from there and they lie in the Bishop of Bayeux's
    Holding. Before 1066, 1 plough in lordship, now 2. Always 9
    villagers' ploughs;
        12 villagers. Then 14 smallholders, now 25; then 4 slaves,
        now none.
    Woodland, 300 pigs; pasture, 300 sheep; meadow, 40 acres;
        now 1 mill; 1 fishery. 10 cattle, 2 cobs, 18 pigs, 250 sheep.
    Value always £10.

2   St. Mary's holds BULPHAN for 7 hides. Then 1 plough in lordship,
    now 2. Then 7 men's ploughs, now 10.
        Then 10 villagers, now 16; then 5 smallholders, now 16;
        3 slaves.
    Woodland, 500 pigs. 8 cattle, 15 pigs, 1 cob, 80 sheep.
    Value then £8; now [£] 10.
    Of this land, Ravengar took 24 acres.

3   In FANTON (Hall) 1 villager holds 40 acres of land. Always ½ plough.
    Value 40d.

4   William holds ½ hide and 30 acres of the above-mentioned manor,
    namely MUCKING.
        3 smallholders.
    Value 18s in the above-mentioned assessment of the same manor.

In hoc hund st̃ . vi . lib̃i hões tenentes . ii . hid̃ . 7 . l . ac̃ . Sep . ii . car . Tc̃ . iii .
bor . m̃ . vi . Tc̃ . i . ser̃ . m̃ . ñ . Tc̃ silũ . c . por . M̃ . lv . xiii . pars uni⁹ piscinæ . Totũ
ual xxx . sol . Isti hões lib̃e exstiterunt ad berchingũ s̃; rex m̃ ex ipsis
pot̃ facere qd̃ sibi placuerit . De silũ huis tr̃æ h̃t Rob̃ grinon . l . porc .
Et de sup̃dicta tr̃a ten& Goduin cudhen . iii . uir̃g . 7 ual . x . sol .

⎰ Dimidiũ Hund de herlaua . In Perenduna ten& sep . sc̃a mar̃ . dim̃
hid̃ . dim̃ . car̃ . i . bor . silũ . x . por . v . ac̃ . p̃ti . Val . x . sol .

⎰ Hund de beuentreu .   Berchingas ten& sep sc̃a . M̃ . p̃ xxx . hid̃ .
Tc̃ . iiii . car in dñio . m̃ . iii . 7 . iiii pos̃s& fieri . Tc̃ . lxx . car hom̃ . m̃ lxviii .
Tc̃ . c . uill̃ . m̃ . cxl . Tc̃ . l . bor M̃ . lxxxx Tc̃ . x . ser̃ . m̃ . vi . Silũ . M̃ . porc̃ .
. c . ac̃ . p̃ti . ii . mol̃ . i . pisc̃ . ii . runc̃ . xxxiiii . an̄ . cl . por . cxiiii . oues .
xxiiii . cap̃ . x . uasa apũ .   In Londonia . xxviii . dom quæ reddt . . .

18 a
xiii . sol . 7 . viii . d̃ . 7 dim̃ ecc̃lia quæ t̃ . r̃ . e . reddebat vi . sol . 7 . viii . d̃ . 7
m̃ ñ reddit . Hoc maneriũ ual t̃ . r̃ . e . lxxx . lib̃ . 7 m̃ similit̃ ut dicunt
anglici . s̃; franci app̃tiant̃ . c . lib̃ . Huic manerio p̃tinebant t̃ . r̃ . e .
xxiiii . ac̃ . qs inde tulit Goscelin . Loremari . 7 . iii . milit̃ . ten̄ . ii . hid̃ . 7 . iii . car̃ ⎰

⎰ Hund de Wensistreu . Wicghebg̃a ten& sep . sc̃a maria p̃ . xi . hid̃
7 . dim̃ . 7 . xiii . ac̃ . Tc̃ . ii . car 7 d̃ . in dñio ꞓ m̃ . ii . Tc̃ . x . car hom̃ . m̃ . ix . Tc̃
ix . uill̃ . m̃ . x . Tc̃ . xxiiii . bor . m̃ xxxiii . Sep . viii . fer̃ . Silũ . c . por . Past̃
. c . ou̇ . quæ redd̃ . xvi . d̃ . vi . sal̃ . Tc̃ . xii . an̄ . 7 m̃ similt̃ . ii . runc̃ . xiiii .
por . ccxxx . ou̇ . Tc̃ ual . xii . lib̃ . m̃ . x . Huic man̄ . p̃tinent . iii . dom
in colecastro .

5 In this Hundred are 6 free men who hold 2 hides and 50 acres.
Always 2 ploughs.
    Then 3 smallholders, now 6; then 1 slave, now none.
    Then woodland, 100 pigs, now 55; the thirteenth part of 1
        fishery.
Total value 30s.
    These men existed freely at Barking; but the King might now
do with them as he pleases.
    Of the woodland of this land, Robert Gernon has 50 pigs.
    Of the above land, Godwin Woodhen holds 3 virgates; value 10s.

Half-Hundred of HARLOW
6 St. Mary's has always held ½ hide in PARNDON.
½ plough.
    1 smallholder.
    Woodland, 10 pigs; meadow, 5 acres.
Value 10s.

Hundred of BECONTREE
7 St. Mary's has always held BARKING for 30 hides. Then 4 ploughs
in lordship, now 3; 4 possible. Then 70 men's ploughs, now 68.
    Then 100 villagers, now 140; then 50 smallholders, now 90;
        then 10 slaves, now 6.
    Woodland, 1000 pigs; meadow, 100 acres; 2 mills; 1 fishery.
    2 cobs, 34 cattle, 150 pigs, 114 sheep, 24 goats, 10 beehives.
    In London 28 houses which pay 13s 8d and ½ church which   18 a
    paid 6s 8d before 1066 and now does not pay.
The value of this manor before 1066 was £80; now the same, as
the Englishmen state, but the Frenchmen assess it at £100.
    To this manor before 1066 belonged 24 acres which Jocelyn
Lorimer took away from it.
    3 men-at-arms hold 2 hides and 3 ploughs.
    3 villagers and 10 smallholders.
Value 45s in the same assessment.

Hundred of WINSTREE
8 St. Mary's has always held WIGBOROUGH for 11½ hides and 13 acres.
Then 2½ ploughs in lordship, now 2. Then 10 men's ploughs,
now 9.
    Then 9 villagers, now 10; then 24 smallholders, now 33;
        always 8 slaves.
    Woodland, 100 pigs; pasture, 100 sheep, which pays 16d;
        6 salt-houses. Then 12 cattle, now the same; 2 cobs,
        14 pigs, 230 sheep.
Value then £12; now [£] 10.
    To this manor belong 3 houses in Colchester.

ꝟHunđ de Ceffeorda. Wareleiã ten& ſep ſca maria . ꝓ . ɪɪɪ . hiđ
ſep . ɪx . uiƚƚ . Tc̄ . vɪɪɪ . bor . m̄ . x . Tc̄ . ɪɪɪ . ſer . m̄ . v . ſep . ɪɪ . car . in dnio . Tc̄ꞏ
vɪɪɪ . car hom . m̄ . vɪ . ſilu . cc . por . paſt . c . oꞹ . vɪɪɪ . an . xɪ . porc . cʟ.
oꞹ . ɪ . uas aꝑ . ſep uaƚ . vɪɪ . liɓ . In Stiforda ħt ſ̄ . ꝏ . xʟ . ac̄ . Tc̄ . ɪ . uiƚƚ.
M̄ . ɪɪ . 7 . ɪɪ . bor . ɪ . ac̄ ꝓti . Tc̄ . ɪ . car . m̄ . dim̄ . 7 uaƚ . ɪɪɪ . ſoƚ . Fuere &ia̅
ad hanc tr̄a xxx . ac̄ . q̄s ħt Wiƚƚ de war̄ ꝓ eſcangio ut ipſe dicit.
Sunt adhuc . aliæ . xxx . ac̄ . 7 . ɪɪ . ac̄ . 7 dim̄ ꝓti . 7 uaƚ . ɪɪɪ . ſoƚ
ꝟHunđ de celmereſfort . Ingã ten& ſep ſc̄ . ꝏ . ꝓ . ɪɪɪ . hiđ . 7 .
dim̄ . 7 . x . ac̄ . ſep . ɪɪ . uiƚƚ . Tc̄ . vɪ . bor . m̄ . vɪɪ . ſep . ɪ . ſer . 7 . ɪ . car . in dnio.
Tc̄ . ɪ . car 7 đ . hom . m̄ . ɪ . ſilu . ɒ . por . 7 . ɪ . ſoc de . xxx . ac̄ . ɪ . runc . ɪx.
an . ɪx . an . xx . porc . xvɪ . oꞹ . Tc̄ uaƚ . ʟxx . ſoƚ . m̄ ʟx.
            ꝟFeſtinges ten& ſc̄ . ꝏ . ꝓ . ɪ . uirḡ 7 . dim̄ . Tc̄ . ɪɪɪ.
bor . m̄ . ɪɪɪɪ . Tc̄ . ɪ . ſer . m̄ nuƚƚ . ſep . ɪ . car . ſilu . cc . por . ɪɪɪɪ . an . xxxvɪɪ.
oꞹ . x . cap . Tc̄ uaƚ . vɪɪɪ . ſoƚ . m̄ . x.

18 b

ꝟHunđ de Rochefort . Hocheleiã ten& ſep . ſ̄ . ꝏ . ꝓꝏ . 7 . vɪɪ . hiđ
7 . dim̄ . Tc̄ xxɪɪɪɪ . uiƚƚ . m̄ . xxvɪɪ . ſep . xɪɪ . bor . Tc̄ . ɪɪɪ . ſer . m̄ . nuƚƚ . Sep
. ɪɪ . car in dnio . 7 . xv . car hom . paſt . cc . oꞹ . ɪ . moƚ . ɪɪ . runc . vɪɪɪ . an.
cʟɪ . oꞹ . xxvɪ . por . Sep uaƚ . x . liɓ . De hoc man ten& Wiƚƚ de burfigni
de eccƚa . ɪɪɪ . uirḡ . 7 . ɪ . car . 7 uaƚ . xxɪ . ſoƚ . in eođ . ꝓtio.

18 a, b

Hundred of CHAFFORD

9 St. Mary's has always held (Great) WARLEY for 3 hides.
    Always 9 villagers. Then 8 smallholders, now 10; then 3
        slaves, now 5. Always 2 ploughs in lordship. Then 8 men's
        ploughs, now 6.
    Woodland, 200 pigs; pasture, 100 sheep. 8 cattle, 11 pigs,
        150 sheep, 1 beehive.
    Value always £7.

10 In STIFFORD St. Mary's has 40 acres.
    Then 1 villager, now 2. 2 smallholders.
    Meadow, 1 acre. Then 1 plough, now ½.
    Value 3s.
    There were also 30 acres (belonging) to this land which William
  of Warenne has by exchange, as he himself states.
    There are besides another 30 acres.
        Meadow, 2½ acres.
    Value 3s.

Hundred of CHELMSFORD

11 St. Mary's has always held INGATESTONE for 3½ hides and 10 acres.
    Always 2 villagers. Then 6 smallholders, now 7. Always 1
        slave; 1 plough in lordship. Then 1½ men's ploughs, now 1.
    Woodland, 500 pigs; 1 Freeman with 30 acres. 1 cob, 9 cattle,
        9 cattle, 20 pigs, 16 sheep.
    Value then 70s; now 60[s].

12 St. Mary's holds FRISTLING for 1½ virgates.
    Then 3 smallholders, now 4; then 1 slave, now none. Always
        1 plough.
    Woodland, 200 pigs. 4 cattle, 37 sheep, 10 goats.
    Value then 8s; now 10[s].

Hundred of ROCHFORD   18 b

13 St. Mary's has always held HOCKLEY as a manor; 7½ hides.
    Then 24 villagers, now 27; always 12 smallholders; then 3
        slaves, now none. Always 2 ploughs in lordship; 15 men's
        ploughs.·
    Pasture, 200 sheep; 1 mill. 2 cobs, 8 cattle, 151 sheep, 26 pigs.
    Value always £10.
    Of this manor, William of Boursigny holds 3 virgates from the
  Church. 1 plough.
    Value 21s in the same assessment.

Hund de Tureſtapla. Tolesbiam ten& ſep.S.M̃.p.m̃.7.VIII.
hiḋ.Tc̃.XI.uiłł.m̃.XII.Tc̃ XIIII.bor.M̃.XVI.Tc̃.V.ſer.m̃.VII.Sep.II.
car in dñio.Tc̃.VIII.car.hom.m̃.VII.ſilu.ḃ.porc̃.Paſt.CCCC.ou.
m̃.I.moł.7.I.piſcina.7.II.ſal.II.runc̃.X.an̄.XXVIII.por.CCC.ou.
Sep.u.ał.X.liḃ.Ranulf piperełł.ten&.I.hiḋ.qm̃ tenuit Siuuarḋ.
de abb.7 ipſe uult facere tale ſeruitiũ qle ſuus anteceſſor fecit.ſ;
abbatiſſa non uult.q̃a erat de uictu eccłiæ.Odo ho ſuani accepit
X.ac̃.quæ fuer̄ de eccła.7 hund hoc teſtat̄.ſ; inde uocat dm̃m ſuũ
ad tutore.Sep ualent.XVI.ḋ.

.X. TERRE Sc̃e Adeldredæ de eli. Hund de dommauua.
Broccheſheuot ten& ſep Sc̃a.A.p.m̃.7.III.hiḋ.ſep.II.car ɪ dñio
7.IIII.car hom.XVI.uiłłi.Tc̃.II.bor.m̃.V.V.ſer.Silu.CCL.por.
.XXX.ac̃.p̃ti.Tc̃ 7 m̃.XVI.an̄.II.runc̃.LXX.ou.
.II.uaſa apũ.Tc̃ uał.X.liḃ.m̃.VIII.De hoc manerio
ablatæ ſunt IX.ac̃ tr̄e.t.r.Wiłłi.qs ten& Eudo dapifer.7 adhuc
.II.car tr̄æ de dominio quas ten&.Idē Eudo.7 uał.IIII.liḃ.

19 a
Rodinges ten& ſep.ſc̃a.A.7 t.r.e.p.III.hiḋ.7.XLV.ac̃.m̃.p.II.hiḋ.
7.XLV.ac̃.7 t̄ciã hidā de dñio tulit Wiłł de uuarenna.quæ ibi jacebat
t.r.e; Sep.VIII.uiłł.7.I.pbr̄.II.bor.IIII.ſer.Tc̃.III.car in dñio.m̃.II.Sep
IIII.car hom.Silu.C.por.XX.ac̃.p̃ti.II.runc̃.IX.an̄.XVIIII.porc̃.XV.ou.
7 tres ſoc̃ attinent huic manerio.7.XI.bor.7.III.ſer.Tc̃ uał.IIII.li.m̃.VI;
Ratendunã tenuit Sc̃a.A.t.r.e.p.I.m̃.7.p.XX.hiḋ.M̃.ten& p XVI.
hiḋ.7.dim.Sep XXVI.uiłł.7 VI.bor.Tc̃.VII.ſer.m̃.VI.Sep.III.car in
dñio.7.XII.car hom.Silu.CCC.porc̃.IX.an̄.XLI.porc̃.CLX.ou.7.IIII.

Hundred of THURSTABLE

14 St. Mary's has always held TOLLESBURY as a manor; 8 hides.
Then 11 villagers, now 12; then 14 smallholders, now 16;
then 5 slaves, now 7. Always 2 ploughs in lordship. Then
8 men's ploughs, now 7.
Woodland, 500 pigs; pasture, 400 sheep; now 1 mill;
1 fishery; 2 salt-houses. 2 cobs, 10 cattle, 28 pigs, 300 sheep.
Value always £10.
Ranulf Peverel holds 1 hide which Siward held from the Abbey.
He himself wants to perform such service as his predecessor
performed; but the Abbess did not want (it so), because it was
for the Church's supplies.
Odo, a man of Swein's, received 10 acres which were the
Church's. The Hundred testifies to this but he vouches his lord
as guarantor for it.
Value always 16d.

10   LANDS OF ST. ETHELDREDA'S, ELY

Hundred of DUNMOW

1 St. Etheldreda's has always held BROXTED as a manor; 3 hides.
Always 2 ploughs in lordship; 4 men's ploughs.
16 villagers; then 2 smallholders, now 5; 5 slaves.
Woodland, 250 pigs; meadow, 30 acres. Then and now 16
cattle, 2 cobs, 70 sheep, 2 beehives.
Value then £10; now [£] 8.
From this manor, 9 acres of land were taken away after 1066,
which Eudo the Steward holds. Also 2 carucates of land from the
lordship which Eudo also holds.
Value £4.

2 St. Etheldreda's has always held (Aythorp) RODING; before 1066   19 a
for 3 hides and 45 acres, now for 2 hides and 45 acres. William of
Warenne took the third hide from the lordship which lay there
before 1066.
Always 8 villagers; 1 priest; 2 smallholders; 4 slaves. Then
3 ploughs in lordship, now 2. Always 4 men's ploughs.
Woodland, 100 pigs; meadow, 20 acres. 2 cobs, 9 cattle,
23 pigs, 15 sheep.
3 Freemen belong to this manor; 11 smallholders; 3 slaves.
Value then £4; now [£] 6.

[Hundred of CHELMSFORD]

3 St. Etheldreda's held RETTENDON before 1066 as 1 manor, for 20
hides. Now it holds (it) for 16½ hides.
Always 26 villagers; 6 smallholders. Then 7 slaves, now 6.
Always 3 ploughs in lordship; 12 men's ploughs.
Woodland, 300 pigs. 9 cattle, 41 pigs, 164 sheep.

Tc ual . xvii . lib . m̃ . xx . ⁊ . i . hid ⁊ . xxx . ac . ten& Siuuard de sc̃a . A.
M̃ ten& Ranulf piperell de rege . f; hund̃ testat̃ de abbatia.
⁊ . ii . hid . ⁊ . xxx . ac . q² tenuit ecclia ⁊ Leuesun de ea . t̃ . r̃ . ẽ . M̃ ten&
eudo de abbe . q² antecessor ej tenuit eã . f; hund̃ testat̃ . qd non
poterat uende eã sine licentia abbis.

⌐Dimidium Hund̃ de Frossewella . Cadenhov ten& sep . sc̃a.
A . p . i . m̃ . ⁊ . ii . hid . Tc . viii . uill . m̃ . xii . Tc . iiii . bor . m̃ . xiii . Tc . iiii.
ser . m̃ . ii . Sep . ii . car . in dñio . Tc . iii . car . hom . m̃ . iiii . Silu . c . porc.
vi . ac . p̃ti . Tc . i . mol . m̃ . null . i . runc . iiii . an . xvi . por . xxxvi . oues
viii . cap . Tc ual . vi . lib . m̃ . x.

⌐Hund̃ de udelesfort   Litelbyria ten& sep . S . A . p . i . maner.
⁊ . xxv . hid . Sep . xxxix . uill . ⁊ . xix . bor . vii . ser . Tc . v . car in
dñio . m̃ . iiii . Tc . xvii . car . hom . m̃ . xv . Silu . clx . por . lv . ac . p̃ti.
sep . iiii . mol . ii . runc . xxxii . porc . lxxx . ou . iii . uasa apum.
Val . xx . lib . Est &iã . i . bereuuita que vocat̃ Strathala quã
tenuer . ii . hões . Wills . Eluui . p . v . hid . ⁊ n̄ poterant recede

19 b

a t̃ra sine licentia abbis . m̃ ten& hugo sub abbe . Tc . vii . uill . m̃ . vi.
Tc . iiii . bor . m̃ . vii . Sep . vi . ser . ⁊ . iii . car . in dñio . Tc . iiii . car . hom . M̃ . v.
silu . x . por . xii . ac . p̃ti . i . mol . Tc . ual . vii . lib . m̃ . viii . In dñio . vii . an . c . ou.
xxii . porc . ii . uasa apũ.
Est adhuc . i . bereuuita que uocat̃ . hamdena quã Eluui p d̃ . hid . ⁊
xv . ac . Tc . ii . car . in dñio . m̃ . i . Tc . iiii . ser . m̃ null . Tc . lv . ou . ⁊ m̃;
Tc . ual . lx . sol . m̃ . xxx . De hoc maner accepit Will cardon : hõ . G.
de magna uill . xxiiii . ac . siluæ . q̄n Suan erat uicecomes . ut hundret
⌐testatur

Value then £17; now [£] 20.

Siward holds 1 hide and 30 acres from St. Etheldreda's. Now Ranulf Peverel holds (it) from the King; but the Hundred testifies that (it is) the Abbey's.

2 hides and 30 acres, which the Church held and Leofson from it before 1066. Eudo now holds from the Abbot, because his predecessor held it; but the Hundred testifies that he could not sell it without the Abbot's permission.

Half-Hundred of FRESHWELL

4 St. Etheldreda's has always held HADSTOCK as 1 manor; 2 hides.

Then 8 villagers, now 12; then 4 smallholders, now 13; then 4 slaves, now 2. Always 2 ploughs in lordship. Then 3 men's ploughs, now 4.

Woodland, 100 pigs; meadow, 6 acres; then 1 mill, now none. 1 cob, 4 cattle, 16 pigs, 36 sheep, 8 goats.

Value then £6; now [£] 10.

Hundred of UTTLESFORD

5 St. Etheldreda's has always held LITTLEBURY as 1 manor; 25 hides.

Always 39 villagers; 19 smallholders; 7 slaves. Then 5 ploughs in lordship, now 4. Then 17 men's ploughs, now 15.

Woodland, 160 pigs; meadow, 55 acres; always 4 mills. 2 cobs, 32 pigs, 80 sheep, 3 beehives.

Value £20.

There is also 1 outlier which is called STRETHALL, which 2 men, William (and) Alwin, held for 5 hides; they could not withdraw from the land without the Abbot's permission. Now Hugh holds 19 b (it) under the Abbot.

Then 7 villagers, now 6; then 4 smallholders, now 7. Always 6 slaves; 3 ploughs in lordship. Then 4 men's ploughs, now 5.

Woodland, 10 pigs; meadow, 12 acres; 1 mill.

Value then £7; now [£] 8.

In lordship 7 cattle, 100 sheep, 22 pigs, 2 beehives.

There is also 1 outlier which is called HEYDON, which Alwin [held] for ½ hide and 15 acres. Then 2 ploughs in lordship, now 1.

Then 4 slaves, now none.

Then and now 55 sheep.

Value then 60s; now 30[s].

From this manor, William Cardon, a man of G(eoffrey) de Mandeville's, wrongfully received 24 acres of woodland when Swein was Sheriff, as the Hundred testifies.

Terra Sci Edmundi.   Hund de Witham.

Breddinchou ten& Witt fili groffe de abbe. p. 1. hid. 7. xv. ac. Tc. 11.
car in dnio. m. 1. Sep. 1. car. hom. 1111. uitt. 111. bor. m. 1. mot. Silu. L. por.
. xx. ac. pti. 11. runc. vi. an. xii. por. v. cap. Vat. L. fot.

Dimidiu Hund de Herlaua   Herlaua ten& fep. fcs. E. p. 1.
Man. 7. 1. hid. 7. d. Sep. 11. car. in dnio. 7. vi. car hom. 7. xii. uitt. xv. bor.
7. 1111. fer. Silu. cL. por. xxx. ac. pti. 1. molin. 1111. runc. xxv. an.
. 111. pulli. L. porc. Lx. ou. v. uafa apu.   Huic manerio addite funt.
. 111. hid. t. r. Witti. qs tenebant. v. libi hoes. t. r. e. In qb; ft fep. vi. car
in dnio viii. bor. 1111. fer. Silu. c. por. xiiii. ac. pti. Sep. uat. maner.
viii. lib. 7. 111. hid. uat. tc. Lxx. fot. m. 1111. lib.

Lattuna ten& fcs. E. p. man. 7. p. 1111. hid. 7. d. qd tenuit Turgot
. 1. lib ho. t. r. e. Sep. 11. car in dnio. 7. 1. car. hom. 1111. uitt. Tc. 1111t

20 a

bor. m. v. fep. 1111. fer. filu. cc. por. xxxv. ac. pti. 1111. an. L. por. xxx. ou. xxv
cap. Sep. uat. vi. lib.

Hund de hidinghefort.   In Alfelmeftuna ten&. S. E. dim. hid. 1. car
in dnio. Tc. 1. fer. M. 111. bor. 11. ac. pti. Tc. uat. x. fot. M. xx.

Hund de Laxefelda   In Colu ten&. S. E. xxxvi. ac. Tc. 111. bor.
m. 1111. Sep. dim. car. filu. xL. por. 111. ac. pti. Vat. xx. fot.

Hund de Angra.   Staplefort ten& fep. S. E. p. 111. hid. 7. dim.
7. vi. ac. 7. dim. Tc. viii. uitt. m. ix. Sep. v. bor. 7. 11. fer. 7. 1. car. in
dnio. Tc. 1111. car. hom. m. 111. Silu. ccL. por. xii. ac. pti. xx. an. 1. r.

Hundred of WITHAM
1   William son of Gross holds BENTON (Hall) from the Abbot for 1
hide and 15 acres. Then 2 ploughs in lordship, now 1. Always 1
men's plough.
    4 villagers and 3 smallholders.
    Now 1 mill; woodland, 50 pigs; meadow, 20 acres. 2 cobs,
        6 cattle, 12 pigs, 5 goats.
Value 50s.

Half-Hundred of HARLOW
2   St. Edmund's has always held HARLOW as 1 manor; 1½ hides.
Always 2 ploughs in lordship; 6 men's ploughs;
    12 villagers; 15 smallholders; 4 slaves.
    Woodland, 150 pigs; meadow, 30 acres; 1 mill. 4 cobs, 25
        cattle, 3 foals, 50 pigs, 60 sheep, 5 beehives.
To this manor were added 3 hides after 1066, which 5 free men
held before 1066. In them have always been 6 ploughs in lordship.
    8 smallholders and 4 slaves.
    Woodland, 100 pigs; meadow, 14 acres.
Value of the manor always £8. Value of the 3 hides then 70s;
now £4.

3   St. Edmund's holds LATTON as a manor, for 4½ hides which 1 free
man, Thorgot, held before 1066. Always 2 ploughs in lordship; 1
men's plough.
    4 villagers; then 4 smallholders, now 5; always 4 slaves.   20 a
    Woodland, 200 pigs; meadow, 35 acres. 4 cattle, 50 pigs,
        30 sheep, 25 goats.
Value always £6.

Hundred of HINCKFORD
4   In ALPHAMSTONE St. Edmund's holds ½ hide. 1 plough in lordship.
    Then 1 slave; now 3 smallholders.
    Meadow, 2 acres.
Value then 10s; now 20[s].

Hundred of LEXDEN
5   In COLNE St. Edmund's holds 36 acres.
    Then 3 smallholders, now 4. Always ½ plough.
    Woodland, 40 pigs; meadow, 3 acres.
Value 20s.

Hundred of ONGAR
6   St. Edmund's has always held STAPLEFORD (Abbotts) for 3½ hides
and 6½ acres.
    Then 8 villagers, now 9. Always 5 smallholders; 2 slaves;
        1 plough in lordship. Then 4 men's ploughs, now 3.
    Woodland, 250 pigs; meadow, 12 acres. 20 cattle, 1 cob,

XLVIII.oves.XLIII.por.III.pulli.7.II.libi hões in ſocã manerij.de
XXXVI.ac̄.7.dim̄.I.car̄.ſilu.XL.por.II.ac̄ p̃ti.Tc̄ ual.XLV.ſol.m̄.L.

⌐Hund de Celmeresfort.   Waltham ten& Albt de abbe.qd̄
tenuit Stanhard.t.r.e.p.I.Man̄ 7.II.hid.xv.ac̄.min̄.7.ſc̄s.E.de.
dono regis.Sep̄.I.uilt 7.VII.bor.7.II.ſer.7.II.car̄.in dn̄io.7.I.car̄
hom̄.Silu.xxx.por.VII.ac̄.p̃ti.I.an̄.L.ou.II.por.x.cap.Tc̄ ual XL ſol.
M̄.LX.

⌐Hund de tendringa   Wrabenaſã ten& ſep̄.ſc̄s.E.p̄.I.Man̄.7 p̄
.v.hid Sep̄.VI.uilt.VIII.bor.VI.ſer.Tc̄.IIII.car̄.in dn̄io.m̄.II.Tc̄.VI.ca̅
hom̄.m̄.v.7.dim̄.I.ac̄.p̃ti.m̄.I.mot.7.I.ſal.II.pulli.xxx.porc̄.
cc.ou.v.uaſa ap̄.Ual.VI.lib̄.

★

.XII.⌐TERRA Sc̄i martini Londoniæ. Eſtrã tenuit Ailmar.I.teinn
regis.E. 7 conſul Euſtachi dedit ſc̄o martino.p̄.I.m̄.7.IIII.hid.7.L.ac̄.
Tc̄.III.car̄.in dn̄io.m̄.II.Sep̄.VIII.car̄.hom̄.VIII.uilt.Tc̄.xvi.bor.m̄.
xxi.Tc̄.VIII.ſer.m̄.III.Silu.LX por.xx.ac̄.p̃ti.M̄.I.mot.Tc̄.ual.VIII.
lib̄.m̄.x.   Huic manerio attinebat.I.bereuuita de dim̄.hid.7
xx.ac̄.t.r.e.ſ; conſul.E.eã fibi retinuit.7 jac& in hund de cel
meresfort.

XIII.⌐TERRA Sc̄i Martini de bello.   Hund de b̄deſtapla.Atahov
tenuit Goti lib̄ hō.t.r.e.p̄.I.Man̄.7.III.hid.xx.ac̄.min̄.ſep̄.II.car̄
in dn̄io.7.III.car̄ hom̄.Tc̄.I.uilt.m̄.II.Tc̄.x.bor.m̄.xv.IIII.ſer.
ſilu.m̄.porc̄.Tc̄.I.piſc̄.m̄ n̄.Tc̄.II.runc̄.m̄.III.Tc̄.IIII.an̄.m̄ xix.
.c.ou.Tc̄.LX.porc̄.m̄.c.VIII.min̄.IIII.uaſa apū.7.III.ſoc̄.de.I.
hid.7.xxx.ac̄.ſep̄.I.car̄.7.xv.ac̄.libæ trã.Tc̄.ual.c.ſol.m̄.vi.
lib̄.7.illæ.xv.ac̄.ual.xxx.d̄.

48 sheep, 43 pigs, 3 foals.
2 free men in the jurisdiction of the manor with 36½ acres.
1 plough. Woodland, 40 pigs; meadow, 2 acres.
Value then 45s; now 50[s].

Hundred of CHELMSFORD
7   Albert holds (Little) WALTHAM from the Abbot, which Stanhard
held before 1066 as 1 manor, 2 hides less 15 acres. St. Edmund's
(holds) by the King's gift.
Always 1 villager; 7 smallholders; 2 slaves; 2 ploughs in
lordship; 1 men's plough.
Woodland, 30 pigs; meadow, 7 acres. 1 (head of) cattle,
50 sheep, 2 pigs, 10 goats.
Value then 40s; now 60[s].

Hundred of TENDRING
8   St. Edmund's has always held WRABNESS as 1 manor, for 5 hides.
Always 6 villagers; 8 smallholders; 6 slaves. Then 3 ploughs
in lordship, now 2. Then 6 men's ploughs, now 5½.
Meadow, 1 acre; now 1 mill and 1 salt-house. 2 foals, 30 pigs,
200 sheep, 5 beehives.
Value £6.

12   **LAND OF ST. MARTIN'S, LONDON**   20 b

[Hundred of DUNMOW]
1   Aelmer, 1 thane of King Edward's, held (Good) EASTER. Count
Eustace gave (it) to St. Martin's as 1 manor, 4 hides and 50 acres.
Then 3 ploughs in lordship, now 2. Always 8 men's ploughs.
8 villagers; then 16 smallholders, now 21; then 8 slaves, now 3.
Woodland, 60 pigs; meadow, 20 acres; now 1 mill.
Value then £8; now [£] 10.
To this manor belonged 1 outlier with ½ hide and 20 acres
before 1066, but Count Eustace kept it for himself.
It lies in the Hundred of CHELMSFORD.

13   **LAND OF ST. MARTIN'S, BATTLE**

Hundred of BARSTABLE
1   Goti, a free man, held HUTTON before 1066 as 1 manor, 3 hides
less 20 acres. Always 2 ploughs in lordship; 3 men's ploughs.
Then 1 villager, now 2; then 10 smallholders, now 15; 4 slaves.
Woodland, 1000 pigs; then 1 fishery, now none. Then 2 cobs,
now 3; then 4 cattle, now 19; 100 sheep; then 60 pigs, now
100 less 8; 4 beehives.
3 Freemen with 1 hide and 30 acres. Always 1 plough. 15 acres
of free land.
Value then 100s; now £6. Value of the 15 acres 30d.

Hund de hidingforda. Hersā tenuit Orgar lib hō . t . r . e . ꝑ . Ma.
7 . ꝑ . ɪ . hid . Sēp . ɪɪ . car . in dn̄io . 7 . ɪ . car hom . Tc 7 . ꝑ . v . uilt . m̄ . ɪɪɪ.
Tc . ɪ . bor . m̄ . ɪɪɪ . Tc . ɪɪɪ . ſer . m̄ . ɪɪ . xɪɪɪ . ac . p̄ti . vɪɪɪ . an . x . por . Tc.
xxx ou . m̄ . xxv . ɪɪɪ . uaſa apū . Val . xl . ſol.

XIIII. TERRA SC̄I Walerici.   Hund de herLAVA.
Metcingā tenuit Godric . ɪ . lib hō . t . r . e . ꝑ . xl . ac . Tc . ɪ . car
m̄ . nulla . Val . x . ſol . 7 . vɪɪɪ . d.
Lindeſelā tenuit Horolf . ɪ . lib hō . t . r . e . ꝑ . ɪ . m̄ . 7 . ꝑ . ɪ . hid.

21 a
m̄ Sc̄s Wal . Sēp . ɪɪ . car in dn̄io . 7 . ɪɪɪ . car hom . Tc . vɪɪɪ . uilt . m̄ . ɪx.
Tc . ɪɪɪɪ . bor . m̄ . xv . Tc . ɪɪɪɪ . ſer . m̄ null . Silu . l . por . vɪ . ac . p̄ti.
. ɪɪɪɪ . an . xl . por . xxvɪɪɪ . ou . v . uaſa apū . Tc . 7 p ual . c . ſol.
M̄ . vɪ . lib.
Hund de Vdelesfort.   Tacheleiā ten& . Sc̄s
Wal . qd tenuit Turchill lib hō . t . r . e . ꝑ . dim . hid.
Sēp . ɪɪ . car in dn̄io . 7 . ɪɪɪ . car hom . vɪɪɪ . uilt . Tc . 7 . ꝑ . ɪɪɪ.
bor . m̄ . v . Sēp . ɪɪ . ſer . Tc 7 p ſilu . Ⓜ . por . m̄ . dc . xxɪɪɪɪ . ac . p̄ti . Tc.
7 p . ɪ . mol . m̄ . d . ɪɪɪ . runc . ɪɪɪɪ . an . xxx . por . xxvɪɪɪ . ou . l . cap . v . uas
apū . Tc 7 p ual . vɪ . lib . m̄ . vɪɪ.
Bilichangrā tenuit Idē Turchill . ꝑ . ɪɪ . hid . 7 . ꝑ . ɪ . Man . Tc . 7 . p.
. ɪɪ . car in dn̄io . m̄ . ɪ . Sēp . ɪɪ . car hom . ɪ . uilt . v . bor . Tc . ɪɪ . ſer . Tc ſilu
. c . por . M̄ . l . vɪ . ac . p̄ti . ɪ . mol . ɪɪ . runc . vɪ . an . xxvɪɪɪ . por . xxxvɪ.
cap . Tc 7 p . ual . lx . ſol . m̄ . l.

Hundred of HINCKFORD
2 Ordgar, a free man, held HORSEHAM (Hall) before 1066 as a manor, for 1 hide. Always 2 ploughs in lordship; 1 men's plough.
　　Then and later 5 villagers, now 3; then 1 smallholder, now 3; then 3 slaves, now 2.
　　Meadow, 13 acres. 8 cattle, 10 pigs; then 33 sheep, now 25; 3 beehives.
Value 40s.

14   LAND OF ST. VALERY'S

Hundred of HARLOW
1 1 free man, Godric, held MATCHING before 1066 for 40 acres.
Then 1 plough, now none.
Value 10s 8d.

[Hundred of DUNMOW]
2 1 free man, Horwulf, held LINDSELL before 1066 as 1 manor, for 1 hide. Now St. Valéry's (holds it). Always 2 ploughs in   21 a
lordship; 3 men's ploughs.
　　Then 8 villagers, now 9; then 4 smallholders, now 15; then 4 slaves, now none.
　　Woodland, 50 pigs; meadow, 6 acres. 4 cattle, 40 pigs, 28 sheep, 5 beehives.
Value then and later 100s; now £6.

Hundred of UTTLESFORD
3 St. Valéry's holds TAKELEY which Thorkell, a free man, held before 1066, for ½ hide. Always 2 ploughs in lordship; 3 men's ploughs.
　　8 villagers; then and later 3 smallholders, now 5; always 2 slaves.
　　Woodland then and later, 1000 pigs, now 600; meadow, 24 acres; then and later 1 mill, now ½. 3 cobs, 4 cattle, 30 pigs, 28 sheep, 50 goats, 5 beehives.
Value then and later £6; now [£] 7.

4 Thorkell also held BIRCHANGER for 2 hides, as 1 manor. Then and later 2 ploughs in lordship, now 1. Always 2 men's ploughs.
　　1 villager, 5 smallholders; then 2 slaves.
　　Woodland, then 100 pigs, now 50; meadow, 6 acres; 1 mill. 2 cobs, 6 cattle, 28 pigs, 36 goats.
Value then and later 60s; now 50[s].

⌐Widitunā tenuit Idē Turchill. ᵱ.m.7.IIII.hid.7.đ.Tc.7.ᵱ.III.

car̄.in dn̄io.M.II.Sēp.VI.car̄.hom.Tc.7.ᵱ.VIII.uiłł.M.XI.xx.ou̇.

VI.ſer.ſilu.X.por.XII.ac.ᵱti.V.an.XXIIII.por.L.ou̇.Sēp uał.

VII.liƀ. huic t̄ræ.jacent.II.hid.q̄s sēp.tenent.IIII.ſoc.7.uał.xxx.ſoł.

⌐Hund de Witbrictesherna. Effeceſtrā tenuit Turchill.

liƀ hō.t.r.e.ᵱ.I.hid.7.dim.7.xx.ac.Tc.II.bor.m̄.III.sēp.II.ſer.

7.I.car̄.past.ccc.ou̇.I.piſc.III.an.xx.porc.ccxvI.ou̇.Tc uał

XL.ſoł.M.LXX. In Ead.III.liƀi hōes.de.I.hid.7.đ.I.car̄.Vał.xx.ſoł.

⌐Daneſeiā ten Idē.ᵱ.II.hid.7 đ.IIII.uiłł.Tc.I.bor.m̄.VIII.sēp.IIII.ſer.

.II.ca.i dio.7 II.ca.hom.Past.cc.ou̇.Tc.IIII.liƀ.m̄.c.ſoł.In Ead uiłł

21 b

tenent.IIII.liƀi hōes.L.ac.7 uał.V.ſoł.

.XV.⌐Terra ſc̄e trinitatis de Cadomo. Hund de hidingfort

Phenſtedā tenuit.Comes Algar.t.r.e.ᵱ.V.hid.m̄ ten& ſc̄a trin.

ᵱ.IIII.hid.Sēp.III.car̄ in dn̄io.7.xvI.car̄ hom.Tc.xxII.uiłł.Poſt

7.m̄.xx.Tc 7 ᵱ xxIII.bor.m̄.xxxIII.sēp.xI.ſer.Silu.đc.porc.

xxxvI.ac.ᵱti.II.moł.xxI.an.cc.porc.LvIII.ou̇.xxx.cap.I.runc.

Huic manerio jacebant.t.r.e.LV.ac.q̄s tenebant.III.ſoc.m̄.IIII.

tc.II.car̄.m̄.III.M.II.bor.Silu.xxx.por.xII.ac.ᵱti.Tc uał.xx.

liƀ.Poſt.xxx.m̄.xxxII.Quinta hida n̄ ē huic manerio.rex

eni Wiłł dedit Roḡo đs ſaluæt dn̄as.III.uirḡ.7 Giſleƀto filio Sa

lomonis.IIII.

21 a, b

5   Thorkell also held WIDDINGTON as a manor, 4½ hides. Then and
later 3 ploughs in lordship, now 2. Always 6 men's ploughs.
>Then and later 8 villagers, now 11; 20 sheep; 6 slaves.
>Woodland, 10 pigs; meadow, 12 acres. 5 cattle, 24 pigs,
>>50 sheep.
>Value always £7.
>To this land belong 2 hides which 4 Freemen have always held.
Value 33s.

Hundred of 'WIBERTSHERNE'

6   Thorkell, a free man, held ST. PETER'S CHAPEL before 1066 for 1½
hides and 20 acres.
>Then 2 smallholders, now 3. Always 2 slaves; 1 plough.
>Pasture, 300 sheep; 1 fishery. 3 cattle, 20 pigs, 216 sheep.
>Value then 40s; now 70[s].
>In the same (Bradwell) 3 free men with 1½ hides. 1 plough.
Value 20s.

7   He also held DENGIE for 2½ hides.
>>4 villagers; then 1 smallholder, now 8. Always 4 slaves;
>>>2 ploughs in lordship; 2 men's ploughs.
>>Pasture, 200 sheep.
>[Value] then £4; now 100s.
>In the same village 4 free men hold 50 acres.   21 b
Value 5s.

15   LAND OF HOLY TRINITY, CAEN

Hundred of HINCKFORD

1   Earl Algar held FELSTED before 1066 for 5 hides. Now Holy Trinity
holds (it) for 4 hides. Always 3 ploughs in lordship; 16 men's
ploughs.
>Then 22 villagers, later and now 20; then and later 23
>>smallholders, now 33; always 11 slaves.
>Woodland, 600 pigs; meadow, 36 acres; 2 mills. 21 cattle,
>>200 pigs, 58 sheep, 30 goats, 1 cob.
>To this manor belonged 55 acres before 1066 which 3 Freemen
held, now 4.
>Then 2 ploughs, now 3.
>Now 2 smallholders.
>Woodland, 30 pigs; meadow, 12 acres.
Value then £20; later [£] 30; now [£] 32.
>The fifth hide is not in this manor; for King William gave 3
virgates to Roger God-Save-Ladies and the fourth to Gilbert son
of Solomon.

⁊Hund de Celmeresforda . Baduuen . tenuit Comes . Algar⁹
ꝓ . I . Man . ⁊ ꝓ . VIII . hid . m̃ . Sc̃a . Trin⁷ . ꝓ tantundẽ . Sẽp . XVI . uiłł . Tc̃
VIII . bor . m̃ . XV . sẽp . VI . ser . ⁊ . III . car in dñio . Tc̃ . VIII . car̃ hom̃ .
m̃ . XII . Silũ . CCCC . porc̃ . XLV . ac̃ . ꝑti . I . moł . I . runc̃⁷ . ⁊ . I . pull⁹ . ⁊
XIIII . an̄⁷ . C . porc̃ . IIII . min⁹ . XXXVIII . ou . XIII . cap̃⁷ . ⁊ . III . foch̃ .
ꝗ ñ potant recede . de . I . uirg̃ . ⁊ . XX . ac̃ . ⁊ . d . Tc̃ reddidit . VIII . noct̃ .

22 a
de firma . m̃ . XVII . łib .

⁊TERRA Sci Stephani de cadomo . Hund de hidinghfort ;   ˌXVIˌ
Penfeldā tenuit . I . libā fem⁷ . t . r . e . ꝓ . I . hid . ⁊ . III . uirg⁷ . t . r . e . Tc̃
. IIII . car̃ . in dñio . m̃ . III . Tc̃ . II . car̃ . hom̃ . qñ recep̃ nulla . m̃ . dimid⁷ .
Tc̃ . IIII . uiłł . m̃ null⁹ . Sẽp . VIII . bor . Tc̃ . VIII . ser⁷ . m̃ . VII . Silũ . CC . por .
XII . ac̃⁷ . ꝑti . II . runc̃ . XII . an̄⁷ . CLXV . ou⁷ . XXXVII . porc̃ . Tc̃ uał . X . łib .
Poſt . C . soł . m̃ . X . łib .

⁊Tra sci Audoeni . Hund de Wenfiſtreu . Meresaiam tenuit   ˌXVIIˌ
Sc̃s Audoen . t . r . e . ꝓ . XX . hid . Tc̃ . IIII . car̃ in dñio . m̃ . VI . Sẽp . XVI . car̃
hom̃ . XXXVI . uiłł . LXII . bor . Tc̃ . X . ser . m̃ . III . XI . runc̃ . ⁊ . II . pulli . XVIˌ
an̄⁷ . XXXIIII . porc̃ . CCC . ou . Huic manerio adjac& dim̃ hid⁷ . ꝗ sẽp . ten&
. I . pbr̃ . ⁊ . uał . X . soł . ⁊ . silũ . CC . por . Paſt . CCC . ou⁷ . Tc̃ . I . pisc̃ . Tc̃ uał
XXVI . łib . m̃ . XXII . Eſt & iā in Coleceſtra . I . dom⁹ . quæ ꝑtinuit huic trǣ .
ſ; Waleram eā abſtulit ; Et in Hund de Wenfiſtreu | VIII . soch̃m
regis tenentes . CVII . ac̃ . ⁊ uał . X . soł de his h̃t sc̃s Audoen . II . partes .
Et . II . soc̃ . tulit Ingelric̃ . de . dim̃ hid . ⁊ . XXX . ac̃ . m̃ h̃t eos comes . E .
Et . II . soc̃ ꝗ st̃ additi ad Legrā maneriū regis in alio hund⁷ . & de tota
hac soca h̃t sc̃s . Audoen⁹ . duas partes . ⁊ . rex . t̃ciā . Et sẽp . ͆ . partes
de forisfacturis de hundret

Hundred of CHELMSFORD

2 Earl Algar held (Great) BADDOW as 1 manor, for 8 hides. Now
Holy Trinity (holds it) for as much.
    Always 16 villagers. Then 8 smallholders, now 15. Always 6
        slaves; 3 ploughs in lordship. Then 8 men's ploughs, now 12.
    Woodland, 400 pigs; meadow, 45 acres; 1 mill. 1 cob, 1 foal,
        14 cattle, 100 pigs less 4, 38 sheep, 13 goats.
    3 Freemen, who cannot withdraw, with 1 virgate and 20½
        acres.
    Then it paid 8 nights' provisions; now £17.   22 a

16 LAND OF ST. STEPHEN'S, CAEN

Hundred of HINCKFORD

1 1 free woman held PANFIELD before 1066, for 1 hide and 3 virgates
before 1066. Then 4 ploughs in lordship, now 3. Then 2 men's
ploughs, when acquired none, now ½.
    Then 4 villagers, now none; always 8 smallholders; then 8 slaves,
        now 7.
    Woodland, 200 pigs; meadow, 12 acres. 2 cobs, 12 cattle,
        165 sheep, 37 pigs.
    Value then £10; later 100s; now £10.

17 LAND OF ST. OUEN'S

Hundred of WINSTREE

1 St. Ouen's held (West) MERSEA before 1066 for 20 hides. Then 4
ploughs in lordship, now 6. Always 16 men's ploughs.
    36 villagers, 62 smallholders. Then 10 slaves, now 3.
    11 cobs, 2 foals, 16 cattle, 34 pigs, 300 sheep.
    To this manor is attached ½ hide which 1 priest has always
held; value 10s.
    Woodland, 200 pigs; pasture, 300 sheep; then 1 fishery.
    Value then £26; now [£] 22.
    There is also 1 house in Colchester which belonged to this land;
but Waleran took it away.

2 Also in Winstree Hundred 8 King's Freemen who hold 107 acres.
Value 10s; of these, St. Ouen's has two parts.
    Engelric took 2 Freemen with ½ hide and 30 acres. Count
E(ustace) has them now. Also 2 Freemen who have been added
to the King's manor at Layer in another Hundred. Of all this
jurisdiction St. Ouen's has two parts and the King (has) the third
part; and always two parts of the forfeitures of the Hundred.

XVIII. ꝟTERRE EPI Baiocenſis in Exſeſſa Hundret de

Berdeſtapla. Phenge ten& . fili̇ turoldi de eꝓ qđ tenueꝛ . II . liƀi
hões .p . v . hid . 7 . dim̃ . Sep̃ . II . caꝛ in dñio 7 . IIII . caꝛ hom̃ . VI . uiłt.
IX . bor . I . ſeꝛ . dimidia hid̃ ſiluæ . Paſt . CXX . ou̇ . I . piſcina . m̃ . I . moł.
. II . runc̃ . IIII . an̂ . IIII . porc̃ . Tc̃ . LXVII . ou̇ . M̃ . CCLXX . De hac tꝛa tenebat
. I . liƀ hõ . XXX . ac̃ . quæ . t̂ . r . Wiłłi addite ſt ad p̃dic̃ta tꝛa . 7 neſcit̂ q̃m̃.
Tc̃ ual . c . ſoł . m̃ . VIII . liƀ.

ꝟBurgheſtedã ten& Epc̃ in dñio qđ tenuit Ingar teinn̄ . t . r̂ . e . .p
. I . Man̂ . 7 . x . hid̃ . Sep̃ . III . caꝛ in dñio . Tc̃ . XII . caꝛ hom̃ . m̃ . XI . Tc̃ . XX.
uiłt . m̃ . XXII . Tc̃ . v . bor . m̃ . x . Dim̃ hid̃ . ſiluæ paſt . CL . ou̇ . II . runc̃.
XI . an̂ . c̄'' · porc̃ . CCXVIIII . ou̇ . Val . XX . liƀ . Huic manerio additi
ſunt . t̂ . r . Wiłłi XXVIII . liƀi hões . tenentes . XXVIII . hid̃ . 7 . v . ac̃ . in
quiłꝫ erant . tc̃ . XVI . caꝛ . m̃ . XIII . v . hid̃ . ſiluæ . XXIII . ac̃ p̃ti . Paſtura
. CCL . ou̇ . LIIII . bor . IIII . ſeꝛ . hoc additam̃tu ual . tc̃ . XX . liƀ . M̃ XVI.

ꝟDantunã ten& epc̃ in dñio qđ tenuit . I . p̃br liƀ hõ . t̂ . r̂ . e . .p . VII.
hid̃ . 7 . XL . ac̃ . Tc̃ . IIII . caꝛ . in dñio . m̃ . II . ſep̃ . IIII . caꝛ hom̃ . Tc̃ . VII . uiłt
m̃ . II . 7 . VI . bor . Tc̃ . v . ſeꝛ . m̃ . II . II . runc̃ . II . an̂ . XV . por . XXXIIII . ou̇.
Tc̃ ual . XII . liƀ . m̃ . VII.

ꝟBerdeſteſtapla ten& fili̇ Turoldi . đeꝓ qđ tenuit . I . liƀ hõ . .p . v . hid̃.
7 dim̃ . 7 . XXX . ac̃ . Sep̃ . III . caꝛ̂ . in dñio . 7 . II . hom̃ . VI . uiłt . XI . bor . Tc̃
ual . IIII . liƀ . m̃ . c . ſoł . In dñio . II . runc̃ . v . anim̃ . XVIII por . XXXVI . ou̇.
M̃ . I . runc̃ . IX . an̂ . XXIIII . porc̃ . LXXX . ou̇ ;

LANDS OF THE BISHOP OF BAYEUX IN ESSEX

Hundred of BARSTABLE

1　Thorold's son holds VANGE from the Bishop. 2 free men held it
for 5½ hides. Always 2 ploughs in lordship; 4 men's ploughs.
　　6 villagers; 9 smallholders; 1 slave.
　　Woodland, ½ hide; pasture, 120 sheep; 1 fishery; now 1 mill.
　　　2 cobs, 4 cattle, 4 pigs; then 67 sheep, now 270.
　　Of this land, 1 free man held 30 acres which were added to the
aforesaid land after 1066; it is not known how.
Value then 100s; now £8.

2　The Bishop holds (Great) BURSTEAD in lordship. Ingvar, a thane,
held it before 1066 as 1 manor, 10 hides. Always 3 ploughs in
lordship. Then 12 men's ploughs, now 11.
　　Then 20 villagers, now 22; then 5 smallholders, now 10.
　　Woodland, ½ hide; pasture, 150 sheep. 2 cobs, 11 cattle,
　　　106 pigs, 219 sheep.
Value £20.
　　28 free men were added to this manor after 1066; they hold
28 hides and 5 acres. On these there were then 16 ploughs, now 13.
　　Woodland, 5 hides; meadow, 23 acres; pasture, 250 sheep.
　　54 smallholders, 4 slaves.
Value of this addition then £20; now [£] 16.

3　The Bishop holds DUNTON in lordship. 1 priest, a free man, held it
before 1066 for 7 hides and 40 acres. Then 4 ploughs in lordship,
now 2. Always 4 men's ploughs.
　　Then 7 villagers, now 2; 6 smallholders; then 5 slaves, now 2.
　　2 cobs, 2 cattle, 15 pigs, 34 sheep.
Value then £12; now [£] 7.

4　Thorold's son holds BARSTABLE (Hall) from the Bishop. 1 free
man held it for 5½ hides and 30 acres.
　　Woodland, 30 acres; pasture, 100 sheep.
　　Always 3 ploughs in lordship; 2 men's [ploughs].
　　　6 villagers, 11 smallholders.
Value then £4; now 100s.
　　In lordship then 2 cobs, 5 cattle, 18 pigs, 36 sheep; now 1 cob,
9 cattle, 24 pigs, 80 sheep.

Ingā ten& fili Turoldi de epo. q̄d tenuit.ɪ.lib̄ hō.t.r.e.p.ɪɪ.hid.
Sēp.ɪ.car in dn̄io.7.ɪ.car hom.ɪ.uillt.Tc.ɪ.bor.m̄.v.ɪɪɪ.ser.ɪ.hid̄.7.d

.ɪɪɪ.runc.vɪɪɪ.an.Tc.xxx.por.m̄.lvɪɪɪ.Tc.xl.ou.m̄.lxxvɪ.Tc
xxxɪɪ.cap.m̄.xɪɪɪɪ.Tc uat.lx.sot.m̄.lxx.huic manerio additi
st̄ vɪɪ.lib̄i hoes.de.v.hid.t.r.Willt.Sēp.v.car.ɪ.hid̄.7.d.siluæ.
xɪ.bor.ɪɪɪɪ.ac.p̄ti.Tc.uat.ɪɪɪɪ.lib̄.m̄.xl.sot.

Ramesdanā tenent.ɪɪ.milit.de epo.q̄d tenuer.ɪɪ.lib̄i hoēs.p.ɪɪɪ.
hid̄.& sic anglici dicunt Rauengari abstulit.tr̄a ab uno illoꝗ
7 Rob̄ fili Wimarc altam tr̄a ab alto.m̄ ū n̄esciunt q̄m uenerit
ad epm.Tc.habuer.ɪɪ.car.m̄ ibi nulla ē.Tc.v.bor.m̄.vɪɪ.dim
hid̄ siluæ.Pastura.c.ou.Tc uat.ɪɪɪ.lib̄.m̄.ɪɪɪɪ.

In Wateleia.7.in Wincfort.tenent.Pointel.7 Osb̄n.ɪɪ.hid̄.quas
tenuer.ɪɪ.lib̄i hoēs.t.r.e Tc.ɪɪ.car.m̄.ɪ.ɪɪɪɪ.bor.ɪ.hid̄.Siluæ.xxv.
ac.p̄ti.Past.xl.ou.Tc.uat.xl.sot.m̄.xxx.Et ist̄a tr̄a abstulit eis
Rauengari.7 m̄ nesciunt angli q̄m uenerit in manu epi

Wicfort ten& fili turoldi.de epo.q̄d tenuer.v.lib̄i hoēs.t.r.e.
p.ɪɪ.hid̄.7.xlvɪɪɪ.ac.sēp.ɪɪ.car.v.bor.ɪɪ.ser.Silu.xxx.porc.Vat
xl.sot. Wicfort ten& Teher de epo.q̄d tenuit.Godric.ɪ.lib̄ hō
.t.r.e.p.ɪ.hid̄.Sēp.ɪ.car.Tc.ɪ.bor.m̄.ɪɪ.Silu.xxx.por.vɪɪɪ.ac.
p̄ti Vat.xx.sot.

Hasinghebroc ten& fili turoldi.q̄d tenuer.xvɪ.lib̄i hoēs.t.r.e
p.xɪɪ.hid̄.7.xɪɪɪ.ac.7.dim.Tc.xɪ.car.m̄.vɪɪ.m̄.xɪɪɪɪ.bor
xx.soc.Silu.cc.por.xvɪ.ac.p̄ti.Past.cccc.ou.Vat.x.lib̄.

5 Thorold's son holds INGRAVE from the Bishop. 1 free man held it
before 1066 for 2 hides. Always 1 plough in lordship; 1 men's
plough.

> 1 villager. Then 1 smallholder, now 5; 3 slaves.
> Woodland, 1½ hides. 3 cobs; 8 cattle; then 30 pigs, now 58;   23 a
>> then 40 sheep, now 76; then 32 goats, now 14.

Value then 60s; now 70[s].

> 7 free men with 3 hides have been added to this manor after
1066. Always 5 ploughs.
> Woodland, 1½ hides. 11 smallholders. Meadow, 4 acres.

Value then £4; now 40s.

6 2 men-at-arms hold RAMSDEN (Cray) from the Bishop, which 2
free men held for 3 hides. So the English state, Ravengar took
the land away from one of them and Robert son of Wymarc took
the other land away from the other one; but now they do not
know how it has come to the Bishop. Then they had 2 ploughs,
now there is none there.

> Then 5 smallholders, now 7.
> Woodland, ½ hide; pasture, 100 sheep.

Value then £3; now [£]4.

7 In WHEATLEY and in WICKFORD Pointel and Osbern hold 2 hides
which 2 free men held before 1066. Then 2 ploughs, now 1.

> 4 smallholders.
> Woodland, 1 hide; meadow, 25 acres; pasture, 40 sheep.

Value then 40s; now 30[s].

> Ravengar took this land away from them; now the English do
not know how it came into the Bishop's hand.

8 Thorold's son holds WICKFORD from the Bishop, which 5 free men
held before 1066, for 2 hides and 48 acres. Always 2 ploughs.

> 5 smallholders, 2 slaves.
> Woodland, 30 pigs.

Value 40s.

9 Teher holds WICKFORD from the Bishop, which 1 free man, Godric,
held before 1066, for 1 hide. Always 1 plough.

> Then 1 smallholder, now 2.
> Woodland, 30 pigs; meadow, 8 acres.

Value 20s.

10 Thorold's son holds HASSENBROOK (Hall), which 16 free men held
before 1066, for 12 hides and 13½ acres. Then 11 ploughs, now 7.

> Now 14 smallholders, 20 Freemen.
> Woodland, 200 pigs; meadow, 16 acres; pasture, 400 sheep.

Value £10.

Celdewellā ten&. Idē de eɓo qđ tenuit Eduuolt ꝑpoſit regis . E . ꝑ
. I . hiđ . 7 . dim̄ . Seᵖ . I . car̄ . 7 . đ . in dn̄io . dim̄ . car̄ hom̄ . Tc̄ . VI . bor . m̄ . VII .
Tc̄ . II . ſer̄ . m̄ . I ; Qđā ſoc̄ . đe . xxx . ac̄ . Silu . LXXX . por . Paſt̄ . c . ou.

Tc̄ . I . piſc̄ . m̄ n̄ ſ; poꝛ fieri . Dē hac tr̄a fuer̄ t . r . e . xxx . ac̄ . ad aliā tr̄a
Tc̄ ual . XL . ſot . m̄ totū ſimul . xxx . ſot . In Torinduna ħt eɓc . xx .
ac̄ . qs ten̄ . I . lib hō . t . r̄ i e . Val . xxx . đ . .

Hund de Witham . In Hafelda . xv . ac̄ . q̄s tenuit . I . ſoc̄ . Tc̄ ual
. III . ſot . m̄ . IIII .

Hund de Rochefort . Stanbruge ten& Suen̄ de eɓo : q̄m ten̄
Oſuuard . t . r . e . ꝑ . III . hiđ . 7 . dim̄ . 7 . xxx . ac̄ . Tc̄ . VII . ult . m̄ . null . Tc̄ . v.
bor . m̄ . x . Tc̄ . III . ſer̄ . m̄ null . Seᵖ . II . car̄ . in dn̄io . Tc̄ . III . car̄ homin̄ .
m̄ . IIII . Paſt̄ . ccc . ou . I . mot . M̄ . I . runc̄ . Tc̄ . IIII . am̄ . M̄ . II . Tc̄ . xv.
por . m̄ . xxv . Tc̄ . c . ou . m̄ LVIII . Seᵖ . ual . VI . lib.

Bacheneiā ten̄ . Rauengar̄ . m̄ eɓc . in dn̄io . ꝑ . dim̄ . hiđ . Tc̄ . I . ſer̄ . m̄
. I . bor . Seᵖ . I . car̄ in dn̄io . Paſtur̄ . xxx . ou . Tc̄ ual . xx . ſot . m̄ . xxx .
In ꝑtio de his . xxx . ſot ſꝛ adhuc . xxx . ac̄ . 7 . I . bor . 7 . dim̄ . car̄ .

Berlingā ten& eɓc in dn̄io qđ tenuit . I . lib hō . ꝑ . dim̄ . hiđ . Seᵖ . I .
bor . Tc̄ . I . car̄ . m̄ . nulla . ſed poꝛ fieri . Val . x . ſot.

Sobiam ten& eɓc in dio . qđ tenuit . I . lib hō ꝑ . I . hiđ . 7 . xxx . ac̄ . Sep
. II . uilt . Tc̄ . II . bor . m̄ . III . Tc̄ . I . car̄ . in dn̄io . m̄ . II . bou . Seᵖ . I . car̄ hou.
Paſt̄ . XL . ou . Tc̄ ual . XL . ſot . m̄ . LV.

11 He also holds CHADWELL from the Bishop, which Edwold, King
Edward's reeve, held for 1½ hides. Always 1½ ploughs in lordship;
½ men's plough.
> Then 6 smallholders, now 7; then 2 slaves, now 1. A Freeman
> with 30 acres.
> Woodland, 80 pigs; pasture, 100 sheep; then 1 fishery, now   23 b
> none, but (1) possible.
> Before 1066, 30 acres of this land (belonged) to another land.
Value then 40s; now altogether 30s.

12 In HORNDON the Bishop has 20 acres, which 1 free man held
before 1066.
Value 30d.

Hundred of WITHAM
13 In HATFIELD (Peverel) 15 acres, which 1 Freeman held.
Value then 3s; now 4[s].

Hundred of ROCHFORD
14 Swein holds (Great) STAMBRIDGE from the Bishop, which Osward
held before 1066, for 3½ hides and 30 acres.
> Then 7 villagers, now none; then 5 smallholders, now 10;
> then 3 slaves, now none. Always 2 ploughs in lordship.
> Then 3 men's ploughs, now 4.
> Pasture, 300 sheep; 1 mill. Now 1 cob; then 4 cattle, now 2;
> then 15 pigs, now 25; then 100 sheep, now 58.
Value always £6.

15 Ravengar held BECKNEY. Now the Bishop (holds it) in lordship for
½ hide.
> Then 1 slave; now 1 smallholder. Always 1 plough in lordship.
> Pasture, 30 sheep.
Value then 20s; now 30[s]. In the same assessment of these 30s
are a further 30 acres and
> 1 smallholder; ½ plough.

16 The Bishop holds BARLING in lordship, which 1 free man held, for
½ hide.
> Always 1 smallholder. Then 1 plough, now none, but (1)
> possible.
Value 10s.

17 The Bishop holds SHOEBURY in lordship, which 1 free man held,
for 1 hide and 30 acres.
> Always 2 villagers. Then 2 smallholders, now 3. Then 1 plough
> in lordship, now 2 oxen. Always 1 men's plough.
> Pasture, 40 sheep.
Value then 40s; now 55[s].

⊦Hund de Witbricteſherna   Criccheſeiã ten& Suen de epo

qd̃ tenuit Edric lib̃ hõ.t.r.e.p.ı.m̃.7.p.ı.hid.Tc̃ıı.bor.m̃.ııı.
ſẽp.ıı.ſer.7.ı.car.in dñio.filu.xx.porc.Paſt.xx.ou.Tc̃.ıııı.an.7 m̃;
ſimil.Tc̃ 7 p̃ ual.xııı.ſol m̃.xxx.

⊦Criccheſeiam ten&.Pointel de epo.qd̃ tenuit Leuric.t.r.e.p.d.
hid.Tc̃.dim.car.m̃.n̄.Tc̃.ual.x.ſol.m̃.v.

24 a

⊦Hund de Wenſiſtrev.   Samantunã ten& Rad̃ fili turoldi
de epõ.qd̃ tenuer.ıı.libi hões.p.dim.hid.7 xxxᵛ.ac.Sẽp.dim.car.M̃.ıı.
bor.Tc̃ ual.xvı.ſol.m̃.xv.

⊦Hund de Hidincfort.   Nepſtedã ten& Vxor albici de epõ qd̃
tenuer.vııı.libi hões.t.r.e.p.xxıı.ac.7.d̃.Sẽp.ı.car.filu.xx.porc.vı.
ac.p̃ti.Sẽp.ual.xxx.ſol. ⎰ In Hoc hundret ten& Tiheli de herion
xxıı.libos hões.de.ıı.hid.7.xııı.ac.7.dim.ſẽp.v.car.Tc̃ 7 p̃.ı.bor.
m̃.ıx.ſẽp.ı.ſer.filu.ıııı.porc.xxxı.ac.p̃ti.Tc̃ 7 p̃ ual.lx.ſol m̃.ıııı.lib̃.

⊦Hund de Witbricteſherna. Daneſceiã ten&.ı.mil epiſcopi.qd̃
tenuit Siric.t.r.e.p.ıı.hid.7.dim.Sẽp.ıı.uill.m̃.vı.bor.Sẽp.ııı.ſer
7.ıı.car.in dñio.7.ı.car.hom.Paſt.clx.ou.Tc̃ ual.ıııı.lib̃.m̃.c.ſol
in dñio.cl.ou.ı.runc.xııı.por. Ad hoc manerıũ erant t.r.e.ıı.
libi homines.de xlvıı.ac.q̃s occupaũ Idẽ miles ep̃i.Sẽp.ual.ıııı.
ſol.

Hundred of 'WIBERTSHERNE'

18 Swein holds CREEKSEA from the Bishop, which Edric, a free man, held before 1066, as 1 manor, for 1 hide.
    Then 2 smallholders, now 3. Always 2 slaves; 1 plough in lordship.
    Woodland, 20 pigs; pasture, 20 sheep. Then 4 cattle, now the same.
Value then and later 23s; now 30[s].

19 Pointel holds CREEKSEA from the Bishop, which Leofric held before 1066, for ½ hide. Then ½ plough, now none.
Value then 10s; now 5[s].

Hundred of WINSTREE

20 Ralph son of Thorold holds SAMPSON'S (Farm) from the Bishop, which 2 free men held for ½ hide and 35 acres. Always ½ plough.
    Now 2 smallholders.
Value then 16s; now 15[s].

Hundred of HINCKFORD

21 Aubrey's wife holds 'NAPSTED' from the Bishop, which 8 free men held before 1066, for 22½ acres. Always 1 plough.
    Woodland, 20 pigs; meadow, 6 acres.
Value always 30s.

21a In this Hundred Tihel of Helléan holds 22 free men with 2 hides and 13½ acres. Always 5 ploughs.
    Then and later 1 smallholder, now 9; always 1 slave.
    Woodland, 4 pigs; meadow, 31 acres.
Value then and later 60s; now £4.

Hundred of 'WIBERTSHERNE'

22 1 man-at-arms of the Bishop's holds DENGIE, which Siric held before 1066, for 2½ hides.
    Always 2 villagers. Now 6 smallholders. Always 3 slaves; 2 ploughs in lordship; 1 men's plough.
    Pasture, 160 sheep.
Value then £4; now 100s.
    In lordship 150 sheep, 1 cob, 13 pigs.
    In this manor before 1066 were 2 free men with 47 acres, whom the Bishop's man-at-arms also appropriated.
Value always 4s.

Hacflet ten& . I . miɫ epi . q̃d tenuit Aluuard lib hō

.p.II.hid.7.xxx.ac.Tc.IIII.bor.m̃.x.Sep.I.car.Past.

.cc 7 LX.ou.I.pisc.Ecclia ten& xL.ac.Tc uaɫ.LX.soɫ.m̃.

.IIII.lib.7.xI.soɫ.In hac uilla erat.I.lib hō de.xxx.ac.7 udlagaũ

m̃ hōes sueni accepunt trã 7 adhuc tenent.

Hund de Laſſendene. Aldeham tenuit Leueua.p.I.hid.v.

ac min.t.r.e.M ten& vxor albici de epo.Tc.I.uiɫɫ.m̃ nuɫɫ.Sep

.IIII.ser.7.II.car in dñio.Silu.xII.por.III.ac.p̃ti.I.runc.vI.an.Tc 7 poſt

uaɫ.xxx.soɫ.m̃.LX.

Hund de Angra. Kelendunã ten& nepos herbti de epo q̃d tenuit

Algar lib hō.p.dim.hid.7.xx.ac.Sep.IIII.bor.7.I.car.Silu.LX.por

24 b

vII.ac.7.dim p̃ti.I.an.v.porc.xLvII.ou.Vaɫ.xx.soɫ.

Hund de Ceſſeorda. Vpmunſtrã ten& Malger de epo q̃d tenuit Vluuin

.p.I.hid.7 dim.Tc.II.bor.7 m̃ similiꝉ.Sep.I.car.Tc uaɫ.xx.soɫ.m̃ xxx.

Aluitheleam ten& Idē Malger.q̃d tenuit Eduuard un lib homo.p.I.hid.7 xxx.ac.

Sep.vI.bor.7.I.car in dñio.7.I.car hominũ.Tc uaɫ.xx.soɫ.m̃.xxx.

Turocham ten& Hugo de epo.q̃d tenuit Aluuard lib hō.p.I.hid.7.xL.ac.Sep

.II.bor.Tc.II.car.m̃.I.silu.x.porc.vIII.ac.p̃ti.Paſtur.L.ou.Tc.uaɫ.xxx.soɫ.

m̃ xL.Tc.I.runc.Tc.I.an.m̃.II.Tc.xxv.por.m̃.Ix.Tc.L.ou.m̃ xLvIII.

23   1 man-at-arms of the Bishop's holds BRADWELL QUAY, which Alfward, a free man, held for 2 hides and 30 acres.

      Then 4 smallholders, now 10. Always 1 plough.

      Pasture, 260 sheep; 1 fishery. The church holds 40 acres.

      Value then 60s; now £4 11s.

      In this village there was 1 free man with 30 acres and he was outlawed; now Swein's men have received the land and still hold (it).

Hundred of LEXDEN

24   Leofeva held ALDHAM for 1 hide less 5 acres before 1066. Now Aubrey's wife holds (it) from the Bishop.

      Then 1 villager, now none. Always 4 slaves; 2 ploughs in lordship.

      Woodland, 12 pigs; meadow, 3 acres. 1 cob, 6 cattle.

      Value then and later 30s; now 60s.

Hundred of ONGAR

25   Herbert's nephew holds KELVEDON (Hatch) from the Bishop, which Algar, a free man, held for ½ hide and 20 acres.

      Always 4 smallholders; 1 plough.

      Woodland, 60 pigs; meadow, 7½ acres. 1 (head of) cattle,   24 b
      5 pigs, 47 sheep.

      Value 20s.

Hundred of CHAFFORD

26   Mauger holds UPMINSTER from the Bishop, which Wulfwin held for 1½ hides.

      Then 2 smallholders, now the same. Always 1 plough.

      Value then 20s; now 30[s].

27   Mauger also holds AVELEY, which Edward, a free man, held for 1 hide and 40 acres.

      Always 6 smallholders; 1 plough in lordship; 1 men's plough.

      Value then 20s; now 30[s].

28   Hugh holds THURROCK from the Bishop, which Alfward, a free man, held for 1 hide and 40 acres.

      Always 2 smallholders. Then 2 ploughs, now 1.

      Woodland, 10 pigs; meadow, 8 acres; pasture, 50 sheep.

      Value then 30s; now 40[s].

      Then 1 cob; then 1 (head of) cattle, now 2; then 25 pigs, now 9; then 50 sheep, now 48.

Turochā ten& Anſchetill. de epo . qđ tenuit Mannic lib hō . t . r . e . ꝓ . ıı . hıđ
. 7 . dım . 7 . xl . ac . M . ıı . uıłł . Tc . ııı . bor . m̄ . vııı . Tc . vı . ſer . m̄ nułł . Sep . ı . car in dn̄io .
7 . ı . car homınū . vııı . ac . p̄ti . Tc uał . ııı . lıb . m̄ . ıııı .

Reneham ten& Hugo de epo . qđ tenuit Alſı lıb hō . ꝓ . Man̄ . 7 . ꝓ . ıııı . hıđ
t . r . e . Sep . vııı . uıłł . Tc . ııı . bor . m̄ . v . Tc . ıııı . ſer . m̄ nułł . Tc . ııı . car . in dn̄io
7 . qn̄ recep̄ . ıı . m̄ nulla . Tc . 7 . ꝓ . ııı . car hom̄ . m̄ . ıı . Tc . 7 p̄ uał
vı . lıb . m̄ . xl . ſoł . In Turoc tenuit Vluuın̄ . dımıđ . hıđ . M̄ . hugo
de epo Tc . ı . car . m̄ n̄ . Sıłu . v . por . vııı . ac . p̄ti . Paſt . l . ou . Vał . xx . ſoł.   ★

Eſtınfort tenuit Aluric . lıb hō . ꝓ . ı . hıđ . 7 . xxx . ac . m̄
ten&   Ide hugo . ſep . ı . bor . 7 . ı . car . v . ac . p̄ti . Vał . xxx . ſoł.   ★
De hǎc tr̄a ſt̄ xv . ac . in Soca Wıłłı pıperellı . de turoc . ſicut
comıtaꞇ teſtaꞇ . Ad eccłıā huꝯ manerıj jacent . xxx . ac . q̄s uıcıni de
deꝝ in elemoſina .

Craohv . ten& hugo de epo qđ ꞇenuit Aluuın̄ lıb hō . ꝓ . m̄ . 7 . ꝓ . ı . hıđ . 7 . đ .
Sep . ı . uıłł . 7 . ı . bor . Tc . ı . car . M̄ . dım . Sıłu . c . porc . ı . ac . 7 . dım . p̄ti . Tc
7 poſt uał . l . ſoł . m̄ . xx . In Eſtınfort . tenuit Gıſłeꞇ hō epi baıoc.

25 a
. ı . hıđ . 7 . dım . qđ ten& fılı turoldi de epo . Sep . ııı . uıłł . 7 . ıııı . bor . 7 . ıı . car in đio .
Vał . xxx . ſoł . Hoc teſtatur hund qđ hec hıđ jacuıt t . r . e . in Turroc maner̄
Wıłłı pıperellı . exceptıs . x . ac .

Lımpwełłā ten& Hugo de ~~comıte~~ epo qđ tenuit Edric lıb hō . ꝓ . ı . Man̄ . 7
dım hıđ . Tc . ı . bor . m̄ . ıı . Tc . ı . car . m̄ . dım . Sıłu . xx . porc . Paſtura xx . ou .
Tc uał . x . ſoł . m̄ . xx .

29 Ansketel holds THURROCK from the Bishop, which Manning, a free
man, held before 1066, for 2½ hides and 40 acres.
   Now 2 villagers; then 3 smallholders, now 8; then 6 slaves,
      now none. Always 1 plough in lordship; 1 men's plough.
   Meadow, 8 acres.
Value then £3; now [£] 4.

30 Hugh holds RAINHAM from the Bishop, which Alfsi, a free man,
held as a manor, for 4 hides before 1066.
   Always 8 villagers. Then 3 smallholders, now 5; then 4 slaves,
      now none. Then 3 ploughs in lordship, when acquired 2,
      now none. Then and later 3 men's ploughs, now 2.
Value then and later £6; now 40s.

31 Wulfwin held ½ hide in THURROCK. Now Hugh (holds it) from the
Bishop. Then 1 plough, now none.
   Woodland, 5 pigs; meadow, 8 acres; pasture, 50 sheep.
Value 20s.

32 Aelfric, a free man, held STIFFORD for 1 hide and 30 acres. Now
Hugh also holds it.
   Always 1 smallholder; 1 plough.
   Meadow, 5 acres.
Value 30s.
   Of this land, 15 acres are in William Peverel's jurisdiction of
(Grays) Thurrock, as the County testifies. 30 acres, which
neighbours gave in alms, lie in (the lands of) this manor's church.

33 Hugh holds CRANHAM from the Bishop, which Alwin, a free man,
held as a manor, for 1½ hides.
   Always 1 villager; 1 smallholder. Then 1 plough, now ½.
   Woodland, 100 pigs; meadow, 1½ acres.
Value then and later 50s; now 20[s].

34 In STIFFORD Gilbert, a man of the Bishop of Bayeux's, held 1½   25 a
hides, which Thorold's son holds from the Bishop.
   Always 3 villagers; 4 smallholders; 2 ploughs in lordship.
Value 30s.
   This Hundred testifies that these hides lay in (the lands of)
Grays) Thurrock, William Peverel's manor, before 1066, apart
from 10 acres.

35 Hugh holds LIMPWELLA from the Bishop, which Edric, a free man,
held as 1 manor; ½ hide.
   Then 1 smallholder, now 2. Then 1 plough, now ½.
   Woodland, 20 pigs; pasture, 20 sheep.
Value then 10s; now 20[s].

⌐Hund de Celmeresfort. Haneghefeldā tenuit Friebť ꝑ.ı.Man.ꝶ

ꝑ.ıx.hıd.t.r.e.m̄ ten& Rađ fili Turoldi de epō.Sēp.ııı.uıłł.Tc̄.ıı.boř.m̄.v.
Tc̄.ıııı.fer.m̄.vııı.Tc̄.ıı.cař in dn̄io.m̄.ııı.Sēp.ıı.cař.hom̄.Sılu.ʟx.por.ııı.runc̄.
xvı.an̄.xxxıı.por.Tc̄.cxvıı.ou.m̄.ꝺcccx.Tc̄ uał.c.foł.m̄.vıı.In eađ
tenuer xxııı.libi hōes xıııı.hıd.q̄ poſſent recede fine licentia dn̄i ıpſi manſioıs
Hos ten& Epc̄.ſ; comitat neſcit q̄ m̄ eos habuerit.Sēp.ı.uıłł.ꝶ.xvııı.bor.
ꝶ.vııı.fer.Tc̄.xı.cař.m̄.x.Sılu.cʟ.por.Tc̄ uał.vııı.lıb.m̄.vıı.lıb.ꝶ.
.ıı.foł.has hıd.p̄occupau turold de Roueceſtra.ꝶ abbatia de eli calump
niať.ıı.hıd.ꝶ.ııı.uırg̃.q̄s tenebant.ıı.hōes.ꝶ hund teſtať.q̄d ıpſi tenebant
lıbe trā fuā.ꝶ tantū m̄ erant cōmdati abbi de eli.

⌐Berewic tenuit Oın̄ dac̄:lıb hō.t.r.e.M Turolđ de epō.ꝑ.vı.hıd.ꝶ.xxxvıı.
ac̄.Tc̄.ıııı.uıłł.m̄.vı.Tc̄.ıııı.bor.m̄.vı.Tc̄.ııı.fer.m̄.v.Sēp.ııı.cař in dn̄io ꝶ.ıı.cař
hom̄.Sılu.c.porc̄.ııı.ac̄.p̄ti.Tc̄.ıııt.runc̄.m̄:v.| Tc̄.ıııı.an̄:m̄r.xvııı.Tc̄.xvı.porc̄
m̄.ʟxı.Tc̄.ʟx.ou.m̄.cxxvı.Tc̄ uał.ıııt.lıb.m̄.vı.

⌐Laghenbiam.tenuit Turchıłł ꝑ:m̄.t.r.e:ꝑ.ıı.hıd.ꝶ.dım̄.ꝶ.vı.ac̄.M
.R.ꝑ tantundē.de epō.Tc̄.ıı.uıłł.m̄.ı.Sēp.v.bor ꝶ.ıı.fer.ꝶ.ı.cař in dn̄io.
ꝶ.ı.cař.hom̄.Sılu.c.porc̄.xvıı.ac̄:p̄ti.Tc̄.ııı.runc̄.m̄.ı.Tc̄.v.an̄.m̄.ıx.
Tc̄:xıx.por.m̄.xʟ.Tc̄.xʟv.ou.M.cx.Tc̄ ꝶ uał.xʟ.foł.m̄.ʟx.

25 b

Walfarā.tenuit.Anunt dac̄:t.r.e.ꝑ.ııı.ꝶ.ꝑ.ı.hıd.ꝶ.dım̄.m̄.R.de epō.
Sēp.ıı.bor.ꝶ.ı.fer.ꝶ.ı.cař.Sılu.ʟx.porc̄.xv.ac̄.p̄ti.ı.runc̄.Tc̄.v.an̄.m̄.ıııı.
Tc̄.xv.ou.m̄.ʟ.Tc̄:xı.por.m̄.xvıı:ı.cap̄.Tc̄ uał.xx.foł.m̄.xxx.

Hundred of CHELMSFORD

36 Fridebert held (South) HANNINGFIELD as 1 manor, for 9 hides before 1066. Now Ralph son of Thorold holds (it) from the Bishop.

> Always 3 villagers. Then 2 smallholders, now 5; then 4 slaves, now 8. Then 2 ploughs in lordship, now 3. Always 2 men's ploughs.
>
> Woodland, 60 pigs. 3 cobs, 16 cattle, 32 pigs; then 117 sheep, now 810.

Value then 100s; now £7.

> In the same (Hanningfield), 23 free men, who could withdraw without the lord of the place's permission, held 14 hides. The Bishop holds these, but the County does not know how he has them.
>
> Always 1 villager; 18 smallholders; 8 slaves. Then 11 ploughs, now 10.
>
> Woodland, 150 pigs.

Value then £8; now £7 2s.

> Thorold of Rochester misappropriated these hides. Ely Abbey claims 2 hides and 3 virgates, which 2 men held; the Hundred testifies that they held their land freely and were nevertheless under the Abbot of Ely's patronage.

37 Odin the Dane, a free man, held *BEREWIC* before 1066. Now Thorold (holds it) from the Bishop for 6½ hides and 37 acres.

> Then 4 villagers, now 6; then 4 smallholders, now 6; then 3 slaves, now 5. Always 3 ploughs in lordship; 2 men's ploughs.
>
> Woodland, 100 pigs; meadow, 3 acres. Then 3 cobs, now 5 and 10 foals; then 4 cattle, now 18; then 16 pigs, now 61; then 60 sheep, now 126.

Value then £4; now [£] 6.

38 Thorkell held LAWN (Hall) as a manor before 1066, for 2½ hides and 6 acres. Now R(alph holds it) from the Bishop for as much.

> Then 2 villagers, now 1. Always 5 smallholders; 2 slaves; 1 plough in lordship; 1 men's plough.
>
> Woodland, 100 pigs; meadow, 17 acres. Then 3 cobs, now 1; then 5 cattle, now 9; then 19 pigs, now 40; then 45 sheep, now 110.

Value then and later 40s; now 60[s].

39 Anand the Dane held WALTER (Hall) before 1066 as a manor, for 25 b 1½ hides. Now R(alph holds it) from the Bishop.

> Always 2 smallholders; 1 slave; 1 plough.
>
> Woodland, 60 pigs; meadow, 15 acres. 1 cob; then 5 cattle, now 4; then 15 sheep, now 50; then 11 pigs, now 17; 1 goat.

Value then 20s; now 30[s].

⌐Pacingas tenuit Segar̃ ꝑ. M̃.7.ꝑ.ii.hid̃. 7.xxx ⸝ac̃. t́. r̃. ẽ. m̃. R. de eꝑo. Tc̃
.i.uill̃. m̃. iii. Sep̃. iiii. bor̃. 7. i. ſer̃. 7. i. car̃. in dĩo. 7. i. car̃. hom̃. Silũ. xv. porc̃.
viii. ac̃. ꝑti. i. mol̃. Tc̃. iii. runc̃. m̃. iiii. Tc̃. ii. añ. m̃. iiii. Tc̃. xi. ou̇. m̃. xxiii.
Val̃. xl ſol̃. ⌐ M

⌐Meleſham tenuit Godric̃ ꝑ m̃. 7. ꝑ. ii. hid̃. 7. dim̃. 7 xxx. ac̃. M̃. R. de eꝑo.
Tc̃. i. uill̃. m̃. ii. Tc̃. i. bor̃. m̃. vi. Tc̃. iiii. ſer̃. m̃. iii. Sep̃. ii. car̃. in dñio. Tc̃. i. car̃
7. dim̃. hom̃. m̃. i. ſilũ. lx. porc̃. x. ac̃. ꝑti. Sep̃. i. mol̃. Tc̃. iii. runc̃. 7. i. pull̃.
m̃. ii. runc̃. 7. iiii. pull̃. Tc̃. ix. añ. m̃. xxviii. Tc̃. xlvii. ou̇. m̃. cxl. Tc̃ ual̃
.l. ſol̃. m̃. iiii. lib̃.

⌐Aliã Meleſham tenuit Vlmar̃ lib̃ ho̅. ꝑ. M̃. 7. ꝑ. i. hid̃. 7. xl. ac̃. M̃. R.
de eꝑo. Tc̃. i. bor̃. Sep̃. ii. ſer̃. 7. i. car̃. Silũ. xl. porc̃. x. ac̃. ꝑti. Val̃. xx. ſol̃.

⌐Hund de Tendringe. Torindunã tenuit Adſtan̄ ꝑ. uno maner̃.
7. ꝑ. iiii. hid̃. M̃. Rad̃. de eꝑo ꝑ tantundẽ. 7 hanc trã inuaſit Turoldus
de ruueceſtra. Sep̃. iii. uill̃. 7. ix. bor̃. 7. v. ſer̃. Tc̃. ii. car̃. in dñio. m̃. i. 7. d̃.
ſ; tcia poteſt eſſe. Tc̃ iñt hoẽs. ii. car̃ 7. dim̃. m̃. i. 7. dim̃. Silũ. c. porc̃.
. i. ac̃. ꝑti. Paſt̃. c. ou̇. M̃. i. mol̃. i. ſal̃. Sep̃. ual̃. iiii. lib̃.

Quidam lib̃ homo tenuit in Eileſforda dim̃ hidã. quẽ inuaſit Torold̃ ſic̃
alia trã. 7. qñ recepit. dim̃. car̃. m̃ nulla. ſ; pot̃ eſſe. 7 hund̃ neſcit q̃m
l̃it hanc trã. 7 q̃a neq; Legat̃ neq̃ ali̇ ho̅ uenit ex parte ſua q̇ derationaſſ̃&
hanc. trã. ideo ẽ in manu regis cũ alia. Tc̃ 7 ꝑ ual̃. x. ſol̃. m̃. v. 7. iiii. d̃.

⌐Hund de Tureſtapla. Toleſhuntã tenuit Oſlac̃ lib̃ ho̅ ꝑ. i. hid̃. M̃. eꝑc̃

ꝑ tantundẽ. Tc̃. ii. bor̃. m̃. iii. m̃. i. ſer̃. Tc̃. i. car̃. m̃. dim̃. Silũ. xxx. porc̃.
paſt̃. lx. ou̇. Tc̃ ual̃ xx. ſol̃. Poſt 7. m̃. xxx.

40 Saegar held PATCHING (Hall) as a manor, for 2 hides and 30 acres
before 1066. Now R(alph holds it) from the Bishop.
Then 1 villager, now 3. Always 4 smallholders; 1 slave;
1 plough in lordship; 1 men's plough.
Woodland, 15 pigs; meadow 8 acres; 1 mill. Then 3 cobs,
now 4; then 2 cattle, now 4; then 11 sheep, now 23.
Value 40s.

41 Godric held MOULSHAM (Hall) as a manor, for 2½ hides and 30
acres. Now R(alph holds it) from the Bishop.
Then 1 villager, now 2; then 1 smallholder, now 6; then 4
slaves, now 3. Always 2 ploughs in lordship. Then 1½ men's
ploughs, now 1.
Woodland, 60 pigs; meadow, 10 acres; always 1 mill. Then 3
cobs and 1 foal, now 2 cobs and 4 foals; then 9 cattle,
now 28; then 47 sheep, now 140.
Value then 50s; now £4.

42 Wulfmer, a free man, held the other MOULSHAM (Hall) as a manor
for 1 hide and 40 acres. Now R(alph holds it) from the Bishop.
Then 1 smallholder. Always 2 slaves; 1 plough.
Woodland, 40 pigs; meadow, 10 acres.
Value 20s.

Hundred of TENDRING

43 Aethelstan held THORRINGTON as 1 manor, for 4 hides. Now Ralph
(holds it) from the Bishop for as much. Thorold of Rochester
annexed this land.
Always 3 villagers; 9 smallholders; 5 slaves. Then 2 ploughs in
lordship, now 1½; but 3 possible. Then among the men 2½
ploughs, now 1½.
Woodland, 100 pigs; meadow, 1 acre; pasture, 100 sheep;
now 1 mill; 1 salt-house.
Value always £4.

44 A free man held ½ hide in ALRESFORD, whom Thorold annexed,
like the other land. When acquired, ½ plough, now none; but (1)
possible. The Hundred does not know how he has this land and
because neither a Commissioner nor another man came on his
behalf to adjudge this land, it is now in the King's hand with the
other (land).
Value then and later 10s; now 5s 4d.

Hundred of THURSTABLE

45 Oslac, a free man, held TOLLESHUNT for 1 hide. Now the Bishop
(holds it) for as much.   26 a
Then 2 smallholders, now 3; now 1 slave. Then 1 plough, now ½.
Woodland, 30 pigs; pasture, 60 sheep.
Value then 20s; later and now 30[s].

⌐Terra Ep̄i Herefordenſis.   In Writa . ten& Epc̄ . ii . hid̄ . 7 . xx . ac̄ . qrū
una fuit in eccl̄a t̄ . r̄ . e . 7 alia feudo haroldi . Sēp . iii . uiƚƚ . 7 . i . pƀr . Tc̄ . ii . bor.
m̄ . viii . Tc̄ . ii . ſer̄ m̄ nuƚƚ . ſēp . i . car̄ in dn̄io . 7 . ii . car̄ hom̄ . ſiƚu . c . porc̄ . viii.
ac̄ . p̄ti . Vaƚ . l . ſoƚ.

⌐TERRE Comitis Euſtachij In Exſſeſſa .   Hund̄ de berdeſtapla.
Phobinge tenuit Brictmar̄ un teinn̄ regis Eadūuardi p̄ . v . hid̄ . 7 . p̄ uno man̄.
m̄ ten& comes . E . in dn̄io . Sēp . iiii . car̄ in dn̄io . 7 . v . carruc̄ . hominū . Tc̄ . viii . uiƚƚ
m̄ . iii . Tc̄ . viii . bor . m̄ . xxii . Tc̄ . xii . ſer̄ . m̄ . vi . Siƚu . ɔcc . porc̄ . Paſt̄ . ɔcc . ouib; . dim̄
piſcina . xxxi . porc̄ . ɔcc . ou̇ . 7 xvii . Ex hac tr̄a tulit Turold̄ . xxx . ac̄ . quæ ſt̄
ad feudū ep̄i baiocenſis . Pt̄ hoc addidit Ingelric̄ huic manerio . xxii . liƀos hōes
tenentes . xv . hid̄ . 7 . dimid̄ . 7 . xv . ac̄ . 7 . dim̄ . In q̄ tr̄a . ſt̄ ſēp . xii . car̄ . 7 . xx . bord̄.
7 . iii . ſer̄ . Siƚu . l . porc̄ . x . ac̄ . p̄ti . Paſt̄ . cccc . ou̇ . T̄cia pars uni piſcinæ . 7 poſſt̄
addi . iii . car̄ . 7 . dim̄ . Tc̄ uaƚ . maneriū . xx . liƀ . 7 tr̄a . ſochemanoᷱ . xii . liƀ . Ṁ
int̄ totū . xxxvi . liƀ.
⌐Hornindunā ten& Garner̄ de comite qd̄ tenuit Vluric̄ liƀ hō . p̄ . uno
manerio . 7 . p̄ . ii . hid̄ . 7 . l . ac̄ . Sēp . ii . car̄ . in dn̄io . Tc̄ . ii . uiƚƚ . m̄ nuƚƚ . Tc̄ . vii.

26 b

bord̄ . m̄ . xii . Tc̄ . ii . ſer̄ . m̄ . iii . xii . ac̄ . p̄ti . Paſt̄ . lx . ou̇ . ii . uac̄ . x . por . cx . ou̇.
Pt̄ hoc xv . ac̄ . ad elemoſinā ecclæ . Tc̄ uaƚ . lx . ſoƚ . m̄ . l.
⌐Scenefeldā ten& Roḡ de comite qd̄ tenuit Bodd̄ . i . liƀ hō . t̄ . r̄ . e . p̄ . i . Man̄ . 7
p̄ . ii . hid̄ . Tc̄ . ii . carrc̄ . in dn̄io . m̄ . i . m̄ dim̄ . car̄ hom̄ Tc̄ . i . bor . m̄ . vi . Tc̄ . ii . ſer̄
m̄ nuƚƚ . Siƚu . xl . porc̄ . ii . animalia . xx . porc̄ . xv . cap̄ . Vaƚ . lx . ſoƚ.

19   LAND OF THE BISHOP OF HEREFORD

[Hundred of CHELMSFORD]

1   In WRITTLE the Bishop holds 2 hides and 20 acres of which 1
(hide) was in the (lands of the) Church before 1066 and the other
(was) in Harold's Holding.
> Always 3 villagers; 1 priest. Then 2 smallholders, now 8;
>   then 2 slaves, now none. Always 1 plough in lordship;
>   2 men's ploughs.
> Woodland, 100 pigs; meadow, 8 acres.

Value 50s.

20   LANDS OF COUNT EUSTACE IN ESSEX

Hundred of BARSTABLE

1   Brictmer, a thane of King Edward's, held FOBBING for 5 hides, as
one manor. Now Count Eustace holds it in lordship. Always 4
ploughs in lordship; 5 men's ploughs.
> Then 8 villagers, now 3; then 8 smallholders, now 22; then
>   12 slaves, now 6.
> Woodland, 700 pigs; pasture, 700 sheep; ½ fishery. 31 pigs,
>   717 sheep.

From this land, Thorold took 30 acres which are in the Bishop
of Bayeux's Holding. Besides this, Engelric added to this manor
22 free men who hold 15½ hides and 15½ acres. In this land have
always been 12 ploughs;
> 20 smallholders; 3 slaves.
> Woodland, 50 pigs; meadow, 10 acres; pasture, 400 sheep; the
>   third part of 1 fishery. 3½ ploughs could be added.

Value then of the manor £20, of the Freemen's land £12; now
£36 in total.

2   Warner holds HORNDON (-on-the-Hill) from the Count which
Wulfric, a free man, held as one manor, for 2 hides and 50 acres.
Always 2 ploughs in lordship.
> Then 2 villagers, now none; then 7 smallholders, now 12; then   26 b
>   2 slaves, now 3.
> Meadow, 12 acres; pasture, 60 sheep. 2 cows, 10 pigs, 110
>   sheep.

Besides this, 15 acres in the church's alms.

Value then 60s; now 50[s].

3   Roger holds SHENFIELD from the Count which 1 free man, Budd,
held before 1066 as 1 manor, for 2 hides. Then 2 ploughs in
lordship, now 1. Now ½ men's plough.
> Then 1 smallholder, now 6; then 2 slaves, now none.
> Woodland, 40 pigs. 2 cattle, 20 pigs, 15 goats.

Value 60s.

⌐Dorſedā ten& Comes q̄d tenuit Epc̄ Londonienſis . t̄ . r . e . p̄ . ı . hīd . quā tene
bat InGelric̄ de eccła . Sēp . ı . car̄ in dn̄io . 7 . ı . pbr̄ . ħt ibi . ı . carc̄ . Val̄ . xx . ſol.
hec hīd n̄ jac& ad ſuos . c . man̄.

⌐Grauesandā Tenuit Harold . 7 Ingelric̄ de eo . p̄ . man̄ . 7 . p̄ . ı . hīd . Sēp . ı . car̄.
Tc̄ . ı . uill̄ . m̄ . ıı . Tc̄ . ual̄ . x . ſol̄ . m̄ . xx . 7 hec hīd n̄ adjac& ſuis . c . manerijs.

⌐Hund de Witham.   Nutleam Tēn ał Aluric̄ teinn̄ . p̄ . uno manerio.
de comite q̄d tenuit Harold . t̄ . r̄ . e . Tc̄ 7 poſt . ııı . car̄ in dn̄io . m̄ . ıı.
Tc̄ 7 poſt . v . car̄ hom̄ . m̄ . ııı . Tc̄ 7 poſt . x . uilłi . m̄ . vı . Tc̄ . ııı . bor̄ . Poſt.
7 m̄ . xvı . Tc̄ ıx . ſer̄ . m̄ . ıııı . Tc̄ ſilu̅ . cc . por̄ . M̄ . c . xxx . ac̄ . p̄ti . paſt . c . ou̅.
m̄ . ıı . moł . v . uacas . xıııı . porc̄ . c . ou̅ . vıı . cap̄ . ııı . eq̄s . De hoc manerio
tulit Rad̄ de marci . xxx . ac̄ . 7 . jacent in feudo filij . hamonis . Sēp ual̄.
. x . lib̄.

⌐Cogheſhalā ten& Comes in dn̄io q̄d tenuit Colo . lib̄ hō . t̄ . r̄ . e . p̄ uno
manerio . 7 . p̄ . ııı . hīd . 7 . dim̄ . 7 . xxxııı . ac̄ . Sēp . ııı . car̄ in dn̄io . 7 . qn̄ eam
recepit . ı . carrc̄ . Tc̄ . xvı . car̄ hominū̸ poſt 7 m̄ . xıııı . Tc̄ . xı . uilł . Poſt
7 . m̄ . ıx . Tc̄ . xxıı . bor̄ . m̄ . xxxı . M̄ . ıııı . ſer̄ . Tc̄ . ſilu̅ . ɔc . porc̄ . m̄ . ɒ.
xxxvııı . ac̄ . p̄ti . Tantū paſturæ que ual̄ . x . d̄ . Sēp . ı . moł . ı . runc̄.
xv . porc̄ . ıııı . cap̄ . ıııı . uaſa apū . huic maɒerio p̄tinent . xı . ſochem̄
7 . ı . pbr̄ . 7 . ı . porcari̅ . 7 . ı . mercennari̅ . huic tr̄e . additæ ſt̄ . xxxvııı.
ac̄.

27 a
q̄s . ı . lib̄ hō ten& de rege ⸴ Tc̄ ual̄ hoc manerium . x . lib̄ . M̄ . xıııı.
ſ; tam̄ reddit ⸴ xx . lib̄ . 7 ſup̄dictæ xxxvııı . ac̄ . ual̄ ⸴ x . ſol̄.

⌐Ruenhalē ⸴ ten& Comes in̄ dn̄io q̄d tenuit Edeua regina t̄ . r̄ . c̄
p̄ . uno manerio . 7 . p̄ . ıı . hīd . 7 . dim̄ . Tc̄ . ııı . car̄ in dn̄io . M̄ . ıı ⸴ Tc̄ . vııı.
car̄ . hom̄ . m̄ . vı . Tc̄ . xıı . uilł . m̄ . xııı . Tc̄ . vııı . bor̄ . m̄ . xıııı . Sēp . vı ⸴ ſer̄.

4 The Count holds ORSETT which the Bishop of London held before 1066 for 1 hide, which Engelric held from the Church.
Always 1 plough in lordship.
1 priest has 1 plough there.
Value 20s.
This hide does not lie in his 100 manors.

5 Harold held 'GRAVESEND' and Engelric from him as a manor, for 1 hide. Always 1 plough.
Then 1 villager, now 2.
Value then 10s; now 20[s].
This hide does not lie in his 100 manors.

Hundred of WITHAM
6 Aelfric, a thane, holds (White) NOTLEY as one manor from the Count, which Harold held before 1066. Then and later 3 ploughs in lordship, now 2. Then and later 5 men's ploughs, now 3.
Then and later 10 villagers, now 6; then 3 smallholders, later and now 16; then 9 slaves, now 4.
Woodland, then 200 pigs, now 100; meadow, 30 acres; pasture, 100 sheep; now 2 mills. 5 cows, 14 pigs, 100 sheep, 7 goats, 3 horses.
From this manor Ralph of Marcy took 30 acres; they lie in the Holding of Hamo's son.
Value always £10.

7 The Count holds COGGESHALL in lordship, which Cola, a free man, held before 1066 as one manor, for 3½ hides and 33 acres. Always 3 ploughs in lordship. When acquired, 1 plough. Then 16 men's ploughs, later and now 14.
Then 11 villagers, later and now 9; then 22 smallholders, now 31; now 4 slaves.
Woodland, then 600 pigs, now 500; meadow, 38 acres; pasture to the value of 10d; always 1 mill. 1 cob, 15 pigs, 4 goats, 4 beehives.
To this manor belong 11 Freemen, 1 priest, 1 pigman and 1 hired man.
To this land have been added 38 acres, which 1 free man holds   27 a
from the King.
Value of this manor then £10; now [£] 14, but however it pays £20.
Value of the above 38 acres 10s.

8 The Count holds RIVENHALL in lordship, which Queen Edith held before 1066 as one manor, for 2½ hides. Then 3 ploughs in lordship, now 2. Then 8 men's ploughs, now 6.
Then 12 villagers, now 13; then 8 smallholders, now 14; always 6 slaves.

Tc̄.ſilu̅.cccc.porc̄.m̄.ccc.7.dim̄.xxx.ac̄.p̄ti.Paſtura de q̄ accipi
un̄t.iii.ſol.Tc̄.i.mol̄.m̄.dim̄.i.ſoc̄.de.xv.ac̄.i.burgēſis de colē
caſtro.7 medietatē molini.abſtulit Ricard̄ de Sacheuilla.i.runc̄.
vi.an̄.xl.porc̄.viii.cap̄.ii.uaſa apū.Tc̄.ual̄.ix.lib̄.M.xii.ſ; tn̄
reddit.xx.lib̄.

Ruenhala ten̄& comes in dn̄io.qd̄ tenuit harold̄.p.i.maner.7.p.i.
hid̄.7.xv.ac̄.Tc̄.ii.car.in dn̄io.m̄.i.Sep.i.car.hom̄.Tc̄.ii.uil̄t.m̄.v.
Tc̄.i.bor.m̄.ii.Tc̄.v.ſer.m̄.iiii.& xxi.ac̄.7.d̄.p̄ti.Paſt.de.vi.d̄.
.x.porc̄.xxvii.ou̅.Tc̄ ual̄.lx.ſol̄.m̄.xxx.

⁊Blundeſhala ten̄& Comes in dn̄io.qd̄ tenuit.i.lib̄a femina.t.r.e
.p.i.Man̄.7.dim̄.hid̄.Sep.i.car in dn̄io.7.i.bor.vi.ac̄.p̄ti.Tc̄.ual̄
xx.ſol̄.m̄.x.

⁊Witham ten̄& Ricard̄ de comite qd̄ tenuit harold̄.p.li.ac̄.Sep.i.car.
7.i.bord̄.ii.ac̄.7.dim̄.p̄ti.Val̄.xx.ſol̄.

⁊Hund̄ de herlaua.Perendu̅na ten̄& Junain de comite qd̄ tenuit
Vlf teinn reḡ t.r.e.p uno manerio.7.p.iii.hid̄.7.dim̄.Sep.ii.car
in dn̄io.7.ii.car.hom̄.Tc̄.iiii.uil̄t.m̄.iii.Tc̄.iiii.bor.m̄.v.Sep.ii.
ſer.Silu̅.cc.porc̄.xiiii.ac̄.p̄ti.Val̄.iiii.lib̄.

⁊Lattuna ten̄& Adelolf̄.de comite qd̄ tenuit Ernulf̄ lib̄ ho̅.t.r.e

.p uno manerio.7.p.i.hid̄.7.dim̄.7.xxx.ac̄.ii.car in dn̄io.tc̄⸍.m̄.i.Sep.i.
uillanus.7.ii.bor.Tc̄.iiii.ſer.m̄.ii.Silu̅.ccc.porc̄.xxxv.ac̄.p̄ti.7.i.pbr q̄
ten̄& dim̄.hida ad una̅ eccl̄iam.Tc̄ ual̄.l.ſol̄.m̄ lx.

⁊Herlaua ten̄& Goisfrid̄ de comite qd̄ tenuit Brictnar̄ lib̄ ho̅.t.r.e.
7 dim̄ hid̄.Sep.dim̄.car.Silu̅.xl.porc̄.iii.ac̄.p̄ti.Val̄.xi.ſol̄.   ★

Woodland, then 400 pigs, now 300 and a half; meadow, 30 acres; pasture, from which 3s are received; then 1 mill. now ½. 1 Freeman with 15 acres. 1 burgess of Colchester. Richard of Sackville took away ½ mill. 1 cob, 6 cattle, 40 pigs, 8 goats, 2 beehives.

Value then £9; now [£] 12, but however it pays £20.

9 The Count holds RIVENHALL in lordship, which Harold held as 1 manor, for 1 hide and 15 acres. Then 2 ploughs in lordship, now 1.
  Always 1 men's plough.
  Then 2 villagers, now 5; then 1 smallholder, now 2; then 5 slaves, now 4.
  Meadow, 21½ acres; pasture at 6d. 10 pigs, 27 sheep.
Value then 60s; now 30[s].

10 The Count holds BLUNT'S HALL in lordship, which 1 free woman held before 1066 as 1 manor; ½ hide. Always 1 plough in lordship; 1 smallholder.
  Meadow, 6 acres.
Value then 20s; now 10[s].

11 Richard holds WITHAM from the Count, which Harold held for 51 acres. Always 1 plough; 1 smallholder.
  Meadow, 2½ acres.
Value 20s.

Hundred of HARLOW

12 Iwain holds (Great) PARNDON from the Count, which Ulf, a King's thane, held before 1066 as one manor, for 3½ hides. Always 2 ploughs in lordship; 2 men's ploughs.
  Then 4 villagers, now 3; then 4 smallholders, now 5; always 2 slaves.
  Woodland, 200 pigs; meadow, 14 acres.
Value £4.

13 Adelulf holds LATTON from the Count, which Ernulf, a free man, held before 1066 as one manor, for 1½ hides and 30 acres.   27 b
2 ploughs in lordship then, now 1.
  Always 1 villager; 2 smallholders. Then 4 slaves, now 2.
  Woodland, 300 pigs; meadow, 35 acres. 1 priest who holds ½ hide at a church.
Value then 50s; now 60[s].

14 Geoffrey holds HARLOW from the Count, which Brictmer, a free man, held before 1066; ½ hide. Always ½ plough.
  Woodland, 40 pigs; meadow, 3 acres.
Value 11s.

Hund . de Dommauua .   Dommauuā ten& Adelolf de merc de comite
qd tenuit Edmar . 1 . lib hō . t̄ . r̄ . ē . p̄ uno manerio . 7 . p̄ . 11 . hid̄ . 7 . xxx .
ac̄ . Tc̄ . 111 . car̄ . in dn̄io . m̄ . 11 . Tc̄ . 1 . car̄ . hom̄ . m̄ . 111 . Tc̄ . 111 . uilt̄ . m̄ . x111 .
m̄ . 1x . bor . Tc̄ . x . fer̄ . m̄ . 1111 . Silu . ccc . porc̄ . xxxvi . ac̄ . p̄ti . 7 . una carr̄
pot̄ . reftaurari . x11 . an̄ . l . por . c . ou . 1 . runc̄ . 1111 . uafa apū . Val . v111 .
lib̄ .

Hund de Witbricteſherna .   Eltenai . ten& Comes in dn̄io . qd tenuit
Ingelric̄ . t̄ . r̄ . ē . p̄ uno manerio . 7 . p̄ . 11 . hid̄ . Tc̄ . 1 . fer̄ . m̄ . 11 . bor . ſep . 1 . car̄
in dn̄io . Paftur̄ . l . ou . Val . xxx . fol .
Purlai tenuit Edeua t̄ . r̄ . ē . p̄ uno man̄ . 7 . p̄ . 1 . hid̄ . 7 . xxx . ac̄ . ſ; non
fuit de feudo Ingelrici . 7 . nc̄ ht̄ Euftachi . Tc̄ . ual . xvi . fol . 7 . v111 . d̄ .
m̄ . xx111 . fol . Tc̄ . 1 . bi . manfer̄ . 11 . hōes . m̄ . 1 . pbr̄ .

Hund de Dommauua .   Pleſinchov ten& Bernard de comite .
qd tenuit . 1 . lib̄ hō . t̄ . r̄ . e . p̄ dim̄ . hid̄ . Sep . dim̄ . car̄ . Tc̄ . 11 . bor . m̄ . 1 . fer̄ .
Silu . xx . pocc̄ . v . ac̄ . p̄ti . Val . x . fol .

Hund de Wenfiſtrev .   Langhou tenuit Ingelric̄ . t̄ . r̄ . ē . p̄ uno
manerio . 7 . p̄ . v11 . hid̄ . M̄ ten& Comes in dn̄io . Tc̄ . v . car̄ in
dn̄io . Poft . 1111 . M̄ . 111 . Tc̄ 7 p̄ . 1 . car̄ . 7 . dim̄ . hominū . m̄ . 11 . Tc̄
v . uilt̄ . m̄ . 1x . Sep . v11 . bor . Tc̄ . x11 . fer̄ . m̄ . v111 . Silu . cc . por .

★

28 a
. 1 . ac̄ . p̄ti . Paftura . δ . ou . 1 . mot̄ . 1 . fal̄ . 11 . an̄ . ccc . ou . x111 . porc̄ . 7 . 111 . runc̄ .
huic manerio addidit Ingelric̄ . t̄ . r̄ . Willi . 11 . hid̄ . qs tenuit . 1 . lib̄ homo
t̄ . r̄ . e . 7 . dim̄ . hid̄ quā tenuer̄ . 111 . libi hōes . t̄ . r̄ . ē . In his hid̄ . 7 dim̄ . ſt̄ ſ̄cp . 11 .
car̄ . M̄ . 1111 . bor . Paft . c . ou . Tc̄ . totū ſimul . ual : xv11 . lib̄ . 7 m̄ . xv11 . 7 . v . fol
7 . qn̄ recep̄ ſimilit̄ .

Hundred of DUNMOW

15 Adelulf of Marck holds DUNMOW from the Count, which 1 free
man, Edmer, held before 1066 as one manor, for 2 hides and 30
acres. Then 3 ploughs in lordship, now 2. Then 1 men's plough,
now 3.

   Then 3 villagers, now 13; now 9 smallholders; then 10 slaves,
   now 4.

   Woodland, 300 pigs; meadow, 36 acres; 1 plough could be
   restored. 12 cattle, 50 pigs, 100 sheep, 1 cob, 4 beehives.

   Value £8.

Hundred of 'WIBERTSHERNE'

16 The Count holds ILTNEY (Farm) in lordship, which Engelric held
before 1066 as one manor, for 2 hides.

   Then 1 slave; now 2 smallholders. Always 1 plough in lordship.
   Pasture, 50 sheep.

   Value 30s.

17 Edeva held PURLEIGH before 1066 as one manor, for 1 hide and
30 acres. But it was not of Engelric's Holding. Now Eustace has it.
Value then 16s 8d; now 23s.

   Then 2 men dwelt there, now 1 priest.

Hundred of DUNMOW

18 Bernard holds 'PLESINGHO' from the Count, which 1 free man held
before 1066 for ½ hide. Always ½ plough.

   Then 2 smallholders; now 1 slave.
   Woodland, 20 pigs; meadow, 5 acres.

   Value 10s.

Hundred of WINSTREE

19 Engelric held LANGENHOE before 1066 as one manor, for 7 hides.
Now the Count holds it in lordship. Then 5 ploughs in lordship,
later 4, now 3. Then and later 1½ men's ploughs, now 2.

   Then 5 villagers, now 9; always 7 smallholders; then 12 slaves,
   now 8.

   Woodland, 200 pigs; meadow, 1 acre; pasture, 500 sheep; 1 mill;   28 a
   1 salt-house. 2 cattle, 300 sheep, 13 pigs and 3 cobs.

   To this manor after 1066 Engelric added 2 hides which 1 free
man held before 1066, and ½ hide which 3 free men held before
1066. On these hides and the half have always been 2 ploughs.

   Now 4 smallholders.
   Pasture, 100 sheep.

   Value altogether then £17; now [£]17 5s; when acquired the same.

Edburghetunā ten& Rad de marci . qd̄ tenuit Siuuard . lib̄ hō . t̄ . r̄ . c̄.
p̄ uno manerio . 7 . p̄ . i . hid̄ . 7 . dim̄ . 7 . i . uirg̃ . Sēp . i . car̄ in dn̄io . Tc̄ . dim̄ . car̄.
hom̄ . 7 m̄ ſimiliſ . Tc̄ . iiii . bor . m̄ . iii . Tc̄ . i . ſer̄ . m̄ null̄ . ſilu . c . porc̄ . iiii . ac̄
p̄ti . iiii . an̄ . c . ou̇ . xxx . porc̄ . ii . runc̄ . Val . lx . ſol.
Legrā tenuit . i . lib̄ hō . Alric . t̄ . r̄ . c̄ . p̄ . ii . hid̄ . 7 . dim̄ . 7 . i . uirg̃ . Tc̄ . i . car̄ . 7 . d̄.
in dn̄io . m̄ . ii . Tc̄ . i . bor . m̄ . iii . Tc̄ . ii . ſer̄ . m̄ . i . Silu . xl . porc̄ . m̄ . i . mol̄ . Tc̄.
. i . runc̄ . m̄ . ii . Tc̄ . iii . an̄ . m̄ . v . xxxviii . ou̇ . m̄ . cxlvi . vi . uaſa apū . Tc̄
ual . iiii . lib̄ . m̄ . iii.

Hund de Odelesforda . Sortegrauā tenuit . i . lib̄ hō . t̄ . r̄ . c̄ . m̄ ten&
Adelolf de comite . p̄ uno Man̄ . 7 . p̄ . i . hid̄ . 7 . xxx . ac̄ . Tc̄ . 7 . p̄ . i . car̄ . in dn̄io.
m̄ . ii . Tc̄ . 7 . p̄ . i . uilt̄ . m̄ null̄ . Tc̄ . 7 p̄ . i . bor . m̄ . iii . Tc̄ . i . ſer̄ . m̄ n̄ . ix . ac̄ . p̄ti . iii.
an̄ . ii . runc̄ . xi . por . lxxxx . ou̇ . Val . xl . ſol . hanc tr̄ā occupauit Ingelric̄.
tēpore regis Witti ;

Hund de Hidincforda . Rideuuellā tenuit . t̄ . r̄ . c̄ . i . lib̄ hō . nōe Godu
in . p̄ uno man̄ . 7 . p̄ . ii . hid̄ . 7 . iii . uirg̃ . Tc̄ . v . car̄ . in dn̄io . poſt . 7 . m̄ . iiii.
xiiii . uilti . xiiii . ſer̄ . iii . bord . Silu . lxxx . por . xxxvi . ac̄ . p̄ti . xxii . an̄
xliiii . porc̄ . cii . ou̇ . xxx . cap̄ . 7 . ii . runc̄ . Huic manerio adjacent ſēp . xiiii.
ſoc̄ . de lxvii . ac̄ . 7 . dim̄ . hn̄tes . i . car̄ . 7 . dim̄ . vi . ac̄ . p̄ti . Tc̄ totū ual xviii.
lib̄ . Poſt 7 m̄ . xxiiii . hoc ten& Comes in dn̄io ;

Sortegrauā ten& Adelolf dè comite qd̄ tenuit . i . lib̄ hō . t̄ . r̄ . c̄ . p̄ uno
Man̄ . 7 . p̄ . i . hid̄ . 7 . xxx . ac̄ . Tc̄ . i . car̄ . in dn̄io . m̄ nulla . Sēp . i . uilt̄ . 7 . i . bor.
7 . i . ac̄ . p̄ti . Tc̄ 7 p̄ ual . xxx . ſol . M̄ . xxxiii.

20 Ralph of Marcy holds ABBERTON which Siward, a free man, held before 1066 as one manor, for 1½ hides and 1 virgate. Always 1 plough in lordship. Then ½ men's plough, now the same.
Then 4 smallholders, now 3; then 1 slave, now none.
Woodland, 100 pigs; meadow 4 acres. 4 cattle, 100 sheep, 30 pigs, 2 cobs.
Value 60s.

21 1 free man, Alric, held LAYER (de la Haye) before 1066 for 2½ hides and 1 virgate. Then 1½ ploughs in lordship, now 2.
Then 1 smallholder, now 3; then 2 slaves, now 1.
Woodland, 40 pigs; now 1 mill. Then 1 cob, now 2; then 3 cattle, now 5; then 38 sheep, now 146; 6 beehives.
Value then £4; now [£] 3.

Hundred of UTTLESFORD
22 1 free man held SHORTGROVE before 1066. Now Adelulf holds (it) from the Count as one manor, for 1 hide and 30 acres. Then and later 1 plough in lordship, now 2.
Then and later 1 villager, now none; then and later 1 smallholder, now 3; then 1 slave, now none.
Meadow, 9 acres. 3 cattle, 2 cobs, 11 pigs, 90 sheep.
Value 40s.
Engelric appropriated this land after 1066.

Hundred of HINCKFORD
23 1 free man, Godwin by name, held RIDGEWELL before 1066 as one manor, for 2 hides and 3 virgates. Then 5 ploughs in lordship, later and now 4.
14 villagers; 14 slaves; 3 smallholders.
Woodland, 80 pigs; meadow, 36 acres. 22 cattle, 44 pigs, 102 sheep, 30 goats and 2 cobs.
To this manor have always been attached 14 Freemen with 67½ acres, who have 1½ ploughs.
Meadow, 6 acres.
Value of the whole then £18; later and now [£] 24.
The Count holds it in lordship.

[Hundred of UTTLESFORD]   28 b
24 Adelulf holds SHORTGROVE from the Count, which 1 free man held before 1066 as one manor, for 1 hide and 30 acres. Then 1 plough in lordship, now none.
Always 1 villager; 1 smallholder.
Meadow, 1 acre.
Value then and later 30s; now 33[s].

Clare tenuit Ledmar . i . lib hō . t . r . e . p . i . hid . 7 . dim . 7 . xxxv . ac.
Tc . v . car in dnio P 7 m . iii . Sep . ii . car hominu . Tc . vii : uilt : Poſt 7 m
. iiii . Poſt 7 m . xii . bord . Tc . x . ſer . Poſt 7 m . iiii . xxvii . ac . pti . i . mot.
. iii . runc . viii . an . xl . porc . ccxxxix . ou . Huic manerio adjac& ſeper
. i . bereuuita . que uocat . geldeham de . ii . hid . 7 . xviii . ac . Tc . iii . car
in dnio . Poſt . 7 . m . ii . Sep . ii . car hom . Tc . viii . uilt . Poſt 7 . m . vi . Poſt
7 . m . viii . bor . viii . ſer . tc . Poſt 7 m . vi . xviii . ac . pti . Adhuc adjac&
huic manerio . vii . ſoc . de xxxv . ac . trę . hntes . i . car . Tc ual . xviii.
lib hoc maner . Poſt 7 m . xxii . Huic &ia manerio addidit Ingelric.
. i . libum hōem . t . r . Witti . 7 habebat . xv . ac . 7 . i . car . 7 . ual . x . ſol . hoc
maneriu ten& Comes in dnio.

Belcham tenuit Ledmar . lib hō . t . r . e . p . i . hid . 7 . xlv . ac . m ten&
Vlmar de comite . Sep . ii . car . in dnio . 7 . ii . car houm . 7 . iiii . uilt.
Tc . 7 p . iiii . bor . m . v . Tc . 7 p . iiii . ſer . m . ii . Silu . xx . porc . viii . ac pti.
huic manerio jacent . v . ſochem . qʒ . ii . occupauit Ingelric tępore
regis Witti . q tc erant libi hōes . 7 hnt . xxxv . ac . trę . In dnio . ix.
anim . ii . runc . xx . porc . c . ou . Tc . ual . xl . ſol . Poſt 7 m . iiii . lib.

Bummeſtedā ten& Adeloſi de Merc de comite . qd tenuit . i . lib
hō . t . r . e . p . ʘ . 7 . p . dim . hid . Tc . iii . car . in dnio . Poſt 7 . m . ii.
Sep . ii . car hom . vii . uilt . xi . bord . iiii . ſer . xv . ac . pti . i . runc.
. iii . anim . Tc ual . iiii . lib . Poſt 7 m . c . ſol.

Belcham ten& Bernard de comite qd ~~tenuit~~ qd tenuit Etnod lib hō
t . r . e . p . dim hid . 7 . x . ac . Sep . i . car . in dnio . M . ii . bor . ii . ſer . iiii . ac . pti.
. i . ſochem de . xx . ac . i . runc . iiii . uac . Tc . xiiii . porc . m null . Sep . l . ou.
Val . xxx . ſol.

[Hundred of HINCKFORD]

25   1 free man, Ledmer, held CLARET (Hall) before 1066 for 1½ hides
and 35 acres. Then 5 ploughs in lordship, later and now 3. Always
2 men's ploughs.
> Then 7 villagers, later and now 4; later and now 12 smallholders;
>   then 10 slaves, later and now 4.
>
> Meadow, 27 acres; 1 mill. 3 cobs, 8 cattle, 40 pigs, 239 sheep.
>
> To this manor has always been attached 1 outlier, which is
called (Little) YELDHAM, with 2 hides and 18 acres. Then 3 ploughs
in lordship, later and now 2. Always 2 men's ploughs.
>
> Then 8 villagers, later and now 6; later and now 8 smallholders;
>   then 8 slaves, later and now 6.
>
> Meadow, 18 acres.
>
> Besides, attached to this manor are 7 Freemen with 35 acres of
land, who have 1 plough.
>
> Value of this manor then £18; later and now [£] 22.
>
> To this manor Engelric also added 1 free man after 1066; he
had 15 acres. 1 plough. Value 10s.
>
> The Count holds this manor in lordship.

26   Ledmer, a free man, held BELCHAMP (Otten) before 1066 for 1
hide and 45 acres. Now Wulfmer holds (it) from the Count.
Always 2 ploughs in lordship; 2 men's ploughs;
> 4 villagers. Then and later 4 smallholders, now 5; then and
>   later 4 slaves, now 2.
>
> Woodland, 20 pigs; meadow, 8 acres.
>
> Attached to this manor are 5 Freemen, 2 of whom Engelric
appropriated after 1066. They were then free men; they have 35
acres of land.
>
> In lordship 9 cattle, 2 cobs, 20 pigs, 100 sheep.
>
> Value then 40s; later and now £4.

27   Adelulf of Marck holds (Steeple) BUMPSTEAD from the Count,
which 1 free man held before 1066 as 1 manor, for ½ hide. Then
3 ploughs in lordship, later and now 2. Always 2 men's ploughs;
> 7 villagers; 11 smallholders; 4 slaves.
>
> Meadow, 15 acres. 1 cob, 3 cattle.
>
> To this manor Engelric added 1 free man (with) 3½ acres.
>
> Value then £4; later and now 100s.

28   Bernard holds BELCHAMP from the Count which Ednoth, a free   29 a
man, held before 1066 for ½ hide and 10 acres. Always 1 plough
in lordship.
> Now 2 smallholders; 2 slaves.
>
> Meadow, 4 acres. 1 Freeman with 20 acres. 1 cob, 4 cows;
>   then 14 pigs, now none; always 50 sheep.
>
> Value 30s.

⁌ Vueſtunā ten& ~~ten&~~ Adelolf de comite qd tenuit . ı . liƀ hō . t̅ . r̅ . e̅ . ꝓ.
xxx . ac̅ . ſēp . ı . car̅ . 7 . ııı . ac̅ p̅ti Tc̅ . ual̅ . xx . ſol̅ . m̅ . xxv .

⁌ Phincingefeldā ten& Wido de comite qd tenuit Normann . t̅ . r̅ . e̅ .
ꝓ . Man̅ . 7 . ꝓ . dim hid̅ . 7 . x . ac̅ . Sēp . ı . car̅ in dn̅io . 7 . ı . bor . 7 . ı . ſer̅ . Silua
xx . porc̅ . ıx . ac̅ p̅ti . ııı . an̅ . xx . ı . min . Tc̅ ual̅ . xx . ſol̅ . m̅ . xl .

⁌ Phincinghefeldā tenuit Vluric̅ liƀ hō . t̅ . r̅ . e̅ . M̅ . Idē Wido de
comite ꝓ . xxxvıı . ac̅ . Sēp . ı . car̅ . Tc̅ . ı . ſer̅ . m̅ . ıı . bor . Tc̅ . ſilu̅ . xx . porc̅ .
m̅ . v . ıııı . ac̅ . p̅ti . ı . mol̅ . val̅ . xvı . ſol̅ .

⁌ Smedetunā ten& Raner̅ de comite qd . tenuit . ı . liƀa femina . t̅ . r̅ . e̅ .
ꝓ uno manerio . 7 . ꝓ . ııı . hid̅ . Tc̅ . ıııı . car̅ . in dn̅io Poſt . 7 . m̅ . ıı . Tc̅ . 7 p̅
. ı . car̅ . 7 . dim . hom . m̅ . ı . Tc̅ . 7 . p̅ . ıııı . uilt̅ . m̅ . ııı . Sēp . xıııı . bor . 7
. ıı . ſer̅ . Silu̅ . xx . porc̅ . xx . ac̅ . p̅ti . Tc̅ ual̅ . vıı . liƀ . m̅ . vııı . Hec̅ .
maneria tenuit Ingelric̅ .

⁌ Topesfeldā ten& Bernard de comite qd tenuit . ı . liƀ hō . ꝓ . xv . ac̅ .
t̅ . r̅ . e̅ . Sēp . ı . car̅ in dn̅io . 7 . ı . uilt̅ . 7 . ı . bor . Tc̅ . ı . ſer̅ . m̅ null̅ . Silua .
. x . porc̅ . vı . ac̅ . p̅ti . Val̅ . xx . ſol̅ .

⁌ Hund de Witbriċteſherna . Meldunā ten& Sc̅s Martin̅
Londoniæ de comite . qd tenuit . ı . liƀ . hō . t̅ . r̅ . e̅ . ꝓ . ı . hid̅ . 7 . dim̅ . 7 . xxx . ac̅ .
poſtea tenuit Ingelric̅ . Sēp . vı . bor . 7 . ıı . ſer̅ . 7 . ıı . car̅ . Silu̅ . xxx . porc̅ .
Paſtura . c . ou̅ . ~~Tc̅ ual̅ . ıııı . liƀ . M̅ . c . ſol̅ .~~ In dn̅io . ıı . uac̅ . xıııı .
. porc̅

29 b

. c . ou̅ . Tc̅ ual̅ . ıııı . liƀ . m̅ . c . ſol̅ . In Ead̅ . ı . liƀ hō tenuit . xxx . ac̅ . t̅ . r̅ . e̅ . quē
occupauit Ingelric̅ . m̅ ten& Sc̅s Martin̅ de comite . 7 aliū liƀum hominē .
de . xxx . ac̅ . Iſtos hōes poſuit Ingelric̅ ad ſuā hallā . In tr̅a eoꝝ e̅ ſēp . ı .
car̅ . 7 . ual̅ . xx . ſol̅ .

29 Adelulf holds WESTON (Hall) from the Count, which 1 free man held before 1066 for 30 acres. Always 1 plough.

Meadow, 4 acres.

Value then 20s; now 25[s].

30 Guy holds FINCHINGFIELD from the Count, which Norman held before 1066 as a manor, for ½ hide and 10 acres. Always 1 plough in lordship;

1 smallholder; 1 slave.

Woodland, 20 pigs; meadow, 9 acres. 3 cattle, 20 ... less 1.

Value then 20s; now 40[s].

31 Wulfric, a free man, held FINCHINGFIELD before 1066. Now Guy also (holds it) from the Count for 37 acres. Always 1 plough.

Then 1 slave; now 2 smallholders.

Woodland, then 20 pigs, now 5; meadow, 4 acres; 1 mill.

Value 16s.

32 Rainer holds SMEETHAM (Hall) from the Count, which 1 free woman held before 1066 as one manor, for 3 hides. Then 4 ploughs in lordship, later and now 2. Then and later 1½ men's ploughs, now 1.

Then and later 4 villagers, now 3. Always 14 smallholders; 2 slaves.

Woodland, 20 pigs; meadow, 20 acres.

Value then £7; now [£] 8.

Engelric held these manors.

33 Bernard holds TOPPESFIELD from the Count, which 1 free man held for 15 acres before 1066. Always 1 plough in lordship;

1 villager; 1 smallholder. Then 1 slave, now none.

Woodland, 10 pigs; meadow, 6 acres.

Value 20s.

Hundred of 'WIBERTSHERNE'

34 St. Martin's, London, holds MALDON from the Count, which 1 free man held before 1066 for 1½ hides and 30 acres. Later on Engelric held it.

Always 6 smallholders; 2 slaves; 2 ploughs.

Woodland, 30 pigs; pasture, 100 sheep.

In lordship 2 cows, 14 pigs, 100 sheep.

29 b

Value then £4; now 100s.

In the same (Maldon) 1 free man held 30 acres before 1066, which Engelric appropriated. Now St. Martin's holds it from the Count and another free man with 30 acres. Engelric placed these men in his hall. On their land, has always been 1 plough. Value 20s.

Vleham ten& Roᵬ. de comite qđ tenuit . ɪ . liᵬ hō . t̃ . r̃ . ẽ . Poſt Ingelric̓.
p̃ . ɪ . hiđ . Tc̃ . uaĺ . vɪɪɪ . ſoĺ . 7 . ɪɪɪɪ . đ . m̂ . xɪɪɪɪ . ſoĺ.

Hund̃ de Laſſendena . Teiam tenuit . ɪ . liᵬ homo . t̃ . r̃ . ẽ . p̃ . ɪɪɪ . hiđ
7 . dim̃ . m̂ comes . E . Tc̃ . vɪ . uiłłi . m̂ . ɪɪ . Tc̃ . xvɪ . bor̃ . m̂ . xxxv . Tc̃ . ɪx . ſer̃.
m̂ . x . Tc̃ . ɪɪɪɪ . car̃ in dñio . m̂ . ɪɪ . Tc̃ . inᵗ hõẽs . vɪ . car̃ . m̂ . ɪɪɪɪ . Siłu . cʟx.
porc̃ . xx . ac̃ . p̃ti . ɪɪɪɪ . runc̃ . vɪɪ . an . ʟxvɪɪɪ . porc̃ . ʟxxx . oũ . xxxɪɪɪɪ . cap̃.
huic manerio jac& una ᵬiuuita . de . ɪ . hiđ . 7 . dim̃ . x . ac̃ . min . Sẽp . ɪ . bor.
7 . ɪɪ . ſer̃ . Tc̃ . ɪɪ . car̃ . in dñio . m̂ . ɪ . ſilu . xxɪɪɪɪ . porc̃ . 7 . xvɪɪ : ſoc̃ . tenentes.
. ɪɪ . hiđ . 7 . v . ac̃ . in iſto manerio . m̂ tenent iłłā tr̄a xvɪ . ſoc̃ . Sẽp . ſub ipſis
vɪ . bor . Tc̃ . ɪɪ . ſer̃ . m̂ nułł . Tc̃ . inᵗ eos . vɪ . car̃ . m̂ . ɪɪɪɪ . Siłu . xxx . porc̃.
xɪɪ . ac̃ . p̃ti . ſep . ɪ . moł . 7 . iſti ſoc̃ . n̄ poᵗant recede ab hoc manerio . 7 . ad
huc jac& huic manerio . ɪ . dom in coleceſtra . Tc̃ uaĺ hoc maneriũ . xvɪ . liᵬ.
7 qn̄ recep̃ ſimiliᵗ . m̂ uaĺ . xxɪɪ . liᵬ . candidas.

In Ead̃ tenuer̃ . v . libi hõẽs ʟx . ac̃ . 7 xxvɪɪɪ . ac̃ . q̃ n̄ erant de iſto man.
q̃s m̂ h̃t comes . q̃a antec̃ ſuus faiſiᵗ fuit . 7 p̃tiũ iſti tr̃e ẽ in ſup̃dicᵗo
p̃tio . Boccheſted̃a tenuit Aluric̃ . p̃ . ɪɪɪɪ . hiđ . 7 . dim̃ . m̂ . Comes.
in dñio . Sẽp . v . uiłł . 7 . xvɪɪɪ . bor . Tc̃ . ɪɪ . ſer̃ . m̂ . nułł . Tc̃ . ɪɪ . car̃ . in dñio . m̂
ſimiliᵗ . Sẽp . vɪ . car̃ . hom . Siłu . ccc . porc̃ . vɪɪɪ . ac̃ . p̃ti . Tc̃ . ɪ . moł . m̂
nułł . 7 . ɪ . ſoc̃ . q̃ n̄ potuit recede . tenens dim̃ . hiđ . Tc̃ . dim̃ . car̃ . m̂ nulla.
. ɪɪ . ac̃ . p̃ti . xɪɪɪ . an . xxxv . porc̃ . 7 . cxʟ . oũ . 7 xxv . cap̃ . 7 . ɪɪ . runc̃.

30 a
Tc̃ . 7 p̃ uaĺ . vɪɪɪ . liᵬ . M̂ . xɪɪ . blanc̃.
Dunulanda tenuit Edric p̃ . man̂ . 7 . p̃ . ɪ . hiđ . 7 . dim̃ . m̂ . ten& Comes i̅ dñio.
Sẽp . x . bor . Tc̃ . ɪɪɪɪ . ſer̃ . m̂ . ɪ . Tc̃ . ɪɪ . car̃ in dñio . m̂ . ɪ . Tc̃ . ɪɪ . car̃ . hom . m̂ . ɪ.

35   Robert holds ULEHAM ('s Farm) from the Count, which 1 free man held before 1066. Later Engelric (held it) for 1 hide.
Value then 8s 4d; now 14s.

Hundred of LEXDEN

36   1 free man held TEY before 1066 for 3½ hides. Now Count Eustace (holds it).

> Then 6 villagers, now 2; then 16 smallholders, now 35; then 9 slaves, now 10. Then 4 ploughs in lordship, now 2. Then among the men 6 ploughs, now 4.
> Woodland, 160 pigs; meadow, 20 acres. 3 cobs, 7 cattle, 68 pigs, 80 sheep, 34 goats.
> Attached to this manor is one outlier of 1½ hides less 10 acres.
> Always 1 smallholder; 2 slaves. Then 2 ploughs in lordship, now 1.
> Woodland, 24 pigs.
> In this manor, 17 Freemen who held 2 hides and 5 acres; now 16 Freemen hold this land.
> Always 6 smallholders under them. Then 2 slaves, now none. Then among them 6 ploughs, now 4.
> Woodland, 30 pigs; meadow, 12 acres; always 1 mill.
> These Freemen could not withdraw from this manor.
> Also attached to this manor is 1 house in Colchester.

Value of this manor then £16; when acquired, the same; value now £22 blanched.

In the same (Tey) 5 free men, who were not part of this manor, held 60 acres and 28 acres, whom the Count now has, because his predecessor was in possession. The assessment of this land is in the above assessment.

37   Aelfric held BOXTED for 4½ hides. Now the Count (holds it) in lordship.

> Always 5 villagers; 18 smallholders. Then 2 slaves, now none. Then 2 ploughs in lordship, now the same. Always 6 men's ploughs.
> Woodland, 300 pigs; meadow, 8 acres; then 1 mill, now none.
> 1 Freeman, who could not withdraw, who holds ½ hide. Then ½ plough, now none.
> Meadow, 2 acres. 13 cattle, 35 pigs, 140 sheep, 25 goats and 2 cobs.

Value then and later £8; now [£] 12 blanched.   30 a

38   Edric held (East) DONYLAND as a manor, for 1½ hides. Now the Count holds it in lordship.

> Always 10 smallholders. Then 4 slaves, now 1. Then 2 ploughs in lordship, now 1. Then 2 men's ploughs, now 1.

Silu̅.c.porc̃.vi.ac̃.p̃ti.Paſtura.c.ou̅.Tc̃ 7 p̃ ual.xl.ſol.m̃.iii.lib.In dn̅io
lxxx.oues.In Ead tenuit.i.lib h̅o dim̅ hid.qua̅ m̃ ten& Comes ſed In
gelric̃ eam habuit.7 hund neſcit q̃m eam habuerit.Val.v.ſol.

Bricceia̅ ten& Hugo de comite qd tenuit Edric.p.uno manerio.
7.p.iii.hid.7 poſt tenuit Ingelric̃.Tc̃.xiii.uitt.m̃.vi.Tc̃.v.bor.
m̃.xvii.Tc̃.vi.ſer.m̃.iiii.Tc̃.iii.car̃.in dn̅io.m̃.ii.7.d.Tc̃.viii.car̃ ho̅u̅
m̃.vi.Silu̅.c.por̃.xvi.ac̃.p̃ti.7.ii.dom in colecaſtro.que jacent huic
manerio.7.i.ſoc̃.q̃ n̅ pot̅at rece∂e.de.xiii.ac̃.Sẽp h̅t.dim̅.car̃.
In dn̅io.Tc̃.i.runc̃.m̃.iii.Tc̃.xx.an̅.m̃.x.Tc̃.xxxv.por.m̃.xxxiiii.
Tc̃.cxl.ou̅.m̃.cxx.Tc̃.xl.cap̃.m̃.xx.Tc̃.7 p̃ ual.vi.lib.m̃.c.ſol.

Eſtorp ten& Id̅e de comite.qd tenuit.Edric̃.lib h̅o.t.r̅.e.p.m̅.
7.p.i.hid.7.xxv.ac̃.Tc̃.ii.bor.m̃.viii.Tc̃.iiii.ſer.m̃.ii.Tc̃.ii.car̃ in
dn̅io.m̃.i.Tc̃.int̃ h̅oes.i.car̃.m̃.iii.Silu̅.xxx.por.vi.ac̃.p̃ti.Tc̃.i.
runc̃.7.xvi.an̅.7.xv.porc̃.7.xxx.ou̅.M.x.por.7.i.runc̃.Tc̃ ual.
xl.ſol.m̃.xxx.

Colu̅ tenet.Rob de comite qd tenuit Aluric̃ biga.p.i.uirg̅.7.x.ac̃.
t̅.r̅.e.Tc̃.i.bor.m̃.iii.Sẽp.ii.car in dn̅io.m̃.int̃ h̅oes.i.car̃.Tc̃.v.
ſer.m̃.iii.xiii.ac̃.p̃ti.ſilu̅.xl.porc̃.Tc̃.ual.xxx.ſol.m̃.xl.Hic
Aluric̃ libe tenuit iſta̅ tr̅a.ſed Ingelric̃.habuit ea̅ pq̅ rex uenit.7
hund neſcit q̃m.

Dunilanda̅ ten& Id̅e qd tenuit Godric̃ de cola̅ caſtro.p.xxv.ac̃.
.Val.xii.d.

Woodland, 100 pigs; meadow, 6 acres; pasture, 100 sheep.
Value then and later 40s; now £3.

In lordship 80 sheep.

In the same (Donyland) 1 free man held ½ hide which the Count now holds but Engelric had it and the Hundred does not know how he should have it.
Value 5s.

39 Hugh holds (Great) BIRCH from the Count, which Edric held as one manor, for 3 hides. Later Engelric held it.

Then 13 villagers, now 6; then 5 smallholders, now 17; then 6 slaves, now 4. Then 3 ploughs in lordship, now 2½. Then 8 men's ploughs, now 6.

Woodland, 100 pigs; meadow, 16 acres. 2 houses in Colchester which lie (in the lands of) this manor. 1 Freeman who could not withdraw, with 13 acres; he has always had ½ plough.
In lordship then 1 cob, now 3; then 20 cattle, now 10; then 35 pigs, now 34; then 140 sheep, now 120; then 40 goats, now 20.

Value then and later £6; now 100s.

40 He also holds EASTHORPE from the Count which Edric, a free man, held before 1066 as a manor, for 1 hide and 25 acres.

Then 2 smallholders, now 8; then 4 slaves, now 2. Then 2 ploughs in lordship, now 1. Then among the men 1 plough, now 3.

Woodland, 30 pigs; meadow, 6 acres. Then 1 cob, 16 cattle, 15 pigs, 30 sheep; now 10 pigs, 1 cob.

Value then 40s; now 30[s].

41 Robert holds COLNE from the Count, which Aelfric Big held for 1 virgate and 10 acres before 1066.

Then 1 smallholder, now 3. Always 2 ploughs in lordship. Now among the men 1 plough. Then 5 slaves, now 3.

Meadow, 13 acres; woodland, 40 pigs.

Value then 30s; now 40[s].

This Aelfric held this land freely but Engelric had it after the King came and the Hundred does not know how.

42 He also holds (East) DONYLAND, which Godric of Colchester held for 25 acres.
Value 12d.

Hund de Angra . Stanfort tenuit Leuuin . t . r . e . 7 poſt . Ingelric
p . uno manerio . 7 . p . ix . hid . M ten& Comes in dnio . p tantūnde . Sẽp.
xxiiii . uilt . Tc . ii . bor . m̃ . xvii . Tc . xxii . ſer . m̃ . xvi . Tc . x . car . in dnio.
7 . qñ recep . vii . m̃ . v . Sẽp . xv . car . hom . Silu . cccc . porc . l . ac . p̃ti.
Sẽp . i . mol . iiii . runc . xl . añ . xi . porc . ccxxxiii . ou . Tc ual . xxiiii . lib
7 . qñ recep . ſimiliſ . M . xl . lib . blancas.

In Ead tenuit qdã lib hõ . xl . ac . ſ; Ingelric accep eũ adjungens iſti trãe.
Sẽp . ibi ẽ dim . car . ſilua . xx . porc . Sẽp . ~~v . ſol.~~ uat . v . ſol. Et briſtuuin . tenuit
xx . ac . qs ingeiric adjunxit ſuæ trãe . 7 . adp̃tiatũ ẽ in ſup̃diſtis lib.

Paruã Stanfort ten Paſ Alurici . t . r . e . p . uno manerio . 7 . p . i . hid . 7
lxxx . ac . M ten& Comes . E . p tantũ de feudo ingelrici . Tc . iii . uilt . 7 . qñ
recep . v . M . ſimiliſ . Sẽp . iii . ſer . Tc . ii . car . in dnio . m̃ null . Sẽp . i . car . hõu.
Silu . c . porc . vi . ac . p̃ti . vi . añ . ccxiii . ou . Val . xl . ſol.

De hoc manerio ten& Aluric . dim hid . de comite . 7 ual . x . ſol . in eod p̃tio.

Lagafarã tenuit Leuuin t . r . e . p . i . hid . 7 . xl . ac . 7 Aluuin tenuit aliã
partẽ illi manerij . p . i . hid . 7 . xl . ac . p . Man . ſ; Ingelric adjunxit ſuo Man.
m̃ ten& Comes . E . in dnio . Sẽp . vii . uilt . 7 . x . bor . 7 . xv . ſer . 7 . v . car.
7 . dim . in dnio . 5 . v . car . hom . Silu . cc . por . xxxvii . 7 . dim . p̃ti . ii . añ.
xi . porc . lxxx . ou . iii . runc . Tc 7 p ual . xvi . lib . m̃ . xx . cañdidas.
De hoc manerio ten& Rad lxxx . ac . 7 . i . uilt . 7 . iii . bor . 7 . i . car . 7 . ual
xx . ſol . in eod . p̃tio.

In Ead tenuit qdã . lib hõ . xl . ac . qs adjunx̃ Ingelric iſti trãe . M.
ten& Rad de comite . 7 ẽ in eod p̃tio . 7 ual . x . ſol.

Angrã tenuit Ailida p . i . hid . 7 . p uno Man . M comeſ iñ dnio . Sẽp

viii . uilt . 7 . viii . bor 7 . iii . ſer . 7 . ii . car in dnio . 7 . iii . car hominũm

43 Leofwin, and later Engelric, held STANFORD (Rivers) before 1066
   as one manor, for 9 hides. Now the Count holds it in lordship for
   as much.
   Always 24 villagers. Then 2 smallholders, now 17; then 22
      slaves, now 16. Then 10 ploughs in lordship, when acquired
      7, now 5. Always 15 men's ploughs.
   Woodland, 400 pigs; meadow, 50 acres. Always 1 mill. 4 cobs,
      40 cattle, 11 pigs and 233 sheep.
   Value then £24; when acquired, the same; now £40 blanched.
   In the same (Stanford) a free man held 40 acres, but Engelric
   acquired him, adding him to this land. Always ½ plough there.
   Woodland, 20 pigs.
   Value always 5s.
   Also Brictwin held 20 acres, which Engelric added to his land.
   It is assessed in the above pounds.

44 Aelfric's father held STANFORD (Rivers) before 1066 as one manor,
   for 1 hide and 80 acres. Now Count Eustace holds it (as) of
   Engelric's Holding for as much.
   Then 3 villagers, when acquired 5, now the same. Always 3
      slaves. Then 2 ploughs in lordship, now none. Always 1
      men's plough.
   Woodland, 100 pigs; meadow, 6 acres. 6 cattle, 213 sheep.
   Value 40s.
   Of this manor, Aelfric holds ½ hide from the Count. Value 10s
   in the same assessment.

45 Leofwin held LAVER before 1066 for 1 hide and 40 acres. Alwin
   held another part of that manor for 1 hide and 40 acres as a
   manor. But Engelric added them to his manor. Now Count
   Eustace holds them in lordship.
   Always 7 villagers, 10 smallholders and 15 slaves; 5½ ploughs
      in lordship; 5 men's ploughs.
   Woodland, 200 pigs; meadow, 37½ acres. 2 cattle, 11 pigs,
      80 sheep, 3 cobs.
   Value then and later £16; now [£] 20 blanched.
   Of this manor Ralph holds 80 acres.
   1 villager, 3 smallholders. 1 plough.
   Value 20s in the same assessment.
   In the same (Laver) a free man held 40 acres which Engelric
   added to this land. Now Ralph holds (them) from the Count and
   he is in the same assessment.
   Value 10s.

46 Aethelgyth held (Chipping) ONGAR for 1 hide, as one manor. Now
   the Count (holds it) in lordship.
   Always 8 villagers, 8 smallholders, 3 slaves; 2 ploughs in
      lordship; 3 men's ploughs.

Silu̅ . ꟽ . porc̅ . xxviii . ac̅ . p̅ti . ii . runc̅ . x . an̅ . xxxvi . porc̅ . cxii . ou̅.
Tc̅ ua̅t . c . ſot . m̅ . viii . li̅b.

In Ead . tenuit . i . li̅b ho̅ . dim̅ . hid . que fuit de hoc manerio . m̅ ten&
Rad̅ baignard̅.

/ Laghefara̅ ten& Ricard̅ de comite qd̅ tenuit bri̅ctmar̅ . ꝑ . xl.
ac̅ . 7 . ꝑ uno Maner̅ . Se̅p . i . ſer̅ . 7 . i . car̅ . vi . ac̅ . p̅ti . Va̅t . x . ſot.

/ Lamburna̅ ten& Dauid de Comite qd̅ tenuit Lefſi̅ . ꝑ uno Man̅.
7 . ꝑ . ii hid̅ . 7 . lxxx . ac̅ . Se̅p . i . uitt . Tc̅ . x . bor̅ . m̅ . xii . Se̅p . i . ſer̅ . 7 . ii .
car̅ . in d̅nio . 7 . i . car̅ . hom̅ . Silu̅ . c . porc̅ . xx . ac̅ . p̅ti . Tc̅ ua̅t xl . ſot . m̅ . lx.

In d̅nio . ix . an̅ . 7 . lxxx . ou̅.

/ Fifhida̅ . ten& Ricard̅ . de comite qd̅ tenuit Bri̅ctmar̅ . ꝑ . xl . ac̅ . t̅ . r̅ . e̅ .
7 . ꝑ uno maner̅ . Se̅p . iii . ſer̅ . 7 . i . car̅ . in d̅nio . Silu̅ . xxiiii . porc̅ . xx . ac̅
p̅ti . Tc̅ . ua̅t . x . ſot . m̅ . xx . Qda̅ li̅b ten̅ . x . ac̅ . ſ; Ing̅ . iuaſit . ſe̅p . iii . ſer̅ . ſilu̅ . xxiiii . por.

/ Fifhida̅ ten& Junan̅ de comite qd̅ tenuit Aluuin . t̅ . r̅ . e̅ . ꝑ . uno . ꟽ.
/ iiii . ac̅ p̅ti . tc̅ uat̅ . v . ſot . m̅ . x.
7 . ꝑ . lxxx . ac̅ . Se̅p . i . uitt . Tc̅ . iiii . bor̅ . m̅ . vi . Se̅p . ii . ſer̅ . 7 . i . car̅ . in d̅io .
7 . i . car̅ . hom̅ . Silu̅ . l . porc̅ . x . ac̅ . p̅ti . Tc̅ ua̅t . xxx . ſot . m̅ . xl.

/ Hund̅ de Celmeresfort . Neuuelanda̅ ten& . Malger̅ de com̅ .
qd̅ tenuit Harold̅ . t̅ . r̅ . e̅ . ꝑ uno Man̅ 7 . ꝑ . iii . hid̅ . Se̅p . xv . uitt .
7 . vii . bor̅ . 7 . ii . ſer̅ . 7 . ii . car̅ . in d̅nio . ii . car̅ . hom̅ . Silu̅ . c . porc̅ . xx .
ac̅ . p̅ti . Tc̅ ua̅t . c . ſot . m̅ . vii . li̅b . Ingelr̅ iua̅s hoc ꟽ . 7 hund̅ teſta̅t q̅ jacuit /
/ in Wiretett . t̅ . r̅ . e̅ . 7 m̅ ten& Comes . E.

Woodland, 1000 pigs; meadow, 28 acres. 2 cobs, 10 cattle,
36 pigs, 112 sheep.
Value then 100s; now £8.
In the same (Ongar) 1 free man held ½ hide which was this
manor's. Now Ralph Baynard holds it.

47 Richard holds LAVER from the Count, which Brictmer held for
40 acres, as one manor.
Always 1 slave; 1 plough.
Meadow, 6 acres.
Value 10s.

48 David holds LAMBOURNE from the Count, which Leofsi held as
one manor, for 2 hides and 80 acres.
Always 1 villager. Then 10 smallholders, now 12. Always 1
slave; 2 ploughs in lordship; 1 men's plough.
Woodland, 100 pigs; meadow, 20 acres.
Value then 40s; now 60[s].
In lordship 9 cattle and 80 sheep.

49 Richard holds FYFIELD from the Count, which Brictmer held for
40 acres before 1066, as one manor.
Always 3 slaves; 1 plough in lordship.
Woodland, 24 pigs; meadow, 20 acres.
Value then 10s; now 20[s].
A free [man] held 10 acres, but Engelric annexed (him).
Always 3 slaves.
Woodland, 24 pigs; meadow, 4 acres.
Value then 5s; now 10[s].

50 Iwain holds FYFIELD from the Count, which Alwin held before
1066 as one manor, for 80 acres.
Always 1 villager. Then 4 smallholders, now 6. Always 2
slaves; 1 plough in lordship; 1 men's plough.
Woodland, 50 pigs; meadow, 10 acres.
Value then 30s; now 40[s].

Hundred of CHELMSFORD
51 Mauger holds NEWLAND (Hall) from the Count, which Harold held
before 1066 as one manor, for 3 hides.
Always 15 villagers, 7 smallholders, 2 slaves; 2 ploughs in
lordship; 2 men's ploughs.
Woodland, 100 pigs; meadow, 20 acres.
Value then 100s; now £7.
Engelric annexed this manor and the Hundred testifies that it
lay in (the lands of) Writtle before 1066. Now Count Eustace
holds it.

Baduuen tenuit Leuuiñ ᵽ.v.hid.t.r.e. M ten& Labᵗ de coñ. ᵽ tantund. Hanc &iã t̃ra inuaſit Ingelric. poſt q̃ rex aduenit. Tc̃ 7 ᵽ.iii.uiłł. m̃ null. Tc̃ 7 ᵽ.iiii.bor.m̃.viii. Tc̃ 7 ᵽ.vi.ſer.m̃.iii.

Sẽp.iii.car.in dñio. Tc̃.7 ᵽ.i.car hom.m̃.null. Silu.c.porc.xxiiii.ac.ᵽti. .i.runc.xv.an.l.porc.cxxxv.ou. Tc̃ 7 ᵽ uał.c.ſoł.m̃.vi.lib.

Runewellã ten& Idẽ Labᵗ de comite. qd̃ ten. Lefſtan.t.r.e.ᵽ.ℳ. 7.ᵽ.i.hid.7 hoc inuaſit Ingelric. Tc̃.ii.bor.m̃.iii. Sẽp.i.car. Silu.l. porc.ii.ac.ᵽti.xiii.an.xx.porc.xxxvi.ou. Vał.xx.ſoł.

Runeuuellã ten& Adelolf de comite qd̃ tenuit Edeua t.r.e. ᵽ.uno Man.7.ᵽ.iiii.hid.7 hoc inuaſit Ingelric. Tc̃.iiii.bor.m̃.v. Tc̃.ii.ſer.m̃.i. Tc̃.7.ᵽ.dim.car in dñio.m̃.ii.7.dim. Sẽp.dim.car hominũ. Silu.lxxx.porc. Tc̃ 7 ᵽ.uał.c.ſoł.m̃.vi.lib.

Waltham ten& Labᵗ de comite q̃ tenuit Lefſtan.t.r.e.ᵽ.uno.ℳ. 7.ᵽ.ii.hid.7.i.uirg.7 hanc inuaſit.ingelric. Tc̃ 7 ᵽ.iiii.bor.m̃.vii. Tc̃.ii.ſer.m̃.i. Tc̃.7.ᵽ.ii.car.in dñio.m̃.i.7.d. Sẽp.dim.car.hom. Silu.x.porc.xii.ac.ᵽti.i.runc.viii.an.c.ou. Tc̃ 7 ᵽ uał.l.ſoł m̃.lx.

Borham ten& Idẽ Lambᵗ de comite.qd̃ tenuer.xiiii.libi hões ᵽ.viii.hid.7.xxiii.ac.7 hoc inuaſit Ingelric poſt q̃ rex uenit in hanc t̃ra. Tc̃.ſub ipſis.iiii.bor.m̃.viii. Sẽp.iii.ſer.7.ii.car.in dñio. Tc̃.inꝑ hões.xiii.car; q̃n recep.7.m̃.ii. Silu.x.porc.liiii.ac.ᵽti. m̃.i.moł.i.runc.xv.an.cxxxii.ou. Tc̃.uał.xii.lib.7.q̃n rec. vi.lib.m̃.viii.

52 Leofwin held (Little) BADDOW for 5 hides before 1066. Now
Lambert holds it from the Count for as much. This land also
Engelric annexed after the King arrived.
> Then and later 3 villagers, now none; then and later 4
> smallholders, now 8; then and later 6 slaves, now 3.
> Always 3 ploughs in lordship. Then and later 1 men's   31 b
> plough, now none.
> Woodland, 100 pigs; meadow, 24 acres. 1 cob, 15 cattle,
> 50 pigs, 135 sheep.

Value then and later 100s; now £6.

53 Lambert also holds RUNWELL from the Count, which Leofstan
held before 1066 as a manor, for 1 hide. Engelric annexed this.
> Then 2 smallholders, now 3. Always 1 plough.
> Woodland, 50 pigs; meadow, 2 acres. 13 cattle, 20 pigs,
> 36 sheep.

Value 20s.

54 Adelulf holds RUNWELL from the Count, which Edeva held before
1066 as one manor, for 4 hides. Engelric annexed this.
> Then 4 smallholders, now 5; then 2 slaves, now 1. Then and
> later ½ plough in lordship, now 2½. Always ½ men's plough.
> Woodland, 80 pigs.

Value then and later 100s; now £6.

55 Lambert holds (Little) WALTHAM from the Count, which Leofstan
held before 1066 as one manor, for 2 hides and 1 virgate. Engelric
annexed this.
> Then and later 4 smallholders, now 7. Then 2 slaves, now 1.
> Then and later 2 ploughs in lordship, now 1½. Always ½
> men's plough.
> Woodland, 10 pigs; meadow, 12 acres. 1 cob, 8 cattle, 100
> sheep.

Value then and later 50s; now 60[s].

56 Lambert also holds BOREHAM from the Count, which 14 free men
held for 8 hides and 23 acres. Engelric annexed this after the King
came to this land.
> Then 4 smallholders under them, now 8. Always 3 slaves;
> 2 ploughs in lordship. Then among the men 13 ploughs,
> when acquired and now 2.
> Woodland, 10 pigs; meadow, 54 acres. Now 1 mill. 1 cob,
> 15 cattle, 132 sheep.

Value then £12; when acquired £6; now [£] 8.

In Ead ten& . ı . liɓ hõ . v . aċ . 7 uaɫ . x . đ.

Ranulꝼ piperelɫ calumpniaᵗ dim . hid . 7 . xvııı . aċ . que jacent
ad eccliam huj manerij 7 dim ecclıam . 7 Ingelric n̄ fuit ſaiſiᵗ.

ſ; comes . E . dedit cuidã ſuo militi unde reuocat eã ad defenſorē.

          ★

7 . xxx . aċ . que reddebant p annũ . xıı . đ . anteceſſori Ranulfi piperelli.
u hunđ teſtaᵗ.

⌐Hunđ de Tureſtapla . Toleſhuntã ten& Adelolꝼ de comite . qđ
tenuit Torɓn ꝑ uno manerio . 7 . ꝑ . vııı . hid . 7 . đ . Tc̄ . v . uiɫɫ . m̄ . ııı . Tc̄ . xvı.
bor . m̄ . xıııı . tc̄ . vııı . ſeꝛ . m̄ . ıııı . Tc̄ . ıııı . caꝛ . in dn̄io . m̄ . ııı . Tc̄ . ıııı . caꝛ
hom̄ . m̄ . ıı . Siɫu . ɫx . porċ . Paſt . ccc . oū . Tc̄ . xıı . ſalinæ . m̄ . v . ıı . runċ.
xvı . an . xɫ . porċ . cccc . oū . Tc̄ . 7 ꝑ uaɫ . x . liɓ . m̄ . c . ſoɫ.

In Ead . tenueꝛ . ııı . liɓi hões . dim . hid . 7 . ı . aċ . 7 uaɫ . x . ſoɫ.

⌐Goldhangram ten& Idē Adelolꝼ de comite . qđ tenuit Elric̄.
ꝑ . ı . hid . 7 . xv . aċ . m̄ . ıııı . bor . Tc̄ . ıı . ſeꝛ . m̄ null . Sēp . ı . caꝛ . in dn̄io . m̄
dim . caꝛ . hom̄ . Siɫu . xɫ . por . ııı . aċ . 7 . dim . ꝑti . Paſt . ɫ . oū . Tc̄ uaɫ . xx . ſoɫ
. m̄ . xxx.

⌐Toleſhunta . ten . comes in dn̄io . qđ tenuit Almaꝛ . ꝑ . ıı . hid . 7 . v . aċ.
Tc̄ . ııı . bor . m̄ . v . Sēp . ıı . ſeꝛ . 7 . ı . caꝛ . in dn̄io . 7 . ı . caꝛ . hom̄ . Siɫu . c . porċ.
paſt . cɫx . oū . ɫ . oū . Tc̄ . uaɫ . xɫ . ſoɫ . 7 qn̄ recep . xv . ſoɫ . m̄ . xx.

⌐Toleſhuntã ten& Sc̄s Martin de comite qđ tenuit Vluric̄ . liɓ
hõ . ꝑ uno Manerio . 7 . ꝑ . ı . hid . 7 . xxxv . aċ . Sēp . ıı . bor . 7 . ı . caꝛ . Siɫu . xxx.
porċ . ı . animaɫ . Vaɫ . xxx . ſoɫ.

⌐In Blacham tenueꝛ . ıııı . liɓi hões . dim . hid . 7 poᵗant eã uenđe . M
ten& Comes . E . Sēp . ı . caꝛ . Vaɫ . x . ſoɫ . 7 . qn̄ rec̄ . x . ſoɫ . m̄ . vıı . ſoɫ.

In the same (Boreham) 1 free man holds 5 acres. Value 10d.

Ranulf Peverel claims ½ hide and 18 acres which lie (in the lands of) the church of this manor and ½ church. Engelric was not in possession. But Count Eustace gave it to one of his men-at-arms who calls him as his defender.

30 acres which paid 12d a year to Ranulf Peverel's predecessor, 32a as the Hundred testifies.

Hundred of THURSTABLE

57 Adelulf holds TOLLESHUNT from the Count, which Thorbern held as one manor, for 8½ hides.

Then 5 villagers, now 3; then 16 smallholders, now 14; then 8 slaves, now 4. Then 4 ploughs in lordship, now 3. Then 4 men's ploughs, now 2.

Woodland, 60 pigs; pasture, 300 sheep; then 12 salt-houses, now 5. 2 cobs, 16 cattle, 40 pigs, 400 sheep.

Value then and later £10; now 100s.

In the same (Tolleshunt) 3 free men held ½ hide and 1 acre. Value 10s.

58 Adelulf also holds GOLDHANGER from the Count, which Alric held for 1 hide and 15 acres.

Now 4 smallholders; then 2 slaves, now none. Always 1 plough in lordship. Now ½ men's plough.

Woodland, 40 pigs; meadow, 3½ acres; pasture, 50 sheep. Value then 20s; now 30[s].

59 The Count holds TOLLESHUNT in lordship, which Aelmer held for 2 hides and 5 acres.

Then 3 smallholders, now 5. Always 2 slaves; 1 plough in lordship; 1 men's plough.

Woodland, 100 pigs; pasture, 160 sheep. 50 sheep. Value then 40s; when acquired 15s; now 20[s].

60 St. Martin's holds TOLLESHUNT from the Count which Wulfric, a free man, held as one manor for 1 hide and 35 acres.

Always 2 smallholders; 1 plough.

Woodland, 30 pigs. 1 (head of) cattle. Value 30s.

61 4 free men held ½ hide in 'BLATCHAMS' and could sell it. Now Count Eustace holds it. Always 1 plough.

Value 10s; when acquired 10s; now 7s.

Tolesbīā ten& Almfrid de comite q̄d tenuit Gudmund lib
lib hō . p̄ uno manerio . 7 . p̄ . III . hid . t . r . e . 7 hoc ē de feudo ingelrici.
Tc̄ . IIII . bor . M̄ . III . Tc̄ . IIII . ſer . m̄ . II . Tc̄ . in dn̄io . III . car̄ . m̄ . II.
Sēp . dim̄ . car̄ hom̄ . Paſt . c . ou . I . ſal . Tc̄ ual . IIII . lib . P̄ 7 m̄ . III.

Hund̄ de Tenderinga . Cītā ten& . Comes in dn̄io . q̄d ten
Eduuard p̄ uno man . 7 . p̄ . III . hid . 7 . XL . ac̄ . t . r . e . Poſt Ingelric̄ . Tc̄.
IX . uiłł . Poſt 7 m̄ . VII . m̄ . II . bor . Tc̄ . VIII . ſer . P̄ 7 m̄ . II . Tc̄ . in dn̄io . I . car̄.
7 . q̄n recep̄ . nichil . m̄ . I . Tc̄ . VI . car̄ hominū Poſt 7 m̄ . III . Silu̅ . cccc.
porc̄ . VI . ac̄ . p̄ti . I . uac̄ . XI . ou . Tc̄ . ual . XII . lib . 7 . q̄n recep̄ . XL . ſoł.
m̄ . X . lib . Huic manerio jac& . I . bereuuita que uocat̄ . Fratinga.
de . XL . ac̄ . m̄ . dim̄ . car̄ . App̄tiatū ē ſup̄i . 7 Ad Burnā . XXX . ac̄.
Tc̄ . I . car̄ . m̄ . dim̄ . Val . XX . ſoł . 7 In Froruuica . L . ac̄ . 7 Sēp . III . bor̄
7 . I . ſer . 7 . I . ac̄ . 7 . d̄ . p̄ti . m̄ . I . car̄ . Silu̅ . XII . porc̄ . Val . X . ſoł.
Tendringā tenuit Freuuin . t . r . e . p̄ . uno maner̄ . 7 . p̄ . d̄ . hid̄ . M̄
ten& Comes in dn̄io . p̄ tantudē . Sēp . I . uiłł . 7 . II . bor . 7 . II . ſer . Tc̄ . II.
car̄ . in dn̄io . Poſt 7 m̄ . I . Sēp . I . car̄ . hoūm . Silu̅ . XXX . porc̄ . II . ac̄ . p̄ti.
Tc̄ . II . runc̄ . m̄ . IIII . Tc̄ . IIII . an . m̄ . VII . Sēp . XX . porc̄ . Tc̄ . XL . ou . m̄ . c.
Tc̄ . XIIII . cap̄ . m̄ . XX . Tc̄ . ual . XL . ſoł . m̄ . LX.
Elesfordam ten& Hato de comite q̄d tenuit Eduuard . p̄ uno
manerio . 7 . p̄ . II . hid̄ . 7 . L . ac̄ . Tc̄ . IIII . bor . m̄ . VII . Tc̄ . VI ſer . m̄ . II . Tc̄ . in dı̄o
. II . car̄ . 7 . q̄n recep̄ . nułł . M̄ . dim̄ . Tc̄ . I . car̄ . hominū . m̄ . dim̄ . Silu̅ . c . por.
. III . ac̄ . p̄ti . Paſt . XX . ou . Val . LX . ſoł.

62 Amalfrid holds TOLLESBURY from the Count which Guthmund, a free man, held as one manor for 3 hides before 1066. This is (part) of Engelric's Holding.

  Then 4 smallholders, now 3; then 4 slaves, now 2. Then 3 ploughs in lordship, now 2. Always ½ men's plough.

  Pasture, 100 sheep; 1 salt-house.

Value then £4; later and now [£] 3.

Hundred of TENDRING

63 The Count holds ST. OSYTH in lordship, which Edward held as one manor, for 3 hides and 40 acres before 1066. Later Engelric (held it).

  Then 9 villagers, later and now 7; now 2 smallholders; then 8 slaves, later and now 2. Then 1 plough in lordship, when acquired nothing, now 1. Then 6 men's ploughs, later and now 3.

  Woodland, 400 pigs; meadow, 6 acres. 1 cow, 11 sheep.

Value then £12; when acquired 40s; now £10.

  1 outlier, which is called FRATING, lies in (the lands of) this manor, with 40 acres. Now ½ plough. It is assessed above.

  At BURNA 30 acres. Then 1 plough, now ½.

Value 20s.

  In FROWICK (Hall) 50 acres.

  Always 3 smallholders; 1 slave.

  Meadow, 1½ acres; now 1 plough; woodland, 12 pigs.

Value 10s.

64 Frewin held TENDRING before 1066 as one manor, for ½ hide. Now the Count holds it in lordship for as much.

  Always 1 villager; 2 smallholders; 2 slaves. Then 2 ploughs in lordship, later and now 1. Always 1 men's plough.

  Woodland, 30 pigs; meadow, 2 acres. Then 2 cobs, now 4; then 4 cattle, now 7; always 20 pigs; then 40 sheep, now 100; then 14 goats, now 20.

Value then 40s; now 60[s].

65 Hato holds ALRESFORD from the Count, which Edward held as one manor, for 2 hides and 50 acres.

  Then 4 smallholders, now 7; then 6 slaves, now 2. Then 2 ploughs in lordship, when acquired none, now ½. Then 1 men's plough, now ½.

  Woodland, 100 pigs; meadow, 3 acres; pasture, 20 sheep.

Value 60s.

⌐Frietunā ten& Rað de marci . de comite . qð tenuit Harolð ⍴ . ı .
maneř . 7 . ⍴ . ııı . hið . t . r . e . poſt tenuit Ingelric . Tc . vı . uiłł . m̂ . ıııı .
Tc . ııı . bor . m̂ nulł . tc . ıı . ſer . m̂ . ı . Sep . ı . car . in dn̄io . Tc . ıı . car . hoūm .
m̂ . dim . Paſt . ʟx . ou . ıı . an̄ . vıı . por . xx . ou . Tc uał . ʟx . ſoł . m̂ . ıııı .
lıb . 7 . x . ſoł .

⌐Birichou ten& Rob de comite . qð tenuit Ingelric de ſc̄o Paulo

Londoniæ . ⍴ uno manerio 7 . ⍴ . ııı . hið . Tc . vı . bor . M̂ vııı . Tc . ıı . ſer . M̂ . ı .
Tc . in dn̄io . ıı . car . m̂ nulla . Tc . in̄t hōes . ı . car . m̂ . ıı . Sılu . x . por . Paſt .
. c . ou . Tc . ıı . runc . m̂ nulł . Tc . vııı . an̄ . m̂ nulla . Tc . xııı . ou . m̂ nułł .
Tc . vı . porc . m̂ nulł . Tc uał . ʟx . ſoł . M̂ . ıııı . lıb . 7 . vıı . ſoł .

⌐Hoilandam ten& Adelolf de comite qð tenuit Leſtan̄ ⍴ uno
Manerio . 7 . ⍴ . ıııı . hið . t . r . e . poſtea tenuit Ingelric . Tc . xı . uiłł . m̂ .
vııı . Sep . v . bor . Tc . ıı . ſer . m̂ . ı . Tc . ıı . car . in dn̄io . m̂ . ı . Tc . in̄t hōes . vı .
car . m̂ . ıı . Sılu . ʟ . porc . Paſt . c . ouıb; . xııı . porc . xıııı . ou . Tc uał . vı .
lıb . m̂ . ıııı .

⌐Leleforðā ten& Idē de comite . qð tenuit Aluric lıb hō . t . r . e . Poſt
Ingelric . ⍴ . m̄ . 7 . ⍴ . ıı . hið . Tc . ıııı . uiłł . m̂ . ı . Tc . vıı . bor . m̂ . x . Tc . ıııı .
ſer . m̂ . ⌵ . Tc . in dn̄io . ıı . car . m̂ . ı . Tc . in̄t homines . ıııı . car . m̂ . ıı .
Sılu . x . por . vı . ać . p̄ti . Paſt . cc . ou . ıııı . animal . ʟxxx . ou . ı . r
vııı . porc . Sep . uał . x . lıb . In Ead . tenueř . ııı . ſoc . dim . hið . 7 .
xxx . ać . q̂s inuaſit Ingelric . 7 . m̂ ten& eos comes . E . 7 . Idē ade
lolf de eo . Tc . in̄t eos . ıı . car . m̂ . ı . ıı . ać . p̄ti . Vał . xx . ſoł

⌐Tendringe ten& b̄nard de comite qð . tenuit Ætnoð . ⍴ . Man .
7 . ⍴ . ı . hið . xv . ać . mın . 7 hoc ē de feudo Ingelrici . Tc . vııı . uiłł .
m̂ . vı . m̂ . vı . bor . Tc . vı . ſer . m̂ . ı . Sep . ıı . car . in dn̄io . 7 . ııı . car
homınū . Sılu . cc . porc . ıı ać . p̄ti . Sep . uał . ıııı . lıb .

66 Ralph of Marcy holds FRINTON from the Count, which Harold held as 1 manor, for 3 hides before 1066. Later Engelric held it.

Then 6 villagers, now 4; then 3 smallholders, now none; then 2 slaves, now 1. Always 1 plough in lordship. Then 2 men's ploughs, now ½.

Pasture, 60 sheep. 2 cattle, 7 pigs, 20 sheep.

Value then 60s; now £4 10s.

67 Robert holds BIRCH HALL from the Count, which Engelric held from St. Paul's, London, as one manor for 3 hides.

Then 6 smallholders, now 8; then 2 slaves, now 1. Then 2 ploughs in lordship, now none. Then among the men 1 plough, now 2.

Woodland, 10 pigs; pasture, 100 sheep. Then 2 cobs, now none; then 8 cattle, now none; then 13 sheep, now none; then 6 pigs, now none.

Value then 60s; now £4 7s.

68 Adelulf holds (Little) HOLLAND from the Count, which Leofstan held as one manor, for 4 hides before 1066. Later on Engelric held it.

Then 11 villagers, now 8; always 5 smallholders; then 2 slaves, now 1. Then 2 ploughs in lordship, now 1. Then among the men 6 ploughs, now 2.

Woodland, 50 pigs; pasture, 100 sheep. 13 pigs, 14 sheep.

Value then £6; now [£] 4.

69 He also holds LAWFORD from the Count, which Aelfric, a free man, held before 1066. Later Engelric (held it) as a manor, for 2 hides.

Then 4 villagers, now 1; then 7 smallholders, now 10; then 4 slaves, now 1. Then 2 ploughs in lordship, now 1. Then among the men 4 ploughs, now 2.

Woodland, 10 pigs; meadow, 6 acres; pasture, 200 sheep. 4 cattle, 80 sheep, 1 cob, 8 pigs.

Value always £10.

In·the same (Lawford) 3 Freemen held ½ hide and 30 acres, which Engelric annexed. Now Count Eustace holds them and Adelulf also from him. Then among them 2 ploughs, now 1.

Meadow, 2 acres.

Value 20s.

70 Bernard holds TENDRING from the Count, which Ednoth held as a manor, for 1 hide less 15 acres. This is (part) of Engelric's Holding.

Then 8 villagers, now 6; now 6 smallholders; then 6 slaves, now 1. Always 2 ploughs in lordship; 3 men's ploughs.

Woodland, 200 pigs; meadow, 2 acres.

Value always £4.

⌐Hund.de Vdelesfort.Cristeshalā tenuit Inguar꞉.p̄
uno manerio.7.p̄.vi.hid.t.r.e.m̄ ten& comes.E.in dn̄io
de feudo Ingelrici.Sēp.xxxii.uill.Tc.vi.bor.m̄.xiii.

33 b

Sēp.vi.ser.7.iii.car.in dn̄io.7.xvi.car.hominū.Silu꞉.cc.por.7
viii.ac.p̄ti.i.runc.xl.porc.cl.ou.xxiiii.cap.iiii.uasa.apū.
Sēp.ual.xv.lib.Huic manerio ptinent.ii.soc.de.viii.ac.7.i.soc.
de.viii.ac.quē occupau Ingelric.t.r.Witti.In istis.viii.ac.st̄
.iii.bor.7.ual.xvi.đ.Huic manerio attinebat.i.soc.de.iii.uirg꞉.
t.r.e.quē m̄.ten& Witt cardun ad feudū.G.de magna uilla.
7.reddebat.p.annū.ii.đ.

⌐Cishellā ten& Wido de comite.qđ tenuit Si꞉ꞏ꞉ard͏꞊ꝺ.lib hō.t.r.e.
p̄.m̄.7.p̄.vi.hid.7.xxx.ac.Tc.v.uill.m̄.vi.Tc.iii.bor.m̄.v.Sēp̄꞉
vi.ser.7.iii.car.in dn̄io.7.v.car.hom.7.viii.ac.p̄ti.xxiiii.porc꞉
ccl.ou.Tc.7 p̄.ual.c.sol.7.m̄.vi.lib.

⌐Cishellā tenuit.Godric lib hō.t.r.e.m̄.ten&.Idē Wido de comite
p̄.uno manerio.7.p̄.ii.hid.7.dim.Val.lx.sol.⌐In Eadē tenuit.
.i.lib hō.dim hid.quā occupauit Ingelric.t.r.Witti.7 m̄ ten&
Enselm de comite.In illa tr̄a st̄ sēp.ii.bor.7.i.car.7.ii.ac.p̄ti.
Val.x.sol.

⌐Elmdunā ten& Rog de Sumeri de comite.q̄ tenuit.Almar꞉.
lib hō.t.r.e.7 Ingelric occupau hoc maneriū t.r.Witti.Sēp ibi
st̄.xiiii.hid.7.xxvi.uill.7.xv.bor.Tc.xii.ser.m̄ nuli.Tc.vi.
car.in dn̄io.7.qn̄ recep̄.iii.m̄.iiii.Sēp.x.car.hominū.Silu꞉.
.ccl.porc.vii.ac.p̄ti.xx.porc.cc.ou.7.lxxxviii.ou.Tc ual
xvi.lib.7 qn̄ recep̄.M.xx.lib.

Hundred of UTTLESFORD

71 Ingvar held CHRISHALL as one manor, for 6 hides before 1066.
Now Count Eustace holds it in lordship (as) of Engelric's Holding.

> Always 32 villagers. Then 6 smallholders, now 13. Always 6
slaves; 3 ploughs in lordship; 16 men's ploughs.
Woodland, 200 pigs; meadow, 8 acres. 1 cob, 40 pigs, 150
sheep, 24 goats, 4 beehives.

Value always £15.

> To this manor belong 2 Freemen with 8 acres, and 1 Freeman
with 8 acres whom Engelric appropriated after 1066.
On these 8 acres are 3 smallholders.

Value 16d.

> To this manor was attached 1 Freeman with 3 virgates before
1066, whom William Cardon holds for G(eoffrey) de Mandeville's
Holding.
He paid 2d a year.

72 Guy holds CHISHILL from the Count, which Sired, a free man, held
before 1066 as a manor for 6 hides and 30 acres.

> Then 5 villagers, now 6; then 3 smallholders, now 5. Always 6
slaves; 3 ploughs in lordship; 5 men's ploughs.
Meadow, 8 acres. 24 pigs, 250 sheep.

Value then and later 100s; now £6.

73 Godric, a free man, held CHISHILL before 1066. Now Guy also
holds it from the Count as one manor, for 2½ hides.
Value 60s.

> In the same (Chishill) 1 free man held ½ hide which Engelric
appropriated after 1066. Now Anselm holds it from the Count.
On that land have always been 2 smallholders; 1 plough.
Meadow, 2 acres.

Value 10s.

74 Roger of Sommery holds ELMDON from the Count, which Aelmer,
a free man, held before 1066. Engelric appropriated this manor
after 1066. There have always been 14 hides there;

> 26 villagers; 15 smallholders. Then 12 slaves, now none.
Then 6 ploughs in lordship, when acquired 3, now 4.
Always 10 men's ploughs.
Woodland, 250 pigs; meadow, 7 acres. 20 pigs, 200 sheep and
88 sheep.

Value then and when acquired £16; now £20.

⌐Leam tenuit . Brictulf . liɓ hō . t̃ . r̃ . e . p̃ . manerio . 7 . p̃ . ii . hiꝺ

34 a
7 dim̃ . Poſtea . tenuit Ingelric̃ . m̃ . Idē Roḡ de comite . Sẽp .
v . uiɫɫ . Tc̃ . i . bor̃ . P̃ 7 m̃ . viii . Tc̃ . iiii . ſer̃ . M̃ null̃ . Tc̃ . iii . car̃ . in
dñio . P̃ 7 m̃ . ii . Tc̃ . iiii . car̃ . hom̃ . 7 . qñ rec̃ . iii . 7 . m̃ ſimiliꞇ . Silũ .
. l . porc̃ . Tc̃ . 7 . p̃ uaɫ . iiii . liɓ . m̃ . c . ſoɫ .

⌐Crauuelæam . ten& . Idē de comite . qꝺ tenuit Lefſi liɓ hō . t̃ . r̃ . e . p̃ xxx . ac̃ .
7 Ingelric̃ . occupauit . t̃ . r . Wiɫɫi . Sẽp . ii . bor̃ . Tc̃ . i . ſer̃ . Sẽp . i . car̃ . ii . ac̃ .
p̃ti . Vaɫ . x . ſoɫ .

⌐Hunꝺ de Froſſeuuella . dimidiũ ; Benediſc̃ . tenuit Ledmar̃
pɓr̃ . t̃ . r̃ . e . p̃ . m̃ . 7 . p̃ . iiii . hiꝺ . 7 . dim̃ . Poſt tenuit Ingelric̃ . m̃ . ten&
comes in dñio . Sẽp . viii . uiɫɫ . 7 . iii . bor̃ . 7 . viii . ſer̃ . 7 . iiii . car̃ in
dñio . Tc̃ . inꞇ hōes . iiii . car̃ . Poſt 7 m̃ . iii . Silũ . c . por̃ . viii . ac̃ . p̃ti .
xxviii . por̃ . c . 7 xii . oů . 7 . i . ſoc̃ . tenuit . i . ac̃ . 7 . i . pertic̃ . quē in
uaſit Ingelric̃ . M̃ ten& comes . Tc̃ uaɫ . totũ . xi . liɓ . m̃ . xii .

⌐Neuuham tenuit . Alſi . p̃ . i . hiꝺ . t̃ . r̃ . e . Poſt ten̄ . Ingelric̃ . m̃ . ten&
comes in dñio . Tc̃ . vi . uiɫɫ . m̃ . ix . Tc̃ . ii . bor̃ . P̃ 7 m̃ . vii . Sẽp . vi .
ſer̃ . 7 . iii . car̃ . in dñio , Tc̃ . iiii . car̃ . hominũ . P̃ 7 m̃ . iii . Silũ . xx .
por̃ . v . ac̃ p̃ti . xiiii . por̃ . lvi . oů . i . runc̃ . Huic manerio fuer̃ .
v . ſoc̃ . tenentes . dim̃ . hiꝺ . 7 . xxxv . ac̃ . remanentes . cũ ſoca . Tc̃ .
. iii . car̃ . P̃ 7 m̃ . ii . v . ac̃ . p̃ti . Tc̃ . uaɫ . xi . liɓ . m̃ . xii .

⌐Birdefelda . ten& Adolof̃ . de comite . qꝺ tenuit . Normann̄ . t̃ . r . e .
p̃ . ii . hiꝺ . 7 . i . uirg̃ . poſt ea . tenuit Ingelric̃ . 7 inuaſit eũ . Sẽp
vi . uiɫɫ . Tc̃ . 7 p̃ . i . bor̃ . m̃ . xii . Sẽp . iiii . ſer̃ . 7 . iii . car̃ . in dñio . 7 . ii .
car̃ . hom̃ . Silũ . cc . por̃ . xlix . ac̃ p̃ti . v . añ . xxv . porc̃ . ii . uaſa . ap̃ .

34 b
xxx . cap̃ . i . runc̃ . Sẽp . i . moɫ . m̃ . i . piſcina . Tc̃ . uaɫ . viii . liɓ . m̃
x . liɓ .

75 Brictwulf, a free man, held (Elmdon) LEE before 1066 as a manor, for 2½ hides. Later on Engelric held it. Now Roger also (holds it) 34 a from the Count.

 Always 5 villagers. Then 1 smallholder, later and now 8; then 4 slaves, now none. Then 3 ploughs in lordship, later and now 2. Then 4 men's ploughs, when acquired 3, now the same.

 Woodland, 50 pigs.

Value then and later £4; now 100s.

76 He also holds CRAWLEYBURY from the Count, which Leofsi, a free man, held before 1066 for 30 acres. Engelric appropriated it after 1066.

 Always 2 smallholders. Then 1 slave. Always 1 plough.

 Meadow, 2 acres.

Value 10s.

Half-Hundred of FRESHWELL

77 Ledmer the priest held BENDYSH (Hall) before 1066 as a manor, for 4½ hides. Later Engelric held it. Now the Count holds it in lordship.

 Always 8 villagers, 3 smallholders, 8 slaves; 4 ploughs in lordship. Then among the men 4 ploughs, later and now 3.

 Woodland, 100 pigs; meadow, 8 acres. 28 pigs, 112 sheep.

 1 Freeman held 1 acre and 1 perch, whom Engelric annexed.

Now the Count holds it.

Value of the whole then £11; now [£] 12.

78 Alfsi held NEWNHAM (Hall) for 1 hide before 1066. Later Engelric held it. Now the Count holds it in lordship.

 Then 6 villagers, now 9; then 2 smallholders, later and now 7.

 Always 6 slaves; 3 ploughs in lordship. Then 4 men's ploughs, later and now 3.

 Woodland, 20 pigs; meadow, 5 acres. 14 pigs, 56 sheep, 1 cob.

 (Belonging) to this manor were 5 Freemen who hold ½ hide and 35 acres (and) who remain with the jurisdiction. Then 3 ploughs, later and now 2.

 Meadow, 5 acres.

Value then £11; now [£] 12.

79 Adelulf holds (Little) BARDFIELD from the Count, which Norman held before 1066 for 2 hides and 1 virgate. Later on Engelric held it and annexed him.

 Always 6 villagers. Then and later 1 smallholder, now 12.

 Always 4 slaves; 3 ploughs in lordship; 2 men's ploughs.

 Woodland, 200 pigs; meadow, 49 acres. 5 cattle, 25 pigs, 2 beehives, 30 goats, 1 cob. Always 1 mill. Now 1 fishpond. 34 b

Value then £8; now £10.

Hund̄ de Rochefort . Scopelandā . tenuit . I . lib̄ hō . t . r̄ . e.

p̄ . v . hid̄ . Poſt tenuit Ingelric̄ . m̄ . comes . E . in dn̄io . Sēp . v . uiłł . 7

. II . ſoc̄ . 7 . dn̄s eoɀ habebat focā 7 . ſacā . Sēp . IX . bord̄ . 7 . II . car̄ . in dn̄io.

7 . v . car̄ . hom̄ . Silu . XL . porc̄ . Paſt . CCCC . ou . II . an̄ . LIIII . ou . XIIII.

porc̄ . XIII . cap̄ . IIII . runc̄ . Tc̄ uał . vI . lib̄ . m̄ . x . In ead̄ tenuit . I . lib̄ hō

dim̄ . hid̄ . 7 . xxx . ac̄ . qd̄ occupauit Ingelric̄ . Sēp . I . car̄ . 7 . III . bor 7 hoc eſt

ap̄p̄tiatū in x . lib̄.

TERRA COMITIS ALANI.

Hund̄ de Herlaua . Eppingam tenuit

Wiſgarus lib̄ homo tēpore regis . E . p̄ uno maner̄.

7 . p̄ . I . hid̄ . 7 . dim̄ . 7 dim̄ uirḡ . Semp . I . car̄ in dn̄io.

7 . dim̄ . car̄ hom̄ . 7 . II . uiłł . 7 . II . bor . Silu . c . porc̄ . vIII . ac̄.

p̄ti . Tc̄ uał . xx . ſoł . m̄ . xxx . hoc . m̄ . ten̄& Osb̄n̄ . de Comite.

Hund̄ de Dommauua . Vlinghehalam ten̄& Herueus

de comite qd̄ tenuit Edeua t . r̄ . e . p̄ uno . m̄ . 7 . p̄ . I . hid̄ . 7 . I.

uirḡ . 7 . dim̄ . Sēp . III . car̄ in dn̄io . 7 . I . car̄ 7 . dim̄ hominū.

7 . IIII . uiłł . 7 . vIII . bord̄ . 7 . IIII . ſer̄ . Silu . ccL . porc̄ . xII . ac̄

p̄ti . Tc̄ uał Lx . ſoł . m̄ . c.

Canefeldā ten̄& Albic̄ deuer̄ de comite qd̄ tenuit

Edeua t . r̄ . e . p̄ . I . hid̄ . 7 . xxx . ac̄ . Sēp . I . car̄ . in dn̄io.

7 . I . car̄ . hom̄ . Tc̄ . III . uiłł . m̄ . I . Tc̄ . v . bord̄ . m̄ . x . Silu.

. c . porc̄ . xLvIII . ac̄ . p̄ti . in̄ p̄tū 7 mareſc̄ . Sēp uał . Lx . ſoł.

Hund̄ de Hidinghafort . Phincingefeldam ten̄&

Herueus de Comite qd̄ ten̄ . III . lib̄i hōes . t . r̄ . e . p̄ . II . hid̄.

7 . dim̄ . ſub Edeua . Sēp . v . car̄ . in dn̄io . 7 vII . car̄ hōu

7 . III . uiłł . 7 . L . bord̄ . v . ſer̄ . Silu . cLx . porc̄ . xvI . ac̄ . p̄ti.

Tc̄ uał . c . ſoł . m̄ . vIII . lib̄.

Hundred of ROCHFORD

80 1 free man held SHOPLAND before 1066 for 5 hides. Later Engelric held it. Now Count Eustace (holds it) in lordship.

Always 5 villagers; 2 Freemen, their lord had full jurisdiction.
Always 9 smallholders; 2 ploughs in lordship; 5 men's ploughs.
Woodland, 40 pigs; pasture, 400 sheep. 2 cattle, 54 sheep, 14 pigs, 13 goats, 3 cobs.
Value then £6; now [£] 10.
In the same (Shopland) 1 free man held ½ hide and 30 acres, which Engelric appropriated. Always 1 plough;
3 smallholders.
This is assessed in the £10.

21   **LAND OF COUNT ALAN**   35 a

Hundred of HARLOW

1 Withgar, a free man, held EPPING before 1066 as one manor, for 1½ hides and ½ virgate. Always 1 plough in lordship; ½ men's plough;
2 villagers; 2 smallholders.
Woodland, 100 pigs; meadow, 8 acres.
Value then 20s; now 30[s].
Osbern holds this manor from the Count.

Hundred of DUNMOW

2 Hervey holds WILLINGALE (Spain) from the Count, which Edeva held before 1066 as one manor, for 1 hide and 1½ virgates. Always 3 ploughs in lordship; 1½ men's ploughs;
4 villagers; 8 smallholders; 4 slaves.
Woodland, 250 pigs; meadow, 12 acres.
Value then 60s; now 100[s].

3 Aubrey de Vere holds (Great) CANFIELD from the Count, which Edeva held before 1066 for 1 hide and 30 acres. Always 1 plough in lordship; 1 men's plough.
Then 3 villagers, now 1; then 5 smallholders, now 10.
Woodland, 100 pigs; meadow, 48 acres among meadow and marsh.
Value always 60s.

Hundred of HINCKFORD

4 Hervey holds FINCHINGFIELD from the Count, which 3 free men held before 1066 for 2½ hides under Edeva. Always 5 ploughs in lordship; 7 men's ploughs;
3 villagers; 50 smallholders; 5 slaves.
Woodland, 160 pigs; meadow, 16 acres.
Value then 100s; now £8.

In Bumeſteda ten& . I . miɫ . VII . ac�‍ . 7 . dim͛ . qđ tenuit
. I . ſoc͛ . ſub Edeua . t . r . e . 7 . I . ac͛ . 7 . dim͛ . p̄ti . Tc͞ uaɫ . II . ſoɫ.
M̊ . III . In Gerham . XLII . ac͛ . qs tenuit . I . liƀ ho͞ . t . r . e.

35 b
Sep͞ . I . car͛ . 7 . III . bor . Tc͞ . II . ſer͛ . m̊ . I . Silu͛ . XV . porc͛ . V . ac͛
p̄ti . m̊ . I . moɫ . Tc͞ uaɫ . XX . ſoɫ . m̊ . XXV.
In Phincingefelda . ten& Comes in dn̄io . XXXVIII . ac͛ . 7 dim͛.
qs tenuer͛ . II . ſoc͛ . 7 . I . liƀ ho͞ . t . r . e . Sep͞ . dim . car͛ . 7 . II . borđ
. II . ac͛ . p̄ti . Vaɫ . V . ſoɫ.
〵Hunđ de Angra   Roinges ten& Albic͛͠ de uer de com͛.
qđ tenuit Leuuin͛ 7 Etſi͛ p̄ . M̊ . t . r . e . 7 . p̄ . I . hiđ . 7 . dim͛.
Sep͞ . II . uiɫɫ . 7 . XIII . borđ . 7 . III . car͛ . in dn̄io . 7 . I . car͛ hominu͞
Silu͛ . CC . porc͛ . L . ac͛ p̄ti Tc͞ uaɫ . IIII . liƀ . p̄ . 7 m̊ . C . ſoɫ.
〵Hunđ de Tendringa . Benetlea͞ ten& Herueus de iſpa
nia de comite q͛ tenuit Eluuin͛ p̄ . XLII . ac͛ . 7 . dim͛ . liƀe han t̄r̄a
tenuit Comes . R . Sep͞ . III . uiɫɫ . 7 . dim͛ . car͛ . 7 . I . ac͛ p̄ti . Silu͛.
VI . porc͛ . Vaɫ . III . ſoɫ . Iſte Idé tenuit dim͛ hiđ . Sep͞ . IIII . uiɫɫ.
7 . I . car͛ . Silu͛ . VI . porc͛ . dim͛ . ac͛ . p̄ti . Vaɫ . X . ſoɫ.
〵Hunđ de Udeleſforda   Monehala͞ ten& Idé . H . de com͛.
qđ ten͛ . Siuuarđ . p̄ . I . hiđ . Sep͞ . II . uiɫɫ . Tc͞ . I . ſer͛ . m̊ . nuɫɫ.
m̊ . I . borđ . Sep͞ . dim͛ . car͛ . VII . ac͛ p̄ti . 7 . II . part moɫ . uaɫ.
XX . ſoɫ.

5 In (Steeple) BUMPSTEAD 1 man-at-arms holds 7½ acres, which 1
Freeman held under Edeva before 1066.
>   Meadow, 1½ acres.

Value then 2s; now 3[s].

6 In YELDHAM 42 acres which 1 free man held before 1066. Always   35 b
1 plough;
>   3 smallholders. Then 2 slaves, now 1.
>   Woodland, 15 pigs; meadow, 5 acres; now 1 mill.

Value then 20s; now 25[s].

7 In FINCHINGFIELD the Count holds 38½ acres in lordship, which
2 Freemen and 1 free man held before 1066. Always ½ plough;
>   2 smallholders.
>   Meadow, 2 acres.

Value 5s.

Hundred of ONGAR

8 Aubrey de Vere holds (Beauchamp) RODING from the Count,
which Leofwin and Edsi held as a manor before 1066, for 1½
hides.
>   Always 2 villagers; 13 smallholders; 3 ploughs in lordship;
>   1 men's plough.
>   Woodland, 200 pigs; meadow, 50 acres.

Value then £4; later and now 100s.

Hundred of TENDRING

9 Hervey of 'Spain' holds (Little) BENTLEY from the Count, which
Alwin held freely for 42½ acres. Earl R(alph) held this land.
>   Always 3 villagers; ½ plough.
>   Meadow, 1 acre; woodland, 6 pigs.

Value 3s.
>   This same man also held ½ hide.
>   Always 4 villagers; 1 plough.
>   Woodland, 6 pigs; meadow, ½ acre.

Value 10s.

Hundred of UTTLESFORD

10 Hervey also holds EMANUEL (Wood) from the Count, which Siward
held for 1 hide.
>   Always 2 villagers. Then 1 slave, now none; now 1 smallholder.
>   Always ½ plough.
>   Meadow, 7 acres; 2 parts of a mill.

Value 20s.

Dim̄ Hund de Froffeuuella . In Rodā ten& Idē xxx.
ac̄ . qđ tenuit Edeua S̄ep . dim̄ . car̄ . Silū . viii . porc̄ . ii . ac̄ . 7
dim̄ . p̄ti . Tc̄ . ual̄ . v . fol̄ . m̄ . x . In Stauintuna tenuit Edeua
. v . ac̄ . qđ ten& Herueu . val̄ . ii . fol̄

Γ Terra Witti de Warenna in Exffeffa.   Hund de b̄deftapla .   . XXII .

Γ Vpham tenuit Edeua quedā femina t̄ . r̄ . e . p̄ dim̄ hid̄ . 7 . xxx . ac̄ .
m̄ ten& Witt in dn̄io . val̄ . x . fol̄ .

Γ Tilibiam ten& Ranulf̄ de Witto qđ tenuit Sueting lib̄ hō . t̄ . r̄ . e .
p̄ . xxx . ac̄ . s̄ep . i . bor̄ . Paſt̄ . xl . ou̅ . i . ac̄ . p̄ti . Tc̄ . ual̄ . vii . fol̄ . m̄ . xiiii .

Γ Dim̄ Hund de herlaua Ouefham ten& Ricard . de . W . qđ tenuit
Holefeſt . lib̄ hō . t̄ . r̄ . e . p̄ uno manerio . 7 . p̄ . i . hid̄ . 7 . iii . uirḡ . Tc̄ . ii . car̄
in dn̄io . m̄ . i . Tc̄ . iii . car̄ . 7 . dim̄ hou̅m . m̄ . v . Tc̄ . vi . uitt . m̄ . x . S̄ep .
. iii . bor̄ . Tc̄ . iii . fer̄ . m̄ . i . Silū . l . porc̄ . x . ac̄ . p̄ti . Qn̄ recepit . v . anim̄ .
7 . i . uitul̄ . 7 . xl . porc̄ . xl . ou̅ . M̄ . vi . an̄ . 7 . l . porc̄ . xc . ou̅ . iii . uaſa
apu̅ . Huic manerio addita . i . uirḡ . t̄ . r . Witti . quā tenuit Vluric̄ .
lib̄ hō . t̄ . r̄ . e . Tc̄ . dim̄ . car̄ . m̄ . nulla . s̄ep . i . bor̄ . Silū . x . porc̄ . ii . ac̄ . p̄ti .
tc̄ ual̄ . iiii . fol̄ . m̄ . vi . 7 maneriū ual̄ . tc̄ . vi . lib̄ . m̄ . vii .

Γ Cuicā ten& Idē Ricard de Witto . qđ tenuſt Aluuin godtuna . t̄ .
r̄ . e . p̄ . iii . hid̄ . S̄ep . ii . car̄ . in dn̄io . Tc̄ . iii . car̄ . 7 . dim̄ . hominū . m̄ . iii .
Tc̄ . vii . uitt . m̄ . vi . m̄ . vi . bord̄ . tc̄ . v . fer̄ . m̄ . ii . xx . ac̄ . p̄ti . S̄ep . i .
mol̄ . Tc̄ . xlvii . ou̅ . m̄ . lii . 7 . ii . putti . Val̄ . c . fol̄

Half-Hundred of FRESHWELL

11 He also holds 30 acres in ROTH(END), which Edeva held. Always ½ plough.
    Woodland, 8 pigs; meadow, 2½ acres.
    Value then 5s; now 10[s].

12 In STEVINGTON (End) Edeva held 5 acres, which Hervey holds.
    Value 2s.

22   LAND OF WILLIAM OF WARENNE IN ESSEX

Hundred of BARSTABLE

1 Edeva, a woman, held *UPHAM* before 1066 for ½ hide and 30 acres.
    Now William holds it in lordship.
    Value 10s.

2 Ranulf holds TILBURY from William, which Sweeting, a free man,
    held before 1066 for 30 acres.
    Always 1 smallholder.
    Pasture, 40 sheep; meadow, 1 acre.
    Value then 7s; now 14[s].

Half-Hundred of HARLOW

3 Richard holds HOUSHAM (Hall) from William, which Holdfast, a
    free man, held before 1066 as one manor for 1 hide and 3 virgates.
    Then 2 ploughs in lordship, now 1. Then 3½ men's ploughs, now 5.
       Then 6 villagers, now 10. Always 3 smallholders. Then 3 slaves,
          now 1.
       Woodland, 50 pigs; meadow, 10 acres. When acquired 5 cattle,
          1 calf, 40 pigs, 40 sheep; now 6 cattle, 50 pigs, 90 sheep,
          3 beehives.
    To this manor was added 1 virgate after 1066 which Wulfric, a
    free man, held before 1066. Then ½ plough, now none.
    Always 1 smallholder.
    Woodland, 10 pigs; meadow, 2 acres.
    Value then 4s; now 6[s].
    Value of the manor then £6; now [£] 7.

4 Richard also holds QUICK(SBURY Farm) from William, which Alwin
    Gotton held before 1066 for 3 hides. Always 2 ploughs in
    lordship. Then 3½ men's ploughs, now 3.
       Then 7 villagers, now 6; now 6 smallholders; then 5 slaves,
          now 2.
       Meadow, 20 acres. Always 1 mill. Then 47 sheep, now 52;
          2 foals.
    Value 100s.

⌐Hund de Dommauua . Eſtanes tenuit Ďuua . liƀa femina
t . r . e . p . man . 7 . p . ii . hid . m̂ . Wiłł in dñio . Sep . ii . car in dñio
te . iiii . car . hominū . m̂ . ii . Sep . iiii . uiłł . Te . iii . bor . m̂ . viii . Te
iii . ſer . m̂ . ii . Silua te . ad . cc . porc . m̂ . cl . lii . ac . p̂ti . Te . i . r̂ .
7 . vii . an . 7 . lx . porc . 7 . lx . oũ . M . i . r̂ . xxiii . an . xx . por .
lxx . oũ . iiii . uaſa apū . Val . c . ſoł .

36 b

⌐Caneſeldā tenuierunt . ii . liƀi hões . t . r̂ . e . p . ii . hid . viii . ac .
min . m̂ . Wiłł in dñio Te . iiii . car . in dñio m̂ . ii . Te . viii . car . hoũ
m̂ . vi . Te . i . pƀr . 7 . vii uiłł . m̂ . i . pƀr . 7 . vii . uiłł . Te . iii . bor . m̂ .
xvii . Sep . ii . ſer . M . i . moł . Te . ſiłu . clx . porc . m̂ . cxx . lxx . ac . p̂ti .
Te . i . runc . 7 . viii . an . 7 . c . porc . 7 . cc . oũ . M . i . runc . xv . an .
. l . porc . lxx . oũ . ix . cap . Te ual . viii . liƀ . m̂ . ix .

⌐Rodinges ten& . W . de uuateuiłł . de Wiłło . qđ tenuit Abbas de
eli . t . r̂ . e . p uno manerio . 7 . p . ii . hid . 7 . dim . Sep . iii . car . in dñio .
7 . iii . car . hom . & . i . pƀr . 7 . viii . uiłł . Te . xii . bor . m̂ . xi . Sep . vii . ſer .
Siłu . ccc . porc . xlii . ac . p̂ti . Sep . iii . runc . viii . an . 7 . cxx . oũ . m̂ .
. vii . porc . Te ual . x . liƀ . 7 . qñ rec . xii . m̂ . xviii .

⌐Rodinges ten& Galt de Wiłło . qđ tenuit . liƀa femina . t . r̂ . e
p . uno maner . 7 . p . ii . hid . 7 . dim . 7 M st . iii . hid . 7 . dim ; Te . iii . car .
in dñio . m̂ . ii . 7 qñ rec . iii . Sep . i . car . hom . Te . iii . uiłł . M . i . pƀr .
7 . iiii . uiłł . Te . iiii . bor . m̂ . xiii . Te . iiii . ſer . m̂ . ii . Siłu . l . por . xxx . ac .
p̂ti . m̂ . iiii . an . 7 . xl . porc . lxxx . oũ . 7 . iii ; i . uas . ap . Val . viii . liƀ .
Et illa hid . que huic manerio addita e . adjacebat . t . r̂ . e . abbatiæ
de eli ut hund teſtat .

⌐Dommauuā ten& Guiƀt de . W . qđ tenuit comes Algar . t . r̂ . e .
p . dim . hid . Sep . dim . car . in dñio . m̂ . iii . bor te . iii . ſer . m̂ nulł .
Siłu . xl . porc . vii . ac . p̂ti . Te . x . porc . xxx . oũ . M . ix . an . xxx .
porc . lxxx . oũ . xii . cap . viii . uaſa . ap . Te ual . xx . ſoł . 7 qñdo rec .
xxx . ſoł . M ual xxxv . ſoł .

Hundred of DUNMOW

5 Dove, a free woman, held (Great) EASTON before 1066 as a manor,
for 2 hides. Now William (holds it) in lordship. Always 2 ploughs
in lordship. Then 4 men's ploughs, now 2.
  Always 4 villagers. Then 3 smallholders, now 8; then 3 slaves,
  now 2.
  Woodland, then for 200 pigs, now 150; meadow, 52 acres.
  Then 1 cob, 7 cattle, 60 pigs, 60 sheep; now 1 cob, 23
  cattle, 20 pigs, 70 sheep, 4 beehives.
Value 100s.

6 2 free men held (Little) CANFIELD before 1066 for 2 hides less 8   36 b
acres. Now William (holds it) in lordship. Then 4 ploughs in
lordship, now 2. Then 8 men's ploughs, now 6.
  Then 1 priest and 9 villagers, now 1 priest and 7 villagers;
  then 3 smallholders, now 17; always 2 slaves.
  Now 1 mill; woodland, then 160 pigs, now 120; meadow, 70
  acres. Then 1 cob, 8 cattle, 100 pigs, 200 sheep; now 1 cob,
  15 cattle, 50 pigs, 70 sheep, 9 goats.
Value then £8; now [£] 9.

7 W(illiam) of Vatteville holds (High) RODING from William, which
the Abbot of Ely held before 1066 as one manor, for 2½ hides.
Always 3 ploughs in lordship; 3 men's ploughs;
  1 priest, 8 villagers. Then 12 smallholders, now 11; always 7
  slaves.
  Woodland, 300 pigs; meadow, 42 acres. Always 3 cobs, 8
  cattle, 120 sheep; now 7 pigs.
Value then £10; when acquired [£] 12; now [£] 18.

8 Walter holds (Leaden) RODING from William, which a free woman
held before 1066 as one manor, for 2½ hides. Now there are 3½
hides. Then 3 ploughs in lordship, now 2; when acquired 3.
Always 1 men's plough.
  Then 3 villagers, now 1 priest and 4 villagers; then 4
  smallholders, now 13; then 4 slaves, now 2.
  Woodland, 50 pigs; meadow, 30 acres. Now 4 cattle, 40 pigs,
  83 sheep, 1 beehive.
Value £8.
  The hide which was added to this manor lay in (the lands of)
Ely Abbey before 1066, as the Hundred testifies.

9 Wulfbert holds DUNMOW from William, which Earl Algar held
before 1066 for ½ hide. Always ½ plough in lordship.
  Now 3 smallholders; then 3 slaves, now none.
  Woodland, 40 pigs; meadow, 7 acres. Then 10 pigs, 30 sheep;
  now 9 cattle, 30 pigs, 80 sheep, 12 goats, 8 beehives.
Value then 20s; when acquired 30s. Value now 35s.

Dim̃ Hund de Clauelinga. Pachen hov̄ . ten& Simond.

de Witto qd ten . i . lib hō . p . m̃ . 7 . p . i . hid . 7 xxx . ac̄ . t . r . e . Sep̄.
. i . car̄ in dñio . 7 . i . car̄ hom̃ . Tc̄ 7 p̄ . iii . uitt . m̃ . ii . Tc̄ . 7 p̄ . iii . bor . m̃ . vii .
vii . ac̄ . p̄ti . i . runc̄ . tc̄ . 7 . ix . por . M . i . runc̄ . ix . por . xl . ou . Tc̄ uat
xx . fot . m̃ . xxv.

Hund de Hidingforda . In Haltefteda . ten& Witt de gar̄.
. ii . hid . iiii . ac̄ . min . qs tenuer̄ . xxx . libi hōes . t . r . e . In q̃ tr̃a st
sep̄ . x . car̄ in dñio . 7 . iii . car̄ . hom̃ . 7 . viii . uitt . 7 . xxiii . bor . 7 . vi . fer.
Silu . cxl . porc̄ . xlvi . ac̄ . p̄ti . ii . mot . Tc̄ . vi . an̄ . xl . ou . xii . porc̄ . m̃.
xiiii . an̄ . xxxvi . ou . xx . porc̄ . ii . runc̄ . ii . uafa . ap̄ . Tc̄ . 7 p̄.
uat . x . lib . m̃ . xiii . lib . 7 . xvii . fot . 7 . iiii . d̄ . De hac tr̃a ten&
Ricard . xxxiiii . ac̄ . 7 . uat . x . fot . in eod̄ p̄tio.

In Bumefteda . ten& Gulbt̄ . iii . hid . 7 . xviii . ac̄ . qs tenuer̄
. xii . libi hōes . t . r . e . In illa tr̃a st sep̄ . ix . car̄ . 7 . iii . uitt . 7 . xviii .
bord . 7 . v . fer . Silu . xx . porc̄ . xl . ac̄ . p̄ti . Tc̄ . i . runc̄ . xl . ou . xxx
porc̄ . M . i . runc̄ . xvi . an̄ . c . porc̄ . c . ou . iiii . uafa . ap̄ . Tc̄ . 7 p̄ uat
. x . lib . m̃ . xii.

In Polheia . ten& Witt . iii . hid . 7 . dim̃ . 7 . xiii . ac̄ . Ex hac tr̃a . ten&
Ricard . xxv . ac̄ . 7 . Gladiou . iii . uirḡ . Totã hanc tr̃a tenuer̄
xxiii . hōes . t . r . e . Tc̄ . habebant . x . car̄ . Poft . 7 . m̃ . st . ibi . viii.
car̄ . m̃ . vi . bor . Tc̄ . vii . fer . m̃ null . v . M . i . mot Tc̄ . filu . lx.
porc̄ . M . xl . xxx . ac̄ . p̄ti . viii . an̄ . xx . porc̄ . xx . ou . m̃ . xii.
an̄ . xxx . porc̄ . lx . ou . ii . uafa ap̄ . Tc̄ uat . x . lib . m̃ . xiiii . lib

7 . xvi . fot . Iftas tr̃as reclamat Witt p̄ efcangio.

Half-Hundred of CLAVERING

10 Simond holds PEYTON (Hall) from William, which 1 free man held
as a manor for 1 hide and 30 acres before 1066. Always 1 plough
in lordship; 1 men's plough.
　　Then and later 3 villagers, now 2; then and later
　　　3 smallholders, now 7.
　　Meadow, 7 acres. 1 cob then and 9 pigs; now 1 cob, 9 pigs,
　　　40 sheep.
　　Value then 20s; now 25[s].

Hundred of HINCKFORD

11 In HALSTEAD William of Warenne holds 2 hides less 4 acres, which
30 free men held before 1066. In this land there have always been
10 ploughs in lordship; 3 men's ploughs;
　　8 villagers; 23 smallholders; 6 slaves.
　　Woodland, 140 pigs; meadow, 46 acres; 2 mills. Then 6 cattle,
　　　40 sheep, 12 pigs; now 14 cattle, 36 sheep, 20 pigs, 2 cobs,
　　　2 beehives.
　　Value then and later £10; now £13 17s 4d.
　　Richard holds 34 acres of this land.
　　Value 10s in the same assessment.

12 In (Steeple) BUMPSTEAD Wulfbert holds 3 hides and 18 acres,
which 12 free men held before 1066. In this land have always
been 9 ploughs;
　　3 villagers; 18 smallholders; 5 slaves.
　　Woodland, 20 pigs; meadow, 40 acres. Then 1 cob, 40 sheep,
　　　30 pigs; now 1 cob, 16 cattle, 100 pigs, 100 sheep, 4 beehives.
　　Value then and later £10; now [£] 12.

13 In HUNT'S HALL William holds 3½ hides and 13 acres. Of this land
Richard holds 25 acres and Gladiou 3 virgates. 23 men held all
this land before 1066. Then they had 10 ploughs, later and now
there are 8 ploughs.
　　Now 6 smallholders; then 7 slaves, now 5.
　　Now 1 mill; woodland, then 60 pigs, now 40; meadow, 30 acres.
　　　[Then] 8 cattle, 20 pigs, 20 sheep; now 12 cattle, 30 pigs,
　　　60 sheep, 2 beehives.
　　Value then £10; now £14 16s.
　　William claims these lands by exchange.

⁊Hund de Cesseurda. Kelitunā tenuer̃. iii. libi hōes ⱣΡ. iiii. hid.
t̃. r̃. ē. M ten& Will̃. Ᵽ tantundē Ᵽ escangio. ut dicit. ⁊ Wlbt
de illo. Tc̃. i. uill̃. m̃. vii. m̃. i. bor. Tc̃. iii. ser̃. m̃. i. Tc̃. int totū. iii. car̃
m̃. i. ⁊ dim̃. Silu̇. c. porc. viii. ac̃. pti. Tc̃. ii. añ. ⁊. xv. porc. xx. ou.
m̃. ii. añ. xv. por. L. ou. Tc̃. ual̃. sol̃. ⁊ qn̄ rec̃. xxx. m̃. c. sol̃. iii. sol̃
min. Hĩ &iam. Ranulf̃. dim̃. hid. quam tenuit Vluuin lib hō. t̃. r̃. ē.
Tc̃. i. car̃. m̃. dim̃. Val̃. vi. sol̃.

⁊Hund de celmeresfort   Haningefeldā tenuer̃. iii. libi. hōes. Ᵽ
. iii. Mañ. ⁊. Ᵽ. iiii. hid. ⁊. xxvii. ac̃. m̃. Will̃ Ᵽ tantundē. Ᵽ suo escan
gio. ⁊ Vlbt de eo. Sep. iii. bor. ⁊. ii. ser̃. Tc̃. iii. car̃. in dñio. m̃. iiii.
Silu̇. xl. por. ii. ac̃. pti. Past. c. ou. Tc̃. ii. runc̃. ⁊. xii. añ. lx ou. xl.
por. m̃. ii. runc̃. xxx. añ. c. ou. xv. porc. Tc̃. ual̃. lx. sol̃. m̃.
. iiii. lib̃.

⁊Haningefeldā ten& Ranulf de uuitto. qd̃ tenuit Godric̃ scipri.
t̃. r̃. ē. Ᵽ uno manerio. ⁊. Ᵽ. ii. hid. xxx. ac̃. min. Tc̃. ii. ser̃. m̃ null̃.
Sep. i. car̃. iii. ac̃. pti. Tc̃. ual̃. xxx. sol̃. m̃. xl.

⁊Borham ten& Will̃ in dñio. qd̃ tenuit Anschill̃ Ᵽ. m̃. ⁊ Ᵽ. dim̃.
hid. Sep. i. bor. Tc̃. i. ser̃. m̃. null̃. Tc̃. i. car̃. m̃. dim̃. v. ac̃. pti. Silua
xx. por. Val̃. x. sol̃.

⁊Belestedam ten& Ricard̃ de Witto. qd̃ tenuit Godric̃ poinc
Ᵽ. m̃. ⁊. Ᵽ. i. hid. x. ac̃. min. Tc̃. ii. ser̃. m̃. i. Tc̃. ii. car̃ in dñio. M. i.
vi. ac̃. pti. Silu̇. xx porc̃. Val̃. xl sol̃

Hundred of CHAFFORD

14 3 free men held KENNINGTONS for 4 hides before 1066. Now
William holds them for as much by exchange, as he states, and
Wulfbert from him.
  Then 1 villager, now 7; now 1 smallholder; then 3 slaves,
    now 1. Then in total 3 ploughs, now 1½.
  Woodland, 100 pigs; meadow, 8 acres. Then 2 cattle, 15 pigs,
    20 sheep; now 2 cattle, 15 pigs, 50 sheep.
  Value then ... s; when acquired 30[s] ; now 100s less 3s.
  Also Ranulf has ½ hide which Wulfwin, a free man, held
before 1066. Then 1 plough, now ½.
  Value 6s.

Hundred of CHELMSFORD

15 3 free men held (West) HANNINGFIELD as 3 manors, for 4 hides and
27 acres. Now William (holds it) for as much by his exchange,
and Wulfbert from him.
  Always 3 smallholders; 2 slaves. Then 3 ploughs in lordship,
    now 4.
  Woodland, 40 pigs; meadow, 2 acres; pasture, 100 sheep.
    Then 2 cobs, 12 cattle, 60 sheep, 40 pigs; now 2 cobs,
    30 cattle, 100 sheep, 15 pigs.
  Value then 60s; now £4.

16 Ranulf holds (West) HANNINGFIELD from William, which Godric
Skipper held before 1066 as one manor, for 2 hides less 30 acres.
  Then 2 slaves, now none. Always 1 plough.
  Meadow, 3 acres.
  Value then 30s; now 40[s].

17 William holds BOREHAM in lordship, which Ansketel held as a
manor, for ½ hide.
  Always 1 smallholder. Then 1 slave, now none. Then 1 plough,
    now ½.
  Meadow, 5 acres; woodland, 20 pigs.
  Value 10s.

18 Richard holds BELSTEAD (Hall) from William, which Godric Poinc
held as a manor, for 1 hide less 10 acres.
  Then 2 slaves, now 1. Then 2 ploughs in lordship, now 1.
  Meadow, 6 acres; woodland, 20 pigs.
  Value 40s.

Hund de Vdelesfort. Wendenā ten& Ricard̄ . de Wilto . qd̄ ten̄.

Vlmar̄ ,p . m̄ . 7 . ,p . I . hid̄ . 7 . dim̄ . 7 . xxx . ac̄ . 7 hoc ē ,p eſcangio . Sēp . II.
uilt . 7 . VII . bor . Tc̄ . 7 . p̄ . I . car̄ . in dn̄io . m̄ . I . 7 . dim̄ . Sēp . I . car̄ . 7 . dim̄ . houm̄
XVI . ac̄ . p̄ti . Tc̄ . XVII . por . m̄ null̄ . Sēp . L . ou . Tc̄ . ual . XL . ſol . m̄ . LX.

Eineſuurdam ten& Ide . R . qd̄ tenuit Vlmar̄ . p . m̄ . 7 . ,p . II . hid̄ . 7 . dim̄ .
Tc̄ . IIII . uilt . m̄ . III . Tc̄ . bor . m̄ . VIII . Tc̄ . II . ſer . Tc̄ . I . car̄ . 7 . dim̄ . in d̄io .
7 qn̄ rec̄ . nich . m̄ . I . car̄ . 7 . dim̄ . Sēp . I . car̄ . 7 . dim̄ . hominū . x . ac̄ . p̄ti .
Tc̄ nichil recep̄ . M . XXXII . porc̄ . LII . ou . II . an̄ . III . uas . ap . Tc̄ . ual
XL . ſol . m̄ . LX . In Ciſhella tenuer̄ . VIII . libi . hoēs . I . hid̄ . 7 . XLV . ac̄ .
m̄ ht . Wilt de uuar̄ . p eſcangio , 7 Ide . R . de eo . Tc̄ . III . car̄ . m̄ . II .
7 qn̄ recep̄ . nichil . II . ac̄ . p̄ti . Val . XXX . ſol .

Hund de . Rochefort . I Pacheſham ten& Wilt de gar̄ . I . hid̄ . in
dn̄io . qd̄ tenuit . I . lib̄ hō . t . r . e . Sēp . I . car̄ . in dn̄io . Tc̄ . IIII . ſer . m̄
. III . Paſt . c . ou . Val . xx . ſol .

In Plūbga . ten& Ranulf de W . xxx . ac̄ . qd̄ . ten̄ . I . lib̄ . hō . t . r . e
Tc̄ dim̄ . car̄ . m̄ . I . Tc̄ . v . ſol . m̄ . x . has tr̄as reclamat . pro eſcangio
de normannia .

Hund de Lexſendena . In Forham tenuit . Aluric̄ xxv . ac̄ .
libe . M Wilt ,p eod eſcangio . Sēp dim̄ . car̄ . I . ac̄ . 7 . dim̄ . p̄ti . Tc̄
ual . x . ſol . m̄ . VI . ſol . 7 . VIII . d̄ . hec tr̄a ē de ſocna regis .

19 Richard holds WENDENS (Ambo) from William, which Wulfmer
held as a manor, for 1½ hides and 30 acres. This is by exchange.
Always 2 villagers; 7 smallholders. Then and later 1 plough
in lordship, now 1½. Always 1½ men's ploughs.
Meadow, 16 acres. Then 17 pigs, now none; always 50 sheep.
Value then 40s; now 60[s].

20 Richard also holds CHARDWELL, which Wulfmer held as a manor,
for 2½ hides.
Then 4 villagers, now 3; then ... smallholders, now 8; then 2
slaves. Then 1½ ploughs in lordship; when acquired, nothing;
now 1½ ploughs. Always 1½ men's ploughs.
Meadow, 10 acres. Then (when) acquired nothing; now 32 pigs,
52 sheep, 2 cattle, 3 beehives.
Value then 40s; now 60[s].

21 In (Great) CHISHILL 8 free men held 1 hide and 45 acres. Now
William of Warenne has it by exchange and Richard also from
him. Then 3 ploughs, now 2; when acquired, nothing.
Meadow, 2 acres.
Value 30s.

Hundred of ROCHFORD
22 In PAGLESHAM William of Warenne holds 1 hide in lordship, which
1 free man held before 1066. Always 1 plough in lordship.
Then 4 slaves, now 3.
Pasture, 100 sheep.
Value 20s.

23 In PLUMBEROW Ranulf holds 30 acres from William, which 1 free
man held before 1066. Then ½ plough, now 1.
[Value] then 5s; now 10[s].
He claims these lands by exchange in Normandy.

Hundred of LEXDEN
24 In FORDHAM Aelfric held 25 acres freely. Now William (holds
them) by the same exchange. Always ½ plough.
Meadow, 1½ acres.
Value then 10s; now 6s 8d.
This land is of the King's jurisdiction.

.XXIII. ꝔRA Ricardi filij comitis Giſlebti .   Hundret de

Herlaua . Wallā ten& Ricard in dñio . Qđ tenuit Toti . I . liƀ hō . t . r . e
p . uno maneꝛ . 7 . p . I . hiđ . Tc . II . car . in dñio . m̄ . I . Sēp . I . car . hom̄ . Tc . II .
bor . m̄ . vI . Tc . II . ſeꝛ . m̄ null . Silu . c . porc . xxIIII . ac . apti . Tc . ual .
xxx . ſol . m̄ . xL .

Hunđ . de Dommauua . Tacheſteđa tenuit Wiſgar . t . r . e . m̄ . R .
in dñio . p . uno manerio . 7 . p . Ix . hiđ . 7 . dim̄ . Tc . vIII . car . in dñio . m̄ . vII .
Tc . xxxIIII . car . hom̄ . M̄ . xvIII . Tc . Lv . uilt . m̄ . LII . Sēp . xxIIII . bor .
7 . xvI . ſeꝛ . Tc ſilu . ꝏ . porc . m̄ . ꝺccc . cxx . ac . pti . Tc . I . mol . m̄ . II .
Adhuc poſſꝼ reſtaurari . xvI . car . Sēp . IIII . runc . 7 . xxxvI . an .
cxxvIII . porc . Tc . cc . ou . m̄ . cccxx . Tc . x . uaſa . ap . m̄ . xvI . Tc .
ual . xxx . liƀ . 7 qn̄ recep . ſimilit̄ . M ual . L . liƀ . ut đic franci . 7 . an
glici . S; Ricard dedit cuidā anglico . ad . Censū . p . Lx . liƀ . ſ; uno q̊q;
anno deficiunt illi ađ min . x . liƀ .   Huic manerio adjacent ſēp .
. III . ſoc . de . II . hiđ . 7 . xv . ac . q̊s ten& Garner de . R . Tc . IIII . car . m̄ .
. III . 7 . dim̄ . Tc . x . uilt . m̄ . II . Tc . II . bor . m̄ . x . Tc . IIII . ſeꝛ . m̄ . null .
Silu . L . porc . xxxIIII . ac . pti . Val . vI . liƀ . 7 de hac tꝛa tenuit . I .
ſoc . regis . t . r . e . vII . ac . 7 . dim̄ . que ſꝼ addite huic manerio t . r . Wilt .
7 . n̄ reddiđunt conſuetudinē regis .

Ꝕ Dommauua tenuit Wiſgar . t . r . e . p uno manerio . 7 . p . II . hiđ . 7
xxx . ac . Sēp . II . car . in dñio . 7 . II . car . hom̄ . 7 . v . uilt . Tc . IIII . borđ .
m̄ . vII . Sēp . IIII . ſeꝛ . Tc ſilu . ꝺ . porc . m̄ . ccc . xv . ac . pti . Sēp . I . mol .
Tc . 7 p ual . Lx . ſol . m̄ . c . 7 iſtā tꝛa calūpniat . uital . I . miles . quā ut

teſtat . tenuit . I . liƀ . hō . t . r . e . In Iſto manerio ten& ſēp . I . pƀr . dim̄ .
hiđ . in elemoſina . 7 ſēp . dim̄ . car . 7 . II . bor . hoc . ꝏ . ten& Ernalđ .

Hundred of HARLOW

1 Richard holds WALL(BURY) in lordship which Toti, 1 free man, held before 1066 as one manor, for 1 hide. Then 2 ploughs in lordship, now 1. Always 1 men's plough.

Then 2 smallholders, now 6; then 2 slaves, now none.

Woodland, 100 pigs; meadow, 24 acres.

Value then 30s; now 40[s].

Hundred of DUNMOW

2 Withgar held THAXTED before 1066. Now Richard (holds it) in lordship as one manor, for 9½ hides. Then 8 ploughs in lordship, now 7. Then 34 men's ploughs, now 18.

Then 55 villagers, now 52. Always 24 smallholders; 16 slaves.

Woodland, then 1000 pigs, now 800; meadow, 120 acres; then 1 mill, now 2. 16 ploughs can still be restored. Always 4 cobs, 36 cattle, 128 pigs; then 200 sheep, now 320; then 10 beehives, now 16.

Value then £30; when acquired, the same. Value now £50, as the French and English say; but Richard gave it to an Englishman for £60 for the dues; but each year they are deficient in at least £10.

In (the lands of) this manor have always been 3 Freemen with 2 hides and 15 acres, whom Warner holds from Richard. Then 4 ploughs, now 3½.

Then 10 villagers, now 2; then 2 smallholders, now 10; then 4 slaves, now none.

Woodland, 50 pigs; meadow, 34 acres.

Value £6.

Of this land, 1 Freeman held 7½ acres before 1066 which were added to this manor after 1066. They have not paid the King's customary dues.

3 Withgar held (Great) DUNMOW before 1066 as one manor, for 2 hides and 30 acres. Always 2 ploughs in lordship; 2 men's ploughs; 5 villagers. Then 4 smallholders, now 7; always 4 slaves.

Woodland, then 500 pigs, now 300; meadow, 15 acres; always 1 mill.

Value then and later 60s; now 100[s].

Vitalis, 1 man-at-arms, lays claim to this land which, as he testifies, 1 free man held before 1066. In that manor 1 priest has always held ½ hide in alms. Always ½ plough; 2 smallholders.

Arnold holds this manor.

39 a

⌐Hund̄ de Hidincforda . Gheſtingetorp ten& . W . peccatū
de ; R . qđ tenuit Ledmar p̄br . t . r̄ . e . ꝓ . dim . hid . Sēp . iii . car . in dn̄io.
7 . iii . car̄ . hom̄ . 7 ; viii . uiłł . m̄ . ix . bor . Sēp . vi . ſer̄ . Silŭ . xx . porc̄ . xx . ac̄.
p̄ti . Tc̄ . i . moł . m̄ . nułł . Huic t̄re ſēp jac& . i ; ſoc̄ . de . xv . ac̄ . 7 . ħt . dim̄.
car̄ . 7 . ii . bor . 7 . i ; ac̄ . p̄ti . Tc̄ . ual̄ . c . ſoł . M̄ . vii . liƀ.

⌐Phincinghefeldā tenuer̄ . ii . ſoc̄ . t . r̄ . e . ꝓ . xlviii . ac̄ . m̄ . ten& Elinant
de . R . Sēp . i . car̄ . 7 . dim̄ . Tc̄ . 7 p̄ . iiii ; bor . m̄ . vii . Silŭ . vi . porc̄ . 7
vi . ac̄ . 7 ; dim̄ . p̄ti . Tc̄ . i . runc̄ . 7 . m̄ null . Tc̄ . x . an̄ . m̄ . viii . Tc̄ . xx ;
por . m̄ . xxvi . Tc̄ . c . ou ; M̄ . cxxvii . Tc̄ . ual̄ . x . ſoł . m̄ . xxx.

⌐Penfeldā ten& Roƀ de . R . qđ tenuit Wiſgar̄ . t . r̄ . e . ꝓ uno man̄.
7 . ꝓ . i⸱ hid . 7 . dim̄ . 7 . xxx . ac̄ . Tc̄ . iiii . car̄ . in dn̄io ; Poſt 7 . m̄ . ii.
Sēp . v . car̄ . hominū . Tc̄ . 7 p̄ . x . uiłł . m̄ . viii ; Tc̄ . 7 p̄ . viii . bord.
m̄ . xv . Tc̄ 7 p̄ ; viii ; ſer̄ . m̄ . vii . Silŭ . cxx . porc̄ . xiii . ac̄ . p̄ti.
7 . ii . car̄ . pofſt̄ reſtaurari . Tc̄ 7 p̄ ual̄ . viii . liƀ . m̄ . x.

⌐In Geldham ten& Goiſm̄er . i . hid . 7 . v . ac̄ . qđ tenuer̄ . viii.
ſoc̄ . t . r̄ . e . ſub uuiſgaro Sēp . iii . car̄ . 7 . dim̄ . in dn̄io . 7 . dim̄ . car̄.
hom̄ . Tc̄ . 7 p̄ . v . bor . m̄ . viii ; Tc̄ . 7 ; p̄ . v . ſer̄ . m̄ . ii . Silŭ . xx . porc̄.
xxiii ; ac̄ . p̄ti . Tc̄ . i . moł . Tc̄ 7 p̄ ual̄ . lx . ſoł . m̄ . c . ſoł.

⌐In Wicam ten& Ernald . dim̄ . hid . 7 . x . ac̄ . de . R . qđ tenuer̄
. ii . ſoc̄ ; ſub Wiſgaro . t . r̄ . e . ſēp . ii . car̄ . in dn̄io . Tc̄ . 7 p̄ . v . bor . m̄
; x ; Tc̄ 7 p̄ ; i . ſer̄ . m̄ . null . Tc̄ . ſilŭ . xl . porc̄ . m̄ . xx ; x . ac̄ . p̄ti.

39 b
Tc̄ . 7 p̄ . ual̄ . xxx . ſoł . m̄ . xl.

Hundred of HINCKFORD

4 W(illiam) Peche holds GESTINGTHORPE from Richard, which Ledmer the priest held before 1066 for ½ hide. Always 3 ploughs in lordship; 3 men's ploughs;
8 villagers. Now 9 smallholders; always 6 slaves.
Woodland, 20 pigs; meadow, 20 acres; then 1 mill, now none.
1 Freeman with 15 acres has always lain in (the lands of) this manor and has ½ plough.
2 smallholders.
Meadow, 1 acre.
Value then 100s; now £7.

5 2 Freemen held FINCHINGFIELD before 1066 for 48 acres. Now Elinant holds it from Richard. Always 1½ ploughs.
Then and later 4 smallholders, now 7.
Woodland, 6 pigs; meadow, 6½ acres. Then 1 cob, now none; then 10 cattle, now 8; then 20 pigs, now 26; then 100 sheep, now 127.
Value then 10s; now 30[s].

6 Robert holds PANFIELD from Richard, which Withgar held before 1066 as one manor, for 1½ hides and 30 acres. Then 4 ploughs in lordship, later and now 2. Always 5 men's ploughs.
Then and later 10 villagers, now 8; then and later 8 smallholders, now 15; then and later 8 slaves, now 7.
Woodland, 120 pigs; meadow, 13 acres. 2 ploughs can be restored.
Value then and later £8; now [£] 10.

7 In (Great) YELDHAM Goismer holds 1 hide and 5 acres, which 8 Freemen held before 1066 under Withgar. Always 3½ ploughs in lordship; ½ men's plough.
Then and later 5 smallholders, now 8; then and later 5 slaves, now 2.
Woodland, 20 pigs; meadow, 23 acres; then 1 mill.
Value then and later 60s; now 100s.

8 In WICKHAM (St. Paul's) Arnold holds ½ hide and 10 acres from Richard, which 2 Freemen held under Withgar before 1066. Always 2 ploughs in lordship.
Then and later 5 smallholders, now 10; then and later 1 slave, now none.
Woodland, then 40 pigs, now 20; meadow, 10 acres.
Value then and later 30s; now 40[s].   39 b

In Fincinghefelda ten& Idē Ernald

xxxviii . ac . qđ tenueꝛ . ii . ſoc . ſub Wiſgaro . t . r . e . Sēp . i . car.

m̃ . iii . bóꝛ ; 7 . i . ſeꝛ . 7 . iiii . ac . 7 . dim . p̃ti . Val : x . ſol.

In Bineſlea . ten& Wielard . i . hid qđ tenuit . i . ſoc . ſub Wiſgaro.

ſēp . i . car . in dñio . 7 . dim . car . hom . 7 . ii . uiłt . Tē . 7 . p . xvi . bor . m̃.

vii . Tē . ii . ſeꝛ . m̃ . nułł . Silu . xx . poꝛc . iiii . ac . p̃ti . Tē . ual . xx . ſol.

P̃ 7 m̃ xl. ⸗ In Alreforda . tenent . ii . milit . xxxvi . ac . qs

tenueꝛ . iii . ſoc . ſub Wiſg . Sēp . ii . car . 7 . iiii . bor . Silu . xii . ix . ac . p̃ti.

xxx . oũ . Tē . ual . xl . ſol . Poſt 7 ; m̃ . lx.

⸗ Ad Aſce . ten& Ricard in dñio . dim . hid . 7 . xl . ac . qđ . tenueꝛ . ii.

ſoc . t . r . e . ſub Wiſgaro . Sēp . i . car . Tē . 7 . p ; ii . bor . m̃ . vi . ix . ac ;

p̃ti . m̃ . i . moł . Tē . ual . xx . ſol . P̃ 7 m̃ . xxxv.

⸗ Ad Fincingefeldā tenent . ii . Milit . de . R . xxxvi . ac . qđ tenueꝛ

. iii . ſoc . ſub Wiſg . t . r . e . Sēp . ii . car . 7 . iiii bor . Tē . iii . ſeꝛ . P̃ 7 . m̃ . ii.   ★

Silu . x . poꝛc . vii . ac . p̃ti . Tē . 7 p ual . xl . ſol . m̃ . lxv.

⸗ In Bulenemera ten& Maſcerel . dim . hid . 7 . xxx . ac . qđ tenuit.

. i . ſoc . ſub Wiſg . Sēp . ii . car . m̃ . i . bor . Silu . v . poꝛc . ii . ac . p̃ti . 7

ual . xxii . ſol . 7 . ii . đ.

⸗ Ad Weninchou ten& Germund . xxxii . ac . 7 . dim . qđ tenueꝛ

. iii . ſoc . ſub Wiſg . Sēp . ii . car . 7 . v . bor . 7 . iii . ſeꝛ . Silu xxx . poꝛc .

viii . ac . p̃ti . Tē . v . an . m̃ . viii . Modo . iiii . poꝛc . Tē . xx . oũ . m̃ . lxxx.

7 . iii ; M̃ . xxxii . cap . Tē 7 p Val . xxx . ſol . m̃ . l.

⸗ In buro . ħt . R . in dñio . xiii . ſoc . de . xxxv . ac . Sēp . iiii . car.

Tē . ix . bor . m̃ . xvi . Tē . i . ſeꝛ . m̃ . nułł . Silu . xx . poꝛc . xi . ac . p̃ti.

9 In FINCHINGFIELD Arnold also holds 38 acres, which 2 Freemen held under Withgar before 1066. Always 1 plough.
　　Now 3 smallholders; 1 slave.
　　Meadow, 4½ acres.
　Value 10s.

10 In 'BINSLEY'Widelard holds 1 hide, which 1 Freeman held under Withgar. Always 1 plough in lordship; ½ men's plough;
　　2 villagers. Then and later 16 smallholders, now 7; then 2 slaves, now none.
　　Woodland, 20 pigs; meadow, 4 acres.
　Value then 20s; later and now 40[s].

11 In ALDERFORD 2 men-at-arms hold 36 acres, which 3 Freemen held under Withgar. Always 2 ploughs;
　　4 smallholders.
　　Woodland, 12 [pigs] ; meadow, 9 acres. 30 sheep.
　Value then 40s; later and now 60[s].

12 At ASHEN Richard holds ½ hide and 40 acres in lordship, which 2 Freemen held before 1066 under Withgar. Always 1 plough.
　　Then and later 2 smallholders, now 6.
　　Meadow, 9 acres; now 1 mill.
　Value then 20s; later and now 35[s].

13 At FINCHINGFIELD 2 men-at-arms hold 36 acres from Richard, which 3 Freemen held under Withgar before 1066. Always 2 ploughs;
　　4 smallholders. Then 3 slaves; later and now 2.
　　Woodland, 10 pigs; meadow, 7 acres.
　Value then and later 40s; now 65[s].

14 In BULMER Mascerel holds ½ hide and 30 acres, which 1 Freeman held under Withgar. Always 2 ploughs.
　　Now 1 smallholder.
　　Woodland, 5 pigs; meadow, 2 acres.
　Value 22s 2d.

15 At HOWE Germund holds 32½ acres, which 3 Freemen held under Withgar. Always 2 ploughs;
　　5 smallholders; 3 slaves.
　　Woodland, 30 pigs; meadow, 8 acres. Then 5 cattle, now 8; now 4 pigs; then 20 sheep, now 83; now 32 goats.
　Value then and later 30s; now 50[s].

16 In BURES Richard has in lordship 13 Freemen with 35 acres. Always 4 ploughs.
　　Then 9 smallholders, now 16; then 1 slave, now none.　　　　40 a
　　Woodland, 20 pigs; meadow, 11 acres.

In Focfearde.xix.foc.de.i.hid.7.dim.7.xv.ač.Sẽp.v.car.7.

x.bor.7.i.fer.xxii.ač.p̃ti.7 In Pebenhers.xviii.foc.de dim hid.

7.xii.ač.Sẽp.iii.car.7.iii.bord.7.iii.ač.p̃ti.

In Alfelmeftuna.i.hid.v.ač.min.tenent sẽp.xv.foc.7.hnt.ii.car.

7.iii.bord.Silu.v.porc.iiii.ač.p̃ti.

In Mildeltuna.xiii.foc.de.i.hid.7.dim.7.xxx.ač.Sẽp.iii.car.7.viii.

bor.Silu.viii.porc.xiii.ač.p̃ti.

In Bumefteda.iii.foc.q̃ tenent sẽp.xxv.ač.Sẽp.i.car.7.ii.bor.

7.vi.ač.p̃ti. In Phincinghefelda.xi.foc.de.dim.Sẽp.i.car.7.iii.ač.p̃ti.

In Celueftuna.v.foc.de dim.hid.v.ač.min.sẽp.i.car.ii.ač.p̃ti.

In Tumefteda xviii.foc.de dim hid.7.xv.ač.sẽp.ii.car.7.vii.bor.

Silu.viii.porc.iii.ač.p̃ti. In Cheneboltuna xv.foc.dim.hid.7 v.

ač.Sẽp.i.car.7.dim.iii.bord.iiii.ač.p̃ti.

In Halfteda tenent.xxii.foc.dim.hid.7.xi.ač.Sẽp.v.car.7.i.

uilt.xv.bor.ii.fer.Silu.l.porc.xix.ač.p̃ti.i.mol.

In Sudbia.v.burgenfes.tenentes.ii.ač. Ifti cũ omnib; fup̃dictis.

reddt.xv.lib.7.vi.fol.7.vi.d.7 totũ ẽ in dñio Ricardi.

40 a

17 In FOXEARTH 19 Freemen with 1½ hides and 15 acres. Always 5 ploughs;
    10 smallholders; 1 slave.
    Meadow, 22 acres.

18 In PEBMARSH 18 Freemen with ½ hide and 12 acres. Always 3 ploughs;
    3 smallholders.
    Meadow, 3 acres.

19 In ALPHAMSTONE 15 Freemen have always held 1 hide less 5 acres and have 2 ploughs.
    3 smallholders.
    Woodland, 5 pigs; meadow, 4 acres.

20 In MIDDLETON 13 Freemen with 1½ hides and·30 acres. Always 3 ploughs;
    8 smallholders.
    Woodland, 8 pigs; meadow, 13 acres.

21 In (Steeple) BUMPSTEAD 3 Freemen who have always held 25 acres. Always 1 plough;
    2 smallholders.
    Meadow, 6 acres.

22 In FINCHINGFIELD 11 Freemen with ½ hide. Always 1 plough.
    Meadow, 3 acres.

23 In COUPALS FARM 5 Freemen with ½ hide less 5 acres. Always 1 plough.
    Meadow, 2 acres.

24 In TWINSTEAD 18 Freemen with ½ hide and 15 acres. Always 2 ploughs;
    7 smallholders.
    Woodland, 8 pigs; meadow, 3 acres.

25 In *CHENEBOLTUNA* 15 Freemen. ½ hide and 5 acres. Always 1½ ploughs;
    3 smallholders.
    Meadow, 4 acres.

26 In HALSTEAD 22 Freemen hold ½ hide and 11 acres. Always 5 ploughs;
    1 villager; 15 smallholders; 2 slaves.
    Woodland, 50 pigs; meadow, 19 acres; 1 mill.

27 In SUDBURY 5 burgesses who hold 2 acres.
They with all the above pay £15 6s 6d. The whole is in Richard's lordship.

In Boituna tenuit Colſege. liƀ hō. t. r. e. dim. hid. 7. x. ac. Sep. ii.
car. in dnio. Tc. iii. car. hom. P 7 m. ii. Sep. i. uilt. Tc. vii. bor. P 7 m. viii.
Tc. 7 p. iiii. ſer. m. ii. Silu. xxx. porc. viii. ac. pti. Tc 7 uat xl.
ſot. P 7 m. iiii. liƀ. Huic manerio addite ſt t. r. Witti. xlv. ac. quæ
jacebant ad uueſtrefeldā. maneriū regis. Tc. dim. car. m nulla.

40 b

Tc 7 p. i. bor. m. ii. Silu. x. porc. ii. ac. pti. Vat. viii. ſot.
In Bura tenuit Leueua. liƀa femina xl. ac. Sep. i. car. 7. dim. hom.
7. i. uilt. Tc. 7 p. ii. bor. m. iii. Sep. ii. ſer Silu. xx. porc. v. ac. pti. Vat.
xxx. ſot. Hanc trā ſcit boitunā. 7. buro. ht Ricard p eſcangio ut dict
ſui hōes.

Roinges tenuit Coleman. t. r. e. p. iii. uirg. m. R. p tantundē in dnio.
7. iſte fuit ita liƀ. qđ poſſ& ire q̃ uell& cū ſoca. 7. ſacna. ſ; tm fuit homo.
Wiſgari anteceſſoris Ricardi. Sep. i. uilt. 7. ii. bor. Tc. iiii. ſer. m. i. Sep.
. ii. car. in dnio. 7. dim. car. hom. Silu. cc. porc. xx. ac. pti. Tc. uat.
lx. ſot. Poſt. xl. M. iiii. liƀ.

Hund de tendringe. Menetleam tenuit Wiſgar p. i. hid. 7 p. i.
man. M ten& Rog de Ricardo. Sep. iii. uilt. 7. iiii. bord. Tc. i. ſer. m
null. Sep. i. car. in dnio. 7. i. car. hom. Silu. c. porc. iii. ac. pti. Tc uat.
xl. ſot. m. L.

Brumleā tenuit Aluuin liƀe. p. uno man. 7. p. dim. hid. 7 erat cō
mdat Wiſgaro potens trā ſuā uende. Modo ten& . R. ſub. Ricardo. Sep. i.
uilt. m. ii. bor. Tc. in dnio. i. car. m nult. Silu. c. porc. ii. ac. pti. m.
xi. oues. Vat. xl. ſot.

40 a, b

28 In BOYTON (Hall) Colsege, a free man, held ½ hide and 10 acres
before 1066. Always 2 ploughs in lordship. Then 3 men's ploughs,
later and now 2.
    Always 1 villager. Then 7 smallholders, later and now 8; then
      and later 4 slaves, now 2.
    Woodland, 30 pigs; meadow, 8 acres.
Value then 40s; later and now £4.
    To this manor 45 acres were added after 1066 which lie in (the
lands of) the King's manor of Wethersfield. Then ½ plough, now
none.
    Then and later 1 smallholder, now 2.   40 b
    Woodland, 10 pigs; meadow, 2 acres.
Value 8s.

29 In BURES Leofeva, a free woman, held 40 acres. Always 1½ men's
ploughs;
    1 villager. Then and later 2 smallholders, now 3; always 2
      slaves.
    Woodland, 20 pigs; meadow, 5 acres.
Value 30s.
    Richard has this land, namely Boyton (Hall) and Bures, by
exchange, as his men state.

[Hundred of ONGAR]
30 Colman held ('Morrell') RODING before 1066 for 3 virgates. Now
Richard (holds it) for as much in lordship. That man was so free
that he could go whither he would with full jurisdiction, although
he was the man of Withgar, Richard's predecessor.
    Always 1 villager; 2 smallholders. Then 4 slaves, now 1.
      Always 2 ploughs in lordship; ½ men's plough.
    Woodland, 200 pigs; meadow, 20 acres.
Value then 60s; later 40[s]; now £4.

Hundred of TENDRING
31 Withgar held (Little) BENTLEY for 1 hide, as 1 manor. Now Roger
holds it from Richard.
    Always 3 villagers; 4 smallholders. Then 1 slave, now none.
      Always 1 plough in lordship; 1 men's plough.
    Woodland, 100 pigs; meadow, 3 acres.
Value then 40s; now 50[s].

32 Alwin held (Little) BROMLEY freely as one manor, for ½ hide. He
was under the patronage of Withgar (and) able to sell his land.
Now R(oger) holds it under Richard.
    Always 1 villager. Now 2 smallholders. Then 1 plough in
      lordship, now none.
    Woodland, 100 pigs; meadow, 2 acres. Now 11 sheep.
Value 40s.

Aleforda ten̅ . Algar̅ . p̅ . xxxvii . ac̅ . t . r . e̅ . m̅ ten& Ide̅ fub . R.

7 . hoc e̅ de focha regis . de laleforda . ut hund teftar̅ . Tc̅ . i . car̅ . m̅.

nulla . Paft . xl . ou̅ . Tc̅ . ual . x . fol . m̅ . vi.

Hund de Laxedana . In te̅pr̅ reg̅ Eduuardi fuer̅ . v . foc.

q̅s tenuit Wifgar̅ . Vluuin 7 . ii . forores ej in colun ~~tenentes~~

tenentes lxiiii . ac̅ . 7 Leuric̅ . tenens . xxx . ac̅ ʑ in ead̅ uilla . 7 . ifti n̅

poterant recede a foca Wifgari . Se̅p . fub ipfis . ii . bor . 7 . i . car̅ . Silu̅ . xii.

porc̅ . ix . ac̅ . p̅ti . sᵉp . i . mol̅ Val̅ . xx fol . In Sordeha̅ tenuit Vlmar̅ fub Wifgaro . xl . ac̅.

& ten& fub . R . 7 n̅ poᵣat recede de foca tc̅ . iii . bor . m̅ . vi . dim̅ . car̅ . filu̅ . x . par . iii . ac̅ p̅ti . val . x . fol. In bcolta tenuit Lefcild⁹ . xxxi . ac̅ . 7 . dim̅ . ⊙° ten& Goding⁹ fub . R.

Tc̅ . ii . bor . m̅ . vi . m̅ . i . fer̅ . Se̅p . dim̅ . car̅ . Silu̅ . xvi . porc̅ . iii . ac̅ . p̅ti.

Tc̅ . i . mol̅ . m̅ . null̅ . Val̅ . x . fol.

In Witefuuorda . tenuit Algar̅ fub Wifgaro . xii . ac̅ . 7 . dim̅ . qui

n̅ potat . recede de . foca . m̅ . i . bor . 7 . i . ac̅ . p̅ti . Val̅ . iii . fol.

Laingaham ten& Walt̅ tirelde . R . q̅d tenuit Phin . dac̅ . p . ii . hid̅.

7 . dim̅ . 7 p uno manerio . Tc̅ . xxii . uilt̅ . m̅ . xvii . Tc̅ . ix . bor . m̅ . xxvii.

Tc̅ . iiii . fer̅ . m̅ null⁹ . Se̅p . i . car̅ . in d̅nio . Tc̅ . xi . car̅ . hominu̅ . m̅ . vii.

Silu̅ . ⊙ . porc̅ . xl . ac̅ . p̅ti . Tc̅ . i . mol̅ . m̅ . ii . Tc̅ . vi . runc̅ . m̅ . null⁹.

Se̅p . xxii . an̅ . Tc̅ . xlvi . porc̅ . M lxxx . Tc̅ . liiii . ou̅ . m̅ . cc . Tc̅ . lxii.

cap̅ . m̅ . lxxx . Tc̅ . iii . uafa ap̅ . m̅ . n̅ . Tc̅ ual̅ . xii . lib̅ . m̅ . xv.

33 Algar held ALRESFORD for 37 acres before 1066. Now he also
holds it under Richard. This is in the King's jurisdiction of
Lawford, as the Hundred testifies. Then 1 plough, now none.
  Pasture, 40 sheep.
Value then 10s; now 6[s].

Hundred of LEXDEN

34 Before 1066 there were 5 Freemen whom Withgar held. Wulfwin
and 2 of his sisters who hold 64 acres in COLNE and Leofric who   41 a
holds 30 acres in the same village. They could not withdraw from
Withgar's jurisdiction.
  Under them always 2 smallholders; 1 plough.
  Woodland, 12 pigs; meadow, 9 acres; always 1 mill.
Value 20s.

35 In FORDHAM Wulfmer held 40 acres under Withgar and holds under
R(ichard). He could not withdraw from the jurisdiction.
  Then 3 smallholders, now 6. ½ plough.
  Woodland, 10 pigs; meadow, 3 acres.
Value 10s.

36 In (West) BERGHOLT Leofcild held 31½ acres. Now Goding holds
it under Richard.
  Then 2 smallholders, now 6; now 1 slave. Always ½ plough.
  Woodland, 16 pigs; meadow, 3 acres; then 1 mill, now none.
Value 10s.

37 In *WITESUUORDA* Algar, who could not withdraw from the
jurisdiction, held 12½ acres under Withgar.
  Now 1 smallholder.
  Meadow, 1 acre.
Value 3s.

38 Walter Tirel holds LANGHAM from Richard, which Finn the Dane
held for 2½ hides, as one manor.
  Then 22 villagers, now 17; then 9 smallholders, now 27;
    then 4 slaves, now none. Always 1 plough in lordship.
    Then 11 men's ploughs, now 7.
  Woodland, 1000 pigs; meadow, 40 acres; then 1 mill, now
    2. Then 6 cobs, now none; always 22 cattle; then 46 pigs.
    now 80; then 54 sheep, now 200; then 62 goats, now 80;
    then 3 beehives, now none.
Value then £12; now [£] 15.

⌐Dim̃ . Hund̃ de Froſſeuuella . B̃irdefeldã tenuit Wiſgar̃ ₚ
uno mañ . 7 . ₚ . IIII . hid̃ . M̃ ten& Ricard̃ in dñio . Tc̃ . xxIIII . uiłł .
m̃ . xx . Tc̃ 7 p̃ . vII . bor . m̃ . xxII . Sep̃ . vIII . fer̃ . Sep̃ . IIII . car̃ . in dñio .
Tc̃ 7 p̃ xxI . car̃ . M̃ . Ix . Siłu . ɒccc . porc̃ . xxxII . ac̃ . p̃ti . Sep̃ . II .
mol . Tc̃ . IIII . runc̃ . M̃ . v . Tc̃ . xxvIII . añ . M̃ . xlI . Tc̃ . lx . porc̃ .
M̃ . cvII . Tc̃ . c . ou . m̃ ; cc . Sep̃ . uał . xvI . lib̃ .

⌐Sanfordã tenuit Wiſgar̃ ₚ . uno mañ . 7 . ₚ . v . hid̃ . M̃ . ten& .
Ricard̃ in dñio . Tc̃ . xxIIII . uiłł . m̃ . xIIII . Tc̃ . II . bor . m̃ . xvIII .
Tc̃ . vI . fer̃ . m̃ . IIII . Sep̃ . III . car̃ . in dñio . Tc̃ . xxI . car̃ hou . m̃ . x .

41 b

Siłu . lx . porc̃ . xxII . ac̃ . p̃ti . Tc̃ . I . mol . m̃ null . Tc̃ uał . xII . lib̃ . m̃ . xvII .
Qñ Ricard̃ recep̃ hoc . m̃ . tc̃ inuenit . ibi . III . runc̃ . m̃ . II . Tc̃ . xIx . añ . m̃
Ix . Tc̃ . l . porc̃ . m̃ . xxx . Tc̃ . c . ou . m̃ . lxxx . 7 vIII ; Tc̃ . III . uaſa ap̃ . m̃ . I .
De hoc manerio 7 de ſup̃dictis . v . hid̃ . tenent . II . franci . I . hid̃ . 7 . dimidiã .
7 . Ix . bord̃ . 7 . II . car̃ . 7 . xvI . ac̃ . p̃ti . App̃tiatũ ẽ ſup̃ .

⌐Hamſtedã tenuit Wiſg̃ . ₚ . I . m̃ . 7 . ₚ . IIII . hid̃ . xxx . ac̃ . min . t . r . e . m̃ .
Rob̃ de uuateuiłł de . R . Sep̃ . xxII . uiłł . Tc̃ . vI . bor . m̃ . x . Tc̃ . vIII . fer̃ . m̃ . vII .
Tc̃ . in d̃io . IIII . car̃ . m̃ . III . Tc̃ . xIIII . car̃ . m̃ . x . Siłu . cc . porc̃ . xv . ac̃ . p̃ti . Tc̃
uał . xII . lib̃ . m̃ . xvI .

⌐In b̃defelda ten& Wielard̃ . I . hid̃ . qm̃ tenuer̃ . II . ſeruientes Wiſgari 7
tc̃ ñ reddebant conſuetudinẽ . ł gelt regi . nec poł̃ant abire ſine juſſu
dñi . ſui . ſic hund̃ teſtat̃ . Sep̃ . I . car̃ . in dñio . Vał . xx . ſoł .

⌐Hund̃ de Rochefort . Berreuuerã tenuit Phin dac̃ . I . hid̃ . 7 . dim̃ .
m̃ . R . in dñio . Sep̃ . III . bord̃ . 7 . III . fer̃ . 7 . II . car̃ . Siłu . xxx . porc̃ . Tc̃ . uał
xl . ſoł . m̃ . IIII . lib̃ .

41 a, b

Half-Hundred of FRESHWELL

39 Withgar held (Great) BARDFIELD as one manor, for 4 hides. Now Richard holds it in lordship.

Then 24 villagers, now 20; then and later 7 smallholders, now 22; always 8 slaves. Always 4 ploughs in lordship. Then and later 21 [men's] ploughs, now 9.

Woodland, 800 pigs; meadow, 32 acres; always 2 mills. Then 4 cobs, now 5; then 28 cattle, now 41; then 60 pigs, now 107; then 100 sheep, now 200.

Value always £16.

40 Withgar held (Little) SAMPFORD as one manor, for 5 hides. Now Richard holds it in lordship.

Then 23 villagers, now 14; then 2 smallholders, now 18; then 6 slaves, now 4. Always 3 ploughs in lordship. Then 21 men's ploughs, now 10.

Woodland, 60 pigs; meadow, 22 acres; then 1 mill, now none.   41 b
Value then £12; now [£] 17.

When Richard acquired this manor, he then found there 3 cobs, now 2; then 19 cattle, now 9; then 50 pigs, now 30; then 100 sheep, now 88; then 3 beehives, now 1.

Of this manor and of the above 5 hides, 2 Frenchmen hold 1½ hides.

9 smallholders. 2 ploughs.

Meadow, 16 acres.

It is assessed above.

41 Withgar held HEMPSTEAD as 1 manor, for 4 hides less 30 acres before 1066. Now Robert of Vatteville (holds it) from Richard.

Always 22 villagers. Then 6 smallholders, now 10; then 8 slaves, now 7. Then 4 ploughs in lordship, now 3. Then 14 [men's] ploughs, now 10.

Woodland, 200 pigs; meadow, 15 acres.

Value then £12; now [£] 16.

42 In BARDFIELD Widelard holds 1 hide, which 2 servants of Withgar held. Then they did not pay customary dues or tax to the King and could not go away without their lord's order; so the Hundred testifies. Always 1 plough in lordship.

Value 20s.

Hundred of ROCHFORD

43 Finn the Dane held BARROW (Hall). 1½ hides. Now Richard (holds it) in lordship.

Always 3 smallholders; 3 slaves; 2 ploughs.

Woodland, 30 pigs.

Value then 40s; now £4.

TERRA SVENI De Exſſeſſa . Hund de ꝺdeſtapla

V Tornindunam tenuit Aluuin teinn reḡ . E . t . r . e . ⁊ Rex Witt
dedit Roɓto . M . ten& Suen̄ . ⁊ Siric de illo . ꝑ uno manerio . ⁊ . ꝑ . v . hid̄ .
⁊ . xv . ac̄ . Sēp . ii . car̄ in dn̄io . ⁊ . iii . car̄ . hom̄ . ⁊ . iii . uitt . Tc̄ . vii . bor̄ . m̄
. x . Tc̄ . iiii . ſer̄ . m̄ . i . ii . hid̄ . ſiluæ . ⁊ . ii . ſoc̄ . de . L . ac̄ . ħntes ſēp . dim̄ . car̄ .
In hoc manerio recep̄ . Suen̄ . i . runc̄ . viii . an̄ . xx . por̄ . Lx . ou̇ . m̄ . iiii .
an̄ . xii . porc̄ . L . ou̇ . Vat . c . ſot .

V Langendunā ten& . Watt de Sueno . qđ tenuit Alric teinn̄ reḡ . e .
ꝑ . m̄ . ⁊ . ꝑ . v . hid̄ . Sēp . ii . car̄ . in dn̄io . ⁊ . iii . car̄ . hom̄ . ⁊ . v . uitt . Tc̄ . iiii . ſer̄ .
m̄ . iiii . ⁊ . i . hid̄ . ſiluæ . Paſt . c . ou̇ . Tc̄ . v . an̄ . ⁊ . x . porc̄ . Lx . ou̇ . m̄ . x . porc̄ .
xLii . ou̇ . Tc̄ uat . c . ſot . m̄ . vi . liɓ .

V Tilibiam tenent . ii . franci de Sueno . ſcit Osɓn̄ . ⁊ . Rad̄ . qđ tenuit
Aluric pɓr liɓ ħo t . r . e . ꝑ uno manerio . ⁊ . ꝑ . ii . hid̄ . Sēp . ii . car̄
in dn̄io . ⁊ . iiii . car̄ hominum . ⁊ . i . uitt . ⁊ . xi . bor̄ . ⁊ . ii . ſer̄ ⁊ . iiii .
hid̄ ſiluæ . Paſt . ccc . ou̇ . ⁊ . i . piſc̄ . Tc̄ . i . runc̄ . ⁊ . Lx . ou̇ . M̄ . i . runc̄ .
⁊ . xii . pulli . ⁊ . xxxi . an̄ . ix . porc̄ . ⁊ . ccLx . ou̇ . Tc̄ uat . viii . liɓ m̄ . c . ſot

V Ciltedic . ten& Osɓn̄ de . S . qđ tenuit Aluuen liɓa femina . t . r . e .
⁊ neſcit q̄ m̄ ueħerit ad Roɓtum filium Wicmarc . Sēp . i . bi ē . i . hid̄ .
⁊ . xL . ac̄ . Sēp . i . car̄ . in dn̄io . Tc̄ . dim̄ . car̄ . hom̄ . m̄ nicħ . Tc̄ . i . uitt
m̄ nuit . Tc̄ . i . bord̄ . m̄ . iiii . Tc̄ . ii . ſer̄ . m̄ . i . Silu̇ . c . porc̄ . Paſt . c . ou̇ .
Tc̄ . i . animal . m̄ . x . an̄ . Vat . xL . ſot .

Hundred of BARSTABLE

1 Alwin, a thane of King Edward's, held (West) HORNDON before
1066. King William gave it to Robert. Now Swein holds it, and
Siric from him, as one manor for 5 hides and 15 acres. Always 2
ploughs in lordship; 3 men's ploughs;
>3 villagers. Then 7 smallholders, now 10; then 4 slaves, now 1.
>Woodland, 2 hides. 2 Freemen with 50 acres who have always
>>had ½ plough.
>In this manor Swein acquired 1 cob, 8 cattle, 20 pigs, 60 sheep;
>>now 4 cattle, 12 pigs, 50 sheep.
Value 100s.

2 Walter holds LANGDON from Swein which Alric, a thane of King
Edward's, held as a manor for 5 hides. Always 2 ploughs in
lordship; 3 men's ploughs;
>5 villagers. Then 4 slaves, now 4.
>Woodland, 1 hide; pasture, 100 sheep. Then 5 cattle, 10 pigs,
>>60 sheep; now 10 pigs, 42 sheep.
Value then 100s; now £6.

3 2 Frenchmen, namely Osbern and Ralph, hold (West) TILBURY
from Swein, which Aelfric the priest, a free man, held before 1066
as one manor for 2 hides. Always 2 ploughs in lordship; 4 men's
ploughs;
>1 villager; 11 smallholders; 2 slaves.
>Woodland, 4 hides; pasture, 300 sheep; 1 fishery. Then 1 cob,
>>60 sheep; now 1 cob, 12 foals, 31 cattle, 9 pigs and 260
>>sheep.
Value then £8; now 100s.

[Hundred of CHAFFORD]

4 Osbern holds CHILDERDITCH from Swein which Alwen, a free
woman, held before 1066 and it is not known how it came to
Robert son of Wymarc. Always 1 hide there and 40 acres. Always
1 plough in lordship. Then ½ men's plough, now nothing.
>Then 1 villager, now none; then 1 smallholder, now 4; then 2
>>slaves, now 1.
>Woodland, 100 pigs; pasture, 100 sheep. Then 1 (head of)
>>cattle, now 10 cattle.
Value 40s.

ᚼHornindunã tenuit Aluric pbr lib hõ . t . r . e . ꝑ uno Man . 7 . ꝑ
. II . hid . 7 . xxx . ac . Sẽp . I . car . in dñio . 7 . dim . car hoũm . 7 . xI . bor

7 . III . ſer . De hac trã dedit Aluric pbr cuidã eccƚe dim . hid . 7 . xxx . ac .
ſed Suen abſtulit de ecƚia Sẽp . I . runc . 7 . II . an . Vaƚ . xxx . ſoƚ . Hoc
maner̄ ten& Pagan de Sueno.

ᚼHaſingebroc ten& Turolđ de . S . qđ tenuit Lefſtan lib hõ . t . r . e .
ꝑ . I . hid . 7 . xxx . ac . Sẽp . I . car . in dñio . Tc . II . bor . m̃ . III . Tc . II . ſer m̃
nulƚ . vI . ac . pti . Tc . x . oũ . m̃ . xIII . 7 . v . porc . Vaƚ . xx . ſoƚ .

ᚼBeleſdunam ten& Idē Turolđ de . S . qđ tenuit Idē Lefſtan . t . r . e
ꝑ . I . hid . 7 . ꝑ . ꝳ . 7 . xv . ac . Sẽp . I . car . Tc . III . bor . m̃ . I . Sẽp . II . ſer . Paſt .
. c . oũ . Tc . II . runc . 7 . vII . porc . 7 . xv . oũ . M . I . runc . 7 . I . uac . 7 . I . por .
7 Lxxxxv . oũ . Tc uaƚ . xx . ſoƚ . M . xxv .

ᚼBerleſduna ten& . W . qđ tenuit God& q̃dã lib hõ . t . r . e . ꝑ . m̃ . 7 . ꝑ .
. III . hid . Tc . III . car . in dñio . m̃ . II . 7 . dim . Tc . I . car . hom . m̃ . I . 7 . dim .
Tc . II . uiƚƚ . m̃ . I . Tc . IIII . borđ . m̃ . III . Tc . IIII . ſer . m̃ nulƚ . Silua
xL . porc . Paſt . c . oũ . Tc . I . runc . 7 . xvII . oũ . M . v . an . 7 . xvI . porc .
7 . xxxIx . oũ . Vaƚ . Lx . ſoƚ .

ᚼWicfort tenet Turchiƚƚ qđ tenuit Lefſtan libe . ꝑ . ꝳ . 7 . ꝑ . dim . hid .
7 . xxxv . ac . Sẽp . I . car . 7 . I . borđ . Tc . I . ſer . m̃ nulƚ . xxx . ac . ſiluæ .
. III . ac . pti . Tc . II . runc . 7 . xvI . an . 7 . III . porc . 7 . c . oũ . m̃ . III . runc .
7 vIII . an . 7 . xI . porc . 7 . Lx . oũ . Pt hanc trã tenuit bricteua liba
femina dim hid . 7 . xv . ac . q̃m Suen addidit p̃dicte træ . in q̃ erat
tc . I . car . m̃ . n̄ . Sẽp . II . borđ . 7 . I . uiƚƚ . xx . ac . ſiluæ . Addidit &iam
. III . libos hões . de xLv . ac . in qbꝫ erat . tc . I . car . m̃ . dim . Addidit
&iam . I . libm hom . de . Ix . ac . Tc uaƚ totũ . t . r . e . Lx . ſoƚ . m̃ . L .

[Hundred of BARSTABLE]

5   Aelfric the priest, a free man, held HORNDON (-on-the-Hill) as one manor, for 2 hides and 30 acres. Always 1 plough in lordship; ½ men's plough;
> 11 smallholders; 3 slaves.

> Of this land, Aelfric the priest gave ½ hide and 30 acres to a church, but Swein took it away from the church.
> Always 1 cob; 2 cattle.

Value 30s.
> Payne holds this manor from Swein.

6   Thorold holds HASSENBROOK (Hall) from Swein, which Leofstan, a free man, held before 1066 for 1 hide and 30 acres. Always 1 plough in lordship.
> Then 2 smallholders, now 3; then 2 slaves, now none.
> Meadow, 6 acres. Then 10 cattle, now 13 and 5 pigs.

Value 20s.

7   Thorold also holds BASILDON from Swein, which Leofstan also held before 1066 as a manor for 1 hide and 15 acres. Always 1 plough.
> Then 3 smallholders, now 1; always 2 slaves.
> Pasture, 100 sheep. Then 2 cobs, 7 pigs, 15 sheep; now 1 cob, 1 cow, 1 pig and 95 sheep.

Value then 20s; now 25[s].

8   W. holds BASILDON, which Godith, a free man, held before 1066 as a manor for 3 hides. Then 3 ploughs in lordship, now 2½. Then 1 men's plough, now 1½.
> Then 2 villagers, now 1; then 4 smallholders, now 3; then 4 slaves, now none.
> Woodland, 40 pigs; pasture, 100 sheep. Then 1 cob, 17 sheep; now 5 cattle, 16 pigs and 39 sheep.

Value 60s.

9   Thorkell holds WICKFORD, which Leofstan held freely as a manor for ½ hide and 35 acres. Always 1 plough;
> 1 smallholder. Then 1 slave, now none.
> Woodland, 30 acres; meadow, 3 acres. Then 2 cobs, 16 cattle, 3 pigs and 100 sheep; now 3 cobs, 8 cattle, 11 pigs and 60 sheep.

> Besides this land, Bricteva, a free woman, held ½ hide and 15 acres which Swein added to the above-mentioned land, in which there was then 1 plough, now none.
> Always 2 smallholders; 1 villager.
> Woodland, 20 acres.
> He also added 3 free men with 45 acres, in which there was then 1 plough, now ½. He also added 1 free man with 9 acres.

Value of the whole then, before 1066, 60s; now 50[s].

⌐Wicfort ten& Suen̅ in dn̅io . qd̅ tenuit Goduin̅ teinnus reg̅.

43 a

ꝑ uno man̅ . 7 . ꝑ . x . hid̅ . Sep̅ . ii . car̅ in dn̅io . Tc̅ . vi . car̅ . hom̅ . m̅ . iiii.
Sep̅ . vii . uill̅ . Tc̅ . ii . bor̅ . m̅ . xii . Tc̅ . vi . ſer̅ . m̅ . null̅ . Tc̅ . xii . hid̅ . ſiluæ
m̅ . vi . ac̅ . Tc̅ . i . runc̅ . 7 . xii . ou̅ . 7 . xvii . cap̅ . 7 . ii . uaſa ap̅ . m̅ . i . uac̅ . 7
xx . ou̅ . 7 . ii . pull̅ . 7 . iiij . uaſa ap̅ . Tc̅ uat̅ . xvi . lib̅ . m̅ . ix.

⌐Wicfort ten& Will̅ fili Odonis qd̅ tenuit Dot lib ho̅ . t . r . E . ꝑ . m̅ . 7 . d̅.
hid̅ . 7 . xlv . ac̅ . Sep̅ . i . car̅ in dn̅io . 7 . i . bor̅ . Silu̅ . x . porc̅ . Val̅ . x . ſot.

⌐Wicfort ten& Mainard̅ . qd̅ tenuit . t . r . e . Godric . ꝑ . xxx . ac̅ . Val̅
. v . ſot.

⌐Benſlet ten& Suen̅ in dn̅io qd̅ tenuit Aluuin̅ . lib ho̅ . t . r . e . ꝑ
m̅ . 7 . ꝑ . ii . hid̅ . Tc̅ . iii . car̅ in dn̅io . m̅ . i . 7 . i . car̅ poſſ& reſtaurari.
m̅ . v . bord̅ . 7 . ii . ſer̅ . Paſt . ccl . ou̅ . Val̅ . xl . ſot.

⌐Wateleam ten& Galt̅ de Sueno . qd̅ tenuit Edric . t . r . e . ꝑ . m̅ . 7
ꝑ . dim hid̅ . Sep̅ . i . car̅ . m̅ . i . bord̅ 7 xv . ac̅ . paſturæ ; Val̅ . x . ſot.

⌐Wateleam ten& Suen̅ in dn̅io . qd̅ tenuit Leuecilt . t . r . e . tegn̅ reg̅.
. ꝑ . i . Man̅ . 7 . ꝑ . v . hid̅ . Tc̅ . ii . car̅ . 7 . i . car̅ . hom̅ . 7 . m̅ ſimit̅ . Tc̅ . i . uill̅ . m̅
null̅ . Tc̅ . x . bor̅ . M̅ xi . dim hid̅ ſilue uaſtatæ . Paſt . c . ou̅ . Tc̅ . i . piſc̅.
m̅ . ii . Tc̅ . iii . runc̅ . 7 . v . an̅ . 7 . xx . porc̅ . 7 . c . ou̅ . m̅ . i . runc̅ . 7 . i . pull̅.
7 . vii . an̅ . 7 . lxx . ou̅ . Tc̅ uat̅ . lx . ſot . m̅ . iiii . lib̅.

⌐Thunreſleam ten& S . in dn̅io . qd̅ tenuit Godric tegn̅ reg̅ . t . r . e.
ꝑ uno Man̅ . 7 . ꝑ . v . hid̅ . 7 . xv . ac̅ . Sep̅ . ii . car̅ . in dn̅io . 7 . ii . car̅ hou̅.
7 . v . uill̅ . 7 . v . bord̅ . Tc̅ . iiii . ſer̅ . m̅ . ii . Paſt . cc . ou̅ . Silu̅ . l . porc̅.
Tc̅ . ii . runc̅ . 7 . vii . an̅ . 7 . xvi . porc̅ . 7 . cc . ou̅ . 7 . ii . uaſa ap̅ . M̅ . iii.
runc̅ . 7 . i . runc̅ . xiiii . an̅ . xxxvi . porc̅ . cc . ou̅ . ii . uaſa ap̅ . Tc̅ uat̅
. cii ſot̅ . M̅ . c . ſot.

10 Swein holds WICKFORD in lordship which Godwin, a King's thane, held as one manor for 10 hides. Always 2 ploughs in lordship. 43 a Then 6 men's ploughs, now 4.

>Always 7 villagers. Then 2 smallholders, now 12; then 6 slaves, now none.

>Woodland, then 12 hides, now 6 acres. Then 1 cob, 12 sheep, 17 goats, 2 beehives; now 1 cow, 20 sheep, 2 foals, 3 beehives.

Value then £16; now [£] 9.

11 William son of Odo holds WICKFORD which Dot, a free man, held before 1066 as a manor. ½ hide and 45 acres. Always 1 plough in lordship;

>1 smallholder.

>Woodland, 10 pigs.

Value 10s.

12 Maynard holds WICKFORD, which Godric held before 1066 for 30 acres.

Value 5s.

13 Swein holds (South) BENFLEET in lordship which Alwin, a free man, held before 1066 as a manor, for 2 hides. Then 3 ploughs in lordship, now 1; 1 plough can be restored.

>Now 5 smallholders; 2 slaves.

>Pasture, 250 sheep.

Value 40s.

14 Walter holds WHEATLEY from Swein, which Edric held before 1066 as a manor, for ½ hide. Always 1 plough.

>Now 1 smallholder.

>Pasture, 15 acres.

Value 10s.

15 Swein holds WHEATLEY in lordship, which Leofcild, a King's thane, held before 1066 as 1 manor for 5 hides. Then 2 ploughs and 1 men's plough; now the same.

>Then 1 villager, now none; then 10 smallholders, now 11.

>Woodland, ½ hide, laid waste; pasture, 100 sheep; then 1 fishery, now 2. Then 3 cobs, 5 cattle, 20 pigs and 100 sheep; now 1 cob, 1 foal, 7 cattle and 70 sheep.

Value then 60s; now £4.

16 Swein holds THUNDERSLEY in lordship, which Godric, a King's thane, held before 1066 as one manor for 5 hides and 15 acres. Always 2 ploughs in lordship; 2 men's ploughs;

>5 villagers; 5 smallholders. Then 4 slaves, now 2.

>Pasture, 200 sheep; woodland, 50 pigs. Then 2 cobs, 7 cattle, 16 pigs, 200 sheep and 2 beehives; now 3 cobs and 1 cob, 14 cattle, 36 pigs, 200 sheep, 2 beehives.

Value then 102s; now 100s.

Hund de Rochefort . Rageneia . ten& Suen in dnĩo ꝑ . uno
Man . 7 ꝑ . v . hid . Tc̃ . II . car in dnĩo . m̃ . III . Sep . x . car . hom . Tc̃ . xxi .
uilł . m̃ . vi . Tc̃ . vi . borḋ . m̃ . xv . Sep . II . fer . x . ac̃ . p̃ti . Silu . xl . porc . m̃
. I . parc . 7 vi . arpenni uineæ . 7 reddit . xx . modios uini ſi bene procedit .
Tc̃ . IIII . runc . 7 . xiii . an . xxv . porc . cv . ou . m̃ . v . runc . 7 . II . pulli .
7 . xx . an . 7 xi . porc . 7 lxxx . ou . 7 . xi . cap . Tc̃ uał . x . lib . m̃ p̃t uinum
tantundẽ . 7 in hoc manerio fecit Suen ſuũ caſtellũ . De hoc manerio
tenent . IIII . franci . II . hid . 7 . IIII . car . 7 . IIII . borḋ . 7 uał . lx . ſoł in
eoḋ p̃tio .

Ragheleiam ten& . S . in dnĩo qḋ tenuit . I . lib hõ . t . r . e . ꝑ . Man . 7 ꝑ .
. II . hid . 7 . dim . Sep . II . car in dnĩo . tc̃ . III . uilł . m̃ . II . Tc̃ . v . bor . m̃ . vi .
hntes tc̃ . II . car 7 dim . m̃ dim tantũ . Tc̃ . I . runc . 7 . II . an . 7 . xv . ou .
m̃ . II . runc . ix . an . ix . por . xx . ou . Tc̃ 7 p uał . xxx . ſoł . m̃ . xl .

Hocheleiam tenent . II . franci de Sueno . Godebolḋ . I . hid . 7 Odo
. xxx . ac̃ . 7 hoc Man tenuit . I . lib hõ . t . r . e . Sep . II . car . 7 . dim . in dnĩo .
Tc̃ . III . borḋ . m̃ . v . Tc̃ . v . fer . m̃ . III . Paſt . c . ou Sep . I . mot . Tc̃ . v .
an . 7 . x . porc . 7 . c . ou . 7 . vii . cap . M . I . runc . 7 . xiii . an . 7 xxii . porc .
7 . c . ou . 7 . IIII . uaſa ap . Tc̃ uał . xxx . ſoł . P 7 m̃ . xl .

Eſtuudã . ten& Suen in dnĩo . qḋ tenuit Pat̃ ſuus . t . r . e . ꝑ uno
Man . 7 ꝑ . III . hid 7 . dim . Sep . III . uilł . 7 . II . car . in dnĩo . Tc̃ . viii . car
hom . m̃ . v . Tc̃ . xxi . bor . m̃ . xxx . Sep . II . fer . IIII . ac̃ . p̃ti . Tc̃ ſilu
. l . porc . m̃ . xxx . m̃ . I . mot̃ Paſt . ccc . ou . Tc̃ . II . runc . 7 . vi . an .
. xxx . porc . ccc . ou . m̃ . II . runc . 7 . II . puł̃ . 7 . xxxiii . an . xl .
porc . cxxxvi . o . Tc̃ uał . vi . lib . m̃ . x . De hoc manerio

ten& Goisfriḋ . dim hid . 7 . I . bor . 7 . I . car . 7 uał xx . ſoł . in eoḋ p̃tio .

17   Swein holds RAYLEIGH in lordship as one manor, for 5 hides. Then
      2 ploughs in lordship, now 3. Always 10 men's ploughs.
          Then 21 villagers, now 6; then 6 smallholders, now 15;
          always 2 slaves.
          Meadow, 10 acres; woodland, 40 pigs; now 1 park; 6 *arpents*
          of vines and it pays 20 measures of wine if it does well.
          Then 4 cobs, 13 cattle, 25 pigs, 105 sheep; now 5 cobs,
          2 foals, 20 cattle, 11 pigs, 80 sheep and 11 goats.
      Value then £10; now, apart from the wine, as much.
      In this manor Swein made his castle.
      Of this manor, 4 Frenchmen hold 2 hides. 4 ploughs.
      4 smallholders.
      Value 60s in the same assessment.

18   Swein holds RAYLEIGH in lordship, which 1 free man held before
      1066 as a manor, for 2½ hides. Always 2 ploughs in lordship.
          Then 3 villagers, now 2; then 5 smallholders, now 6, who
          then had 2½ ploughs and now have only ½.
          Then 1 cob, 2 cattle and 15 sheep; now 2 cobs, 9 cattle,
          9 pigs, 20 sheep.
      Value then and later 30s; now 40[s].

19   2 Frenchmen hold HOCKLEY from Swein, Godbold (holds) 1 hide
      and Odo 30 acres. 1 free man held this manor before 1066.
      Always 2½ ploughs in lordship.
          Then 3 smallholders, now 5; then 5 slaves, now 3.
          Pasture, 100 sheep; always 1 mill. Then 5 cattle, 10 pigs,
          100 sheep and 7 goats; now 1 cob, 13 cattle, 22 pigs, 100
          sheep and 4 beehives.
      Value then 30s; later and now 40[s].

20   Swein holds EASTWOOD in lordship, which his father held before
      1066 as one manor, for 3½ hides.
          Always 3 villagers; 2 ploughs in lordship. Then 8 men's ploughs,
          now 5. Then 21 smallholders, now 30; always 2 slaves.
          Meadow, 4 acres; woodland, then 50 pigs, now 30; now 1 mill;
          pasture, 300 sheep. Then 2 cobs, 6 cattle, 30 pigs, 300
          sheep; now 2 cobs, 2 foals, 33 cattle, 40 pigs, 136 sheep.
      Value then £6; now [£] 10.
      Of this manor, Geoffrey holds ½ hide.   44 a
      1 smallholder. 1 plough.
      Value 20s in the same assessment.

Wachelingam ten& . S . in dñio .p . I . Man . 7 . p . v . hid . 7 dim . Sep.
. II . uilt . 7 . xvIII . bord . 7 . II . car in dñio . 7 tcia poff& fieri . Tc . III.
. car hom . m . v . Silu . xL . porc . Past . ccc . ou . Tc . IIII . runc . Ix.
an . xxxvIII . porc . cxv . ou . M . IIII . runc . II . an . cx . ou . xxvII . porc.
Tc uat . Ix . lib . m . x . De hoc man . tenent Garner 7 . W . I . hidam.
7 . II . car . 7 uat . xxx . fot . in eod ptio.

Pritteuuellã . ten& . S . in dñio . p . vII . hid . 7 . dim . Tc . vII . uilt . m . IIII.
Tc . xIIII . bord . m . xxIII . Tc . II . car . in dñio m . III . Tc . vII . car . hou
m . Ix . Past . xII . porc . Past . cc . ou . Tc . II . runc . vIII . an . xxx . porc.
. c . ou . M . I . runc . III . pult . xIII . an . Lxv . porc . cc . ou . IIII . min.
. Lxvi . cap . Ix . uafa ap . ┌ De hac tra ten& . I . lib hõ . I . uirg quã potat
uende . f; foca jacuit in hoc manerio . 7 ad eccliam huj manerij.
appofuer . II . hões . xxx . ac . de alia tra . Sep uat . xII . lib . De hoc Man
ten& Grapinel dim . hidã . 7 . II . bord . 7 . I . car . 7 . uat . x . fot in eod
ptio.

Effobiam tenuit . R . fili uuimarcæ poft morte reg . E . m . Suen
in dñio . p uno Man . 7 . p . v . hid . Sep . Ix . uilt . Tc . IIII . bor . m . vi.
Sep . II . car . in dñio . 7 . vIII . car . hom . III . ac . pti . Silu . xx . porc.
Tc . II . runc . IIII . an . xII . porc . c . ou . m . II . runc . xvi . porc . Lxiiii.
ou . Tc . 7 p uat . vi . lib . m . x.

Carendunã ten& . S . in dñio . p . vi . hid . 7 . dim . 7 . xxx . ac . Tc . xxii.
uilt . m . xvi . Tc . II . bord . m . vIII . Tc . III . fer . m . I . Tc . II . car i dñio
m . III . 7 qrta pot fieri . Tc . x . car . hom . M . vi . Past . bc . ou . Tc.
. III . runc . x . an . xxIIII . porc . cccxxxvi . ou . m . III . runc . 7 . v . an.

★

44 b
. xx . porc . ccc . xLII . ou . Tc . uat . xII . lib . m . xIII . In hoc manerio
ht Hugo de monteforti . I . hid . 7 . uat . xx . fot . De hoc man . tenent
. II . franci . Girold . I . hid . 7 . ihos . xxx . ac . 7 . III . bord . 7 . I . car . 7 uat . xL.
fot . in eod ptio . Ht &iã . S . I . hid . 7 . IIII . bord . 7 . I . car . qd tenuit . I . lib
hõ t . r . e . cũ foca . Vat . xx . fot.

21 Swein holds (Great) WAKERING in lordship as 1 manor, for 5½ hides.

> Always 2 villagers; 18 smallholders; 2 ploughs in lordship, 3 possible. Then 3 men's ploughs, now 5.
>
> Woodland, 40 pigs; pasture, 300 sheep. Then 4 cobs, 9 cattle, 38 pigs, 115 sheep; now 4 cobs, 2 cattle, 110 sheep, 27 pigs.

Value then £9; now [£] 10.

Of this manor, Warner and W. hold 1 hide. 2 ploughs.

Value 30s in the same assessment.

22 Swein holds PRITTLEWELL in lordship for 7½ hides.

> Then 7 villagers, now 4; then 14 smallholders, now 23. Then 2 ploughs in lordship, now 3. Then 7 men's ploughs, now 9.
>
> Pasture, 12 pigs; pasture, 200 sheep. Then 2 cobs, 8 cattle, 30 pigs, 100 sheep; now 1 cob, 3 foals, 13 cattle, 65 pigs, 200 sheep less 4, 66 goats, 9 beehives.

Of this land, 1 free man holds 1 virgate which he could sell; but the jurisdiction lay in (the lands of) this manor. To (the lands of) this manor's church 2 men added 30 acres of another land. Value always £12.

Of this manor, Grapinel holds ½ hide.

2 smallholders. 1 plough.

Value 10s in the same assessment.

23 Robert son of Wymarc held SHOEBURY after the death of King Edward. Now Swein (holds it) in lordship as one manor, for 5 hides.

> Always 9 villagers. Then 4 smallholders, now 6. Always 2 ploughs in lordship; 8 men's ploughs.
>
> Meadow, 3 acres; woodland, 20 pigs. Then 2 cobs, 4 cattle, 12 pigs, 100 sheep; now 2 cobs, 16 pigs, 64 sheep.

Value then and later £6; now [£] 10.

24 Swein holds CANEWDON in lordship for 6½ hides and 30 acres.

> Then 22 villagers, now 16; then 2 smallholders, now 8; then 3 slaves, now 1. Then 2 ploughs in lordship, now 3; 4 possible. Then 10 men's ploughs, now 6.
>
> Pasture, 600 sheep. Then 3 cobs, 10 cattle, 24 pigs, 336 sheep; now 3 cobs, 5 cattle, 20 pigs, 342 sheep.

44 b

Value then £12; now [£] 13.

In this manor Hugh de Montfort has 1 hide.

Value 20s.

2 Freemen hold (parts) of this manor, Gerald 1 hide and John 30 acres.

3 smallholders. 1 plough.

Value 40s in the same assessment.

Swein also has 1 hide, 4 smallholders and 1 plough, which 1 free man held before 1066 with the jurisdiction.

Value 20s.

⟨Torpeiam ten& Odo de . S . qd̃ tenuit Godric̈ . tegñ reg̃ . E . 7 Rob̃
fili uuimarce habuit p̃ mortẽ reg̃ . E . p̃ uno Mañ . 7 . p̃ . I . hid . 7 . xxx .
ac̈ . Tc̃ . I . uitł . m̃ . II . Tc̃ . IIII . bor . m̃ . vI . tc̃ . IIII . ſer . m̃ . I . Sep̃ . II . car̃ in
dño . 7 . I . car̃ hom̃ . Past . c . ou . Tc̃ . I . runc̈ . 7 . vII . añ . xvIIII . porc̈ .
LX ^{vIII} . ou . m̃ . vI . añ . xxxIIII . porc̈ . cLx . ou . II . uaſa ap̃ . Tc̃ uał .
xL . ſoł . P̃ 7 m̃ . Lx .

⟨Rochefort ten& Alured̃ de . S . qd̃ teñ . I . lib̃ hõ . t . r . e . p̃ . m̃ . 7 p̃ .
. II . hid . 7 . dim . Sep̃ . v . uiłł . Tc̃ . IIII . bor . m̃ . xII . Tc̃ . II . ſer . m̃ . IIII
tc̃ . II . car̃ in dño . m̃ . III . Tc̃ . III . car̃ . hom̃ . m̃ . IIII . 7 . I . lib̃ hõ
ten& . xxx . ac̈ . 7 adhuc jacent huic mañ . II . ac̈ p̃ti . Silu . xx .
porc̈ . I . moł . Tc̃ . I . runc̈ . 7 . vIII . porc̈ . 7 . xI . ou . m̃ . III . runc̈ . 7
. II . pułł . 7 . x . añ . 7 . xxI . porc̈ . 7 . cLx . ou . 7 xxIII . ou . Tc̃ ualuit
. c . ſoł . m̃ . vII . lib̃ .

⟨Stanbruge ten& Wiard̃ de . S . qd̃ tenuit . I . lib̃ hõ . t . r . e .
p̃ . uno mañ . 7 . p̃ . I . hid . 7 . dim 7 . vII . ac̈ . 7 . dim . Sep̃ . II . bord . 7 .
. I . ſer̃ . 7 . dim . car̃ . tc̃ . m̃ . I . Past . c . ou . Tc̃ uał . x . ſoł . m̃ . xxv .

⟨Eſſobiam . ten& Galt̃ de . S . qd̃ tenuit . I . lib̃ hõ . t . r . e . p̃ . I .
Mañ . 7 . p̃ . IIII . hid . Sep̃ . IIII . uitł . Tc̃ . vI . bor . m̃ . vIII . Tc̃ .
. II . ſer . m̃ . nulł . Tc̃ . II . car̃ . in dño . m̃ . III . Sep̃ . II . car̃ hominũ .
Silu . xII . porc̈ . Quartã hidã ex ħ ten& . I . lib̃ hõ   Past . c . ou .

45 a

Tc̃ . I . runc̈ . 7 . II . añ . 7 . xL . ou . m̃ . I . runc̈ . 7 . vI . añ . I . porc̈ . cxv . ou .
tc̃ 7 p̃ uał . vI . lib̃ . m̃ vIII .

⟨Wacheringa ten& . S . qd̃ tenuit . I . lib̃ hõ . t . r . e . p̃ . Mañ . 7 p̃ . II . hid .
7 hoc tenuit Rob̃ fili uuimarcæ p̃ mortẽ reg̃ Eduuardi . Tc̃ . I . bor .
7 . xv . ſer . m̃ . x . bor . Sep̃ . II . car̃ in dño . 7 . I . car̃ hom̃ . Past . ccc . ou .
Tc̃ . II . añ . 7 . c . ou . m̃ . I . runc̈ . 7 . II . añ . cxv . ou . I . uas ap̃ . Tc̃ . uał . III . lib̃
P̃ 7 m̃ . IIII . De hoc eod̃ Mañ . Ten& Rob̃ . I . hid . 7 . Godric̈ . dim . 7 . uał .
xL . ſoł in eod̃ . p̃tio .

25 Odo holds (LITTLE)THORPE from Swein which Godric, a thane of King Edward's, held, and (which) Robert son of Wymarc had after the death of King Edward as one manor, for 1 hide and 30 acres.

> Then 1 villager, now 2; then 4 smallholders, now 6; then 4 slaves, now 1. Always 2 ploughs in lordship; 1 men's plough. Pasture, 100 sheep. Then 1 cob, 7 cattle, 19 pigs, 68 sheep; now 6 cattle, 34 pigs, 160 sheep, 2 beehives.

Value then 40s; later and now 60[s].

26 Alfred holds ROCHFORD from Swein, which 1 free man held before 1066 as a manor, for 2½ hides.

> Always 5 villagers. Then 4 smallholders, now 12; then 2 slaves, now 3. Then 2 ploughs in lordship, now 3. Then 3 men's ploughs, now 4.

1 free man holds 30 acres and they also lie in (the lands of) this manor.

> Meadow, 2 acres; woodland, 20 pigs; 1 mill. Then 1 cob, 8 pigs and 11 sheep; now 3 cobs, 2 foals, 10 cattle, 21 pigs, 160 sheep and 23 sheep.

Value then 100s; now £7.

27 Wicard holds (Great) STAMBRIDGE from Swein, which 1 free man held before 1066 as one manor, for 1½ hides and 7½ acres.

> Always 2 smallholders; 1 slave. ½ plough then, now 1. Pasture, 100 sheep.

Value then 10s; now 25[s].

28 Walter holds SHOEBURY from Swein, which 1 free man held before 1066 as 1 manor, for 4 hides.

> Always 4 villagers. Then 6 smallholders, now 8; then 2 slaves, now none. Then 2 ploughs in lordship, now 3. Always 2 men's ploughs. Woodland, 12 pigs.

1 free man holds the fourth of these hides.

> Pasture, 100 sheep. Then 1 cob, 2 cattle, 40 sheep; now 1 cob, 45 a 6 cattle, 1 pig, 115 sheep.

Value then and later £6; now [£] 8.

29 Swein holds (Little) WAKERING, which 1 free man held before 1066 as a manor, for 2 hides. Robert son of Wymarc held this after the death of King Edward.

> Then 1 smallholder, 15 slaves; now 10 smallholders. Always 2 ploughs in lordship; 1 men's plough. Pasture, 300 sheep. Then 2 cattle and 100 sheep; now 1 cob, 2 cattle, 115 sheep, 1 beehive.

Value then £3; later and now [£] 4.

> Of this manor, Robert holds 1 hide and Godric ½.

Value 40s in the same assessment.

Suttunā ten& Afcelin̾ de . S . q̅d̅ tenueř . II . libi . hōēs . t̾ . r̾ . e̾ . p̾ . m̅ .
7 . p̾ . I . hiđ . 7 . dim̾ . 7 . xxx . ac̾ . m̅ . VIII . borđ . Tē . IIII . ſeř . m̅ null̾ .
Sēp . II . car̾ in dn̅io 7 . dim̾ . car̾ hom̾ . Paſt . ccc . ou̾ . Tē . II . runc̾ .
. & . L . porc̾ . cc . ou̾ . m̅ . VII . an̾ . CLX . ou̾ . Tē 7 p̾ ual̾ . LX . ſol̾ . m̅ . IIII . liƀ .

Plumƀgā ten& Iđē . A . de . S . q̅d̅ tenuit Roƀ fiłi̾ Wimarcæ . p̾ . m̅ . 7 . p̾
. I . hiđ . Tē . I . borđ . 7 . I . ſeř . m̅ . VIII . bor . Tē . I . car̾ 7 dim in dn̅io . m̅ . I .
dim̾ . car̾ . hom̾ . Siłu . xxx . porc̾ . Paſt . c . ou̾ . m̅ . I . mol̾ . Tē . I . runc̾ .
. VII . an̾ . xxx . porc̾ . c . ou̾ . xL . cap̾ . m̅ . II . runc̾ . 7 . I . pull̾ . III . an̾ .
xx . porc̾ . c . ou̾ . xxIII . cap̾ . Tē ual̾ . xx . ſol̾ . m̅ . xL .

Puteſeiam ten& iđē . Aſc̾ . de . S . q̅d̅ tenuit . I . liƀ hõ . t̾ . r̾ . e̾ . p̾ . m̅ .
7 . LII . ac̾ . 7 . dim̾ . Sēp . II . bor . 7 . I . car̾ . Paſt . xxx . ou̾ . m̅ . I . mol̾ .
Tē . I . runc̾ . 7 . I . pull̾ . 7 . I . an̾ . 7 . III . porc̾ . 7 . Lxxx . ou̾ . m̅ ſimilit̾ .
Tē 7 p̾ ual̾ . xx . ſol̾ . m̅ . xxx .

Hacheleiā ten& Pagan̾ de . S . p̾ . I . m̅ . 7 . p̾ . I . hiđ . Sēp . xII . borđ .
7 . I . car̾ . in dn̅io . Tē . II . car̾ . hom̾ . m̅ . I . Siłu . xxx . porc̾ . Paſt .
. cc . ou̾ . M̅ . I . mol̾ . Tē . II . runc̾ . 7 . II . an̾ . 7 . xII . porc̾ . 7 . CLx . ou̾ .
7 . xxx . cap̾ . m̅ . IIII . runc̾ . x . an̾ . xxIIII . porc̾ . ccc . ou̾ . LIII . cap̾ .

45 b
VI . uaſa ap̾ . Tē ual̾ . III . liƀ . m̅ . IIII .

Puteſeiam ten& . joħs de . S . q̅d̅ tenuit . I . liƀ hõ t̾ . r̾ . e̾ . p̾ . m̅ . 7 . p̾ . I . hiđ
7 . dim̾ . 7 . xxx . ac̾ . Sēp . VIII . bor . Paſt . L . ou̾ . Tē . I . runc̾ . 7 . VIII . porc̾ .
7 . xxv . ou̾ . m̅ . xI . porc̾ . LxxxvI . ou̾ . Val̾ . xL . ſol̾ .

Suttunā ten& Aluid queđā anglica de . S . q̅d̅ tenuit Roƀ fiłi̾ uuim̾ .
p̾ morte reḡ . E . p̾ uno Man̾ . 7 . p̾ . I . hiđ . 7 . xv . ac̾ . Sēp . III . borđ . Tē . II . ſeř .
m̅ null̾ . Sēp . I . car̾ in dn̅io . Tē . II . runc̾ . 7 . x . an̾ . 7 . xI . porc̾ . 7 . c . ou̾ .
m̅ . x . an̾ . x . porc̾ . LxIII . ou̾ . Val̾ . xxx . ſol̾ .

30 Ascelin holds SUTTON from Swein, which 2 free men held before
1066 as a manor, for 1½ hides and 30 acres.
> Now 8 smallholders; then 4 slaves, now none. Always 2
> > ploughs in lordship; ½ men's plough.
>
> Pasture, 300 sheep. Then 2 cobs, 50 pigs, 200 sheep; now 7
> > cattle, 160 sheep.

Value then and later 60s; now £4.

31 A(scelin) also holds PLUMBEROW from Swein, which Robert son of
Wymarc held as a manor, for 1 hide.
> Then 1 smallholder and 1 slave; now 8 smallholders. Then 1½
> > ploughs in lordship, now 1. ½ men's plough.
>
> Woodland, 30 pigs; pasture, 100 sheep; now 1 mill. Then 1 cob,
> > 7 cattle, 30 pigs, 100 sheep, 40 goats; now 2 cobs, 1 foal,
> > 3 cattle, 20 pigs, 100 sheep, 23 goats.

Value then 20s; now 40[s].

32 Ascelin also holds PUDSEY (Hall) from Swein, which 1 free man
held before 1066 as a manor, for 52½ acres.
> Always 2 smallholders; 1 plough.
>
> Pasture, 30 sheep; now 1 mill. Then 1 cob, 1 foal, 1 (head of)
> > cattle, 3 pigs and 80 sheep; now the same.

Value then and later 20s; now 30[s].

33 Payne holds HOCKLEY from Swein as 1 manor, for 1 hide.
> Always 12 smallholders; 1 plough in lordship. Then 2 men's
> > ploughs, now 1.
>
> Woodland, 30 pigs; pasture, 200 sheep; now 1 mill. Then 2
> > cobs, 2 cattle, 12 pigs, 160 sheep and 30 goats; now 4 cobs,
> > 10 cattle, 24 pigs, 300 sheep, 53 goats, 6 beehives.   45 b

Value then £3; now [£] 4.

34 John holds PUDSEY (Hall) from Swein, which 1 free man held
before 1066 as a manor, for 1½ hides and 30 acres.
> Always 8 smallholders.
>
> Pasture, 50 sheep. Then 1 cob, 8 pigs, 25 sheep; now 11 pigs,
> > 86 sheep.

Value 40s.

35 Alfith, an Englishwoman, holds SUTTON from Swein, which Robert
son of Wymarc held after the death of King Edward as one manor,
for 1 hide and 15 acres.
> Always 3 smallholders. Then 2 slaves, now none. Always 1
> > plough in lordship.
>
> Then 2 cobs, 10 cattle, 11 pigs and 100 sheep; now 10 cattle,
> > 10 pigs, 63 sheep.

Value 30s.

Puteſeiam ten& Almar de.S.q̛d teñ.ɪ.ſoc.Roƀti.p̄.m̄.7.p̄ dim.
hid.7.xv.ac.Sēp.ɪɪɪ.bord.7.ɪ.car in dn̄io.Paſt.ʟ.ou.Tc̄.ɪ.runc.
7.vɪɪɪ.porc.7.xxv.ou.m̄.xɪ.porc.7.ʟxxxvɪ.ou.Val.xxx.ſol.

Puteſeiam ten& Hugo de.S.q̛d tenuit.ɪ.liƀ.hō.t.r.e.7.Roƀ habebat
ſocā.p̄.m̄.7.xxxvɪɪɪ.ac.Tc̄.ɪ.uilt.m̄.ɪɪ.Sēp.dim.car.Paſt.xxx.ou.
Tc̄.ɪ.runc.7.ɪɪ.an.7.x.porc.ʟxxv.ou.m̄.ɪ.runc.7.ɪ.uac.7
.c.xɪɪɪɪ.ou.Val.x.ſol.

In Neſenduna ten& Roḡ dim.hid.de.S.q̛d tenuit.Roƀ.Sēp.ɪ.bor
Paſt.xʟ.ou.Tc̄.ɪ.car.m̄.dim.7.tota pot.fieri.Val.x.ſol.

In Suttuna ten&.Roḡ.dimid hid.q̛d tenuit.Roƀ.t.r.e.Sēp.ɪ.
car.Paſt.xʟ.ou.Val.xx.ſol.

In Hacheuuella ten& Godefrid.xv.ac.7.dim.car.7.ɪ.bord.Val
x.ſol.

In Neſtuda ten& Roƀ.xxx.ac.de.S.7.v.bord.Tc̄.dim.car.m̄
.ɪ.Tc̄ ual.x.ſol.m̄.xx.7 In hoc p̄dic̄to hund h̄t Sten.de placitis.
.c.ſol.

Hund de Witbric̄teſherna . Altenai ten& Rad de Sueno.

q̛d tenuit Leſtan liƀe p̄ Man.7.p̄ dim hid.7.xʟ.ac.Sēp.ɪ.
uilt.7.ɪ.bord.Tc̄.ɪɪ.ſer.m̄.ɪ.Sēp.ɪ.car in an̄io.7.dim.car hōu
Paſt.ʟ.ou.Tc̄.v.anim.7.xʟ.ou.m̄.v.an.7.ʟx.ou.7.xxvɪ.porc.
7.ɪɪ.runc.Tc̄ 7 p̄ ual.xx.ſol.m̄.xxvɪ.

Hainc̄tuna ten& Garner de.S.q̛d tenuit Godric liƀe.t.r.e.
p̄.m̄.7 p̄ dim.hid.7.xxxvɪɪ.ac.tc̄.ɪɪɪ.bor.m̄.ɪɪ.Sēp.ɪ.car.
v.ac.p̄ti.Tc̄.nichil.m̄.ɪɪɪ.an.ɪɪɪɪ.porc.xɪ.cap.Val.xx.ſol.
hoc.m̄.habuit.R.fili uuimarcæ.p̄ aduentū reḡ Wilti.

36   Aelmer holds PUDSEY (Hall) from Swein, which a Freeman of Robert's held as a manor, for ½ hide and 15 acres.
     Always 3 smallholders; 1 plough in lordship.
     Pasture, 50 sheep. Then 1 cob, 8 pigs and 25 sheep; now 11 pigs and 86 sheep.
   Value 30s.

37   Hugh holds PUDSEY (Hall) from Swein, which 1 free man held before 1066, and Robert had the jurisdiction, as a manor for 38 acres.
     Then 1 villager, now 2. Always ½ plough.
     Pasture, 30 sheep. Then 1 cob, 2 cattle, 10 pigs, 75 sheep; now 1 cob, 1 cow and 114 sheep.
   Value 10s.

38   In ASHINGDON Roger holds ½ hide from Swein, which Robert held.
     Always 1 smallholder.
     Pasture, 40 sheep. Then 1 plough, now ½; a whole one possible.
   Value 10s.

39   In SUTTON Roger holds ½ hide which Robert held before 1066.
     Always 1 plough.
     Pasture, 40 sheep.
   Value 20s.

40   In HAWKWELL Godfrey holds 15 acres. ½ plough.
     1 smallholder.
   Value 10s.

41   In EASTWOOD Robert holds 30 acres from Swein.
     5 smallholders. Then ½ plough, now 1.
   Value then 10s; now 20[s].

41a   In this said Hundred Swein has 100s from pleas.

Hundred of 'WIBERTSHERNE'

42   Ralph holds ILTNEY (Farm) from Swein, which Leofstan held   46 a
freely as a manor, for 1½ hides and 40 acres.
     Always 1 villager; 1 smallholder. Then 2 slaves, now 1.
     Always 1 plough in lordship; ½ men's plough.
     Pasture, 50 sheep. Then 5 cattle, 40 sheep; now 5 cattle, 60 sheep, 26 pigs and 2 cobs.
   Value then and later 20s; now 26[s].

43   Warner holds ASHELDHAM from Swein, which Godric held freely before 1066 as a manor, for ½ hide and 37 acres.
     Then 3 smallholders, now 2. Always 1 plough.
     Meadow, 5 acres. Then nothing; now 3 cattle, 4 pigs, 11 goats.
   Value 20s.
     Robert son of Wymarc had this manor after the arrival of King William.

⟨V⟩Hund de Witham Ruuuenhalā ten& Clarenbald de . S.

qd tenuit Leftan lib hō . ꝑ . xxx . ac . t . r . e . Sep . i . car in dnio . 7 . d

car . hom̄ . Tc . v . bord . m̄ . vi . Sep . ii . ſer . x . ac . pti . Paſt . de . iiii . ſot .

7 . i . ſoc . de . v . ac . tc . ii . an̄ . 7 . ii . runc . 7 . xv . ou̇ . m̄ . ii . an̄ . ii . runc .

. c . ou̇ . vi . porc . viii . cap̄ . ii . uaſa ap̄ . Tc . uat xl . ſot . m̄ . xxx .

⟨V⟩Nuthleam ten& Godebold . dim̄ . hid . 7 . xxx . ac . qd tenuit

Achi lib hō . t . r . e . ꝑ uno man̄ . Tc . ii . car . in dnio . m̄ . i . Tc . ii .

car . hom̄ . m̄ . i . Tc . iiii . uitt . m̄ . ii . Tc . iiii . bord . m̄ . v . Tc . ii . ſer .

m̄ . nutt . Tc . ſilu . xl . porc . m̄ . xxx . x . ac . pti . Tc . i . runc . 7 . ii . uac .

m̄ . ii . runc . 7 . viii . an̄ . xxx . porc . xi . ou̇ . x . uaſa . ap̄ . Tc . uat . xl . ſot .

m̄ . lx .

⟨V⟩Hund de Herlaua . Halingebiam ten& Galt . de . S . qd ten

Godric lib hō . ꝑ uno man̄ . 7 . ꝑ . ii . hid . 7 . dim̄ . Sep . ii . car . in dnio .

Tc . iii . car . hom̄ . m̄ . iiii . Tc . viii . uitt . m̄ . x . m̄ . xvii . bord . Sep

. iiii . ſer . Tc ſilu . cl . porc . m̄ . c . xxx . ac . pti . m̄ dim̄ . mot .

Tc . ii . runc . 7 . vi . an̄ . 7 . xxiiii . porc . xxx . ou̇ . xxx . cap . m̄ . ii .

putt . 7 . vii . an̄ . 7 . xiii . porc . l . ou̇ . xxxii . cap . vii . uaſa . apū .

46 b

Tc uat . c . ſot . m̄ . vi . lib .

⟨V⟩Hund de Dommauua . Willingehalam ten& Garner de

. Sueno qd tenuit . i . lib hō t . r . e . ꝑ . xx . ac . Tc . uat . iiii . ſot . m̄ viii .

⟨V⟩Dommauuā . ten& Edmar de . S . qd tenuit . i . lib hō . t . r . e . ꝑ

xxxvii . ac . 7 illæ . vii . ac . ſt additæ ꝑ aduentū reg̅ Witti . quæ

fuer̄ cujdā alt libi hōis . Tc . dim̄ . car . m̄ . i . Tc . ii . bor . m̄ . iii . Sep

. i . ſer . Silu . xxx . porc . v . ac . pti . m̄ . i . mot . Tc . iiii . an̄ . ix . porc .

xi . ou̇ . v . cap . m̄ . v . anim̄ . viii . porc . xiii . oues . vii . cap .

Tc uat . x . ſot . m̄ . xx .

Hundred of WITHAM

44 Clarenbold holds RIVENHALL from Swein, which Leofstan, a free
man, held for 30 acres before 1066. Always 1 plough in lordship;
½ men's plough.
Then 5 smallholders, now 6; always 2 slaves.
Meadow, 10 acres; pasture at 4s; 1 Freeman with 5 acres.
Then 2 cattle, 2 cobs, 15 sheep; now 2 cattle, 2 cobs,
100 sheep, 6 pigs, 8 goats, 2 beehives.
Value then 40s; now 30[s].

45 Godbold holds NOTLEY, ½ hide and 30 acres, which Aki, a free
man, held before 1066 as one manor. Then 2 ploughs in lordship,
now 1. Then 2 men's ploughs, now 1.
Then 4 villagers, now 2; then 4 smallholders, now 5; then 2
slaves, now none.
Woodland, then 40 pigs, now 30; meadow, 10 acres. Then 1 cob,
2 cows; now 2 cobs, 8 cattle, 30 pigs, 11 sheep, 10 beehives.
Value then 40s; now 60[s].

Hundred of HARLOW

46 Walter holds (Little) HALLINGBURY from Swein which Godric, a
free man, held as one manor for 2½ hides. Always 2 ploughs in
lordship. Then 3 men's ploughs, now 4.
Then 8 villagers, now 10; now 17 smallholders; always 4 slaves.
Woodland, then 150 pigs, now 100; meadow, 30 acres; now ½
mill. Then 2 cobs, 6 cattle, 24 pigs, 30 sheep, 30 goats; now
2 foals, 7 cattle, 13 pigs, 50 sheep, 32 goats, 7 beehives.
Value then 100s; now £6.   46 b

Hundred of DUNMOW

47 Warner holds WILLINGALE from Swein, which 1 free man held
before 1066 for 20 acres.
Value then 4s; now 8[s].

48 Edmer holds DUNMOW from Swein, which 1 free man held before
1066, for 37 acres, and the 7 acres were added after the arrival of
King William (and) were those of another free man. Then ½
plough, now 1.
Then 2 smallholders, now 3; always 1 slave.
Woodland, 30 pigs; meadow, 5 acres; now 1 mill. Then 4
cattle, 9 pigs, 11 sheep, 5 goats; now 5 cattle, 8 pigs, 13
sheep, 7 goats.
Value then 10s; now 20[s].

⌐Hund de Wenfiſtreu Mereſai ten& Sueñ in dñio qđ teñ
Roƀ fili uuimarcæ . t . r̃ . e . ᵱ . ᴔ . 7 . ᵱ . vi . hid . Sẽp . ii . car̃ . in dñio.
Tẽ . viii . car̃ . m̃ . vi . Tẽ . ix . uiƚƚ . m̃ . viii . Tẽ . xii . bor̃ . m̃ . xiiii.
Tẽ . iii . ſer̃ . m̃ nulƚ . Tẽ ſilu̅ . xl . porc̃ . v . ac̃ . pti . iiii . piſcinæ.
Tẽ . i . runc̃ . ix . añ . xxv . porc̃ . cvii . ou̅ . m̃ . iii . runc̃ . xii . añ.
. x . porc̃ . c . ou̅ . i . uas.aᵱ . Vaƚ . x . liƀ.

⌐Peltendunā ten& . Odo de Sueno qđ tenuit . i . liƀ . hõ . t̃ . r̃ . e . ᵱ ᴔ.
7 . ᵱ . dim . hid . Sẽp . dim . car̃ . Vaƚ . x . ſoƚ.

⌐Edburgetunā ten& Idẽ . ᵱ . xv . ac̃ . q̃s tenuit . i . liƀ . hõ . t̃ . r̃ . e.
Tẽ . i . liƀ homo . m̃ . i . borđ . v . ac̃ . pti . Vaƚ . v . ſoƚ

⌐Dimidium Hunđ de clauelinga ẽ ſueni . 7 placita de
eođ hunđ redđ̃ ſibi ᵽ annū . xxv . ſoƚ.

⌐Dimidiū Hunđ de Clauelinga Clauelinga ten&
Sueñ in dñio . qđ tenuit Roƀ fili uuimarcæ . t̃ . r̃ . e . ᵱ uno . Man.
7 . ᵱ . xv . hid . Tẽ . 7 ᵽ . iiii . car̃ in dñio . m̃ . v . Sẽp . xxv . car̃ hou̅.
7 . xvii . uiƚƚ . Tẽ 7 ᵽ . ix . borđ . m̃ . xxxvii . Tẽ 7 ᵽ . viii . ſer̃ . m̃ xii.

Tẽ ſilu̅ . ᴅcccc porc̃ . m̃ . ᴅc . xxxv . ac̃ . pti . Tẽ . i . moƚ . 7 . i . car̃.
poꞇ reſtaurari in hoc mañ . Tẽ . iii . runc̃ . 7 . xxv . añ . l . porc̃ . xl . ou̅
xv . cap̃ . xii . uaſa apū . m̃ . ii . runc̃ . 7 . i . puƚƚ xiiii . añ . xxi . porc̃.
. xc . ou̅ . xxiii . cap̃ . v . uaſa aᵱ . Tẽ uaƚ . xx . liƀ . m̃ . xxx.

⌐Berdane tenuit Godmañ . i . ſoc̃ . Roƀti . t̃ . r̃ . e . m̃ ten& Aluređ.
de . S . ᵱ . ᴔ . 7 . ᵱ . ii . hid . Sẽp . i . car̃ . in dñio . 7 . ii . car̃ . hom̃ . 7 . iiii . uiƚƚ.
7 . v . borđ . Tẽ 7 ᵽ . iiii . ſer̃ . m̃ nulƚ . Silu̅ . x . porc̃ . ii . ac̃ . pti . Tẽ
. xiiii . porc̃ . 7 . xxv . ou̅ . M̃ . iii . runc̃ . 7 . ii . puƚƚ . 7 . xiii . añ . 7 . xxi . porc̃.
. cxxii . ou̅ . viii . cap̃ . i . uas . aᵱ . Tẽ uaƚ . xxx . ſoƚ . m̃ . xl.

⌐Hund de Wibric̃teſherna . Haintunā ten& Rađ de . S.
ᵱ . ᴔ . 7 . ᵱ . dim hid . 7 . xxxvii . ac̃ . qđ tenuit . i . liƀ hõ . t̃ . r̃ . e . Sẽp . i . car̃.

Hundred of WINSTREE

49 Swein holds (East) MERSEA in lordship, which Robert son of Wymarc held before 1066 as a manor, for 6 hides. Always 2 ploughs in lordship. Then 8 [men's] ploughs, now 6.
 Then 9 villagers, now 8; then 12 smallholders, now 14; then 3 slaves, now none.
 Woodland, then 40 pigs; meadow, 5 acres; 4 fisheries. Then 1 cob, 9 cattle, 25 pigs, 107 sheep; now 3 cobs, 12 cattle, 10 pigs, 100 sheep, 1 beehive.
 Value £10.

50 Odo holds PELDON from Swein, which 1 free man held before 1066 as a manor, for ½ hide. Always ½ plough.
 Value 10s.

51 He also holds ABBERTON for 15 acres, which 1 free man held before 1066.
 Then 1 free man; now 1 smallholder.
 Meadow, 5 acres.
 Value 5s.

52 The Half-Hundred of CLAVERING is Swein's. The pleas of this Hundred pay him 25s a year.

Half-Hundred of CLAVERING

53 Swein holds CLAVERING in lordship, which Robert son of Wymarc held before 1066 as one manor, for 15 hides. Then and later 4 ploughs in lordship, now 5. Always 25 men's ploughs;
 17 villagers. Then and later 9 smallholders, now 37; then and later 8 slaves, now 12.
 Woodland, then 800 pigs, now 600; meadow, 35 acres; then   47 a
 1 mill; 1 plough can be restored in this manor. Then 3 cobs, 25 cattle, 50 pigs, 40 sheep, 15 goats, 12 beehives; now 2 cobs, 1 foal, 14 cattle, 21 pigs, 90 sheep, 23 goats, 5 beehives.
 Value then £20; now [£] 30.

54 Godman, a Freeman of Robert's, held BERDEN before 1066. Now Alfred holds it from Swein as a manor, for 2 hides. Always 1 plough in lordship; 2 men's ploughs.
 4 villagers; 5 smallholders. Then and later 4 slaves, now none.
 Woodland, 10 pigs; meadow, 2 acres. Then 14 pigs and 25 sheep; now 3 cobs, 2 foals, 13 cattle, 21 pigs, 122 sheep, 8 goats, 1 beehive.
 Value then 30s; now 40[s].

Hundred of 'WIBERTSHERNE'

55 Ralph holds ASHELDHAM from Swein as a manor, for ½ hide and 37 acres, which 1 free man held before 1066. Always 1 plough.

Tc̄.ɪɪɪ.bor.m̄.ɪɪ.v.ac̄.p̄ti.Val.xx.ſol. Hanc t̄rā habuit Rob
fili uuimarce .p aduentū reḡ Wilti.

⌐De Supdic̄to mancrio ſcilic& de Clauelinga tenet Anſgot.dim.h̄.
7.xxx.ac̄.de Sueno.7 Wicard.ɪɪɪ.uirḡ.7 Rob dim.hid.7.xv.ac̄.
7 Rad.xv.ac̄.7 int̄ totū.xɪɪɪɪ.bord.7.ɪɪɪ.car̄.7.dim.7 totū
ual.ɪɪɪɪ.lib in eod p̄tio.

⌐Hund de Lexendena. Eiland tenuit.R..p uno.Man.7..p.v.
hid.7.dim.m̄ ten&.S.in dn̄io. Sep.xvɪɪɪ.uilt.Tc̄.xxxɪɪɪ.bor.m̄.
.xlɪɪ.Sep.vɪɪ.ſer.7.ɪɪ.car̄.in dn̄io.7.x.car̄.hom̄.Silu.bc.porc̄.
xxɪɪɪɪ.ac̄.p̄ti.Sep.ɪ.mol.Tc̄.ual.x.lib.m̄.xɪɪ.De hoc maner̄.
ten& Godebold de Sueno.ɪ.hid.7.dim.7.xxx.ac̄.7.ɪɪ.uilt.
7.vɪɪɪ.bord.7.ɪɪ.car̄.in dn̄io.7.ɪɪ.car̄.hom̄.7 Val lx.ſol in
eod p̄tio. Adhuc ten& Idem.xxxvɪɪ.libos hōes.manentes.in
.ɪɪɪ.hid t̄ræ.q̄s habuit.Rob.t.r.e.7 Suen poſtea.Tc̄.int̄ eos.ɪɪɪɪ.

47 b

m̄.v.m̄.ɪ.mol.Silu.lx.porc̄.xɪɪɪɪ.ac̄.p̄ti Tc̄ ual.ɪɪɪɪ.lib.m̄
.c.ſol.7 q̄dā lib homo erat cōmdat Robto tenuit.vɪɪ.ac̄.
7.dim.7 pot̄at ire q̄ uell&.7 illā t̄rā ht̄ Suen.Val.v.ſol.

⌐Hund de Celmeresforda.Borham ten&.Osbt.de.S.qd̄ ten.
Turchill .p uno Man.7..p.ɪ.hid.Sep.ɪ.bord.m̄.ɪ.ſer.Tc̄.ɪ.car̄.m̄
null.vɪɪɪ.ac̄ p̄ti. Val.xx.ſol.

⌐Hund de Angra Staplefort ten& Siric̄.de Sueno.qd̄ ten.
Godric̄..p uno man.7..p.v.hid.7 de his.v.hid.dedit ſuis.x.libis
hominib᷒ libe.ɪɪɪɪ.hid.7.ɪ.retinuit in dn̄io.7 pq̄ rex aduenit.

47 a, b

Then 3 smallholders, now 2.
Meadow, 5 acres.
Value 20s.
Robert son of Wymarc had this land after the arrival of King William.

[Half-Hundred of CLAVERING]

56 Of the above manor, namely CLAVERING, Ansgot holds ½ hide and 30 acres from Swein, Wicard 3 virgates, Robert ½ hide and 15 acres, and Ralph 15 acres.
In total 14 smallholders; 3½ ploughs.
Value of the whole £4 in the same assessment.

Hundred of LEXDEN

57 R(obert) held NAYLAND as one manor, for 5½ hides. Now Swein holds it in lordship.
Always 18 villagers. Then 33 smallholders, now 42. Always 7 slaves; 2 ploughs in lordship; 10 men's ploughs.
Woodland, 600 pigs; meadow, 24 acres; always 1 mill.
Value then £10; now [£] 12.
Of this manor, Godbold holds from Swein 1½ hides and 30 acres.
2 villagers; 8 smallholders. 2 ploughs in lordship. 2 men's ploughs.
Value 60s in the same assessment.
He also holds 37 free men who dwell on 3 hides of land, whom Robert had before 1066, and Swein later on.
Then among them 4 [ploughs], now 5.   47 b
Now 1 mill; woodland, 60 pigs; meadow, 14 acres.
Value then £4; now 100s.
A free man was under the patronage of Robert. He held 7½ acres and could go whither he would. Swein has that land.
Value 5s.

Hundred of CHELMSFORD

58 Osbert holds BOREHAM from Swein, which Thorkell held as one manor, for 1 hide.
Always 1 smallholder. Now 1 slave. Then 1 plough, now none.
Meadow, 8 acres.
Value 20s.

Hundred of ONGAR

59 Siric holds STAPLEFORD (Tawney) from Swein, which Godric held as one manor, for 5 hides. Of these 5 hides, he freely gave 4 hides to his 10 free men and kept one in lordship. After the King came,

dono reg̅ tenuit Rob̅ . I . hid̅ . 7 Suen̅ fili̅ ej adjunxit . IIII . hid̅ . cū
ista . post morte̅ patris sui . Te̅ in . I . hida . null̅ bordari erat . 7 te̅
in . IIII . hid̅ . vi . bord̅ . m̅ . II . uilt̅ . 7 xviii . bord̅ . Silu̅ . ccc . porc̅ . xx .
ac̅ . p̅ti . Sep̅ . I . mol̅ . Te̅ . ual̅ . viii . lib̅ . m̅ . x . Te̅ . in dn̅io . I . uac̅ . 7
. xiii . ou̅ . m̅ . viii . an̅ . 7 . xvii . porc̅ . cxviii . ou̅ . II . uasa . apū .

ᐱTeidanam ten& Rob̅ de . S . qd̅ tenuit . Godric̅ . p̅ uno man̅ . 7 . p̅ .
III . hid̅ . 7 . lxxx . ac̅ . 7 . S . ten& hoc Man̅ de dono regis . Wilt̅i qd̅ dedit
patri . suo . Rob̅to . Te̅ . v . uilt̅ . m̅ . I . Te̅ . III . bord̅ . m̅ . xvii . Te̅ . IIII . ser̅ .
m̅ . null̅ . Te̅ . in dn̅io . II . car̅ . m̅ . III . Te̅ . int̅ h̅o̅e̅s . IIII . car̅ . m̅ . III .
Silu̅ . ꝺ . porc̅ . xxviii . ac̅ . p̅ti . Te̅ . I . runc̅ . 7 . xii . an̅ . lx . por . c . ou̅ .
m̅ . III . runc̅ . III . pult̅ . xiii . an̅ . xxxix . porc̅ . cxlviii . ou̅ . Te̅ . ual̅ .
vi . lib̅ . 7 qn̅ rec̅ simit̅ . m̅ ual̅ . ix .

ᐱHund de Ceffeurda . Warleia̅ tenuit Godric̅ lib̅e . p̅ uno Man̅ .
7 . p̅ . II . hid̅ . t̅ . r̅ . e̅ . m̅ . S . simit̅ in suo dn̅io . Te̅ . II . uilt̅ . m̅ . III . Te̅ . II .
bord̅ . m̅ . viii . Te̅ . III . ser̅ . m̅ . I . Sep̅ . II . car̅ . in dn̅io . Te̅ . int̅ h̅o̅es . I . car̅ .
m̅ . II . 7 . dim̅ . Silu̅ . cl . porc̅ . III . ac̅ . p̅ti . Te̅ . II . runc̅ . 7 . vii . an̅ . 7 . xvii . porc̅ .

★

48 a
Te̅ ual̅ . IIII . lib̅ . 7 . qn̅ rec̅ . similit̅ . m̅ . vi . lib̅ .

★

ᐱHelitunā ten& Leuuin̅ de . S . qd̅ tenuit Vstan̅ . lib̅e . p̅ . ꝯ . 7 . p̅ . I .
hid̅ . t̅ . r̅ . e̅ . Te̅ . III . bord̅ . m̅ . IIII . 7 . I . car̅ . I . uac̅ . 7 . II . an̅ . xvi . porc̅ .
. xxx . ou̅ . Val̅ . xx . sol̅ .

ᐱDim̅ Hund de Melduna . In Melduna tenuit . Rob̅ . dim̅ .
hid̅ . m̅ ten& . S . 7 . Guner̅ de . eo . 7 . in hac t̅ra hab& rex . IIII . sol̅ de
consuetudine . 7 facit̅ adjutorium cum alijs burgensib̅z . inuenire
caballū in exercitu . 7 ad naue̅ faciendā . c&as uero consuetudines . ħt
Suen̅ . Sep̅ . I . bor̅ . 7 . I . car̅ . 7 . ual̅ . xx . sol̅ .

Robert held 1 hide as a gift of the King; Swein, his son, joined 4 hides with that one after his father's death.

Then on 1 hide there were no smallholders, then on 4 hides 6 smallholders; now 2 villagers and 18 smallholders.

Woodland, 300 pigs; meadow, 20 acres; always 1 mill.

Value then £8; now [£] 10.

Then in lordship 1 cow and 13 sheep; now 8 cattle, 17 pigs, 118 sheep, 2 beehives.

60 Robert holds THEYDON (Mount) from Swein, which Godric held as one manor, for 3 hides and 80 acres. Swein holds this manor as a gift of King William, which he gave to his father, Robert.

Then 5 villagers, now 1; then 3 smallholders, now 17; then 4 slaves, now none. Then 2 ploughs in lordship, now 3.

Then among the men 4 ploughs, now 3.

Woodland, 500 pigs; meadow, 28 acres. Then 1 cob, 12 cattle, 60 pigs, 100 sheep; now 3 cobs, 3 foals, 13 cattle, 39 pigs, 148 sheep.

Value then £6; when acquired, the same. Value now [£] 9.

Hundred of CHAFFORD

61 Godric held WARLEY freely as one manor, for 2 hides before 1066. Now Swein (holds it) likewise in his lordship.

Then 2 villagers, now 3; then 2 smallholders, now 8; then 3 slaves, now 1. Always 2 ploughs in lordship. Then among the men 1 plough, now 2½.

Woodland, 150 pigs; meadow, 3 acres. Then 3 cobs, 7 cattle and 17 pigs.

Value then £4; when acquired, the same; now £6.   48 a

62 Leofstan holds KENNINGTONS from Swein, which Wulfstan held freely as a manor, for 1 hide before 1066.

Then 3 smallholders, now 4. 1 plough.

1 cow, 2 cattle, 16 pigs, 30 sheep.

Value 20s.

Half-Hundred of MALDON

63 Robert held ½ hide in MALDON. Now Swein holds it and Gunner from him. In this land the King has 3s from customary dues; and he aids the other burgesses to find a horse on campaign and to make a ship. But Swein has the other dues.

Always 1 smallholder; 1 plough.

Value 20s.

⊦Hund de Tendringe . Almeſtedā tenuit Roƀ fiłꝰ uuimąrc.

m̄ Suen̄ . 7 Siric de eo . ꝑ uno Man̄ . 7 . ꝑ . viii . hiđ . Tc̄ . xiiii . uiłł

m̄ . xiii . Tc̄ . xxxi . borđ . m̄ . xxxvi . Tc̄ . vi . ſer . m̄ . i . Tc̄ . in dn̄io.

. iii . car . m̄ . iiii . Tc̄ . xix . car hom̄ . m̄ . xviii . Siłu . ᶗ . porc.

xxii . ac . p̃ti . Paſt . lx . ou . Sēp . i . moł . 7 . i . ſał . Tc̄ . iii . runc.

7 . xviii . an̄ . 7 xxx . porc . cl . ou . xl . cap . v . uaſa aꝑ . m̄ . v.

runc . x . an̄ . xxxii . porc . cxc . ou . lxxx . cap . ii . uaſa apū.

Tc̄ uał . ix . liƀ . m̄ . x.

⊦Fuletunā ten& Odarđ . de . S . qđ tenuit Bricſi . ꝑ . i . hiđ.

x . ac . min̄ . 7 . ꝑ . uno Man̄ . Hanc tr̄a tenuit Iſte liƀe . & q̃ndo

rex uenit in hanc tr̄a ꞉ utlagauit . 7 . R . acceꝑ . tr̄a ſuam . pea

habuit . S . Sēp . ibi . ē . i . borđ . 7 . i . ſer . 7 . i . car . 7 . ii . ac . p̃ti . paſt.

. c . ou . Tc̄ . nichil rec . m̄ . vi . an̄ . 7 . x . porc . 7 . xx . ou . 7 . ii.

uaſa apū . Tc̄ . uał . x . soł . m̄ . xx.

⊦Hund de Tureſtapla . Toleſhuntā ten& Odo . de Sueno

qđ tenuit Bru̅n ꝑ . Man̄ . 7 . ꝑ . i . hiđ . 7 . dim̄ . 7 . xl . ac . ſ̧ Roƀ habuit

48 b

pquam rex uenit in hanc tr̄a . 7 m̄ ħt . S . M̄ . ibi . sꝚ . iiii . borđ

Tc̄ . ii . ſer . m̄ . i . Siłu . xii . porc . Paſt . xx . ou . Tc̄ . ii . an̄ . 7 . i . runc . 7

. xx . ou . m̄ . xii . an̄ . ii . runc . xii . porc . lxxx . ou . Tc̄ uał . xx . soł.

m̄ . xxv.

⊦Totham tenuit Gunner . t . r . e . 7 adhuc ten& ſub Sueno . ꝑ . xxx.

ac . Sēp . iii . borđ . Tc̄ . dim̄ . car . m̄ ſimił . Siłu . xx . porc . Paſt . lx . ou.

uał . x . soł.

Hundred of TENDRING

64   Robert son of Wymarc held ELMSTEAD. Now Swein (holds it) and
     Siric from him as one manor, for 8 hides.
         Then 14 smallholders, now 13; then 31 smallholders, now 36;
             then 6 slaves, now 1. Then 3 ploughs in lordship, now 4.
             Then 19 men's ploughs, now 18.
         Woodland, 500 pigs; meadow, 22 acres; pasture, 60 sheep.
             Always 1 mill; 1 salt-house. Then 3 cobs, 18 cattle, 30 pigs,
             150 sheep, 40 goats, 5 beehives; now 5 cobs, 10 cattle,
             32 pigs, 190 sheep, 80 goats, 2 beehives.
     Value then £9; now [£] 10.

65   Odard holds FOULTON from Swein, which Brictsi held for 1 hide
     less 10 acres, as one manor. He held this land freely and when the
     King came to this land, he was outlawed and Robert received his
     land; later on Swein had (it).
         Always 1 smallholder there; 1 slave; 1 plough.
         Meadow, 2 acres; pasture, 100 sheep. Then he acquired
             nothing; now 6 cattle, 10 pigs, 20 sheep and 2 beehives.
     Value then 10s; now 20[s].

Hundred of THURSTABLE

66   Odo holds TOLLESHUNT from Swein, which Brown held as a manor,
     for 1½ hides and 40 acres. But Robert had it after the King came   48 b
     to this land and now Swein has it.
         Now 4 smallholders there; then 2 slaves, now 1.
         Woodland, 12 pigs; pasture, 20 sheep. Then 2 cattle, 1 cob and
             20 sheep; now 12 cattle, 2 cobs, 12 pigs, 80 sheep.
     Value then 20s; now 25[s].

67   Gunner held (Little) TOTHAM before 1066 and still holds it under
     Swein for 30 acres.
         Always 3 smallholders. Then ½ plough, now the same.
         Woodland, 20 pigs; pasture, 60 sheep.
     Value 10s.

TERRA EudoniS dapiferi.

〉Hunð de Witham Brachestedam ten& Ricarð de . E.

qð tenuit tegn reg̃ . p uno man̄ . 7 . p . ii . hið . xv . ac̃ . min̄ . Sẽp . ii .

car in dñio . 7 . iii . car̄ . hoū . Tc̃ . v . uilt̃ . m̃ . vi . Tc̃ . iiii . borð . m̃ . vi .

Tc̃ . ii . ser̄ . m̃ null̄ . Silua . ccc . porc̃ . xxx . ac̃ . p̃ti . m̃ dim̄ mol̄ .

. i . soc̃ . de . iiii . ac̃ . Tc̃ . ii . runc̃ . 7 . xiiii . an̄ . xl . porc̃ . lxxx . ou . m̃ . i .

runc̃ . vi . an̄ . xlvi . porc̃ . cx . ou . iiii . uasa apū . Val̄ . viii . lib̄ .

〉Dim̄ Hunð de Herlaua . Herlauā ten& Turgis de . Eudone

qð tenuit Goduin̄ lib̄ homo . t . r . e . p . M̃ . 7 . p . i . hið . 7 . iii . uirg̃ . Tc̃ .

. ii . car in dñio . m̃ . i . Tc̃ . i . car̄ hom . m̃ nulla . Tc̃ . iii . uilt̃ . m̃ . null̄ .

m̃ . ii . borð . Tc̃ . ii . ser̄ . m̃ . i . Silū . l . porc̃ . x . ac̃ . p̃ti . Tc̃ . i . an̄ . 7

xxx . ou . m̃ . xviii . an̄ . iiii . runc̃ . xviiii . porc̃ . lxxv . ii . uasa ap̄ .

De hac t̃ra st̃ . l . ac̃ . que fuer̄ additæ . t . r . Willi . 7 eas addidit Lefsi huic

t̃ræ . Sẽp ual̄ . xl . sol̄ .

〉Hunð de dommauua . Rodinges ten& turgisus de Eudone

qð tenuit Samar̄ lib̄ hõ . t . r . e . p . i . hið . 7 . dim̄ . 7 . xlv . ac̃ . Sẽp . ii . car̄

in dñio . Tc̃ . ii . car̄ . hom . m̃ . i . Tc̃ . ix . uilt̃ . m̃ . iii . tc̃ . i . borð . m̃

. iii . Tc̃ . iii . ser̄ . m̃ . i . Silū . c . porc̃ . xix . ac̃ . p̃ti . Tc̃ . i . runc̃ . m̃ .

. vii . Tc̃ . x . an̄ . m̃ . xxv . Tc̃ . vi . porc̃ . m̃ lxxxix . Tc̃ . l . ou . m̃ . ccxxv .

m̃ . lv . cap̃ . 7 . viii . uasa ap̄ . Tc̃ ual̄ . c . sol̄ . m̃ . vi . Hoc Man̄ . calūpniat̃ abb̄ de eli .

〉Lindeseles ten& Eudo in dñio . qð tenuit Ulmar̄ lib̄ hõ . t . r . e . | teste hunð̄ .

. p uno Man̄ . 7 . p . i . hið . Sẽp . ii . car̄ . in dñio . 7 . iii . car̄ . hom . ix . uilt̃ .

7 . i . pbr̄ . Tc̃ . i . borð . m̃ . ix . Tc̃ . iiii . ser̄ . m̃ . i . Silū . xxx . porc̃ .

vi . ac̃ . p̃ti . m̃ . i . mol̄ . Tc̃ . i . runc̃ . 7 . v . an̄ . 7 . lx . porc̃ . M̃ . i . runc̃ . 7

Tc̃ ual̄ . c . sol̄ . m̃ . vi . lib̄ Et hoc manerium tale erat qū recep̄ .

Hundred of WITHAM

1   Richard holds (Great) BRAXTED from Eudo, which a King's thane held as one manor, for 2 hides less 15 acres. Always 2 ploughs in lordship; 3 men's ploughs.

> Then 5 villagers, now 6; then 4 smallholders, now 6; then 2 slaves, now none.
>
> Woodland, 300 pigs; meadow, 30 acres; now ½ mill; 1 Freeman with 4 acres. Then 2 cobs, 14 cattle, 40 pigs, 80 sheep; now 1 cob, 6 cattle, 46 pigs, 110 sheep, 4 beehives.

Value £8.

Half-Hundred of HARLOW

2   Thorgils holds HARLOW from Eudo which Godwin, a free man, held before 1066 as a manor, for 1 hide and 3 virgates. Then 2 ploughs in lordship, now 1. Then 1 men's plough, now none.

> Then 3 villagers, now none; now 2 smallholders; then 2 slaves, now 1.
>
> Woodland, 50 pigs; meadow, 10 acres. Then 1 (head of) cattle and 30 sheep; now 18 cattle, 4 cobs, 19 pigs, 75 [sheep], 2 beehives.

Of this land, there are 50 acres which were added after 1066 and Leofsi added them to this land.

Value always 40s.

Hundred of DUNMOW

3   Thorgils holds ('Morrell') RODING from Eudo which Saemer, a free man, held before 1066 for 1½ hides and 45 acres. Always 2 ploughs in lordship. Then 2 men's ploughs, now 1.

> Then 9 villagers, now 3; then 1 smallholder, now 3; then 3 slaves, now 1.
>
> Woodland, 100 pigs; meadow, 19 acres. Then 1 cob, now 7; then 10 cattle, now 25; then 6 pigs, now 89; then 50 sheep, now 225; now 55 goats and 8 beehives.

Value then 100s; now £6.

The Abbot of Ely lays claim to this manor as the Hundred testifies.

4   Eudo holds LINDSELL in lordship which Wulfmer, a free man, held before 1066 as one manor, for 1 hide. Always 2 ploughs in lordship; 3 men's ploughs;

> 9 villagers; 1 priest. Then 1 smallholder, now 9; then 4 slaves, now 1.
>
> Woodland, 30 pigs; meadow, 6 acres; now 1 mill. Then 1 cob, 5 cattle, 60 pigs; now 1 cob, ...

Value then 100s; now £6. And this manor was worth that much when acquired.   49 b

⁊Hund̄ de Witbricteſherna   Mundunā tenuit Goduin⁹ teinn⁹

reḡ . ꝑ uno man̄ . 7 . ꝑ . x . hid . M̄ ten& Eudo in dn̄io . Tc̄ . x . uitt . m̄ . xv .

Tc̄ . viii . bord̄ . m̄ . xiiii . Tc̄ . ix . ſer . m̄ . vii . 7 . ii . franci hōes hn̄tes . dim̄ . hid .

quā occupauit Liſois . q̇a un illoꝗ utllagauit . In hoc manerio . ſt̄ . iiii .

car̄ . in dn̄io . Tc̄ . viii . car̄ . hom̄ . m̄ . x . 7 . ii . arpenni uineæ . Silu . xxiiii .

porc̄ . Paſt̄ . cc . oů Tc̄ . iiii . runc̄ . 7 . viii . an̄ . xl . porc̄ . ccl . m̄ . iiii . runc̄ .

7 . xv . an̄ . 7 . lxv . porc̄ . cccliiii . oů . iiii . uaſa ap̄ . Tc̄ . uat̄ . x . litt .

m̄ . xvii : | huic manerio adjacent . xxx . ac̄ . Tc̄ . ualebant . xxx . đ .

m̄ . xxxvi . Adjacent adhuc . xx . ac̄ . de Wringehala . q̇s ten& . i . ſoc̄ .

Tc̄ . uat̄ . xx . đ . m̄ . iii . ſot .

⁊Lalinge ten& Ricard̄ de . E . q̇đ tenuit Vluric̄ caſſa ꝑ . m̄ . 7 . ꝑ . iii

hid . t̄ . r̄ . e̅ . 7 dim̄ ; Tc̄ . iiii . ſer . m̄ . iii . m̄ . i . bord̄ . Tc̄ . ii . car̄ in dn̄io . m̄

. i . Tc̄ . i . runc̄ . m̄ n̄ . Tc̄ . lxxxvii . oů . m̄ . lxiii . Tc̄ . uat̄ . lx . ſot . qn̄ rec̄ .

. xl . ſot . m̄ . iiii . litt .

Steplam ten& Idē . R . de . E . q̇đ tenuit Normann . t̄ . r̄ . e̅ . ꝑ . m̄ . 7 . pro

. iii . hid . 7 . xxxv . ac̄ . Sēp . i . bord̄ . 7 . ii . ſer . 7 . ii . car̄ . Silu . x . porc̄ . Tc̄ . vi .

anim̄ . m̄ . xxvii . Sēp . i . runc̄ . 7 . xv . porc̄ . Tc̄ . cxx . oů . m̄ . clx . Vat̄

. iiii . litt .

⁊Donā ten& Idē . R . de . E . q̇đ tenuit Modinc̄ . t̄ . r̄ . e̅ . ꝑ . m̄ . 7 . ꝑ . ii .

hid . 7 . xx . ac̄ . Sēp . ii . bord̄ . 7 . ii . ſer . 7 . i . car̄ . Paſtura . c . oů . Tc̄ . i . runc̄ .

m̄ . iii . m̄ . iii . an̄ . Tc̄ . cxx . oů . m̄ . clx . i . min̄ . Vat̄ . lx . ſot .

⁊Landunā ten& Idē . R . de . E . q̇đ tenuerunt . iiii . libi hōes . t̄ . r̄ . e̅ .

ꝑ . dim̄ hid . 7 . xx . ac̄ . Sēp . dim̄ . car̄ . Vat̄ . x . ſot . ⁊ Acletā ten& Idē

de . E . q̇đ ten̄ . Modinc̄ ꝑ . m̄ . 7 . ꝑ . i . 7 dim̄ . 7 . x . ac̄ . Sēp . i . bord̄ . 7 . i . car̄ .

50 a

paſtura . c . ouibꝗ Sēp . ii . animat̄ . 7 . lxxx . oů . 7 . ix . porc̄ . Tc̄ 7 poſt uat̄ . xl .

ſot . m̄ . l .

Hundred of 'WIBERTSHERNE'

5 Godwin, a King's thane, held MUNDON as one manor, for 10 hides. Now Eudo holds it in lordship.

Then 10 villagers, now 15; then 8 smallholders, now 14; then 9 slaves, now 7. 2 freemen who have ½ hide which Lisois appropriated because one of them was outlawed. In this manor are 4 ploughs in lordship. Then 8 men's ploughs, now 10.

2 *arpents* of vines; woodland, 24 pigs; pasture, 200 sheep. Then 4 cobs, 8 cattle, 40 pigs, 250 [sheep]; now 4 cobs, 15 cattle, 65 pigs, 354 sheep, 4 beehives.

Value then £10; now [£] 17. It was at a revenue under Eudo himself for £19.

30 acres are attached to this manor.

Value then 30d; now 36[d].

A further 20 acres of *Wringehala* are attached, which 1 Freeman holds.

Value then 20d; now 3s.

6 Richard holds LAWLING from Eudo, which Wulfric Cave held as a manor, for 3½ hides before 1066.

Then 4 slaves, now 3; now 1 smallholder. Then 2 ploughs in lordship, now 1.

Then 1 cob, now none; then 87 sheep, now 63.

Value then 60s; when acquired, 40s; now £4.

7 Richard also holds STEEPLE from Eudo, which Norman held before 1066 as a manor, for 3 hides and 35 acres.

Always 1 smallholder; 2 slaves; 2 ploughs.

Woodland, 10 pigs. Then 6 cattle, now 27. Always 1 cob; 15 pigs. Then 120 sheep, now 160.

Value £4.

8 Richard also holds DOWN (Hall) from Eudo, which Moding held before 1066 as a manor, for 2 hides and 20 acres.

Always 2 smallholders; 2 slaves; 1 plough.

Pasture, 100 sheep. Then 1 cob, now 3; now 3 cattle; then 120 sheep, now 160 less 1.

Value 60s.

9 Richard also holds *LANDUNA* from Eudo, which 4 free men held before 1066 for ½ hide and 20 acres. Always ½ plough.

Value 10s.

10 He also holds *ACLETA* from Eudo, which Moding held as a manor, for 1½ [hides] and 10 acres.

Always 1 smallholder; 1 plough.

Pasture, 100 sheep. Always 2 cattle, 80 sheep and 9 pigs.

Value then and later 40s; now 50[s].

50 a

Hund de Rochefort. Hechuuellā ten& Pirot de . Eudone qđ teñ
Vlmer . t . r . e . ꝑ Man . 7 . ꝑ . III . hid . 7 . dim . xv . ac . miñ . Tc . xI . uilli . m̃
VIII . Sep . v . bord . Tc . II . ser . m̃ . III . Sep . II . car . in dñio . Tc . vI . car . hominū . m̃
v . IIII . ac . ꝑti . Silu . x . porc . Tc . II . runc . 7 . v . añ . cII . ou . xx . porc . m̃ . xvI .
añ . cvI . ou . xx . porc . II . uasa apū . Tc 7 ꝑ ual . vI . liƀ . m̃ . vII .

In Supđicto hund de đomauua ten& . Ricard de Eudone . I . Man
de . Ix . ac . qđ uocat . Brochesheuot . qđ tenuer . II . sochem . t . r . e . de abƀe
de eli . Tc . III . car in dnio . m̃ . II . 7 . dim . M . I . car hom . 7 . II . uilt . Tc . III . bor
m̃ . v . Tc . III . ser . m̃ . I . Silu . c . porc . vI . ac . ꝑti . Tc . I . runc . 7 . III . añ . 7 . xvI .
porc . m̃ . v . añ . xxxIII . porc . Tc 7 ꝑ ual . Lx . sol . m̃ . IIII . liƀ .

Scelgā ten& Eudo in dñio qđ tenuit Vlmar liƀ hō . t . r . e . ꝑ . M̃ . 7 . ꝑ . dim
hida . Sep . dim car in dñio . m̃ . II . bord . Silu . xvI . porc . IIII . ac . ꝑti . Val
sep . x . sol .

Dommauuā ten& . Rad de . E . qđ tenuit . I . liƀ hō . t . r . e . ꝑ Man .
7 . ꝑ . xxxvII . ac . 7 dim . Sep . dim . car in dñio . 7 . dim . car . hom . 7 . II .
uilt . m̃ . II . bor . Tc . I . ser . m̃ null . Silu . xv . porc . IIII . ac . ꝑti . Tc 7 ꝑ ual . x . sol
m̃ . xx . 7 in ead uilla alie . xxx . ac . 7 dim . qs tenuit ali liƀ hō . in qƀ ꝫ idē
ē qđ in alijs . 7 . tantundē ualent .

Hund de Vdelesfort . Tacheleiam ten& . E . in dñio qđ tenuit
Vlmar liƀ hō . t . r . e . ꝑ . Man . 7 . ꝑ . I . hid . 7 . xv . ac . Sep . II . car in dñio .
7 . II . car hom . Tc . III . uilt . m̃ . v . 7 . I . pƀr . Tc . III . bor . P 7 . m̃ . x . Sep . II .
ser . Tc silu . M̃ . porc . Post 7 m̃ . dc . xvI . ac . ꝑti . Tc . I . runc . 7 . xIIII . anim .
xxx . porc . xxx . cap . Lxxx . ou . m̃ . II . runc xx . añ . xLIII . porc cIII . ou

50 b
xL . caꝑ . Tc 7 post ual . vIII . liƀ . m̃ x .

Hundred of ROCHFORD

11 Pirot holds HAWKWELL from Eudo, which Wulfmer held before
1066 as a manor, for 3½ hides less 15 acres.
  Then 11 villagers, now 8; always 5 smallholders. Then 2
    slaves, now 3. Always 2 ploughs in lordship. Then 6 men's
    ploughs, now 5.
  Meadow, 4 acres; woodland, 10 pigs. Then 2 cobs, 5 cattle,
    102 sheep, 20 pigs; now 16 cattle, 106 sheep, 20 pigs,
    2 beehives.
Value then and later £6; now [£] 7.

In the above Hundred of DUNMOW

12 Richard holds from Eudo 1 manor with 9 acres which is called
BROXTED, which 2 Freemen held before 1066 from the Abbot of
Ely. Then 3 ploughs in lordship, now 2½. Now 1 men's plough;
  2 villagers. Then 3 smallholders, now 5; then 3 slaves, now 1.
Woodland, 100 pigs; meadow, 6 acres. Then 1 cob, 3 cattle,
    16 pigs; now 5 cattle, 33 pigs.
Value then and later 60s; now £4.

13 Eudo holds SHELLOW (Bowells) in lordship which Wulfmer, a free
man, held before 1066 as a manor, for ½ hide. Always ½ plough
in lordship.
  Now 2 smallholders.
  Woodland, 16 pigs; meadow, 4 acres.
Value always 10s.

14 Ralph holds DUNMOW from Eudo, which 1 free man held before
1066 as a manor, for 37½ acres. Always ½ plough in lordship;
½ men's plough;
  2 villagers. Now 2 smallholders; then 1 slave, now none.
  Woodland, 15 pigs; meadow, 4 acres.
Value then and later 10s; now 20[s].
  In the same village another 37½ acres which another free man
held and on which there is the same as on the others.
Value as much.

Hundred of UTTLESFORD

15 Eudo holds TAKELEY in lordship which Wulfmer, a free man, held
before 1066 as a manor, for 1 hide and 15 acres. Always 2 ploughs
in lordship; 2 men's ploughs.
  Then 3 villagers, now 5 and 1 priest; then 3 smallholders,
    later and now 10; always 2 slaves.
  Woodland, then 1000 pigs, later and now 600; meadow, 16
    acres. Then 1 cob, 14 cattle, 30 pigs, 30 goats, 80 sheep;
    now 2 cobs, 20 cattle, 43 pigs, 103 sheep, 40 goats. 50 b
Value then and later £8; now [£] 10.

Hund de Clauelinga . Plicedanā ten& Ricard̄ de . E . q̄d tenuer̄ . II .
liƀi hōes . t . r . e . p̄ . Man̄ . 7 . p̄ . v . hid̄ . xx . ac̄ . min̄ . Tc̄ . IIII . car̄ . in dn̄io . Poſt
7 m̄ . II . Tc̄ . 7 poſt . I . car̄ . hom̄ . m̄ . III . Tc̄ . 7 . p̄ . II . uiƚƚ . m̄ . vi . tc̄ . 7 poſt . II .
bord̄ . m̄ . xvi . tc̄ . 7 p̄ . II . ſer̄ . m̄ . nulƚ . Silu̅ . xx . porc̄ . xx . ac̄ . p̄ti . Tc̄ . II .
runc̄ . m̄ . nulƚ . tc̄ . II . anim̄ . M̄ . lxvi . porc̄ . Tc̄ . ccc . oū . m̄ . cc . vi . uaſa ap̄ .
Tc̄ . 7 p̄ uaƚ . c . ſoƚ . m̄ . viii . liƀ . de hac tr̄a calumpniat̄ . G . de magna
uiƚƚa . II . hid̄ . xx . ac̄ . min̄ . 7 . hund̄ teſtat̄ ei .

Hund de Laxendena . Buccheſted̄a ten& Artur̄ de . E . q̄d ten̄
Grim . p̄ . m̄ . 7 . p̄ . I . hid̄ . Tc̄ . I . uiƚƚ . m̄ null̄ . Tc̄ . II . bord̄ . m̄ . ix . Sēp . I .
car̄ in dn̄io . tc̄ . II . car̄ . hom̄ . m̄ . I . Silu̅ . xlii . porc̄ . II . ac̄ . p̄ti . Tc̄ . vi .
anim̄ . m̄ . IIII . Tc̄ . xxx . oū . m̄ . lxiiii . Tc̄ . x . porc̄ . m̄ . xiii . m̄ . xiii . cap̄ .
7 . I . uas̄ . ap̄ . Tc̄ uaƚ . xx . ſoƚ . m̄ . xl . 7 q̄d̄a liƀ tenuit . v . ac̄ . m̄ ten& Id̄e
Artur̄ de . E . Sēp . dim̄ . car̄ . ual̄ . v . ſoƚ .

Hund de Angra . Taindn̄a ten& . Eudo in dn̄io q̄d tenuit
Vlmar̄ p̄ . I . hid̄ . 7 . xl . ac̄ . t . r . e . Tc̄ . IIII . uiƚƚ . m̄ . vi . tc̄ . II . bor̄ . m̄ . IIII .
tc̄ . IIII . ſer̄ . m̄ . I . Sēp . II . car̄ in dn̄io . 7 . II . car̄ . hom̄ . Silu̅ . cccc . porc̄ .
. v . ac̄ . p̄ti . Sēp . II . runc̄ . Tc̄ . viii . an̄ . m̄ . xiii . Tc̄ . xxxv . porc̄ . m̄ . lxvi .
tc̄ . lxxxvii . oū . m̄ . c . 7 . xv . cap̄ . Tc̄ . II . uaſa ap̄ . m̄ . vi . Tc̄ 7 p̄ uaƚ .
xl . ſoƚ . m̄ . IIII . liƀ . 7 . I . ſoc̄ tenuit . vi . ac̄ . q̄ pot̄at uend̄e ſuā tr̄a
ſ; ſoca remanebat in manerio . Vaƚ . xii . d̄

Roinges ten& . E . in dn̄io . q̄d tenuit Vlmar̄ p̄ . m̄ . 7 . p̄ . III . hid̄ . t . r . e .
Sēp . vii . uiƚƚ . m̄ . II . bord̄ . Sēp . IIII . ſer̄ . 7 . II . car̄ . in dn̄io . 7 III . car̄ . hoū .

Hundred of CLAVERING

16 Richard holds PLEDGDON (Hall) from Eudo, which 2 free men held
before 1066 as a manor, for 5 hides less 20 acres. Then 4 ploughs
in lordship, later and now 2. Then and later 1 men's plough, now 3.
  Then and later 2 villagers, now 6; then and later 2
    smallholders, now 16; then and later 2 slaves, now none.
  Woodland, 20 pigs; meadow, 20 acres. Then 2 cobs, now none;
    then 2 cattle; now 66 pigs; then 300 sheep, now 200;
    6 beehives.
Value then and later 100s; now £8.
  Of this land, G(eoffrey) de Mandeville lays claim to 2 hides
less 20 acres. The Hundred testifies to it.

Hundred of LEXDEN

17 Arthur holds BOXTED from Eudo, which Grim held as a manor,
for 1 hide.
  Then 1 villager, now none; then 2 smallholders, now 9. Always
    1 plough in lordship. Then 2 men's ploughs, now 1.
  Woodland, 42 pigs; meadow, 2 acres. Then 6 cattle, now 4;
    then 30 sheep, now 64; then 10 pigs, now 13; now 13
    goats and 1 beehive.
Value then 20s; now 40[s].
  A free man held 5 acres; now Arthur also holds (them) from
Eudo. Always ½ plough.
Value 5s.

Hundred of ONGAR

18 Eudo holds THEYDON (Garnon) in lordship, which Wulfmer held
for 1 hide and 40 acres before 1066.
  Then 4 villagers, now 6; then 2 smallholders, now 4; then
    4 slaves, now 1. Always 2 ploughs in lordship; 2 men's
    ploughs.
  Woodland, 400 pigs; meadow, 5 acres. Always 2 cobs. Then
    8 cattle, now 13; then 35 pigs, now 66; then 87 sheep,
    now 100; 15 goats; then 2 beehives, now 6.
Value then and later 40s; now £4.
  1 Freeman, who could sell his land, held 6 acres; but the
jurisdiction remained in the manor.
Value 12d.

19 Eudo holds (Abbess) RODING in lordship, which Wulfmer held as
a manor, for 3 hides before 1066.
  Always 7 villagers. Now 2 smallholders. Always 4 slaves;
    2 ploughs in lordship; 3 men's ploughs.

Silu̅.xx.porc̅.xx.ac̅.p̅ti.Tc̅.1.runc̅.m̅.111.tc̅.x.an̅.m̅.x1111.

Tc̅.xl.porc̅.m̅.lx.Tc̅.c.ou̅.m̅.cxxx1.7.1.fochem.qui poff&

51 a

uendere t̅ram fuam.f; foca remanebat in manerio tenens dim̅ uirg̅.

7.v111.ac̅.7.dim̅.Tc̅.7 p̅.1.car̅.m̅ dim̅.Se̅p.1.fer̅.Tc̅.7.poft ual totum

.v111.lib̅.m̅.x11.

Hund̅ de Celmeresfort.Ratendun̅a ten&.Ricard̅.de.E.q̅d

tenuit Leuefun̅ p̅.Man̅.t̅.r̅.e̅.7.p̅.11.hid̅.7.xxx.ac̅.7 ift̅a t̅ra calumpni

at̅.Ǣccl̅ia de Eli.7 Hund̅ fert teftimoniu̅.Se̅p.1111.bord̅.7.11.fer̅.7.1.car̅

in d̅nio.7.1.car̅.hom̅.Tc̅.11.runc̅.m̅.1111.Tc̅.1111.an̅.m̅.v11.Tc̅.x.porc̅.

M̅ xxx111.Tc̅.lxxx.ou̅.m̅.c.111.min̅.Tc̅ ual.xl.fol.m̅.lxx.

Leg̅a ten&.Ricard̅ de.E.q̅d tenuit.Edric̅ p̅.Man̅.7.p̅.11.hid̅.Se̅p.111.

uilt̅.Tc̅.11.bord̅.m̅.1x.Tc̅.v11.fer̅.m̅.11.Tc̅.in d̅nio.11.car̅.m̅.1.7.dim̅.Silu̅

ɒccc.porc̅.xv1.ac̅.p̅ti.m̅.1.mol̅.Tc̅.111.runc̅.m̅.1.Tc̅.x.an̅.m̅.1x.tc̅

xl.porc̅.m̅.xxxv.Tc̅.l.ou̅.m̅ lx111.7.x1.cap̅.Tc̅ ual.lx.fol.m̅.1111.lib̅.

Hund̅ de Tendringa Wileiam tenuit Goduin̅ p̅.Man̅.7.p̅.111.hid̅.

7.xxxv111.ac̅.m̅ ten&.E.in d̅nio.Tc̅.x111.uilt̅.m̅.x1.Tc̅.1111.bord̅.

m̅.1x.Tc̅.v111.fer̅.m̅.1111.Silu̅.cc.porc̅.v1.ac̅.p̅ti.Paft.c.ou̅.7.11.

foc̅.tenuer̅.11.hid̅.7.xlv.ac̅.qui adjacebant huic manerio.Se̅p.v.bord̅.

7.11.car̅.Silu̅.xxx.porc̅.111.ac̅.p̅ti.Paft.lx.ou̅.Tc̅ in d̅nio.xv.an̅.

m̅.xv1.Tc̅.lx.porc̅.m̅.xxx.Se̅p.ccxl.ou̅.Tc̅.v.uafa ap̅.m̅.11.

Tc̅ ual.totu̅ fimul.v111.lib̅.m̅.x1x.lib̅.7.1.uncia̅ auri.

Woodland, 20 pigs; meadow, 20 acres. Then 1 cob, now 3; then 10 cattle, now 14; then 40 pigs, now 60; then 100 sheep, now 131.

1 Freeman, who holds ½ virgate and 8½ acres (and) who could sell his land; but the jurisdiction remained in the manor.
Then and later 1 plough, now ½.

Always 1 slave.

Value of the whole then and later £8; now [£] 12.

51 a

Hundred of CHELMSFORD

20 Richard holds RETTENDON from Eudo, which Leofson held as a manor before 1066, for 2 hides and 30 acres. The Church of Ely lays claim to this land and the Hundred bears witness.

Always 4 smallholders; 2 slaves; 1 plough in lordship; 1 men's plough.

Then 2 cobs, now 4; then 4 cattle, now 7; then 10 pigs, now 33; then 80 sheep, now 100 less 3.

Value then 40s; now 70[s].

21 Richard holds LEIGHS from Eudo, which Edric held as a manor, for 2 hides.

Always 3 villagers. Then 2 smallholders, now 9; then 7 slaves, now 2. Then 2 ploughs in lordship, now 1½.

Woodland, 800 pigs; meadow, 16 acres; now 1 mill. Then 3 cobs, now 1; then 10 cattle, now 9; then 40 pigs, now 35; then 50 sheep, now 63; 11 goats.

Value then 60s; now £4.

Hundred of TENDRING

22 Godwin held WEELEY as a manor, for 3 hides and 38 acres. Now Eudo holds it in lordship.

Then 13 villagers, now 11; then 4 smallholders, now 9; then 8 slaves, now 4.

Woodland, 200 pigs; meadow, 6 acres; pasture, 100 sheep.

2 Freemen held 2 hides and 45 acres which were attached to this manor.

Always 5 smallholders; 2 ploughs.

Woodland, 30 pigs; meadow, 3 acres; pasture, 60 sheep.

Then in lordship 15 cattle, now 16; then 60 pigs, now 30; always 240 sheep. Then 5 beehives, now 2.

Value then of the whole altogether £8; now £19 and 1 ounce of gold.

Hund̅ de Vdelesfort. Kuenadanam ten& Ricard̊ . de . E. q̊d̅

tenuit Aldred̅ p̱ . Man̊ . 7 . p̱ . ɪɪ . hid̅ . T̅c . vɪ . uiłł . p̱ 7 m̊ . ɪɪɪ . m̊ . ɪɪɪɪ . bord̊.

S̅ep . ɪɪɪ . ſer̊ . 7 . ɪɪ . car̊ . in d̅nio . 7 . ɪɪɪ . car̊ int h̅oes t̅c̊ꞏ m̊ . ɪɪ . Silu̅ . xʟ . porc̊.

. vɪ . ac̊ . p̊ti . T̅c̊ . runc̊ . m̊ . v . T̅c̊ . vɪ . an̊ . m̊ . ɪx . T̅c̊ . xxxɪɪ . porc̊ . m̊ . ʟ.

T̅c̊ . ʟxxx . oů . m̊ . cc . m̊ . xʟɪɪɪɪ . cap̊ . T̅c̊ . ɪɪɪɪ . uaſa ap̊ . m̊ . xvɪɪ T̅c uał

51 b

vɪɪɪ . lib̊ . m̊ . vɪ.

Dim̊ Hund̅ de Froſſeuuella . In Redeuuintra ten& Ricard̊

. xv . ac̊ . q̊d̅ tenuit Aluric uuand̊ ꞉ S̅ep . ɪ . uiłł . 7 . ɪ . bor̊ . 7 . ɪ . ſer̊ . 7 . ɪ . car̊.

. v . ac̊ . p̊ti . T̅c̊ . v . anim̊ . m̊ . vɪɪɪ . m̊ . ɪɪ . runc̊ . T̅c̊ . v . oů . 7 . ɪɪɪ . porc̊ . m̊

nułł . T̅c uał . x . ſoł . m̊ . xxx.

Hund̅ de Rochefort . ~~Hacuuella ten&~~ . E . in d̅nio . q̊d̅ tenuit

Vlmar̊ . lib̊ h̅o . p̱ . ω̅ . 7 . ~~p̱ . ɪɪɪ . hid̅ . 7 . dim̅~~ . xv . ac̊ . min . t . r . e . T̅c̊ . xɪ . uiłł.

m̊ . vɪɪɪ . S̅ep . v . bord̊ . T̅c̊ . ɪɪ . ſer̊ . m̊ . ɪɪɪ . S̅ep . ɪɪ . car̊ . in dnio . T̅c̊ . vɪ . car̊.

ho̅um m̊ . v . ɪɪɪɪ . ac̊ . p̊ti . Silu̅ . x . porc̊ . T̅c̊ . ɪɪ . runc̊ . m̊ . vɪ . T̅c̊ . v . anim̊.

m̊ . xvɪ . T̅c̊ . cɪɪ . oů . m̊ . cvɪ . S̅ep . xx . porc̊ . m̊ . ɪɪ . uaſa apu̅ . T̅c

uał . vɪ . lib̊ . m̊ . vɪɪ.

Hund̅ de Vdelesforda . Archeſdan̅a ten& . E . in d̅nio . q̊z

tenuit Aluric uuants . p̱ . Man̊ . 7 . p̱ . ɪɪ . hid̅ . xv . ac̊ . min . S̅ep . ɪɪ . uiłł.

7 . vɪɪ . bord̊ . 7 . ɪɪ . ſer̊ . T̅c̊ . 7 p̱ . ɪɪ . car̊ . in d̅nio . m̊ . ɪ . S̅ep . ɪɪ . car̊ . hom̊.

Silu̅ . xx . porc̊ . x . ac̊ . p̊ti . Vał . c . ſoł.

51 a, b

Hundred of UTTLESFORD

23 Richard holds QUENDON from Eudo, which Aldred held as a
manor, for 2 hides.

> Then 6 villagers, later and now 3; now 4 smallholders. Always
3 slaves; 2 ploughs in lordship. Then among the men 3
ploughs, now 2.
Woodland, 40 pigs; meadow, 6 acres. Then ... cobs, now 5;
then 6 cattle, now 9; then 32 pigs, now 50; then 80 sheep,
now 200; now 44 goats; then 4 beehives, now 17.
Value then £8; now [£] 6.

51 b

Half-Hundred of FRESHWELL

24 In RADWINTER Richard holds 15 acres which Aelfric Wand held.

> Always 1 villager; 1 smallholder; 1 slave; 1 plough.
Meadow, 5 acres. Then 5 cattle, now 8; now 2 cobs; then 5
sheep and 3 pigs, now none.
Value then 10s; now 30[s].

Hundred of ROCHFORD

25 Eudo holds HAWKWELL in lordship which Wulfmer, a free man,
held as a manor, for 3½ hides less 15 acres before 1066.

> Then 11 villagers, now 8; always 5 smallholders. Then 2
slaves, now 3. Always 2 ploughs in lordship. Then 6 men's
ploughs, now 5.
Meadow, 4 acres; woodland, 10 pigs. Then 2 cobs, now 6;
then 5 cattle, now 16; then 102 sheep, now 106; always
20 pigs; now 2 beehives.
Value then £6; now [£] 7.

Hundred of UTTLESFORD

26 Eudo holds ARKESDEN in lordship, which Aelfric Wand held as a
manor, for 2 hides less 15 acres.

> Always 2 villagers; 7 smallholders; 2 slaves. Then and later
2 ploughs in lordship, now 1. Always 2 men's ploughs.
Woodland, 20 pigs; meadow, 10 acres.
Value 100s.

TERRA Rogeri de Otburuilla Hund de herlaua

Halingebiam tenuer̄ . ii . lı̄bi hōes . t . r . e . p . Man̄ . 7 . p . iii . hid . 7 .
xxxviii . ac̄ . Tc̄ . vi . car̄ . in dn̄io . m̄ . iii . Tc̄ . x . car̄ . 7 . dim̄ . hōu
m̄ . ii . 7 . dim̄ . Tc̄ . xviii . uiłł . m̄ . viii . Tc̄ . iiii . bord . m̄ . v . Tc̄ . i . ser
m̄ nułł . Silu . ðc . porc̄ . xxv . ac̄ . p̄ti . Past . de . xxviii . ð . i . moł .
7 . ix . carr̄ . pofs̄t̄ reſtaurari . 7 unū maneriū ex iſtis ualebat
. t . r . e . viii . lib . 7 . qn̄ recep̄ . c . soł . m̄ . iiii . lib . 7 aliud uat̄ . tc̄ . lx .
soł . m̄ . xl . In dn̄io recep̄ . Roḡ . i . runc̄ . 7 . iii . an̄ . 7 . xxx . ou . 7 .
xl . porc̄ . m̄ . i . runc̄ . 7 . viii . an̄ . 7 lxxx . porc̄ . 7 . cxx . ou . 7 . iii . uaſa
apū .

Hund de Dommauua . Rodinges tenuit Turchiłł . lı̄b
hō . t . r . e . p . M̄ . 7 . p . ii . hid̄ . Tc̄ . in dn̄io . m̄ . i . 7 . dim̄ . Tc̄ : iii . uiłł .
m̄ . i . p̄r . 7 . ii . uiłł . Tc̄ . ii . bord . m̄ . v . Tc̄ . iiii . ser . m̄ . iii . hn̄tes . i . car̄ .
Silu . xxx . porc̄ . xxiiii . ac̄ . p̄ti . Tc̄ . uat̄ . vi . lib . | . m̄ . c . soł . & qn̄
recep̄ . n̄ inuenit n̄ ſolā trā . 7 . i . carrucā .

Hund de Vdelesfort . Archeſdanā tenuit Leuuin̄ lı̄be
. p . Man̄ . 7 . p . i . hid̄ . 7 Roḡ in ſuo eſcangio . Tc̄ . ii . uiłł . P 7 m̄ . i .
Sēp . iii . bord . Tc̄ . i . car̄ . in dn̄io . Qn̄ rec̄ nulla . m̄ . i . Tc̄ . 7 . p . i . car̄
hominū . m̄ nulla . vii . ac̄ . p̄ti . Silu . x . porc̄ . Tc̄ . i . an̄ . 7 . xix . ou .
m̄ . i . pułł . xiiii . porc̄ . lxxxx . ou . Tc̄ . uat̄ . xl . soł . m̄ . l .

In Ead uilla tenuit Vlfo . i . hid̄ . lı̄bæ . t . r . e . 7 . Roḡ p eſcangio .
Tc̄ . ii . uiłł . P 7 m̄ . i . Sēp . iii . bord . Tc̄ . i . car̄ in dn̄io . 7 qn̄ rec̄
nulla . m̄ . i . Tc̄ . 7 p . i . car̄ . hom̄ . m̄ nułł . vii . ac̄ . p̄ti . Silu . x . porc̄ .
Tc̄ . uat̄ . xl . soł . m̄ . l .

Ciſhellam tenuit Edric̄ p Man̄ . 7 . p . iii . hid̄ . 7 . dim̄ . Tc̄ . viii . uiłł .
P 7 m̄ . vi . Sēp . ii . bord . Tc̄ . ii . ser . m̄ . i . Tc̄ . 7 . p . ii . car̄ in dn̄io . m̄ . i .
tc̄ 7 p . iii . car̄ hom̄ . m̄ . ii . Silu . xl . porc̄ . vi . ac̄ . p̄ti . Tc̄ . i . runc̄ . 7 . ii . porc̄ .
7 . ccxiii . ou . M̄ . ii . runc̄ . 7 . i . anim̄ . xxxii . porc̄ . cc . ou . Sēp uat̄
. iiii . lib .

Hundred of HARLOW

1   2 free men held (Great) HALLINGBURY before 1066 as a manor,
for 3 hides and 38 acres. Then 6 ploughs in lordship, now 3.
Then 10½ men's ploughs, now 2½.
> Then 18 villagers, now 8; then 4 smallholders, now 5; then
> 1 slave, now none.
> Woodland, 600 pigs; meadow, 25 acres; pasture at 28d; 1 mill.
> 9 ploughs can be restored.

Value of one of these manors before 1066 £8; when acquired
100s; now £4. Value of the other then 60s; now 40[s].
In lordship Roger acquired 1 cob, 3 cattle, 30 sheep and 40
pigs; now 1 cob, 8 cattle, 80 pigs, 120 sheep and 3 beehives.

Hundred of DUNMOW

2   Thorkell, a free man, held RODING before 1066 as a manor, for 2
hides. Then ... [ploughs] in lordship, now 1½.
> Then 3 villagers, now 1 priest and 2 villagers; then 2
> smallholders, now 5; then 4 slaves, now 3; who have 1 plough.
> Woodland, 30 pigs; meadow, 24 acres.

Value then £6; later and now 100s; when acquired, he found
only the land and 1 plough.

Hundred of UTTLESFORD

3   Leofwin held ARKESDEN freely as a manor, for 1 hide. Roger (holds
it) by his exchange.
> Then 2 villagers, later and now 1; always 3 smallholders.
> Then 1 plough in lordship, when acquired none, now 1.
> Then and later 1 men's plough, now none.
> Meadow, 7 acres; woodland, 10 pigs. Then 1 (head of) cattle
> and 19 sheep; now 1 foal, 14 pigs, 90 sheep.

Value then 40s; now 50[s].

4   In the same village Wulfa held 1 hide freely before 1066. Roger
(holds it) by exchange.
> Then 2 villagers, later and now 1; always 3 smallholders.
> Then 1 plough in lordship, when acquired none, now 1.
> Then and later 1 men's plough, now none.
> Meadow, 7 acres; woodland, 10 pigs.

Value then 40s; now 50[s].

5   Edric held CHISHILL as a manor, for 3½ hides.   52 b
> Then 8 villagers, later and now 6; always 2 smallholders.
> Then 2 slaves, now 1. Then and later 2 ploughs in lordship,
> now 1. Then and later 3 men's ploughs, now 2.
> Woodland, 40 pigs; meadow, 6 acres. Then 1 cob, 2 pigs and
> 213 sheep; now 2 cobs, 1 (head of) cattle, 32 pigs, 200 sheep.

Value always £4.

⸗TERRA HvGoniS de monteforti. Hundret

de Berdeſtapla. Rameſdanam ten& Osбnus de Hugone qđ tenueř
.III.liбi hões.t.r.e.ꝑ Man.7.ꝑ.II.hid.7.XL.aᴄ.Sēp.I.cař.in đnio.
Tᴄ dim.car hom.m̂.I.Tᴄ.III.borđ.m̂.v.Tᴄ.I.ſeř.m̂.n̄.Silu.LX.porᴄ.
.III.aᴄ.p̂ti.Tᴄ.II.an̂.7.III.porᴄ.7.LX.ou.M.I.runᴄ.7.II.anim.
7.IX.porᴄ.7 LXX.ou.Val.XL.ſol. In Eađ uilla st̄.xxx.aᴄ.q̄
ꝑtinent ad eccliam.7 Val.xxx.đ.

⸗Hund de Witham Chelleuadan̄a ten& Wilłs fili groſſæ.
de hugone.qđ tenuit Gudmund.tegn̂ regis ꝑ.Man.7 ꝑ.III.hid.7.dim.
Sēp.II.cař in đnio.Tᴄ.IIII.cař hom.m̂.I.Sēp.IX.uilł.7.III.ſeř.7.v.
borđ.Silu.L.porᴄ.xxv.aᴄ.p̂ti.I.mol.Tᴄ.I.runᴄ.7.IIII.an̂.7.VII.
porᴄ.7.XL.ou.m̂.II.runᴄ.CXL.ou.Tᴄ ual.VI.liƀ.m̂.VII.

⸗Hund de Beuentrev. Leintun̄a ten& Hugo in đnio qđ tenuit

53 a

Alsi.t.r.e.ꝑ Man.7 ꝑ.III.hid.7.xxx.aᴄ.Tᴄ.II.cař.in đnio.m̂.I.Tᴄ
.I.cař hom.m̂.I.7.dim.Tᴄ.VI.uilł.m̂.I.pƀr.7.I.uilłs.Tᴄ.IIII.borđ.
m̂.III.Tᴄ.II.ſeř.m̂.null.Silu.CL.porᴄ.xxx.aᴄ.p̂ti.Tᴄ LX.ou.m̂.
.IIII.porᴄ.7.LX.ou.Tᴄ ual.xxx.ſol.m̂.XL.7 una iſtarũ hidarũ
reddebat.t.r.e.conſuetudin̄e ad Hauelingas manerium regis.7 m̂
n̄ reddit.

⸗Hund de Witbricteſherna Purlai ten& Hugo in đnio
qđ tenuit Gudmund liƀ hō.t.r.e.ꝑ Man.7.ꝑ.IIII.hid.Sēp.v.uilłi.
Tᴄ.VI.borđ.m̂.VII.Tᴄ.VI.ſeř.m̂.v.Sēp.II.cař in đnio.Tᴄ.III.cař
hom.m̂.II.7.tᴄia pot fieri.Silu.ƀᴄᴄ.porᴄ.Sēp.III.runᴄ.7.XVI.
an̂.Tᴄ.ᴄᴄᴄ.ou.m̂.ᴄᴄᴄVI.Tᴄ.xxx.porᴄ.m̂.xxxv.Tᴄ ual.VIII.liƀ
Poſt 7 m̂.VII.

Hundred of BARSTABLE

1 Osbern holds RAMSDEN from Hugh, which 3 free men held before 1066 as a manor, for 2 hides and 40 acres. Always 1 plough in lordship. Then ½ men's plough, now 1.

Then 3 smallholders, now 5; then 1 slave, now none.

Woodland, 60 pigs; meadow, 3 acres. Then 2 cattle, 3 pigs and 60 sheep; now 1 cob, 2 cattle, 9 pigs and 70 sheep.

Value 40s.

In the same village are 30 acres which belong to the church.
Value 30d.

Hundred of WITHAM

2 William son of Gross holds KELVEDON from Hugh, which Guthmund, a King's thane, held as a manor for 3½ hides. Always 2 ploughs in lordship. Then 4 men's ploughs, now 1.

Always 9 villagers; 3 slaves; 5 smallholders.

Woodland, 50 pigs; meadow, 25 acres; 1 mill. Then 1 cob, 4 cattle, 7 pigs and 40 sheep; now 2 cobs, 140 sheep.

Value then £6; now [£] 7.

Hundred of BECONTREE

3 Hugh holds LEYTON in lordship, which Alfsi held before 1066 as a   53 a
manor, for 3 hides and 30 acres. Then 2 ploughs in lordship, now 1. Then 1 men's plough, now 1½.

Then 6 villagers, now 1 priest and 1 villager; then 4 smallholders, now 3; then 2 slaves, now none.

Woodland, 150 pigs; meadow, 30 acres. Then 60 sheep; now 4 pigs and 60 sheep.

Value then 30s; now 40[s].

One of those hides paid a customary due to the King's manor of Havering (-atte-Bower) before 1066; now it does not pay.

Hundred of 'WIBERTSHERNE'

4 Hugh holds PURLEIGH in lordship which Guthmund, a free man, held before 1066 as a manor, for 4 hides.

Always 5 villagers. Then 6 smallholders, now 7; then 6 slaves, now 5. Always 2 ploughs in lordship. Then 3 men's ploughs, now 2; 3 possible.

Woodland, 700 pigs. Always 3 cobs; 16 cattle. Then 300 sheep, now 306; then 30 pigs, now 35.

Value then £8; later and now [£] 7.

⎸Lachentunam tenuit Gudmund ⍵ .p Man̕ . 7 .p . iii . hid̕ . 7 . dim̕ . 7 . xx . ac̕ .
Sep̄ . ii . uilłi . Tc̄ . ii . bord̕ . m̊ . iiii . tc̄ . v . ſer̕ . m̊ . iiii . Sep̄ . ii . car̕ in dn̄io .
7 . dim̕ . car̕ . hominū . Paſtura . cc . ou̇ . Silu̇ . c . porc̕ . Tc̄ uał . vii . lib̄ .
Poſt 7 m̊ . c . ſoł . De hoc eod̕ manerio ten&̇ . Hunfrid̕ . ii . hid̕ . de hugone
7 Vlmar̕ . i . hid̕ . 7 uał . lx . ſoł in eod̕ p̄tio .

⎸In Purlai tenuer̕ . x . libi hōes . vii . hid̕ . q̇s recep̄ hugo ⍵.p . ii . man̕ .
ſ; hund̕ hoc neſcit . Tc̄ erant in hac tr̄a . iiii . bord̕ . m̊ . viii . Tc̄ . i . ſer̕
m̊ nulł . Tc̄ . viii . car̕ . m̊ . vi . Silu̇ . xv . porc̕ . Paſt . c . ou̇ . Tc̄ 7 p̄ uał
. vi . lib̄ . m̊ . c . ſoł .

Adhuc ten&̇ Hugo in purlai . i . Man̕ . de . i . hid̕ . 7 . dim̕ . 7 . viii . ac̕ . 7 . dim̕ .
q̇d tenuer̕ . iii . libi hōes . t . r . e . cū ſoca . Sep̄ . i . car̕ . 7 . dim̕ . Paſtura
xl . ou̇ . Sep̄ uał . xx . ſoł . Hoc totū ſup̄dict̊ū ualebat . xxx . lib̄ . qn̄
recep̄ .

53 b

⎸Haleſdunam ten&̇ Hugo in dn̄io . q̇d̕ tenuit Aluuin̕ ⍵ teinn̕ . t . r . e .
⍵.p Man̕ . 7 .p . ii . hid̕ . Tc̄ . i . bord̕ . 7 . i . uiłłs . m̊ ſimilit̕ . Sep̄ . i . ſer̕ . 7 . i . car̕ .
in dn̄io . Paſt . xl . ou̇ Tc̄ uał . xxx . ſoł . qn̄ rec̕ . xx . ſoł . m̊ . xxx .

⎸Eſtoleiam ten&̇ . H . in dn̄io . q̇d tenuit ſep̄ . ii . uiłt . Tc̄ . ii . bord̕ . 7 m̊   ★
ſimilit̕ . 7 . i . car̕ 7 . dim̕ . 7 m̊ ſimilit̕ . Vał . xxx . ſoł .

⎸Hund̕ de Wenſiſtreu Legr̄a . ten&̇ Hugo . in dn̄io q̇d tenuit
Liuuin̕ lib̄ hō . t . r . e . ⍵.p Man̕ . 7 .p . i . hid̕ . 7 . dim̕ . 7 . xviii . ac̕ . Sep̄
. i . car̕ 7 dim̕ in dn̄io . M̊ dim̕ . car̕ hom̕ . m̊ . iii . bord̕ . Tc̄ . iii . ſer̕ . m̊
nulł . Sep̄ . iii . uac̕ . Tc̄ . xx . ou̇ . m̊ . lx . m̊ . xiiii . porc̕ . 7 . i . runc̕ .
7 . vii . cap̕ . Tc̄ . uał . l . ſoł . 7 qn̄ rec̕ . xx . ſoł . m̊ . xl . ſoł .

5 Guthmund held LATCHINGDON as a manor, for 3½ hides and 20
acres.
> Always 2 villagers. Then 2 smallholders, now 4; then 5 slaves,
> now 4. Always 2 ploughs in lordship; ½ men's plough.
> Pasture, 200 sheep; woodland, 100 pigs.

Value then £7; later and now 100s.
> Of this same manor, Humphrey holds 2 hides from Hugh and
Wulfmer (holds) 1 hide.

Value 60s in the same assessment.

6 In PURLEIGH 10 free men held 7 hides which Hugh acquired as 2
manors; but the Hundred does not know this.
> Then there were on this land 4 smallholders, now 8; then 1
> slave, now none. Then 8 ploughs, now 6.
> Woodland, 15 pigs; pasture, 100 sheep.

Value then and later £6; now 100s.

7 Hugh holds a further 1 manor in PURLEIGH with 1½ hides and 8½
acres, which 3 free men held before 1066 with the jurisdiction.
Always 1½ ploughs.
> Pasture, 40 sheep.

Value always 20s.

Value of the whole of the above when acquired £30.

8 Hugh holds *HALESDUNA* in lordship which Alwin, a thane, held   53 b
before 1066 as a manor, for 2 hides.
> Then 1 smallholder, 1 villager; now the same. Always 1 slave;
> 1 plough in lordship.
> Pasture, 40 sheep.

Value then 30s; when acquired 20s; now 30[s].

[Hundred of CHELMSFORD]
9 Hugh holds 'STUDLY' in lordship which 2 villagers have always held.
> Then 2 smallholders, now the same. [Then] 1½ ploughs,
> now the same.

Value 30s.

Hundred of WINSTREE
10 Hugh holds LAYER in lordship which Leofing, a free man, held
before 1066 as a manor, for 1½ hides and 18 acres. Always 1½
ploughs in lordship. Now ½ men's plough.
> Now 3 smallholders; then 3 slaves, now none.
> Always 3 cows. Then 20 sheep, now 60; now 14 pigs, 1 cob
> and 7 goats.

Value then 50s; when acquired 20s; now 40s.

Hund de hidingaforda. Raines ten& Alcher de hugone
qđ tenuit Gudmund . ꝑ . Man . 7 . ꝑ . II . hid . xx . ac . min . Sep . III .
car . in dnio . Tc . 7 p . VII . car . hom . m . II . 7 . dim . tc . 7 p . XVIII .
uilt . m . v . Tc . 7 p . VI . bor . m . VII . Tc . 7 p . VI . ſer . m . IIII . Silu .
CL . porc . XVI . ac . pti . ſep . I . mol . 7 . I . runc . Tc . XVIII . an . m . XVII .
Sep . LXX . ou . 7 . x . cap . Tc . 7 p uat . VI . lib . m . VII .

Hund de Witbricteſherna . Effeceſtre ten& Vlmar de . hug
qđ tenuit Ingulf lib ho . t . r . e . ꝑ . Man . 7 . ꝑ . I . hid . 7 . dim . Sep
. II . bord . Tc . I . ſer . m null . I . car . in dnio . 7 . dim . hom . Paſt . cc .
ous . Vat . xxx ſot .

Hund de Laxendena Mercheſhalam ten& Nigell de hugone
qđ tenuit Gudmund t . r . e . ꝑ uno maner . 7 . ꝑ dim hid . 7 . XIII . ac .
Sep . II . uilt . Tc . VII . bord . m . VIII . Sep . v . ſer . Tc . II . car . in dnio
m . I . 7 . dim . Sep . I . car . 7 dim hom . Silu . cc . porc . I . ac . pti . Sep

. I . runc . Tc . II . anim . m . x . Tc . xxx . ou . m . LXXX . Sep . XII .
porc . m . III . uaſa apu . Tc uat . XL . ſot . m LX .

Hund de Celmeresfort . Bedeneſteda ten& . Rob de hug
qđ tenuit Gudmund t . r . e . ꝑ . Man . 7 . ꝑ . IIII . hid . Tc . I . uilt . m
null . Tc . Ix . bord . m . x . Tc . 7 . p . VI . ſer . m . I . Tc . 7 . p . II . car . in
dnio . m . I . Sep . I . car hom . v . ac . pti . Tc . III . runc . m . null . Tc
xxv . an . m . I . uac . Tc . c . porc . m . XIIII . Tc . c . 7 . VIII . ou . m . XXIIII .
tc . LX . cap . m . nulla . Tc uat . VIII . lib . 7 qn rec . ſimilit . m . IIII . lib .
7 . v . libi hoes tenuer . I . hid . 7 . dim . 7 . XXIII . ac . qs ten& Ide Rob de
Hugone . Sep . v . bord . 7 . II . car . 7 . dim . Silu . XL . porc . IIII . ac . pti . Sep
uat . L . ſot . hoc maneriu calumpniant monachi de eli qđ fuit in
abbia in dnio . 7 hoc teſtat hund .

Hundred of HINCKFORD

11 Alchere holds RAYNE from Hugh, which Guthmund held as a manor, for 2 hides less 20 acres. Always 3 ploughs in lordship. Then and later 7 men's ploughs, now 2½.
> Then and later 18 villagers, now 5; then and later 6 smallholders, now 7; then and later 6 slaves, now 4.
> Woodland, 150 pigs; meadow, 16 acres. Always 1 mill; 1 cob. Then 18 cattle, now 17. Always 70 sheep; 10 goats.

Value then and later £6; now [£] 7.

Hundred of 'WIBERTSHERNE'

12 Wulfmer holds ST. PETER'S CHAPEL from Hugh which Ingulf, a free man, held before 1066 as a manor, for 1½ hides.
> Always 2 smallholders. Then 1 slave, now none. 1 plough in lordship; ½ men's (plough).
> Pasture, 200 sheep.

Value 30s.

Hundred of LEXDEN

13 Nigel holds MARKSHALL from Hugh, which Guthmund held before 1066 as one manor, for ½ hide and 13 acres.
> Always 2 villagers. Then 7 smallholders, now 8; always 5 slaves. Then 2 ploughs in lordship, now 1½. Always 1½ men's ploughs.
> Woodland, 200 pigs; meadow, 1 acre. Always 1 cob. Then 2 cattle, now 10; then 30 sheep, now 80. Always 12 pigs. Now 3 beehives.

54 a

Value then 40s; now 60[s].

Hundred of CHELMSFORD

14 Robert holds 'BENSTED' from Hugh, which Guthmund held before 1066 as a manor, for 4 hides.
> Then 1 villager, now none; then 9 smallholders, now 10; then and later 6 slaves, now 1. Then and later 2 ploughs in lordship, now 1. Always 1 men's plough.
> Meadow, 5 acres. Then 3 cobs, now none; then 25 cattle, now 1 cow; then 100 pigs, now 14; then 108 sheep, now 24; then 60 goats, now none.

Value then £8; when acquired the same; now £4.
> 5 free men held 1½ hides and 23 acres which Robert also holds from Hugh.
> Always 5 smallholders; 2½ ploughs.
> Woodland, 40 pigs; meadow, 4 acres.

Value always 50s.
> The monks of Ely lay claim to this manor which was in lordship in the (lands of the) Abbey before 1066. The Hundred testifies to this.

Hund de Tendringa . Wicā tenuit Edeua Regina . t̄ . r̄ . ē.
⅌ Man ̄ | . m̄ ten& Roḡ de huḡ . Sēp . ıı . uill̄ . T̄c . ıı . bord . m̄ . vııı.
T̄c . ıı . ſer . m̄ null . Sēp . ı . car . Silu . x . porc . ııı . ac̄ . p̄ti . Val . x . ſol.
hanc trā ten& Roḡ 7 hund neſcit qm̄ . 7 regina habuit ſocam.

Hund de Tureſtapla . Totham ten& hugo fili Malḡi de
hugone . qd̄ tenuit Cola . Poſt Ricard . ⅌ Man . 7 . ıı . hid . 7 . xxxıı.
ac̄ . T̄c . ıııı . bord . m̄ . ııı . T̄c . ıııı . ſer . m̄ . v . T̄c . ıı . car . in dn̄io
m̄ . ı . Silu . xx . porc . Paſt . c . ou . ııı . ac̄ . p̄ti . T̄c . ı . ſal . m̄ . ııı . T̄c
. ııı . runc . m̄ . ıı . T̄c . xvı . porc . m̄ . xx . T̄c . xlvııı . cap̄ . m̄ lxxxxııı.
m̄ . xvııı . cap̄ . T̄c ual . xl . ſol . 7 . qn̄ rec . x . ſol . m̄ ual . xl . ſol

Goldhangrā . ten& Idē de huḡ . qd̄ tenuit Leuuin poſt hagra
⅌ . Man . 7 . ⅌ . ı . hid . 7 . xv . ac̄ . Sēp . ı . uill̄ . 7 . vı . bord . 7 . ıııı . ſer.

★

54 b

T̄c . ı . car . m̄ . dim . Silu . lx . porc . vıı . ac̄ . p̄ti . Paſt . lx . ou . T̄c . dim
ſalina . m̄ . ı . 7 . dim . T̄c . ual . xxx . ſol . 7 . qn̄ rec . x . ſol . m̄ . ual . xx . ſol.
7 . ıx . libi hōes . manſer in dim hid . 7 . un̄ hō tegn tenuit . xxx . ac̄ . 7 . ıı.
alij libi hōes . tenuer . x . ac̄ . T̄c . ı . car . m̄ . dim . T̄c ual . xxvı . ſol
7 . vııı . d̄ . m̄ . vııı . ſol . Quidā miles hugonis de monte forti . nōe hugo
fili Malgeri ꞉ accepit xv . ac̄ . de uno franco teigno . 7 miſit cū ſua trā . 7
n̄ habuit libatore . ſic hund teſtat . 7 ita ē in manu regis.

Toleſhuntā ten& Humfrid . de hugone qd̄ tenuit Vlsi . t̄ . r̄ . ē.
⅌ Man . 7 . ⅌ dim hid . 7 . xxx . ac̄ . Sēp . ıı . bord . 7 . ı . car . Silu . xxx . porc.
. ıı . ac̄ . 7 . dim . p̄ti . Val . xx . ſol.

XXVIII. TERRA Hamonis dapiferi . Hundret de berdeſtapla
Ateleiam ten& Serlo de hamone qd̄ tenuit Goti de heroldo . t̄ . r̄ . ē
⅌ . Man . 7 . ⅌ . ı . hid . Sēp . ı . car . 7 . ı . bord . 7 . ı . ſer . Val . xx . ſol.

Hundred of TENDRING
15 Queen Edith held WIX before 1066 as a manor, for 1 hide. Now
Roger holds it from Hugh.
> Always 2 villagers. Then 2 smallholders, now 8; then 2 slaves,
> now none. Always 1 plough.
> Woodland, 10 pigs; meadow, 3 acres.
> Value 10s.
> Roger holds this land and the Hundred does not know how.
> The Queen had the jurisdiction.

Hundred of THURSTABLE
16 Hugh son of Mauger holds (Little) TOTHAM from Hugh, which
Cola (and) later Richard held as a manor, 2 hides and 32 acres.
> Then 4 smallholders, now 3; then 4 slaves, now 5. Then 2
> ploughs in lordship, now 1.
> Woodland, 20 pigs; pasture, 100 sheep; meadow, 3 acres;
> then 1 salt-house, now 3. Then 3 cobs, now 2; then 16 pigs,
> now 20; then 48 goats, now 93; now 18 goats.
> Value then 40s; when acquired 10s; value now 40s.

17 He also holds GOLDHANGER from Hugh, which Leofwin (and) later
Hager held as a manor, for 1 hide and 15 acres.
> Always 1 villager; 6 smallholders; 4 slaves. Then 1 plough,   54 b
> now ½.
> Woodland, 60 pigs; meadow, 7 acres; pasture, 60 sheep;
> then ½ salt-house, now 1½.
> Value then 30s; when acquired 10s; value now 20s.
> 9 free men dwelt on ½ hide. One man, a thane, held 30 acres
> and 2 other free men held 10 acres. Then 1 plough, now ½.
> Value then 26s 8d; now 8s.
> One of Hugh de Montfort's men-at-arms, Hugh son of Mauger
> by name, acquired 15 acres from 1 free thane and put it with his
> own land. He did not have a deliverer, so the Hundred testifies;
> therefore it is in the King's hand.

18 Humphrey holds TOLLESHUNT (D'Arcy) from Hugh, which Wulfsi
held before 1066 as a manor, for ½ hide and 30 acres.
> Always 2 smallholders; 1 plough.
> Woodland, 30 pigs; meadow, 2½ acres.
> Value 20s.

28   LAND OF HAMO THE STEWARD

Hundred of BARSTABLE
1   Serlo holds *ATELEIA* from Hamo, which Goti held from Harold
before 1066 as a manor, for 1 hide. Always 1 plough;
> 1 smallholder; 1 slave.
> Value 20s.

⟨Hund de Witham. Falcheburnā ten& Rađ de hamone qđ
tenuit Turbn̄.t.r.e.p.Man.7.p.i.hiđ.7.dim.7.vii.ac̄.7.dim.
Sēp.ii.car̄.in dn̄io.m̄.viii.borđ.Tc̄.vi.fer̄.m̄.iii.v.ac̄.p̄ti.Tc̄.i.
mol.m̄ non.Val.l.fol.

⟨Nutleam ten& Rađ de.H.qđ tenuit Aleſtan̄ lib hō p Man̄.
7.p dim̄ hiđ.7.xxx.ac̄.Sēp.i.car̄.m̄.i.bor.Tc̄.ii.fer̄.m̄.i.i.ac̄ 7 đ
p̄ti.Val.xxx.fol.In Eađ ten& Iđē.xxx.ac̄.qs tenuit Aluric̄
.t.r.e.Sēp dim̄.car̄.7 ual.v.fol.

⟨Raines ten& Iđē.R.de h.qđ tenuit Godinḡ p.Man̄.7 p dim̄ hiđ.
Sēp.i.car̄.7.i.borđ.7.ii.ac̄.p̄ti.Val.xx.fol.

⟨Braccheſtedam ten& Gudmund̄.p.Man̄.7.p.i.hiđ.7.xxxv.ac̄.
qđ tenuit Turbn̄.t.r.e.Tc̄.ii.car̄.in dn̄io.m̄.i.Tc̄.i.car̄ hōu
m̄ nulla.Tc̄.iii.uill.m̄.i.Tc̄.iiii.borđ.m̄.vi.Tc̄.iiii.fer̄.m̄.ii.
Tc̄.filu.c.porc̄.m̄ lxxx.xv.ac̄.p̄ti.Tc̄.xx.ou.m̄.l.Tc̄.xvi.
porc̄.m̄.xi.Tc̄ ual.c.fol.7 qn̄ eā rec̄.iiii.lib.m̄.lx.fol.

⟨Hund de herlaua.Siriceſleam ten&.Rađ.de hamone
qđ tenuit Herold ad maneriū de hatfelde.t.r.e.p.dim̄.hiđ.
Tc̄.i.car̄.in dn̄io.m̄.dim̄.Tc̄.i.fer̄.m̄.i.uill.Silu.xx.porc̄.
.iii.ac̄.7 dim̄.p̄ti.Tc̄ ual.x.fol.m̄.vii.

⟨Hund de Dōmauua.Dommauuā ten& Serlo de hamone
qđ tenuit.i.lib hō.t.r.e.p.xxx.ac̄.7.vii.ac̄.ſt addite.t.r.Willi.
Sēp.dim̄.car̄.in dn̄io.7.ii.borđ.Silu.xl.porc̄.iiii.ac̄.p̄ti.
Val.xvi.fol.

Hundred of WITHAM

2 Ralph holds FAULKBOURNE from Hamo, which Thorbern held before 1066 as a manor, for 1½ hides and 7½ acres. Always 2 ploughs in lordship.
> Now 8 smallholders; then 6 slaves, now 3.
> Meadow, 5 acres; then 1 mill, now none.
Value 50s.

3 Ralph holds NOTLEY from Hamo which Alstan, a free man, held 55 a as a manor, for ½ hide and 30 acres. Always 1 plough.
> Now 1 smallholder; then 2 slaves, now 1.
> Meadow, 1½ acres.
Value 30s.
> In the same (Notley) he also holds 30 acres which Aelfric held before 1066. Always ½ plough.
Value 5s.

[Hundred of HINCKFORD]

4 R(alph) also holds RAYNE from Hamo, which Goding held as a manor, for ½ hide. Always 1 plough;
> 1 smallholder.
> Meadow, 2 acres.
Value 20s.

[Hundred of WITHAM]

5 Guthmund holds (Great) BRAXTED as a manor, for 1 hide and 35 acres, which Thorbern held before 1066. Then 2 ploughs in lordship, now 1. Then 1 men's plough, now none.
> Then 3 villagers, now 1; then 4 smallholders, now 6; then 4 slaves, now 2.
> Woodland, then 100 pigs, now 80; meadow, 15 acres. Then 20 sheep, now 50; then 16 pigs, now 11.
Value then 100s; when he acquired it £4; now 60s.

Hundred of HARLOW

6 Ralph holds RYES from Hamo, which Harold held with the manor of Hatfield (Broad Oak) before 1066 for ½ hide. Then 1 plough in lordship, now ½.
> Then 1 slave; now 1 villager.
> Woodland, 20 pigs; meadow, 3½ acres.
Value then 10s; now 7[s].

Hundred of DUNMOW

7 Serlo holds DUNMOW from Hamo, which 1 free man held before 1066 for 30 acres. 7½ acres were added after 1066. Always ½ plough in lordship;
> 2 smallholders.
> Woodland, 40 pigs; meadow, 4 acres.
Value 16s.

Rodinges ten& Serlo de . H . q̃d tenuit Widi⁹ de Heroldo.
t . r̃ . e . p̃ Man . 7 . p̃ . ı . hid . 7 . dim . m̃ . ı . hid . 7 . xv . ac̃ . Sẽp . ıı . car
in dñio . 7 . ı . car . hom . Tc̃ . ııı ı . uilt . m̃ . ıı ı . Tc̃ . ıı . bord . m̃ . xı.
Tc̃ . ıı . fer . m̃ . ı . Silu . c . porc . xvı . ac̃ . p̃ti . Tc̃ ual . ııı ı . lib . 7
qñ rec̃ . xL . fol . m̃ . c . fol . Ex hac t̃ra ten& Eudo dapifer . xLv . ac̃

q̃s calumpniat̃ Hamo

Hundret de Wenfiftrev . Wighebgam ten& Vital de.
hamone qd tenuit Goti lib hõ . t . r̃ . e . p̃ . Man . 7 . p̃ . vıı . hid . t̃ræ.
7 una filuæ . Sẽp . ıı . car in dñio . Tc̃ . ıı . car . hom . m̃ . ı . Sẽp . ııı . uilt.
7 . ı . bord . Tc̃ . vı . fer . m̃ . ııı ı . paft . cc . ou . Tc̃ . x . anim . m̃ . xıı ıı.
Tc̃ . Lx . ou . m̃ . cc Lx . Sẽp . vı . runc 7 . x . porc . Sẽp ual . vıı.
lib . De hac t̃ra tulit Bernard . fub̃dict̃a hid̃a filuæ . 7 ten& ad feudũ
baignardi 7 Engelric tulit dim hid . t̃ræ . quã ten& Comes . Euft.

Hund de Clauelinga . In Pherneham ten& Serlo dim . hid
de hamone qd tenuit lib hõ . t . r̃ . e . Val . x . fol.

Hund de hidingfort . In Scanburne 7 In Topesfelde ten&
Hamo . ı . hid . in dñio . p̃ Man . qd tenuit Goti . t . r̃ . e . Tc̃ . 7 p̃ . ıı ı ı.
car . in dñio . m̃ . ııı . Sẽp . ııı . car . hom . xıı ıı . uilt . 7 . x . bord . 7.
vı . fer . Silu . xL . porc . xv . ac̃ . p̃ti . Sẽp . ııı . runc . Tc̃ . xxıı ıı.
an . m̃ . xııı . Tc̃ . xL . porc . m̃ . xx . Tc̃ . cxx . ou . m̃ . c . ııı ı . uafa
apũ . Et . xv . foc sẽp adjacent huic manerio . tenentes dim.
hid . x . ac̃ . min . 7 hñt . ııı . car . 7 . xıı . ac̃ . p̃ti . 7 . v . bord . ı . arpen.
uineæ . hec t̃ra fuit in . ıı t̃ . manerijs . t . r̃ . e . Tc̃ ual . Stanburna
. c . fol . Poft 7 m̃ . vı . lib . 7 Topesfelda ualebat . tc̃ . vıı . lib . Poft
7 m̃ . vıı ı . lib . De hoc man tenent . v . milit . Lvııı . ac̃ . 7 ual . xx . fol ĩ eod̃ p̃tio.

55 a, b

8 Serlo holds RODING from Hamo, which Withi held from Harold before 1066 as a manor, for 1½ hides. Now 1 hide and 15 acres. Always 2 ploughs in lordship; 1 men's plough.
> Then 4 villagers, now 3; then 2 smallholders, now 11; then 2 slaves, now 1.
> Woodland, 100 pigs; meadow, 16 acres.
> Value then £4; when acquired 40s; now 100s.
> Of this land, Eudo the Steward holds 45 acres which Hamo claims.

Hundred of WINSTREE

9 Vitalis holds (Little) WIGBOROUGH from Hamo which Goti, a free man, held before 1066 as a manor for 7 hides of land and 1 (hide) of woodland. Always 2 ploughs in lordship. Then 2 men's ploughs, now 1.
> Always 3 villagers; 1 smallholder. Then 6 slaves, now 4.
> Pasture, 200 sheep. Then 10 cattle, now 14; then 60 sheep, now 260. Always 6 cobs; 10 pigs.
> Value always £7.
> From this land Bernard took the above hide of woodland and holds it in Baynard's Holding. Engelric took ½ hide of land which Count Eustace holds.

Hundred of CLAVERING

10 In FARNHAM Serlo holds ½ hide from Hamo, which a free man held before 1066.
> Value 10s.

Hundred of HINCKFORD

11 In STAMBOURNE and in TOPPESFIELD Hamo holds 1 hide in lordship as a manor, which Goti held before 1066. Then and later 4 ploughs in lordship, now 3. Always 3 men's ploughs;
> 14 villagers; 10 smallholders; 6 slaves.
> Woodland, 40 pigs; meadow, 15 acres. Always 3 cobs. Then 24 cattle, now 13; then 40 pigs, now 20; then 120 sheep, now 100; 4 beehives.
> 15 Freemen have always belonged to this manor, who hold ½ hide less 10 acres and have 3 ploughs.
> Meadow, 12 acres.
> 5 smallholders.
> 1 *arpent* of vines.
This land was in 2 manors before 1066.
Value then of Stambourne 100s; later and now £6.
Value then of Toppesfield £7; later and now £8.
> Of this manor, 5 men-at-arms hold 58 acres.
Value 20s in the same assessment.

Hund de Witbricteſherna   Carſeiam ten& Ricard de
hamone q̃d tenuit Turbn lib hō . t̄ . r̄ . ē . p̄ . Man . 7 . p̄ . iiii . hid.
7 . xl . ac̄ . Tc̄ . ii . uill̄ . m̄ . iii . Sẽp . iiii . ſer̄ . 7 . ii . car̄ in dn̄io . 7 . i . car̄
hom̄ . Paſt . lx . ou . Tc̄ ual̄ . lx . ſol̄ . m̄ . iiii . lib̄.

56 a

Hund de Angra .   Gerneſtedam ten& Hamo in dn̄io q̃d
tenuit Gotild p̄ Man̄ . 7 . p̄ . ii . hid . t̄ . r̄ . ē . Sẽp . x . uill̄ . Tc̄ . iiii . bord . m̄ . ix.
Tc̄ vi . ſer̄ . m̄ . iiii . Tc̄ . iii . car̄ . in dn̄io . 7 . qn̄ rec̄ . ii . m̄ . i . Tc̄ 7 p̄ . v . car̄
7 . dim hom̄ . m̄ . iii . 7 . dim . Silu . cccc . porc̄ . xvi . ac̄ . p̃ti . m̄ . i . mol̄.
Tc̄ . ii . runc̄ . m̄ . i . Tc̄ . iiii . anim̄ . m̄ . iii . Tc̄ . xxx . porc̄ . m̄ . xiiii . m̄ . xl.
cap̄ . 7 . xx . ou . Tc̄ ual̄ . iiii . lib̄ . 7 . qn̄ rec̄ . xl . ſol̄ . m̄ ual̄ . c . ſol̄ . de hoc
maner̄ ten& Serlo . xl . ac̄ . 7 ual̄ . x . ſol̄ . in eod̄ . p̃tio . In Ead̄ tenuer̄ . iii.
libi hōes . dim̄ . hid . 7 . xlv . ac̄ . Tc̄ . ſub ipſis . x . bord . m̄ . xvi . Tc̄ . iii . ſer̄ . m̄ . ii.
Sẽp . iii . car̄ . 7 . dim . Silu . cxx . porc̄ . xix . ac̄ . p̃ti . Tc̄ . ual̄ . xxxv . ſol̄ . m̄ lx.
De hac t̄ra ten& Rad̄ dim hid . 7 . v . ac̄ . 7 ual̄ . xl . ſol̄ . in eod̄ p̃tio.
Aſtocam ten& Id̄e de ham̄ q̃d tenuit Gotil . p̄ Man̄ . 7 . p̄ lxxx . ac̄ . t̄ . r̄ . ē
Tc̄ . ii . bord . m̄ . v . Tc̄ . i . car̄ . m̄ nulla . ſ; pot̄ ibi eſſe . Silu . l . porc̄ . ii . ac̄ . p̃ti.
tc̄ ual̄ . xii . ſol̄ . 7 qn̄ rec̄ . viii . ſol̄ . m̄ . xv.
Kalendunam ten& Rad̄ de hamone q̃d tenuit Leueua . p̄ . i . hid.
7 xlv . ac̄ . 7 p̄ uno man̄ . 7 hamo dicit ſe habe iſta t̄ram in ſuo feudo.
Tc̄ . ii . uill̄ . m̄ . i . tc̄ . ii . bord . m̄ . vii . tc̄ . ii . ſer̄ . m̄ . i . tc̄ . in dn̄io . ii . car̄
m̄ . i . 7 . dim . Tc̄ . int̄ hōes . i . car̄ . m̄ . dim . Silu . xx . porc̄ . xvii . ac̄ . p̃ti.
Tc̄ ual̄ . xxx . ſol̄ . 7 . qn̄ rec̄ . xx . m̄ . xxxv . ſol̄.

Hundred of 'WIBERTSHERNE'

12 Richard holds NORTHEY ISLAND from Hamo which Thorbern, a
free man, held before 1066 as a manor, for 4 hides and 40 acres.
> Then 2 villagers, now 3. Always 4 slaves; 2 ploughs in lordship;
> 1 men's plough.
>
> Pasture, 60 sheep.

Value then 60s; now £4.

Hundred of ONGAR

13 Hamo holds GREENSTED in lordship, which Gotild held as a manor,
for 2 hides before 1066.
> Always 10 villagers. Then 4 smallholders, now 9; then 6 slaves,
> now 4. Then 3 ploughs in lordship, when acquired 2, now 1.
> Then and later 5½ men's ploughs, now 3½.
>
> Woodland, 400 pigs; meadow, 16 acres; now 1 mill. Then 2
> cobs, now 1; then 4 cattle, now 3; then 30 pigs, now 14;
> now 40 goats; 20 sheep.

Value then £4; when acquired 40s; value now 100s.
> Of this manor, Serlo holds 40 acres.

Value 10s in the same assessment.
> In the same (Greensted) 3 free men held ½ hide and 45 acres.
> Then 10 smallholders under them, now 16; then 3 slaves, now 2.
> Always 3½ ploughs.
>
> Woodland, 120 pigs; meadow, 19 acres.

Value then 35s; now 60[s].
> Of this land, Ralph holds ½ hide and 5 acres.

Value 40s in the same assessment.

14 He also holds NAVESTOCK from Hamo, which Gotild held as a
manor, for 80 acres before 1066.
> Then 2 smallholders, now 5. Then 1 plough; now none, but it
> could be there.
>
> Woodland, 50 pigs; meadow, 2 acres.

Value then 12s; when acquired, 8s; now 15[s].

15 Ralph holds KELVEDON (Hatch) from Hamo, which Leofeva held
for 1 hide and 45 acres as one manor. Hamo states that he has
this land in his Holding.
> Then 2 villagers, now 1; then 2 smallholders, now 7; then 2
> slaves, now 1. Then 2 ploughs in lordship, now 1½. Then
> among the men 1 plough, now ½.
>
> Woodland, 20 pigs; meadow, 17 acres.

Value then 30s; when acquired 20[s]; now 35s.

⁊Nortunā ten& Wimund̄.de hā᷉m .q̄d tenuit Gotil .ⱷ .Maner᷉.

7 ⱷ .ɪ.hid̄.7 .dim᷉.7 .xv.ac᷉.Tc̄.ɪɪɪɪ.uiłł.m᷉.vɪ.Sēp.ɪɪɪɪ.bord̄.7 .ɪɪɪɪ.
fer᷉.Tc̄.ɪɪ.car᷉.in dn̄io.m᷉.ɪ.Tc̄.inf̄ hōes.ɪ.car᷉.m᷉.ɪ.7 .dim᷉.Silu᷉.
.cc.porc̄.x.ac᷉.ⱷti.Sēp.ɪɪ.an᷉.m᷉.ɪ.runc̄.7 .xL.ou᷉.7 .xx.cap᷉.
tc̄.xvɪ.porc̄.m᷉.xxvɪ.Tc̄ 7 ⱷ uał.xL.foł.m᷉.ɪɪɪɪ.liƀ.

⁊Hūnd̄ de Tureftapla. Toteħam ten& Ricard̄ de hamone

q̄d tenuit Turƀt᷉.ⱷ uno man᷉.7 .ⱷ.v.hid̄.t᷉.r᷉.ę.Tc̄.x.uiłł.m᷉.ɪx.Sēp.xvɪ.
bord̄.Tc̄.xɪɪ.fer᷉.m᷉.xɪɪɪ.Tc̄.ɪɪɪɪ.car᷉.in dn̄io.m᷉.ɪɪɪ.Sēp.v.car᷉.hominū.
Silu᷉.c.porc̄.xvɪ.ac᷉.ⱷti.ɪɪ.falinæ.Sēp.xx.an᷉.7 .xL.porc̄.Tc̄.v.runc̄.
m᷉.ɪɪ.Tc̄.c.ou᷉.m᷉.cL.Sēp.xL.cap᷉.Tc̄ 7 ⱷ uał.c.foł.m᷉.vɪ.liƀ.
In Ead̄ tenuer᷉.vɪɪɪ.liƀi hōes.ɪ.hid̄.7 .dim᷉.q̄d ten& Id̄e Ricard̄.Sēp.ɪɪ.
car᷉.ɪɪɪ.ac᷉.ⱷti.Vał.xx.foł.

⁊Vuefeiam ten& Id̄e q̄d tenuit Turƀt᷉.t᷉.r᷉.ę.ⱷ Man᷉.7 .ⱷ.ɪɪɪɪ.hid̄.Tc̄.ɪ.bord̄.
m᷉ nułł.Sēp.ɪɪɪ.fer᷉.ɪ.pifc̄.Paſt᷉.Lx.ou᷉.Vał.Lx.foł.

.XXIX.⁊TERRA HENRICI dę Ferrerijs Hund̄ de Dōmauua

Tileteiam ten& Henric̄ in dn̄io q̄d tenuit.Doding᷉.t᷉.r᷉.ę.ⱷ Man᷉.7 .ⱷ dim᷉.
hid̄.Sēp.ɪɪ.car᷉.in dn̄io.7 .ɪ.car᷉ hōu᷉.Sēp.ɪɪɪ.uiłł.Tc̄.ɪɪ.bor᷉.m᷉.vɪ.tc̄.
.ɪɪɪ.fer᷉.7 m᷉ fimił.xxx.ac᷉.ⱷti.xx.ac᷉.de marefc̄.m᷉.xL.animalia.Tc̄ uał
.c.foł.m᷉.vɪɪ.liƀ.

⁊Hund̄ de Hidingaforda. Stibingā ten&.H.in dn̄io q̄d tenuit
Siuuard̄ ⱷ Man᷉.7 .ⱷ.ɪɪ.hid̄.7 .xxx.ac᷉.Tc̄.7 ⱷ.ɪɪ.car᷉ in dn̄io.m᷉.ɪɪɪ.Tc̄
inf̄ hōes.ɪɪɪɪ.car᷉.m᷉.vɪ.7 .dim᷉.Tc̄.vɪ.uiłłi.m᷉.vɪɪɪ.Tc̄.xvɪ.bord̄.m᷉.xxxɪɪɪ.

16   Wimund holds NORTON (Mandeville) from Hamo, which Gotild
    held as a manor, for 1½ hides and 15 acres.
> Then 4 villagers, now 6. Always 4 smallholders; 4 slaves.
>> Then 2 ploughs in lordship, now 1. Then among the men
>> 1 plough, now 1½.
> Woodland, 200 pigs; meadow, 10 acres. Always 2 cattle.
>> Now 1 cob, 40 sheep and 20 goats. Then 16 pigs, now 26.

    Value then and later 40s; now £4.

    Hundred of THURSTABLE

17   Richard holds (Great) TOTHAM from Hamo, which Thorbert held   56 b
    as one manor, for 5 hides before 1066.
> Then 10 villagers, now 9; always 16 smallholders. Then 12
> slaves, now 13. Then 4 ploughs in lordship, now 3. Always
> 5 men's ploughs.
> Woodland, 100 pigs; meadow, 16 acres; 2 salt-houses. Always
> 20 cattle; 40 pigs. Then 5 cobs, now 2; then 100 sheep,
> now 150; always 40 goats.

    Value then and later 100s; now £6.
> In the same (Totham) 8 free men held 1½ hides which Richard

    also holds. Always 2 ploughs.
> Meadow, 3 acres.

    Value 20s.

18   He also holds OSEA (Island), which Thorbert held before 1066 as a
    manor, for 4 hides.
> Then 1 smallholder, now none; always 3 slaves.
> 1 fishery; pasture, 60 sheep.

    Value 60s.

29   LAND OF HENRY OF FERRERS

    Hundred of DUNMOW

1   Henry holds TILTY in lordship, which Doding held before 1066 as
    a manor, for ½ hide. Always 2 ploughs in lordship; 1 men's plough.
> Always 3 villagers. Then 2 smallholders, now 6; then 3 slaves,
> now the same.
> Meadow, 30 acres; marsh, 20 acres. Now 40 cattle.

    Value then 100s; now £7.

    Hundred of HINCKFORD

2   Henry holds STEBBING in lordship, which Siward held as a manor,
    for 2 hides and 30 acres. Then and later 2 ploughs in lordship,
    now 3. Then among the men 4 ploughs, now 6½.
> Then 6 villagers, now 8; then 16 smallholders, now 33;

Tc̄.ii.ſer.m̄.i.Silu.cl.porc̄.ix.ac̄.p̄ti.tc̄.Qn̄ rec̄.dim̄ mol.m̄.n̄.Sēp ē.ibi
.i.pbr.Tc̄.vii.anim.7.xl.ou.7.lx.porc̄.7.i.runc̄.m̄.xviii.anim.
7.cxl.ou.7.lxxx.porc̄.7.i.runc̄.Tc̄.ual.x.lib.m̄.xii.7 in tēpr̄ reḡ
.ē.fuit totū ſimilit̄ 7 tantū ualuit qn̄ recep.

Ｖ Hund̄ de Witbric̄teſherna Steplam ten&.H. in dn̄io qd̄ tenuit Bondi
lib hō.t.r.ē.p̄ Man.7.p̄.iii.hid̄.7.dim̄.Sēp.ii.bord̄.Tc̄.iiii.ſer.m̄.iii.Sēp.i.
car in dn̄io.7.dim̄.car.hom̄.Tc̄.c.ou.m̄.cxxx.Val sēp.lx.ſol.

Ｖ Hund̄ de Celmereſfort   Vdeham ten&.H. in dn̄io qd̄ tenuit
Bundi p̄ uno man.7.p̄.xiiii.hid̄ Sēp.xxiiii.uillt.Tc̄.viii.bord̄.m̄.xxxi.
Tc̄.vi.ſer.m̄.iiii.Sēp.iii.car in dn̄io.7.xvi.car.hom̄.Silu.bccc.porc̄.
m̄.i.mol.Tc̄ rec̄.xx.anim.7.xiii.runc̄.7.ccc.ou.7.lx.porc̄.m̄.xxviii.
anim.7.xv.runc̄.7.ccc.ou.7.c.porc̄.7.xxxv.cap̄.Tc̄ ual.xx.lib.m̄
xxviii.

Ｖ Cingam ten& dapiſer Henrici de eo qd̄ tenuit Bondi p̄ Man.7.p̄.v.
hidis.7.dim̄.Tc̄.vi.uillt.m̄.iiii.Tc̄.viii.bord̄.m̄.xii.tc̄.iiii.ſer.m̄.iii.
Sēp.ii.car.in dn̄io.7.iiii.car.hom̄.Silu.b.porc̄.Paſt.c.ou.Tc̄.xx.
anim.7.l.porc̄.7.lx.ou.m̄.vii.an.7.c.ou.7.xl.porc̄.Sēp ual.vii.
lib.

.XXX. Ｖ TERRA Goisfridi de Magna uilla.   Hund̄ de Laxendena.
Teiam ten&.G. in dn̄io qd̄ tenuit Vluric̄.t.r.ē.p̄ Man.7.p̄.i.hid̄.7.d.
7.xx.ac̄.Tc̄.xi.bord̄.m̄.xv.Sēp.iiii.ſer.7.ii.car in dn̄io.Tc̄.int̄ hōes
.iii.car.m̄.ii.7.dim̄.Silu.c.porc̄.xx.ac̄.p̄ti.Tc̄.rec̄.G.ccl.ou.7.viii.
anim.7.vi.uit.7.ii.runc̄.xxviii.porc̄.ii.uaſa apū.m̄ lxvii.ou.7.viii.
anim.7.vi.uit.7.ii.runc̄.7.xxi.porc̄.In Ead̄ tenuer̄.xx.ſoc̄.i.hid̄.7.d.
7.xxxi.ac̄.M tenent.xxx.ſoc̄.illā trā.7 n̄ poſant recede ab illo
manerio.Sēp hn̄t.iii.car.vi.ac̄.p̄ti.Tc̄ 7 qn̄ rec̄ ual.vii.lib.m̄.x.

then 2 slaves, now 1.

Woodland, 550 pigs; meadow, 9 acres; then, when acquired ½ mill, now none. 1 priest has always been there. Then 7 cattle, 40 sheep, 60 pigs and 1 cob; now 18 cattle, 140 sheep, 80 pigs and 1 cob.

Value then £10; now £12. Before 1066 and when acquired it was all the same and the value was as much.

Hundred of 'WIBERTSHERNE'

3 Henry holds STEEPLE in lordship which Bondi, a free man, held before 1066 as a manor, for 3½ hides.

Always 2 smallholders. Then 4 slaves, now 3. Always 1 plough in lordship; ½ men's plough.

Then 100 sheep, now 130.

Value always 60s.

Hundred of CHELMSFORD

4 Henry holds WOODHAM (Ferrers) in lordship, which Bondi held as one manor, for 14 hides.

Always 24 villagers. Then 8 smallholders, now 31; then 6 slaves, now 4. Always 3 ploughs in lordship; 16 men's ploughs.

Woodland, 800 pigs; now 1 mill. Then he acquired 20 cattle, 13 cobs, 300 sheep and 60 pigs; now 28 cattle, 15 cobs, 300 sheep, 100 pigs and 35 goats.

Value then £20; now [£] 28.

5 Henry's steward holds BUTTSBURY from him, which Bondi held as a manor, for 5½ hides.

Then 6 villagers, now 4; then 8 smallholders, now 12; then 4 slaves, now 3. Always 2 ploughs in lordship; 4 men's ploughs.

Woodland, 500 pigs; pasture, 100 sheep. Then 20 cattle, 50 pigs and 60 sheep; now 7 cattle, 100 sheep and 40 pigs.

Value always £7.

30   LAND OF GEOFFREY DE MANDEVILLE

Hundred of LEXDEN

1 Geoffrey holds (Marks) TEY in lordship, which Wulfric held before 1066 as a manor, for 1½ hides and 20 acres.

Then 11 smallholders, now 15. Always 4 slaves; 2 ploughs in lordship. Then among the men 3 ploughs, now 2½.

Woodland, 100 pigs; meadow, 20 acres. Then Geoffrey acquired 250 sheep, 8 cattle, 6 calves, 2 cobs, 28 pigs, 2 beehives; now 67 sheep, 8 cattle, 6 calves, 2 cobs and 21 pigs.

In the same (Tey) 20 Freemen held 1½ hides and 31 acres. Now 30 Freemen hold that land. They could not withdraw from that manor. They have always had 3 ploughs.

Meadow, 6 acres.

Value then and when acquired £7; now [£] 10.

7 ibi fuer̃ . iii . libi . hões tenentes . xii . ac̃ . ſ; ñ fuer̃ de illo man̄ qd . G . h̃t

ſ; ipſe reuocat liberatore . Sẽp . ibi . ē . i . car̃ . 7 ual . xl . ſol .

|̃ Hund de Hangra . Senleiam ten& Rainald . de Goisfrido qd

tenuit Leuedai .p . Man̄ . 7 .p lxxx . ac̃ . 7 . ñ fuit de feudo angari . ſ; tantũ

fuit hõ ſuus . Tc̃ . iiii . uill̃ . m̃ . v . m̃ . v . bord . Tc̃ . ii . ſer . m̃ . iii . Tc̃ . 7 p̃ .

. ii . car̃ . in dñio . m̃ . i . Tc̃ . int̃ hões . i . car̃ . m̃ . ii . Silu . cl . porc̃ . xx . ac̃ . pti .

Tc̃ 7 p̃ ual . lx . ſol . m̃ . iiii . lib̃ .

|̃ Roinges ten& Goisfrid martel . de . G . qd tenuit Leuild .p . M̃ . 7

.p . iii . uirg̃ . Sẽp . i . uill̃ . 7 . ii . bord Tc̃ . i . ſer . m̃ null̃ . Sẽp . i . car̃ . in dñio .

7 . dim . car̃ hom̃ . Silu . xl . porc̃ . xv . ac̃ . pti . Tc̃ 7 p̃ ual . xxx . ſol . m̃ . xl .

7 hec tr̃a qm̃ m̃ ten& . G . fuit in abbia de b̃chingis ſicuti hun̄d teſtat̃ .

ſ; ille q̃ tenuit hanc tr̃a fuit tantũ m̃ hõ anteceſſoris Goisfridi . 7 . ñ

potuit iſtã tr̃a mittere in aliq̃ loco ñ in abbia .

|̃ Hund de Ceſſeorda . Wochadunã ten& Turold de . G . qd ten̄

Freb̃t libe tainn̄ .p uno manerio . 7 . .p . x . hid̃ . 7 dim̃ . 7 . xx . ac̃ .

7 Goisfrid h̃f .p eſcangio ut dicit . Sẽp . iii . uilli . xxxiiii . bord . Tc̃ . iii . ſer

m̃ null̃ . Tc̃ . in dñio . ii . car̃ . m̃ . iii . Tc̃ . int̃ hões . vii . car̃ . m̃ . viii . Silu . cl . porc̃

. viii . ac̃ . pti . Past . c . ou . m̃ . i . mol . Tc̃ . v . anim̃ . 7 . xviii . ou . m̃ . xviii . an̄ .

7 . i . runc̃ . xxxv . porc̃ . ccxx . ou . i . uas apũ . Tc̃ 7 qn̄ rec̃ ual . vii . lib̃ . m̃

ual . xvi . lib̃ . In hac tr̃a ſt̃ . xiii . ſoc̃ . q̃ libe tenent viii . hid̃ . 7 . dim̃ . 7 . xx . ac̃ .

7 . hñt . xii . bord . 7 jacent ad hanc firmã . de xvi . lib̃ . 7 adhuc ſt̃ . xl . ac̃ .

7 . iiii . bor .

There were 3 free men who held 12 acres but they were not of the manor which Geoffrey has; but he himself calls the deliverer. 1 plough has always been there.
Value 40s.

Hundred of ONGAR

2 Reginald holds SHELLEY from Geoffrey, which Leofday held as a manor, for 80 acres. It was not (part) of Asgar's Holding; he was only his man.

> Then 4 villagers, now 5; now 5 smallholders; then 2 slaves, now 3. Then and later 2 ploughs in lordship, now 1. Then among the men 1 plough, now 2.
> Woodland, 150 pigs; meadow, 20 acres.

Value then and later 60s; now £4.

3 Geoffrey Martel holds (Abbess) RODING from Geoffrey, which Leofhild held as a manor, for 3 virgates.

> Always 1 villager; 2 smallholders. Then 1 slave, now none.
> Always 1 plough in lordship; ½ men's plough.
> Woodland, 40 pigs; meadow, 15 acres.

Value then and later 30s; now 40[s].

This land which Geoffrey now holds was in (the lands of) Barking Abbey, as the Hundred testifies. He who held this land was only the man of Geoffrey's predecessor; he could not dispose of that land to any place except the Abbey.

Hundred of CHAFFORD

4 Thorold holds OCKENDON from Geoffrey which Fridebert, a thane, held freely as one manor, for 10½ hides and 20 acres.
Geoffrey has it by exchange, as he states.   58 a

> Always 3 villagers; 34 smallholders. Then 3 slaves, now none.
> Then 2 ploughs in lordship, now 3. Then among the men 7 ploughs, now 8.
> Woodland, 150 pigs; meadow, 8 acres; pasture, 100 sheep; now 1 mill. Then 5 cattle and 18 sheep; now 18 cattle, 1 cob, 35 pigs, 220 sheep, 1 beehive.

Value then and when acquired £7; value now £16.

On this land are 13 Freemen who hold 8½ hides and 20 acres freely and have 12 smallholders. They belong to this revenue of £16.
There are also 40 acres and 4 smallholders.

┌ Hund de Celmeresfort Waldham ten̄& . G . in dn̄io qđ tenuit

Anſgar̄ ꝓ Man̄ . 7 . ꝓ . viii . hid̄ . t . r̄ . e . Sēp . lxxii . uiłłi . 7 xxviii . bor̄ .

Tē . xiiii . ſer̄ . m̄ . xiii . Tē . vi . car̄ . in dn̄io . m̄ . v . Tē . inī hōes . xlii . car̄

m̄ . xxxvi . Silua . Ɔcc . porc̄ . xliiii . ac̄ . p̄ti . Sēp . ii . moł . m̄ . x . arpenni

uineæ . Tē . v . runc̄ . xii . uac̄ . l . porc̄ . lxxx . cap̄ . m̄ . iii . runc̄ . xi . uac̄ .

lx . porc̄ . cxxxii . ou . vii . cap̄ . xx . uaſa apū . Tē uał . l . lib̄ . m̄ . lx .

De hoc manerio ten̄& Hubt . i . uirḡ . 7 . dim̄ . car̄ . 7 uał . v . ſoł i eođ p̄tio

7 Walī . i . uirḡ . 7 . dim̄ . car̄ . 7 uał . v . ſoł . in eođ . p̄tio . Turchill . i . uirḡ .

7 . ii . bord̄ . 7 . dim̄ . car̄ . 7 uał . v . ſoł . in eođ . p̄tio . 7 Galī . xxx . ac̄ . 7 .

Turchill̄ . xxx . ac̄ . 7 Hubt̄ . xxx . ac̄ .

┌ In Waltham tenuit Vluuin̄ . libæ . cū ſoca . i . hid̄ . 7 . l . ac̄ . m̄ ten̄&

. Roḡ . de . G . ꝓ Man̄ . 7 ꝓ tantund̄e . Sēp . iii . uiłłi . tē iiii bor̄ . m̄ . vi .

Tē . in dn̄io . ii . car̄ . m̄ . i . 7 dim̄ . Sēp . i . car̄ hom̄ . 7 . i . ſer̄ . vii . ac̄ . p̄ti .

7 . i . moł . Tē uał . xl . ſoł . m̄ . lx .

┌ Cetham tenuit Eduuard̄ ꝓ man̄ . 7 . ꝓ . ii . hid̄ . & xxx . ac̄ . m̄ ten̄&

Galī de Goisfrido . ꝓ tantund̄e . Sēp . ii . uiłt . Tē . ii . bor̄ . m̄ . v . Sēp

vi . ſer̄ . 7 . ii . car̄ . in dn̄io . 7 . i . car̄ . hom̄ . Silu . c . porc̄ . vi . ac̄ . p̄ti .

58 b

Tē 7 poſt uał . xl . ſoł . m̄ lx .

┌ Pacinges . ten̄ . Id̄e . E . t . r̄ . e . ꝓ man̄ . 7 . ꝓ . ii . hid̄ . m̄ . ten̄& Galī de G .

Sēp . i . ſer̄ . 7 . i . car̄ . Silu . xxx . porc̄ . ix . ac̄ . p̄ti . Vał . xx . ſoł .

┌ Brumfeldam tenuit . Saulf . ꝓ . Ɔ . 7 . ꝓ . iiii . hid̄ . m̄ . Id̄e . Walī de . G .

Sēp . ix . uiłt . Tē . iiii . bord̄ . Tē . v . ſer̄ . m̄ . iiii . Sēp . ii . car̄ . in dn̄io . 7

. iiii . car̄ . hom̄ . silu . l . porc̄ . xiiii . ac̄ . p̄ti . Sēp . i . moł . Tē 7 . ꝓ uał . c .

ſoł . m̄ . vi . lib̄ .

58 a, b

Hundred of CHELMSFORD

5 Geoffrey holds (Great) WALTHAM in lordship, which Asgar held as a manor, for 8 hides before 1066.

Always 72 villagers; 28 smallholders. Then 14 slaves, now 13. Then 6 ploughs in lordship, now 5. Then among the men 42 ploughs, now 36.

Woodland, 1200 pigs; meadow, 44 acres; always 2 mills; now 10 *arpents* of vines. Then 5 cobs, 12 cows, 50 pigs, 80 goats; now 3 cobs, 11 cows, 60 pigs, 132 sheep, 7 goats, 20 beehives.

Value then £50; now [£] 60.

Of this manor Hubert holds 1 virgate. ½ plough.

Value 5s in the same assessment.

Walter (holds) 1 virgate. ½ plough.

Value 5s in the same assessment.

Thorkell (holds) 1 virgate.

2 smallholders. ½ plough.

Value 5s in the same assessment.

Walter (holds) 30 acres, Thorkell 30 acres and Hubert 30 acres.

6 In (Great) WALTHAM Wulfwin held 1 hide and 50 acres freely with the jurisdiction. Now Roger holds it from Geoffrey as a manor, for as much.

Always 3 villagers. Then 4 smallholders, now 6. Then 2 ploughs in lordship, now 1½. Always 1 men's plough; 1 slave.

Meadow, 7 acres; 1 mill.

Value then 40s; now 60[s].

7 Edward held CHATHAM as a manor, for 2 hides and 30 acres. Now Walter holds it from Geoffrey for as much.

Always 2 villagers. Then 2 smallholders, now 5. Always 6 slaves; 2 ploughs in lordship; 1 men's plough.

Woodland, 100 pigs; meadow, 6 acres.

Value then and later 40s; now 60[s].   58 b

8 Edward also held PATCHING (Hall) before 1066 as a manor, for 2 hides. Now Walter holds it from Geoffrey.

Always 1 slave; 1 plough.

Woodland, 30 pigs; meadow, 9 acres.

Value 20s.

9 Saewulf held BROOMFIELD as a manor, for 4½ hides. Now Walter also (holds it) from Geoffrey.

Always 9 villagers. Then 4 smallholders; then 5 slaves, now 4. Always 2 ploughs in lordship; 4 men's ploughs.

Woodland, 50 pigs; meadow, 14 acres; always 1 mill.

Value then and later 100s; now £6.

Cingehalam tenueř . III . liƀi hões . t . r̃ . ẽ . p̃ . I . hiđ . 7 . XV . ac̃ . m̃
Ricarđ . de . G . p̃ Man̄ . 7 p̃ tant̃ . Tc̃ . II . bor . m̃ . X . m̃ . III . uiłł . sep̃ . III .
ser . Tc̃ . 7 p̃ . II . car̃ . hom dñio . m̃ . I . M̃ . int̃ hões . I . car̃ . Silũ . X . porc̃ .
XV . ac̃ . p̃ti . Tc̃ . uał . XXX . sol̃ . m̃ . XLV .   ★

Cingehalam tenuit Goduin̄ diacon̄ t . r̃ . ẽ . p̃ Man̄ . 7 p̃ . I . hiđ . 7 . đ
. V . ac̃ . min̄ . m̃ ten& Ric̃ gernet . p̃ Man̄ . 7 p̃ tant̃ . Sep̃ . I . uiłł . Tc̃ . I .
bor . m̃ . III . Tc̃ . III . ser . m̃ . II . Sep̃ . I . car̃ in dñio . Tc̃ . int̃ hões . I . car̃ . m̃ . dim̃ .   ★
Silũ . XII . porc̃ . XVI . ac̃ . p̃ti . Tc̃ uał . XXX . sol̃ . m̃ . XL .

In Eađ uilla tenuit Vluuin̄ . XLV . ac̃ . t . r̃ . ẽ . m̃ ten& . Rađ de . G .
p̃ Man̄ . 7 p̃ tant̃ . Sep̃ . III . borđ . 7 . I . car̃ . 7 . III . ac̃ . p̃ti . Vał . X . sol̃ .
In Eađ ten& Lefsun̄ de . G . I . uirg̃ . qđ tenuit Iđẽ . t . r̃ . ẽ . Sep̃ . I . car̃ .
. V . ac̃ . p̃ti . Vał . V . sol̃ . 7 Leuric̃ tenuit 7 ten& . XXX . ac̃ . de . G . Tc̃ . dim̃
car̃ . m̃ nułł . VII . ac̃ . p̃ti . vał . III . sol̃ . 7 Leuuin̄ tenuit 7 ten& . XV . ac̃ .
7 . II . ac̃ . p̃ti . Vał . XXX . đ . 7 Alestan̄ ten& sep̃ . X . ac̃ . 7 . III . ac̃ . p̃ti . vał
. II . sol̃ .

In Massebirig tenuit 7 . ten& Eduin̄ . XLV . ac̃ . sub . G . Sep̃ . III . bor .
Tc̃ . dim̃ . car̃ . m̃ nułł . Vał . X . sol̃ .

59 a

Danengeƀiam tenuit Arling̃ p̃ . Man̄ . 7 p̃ . II . hiđ . 7 . dim̃ . m̃ . Wiłłs dẽ
. G . p̃ tant̃ . Sep̃ . I . uiłł . Tc̃ . III . borđ . m̃ . IX . Tc̃ . IIII . ser . m̃ . I . Sep̃ . I . car̃ i dñio ;
7 . I . car̃ . hom̃ . Silũ . c . porc̃ . XVI . ac̃ . p̃ti . Tc̃ uał . XXX . sol̃ . m̃ . XL .

10   3 free men held CHIGNALL before 1066 for 1 hide and 15 acres.
Now Richard (holds it) from Geoffrey as a manor, for as much.
> Then 2 smallholders, now 10; now 3 villagers; always 3 slaves.
> Then and later 2 ploughs in lordship, now 1. Now among
> the men 1 plough.
> Woodland, 10 pigs; meadow, 15 acres.
Value then 30s; now 45[s].

11   Godwin the deacon held CHIGNALL before 1066 as a manor, for
1½ hides less 5 acres. Now Richard Garnet holds it as a manor,
for as much.
> Always 1 villager. Then 1 smallholder, now 3; then 3 slaves,
> now 2. Always 1 plough in lordship. Then among the men
> 1 plough, now ½.
> Woodland, 12 pigs; meadow, 16 acres.
Value then 30s; now 40[s].

12   In the same village Wulfwin held 45 acres before 1066. Now Ralph
holds them from Geoffrey as a manor, for as much.
> Always 3 smallholders; 1 plough.
> Meadow, 3 acres.
Value 10s.
> In the same (Chignall) Leofson holds 1 virgate from Geoffrey
which he also held before 1066. Always 1 plough.
> Meadow, 5 acres.
Value 5s.
> Leofric held and holds 30 acres from Geoffrey. Then ½ plough,
now none. Meadow, 7 acres.
Value 3s.
> Leofwin held and holds 15 acres.
> Meadow, 2 acres.
Value 30d.
> Alstan has always held 10 acres.
> Meadow, 3 acres.
Value 2s.

[Hundred of DUNMOW]
13   In MASHBURY Edwin held and holds 45 acres under Geoffrey.
> Always 3 smallholders. Then ½ plough, now none.
Value 10s.

[Hundred of CHELMSFORD]   59 a
14   Erling held DANBURY as a manor, for 2½ hides. Now William
(holds it) from Geoffrey for as much.
> Always 1 villager. Then 3 smallholders, now 9; then 4 slaves,
> now 1. Always 1 plough in lordship; 1 men's plough.
> Woodland, 100 pigs; meadow, 16 acres.
Value then 30s; now 40[s].

In Cingehala teñ ꞇ Sauin p̄r . xv . ac̄ . m̄ . Ricard̃ de . G . Tc̄ . dim̄ . car̄
m̄ . nich . val . v . fot . In Ead̃ uitt . tenuit Etſin . xv . ac̄ . m̄ . Id̄e . R . 11 . ac̄ꞇ
p̄ti . val . 111 . fot . Iſti ſup̄dicti fuer̄ libi ita qd̄ ipſi poſſent uende tr̄a cũ
ſoca ꞇ ſaca q̃ uellent ut hund̃ teſtat̄.

Legram tenuit Anſgar̄ ꝓ Man̄ . 7 . ꝓ . 11 . hid̃ . 7 dim̄ . 7 xv . ac̄ . m̄ . W . de . G.
ꝓ tant̄ . Tc̄ . 1111 . uitt . m̄ . 11 . Tc̄ . v111 . bord̃ . m̄ . x11 . Tc̄ . 111 . ſer̄ . m̄ . 1111 .
Tc̄ . 11 . car̄ . in dñio . m̄ . 111 . Sēp . 11 . car̄ . hom̄ . Silu̇ . xL . porc̄ . v1 . ac̄ . p̄ti .
Sēp . 1 . mot . M . x . an̄ . x . porc̄ . c . ou̇ . Tc̄ 7 p̄ uat . 1111 . lib̄ . m̄ . 1111 . lib̄
7 . x . fot . Iſtud q̃q; maner̄ t̄ . r̄ . e̓ . dedit Eſgar Haroldo . 7 herold̃ itũm
dedit cuidã ſuo huſcarlo . n̄o̊e ſcalpino . 7 iſte Scalpiñ dedit uxori
ſuæ in dote . uidentib; 11b; h̄oib; ſcit Ro̊go mareſcalco 7 q̊dã anglico .
7 hoc teſtat̄ . hund̃ . qd̄ audier̄ recognoſcere ſcalpino . 7 p̊q̄ rex
uenit in hanc tr̄a tenuit ipſe ꞏ donec iuit ubi mortuus fuit in ebroica .
in utlagaria.

Keuentunã tenuit Toĺi ꝓ Man̄ . 7 . ꝓ . 11 . hid̃ . 7 . 1 . uirḡ . m̄ Osb̄t de . G .
in ſuo eſcangio ut dicit . Sēp . 1 . uitt . Tc̄ . v1 . bord̃ . m̄ . 1111 . Sēp . 111 . ſer̄ꞏ
7 . 11 . car̄ . in dñio . tc̄ . int̄ h̄oe̅s . 1 . car̄ . m̄ . dim̄ . xv111 . ac̄ . p̄ti . Sēp . 1 .
mot . Tc̄ . 11 . uac̄ . x111 . ou̇ . x11 . porc̄ . m̄ . v111 . anim̄ . xxx11 . ou̇ . xx꞉
porc̄ . x1111 . cap . 11 . runc̄ . v . uaſa . ap̄ . Tc̄ uat . xL . fot . m̄ . Lx .

Hund̃ de Tendringa . Moſam tenuit Leueſuñ ꝓ Man̄ . 7 . ꝓ . 1111꞉
hid̃ . m̄ . Goisfrid̃ in dñio ꞏ Sēp . x1111 . uitt . m̄ . x111 . bord̃꞉

Tc̄ . x111 . ſer̄ . 7 . qñ rec̄ . x1 . m̄ . 111 ꞉ Tc̄ 7 p̄ . 1111 . car̄ in dñio m̄ . 11 . Tc̄ 7 p̄
v1 . car̄ hom̄ . m̄ . 1111 . Silu̇ . cL . porc̄ . v1 . ac̄ 7 dim̄ p̄ti . Tc̄ . 1 . mot . m̄ null .
paſt . cL . ou̇ . 111 . ſalinæ . 7 hoc maner̄ . dedit Rex . G . qñ remanſit Londoniæ.

15 In CHIGNALL Saewin the priest held 15 acres. Now Richard (holds them) from Geoffrey. Then ½ plough, now nothing.
Value 5s.

In the same village Edsi held 15 acres. Now Richard also (holds them).
Meadow, 2 acres.
Value 3s.

These above-mentioned people were free to the extent that they themselves could sell the land with full jurisdiction whither they would, as the Hundred testifies.

16 Asgar held (Great and Little) LEIGHS as a manor, for 2½ hides and 15 acres. Now W. (holds it) from Geoffrey for as much.

Then 4 villagers, now 2; then 8 smallholders, now 12; then 3 slaves, now 4. Then 2 ploughs in lordship, now 3. Always 2 men's ploughs.

Woodland, 40 pigs; meadow, 6 acres; always 1 mill. Now 10 cattle, 10 pigs, 100 sheep.
Value then and later £4; now £4 10s.

And Asgar gave this manor to Harold and Harold in turn gave it to one of his Guards, Scalpi by name. This Scalpi gave it to his wife in dowry in the sight of two men, namely Roger the Marshal and an Englishman. The Hundred testifies to this, that they heard (them) acknowledge Scalpi. After the King came to this land, he himself held it until he went to where he died in outlawry in York(shire).

17 Toli held CUTON (Hall) as a manor, for 2 hides and 1 virgate. Now Osbert (holds it) from Geoffrey by his exchange, as he states.

Always 1 villager. Then 6 smallholders, now 4. Always 3 slaves; 2 ploughs in lordship. Then among the men 1 plough, now ½.

Meadow, 18 acres; always 1 mill. Then 2 cows, 13 sheep, 12 pigs; now 8 cattle, 32 sheep, 20 pigs, 14 goats, 2 cobs, 5 beehives.
Value then 40s; now 60[s].

Hundred of TENDRING

18 Leofson held MOZE as a manor, for 4 hides. Now Geoffrey (holds it) in lordship.

Always 14 villagers. Now 13 smallholders; then 13 slaves, when 59 b acquired 11, now 3. Then and later 4 ploughs in lordship, now 2. Then and later 6 men's ploughs, now 4.

Woodland, 150 pigs; meadow, 6½ acres; then 1 mill, now none; pasture, 150 sheep; 3 salt-houses.

The King gave this manor to Geoffrey when he stayed at London.

Tc̄.ii.runc̄.7.ix.anim̄.clxxx.ou.xiiii.porc̄.m̄.ii.runc̄.xiiii.an.
xv.porc̄.clx.ou.l.cap̄.iii.uafa apū.Tc̄ ual.viii.lib.7 qn̄ recepit
fimil.m̄.ual.ix.lib.

⌐ Frientunam ten& Rēnelm de.G.qđ tenuit Leuefun p Man.7.p.
.iii.hiđ.Tc̄.7 p.iii.uilt.m̄.i.Tc̄.7 p.iiii.fer.m̄.iii.Sēp.ii.car in dio.
7.tc̄.ii.car hom.7 qn̄ rec̄;i.7 dim̄.m̄.dim tantū.iii.ac̄.7 dim p̄ti.
Paſt.l.ou.Tc̄.xlix.ou.m̄.ii.runc̄.7.iiii.porc̄.7.xl.ou.Tc̄ 7 poſt
ual.vii.lib.m̄.iiii.

⌐ Erleiam ten& Witt de.G.qđ tenuer̄.ii.libi hōes fr̄es.Bund 7 Alric.
f; non poſant recede.fine licentia illi Algari.p.ii.hiđ.7.p.ii.Man.
Sēp.v.uilt.7.viii.bord.Tc̄.i.fer.m̄ nult.Sēp.ii.car in dnīo.Tc̄.7 p.
.v.car.hom.m̄.iiii.Silu.c.porc̄.xii.ac̄.p̄ti.Paſt.l.ou.Tc̄ 7 p ual
.iiii.lib.m̄.xl.fot.

⌐ In Hund de Berdeſtapla.erant.vi.libi hōes.t̄.r̄.ē.q̄s.G.in
uafit fup regē.Wittm.tenentes.xii.hiđ.tr̄æ.q̄s tenent.v.milites de eo.
Sēp.ix.car.7.dim.Tc̄.i.uilt m̄ nult.tc̄.x.bord.m̄.xxxvi.tc̄.xiiii.
fer.m̄.vii.Tc̄.filu.c.porc̄.m̄.l.Paſt.ccc.ou.x.ac̄.p̄ti.i.pifcina.
De his.xii.hiđ.tulit Rauengari.xii.ac̄.tr̄æ.7 appofuit fuo feudo.
7 Suen inde tulit.xxx.ac̄.7 pofuit in Tilibia fuo manerio.Tc̄ totū
fimul ual.vii.lib.7 m̄ fimilit̄.

⌐ Hund de Witham.Nutleam ten& Galt de.G.

qđ tenuit Efgar.p.man.7.p.i.hiđ.7.dim̄.7.xlv.ac̄.Sēp.ii.car.in dnīo.7.
.iiii.car hom.Sēp.x.uilt.7.v.bord.7.iiii.fer.Silu.c.porc̄.m̄.i.mol.7.ii.
libi hōes de.xl.ac̄.7 de eis clamat regē ad uuarant.Tc̄.vi.anim̄.7.i.runc̄.
7.xii.porc̄.lx.ou.m̄.viii.an.xvi.porc̄.c.ou.i.runc̄.Tc̄.ual.c.fot.m̄
.vi.lib.

Then 2 cobs, 9 cattle, 180 sheep, 14 pigs; now 2 cobs, 14
  cattle, 15 pigs, 160 sheep, 50 goats, 3 beehives.
Value then £8; when acquired, the same. Value now £9.

19 Rainalm holds FRINTON from Geoffrey, which Leofson held as a
manor, for 3½ hides.
  Then and later 3 villagers, now 1; then and later 4 slaves, now 3.
    Always 2 ploughs in lordship. Then 2 men's ploughs; when
    acquired 1½; now only ½.
  Meadow, 3½ acres; pasture, 50 sheep. Then 49 sheep; now 2
    cobs, 4 pigs and 40 sheep.
Value then and later £7; now [£] 4.

20 William holds ARDLEIGH from Geoffrey which 2 free men, the
brothers Bondi and Alric, held for 2 hides as 2 manors; but they
could not withdraw without the permission of a certain Algar.
  Always 5 villagers; 8 smallholders. Then 1 slave, now none.
    Always 2 ploughs in lordship. Then and later 5 men's
    ploughs, now 4.
  Woodland, 100 pigs; meadow, 12 acres; pasture, 50 sheep.
Value then and later £4; now 40s.

In the Hundred of BARSTABLE
21 6 free men were there before 1066 whom Geoffrey annexed
from King William. They held 12 hides of land which 5 men-at-
arms hold from him. Always 9½ ploughs.
  Then 1 villager, now none; then 10 smallholders, now 36;
    then 14 slaves, now 7.
  Woodland, then 100 pigs, now 50; pasture, 300 sheep;
    meadow, 10 acres; 1 fishery.
Of these 12 hides, Ravengar took 12 acres of land and placed
them in his Holding, and Swein took 30 acres from there and
placed them in his manor of (West) Tilbury.
Value of the whole altogether then £7; now the same.

Hundred of WITHAM
22 Walter holds (Black) NOTLEY from Geoffrey, which Asgar held as   60 a
a manor, for 1½ hides and 45 acres. Always 2 ploughs in lordship;
4 men's ploughs.
  Always 10 villagers; 5 smallholders; 4 slaves.
  Woodland, 100 pigs; now 1 mill. 2 free men with 40 acres and
    he claims the King as a warrantor for them. Then 6 cattle,
    1 cob, 12 pigs, 60 sheep; now 8 cattle, 16 pigs, 100 sheep,
    1 cob.
Value then 100s; now £6.

⌐Retleiam ten& Galt de . G . q̄d tenuit Efgar . t . r . ē . p̄ . Man . 7 . p̄ . i . hid.
Sēp . i . car . in dn̄io . 7 . dim̄ . car hom . m̄ . iiii . bord . Tc . iii . ſer . m̄ . i . Silu . x . porc.
. iiii . ac . p̄ti . 7 . xxx . ac adjacebant t . r . ē . huic tr̄æ . ex qb; . G . de magn
uill . h̄t . xx . ac . 7 Ricard fili comitis . Gifletti . x . ac . ſ; hund teſtat
totā recte eſſe ad tr̄a Gosfridi . Totū ſimul . ual . xxx . ſol.

⌐Hund de herlaua . Halingebiam ten& Martel . de . G . q̄d ten.
Efgar . t . r . ē . p̄ . Man . 7 . p̄ . i . hid . Tc . ii . car . in dn̄io . m̄ . i . tc . i . p̄br . 7 . i.
. uill . de . xx . ac . que attinebant ad ecclam ſ; m̄ n̄ ſt ad ecclam . m̄ . iiii.
bord . tc . iii . ſer . m̄ . ii . Silu . c . porc . xx . ac . p̄ti . m̄ . dim . mol . Sēper
ual . xl . ſol.

⌐Matcingā tenuit Efgar p̄ Man . 7 . p̄ . xl . ac . q̄d ten& . G . in dn̄io.
Sēp . i . car . tc . i . ſer . m̄ . n̄ . Silu . x . porc . iii . ac . p̄ti . Val . x . ſol.

⌐Hallingebiam ten& hugo de . G . q̄d tenuit Godid litia femina
. t . r . ē . p̄ Man . 7 p̄ dim̄ . hid . viii . ac min . Tc . dim̄ . car . m̄ . nulla . Tc.
. ii . uill . m̄ . nulli . v . ac . p̄ti . Val . v . ſol.

⌐Hund de Dommaua . Eftram tenuit Efgar . t . r . ē.
p̄ Man . 7 . p̄ . ii . hid . m̄ ten& . G . in dn̄io Sēp . iiii . car in dn̄io . 7.
. xii . car hom . Tc . xlvi . uill . m̄ . xlvii . Tc . xiiii . bor . m̄ . xxxiii.
Sēp . ix . ſer . Silu . tc . porc . xxx . ac . p̄ti . 7 . v . car pot fieri in dn̄io.

tc . iii . runc . 7 . vii . anim . 7 . lx . porc . 7 . lx . ou . xxx . cap . x . uaſa apū.
m̄ . iii . runc . 7 . vii . uac . xxvii . porc . l . ou . &. iiii . cap . xvii . uaſa apū.
Tc 7 p̄ ual . xx . lib . m̄ . xxx.
Huic manerio adjacent femp . vi . ſoc . de . i . hid . 7 dim̄ . tc . ii . car . m̄ . i.

23 Walter holds RIDLEY (Hall) from Geoffrey, which Asgar held before 1066 as a manor, for 1 hide. Always 1 plough in lordship; ½ men's plough.

Now 3 smallholders; then 3 slaves, now 1.

Woodland, 10 pigs; meadow, 4 acres.

30 acres belonged to this land before 1066, of which Geoffrey de Mandeville has 20 acres and Richard son of Count Gilbert (has) 10 acres; but the Hundred testifies that it is all rightly appurtenant to Geoffrey's land.

Value of the whole altogether 30s.

Hundred of HARLOW

24 Martel holds (Little) HALLINGBURY from Geoffrey, which Asgar held before 1066 as a manor, for 1 hide. Then 2 ploughs in lordship, now 1.

Then 1 priest and 1 villager with 20 acres which belonged to the church; but now they are not appurtenant to the church. Now 4 smallholders; then 3 slaves, now 2.

Woodland, 100 pigs; meadow, 20 acres; now ½ mill.

Value always 40s.

25 Asgar held MATCHING as a manor for 40 acres. Geoffrey holds it in lordship. Always 1 plough.

Then 1 slave, now none.

Woodland, 10 pigs; meadow, 3 acres.

Value 10s.

26 Hugh holds HALLINGBURY from Geoffrey which Godith, a free woman, held before 1066 as a manor, for ½ hide less 8 acres. Then ½ plough; now none.

Then 2 villagers; now none.

Meadow, 5 acres.

Value 5s.

Hundred of DUNMOW

27 Asgar held (High) EASTER before 1066 as a manor, for 2 hides. Now Geoffrey holds it in lordship. Always 4 ploughs in lordship; 12 men's ploughs.

Then 46 villagers, now 47; then 14 smallholders, now 33; always 9 slaves.

Woodland, 600 pigs; meadow, 30 acres; 5 ploughs possible in lordship. Then 3 cobs, 7 cattle, 60 pigs, 60 sheep, 30 goats, 10 beehives; now 3 cobs, 7 cows, 27 pigs, 50 sheep, 4 goats, 17 beehives. 60 b

Value then and later £20; now [£] 30.

Attached to this manor have always been 6 Freemen with 1½ hides. Then 2 ploughs, now 1.

m̄ . iii . borđ . viii . ac̄ . p̄ti . Tc̄ uaɫ . xx . foɫ . m̄ . xxx . / Adjacent &iam huic

manerio . ii . hiđ . 7 . i . uirg̃ . q̄s tenuer̃ . ii . foc̄ . t . r . e . In q̄b; s̄t ſep . iiii . car̄

in dn̄io . 7 . i . car̄ 7 dim . hom . Tc̄ . viii . uiɫɫ . m̄ . vii . Tc̄ . vi . borđ . m̄ . vii .

Sep . iii . ſer . Silu . lx . porc̄ . xxiiii . ac̄ . p̄ti . Tc̄ 7 p̄ uaɫ . c . foɫ . m̄ . x . liƀ .

hoc tenent . iiii . miliť de . Gosfrido . 7 adhuc jacent illi manerio . dim .

hiđ . que p̄tinebat ad eccliam manerij . t . r . e . 7 eam m̄ ten& Guťbť de . G .

Sep . i . car̄ tc̄ . i . borđ . m̄ . iii . 7 . i . ſer . Silu . xx . porc̄ . v . ac̄ . p̄ti . Tc̄ uaɫ . xx .

foɫ . m̄ . xxx . 7 hoc ſup̄dict̄u maneriū calumpniať abbas de eli . 7 hund̄

teſtať qđ fuit in abƀia . t . r . e . ſ; Anſgar tenuit hoc maneriū eo die

q̄ Eaduuarđ rex . uiu 7 mortuus fuit.

/ Niuuetun̄a ten& Hugo de ƀneris de . G . qđ tenuit Vluric̄

cauūa t . r . e . p̄ . Man . 7 p̄ . ii . hiđ . 7 . i . uirg̃ . Tc̄ . ii . car̄ in dn̄io . m̄ . i . 7 . dim .

Sep . i . car̄ hom . 7 . v . uiɫɫi . Tc̄ . i . borđ . m̄ . v . ſep . ii . ſer . Silu . clx . porc̄ .

. xii . ac̄ . p̄ti . Tc̄ uaɫ . lx . foɫ . 7 q̄n rec̄ . xl . foɫ . m̄ . iiii . liƀ .

/ Berneſtun̄a ten& Idē qđ tenuit Vluuin t . r . e . p̄ . Man . 7 p̄ . ii .

hiđ . 7 . xxx . ac̄ . Sep . ii . car̄ in dn̄io . 7 . iii . car̄ . hom . Tc̄ . vi . uiɫɫ . m̄ . vii .

tc̄ . v . borđ . m̄ . vii . Sep . ii . ſer . Silu . cc . porc̄ . xx . ac̄ . p̄ti . Tc̄ uaɫ . iiii . liƀ

m̄ . c . foɫ . 7 q̄n rec̄ ſimiɫ .

/ Rodinges ten& Idē . qđ tenuit Vluric̄ . t . r . e . p̄ Man . 7 p̄ . ii . hiđ .

7 . dim . Sep . ii . car̄ in dn̄io . 7 . i . car̄ 7 dim . hom . Sep . iiii . uiɫɫi . 7 . iii . borđ .

7 . iiii . ſer . Silu . c . porc̄ . xxvii . ac̄ . p̄ti . Sep . i . moɫ . Tc̄ . 7 p̄ uaɫ . c . foɫ . m̄ .

vii . liƀ . 7 hec . iii . maneria p̄cep̄ rex . p̄ Robt̄u de Oilleio . ut hugo te-

ner& de . G . de magna uiɫɫ . ſi ipſe . G . poſſ& ea deratiocinari ad ſū feudū .

7 anteq̄ . G . de rationar& ea p̄tinere ſuo feudo ꞉ Hugo ea tenuit de .

Goisfrido.

Now 3 smallholders.

Meadow, 8 acres.

Value then 20s; now 30[s].

Also attached to this manor, 2 hides and 1 virgate which 2 Freemen held before 1066. On them have always been 4 ploughs in lordship and 1½ men's ploughs.

Then 8 villagers, now 7; then 6 smallholders, now 7; always 3 slaves.

Woodland, 60 pigs; meadow, 24 acres.

Value then and later 100s; now £10.

3 men-at-arms hold this from Geoffrey.

Also attached to this manor is ½ hide which belonged to the church of the manor before 1066. Now Gutbert holds it from Geoffrey. Always 1 plough.

Then 1 smallholder, now 3; 1 slave.

Woodland, 20 pigs; meadow, 5 acres.

Value then 20s; now 30[s].

The Abbot of Ely lays claim to the above-mentioned manor and the Hundred testifies that it was in (the lands of) the Abbey before 1066; but Asgar held this manor in 1066.

28 Hugh of Bernières holds NEWTON (Hall) from Geoffrey, which Wulfric Cave held before 1066 as a manor, for 2 hides and 1 virgate. Then 2 ploughs in lordship, now 1½. Always 1 men's plough;

5 villagers. Then 1 smallholder, now 5; always 2 slaves.

Woodland, 160 pigs; meadow, 12 acres.

Value then 60s; when acquired 40s; now £4.

29 He also holds BARNSTON, which Wulfwin held before 1066 as a manor, for 2 hides and 30 acres. Always 2 ploughs in lordship; 3 men's ploughs.

Then 6 villagers, now 7; then 5 smallholders, now 7; always 2 slaves.

Woodland, 200 pigs; meadow, 20 acres.

Value then £4; now 100s; when acquired, the same.

30 He also holds (Berners) RODING, which Wulfric held before 1066 as a manor, for 2½ hides. Always 2 ploughs in lordship; 1½ men's ploughs.

Always 4 villagers; 3 smallholders; 4 slaves. 61 a

Woodland, 100 pigs; meadow, 27 acres; always 1 mill.

Value then and later 100s; now £7.

The King commanded through Robert d'Oilly that Hugh should hold these 3 manors from Geoffrey de Mandeville if Geoffrey himself could prove that they (belonged) to his Holding; and before Geoffrey proved that they belonged to his Holding, Hugh held them from Geoffrey.

Alferestunam ten& Martell de .G. qd tenuit Anfgar .t.r.e. p
uno man. 7 .p. IIII. hid. 7.x. ac. Sep. III. car in dnio. 7.II. car. hom.
tc. XI. uilli. m. VII. Tc. VI. bord. m. XXIIII. Tc. VI. fer. m. IIII. Silua tc
. CCCC. porc. m. CCCL. XXXVI. ac. pti. Sep. I. mol. Tc. 7 p ual. VII. lib.
m. x. lib.

Domauua. ten& Ide de .G. qd tenuit. Ide. Anfgar .t.r.e. p. Man.
7 .p. I. hid. 7. dim. Sep. II. car in dnio. 7. II. car hom. Tc. XIII. uilt. m. v.
Tc. VII. bord. m. VI. Tc. I. fer. m. IIII. Silu. cc. porc. XXVI. ac. pti. Tc ual
. c. fol. m. VII. lib.

Scelgam ten& . Lambt de .G. qd tenuit .A. t.r.e. p. Man. 7 .p. I. hid.
7 dim. Sep. II. car in dnio. Tc. II. uilt. m. I. Tc. V. bord. m. VIII. Tc. II. fer. m. I.
Silu. CL. porc. x. ac. pti. IIII. anim. IIII. porc. XXV. ou. m. I. uafa ap. Tc
7 p ual. XL. fol. m. LX.

Scelga ten& . G. in dnio qd tenuit Vluric lib ho de haroldo. t.r.e.
p. Man. 7 .p. II. hid. Sep. II. car in dnio. Tc. I. car hom. m. dim. Tc. II.
uilt. m. I. Tc. II. bord. m. IIII. tc. IIII. fer. m. VI. Silu. CL. porc. XII. ac pti.
7 adhuc. I. car poff& fieri. Tc ual. IIII. lib m. c. fol. Huic tre adjac&
dim hid tre qm fep ten& . I. foc. Tc. I. car in dnio. m. dim. Sep. I. bord.
7. I. ac. 7 dim. pti. 7. d. car pot reftaurari. Val. x. fol.

Rodinges ten& Martell de .G. qd tenuit Anfgar p Man. 7 .p. II. hid. t.r.e.
Sep. II. car in dnio. tc. III. car hom. m. II. 7. tcia poteft reftaurari. Tc.
. VI. uilt. m. VIII. Tc. I. bor. m. V. Tc. I. fer. m null. Silu. XX. porc. XX. ac.
pti. Tc 7 p ual. c. fol. m. VI. lib.

31 Martel holds BIGODS from Geoffrey, which Asgar held before 1066 as one manor, for 4 hides and 10 acres. Always 3 ploughs in lordship; 2 men's ploughs.
  Then 11 villagers, now 7; then 6 smallholders, now 24; then 6 slaves, now 4.
  Woodland, then 400 pigs, now 350; meadow, 36 acres; always 1 mill.
Value then and later £7; now £10.

32 He also holds (Little) DUNMOW from Geoffrey, which Asgar also held before 1066 as a manor, for 1½ hides. Always 2 ploughs in lordship; 2 men's ploughs.
  Then 13 villagers, now 5; then 7 smallholders, now 6; then 1 slave, now 3.
  Woodland, 200 pigs; meadow, 26 acres.
Value then 100s; now £7.

33 Lambert holds SHELLOW (Bowells) from Geoffrey, which A(sgar) held before 1066 as a manor, for 1½ hides. Always 2 ploughs in lordship.
  Then 2 villagers, now 1; then 5 smallholders, now 8; then 2 slaves, now 1.
  Woodland, 150 pigs; meadow, 10 acres. 3 cattle, 3 pigs, 25 sheep. Now 1 beehive.
Value then and later 40s; now 60[s].

34 Geoffrey holds SHELLOW (Bowells) in lordship which Wulfric, a free man, held from Harold before 1066 as a manor, for 2 hides. Always 2 ploughs in lordship. Then 1 men's plough, now ½.
  Then 2 villagers, now 1; then 2 smallholders, now 4; then 4 slaves, now 6.
  Woodland, 150 pigs; meadow, 12 acres; 1 more plough possible.
Value then £4; now 100s.
  Attached to this land is ½ hide of land which 1 Freeman has always held. Then 1 plough in lordship, now ½.
  Always 1 smallholder.
  Meadow, 1½ acres; ½ plough can be restored.
Value 10s.

35 Martel holds (White) RODING from Geoffrey, which Asgar held as   61 b
a manor, for 2 hides before 1066. Always 2 ploughs in lordship.
  Then 3 men's ploughs, now 2; a third could be restored.
  Then 6 villagers, now 8; then 1 smallholder, now 5; then 1 slave, now none.
  Woodland, 20 pigs; meadow, 20 acres.
Value then and later 100s; now £6.

ᚠDommauua ten& Wilts ᵽ Man 7 ᵽ dim̄ . & xv . ac̄ . q̄ð tenuit . Idē
. A . t . r̄ . e . Sēp . I . car̄ . in dn̄io . Tc̄ . IIII . uilt . m̄ . I . 7 . IIII . bor . Silu̅ . L . porc̄ .
xvi . ac̄ . p̄ti . Tc̄ 7 p̄ uat ; xx . fot . m̄ . LX .

ᚠEſtanes ten& Ricard̄ de ; G . q̄ð tenuit . I . lib̄ hō . t . r̄ . e . ᵽ . Man̄ . 7 . ᵽ
dim̄ hid . Sēp . I . car̄ in dn̄io . Tc̄ . I . ſer̄ . m̄ . I . bord̄ . xII . ac̄ . p̄ti . Tc̄ 7 p̄ uat
. x . fot . m̄ . xxx .

ᚠChenefeldam ten& . Ricard̄ . de ; G . q̄ð tenuit . A . t . r̄ . e . ᵽ . Man̄ . 7 . ᵽ . ð
hid̄ . 7 . xvi . ac̄ . Tc̄ . II . car̄ . in dn̄io . m̄ . I . m̄ . I . car̄ hom̄ . m̄ . II . uilt . Tc̄ .
vIII . bord̄ . m̄ . IIII . Silu̅ . xxx . porc̄ . xvi . ac̄ . p̄ti . Tc̄ uat . xL . fot . 7 . qn̄
rec̄ ſimit . m̄ . LX .

ᚠRoinges ten& Rainalm̄ de . G . q̄ð ten̄ . A . t . r̄ . e . ᵽ . man̄ . 7 . ᵽ . II . hid̄ .
. x . ac̄ min . Sēp . II . car̄ in dn̄io . m̄ . vIII . bord̄ . ſēp . II . ſer̄ . Silu̅ . xx . por̄ .
xxxII . ac̄ . p̄ti . Tc̄ 7 p̄ uat LX . fot . m̄ . c . 7 adhuc poſſ& reſtaurari
. I . car̄ . Huic tr̄e addite ſt̄ . x . ac̄ . q̄s tenuit . I . lib̄ hō . t . r̄ . e . 7 m̄ eas
tot hund̄ teſtat̄ de dn̄io reḡ Wilti .

ᚠRodinges ten& Wilts ; q̄ð tenuit . I . lib̄ hō ; t . r̄ . e . ᵽ . Man̄ . 7 . ᵽ . I . hid̄ .
7 . IIII . uir̄g ; hec tr̄a dimidia reddebat ſoca Anſgaro . 7 alt̄a pars
erat liba qua̅ rex dedit . G . ut ſui hōes dic̄t . Tc̄ . I . car̄ 7 . dim̄ . in
dn̄io ; m̄ . I . m̄ . I . car̄ . hom̄ . Sēp . IIII . uilt . m̄ . II . bord̄ . Tc̄ . II . ſer̄
m̄ null nec qn̄ recep . Silu̅ . xxx . porc̄ . xvi . ac̄ . p̄ti . Tc̄ 7 p̄ uat

62 a
xL . fot . m̄ . IIII . lib̄ .
ᚠScelga̅ ten& Wilts . de . G . q̄ð tenuit . I . lib̄ hō ᵽ xxxv . ac̄ . t . r̄ . e . Silua
xx . porc̄ . IIII . ac̄ p̄ti . Tc̄ . uat . v . fot . m̄ . x . hec tr̄a jacuit ad Rodinges
maneriu̅ Eudonis dapiferi . t . r̄ . e . 7 abbas de eli calumpniat̄ teſte
hundr̄et 7 tr̄a 7 maneriu̅ de Rodingis .

36 William holds DUNMOW as a manor, for ½ hide and 15 acres. Asgar also held it before 1066. Always 1 plough in lordship.
>   Then 4 villagers, now 1; 4 smallholders.
>   Woodland, 50 pigs; meadow, 16 acres.
>   Value then and later 20s; now 60[s].

37 Richard holds EASTON from Geoffrey, which 1 free man held before 1066 as a manor, for ½ hide. Always 1 plough in lordship.
>   Then 1 slave; now 1 smallholder.
>   Meadow, 12 acres.
>   Value then and later 10s; now 30[s].

38 Richard holds (Little) CANFIELD from Geoffrey, which A(sgar) held before 1066 as a manor, for ½ hide and 16 acres. Then 2 ploughs in lordship, now 1. Now 1 men's plough.
>   Now 2 villagers; then 8 smallholders, now 4.
>   Woodland, 30 pigs; meadow, 16 acres.
>   Value then 40s; when acquired, the same; now 60[s].

39 Rainalm holds RODING from Geoffrey, which A(sgar) held before 1066 as a manor, for 2 hides less 10 acres. Always 2 ploughs in lordship.
>   Now 8 smallholders; always 2 slaves.
>   Woodland, 20 pigs; meadow, 32 acres.
>   Value then and later 60s; now 100[s]. 1 more plough could be restored.
>   To this land have been added 10 acres which 1 free man held before 1066. Now the whole Hundred testifies that they are part of King William's lordship.

40 William holds RODING, which 1 free man held before 1066 as a manor, for 1 hide and 3 virgates. Half this land paid suit to Asgar, the other part was free; the King gave it to Geoffrey, as his men state. Then 1½ ploughs in lordship, now 1. Now 1 men's plough.
>   Always 4 villagers. Now 2 smallholders; then 2 slaves, now none, nor when acquired.
>   Woodland, 30 pigs; meadow, 16 acres.
>   Value then and later 40s; now £4.

62 a

41 William holds SHELLOW (Bowells) from Geoffrey, which 1 free man held for 35 acres before 1066.
>   Woodland, 20 pigs; meadow, 4 acres.
>   Value then 5s; now 10[s].
>   This land lay in Eudo the Steward's manor of ('Morrell') Roding before 1066. The Abbot of Ely lays claim to both the land and the manor of ('Morrell') Roding, with the Hundred as witness.

⌐In Dommauua ten& . G . in dñio . xxx . ac̷ . q̅s tenuit . ı . ſoc̷ angari
Sep̅ . dim . car̷ . Tc̅ . ı . bor . m̅ . ııı . Silu . x . porc̷ . ıııı . ac̷ . p̊ti . Tc̅ ual̷
vıı . ſol̷ . m̅ . x.

⌐Rodinges ten& Martell q̷d tenuit Anſg̊ . t . r̊ . e̊ . 7 Leuid
queda̅ femina ſub anſgaro . p . dim . hid . ıııı . ac̷ . p̊ti . Tc̅ . ual̷ . x . ſol̷
m̅ . xıı.

⌐Hund̷ de . Witbric̷teſherna Fenne ten& Hugo . de . G . q̷d
tenuit Friebñ lib̅ homo . t . r̊ . e̊ . p Man . 7 . p . ıııı . hid . t . r̊ . e̊ . Sep̅ .
. ıııı . uilt̷ . Tc̅ . ıı . bor . m̅ . vıı . Tc̅ . ıı . ſer . m̅ null . Sep̅ . ıı . car̷ in
dñio . Tc̅ . ı . car̷ hom . m̅ . dim . Silu . xL . porc̷ . Paſt . xxx . ou̷.
Sep̅ ual̷ . Lx . ſol̷ . h̅t &ıa̅ Id̅e Hugo . ı . hid . quam tenuit lib̅ homo.
Val̷ . xx . ſol̷ . 7 . xxx . ac̷ . h̅t Id̅e q̅s tenuit . ı . lib̅ . h̅o . Tc̅ . dim . car̷
m̅ . nulla . Val̷ . v . ſol̷.

⌐Hund̷ de Vdeleſforda . Waledana̅ ten& . G . in dñio . q̷d ten
Anſgar . t . r̊ . e̊ . p Man . 7 p xvıııı . hid . 7 . dim . Tc̅ 7 p vııı . car̷
in dñio . m̅ . x . Sep̅ xxıı . car̷ hom . Tc̅ 7 p . Lxvı . uilt̷ . m̅ xLvı.
Tc̅ 7 p xvıı . bord̷ . m̅ . xL . Tc̅ 7 p . xvı . ſer . m̅ . xx . Tc̅ 7 p ſilua
. M̅ . porc̷ . m̅ . ɔccc . 7 . Lxxx . ac̷ . p̊ti . Sep̅ . ı . mol̷ . huic manerio
adjacebant . t . r̊ . e̊ . xııı . ſoc̷ . m̅ . xıııı . tenentes . vı . & . dimid̷ hid̷

62 b

Tc̅ 7 poſt . vııı . car̷ 7 dim . m̅ . vııı . Tc̅ 7 p . x . bord̷ . m̅ . xıııı . Tc̅ 7 p filu̷.
. L . porc̷ . m̅ . xxx . xx . ac̷ p̊ti . tc̅ia pars molini . Tc̅ . vı . runc̷ . xı . . . im̅.
. cc . ou̷ . cx . porc̷ . xL . cap . ıııı . uaſa ap̅u . m̅ . ıx . runc̷ . x . an . ccxLııı . ou̷.
. c . porc̷ . xx . cap . xxx . uaſa ap̅u . Tc̅ 7 p ual̷ . xxxvı . lib̅ . m̅ ual̷ . L . lib̅.

⌐De hoc manerio ten& . Odo . ı . hid . 7 . ı . uirg̅ . 7 Renald̷ . ı . hid . xıı . ac̷.
min . 7 . ıı . car̷ . 7 . xııı . bord̷ . 7 ual̷ . L . ſol̷ in eod̷ p̊tio.

62 a, b

42 In DUNMOW Geoffrey holds 30 acres in lordship, which 1 Freeman
of Asgar's held. Always ½ plough.
>Then 1 smallholder, now 3.
>Woodland, 10 pigs; meadow, 4 acres.
>Value then 7s; now 10[s].

43 Martel holds (White) RODING, which Asgar held before 1066.
Leofith, a woman, (held it) under Asgar for ½ hide.
>Meadow, 4 acres.
>Value then 10s; now 12[s].

Hundred of 'WIBERTSHERNE'
44 Hugh holds STOW MARIES from Geoffrey which Fridebern, a free
man, held before 1066 as a manor, for 4 hides before 1066.
>Always 4 villagers. Then 2 smallholders, now 7; then 2 slaves,
>now none. Always 2 ploughs in lordship. Then 1 men's
>plough, now ½.
>Woodland, 40 pigs; pasture, 30 sheep.
>Value always 60s.
>Hugh also has 1 hide which a free man held.
>Value 20s.
>He also has 37 acres which 1 free man held. Then ½ plough,
>now none.
>Value 5s.

Hundred of UTTLESFORD
45 Geoffrey holds (Saffron) WALDEN in lordship, which Asgar held
before 1066 as a manor, for 19½ hides. Then and later 8 ploughs
in lordship, now 10. Always 22 men's ploughs.
>Then and later 66 villagers, now 46; then and later 17
>smallholders, now 40; then and later 16 slaves, now 20.
>Woodland, then and later 1000 pigs, now 800; meadow, 80
>acres; always 1 mill.
>Attached to this manor before 1066 were 13 Freemen, now 14,
who hold 6½ hides. Then and later 8½ ploughs, now 8.   62 b
>Then and later 10 smallholders, now 14.
>Woodland, then and later 50 pigs, now 30; meadow, 20 acres;
>the third part of a mill. Then 6 cobs, 11 cattle, 200 sheep,
>110 pigs, 40 goats, 4 beehives; now 9 cobs, 10 cattle, 243
>sheep, 100 pigs, 20 goats, 30 beehives.
>Value then and later £36; value now £50.
>Of this manor, Odo holds 1 hide and 1 virgate and Reginald
(holds) 1 hide less 12 acres. 2 ploughs.
>13 smallholders.
>Value 50s in the same assessment.

Ciſhellam ten& Wiℓℓ cardon de . G . qð tenuit Vlfeih . lib hõ . t . r . e.
ꝓ Man . 7 ꝑ . ii . hið . 7 . dim . Tc . iii . caꝛ in dnĩo . ꝑ 7 m̃ . ii . Tc 7 ꝑ . iii . caꝛ
hom̃ . m̃ nulla . Tc 7 ꝑ . ix . uiℓℓ . m̃ nuℓℓ . Sep . vi . borð . Tc . 7 ꝑ . vi . ſer.
m̃ . i . ſiℓu . xxx . porc . vi . ac . ꝑti . Tc . cc . ou . 7 . x . porc . m̃ . ccxx . ou.
xxx . porc . lxvi . cap . iii . an . Tc 7 ꝑ uaℓ . vi . lib . m̃ . c . ſoℓ.
In Ead uilla ten& Idẽ . iii . hið . 7 xvii . ac . qs tenueꝛ . v . libi hões
t . r . e Tc . v . caꝛ . 7 qn̄ rec . ii . m̃ nuℓℓ . m̃ . i . uiℓℓ . 7 . iii . borð . iiii . ac.
ꝑti . Tc 7 ꝑ uaℓ . c . ſoℓ . m̃ . xl . Iſtas tᷓas reclamat . G . ꝓ eſcangio.

In Munehala . ten& . qðã angℓic . de . G . iii . uirg̃ . qs tenuit lib hõ
t . r . e . 7 . tēꝓ reg̃ uuiℓℓi . effect ē homo Goisfridi ſponte ſua . 7 dicꝷ
hões Goisfridi . qð ꝑ ea rex conceſſit Goisfrido ꝓ eſcangio . ſ; neꝗ ipſe
homo nec hundret teſtimonium Goisfrido ꝑhibent . In illa tᷓa erat
tc . i . caꝛ . m̃ . dim . Sep . iii . borð . vii . ac . ꝑti . Vaℓ . x . ſoℓ.

Blichangram ten& Germund de . G . qð ten . i . ſoc . Anſgari ꝓ . dim.
hið . t . r . e . Sep . i . caꝛ in dnĩo . 7 . iii . borð . Tc 7 ꝑ ſiℓu . xl . porc . m̃ . xxx.
Tc . uaℓ . xx . ſoℓ . m̃ . x.

Hund de Clauelinga   In Plicedana ten& Ricarð ſoc Angari
. i . hið 7 . xx . ac . t . r . e . Tc . i . caꝛ . m̃ nuℓℓ . Sep . iii . borð . Siℓu . x . porc.

63 a
. x . ac . ꝑti . Sep uaℓ . xxi . ſoℓ.

46 William Cardon holds (Great) CHISHILL from Geoffrey which Wulfheah, a free man, held before 1066 as a manor, for 2½ hides. Then 3 ploughs in lordship, later and now 2. Then and later 3 men's ploughs, now none.

Then and later 9 villagers, now none; always 6 smallholders.
Then and later 6 slaves, now 1.
Woodland, 30 pigs; meadow, 6 acres. Then 200 sheep and 10 pigs; now 220 sheep, 30 pigs, 66 goats, 3 cattle.
Value then and later £6; now 100s.

In the same village he also holds 3 hides and 17 acres which 5 free men held before 1066. Then 5 ploughs, when acquired 2, now none.

Now 1 villager; 3 smallholders.
Meadow, 4 acres.
Value then and later 100s; now 40[s].
Geoffrey claims back these lands by exchange.

47 In EMANUEL (Wood) an Englishman holds 3 virgates from Geoffrey, which a free man held before 1066. After 1066 he was made Geoffrey's man of his own accord. Geoffrey's men state that afterwards the King granted (it) to Geoffrey by exchange; but neither the man himself nor the Hundred bears witness for Geoffrey. On that land there was then 1 plough, now ½.

Always 3 smallholders.
Meadow, 7 acres.
Value 10s.

48 Germund holds BIRCHANGER from Geoffrey, which 1 Freeman of Asgar's held for ½ hide before 1066. Always 1 plough in lordship; 3 smallholders.
Woodland, then and later 40 pigs, now 30.
Value then 20s; now 10[s].

Hundred of CLAVERING

49 In PLEDGDON (Hall) Richard holds. A Freeman of Asgar's ... ; 1 hide and 20 acres before 1066. Then 1 plough, now none.
Always 3 smallholders.
Woodland, 10 pigs; meadow, 10 acres.
Value always 21s.

63 a

Hund de Witbri𝔠teſherna   Phennā ten& hugo de uerli q𝔡
tenuit Friebn̄ ꝓ Man̄ . 7 . ꝓ . iii . Sēp . ii . uilt . Tc̄ . ii . bord . m̄ . vii . Tc̄ . ii . ſer . m̄
nult . Sēp . ii . car in d̄nio . Tc̄ . i . car hom̄ . m̄ . dim̄ . Silu . xl . porc̄ . Paſt .
. xxx . ou . Tc̄ . v . porc̄ . xxx . ou . 7 . m̄ . lxx . porc̄ . Vat . lx . ſot . In Ead̄ ten&
Id̄e xxxvii . ac̄ . Tc̄ . dim̄ . car . m̄ . nult . Vat . v . ſot .

Wenesuuic tenuit Anſgar . t . r . e . ꝓ . Man̄ . 7 . ꝓ . v . hid̄ . 7 xl . ac̄ . q𝔡 tenent
Godefrid̄ 7 Eurard de . G . ſep . ii . uilt . Tc̄ . iiii . bor . m̄ . vii . Sēp . iii . ſer⸝
7 . ii . car̄ . in d̄nio . Tc̄ . ii . car̄ hom̄ . m̄ . i . 7 . dim̄ . vat . iiii . lib̄ . In Ead̄
. vi . libi hōes tenuer̄ . i . hid̄ . 7 . xl . ac̄ . q𝔡 tenent Id̄e . Tc̄ uat . xx . ſot .
m̄ . x .

T̄RA Comitis de . Ov .   Turruc ten& Comes in d̄nio q𝔡 tenuit   . XXXI .
Herold̄ . ꝓ . man̄ . 7 . ꝓ . xiii . hid̄ . Tc̄ . xii . uilt . m̄ . xvii . Tc̄ . xvi . bor . m̄ . xlv .
Tc̄ . xvi . ſer . m̄ . viii . Tc̄ . vi . car̄ in d̄nio . m̄ . v . Tc̄ . x . car̄ hom̄ . m̄ . xiii . Silu .
. cc . porc̄ . xl . ac̄ . ꝓti . Paſt . ɒ . ou . Tc̄ . i . piſc̄ . m̄ . ii . Sēp . v . uac̄ . iii . runc̄ xvi . porc̄ .
ɒl . ou . Tc̄ uat . xii . lib̄ . m̄ . xxx . 7 . vii . dom̄ ſt Londoniæ que jacent huic
manerio 7 . in hac firma .

63 b

. XXXII . T̄ERRE Rob̄ti grenonis .   Hundret de b̄deſtapla .
Rameſdanam ten& Rob̄ in d̄nio q𝔡 tenuer̄ . iii . libi hōes . t . r . e .
ꝓ . Man̄ . 7 . ꝓ . iii . hid̄ . 7 . dim̄ . 7 . xxx . ac̄ . Sēp . ii . car̄ in d̄nio . 7 . i . car̄
hom̄ . Tc̄ . iii . uilt . m̄ . ii . Tc̄ . iii . bord . m̄ . xiii . Tc̄ . iii . ſer . m̄ . iiii .

Hundred of 'WIBERTSHERNE'

50 Hugh of Verly holds STOW MARIES, which Fridebern held as a
manor, for 3 hides.
> Always 2 villagers. Then 2 smallholders, now 7; then 2 slaves,
> now none. Always 2 ploughs in lordship. Then 1 men's
> plough, now ½.
> Woodland, 40 pigs; pasture, 30 sheep. Then 5 pigs, 30 sheep;
> now 70 pigs.

Value 60s.
> In the same (Stow Maries) he also holds 37 acres. Then ½
plough, now none.
Value 5s.

51 Asgar held WENESUUIC before 1066 as a manor, for 5 hides and 40
acres. Godfrey and Evrard hold it from Geoffrey.
> Always 2 villagers. Then 4 smallholders, now 7. Always 3
> slaves; 2 ploughs in lordship. Then 2 men's ploughs, now 1½.
Value £4.
> In the same (*Wenesuuic*) 6 free men held 1 hide and 40 acres
which they also hold.
Value then 20s; now 10[s].

31   LAND OF THE COUNT OF EU

[Hundred of CHAFFORD]

1 The Count holds (West) THURROCK in lordship, which Harold held
as a manor, for 13 hides.
> Then 12 villagers, now 17; then 16 smallholders, now 45;
> then 16 slaves, now 8. Then 6 ploughs in lordship, now 5.
> Then 10 men's ploughs, now 13.
> Woodland, 200 pigs; meadow, 40 acres; pasture, 500 sheep;
> then 1 fishery, now 2. Always 5 cows, 3 cobs, 16 pigs,
> 550 sheep.
Value then £12; now [£] 30.
> There are 7 houses in London which lie in (the lands of) this
manor and in this revenue.

32   LANDS OF ROBERT GERNON   63 b

Hundred of BARSTABLE

1 Robert holds RAMSDEN in lordship, which 3 free men held before
1066 as a manor, for 3½ hides and 30 acres. Always 2 ploughs in
lordship; 1 men's plough.
> Then 3 villagers, now 2; then 3 smallholders, now 13; then 3
> slaves, now 4.

Silua . LXXXX . porc̃ . Tc̃ . I . runc̃ . m̃ . II . Tc̃ . II . an̄ . m̃ . x . Sep̄ . LX . ou.
7 . XL . porc̃ . m̃ . II . uafa apū . Val . L . fol.

Ⅴ Ramefdunā ten& Anfchetill de . Robto . qd̃ tenuit Aluric libe . p̃.
Man̄ . 7 p̃ . II . hid̃ . Sep̄ . I . car in dn̄io . 7 . dim . car hom̃ . Tc̃ . II . uilt . m̃ . I.
Sep̄ . VI . bord̃ . tc̃ . II . fer̃ . m̃ . null . Silu XL . porc̃ . Sep̄ . I . runc̃ . Tc̃ . VII . porc̃.
m̃ . XX . m̃ . VI . an . Tc̃ . XX . ou . m̃ . LXXX . II . uafa apū . val . XXX . fol.

Ⅴ Hund de Witham . Witham ten& Hugo de . R . qd̃ tenuit Burcard
lib hō . t . r . e . p̃ uno Man̄ . 7 p̃ . IIII . hid̃ . Tc̃ . IIII . car in dn̄io . m̃ . II . m̃ . II . car
hom̃ . 7 . II . uilt . 7 . VI . bord̃ . Tc̃ . VI . fer̃ . m̃ . III . VI . ac̃ . pti . I . mot . Tc̃ . I.
runc̃ . 7 . II . anim . 7 . LXXX . ou . 7 . XII . porc̃ . m̃ . I . runc̃ . 7 . IIII . anim.
7 . C . ou . 7 . XX . porc̃ . 7 . III . uafa apū . Sep̄ ual . IIII . lib.

Ⅴ Hobruge ten& Ricãrd de . R . qd̃ tenuit Brictmar . t . r . e . p̃ m̃.
7 p̃ . II . hid̃ . 7 dim . Sep̄ . II . car in dn̄io . 7 . I . car hom̃ . 7 . II . uilt . 7 . VI.
bord̃ . Tc̃ . VI . fer̃ . m̃ null . Silu . XL . porc̃ . XI . ac̃ . pti . I . mot . Tc̃ . II . an.
m̃ . IIII . Tc̃ . I . runc̃ . m̃ null . Tc̃ . XII . porc̃ . m̃ . XL . Tc̃ . XXX . ou . m̃.
LIIII . m̃ . XXIIII . cap . Val . XL . fol.

Ⅴ Riuuehalā . ten& Afcelin̄ . de . R . qd̃ tenuit Aleftan lib hō . t . r . e.
p̃ Man̄ . 7 p̃ . dim . hid̃ . Sep̄ . I . car in dn̄io . Tc̃ . I . bord̃ . m̃ . VIII . Tc̃ . I.
fer̃ . m̃ null . Silu . x . porc̃ . VIII . ac̃ . pti . m̃ . VIII . porc̃ . Val . XX . fol

64 a

Ⅴ Hund de herlaua . Matcingam ten& Hugo de . Rob . qd̃ ten
Aluric cild lib homo t . r . e . p̃ Man̄ . 7 p̃ . I . hid̃ . Sep̄ . I . car . in dn̄io . tc̃ . dim.
car . hom̃ . m̃ nulla . Tc̃ . I . uilt . m̃ . null . Tc̃ . I . bord̃ . m̃ . IIII . Tc̃ . III . fer̃ . m̃
null . Silu . XL . porc̃ . VIII . ac̃ . pti . Tc̃ . I . runc̃ . 7 . VIII . porc̃ . m̃ . XVI . porc̃
7 . XII . ou . 7 . VIII . cap . 7 . IIII . anim . Tc̃ ual . XX . fol . m̃ . XXX.

Woodland, 90 pigs. Then 1 cob, now 2; then 2 cattle, now 10. Always 60 sheep; 40 pigs. Now 2 beehives.
Value 50s.

2 Ansketel holds RAMSDEN from Robert, which Aelfric held freely as a manor, for 2 hides. Always 1 plough in lordship; ½ men's plough.
    Then 2 villagers, now 1; always 6 smallholders. Then 2 slaves, now none.
    Woodland, 40 pigs. Always 1 cob. Then 7 pigs, now 20; now 6 cattle; then 20 sheep, now 80; 2 beehives.
Value 30s.

Hundred of WITHAM

3 Hugh holds WITHAM from Robert which Burghard, a free man, held before 1066 as one manor, for 4 hides. Then 4 ploughs in lordship, now 2. Now 2 men's ploughs;
    2 villagers; 6 smallholders. Then 6 slaves, now 3.
    Meadow, 6 acres; 1 mill. Then 1 cob, 2 cattle, 80 sheep and 12 pigs; now 1 cob, 4 cattle, 100 sheep, 20 pigs and 3 beehives.
Value always £4.

4 Richard holds HOWBRIDGE from Robert, which Brictmer held before 1066 as a manor, for 2½ hides. Always 2 ploughs in lordship; 1 men's plough;
    2 villagers; 6 smallholders. Then 6 slaves, now none.
    Woodland, 40 pigs; meadow, 11 acres; 1 mill. Then 2 cattle, now 4; then 1 cob, now none; then 12 pigs, now 40; then 30 sheep, now 54; now 24 goats.
Value 40s.

5 Ascelin holds RIVENHALL from Robert which Alstan, a free man, held before 1066 as a manor, for ½ hide. Always 1 plough in lordship.
    Then 1 smallholder, now 8; then 1 slave, now none.
    Woodland, 10 pigs; meadow, 8 acres. Now 8 pigs.
Value 20s.

Hundred of HARLOW

6 Hugh holds MATCHING from Robert which Young Aelfric, a free man, held before 1066 as a manor, for 1 hide. Always 1 plough in lordship. Then ½ men's plough, now none.
    Then 1 villager, now none; then 1 smallholder, now 4; then 3 slaves, now none.
    Woodland, 40 pigs; meadow, 8 acres. Then 1 cob and 8 pigs; now 16 pigs, 12 sheep, 8 goats and 4 cattle.
Value then 20s; now 30[s].

Hund de Waltham Cingefort ten& Orgar teinn de . Rob

qd tenuit . I . lib hō . t . r . e . |7 reddit . x . den . de Soca ad uualtham Tc . II .

car in dnio . m . I . Tc . III . car hom̄ . m . II . Sep . VII . uill . 7 . VI . bord . 7 . IIII .

ſer . Silu . ɒ . porc . L . ac . p̄ti . Sep . I . mol . 7 . IIII . piſcinæ . 7 adhuc poſſ̄t

reſtaurari . II . car . una in dnio . 7 alt̄a uittis . Tc . XI . anim̄ . m . nutt .

tc . XXX . porc . m . XXI . Sep uat . LXX . ſot .

Hund de beuentreu . Hame . ten& Rob in dnio . qd tenuit

Aleſtan lib hō . t . r . e . p̄ Man . 7 p̄ . VIII . hid . 7 . XXX . ac . 7 hoc maneriū

Witt rex Ranulfo piperello . 7 Rob grenoni . Tc . v . car in dnio . m

. IIII . tc . VIII . car hom̄ . m XII . tc . XXXII . uitt . m . XLVIII . Tc . XVI .

bord . m . LXXX . I . min . Sep . III . ſer . Silu . c . porc . LX . ac . p̄ti . IX . mol tc .

m . VIII . Tc . uat . XVI . lib . 7 qñ recepunt . XII . lib . m uat . XXIIII . lib .

7 de hoc manerio h̄t . R . piperell medietat̄e . 7 in dnio Robti rec̄ .

. R . I . runc̄ . 7 m . ſimilit ibi ē . Tc . I . uac̄ . m . IX . anim̄ . Tc . VI . oū .

m . XII . Tc . v . porc . m . XI . de hoc manerio tenet Oſb̄n de Robro

XXX . ac . 7 . d . car . 7 uat . x . ſot . in eod . p̄tio .

Hame ten& Rob in dnio qd tenuit Leured lib hō . t . r . e . p̄ Man .

7 p̄ . VII . hid . Sep . III . car in dnio . Tc . VII . car hom̄ . m . XIII . T̄ɇ

XXXIIII . uitt . m . XXXVIII . Tc . III . bord . m . XXVI . Tc . XIX . ſer

m . III . Silu . ɒcc . porc . L . ac . p̄ti . Tc . VIII . anim̄ . m . XV . Tc . XX . porc . m

XXXIIII . m . cc . oū . XX . min . m . IIII . runc̄ . 7 . III . uaſa ap . 7 huic tr̄æ

addite ſ̄ . III . uirg . t . r . Witti . q̄s ten Eduin . lib p̄r . t . r . e . Tc . I . car

m . dim̄ . m . II . bord . Silu . x . porc . IX . ac . p̄tt . 7 hoc man uat t . r . e . x .

lib . 7 qñ rec̄ . VII . tib . m . XVIII . lib . 7 huic maner adjacent . XXX .

ac . q̄s ten . I . ſoc . De hoc man . ten& Ilger . XL . ac . 7 . II . bord . 7 . I . car .

7 uat . XV . ſot . in eod p̄tio .

Hundred of WALTHAM

7　Ordgar, a thane of Robert's, holds CHINGFORD which 1 free man
held before 1066 as a manor, for 5 hides. He pays 10d of suit to
Waltham (Holy Cross). Then 2 ploughs in lordship, now 1. Then
3 men's ploughs, now 2.
　　Always 7 villagers; 6 smallholders; 4 slaves.
　　Woodland, 500 pigs; meadow, 50 acres. Always 1 mill; 4
　　　fisheries. 2 more ploughs can be restored, 1 in lordship, the
　　　other for the villagers. Then 11 cattle, now none; then 30
　　　pigs, now 21.
Value always 70s.

Hundred of BECONTREE

8　Robert holds (West) HAM in lordship which Alstan, a free man,
held before 1066 as a manor, for 8 hides and 30 acres. King
William [gave] this manor to Ranulf Peverel and Robert Gernon.
Then 5 ploughs in lordship, now 4. Then 8 men's ploughs, now 12.
　　Then 32 villagers, now 48; then 16 smallholders, now 80 less 1;
　　　always 3 slaves.
　　Woodland, 100 pigs; meadow, 60 acres; then 9 mills, now 8.
　　Value then £16; when acquired £12. Value now £24.
　　Ranulf Peverel has half of this manor. And in Robert's lordship,
　　R(obert) acquired 1 cob, now the same is there; then 1 cow, now
　　9 cattle; then 6 sheep, now 12; then 5 pigs, now 11.
　　Of this manor, Osbern holds 30 acres from Robert. ½ plough.
Value 10s in the same assessment.

9　Robert holds (East) HAM in lordship which Leofred, a free man,
held before 1066 as a manor, for 7 hides. Always 3 ploughs in
lordship. Then 7 men's ploughs, now 13.
　　Then 34 villagers, now 38; then 3 smallholders, now 26; then
　　　19 slaves, now 3.　　　　　　　　　　　　　　　　　　64 b
　　Woodland, 700 pigs; meadow, 50 acres. Then 8 cattle, now 15;
　　　then 20 pigs, now 34; now 200 sheep less 20; now 4 cobs;
　　　3 beehives.
　　3 virgates were added to this land after 1066 which Edwin, a
　　free priest, held before 1066. Then 1 plough, now ½.
　　Now 2 smallholders.
　　Woodland, 10 pigs; meadow, 9 acres.
　　Value of this manor before 1066 £10; when acquired £7; now £18.
　　　30 acres are attached to this manor which 1 Freeman holds.
　　　Of this manor, Ilger holds 40 acres.
　　　2 smallholders. 1 plough.
Value 15s in the same assessment.

In Leituna ten& Rob . in dñio . dim . hid . qm tenuit . I . lib hõ . t . r . e.
Sep . dim . car . 7 . II . bord . v . ac . pti . val . v . sol.

In Lochetuna ten& . W . corbun . de . R . XLIIII . ac . qd ten . I . lib hõ.
t . r . e . Sep . dim . car . m . II . bord . Silu . xx . porc . I . ac . pti . val . x . sol.

Hund de Witbricteſherna . Purlai . ten& Ricard de . R . qd
tenuit Algar lib hõ . p . Man . 7 . p . II . hid . 7 . xv . ac . Tc . I . ſer . m . I . bord.
Sep . I . car . Tc . ual . x . sol . 7 qñ rec . xx . m . xxx . In dñio ſt m.
xxxIIII . ou . 7 nichil recep.

Witham ten& Anſchetill de . R . qd tenuit Leſtan lib hõ . t . r . e . p
Man . 7 . p . I . hid . 7 . dim . Tc . II . uill . m . null . tc . IIII . bord . m . vIII.
Sep . I . ſer . 7 . II . car in dñio . Tc . I . car 7 dim hom . m . I . Silu . CL . porc.
Tc . II . uac . m . vIII . anim . Tc . e . ou . m . cXL . Tc . xvI . porc . m . xx.
sep . I . runc . Tc . ual . xL . sol . 7 qñ rec . xxx . m . ual . IIII . lib.

Hund de Wenſiſtreu . Lega ten& Rob de uerli de Robto.
qd tenuit Gotre lib hõ . t . r . e . p . Man . 7 . p . IIII . hid . 7 . dim . Tc . IIL
car . in dñio . m . II . Sep . III . car . hom . Tc . vII . uill . m . v . Tc . v.
bord . m . xII . Tc . vII . ſer . m . III . Silu . c . porc . m . I . mol.

65 a

Tc . I . runc . m . vIII . Tc . cLx . ou . m . Lxxx . tc . xx . porc . m null.
Sep ual . IIII . lib.

Salcota ten& Ide . R . de eod . qd tenuit . I . lib hõ . t . r . e . p . Man . 7.
p . I . hid . 7 . dim . Sep . I . car in dñio . Tc . IIII . bord . m . III . Sep . I . ſer . Tc . nick.
m . II . runc . xx . porc . Lxxx . ou . II . anim . Tc . ual . xxvI . sol . m . xxx.

64 b, 65 a

10 In LEYTON Robert holds ½ hide in lordship, which 1 free man held before 1066. Always ½ plough;
2 smallholders.
Meadow, 5 acres.
Value 5s.

11 In LOUGHTON W. Corbun holds 44 acres from Robert, which 1 free man held before 1066. Always ½ plough.
Now 2 smallholders.
Woodland, 20 pigs; meadow, 1 acre.
Value 10s.

Hundred of 'WIBERTSHERNE'
12 Richard holds PURLEIGH from Robert which Algar, a free man, held as a manor, for 2 hides and 15 acres.
Then 1 slave, now 1 smallholder. Always 1 plough.
Value then 10s; when acquired 20[s]; now 30[s].
34 sheep are now in lordship; he acquired nothing.

13 Ansketel holds (Great) WHITMANS from Robert which Leofstan, a free man, held before 1066 as a manor, for 1½ hides.
Then 2 villagers, now none; then 4 smallholders, now 8.
Always 1 slave; 2 ploughs in lordship. Then 1½ men's ploughs, now 1.
Woodland, 150 pigs. Then 2 cows, now 8 cattle; then 100 sheep, now 140; then 16 pigs, now 20; always 1 cob.
Value then 40s; when acquired 30[s]. Value now £4.

Hundred of WINSTREE
14 Robert of Verly holds LEGA from Robert which Gotre, a free man, held before 1066 as a manor, for 4½ hides. Then 3 ploughs in lordship, now 2. Always 3 men's ploughs.
Then 7 villagers, now 5; then 5 smallholders, now 12; then 7 slaves, now 3.
Woodland, 100 pigs; now 1 mill. Then 1 cob, now 8; then 160 sheep, now 80; then 20 pigs, now none.
Value always £4.

65 a

15 Robert also holds VIRLEY from him, which 1 free man held before 1066 as a manor, for 1½ hides. Always 1 plough in lordship.
Then 4 smallholders, now 3; always 1 slave.
Then nothing; now 2 cobs, 20 pigs, 80 sheep, 2 cattle.
Value then 26s; now 30[s].

ᚠHund de Wdelesforda. Stanestedam ten& Rob in dñio. qd

tenuit lib hō.t.r.e.p.Man. 7 p.vi.hid.Tc.iiii.car.in dñio.Poſt.ii.

m̃.iii.Sep.x.car hom.7.xi.uilt.7.i.pbr.Tc 7 p.iiii.bord.m̃

.xviii.tc.viii.ſer.Poſt.iiii.m̃.iii.Silu.Ꝙ.porc.xx.ac.pti.

Sep.i.mol.Tc.viii.an.m̃.xvi.Tc.cxl.ou.m̃.cxx.Tc.xx.porc.

m̃.lx.xl.cap.tc.m̃.xxiiii.m̃.ii.runc.7.v.aſini.huic man.

adjac&.i.bereuuita quæ uocat magghedana.de.i.hid.Sep.i.car.

in dñio.7.ii.bord.Silu.x.porc.Tc 7 p ual.viii.lib.m̃.xi.

ᚠTacheleiam ten&.R.in dñio.qd tenuit.i.lib hō.t.r.e.p.Man.

7.p.iii.hid.7.xv.ac.Sep.ii.car.in dñio.7.iii.car hom.7.iii.

uilt.m̃.viii.bord.Tc 7 p.iiii.ſer.m̃.ii.Silu.cc.porc.7.xx.ac pti.

Tc.ii.runc.m̃.i.Tc.xii.an.m̃.iii.Tc.xvi.ou.m̃.x.Tc.xx.porc.

m̃ xxxviii. Sep ual.c.ſol.Petr ten& de.R.d.hid.7.i.b.ual.xii.ſol.

ᚠWendenā ten& Hugo de.R.qd ten.i.lib hō.t.r.e.p Man.7

p.vii.hid.vi.ac.min.Sep.iiii.car in dñio.Tc.iiii.car hom.

7 qñ rec.m̃.v.Tc 7 p.viii.uilt.m̃.ix.m̃.v.bord.tc 7 p vi.ſer.

m̃.v.xxiiii.ac.pti.Tc 7 p.i.mol.m̃.ii.Tc.v.ou.7.vii.porc.

m̃.iii.pulli.7.xxx.porc.7 lxvii.ou.Tc 7 p ual.vii.lib.m̃.viii.

ᚠDim Hund de Clauelinga. Benedfeldā ten&.R.in dñio

65 b

qd tenuit lib homo.t.r.e.p Man.7 p.v.hid.Sep.iii.car in dñio.Tc

.vii.car.hominũ.Poſt.vi.m̃.iiii.Tc.x.uilt.Poſt 7 m̃.ix.tc.7 p.ii.

bord.m̃.xi.Tc 7 p.vii.ſer.m̃.iiii.Silu.cc.porc.xvi.ac.pti.i.

mol.Tc.ii.runc.m̃.iii.Tc.i.an.m̃.xiiii.Tc.lxxx.ou.m̃.xxx.

Tc.l.porc.m̃.xl.Tc 7 poſt ual.c.ſol.m̃.vii.lib.Huic tre

adjac& sep.i.ſoc.de.xxx.ac.

65 a, b

Hundred of UTTLESFORD

16 Robert holds STANSTED (Mountfitchet) in lordship, which a free
man held before 1066 as a manor, for 6 hides. Then 4 ploughs in
lordship, later 2, now 3. Always 10 men's ploughs;
11 villagers; 1 priest. Then and later 4 smallholders, now 18;
then 8 slaves, later 4, now 3.
Woodland, 1000 pigs; meadow, 20 acres; always 1 mill. Then 8
cattle, now 16; then 140 sheep, now 120; then 20 pigs, now
60; then 40 goats, now 24; now 2 cobs and 5 asses.
Attached to this manor is 1 outlier which is called MANUDEN
with 1 hide. Always 1 plough in lordship;
2 smallholders.
Woodland, 10 pigs.
Value then and later £8; now [£] 11.

17 Robert holds TAKELEY in lordship, which 1 free man held before
1066 as a manor, for 3 hides and 15 acres. Always 2 ploughs in
lordship; 3 men's ploughs;
3 villagers. Now 8 smallholders; then and later 3 slaves, now 2.
Woodland, 200 pigs; meadow, 20 acres. Then 2 cobs, now 1;
then 12 cattle, now 3; then 16 sheep, now 10; then 20 pigs,
now 38.
Value always 100s.
Peter holds ½ hide from Robert.
1 smallholder.
Value 12d.

18 Hugh holds WENDENS (Ambo) from Robert, which 1 free man held
before 1066 as a manor, for 7 hides less 6 acres. Always 3 ploughs
in lordship. Then 4 men's ploughs, and when acquired; now 5.
Then and later 8 villagers, now 9; now 5 smallholders; then
and later 6 slaves, now 5.
Meadow, 24 acres; then and later 1 mill, now 2. Then 5 sheep
and 7 pigs; now 3 foals, 30 pigs and 67 sheep.
Value then and later £7; now [£] 8.

Half-Hundred of CLAVERING

19 Robert holds BENTFIELD (Bury) in lordship, which a free man held   65 b
before 1066 as a manor, for 5 hides. Always 3 ploughs in lordship.
Then 7 men's ploughs, later 6, now 4.
Then 10 villagers, later and now 9; then and later 2 smallholders,
now 11; then and later 7 slaves, now 4.
Woodland, 200 pigs; meadow, 16 acres; 1 mill. Then 2 cobs,
now 3; then 1 (head of) cattle, now 14; then 80 sheep,
now 30; then 50 pigs, now 40.
Value then and later 100s; now £7.
To this land has always been attached 1 Freeman with 30 acres.

In Bolituna ten& Rob in dnio . i . hid 7 . xv . ac . Tc . i . car 7 . dim .

Poſt 7 m . i . Sep . ii . bord . Tc . x . porc . 7 . xxviii . ou . m . i . anim . 7

. ii . porc . 7 . iiii . ou . Sep . ual . xxv . ſol . In hoc manerio ten& .

Rob . de . R . dim . hid . 7 . dim . car 7 . ual . x . ſol . in eod ptio .

Phernham ten& Rob in dnio . qd tenuit . i . lib ho . t . r . e . p . Man .

7 p . ii . hid . Sep . ii . car . in dnio . 7 . ii . car . hom . Tc 7 p . ii . uill . m . i .

Sep . viii . bord . Tc 7 p . viii . ſer . m . i . Tc 7 poſt ſilu . cc . por . m . cl .

. x . ac pti . Tc . iiii . runc . m . ii . Tc . xv . anim . m . null . Tc . xl . por .

m . xvii . Tc . lx . ou . m . xxx . m . xxxix . cap . 7 . iii . uaſa apu .

Tc ual . xl . ſol . m . l .

Menghedana . tenuer . iiii . libi hoes . t . r . e . p . Man . 7 p . iiii . hid

m tenent . iiii . milit de . R . Sep . iii . car . 7 . ii . uill . 7 . v . bord .

7 . i . ſer . Silu . xxx . porc . xiii . ac pti . Tc . viii . anim . 7 lxxx . ou .

7 . xx . cap . 7 . xx . porc . m . v . an . 7 . xxxiii . porc . 7 . i . pull . 7 . xliiii .

ou . 7 . viii . cap . Tc ual . l . ſol . m . lx .

Hund de hidingforda . Mapledeſteda ten& Ilger de . R . qd

tenuit Vluuin lib ho . t . r . e . p . Man . 7 p dim hid . Sep . ii . car in dnio .

7 . iii . car . hom . 7 . v . uilli . tc . 7 p . ii . bord . m . vi . Tc 7 p . iiii . ſer . m . ii .

66 a

Tc ſilua . c . porc . m . lx . xxvi . ac pti . Tc . i . runc . 7 . viii . anim . 7 . x . porc .

7 . xx . ou . 7 . xx . cap . m . i . runc . 7 . xiiii . anim . 7 . xviii . porc . 7 . lxxx .

ou . 7 . xxiii . cap . 7 . ii . uaſa apu . Val . lx . ſol .

20   In BOLLINGTON (Hall) Robert holds 1½ hides and 15 acres in
lordship. Then 1½ ploughs, later and now 1.
    Always 2 smallholders.
    Then 10 pigs and 28 sheep; now 1 (head of) cattle, 2 pigs
      and 4 sheep.
Value always 25s.
    In this manor Robert holds ½ hide from R(obert). ½ plough.
Value 10s in the same assessment.

21   Robert holds FARNHAM in lordship, which 1 free man held before
1066 as a manor, for 2 hides. Always 2 ploughs in lordship; 2
men's ploughs.
    Then and later 2 villagers, now 1; always 8 smallholders.
    Then and later 8 slaves, now 1.
    Woodland, then and later 200 pigs, now 150; meadow, 10
    acres. Then 4 cobs, now 2; then 15 cattle, now none; then
    40 pigs, now 17; then 60 sheep, now 30; now 39 goats;
    3 beehives.
Value then 40s; now 50[s].

22   4 free men held MANUDEN before 1066 as a manor, for 4 hides.
Now 4 men-at-arms hold (it) from Robert. Always 3 ploughs;
    2 villagers; 5 smallholders; 1 slave.
    Woodland, 30 pigs; meadow, 13 acres. Then 8 cattle, 80 sheep,
    20 goats and 20 pigs; now 5 cattle, 33 pigs, 1 foal, 44 sheep
    and 8 goats.
Value then 50s; now 60[s].

    Hundred of HINCKFORD
23   Ilger holds (Great) MAPLESTEAD from Robert which Wulfwin, a
free man, held before 1066 as a manor, for ½ hide. Always 2
ploughs in lordship; 3 men's ploughs;
    5 villagers. Then and later 2 smallholders, now 6; then and
    later 4 slaves, now 2.
    Woodland, then 100 pigs, now 60; meadow, 26 acres. Then   66 a
    1 cob, 8 cattle, 10 pigs, 20 sheep and 20 goats; now 1 cob,
    14 cattle, 18 pigs, 80 sheep, 23 goats and 2 beehives.
Value 60s.

Ⅴ Hund de Laxedana . Widemondefort ten& Ilger de . R.

qđ tenuit Goduin p Man . 7 p . I . hiđ . 7 dim . 7 . x . ac . Tc . III . uilłi

m̃ . IIII . Tc . II . borđ . m̃ . VIII . Sep . IIII . ſer . Tc . III . car in đnĩo.

m̃ . IIII . Sep . II . car hom . Silu . c . porc . XVI . ac . p̃ti . m̃ . I . mol . I.

piſc . Tc . I . runc . m̃ . VI . Tc . V . anim . m̃ . XXXIII . Tc . XL . porc . m̃ . LX.

tc . VI . ou . m̃ . CC . tc . XV . cap . m̃ , XLVII . m̃ . VII . uaſa apũ . Tc ual . IIII.

lib . m̃ . VI . 7 XVIIII . ſoc . t . r . ẽ tenentes . II . hiđ . 7 . dim . VI . ac . min.

q̃s . R . ht in ſuo eſcangio ſic dicit . q̃s tenet Idẽ Ilger . de eo . 7 hñt . VIII.

. bor . Sep . II . car . IIII . ac . p̃ti . Silu . XVI . porc . Sep ual . XL . ſol.

7 iſti ſochemani ſic comitat teſtat . non poſant remouere ab illo man.

7 . I . uiłtm abſtulit Reimund girald de q̃ fuit Robt ſaiſit . 7 adhuc

ht Rog pictauenſis.

Ⅴ Wiunhov ten& Nigełł de . R . qđ tenuit Aluric p Man . 7 p . V . hiđ

XV . ac . min . Sep . V . uiłt . tc . VI . borđ . m̃ . XX . tc . I . ſer . m̃ . II . Sep . II.

car in đnĩo . tc . int h̃oes . III . car . m̃ . II . Silu . c . porc . XII . ac . p̃ti . Paſt.

LX . ou . m̃ . I . mol . Tc . VIII . anim . m̃ . X . tc . I . runc . m̃ . II . tc . LX . ou.

m̃ . LXXXVII . tc . XXX . cap . m̃ . XX . Tc . XX . porc . m̃ XXIIII . Sep

ual . XL . ſol . 7 . I . lib h̃o . tenuit . XX . ac . q̃s ten& Rob de dono reg

7 . Nigełł de eo . Sep . dim . car . ual . III . ſol . 7 alī lib tenuit . XX . ac.

q̃s ht cuſtos hundret ual . III . ſol ; Idẽ Nigełł ten&.

Ⅴ Briciam ten& Rob de . R . qđ tenuit Vluuin p Man . 7 . p . II . hiđ.

. IIII . ac . 7 dim min . Sep . XII . borđ . tc . VI . ſer . m̃ . V . Sep . II . car . in đnĩo . 7 . II.

car hom . Silu . XL . porc . XII . ac . p̃ti . Sep . I . mol . Tc . II . anim . m̃ . VII . Tunc

XXXVIII . ou . m̃ LXXX . m̃ . XXXIII . cap . Tc . V . porc . m̃ . XXXIII . m̃ . II . runc.

Sep ual . LX . ſol.

24 Ilger holds WORMINGFORD from Robert, which Godwin held as a manor, for 1½ hides and 10 acres.

Then 3 villagers, now 4; then 2 smallholders, now 8; always 4 slaves. Then 3 ploughs in lordship, now 4. Always 2 men's ploughs.

Woodland, 100 pigs; meadow, 16 acres; now 1 mill; 1 fishery. Then 1 cob, now 6; then 5 cattle, now 33; then 40 pigs, now 60; then 6 sheep, now 200; then 15 goats, now 47; now 7 beehives.

Value then £4; now [£] 6.

19 Freemen who held 2½ hides less 6 acres before 1066 (and) whom Robert has in exchange, so he states. Ilger also holds them from him.

They have 8 smallholders. Always 2 ploughs.

Meadow, 4 acres; woodland, 16 pigs.

Value always 40s.

These Freemen, so the County testifies, could not move away from this manor.

Raymond Gerald took away 1 villager of whom Robert was in possession. Roger of Poitou still has (him).

25 Nigel holds WIVENHOE from Robert, which Aelfric held as a manor, for 5 hides less 15 acres.

Always 5 villagers. Then 6 smallholders, now 20; then 1 slave, now 2. Always 2 ploughs in lordship. Then among the men 3 ploughs, now 2.

Woodland, 100 pigs; meadow, 12 acres; pasture, 60 sheep; now 1 mill. Then 8 cattle, now 10; then 1 cob, now 2; then 60 sheep, now 87; then 30 goats, now 20; then 20 pigs, now 24.

Value always 40s.

1 free man held 20 acres which Robert holds by the King's gift. Nigel (holds them) from him. Always ½ plough.

Value 3s.

Another free (man) held 20 acres which the Hundred-reeve has.

Value 3s.

Nigel also holds (them).

26 Robert holds (Little) BIRCH from Robert, which Wulfwin held as a manor, for 2 hides less 4½ acres.   66 b

Always 12 smallholders. Then 6 slaves, now 5. Always 2 ploughs in lordship; 2 men's ploughs.

Woodland, 40 pigs; meadow, 12 acres; always 1 mill. Then 2 cattle, now 7; then 38 sheep, now 80; now 33 goats; then 5 pigs, now 33; now 2 cobs.

Value always 60s.

ᚷHund de Angra. Staplefordam ten&.R.in dñio.qd̄ tenueꝛ.v.
liƀi hões ℈.ıı.hid̄.ꝶ.dim̄.ꝶ.vı.ac̄.ꝶ dim̄.Tc̄.vııı.bord̄.m̄.xıııı.Tc̄.inꝼ
eos.v.car̄.m̄.ıııı.Silu̅.cc.porc̄.xxı.ac̄.p̄ti.Tc̄ ꝶ p̄ ual̄.ʟ.fol̄.m̄.ʟx.
De hoc manerio ten& Nigell̄.ı.hid̄.ꝶ.dim̄.ꝶ.ııı.uillt.ꝶ.vı.bord̄.ꝶ.ıı.car̄.
ꝶ ual̄.xxvııı.fol̄.in eod̄ p̄tio.

ᚷHund de Ceffeorda. Renaham ten& Roƀ de.R.qd̄ tenuit Aluard̄.
℈.Man̄.ꝶ.℈.ııı.hid̄.ꝶ.dim̄.Tc̄.ıııı.uillt.m̄.v.Tc̄.ꝶ.p̄.vı.bord̄.m̄.ıııı.
Tc̄.ıı.fer̄.m̄ null̄.Sēp.ıı.car̄ in dñio Tc̄.inꝼ hões.ıı.car̄ ꝶ dim̄.m̄.ı.
Tc̄.ııı.runc̄.ꝶ.xıııı.anim̄.ꝶ.vı.porc̄.ꝶ.c.ou̅.m̄.ıııı.runc̄.ꝶ.xı.
anim̄.ꝶ.xxıııı.porc̄.ꝶ.ʟxxx.ou̅.ꝶ.xıı.uafa.apu̅.Tc̄,ual̄.vı.liƀ.
ꝶ qn̄ rec̄.m̄.ual̄.ıııı.liƀ.ꝶ.ı.hid̄ tenuit.ı.liƀ hõ.qui poſt ea forisfec̄.
eam.q̄a furat̄ e̅.ꝶ fuit in manu regis.ſ; roƀ lafciuus inuaſit ut hund̄.
teſt̄.Tc̄.ı.car̄.Poſt ꝶ m̄ nulla.Sēp ual̄.xx.fol̄.hoc ten& Id̄e Roƀ de.R.
ᚷWaldam ten& Rad̄.de.R.qd̄ tenuit Sprot.℈ Man̄.ꝶ.℈.ı.hid̄.m̄.ı.
uillt.ꝶ.vı.bord̄.ꝶ.ı.car̄.Silu̅ xʟ.porc̄.Val̄.xx.fol̄.hanc trā ht̄.R.
fic dicit ℈ efcangio.℈ hutū de portu.ꝶ numq̄ reddidit geltū ꝶ neq᷑
ultimum

ᚷHund de Celmeresforda. Ingā ten& Roƀ in dñio qd̄ tenuit
Siuuard̄ ℈ man̄.ꝶ.℈.ııı.hid̄.t̄.r̄.e̅.Sēp.ı.uillt.Tc̄.ııı.bord̄.m̄.ıx.
Tc̄.ı.fer̄.m̄.ııı.Sēp.ı.car̄ in dñio.Tc̄.dim̄.car̄ hom̄.m̄.ı.Silua

.cccc.porc̄.Tc̄.v.anim̄.m̄.ıııı.Tc̄.xxvııı.ou̅.m̄.xxvı.Tc̄.xıı.porc̄.
m̄.xvıı.Tc̄ ual̄.xxx.fol̄.m̄.xx.

Hundred of ONGAR

27 Robert holds STAPLEFORD (Abbotts) in lordship, which 5 free men
held, for 2½ hides and 6½ acres.
  Then 8 smallholders, now 14. Then among them 5 ploughs,
    now 4.
  Woodland, 200 pigs; meadow, 21 acres.
  Value then and later 50s; now 60[s].
  Of this manor, Nigel holds 1½ hides.
  3 villagers; 6 smallholders. 2 ploughs.
  Value 28s in the same assessment.

Hundred of CHAFFORD

28 Robert holds RAINHAM from Robert, which Alfward held as a
manor, for 3½ hides.
  Then 4 villagers, now 5; then and later 6 smallholders, now 4;
    then 2 slaves, now none. Always 2 ploughs in lordship. Then
    among the men 2½ ploughs, now 1.
  Then 3 cobs, 14 cattle, 6 pigs and 100 sheep; now 4 cobs, 11
    cattle, 24 pigs, 80 sheep and 12 beehives.
  Value then £6, and when acquired. Value now £4.
  1 free man held 1 hide. He later forfeited it because he had
stolen and was in the King's hand. But Robert the Lascivious
annexed it as the Hundred testifies. Then 1 plough, later and
now none.
  Value always 20s.
  Robert also holds this from Robert.

29 Ralph holds (South) WEALD from Robert, which Sprot held as a
manor, for 1 hide.
  Now 1 villager; 6 smallholders; 1 plough.
  Woodland, 40 pigs.
  Value 20s.
  Robert has this land, so he says, by exchange through Hubert
of Port. It has never paid tax and did not (pay) the last one.

Hundred of CHELMSFORD

30 Robert holds FRYERNING in lordship, which Siward held as a
manor, for 3 hides before 1066.
  Always 1 villager. Then 3 smallholders, now 9; then 1 slave,
    now 3. Always 1 plough in lordship. Then ½ men's plough,
    now 1.
  Woodland, 400 pigs. Then 5 cattle, now 4; then 28 sheep, now   67 a
    26; then 12 pigs, now 17.
  Value then 30s; now 20[s].

⟨ Ingā tenuit Eduin⁹ grut ꝓ Man̄ . 7 . ꝓ . I . hiđ . 7 . xxxɪɪɪ . ac̄ . m̄ ten& Ilger⁹
de . Robto . Sēp . I . borđ . 7 . I . car̄ . Silu̅ . xʟ . porc̄ . ɪɪ, ac̄ . p̄ti . Val̄ . xx . fol̄ . hanc
tr̄a habuit . R . in Suo efcangio.

⟨ Cinguehellam ten& Anfchetill⁹ de . R . qđ tenuit Doth . ꝓ Man̄ . 7
ꝓ . ɪɪ . hiđ . Sēp . I . uill̄ . 7 . ɪɪ . borđ . 7 . ɪɪ . car̄ in dn̄io . 7 . I . car̄ hom̄ . Silu̅ . xxx .
porc̄ . xx . ac̄ . p̄ti . Sēp . I . runc̄ . 7 . vɪ . anim . 7 . xɪɪ . ou̅ . 7 . xɪɪɪɪ . porc̄ . Tc̄ ual̄
xʟ . fol̄ . m̄ . ɪɪɪɪ . lib̄

⟨ Springinghefeldā ten& Cōrp . de . R . qđ tenuit Godric⁹ ꝓ Man̄ . 7 ꝓ.
. ɪɪ . hiđ . 7 . xʟ . ac̄ . Sēp . ɪɪɪɪ . uill̄ . 7 . vɪɪ . borđ . 7 . ɪɪ . car̄ . in dn̄io . 7 . I . car̄
hom̄ . Silu̅ . xxx . porc̄ . xx . ac̄ . p̄ti . I . pifc̄ . Tc̄ . I . runc̄ . m̄ . x . Tc̄ . v . anim .
m̄ . xxx . Tc̄ . ɪɪɪɪ . ou̅ . m̄ . c . Tc̄ . xɪɪɪ . porc̄ . m̄ . xʟ . Tc̄ . ual̄ . xʟ . fol̄ . m̄ ʟx .

⟨ Ingā ten& Will̄ de . R . qđ tenuer̄ . Selua 7 Topi⁹ ꝓ . Man̄ . 7 ꝓ . ɪɪ . hiđ . 7 . đ .
7 . xxxɪ . ac̄ . 7 . Rob̄ h̄t in efcangio . Sēp . I . uill̄ . 7 . xɪɪɪɪ . borđ . 7 . I . car̄ . 7 . đ
in dn̄io . 7 . I . car̄ . 7 . dim . hom̄ . Silu̅ . c . porc̄ . ɪɪɪɪ . ac̄ . p̄ti . Tc̄ . x . anim .
m̄ . fimilit̄ Tc̄ . I . runc̄ . m̄ . v . Sēp . xx . ou̅ . Tc̄ . xxx . porc̄ . m̄ . xvɪ .
m̄ . ɪɪ . uafa apū . Sēp . ual̄ . ɪɪɪɪ . lib̄ . 7 . xxx . ac̄ . ten̄ . borda m̄ . R . Sēp .
dim . car̄ . 7 . ɪɪ . ac̄ 7 đ . p̄ti . ual̄ . x . fol̄ .

⟨ Pacingas ten& Picot . qđ tenuit borda ꝓ Man̄ . 7 . ꝓ . ɪɪ . hiđ . 7 . dim .
t . r . e . Tc̄ . I . uill̄ . m̄ null̄ . m̄ . vɪ . borđ . Tc̄ . ɪɪɪɪ . fer̄ . m̄ null̄ . Tc̄ . ɪɪ . car̄
in dn̄io m̄ . I . Sēp . dim . car̄ hom̄ . Silu̅ . ʟ . porc̄ . x . ac̄ . p̄ti . Tc̄ . ɪɪɪɪ . an .
7 . xx . porc̄ . 7 xx . ou̅ . m̄ nichil Sēp ual̄ . xʟ . fol̄ . Iftā tr̄a h̄t . R .
in Efcangio.

31 Edwin Groat held FRYERNING as a manor, for 1 hide and 33 acres. Now Ilger holds (it) from Robert.
>   Always 1 smallholder; 1 plough.
>   Woodland, 40 pigs; meadow, 2 acres.
>   Value 20s.
>   Robert had this land in exchange.

32 Ansketel holds CHIGNALL from Robert, which Dot held as a manor, for 2 hides.
>   Always 1 villager; 2 smallholders; 2 ploughs in lordship; 1 men's plough.
>   Woodland, 30 pigs; meadow, 20 acres. Always 1 cob, 6 cattle, 12 sheep and 14 pigs.
>   Value then 40s; now £4.

33 Corp holds SPRINGFIELD from Robert, which Godric held as a manor, for 2 hides and 40 acres.
>   Always 4 villagers; 7 smallholders; 2 ploughs in lordship; 1 men's plough.
>   Woodland, 30 pigs; meadow, 20 acres; 1 fishery. Then 1 cob, now 10; then 5 cattle, now 30; then 4 sheep, now 100; then 13 pigs, now 40.
>   Value then 40s; now 60[s].

34 William holds FRYERNING from Robert, which Selva and Topi held as a manor, for 2½ hides and 31 acres. Robert has (it) in exchange.
>   Always 1 villager; 14 smallholders; 1½ ploughs in lordship; 1½ men's ploughs.
>   Woodland, 100 pigs; meadow, 4 acres. Then 10 cattle, now the same; then 1 cob, now 5; always 20 sheep. Then 30 pigs, now 16; now 2 beehives.
>   Value always £4.
>   Borda held 30 acres, now Robert (holds them). Always ½ plough.
>   Meadow, 2½ acres.
>   Value 10s.

35 Picot holds PATCHING (Hall), which Borda held as a manor, for 2½ hides before 1066.
>   Then 1 villager, now none; now 6 smallholders; then 4 slaves, now none. Then 2 ploughs in lordship, now 1. Always ½ men's plough.
>   Woodland, 50 pigs; meadow, 10 acres. Then 4 cattle, 20 pigs and 20 sheep; now nothing.
>   Value always 40s.
>   Robert has this land in exchange.

67 b

⌐p Man̄ . 7 p̃ . ı . hiđ . 7 . dim̄ . Tc̄ . ı . uiłł . 7 . ı . ſer . m̄ . ıı . borđ . Sēp . ı . car̄ . 7 . đ . in
dn̄io . 7 . x . ac̄ . p̃ti . Sēp . ı . moł . Sēp . uał . xxx . ſoł.

⌐In Toleſhunta ten& Rob de ūli . xL . ac̄ . quæ jacent in hoc hunđ . 7 app̃
tiate ſt in manerio.

⌐Hunđ de Tendringa   Accleiam ten& . R . in dn̄io . q̃d tenuit
Aluric cap̃ p manerio . 7 p̃ . x . hiđ . t . r . e . Tc̄ . 7 . p̃ . xıı . uiłł . m̄ . xı . Tc̄ . 7 p̃
xx . borđ . m̄ . xxx . tc̄ . 7 p̃ . x . ſer . m̄ . v . Sēp . ııı . car in dn̄io . Tc̄ ınt hōes
. x . car̄ . m̄ . ıx . Silu . c . porc̄ . vııı . ac̄ . p̃ti . m̄ . ı . moł . ıı . ſalinæ . Paſt . xx .
ou . Tc̄ . x . runc̄ . m̄ . ıııı . tc̄ . x . anim̄ . m̄ . v . Sēp . cc . ou . xx . min̄.
tc̄ . xx . porc̄ . m̄ . xv . Tc̄ . uał . xı . lıƀ . 7 . q̃n rec̄ . M uał . xvı . lıƀ . De hoc
manerio ten& . Rađ . ıı . hiđ . 7 . x . ac̄ . 7 . xııı . borđ . 7 . ı . car̄ . 7 . uał . xxx .
ſoł . in eod p̃tio . 7 tr̄a cujđa lıƀi hōis ten& . Rob . quæ uocat̄ Tendringa
q̃m ten& Galt̄ de eo . p Man̄ . 7 p̃ . ı . hiđ . xv . ac̄ . min̄ . Tc̄ . v . uiłł . m̄ . ıı .
Tc̄ . ııı . borđ . m̄ . vıı . Tc̄ . ııı . ſer . m̄ nułł . Sēp . ı . car̄ . in dn̄io . tc̄ . ınt
hōes . ııı . car̄ . m̄ . ıı . Silu . xx . porc̄ . ı . ac̄ . p̃ti . Tc̄ . ıı . runc̄ . m̄ . ıııı .
tc̄ . ıı . anim̄ . m̄ . x . tc̄ . xx . porc̄ . m̄ . xxvıı . tc̄ . xLıx . ou . m̄ . Lx . tc̄ .
xxıııı . cap̃ . m̄ . xxxvıı . m̄ . ııı . uaſa apū Tc̄ uał . xx . ſoł m̄ . xxx . hoc
recepit . R . in ſuo eſcangio.

⌐Dicheleiam ten& Nigell̄ đe . R . q̃d tenuit Aleſtan̄ . p man̄ . 7 p̃ . ı .
hiđ . 7 . xxxvıı . ac̄ . 7 . dim̄ . Sēp . vııı . borđ . tc̄ . ı . ſer . m̄ nułł . Tc̄ . in dn̄io
. ıı . car̄ . m̄ . ı . 7 . dim̄ . Sēp . ıı . car . hom̄ . Silu . x . porc̄ . ıı . ac̄ . p̃ti . tc̄ .
vıı . anim̄ . m̄ . vııı . tc̄ . ı . runc̄ . m̄ . ıııı . tc̄ . xxxvıı . ou . m̄ . Lı .
tc̄ . vıı . porc̄ . m̄ . xv . Sēp . xx . cap̃ . Vał . xx . ſoł.

36 From the Holding, Azo holds CULVERT'S FARM from Robert,
which Godwin held as a manor, for 1½ hides.
> Then 1 villager; 1 slave. Now 2 smallholders. Always 1½
> ploughs in lordship.
> Meadow, 10 acres; always 1 mill.
> Value always 30s.

37 In TOLLESHUNT (D'Arcy) Robert of Verly holds 40 acres which lie
in (the lands of) this Hundred. They are assessed in the manor.

Hundred of TENDRING
38 Robert holds (Great) OAKLEY in lordship, which Aelfric Kemp
held as a manor, for 10 hides before 1066.
> Then and later 12 villagers, now 11; then and later 20
> smallholders, now 30. Then and later 10 slaves, now 5.
> Always 3 ploughs in lordship. Then among the men 10
> ploughs, now 9.
> Woodland, 100 pigs; meadow, 8 acres; now 1 mill; 2 salt-houses;
> pasture, 20 sheep. Then 10 cobs, now 4; then 10 cattle, now
> 5; always 200 sheep less 20. Then 20 pigs, now 15.
> Value then, and when acquired, £11. Value now £16.
> Of this manor, Ralph holds 2 hides and 10 acres.
> 13 smallholders. 1 plough.
> Value 30s in the same assessment.

38a Robert holds the land of a free man, which is called TENDRING.
Walter holds it from him as a manor, for 1 hide less 15 acres.
> Then 5 villagers, now 2; then 3 smallholders, now 7; then 3
> slaves, now none. Always 1 plough in lordship. Then among
> the men 3 ploughs, now 2.
> Woodland, 20 pigs; meadow, 1 acre. Then 2 cobs, now 4; then
> 2 cattle, now 10; then 20 pigs, now 27; then 49 sheep, now
> 60; then 24 goats, now 37; now 3 beehives.
> Value then 20s; now 30[s].
> Robert acquired this in exchange.

39 Nigel holds DICKLEY from Robert, which Alstan held as a manor,
for 1 hide and 37½ acres.
> Always 8 smallholders. Then 1 slave, now none. Then 2 ploughs
> in lordship, now 1½. Always 2 men's ploughs.
> Woodland, 10 pigs; meadow, 2 acres. Then 7 cattle, now 8;
> then 1 cob, now 4; then 37 sheep, now 51; then 7 pigs,
> now 15; always 20 goats.
> Value 20s.

⌐Erleiam ten& Witt de . R . qd ten̄ . Scapi̇ . p Man̄ . 7 p dim̄ . hid.

7 . xxx . ac . 7 . jac& cuidam manerio in Sudfolc . ſ; in iſto hund ptin&
Tc̄ . 1 . uitt . m̄ nutt . Sēp . 1 . ſer̄ . tc̄ . in dn̄io . 11 . car̄ . qn̄do rec̄ . 1 . m̄ nulla.
tc̄ . 11 . bord̄ . m̄ . nutt . 1 . ac̄ . p̄ti . Tc̄ . uat . xL . ſot . 7 . qn̄ rec̄ . xx . m̄ . v.

⌐Hund de Vdelesfort   Widintuuā ten& . Rob de . R . qd ten̄
Ingutt . p Man̄ . 7 . p . 111 . hid . 7 . 1 . uirḡ . 7 Rob ħt in eſcangio ut dic̄.
Tc̄ . v . uitt . m̄ . 1111 . tc̄ . 111 . bor . m̄ . v . Sēp . v . ſer̄ . 7 . 11 . car̄ . in dn̄io.
Tc̄ . 1111 . car̄ . hom̄ . m̄ . 11 . x . ac̄ . p̄ti . Tc̄ . 111 . ou̅ . m̄ . Lxv . Tc̄ . xx1111.
porc̄ . m̄ . xL1x . Tc̄ uat . Lx . ſot . m̄ . 1111 . lib.

⌐Scortegrauā ten& Idē . R . qd tenuit Vluuin̄ 7 Grīchett . p . Man̄.
7 . p . 11 . hid . 7 Rob ħt in Eſcangio . Tc̄ . 7 p . v1 . ſer̄ . m̄ . 111 . Tc̄ . in dn̄io
. 111 . car̄ . Poſt 7 m̄ . 11 . x11 . ac̄ . pti . Tc̄ . 1 . mot . m̄ nutt . Tc̄ . 111 . runc̄ . m̄
nutt . tc̄ . 111 . uac . m̄ . nutt . Sēp . c . ou̅ . Tc̄ . Lx . porc̄ . m̄ nutt . Tc̄ . xx111.
uaſa apū . m̄ . x1 . Tc̄ uat . 1111 . lib . 7 qn̄ rec̄ . L . ſot . m̄ . Lx.

⌐Archeſdanam ten& Picot de . R . qd tenuit Grīchett . p Man̄ . 7 . p . 1 . hid.
. v111 . ac̄ . min̄ . 7 . Rob . ħt . p eſcangio . m̄ . 1111 . bord̄ . Sēp . 11 . ſer̄ . 7 . 1 . car̄.
. v1 . ac̄ . p̄ti . m̄ . 11 . anim̄ . Sēp . x11 . porc̄ . 7 . xxx11 . ou̅ . m̄ . 11 . uaſa apū
vat . xx . ſot.

⌐Elſenham ten& Petr̄ de . R . qd ten̄ . Leſtan̄ p Man̄ . 7 . p . 1 . hid . 7 . R.
ħt in eſcangio . Tc̄ . 1111 . uitt . P 7 m̄ . 111 . Tc̄ . 7 p . 111 . bor . m̄ . v1 . Tc̄ . 1111.
ſer̄ . m̄ nutt . tc̄ . 7 p . 11 . car̄ . in dn̄io . m̄ . 1 . Tc̄ . 7 p . 11 . car̄ hom̄ . m̄ . 111.
Silu̅ . c . porc̄ . xx . ac̄ . p̄ti . Sēp . 1 . runc̄ . Tc̄ . v11 . anim̄ . m̄ . 1 . uitut . Tc̄
xv1 . ou̅ . m̄ nutt . tc̄ . v111 . porc̄ . m̄ . xv111 . Tc̄ . xx . cap̄ . m̄ . nutt . Sēp.
uat . xL . ſot.

40 William holds ARDLEIGH from Robert, which Scalpi held as a
   manor, for ½ hide and 30 acres. It lies in (the lands of) a manor   68 a
   in Suffolk; but it belongs in this Hundred.
> Then 1 villager, now none; always 1 slave. Then 2 ploughs in
> lordship, when acquired 1, now none. Then 2 smallholders,
> now none.
> Meadow, 1 acre.

Value then 40s; when acquired 20[s] ; now 5[s] .

Hundred of UTTLESFORD

41 Robert holds WIDDINGTON from Robert, which Ingulf held as a
   manor, for 3 hides and 1 virgate. Robert has (it) in exchange as
   he states.
> Then 5 villagers, now 4; then 3 smallholders, now 5. Always 5
> slaves; 2 ploughs in lordship. Then 4 men's ploughs, now 2.
> Meadow, 10 acres. Then 3 sheep, now 65; then 24 pigs, now 49.

Value then 60s; now £4.

42 Robert also holds SHORTGROVE which Wulfwin and Grimkel held
   as a manor, for 2 hides. Robert has (it) in exchange.
> Then and later 6 slaves, now 3. Then 3 ploughs in lordship,
> later and now 2.
> Meadow, 12 acres; then 1 mill, now none. Then 3 cobs, now
> none; then 3 cows, now none; always 100 sheep. Then 60
> pigs, now none; then 23 beehives, now 11.

Value then £4; when acquired 50s; now 60[s] .

43 Picot holds ARKESDEN from Robert, which Grimkel held as a
   manor, for 1 hide less 8 acres. Robert has (it) by exchange.
> Now 4 smallholders. Always 2 slaves; 1 plough.
> Meadow, 6 acres. Now 2 cattle. Always 12 pigs; 32 sheep.
> Now 2 beehives.

Value 20s.

44 Peter holds ELSENHAM from Robert, which Leofstan held as a
   manor, for 1 hide. Robert has (it) in exchange.
> Then 4 villagers, later and now 3; then and later 3 smallholders,
> now 6; then 4 slaves, now none. Then and later 2 ploughs in
> lordship, now 1. Then and later 2 men's ploughs, now 3.
> Woodland, 100 pigs; meadow, 20 acres. Always 1 cob. Then 7
> cattle, now 1 calf; then 16 sheep, now none; then 8 pigs,
> now 18; then 20 goats, now none.

Value always 40s.

68 b

qđ tenuit Gotra ᵽ Man̅ . 7 . ᵱ . v . hiđ . 7 . dim̅ . Tc̅ . iiii . uiłł . m̅ . vii . tc̅ , vi .
borđ . m̅ . xiiii . tc̅ . iii . ſer . m̅ . v . Sēp . ii . caɼ . in dn̅io . 7 . ii . caɼ . hom̅ . Siłu .
. cc . porc . i . ac̅ . ᵽti . Paſt . xl . ou̅ . i . ſat . Tc̅ . iii . runc . m̅ . nułł . Tc̅ . xiiii . an .
m̅ nułł . Tc̅ . xl . porc . m̅ . xx . Tc̅ . c . ou̅ . m̅ . lx . Tc̅ . xxx . cap . m̅ . xx . m̅
. viii . uaſa apu̅ . Tc̅ 7 ᵽ uał . iiii . liƀ . m̅ . c . ſot . 7 . ii . liƀi h̅oes tenuerŧ
xxx . ac̅ . Tc̅ . i . caɼ . m̅ nułł . Sēp uał . x . ſot . 7 hanc tr̅a dicit ſe haƀe
in ſuo eſcangio.

Vltingam . ten& Girarđ de . Radulfo baignardo . qđ tenuit Hacon t . r . e
ᵽ Man̅ . 7 . ᵱ . i . hiđ . 7 . xl . ac̅ . Sēp . iiii . caɼ in dn̅io . Tc̅ . iii . caɼ . hom̅ . m̅ .
. i . 7 dim̅ . Tc̅ . vii . uiłł . m̅ . iiii . m̅ . xii . borđ . tc̅ . vi . ſer . m̅ nułł . Siłu
. c . porc . xx . ac̅ . ᵽti . ſēp . ii . moł . 7 . v . ac̅ tr̅e addite ſŧ t . r . Wiłłi . 7
ſŧ de ſua conſuetudine . Tc̅ . v . runc . xx . an̅ . vii . porc . lxx . ou̅ .
m̅ . iiii . runc . ix . an̅ . xxiiii . porc . xxxv . ou̅ . ii . uaſa Tc̅ uał . iiii .
liƀ . 7 qn̅ rec̅ . m̅ . uał . c . ſot.

⫽In Langeſort ten& Goiſfriđ . v . liƀos h̅oes de . R . de . iii . uirg̅ . tr̅æ .

69 a

7 . i . ac̅ . q̅ reddebant regi . xv . đ . de conſuetudine t . r . e . Sēp . hn̅t . i . caɼ . 7 . đ .
7 . i . bor . iii . ac̅ . Tc̅ . uał . x . ſot . m̅ . xx.

Hundred of THURSTABLE

45 Robert of Verly holds TOLLESHUNT (D'Arcy) from Robert, which 68 b
Gotre held as a manor, for 5½ hides.
   Then 4 villagers, now 7; then 6 smallholders, now 14; then 3
      slaves, now 5. Always 2 ploughs in lordship; 2 men's ploughs.
   Woodland, 200 pigs; meadow, 1 acre; pasture, 40 sheep; 1
      salt-house. Then 3 cobs, now none; then 14 cattle, now
      none; then 40 pigs, now 20; then 100 sheep, now 60; then
      30 goats, now 20; now 8 beehives.
Value then and later £4; now 100s.
2 free men held 30 acres. Then 1 plough, now none.
Value always 10s.
He states that he has this land in exchange.

33   **LAND OF RALPH BAYNARD**

Hundred of WITHAM

1 Gerard holds ULTING from Ralph Baynard, which Hakon held
   before 1066 as a manor, for 1 hide and 40 acres. Always 4
   ploughs in lordship. Then 3 men's ploughs, now 1½.
   Then 7 villagers, now 4; now 12 smallholders; then 6 slaves,
      now none.
   Woodland, 100 pigs; meadow, 20 acres; always 2 mills.
   5 acres of land were added after 1066 and are part of the
   customary due.
   Then 5 cobs, 20 cattle, 7 pigs, 70 sheep; now 4 cobs, 9 cattle,
      24 pigs, 35 sheep, 2 [bee]hives.
Value then, and when acquired, £4. Value now 100s.

[Hundred of THURSTABLE]

2 In LANGFORD Geoffrey holds 5 free men from Ralph with 3
   virgates of land and 1 acre, who paid the King 15d of the   69 a
   customary due before 1066. They have always had 1½ ploughs;
      1 smallholder.
      3 acres.
Value then 10s; now 20[s].

ᚹHund de Witbricteſherna. Nortunā ten& . R . in dñio . qđ tenuit
Vluric . lib hō . t̄ . r̄ . e . p̄ Man . 7 p̄ . viii . hiđ . Sēp . v . uiłł . 7 . xi . borđ . tc̄.
. ii . ſer . m̄ . nulł . Tc̄ . ii . car . in dñio . m̄ . iii . Tc̄ . iiii . car . hom . m̄ . iii . Ex
his hiđ . st̄ . ii . filuæ . Past . xl . ou . m̄ . i . moł . Tc̄ . iiii . runc . 7 . xv . anim.
. xx . porc . cl . ou . m̄ . vi . runc . viii . anim . xx . porc . 7 . ix . ou . Tc̄
uał . vi . lib . m̄ . vii . Ht̄ &iam . R . p̄ Maner . iii . hiđ . 7 . xlv . ac . q̄s sēp
tenent . vi . libi hōes . Tc̄ . v . car . m̄ . iii . Tc̄ uał . xl . soł . m̄ . xxx . hoc
libatū ē p̄ eſcangio . De hoc man . ten& Walicher . dim hiđ . 7 uał x . soł . i eod p̄tio.
ᚹWdeham ten& Pointell de . R . qđ tenuit Leueua p̄ man . 7 . p̄ . vii.
hiđ . Tc̄ . xii . uiłł . m̄ . vi . Sēp . iiii . borđ . Tc̄ . vi . ſer . m̄ . iiii . Sēp . iii . car
in dñio . Tc̄ . iiii . car hom . m̄ . i . xxiiii . ac . p̄ti . Silu . b . porc . Tc̄ . i . moł
m̄ . ii . Tc̄ . ii . an . 7 . vii . porc . xxxvii . ou . m̄ . viii . anim . xxi . porc . vi.
aſini . cxxx . ou . xiii . uaſa apū . Tc̄ uał . viii . lib . 7 . qn̄ rec . xl . soł.
m̄ uał . vii . lib.
ᚹCurlai ten& Idē de eođ . qđ ten Grim t . r̄ . e . p̄ man . 7 p̄ . i . hiđ . Tc̄
. ii . uiłł . m̄ . iiii . Sēp . ix . borđ . Tc̄ . iiii . ſer . m̄ nulł . Sēp . ii . car . in dñio . 7 . i.
car hom . xxii . ac . p̄ti . Silu . xl . porc . Tc̄ . i . moł . m̄ . nulł . Tc̄ 7 poſt
uał . xl . soł . m̄ . iiii . lib . Ht̄ &iam Godric . de . R . dim . hiđ . qm ht̄
p̄ eſcangio . ut dicit s; hunđ neſcit . Sēp dim . car . uał . x . soł.
ᚹHunđ de Dōmmauua . Dōmauuā ten& . R . in dñio qđ tenuit
Ailid q̄dā femina libæ . p̄ man . 7 p̄ . iiii . hiđ . 7 . dim . Sēp . iii . car i dñio.
tc̄ . vii . car hom . m̄ . vi . Sēp . xv . uiłł . 7 . i . pbr . Tc̄ . xii . borđ . m̄ . xvi.

Hundred of 'WIBERTSHERNE'

3 Ralph holds (Cold) NORTON in lordship which Wulfric, a free man, held before 1066 as a manor, for 8 hides.

Always 5 villagers; 11 smallholders. Then 2 slaves, now none. Then 2 ploughs in lordship, now 3. Then 4 men's ploughs, now 3.

2 of these hides are of woodland. Pasture, 40 sheep; now 1 mill. Then 4 cobs, 15 cattle, 20 pigs, 150 sheep; now 6 cobs, 8 cattle, 20 pigs and 60 sheep.

Value then £6; now [£] 7.

Ralph also has as a manor 3 hides and 45 acres which 6 free men have always held. Then 5 ploughs, now 3.

Value then 40s; now 30[s].

This was handed over by exchange.

Of this manor, Walchere holds ½ hide.

Value 10s in the same assessment.

4 Pointel holds WOODHAM (Walter), which Leofeva held as a manor, for 7 hides.

Then 12 villagers, now 6; always 4 smallholders. Then 6 slaves, now 4. Always 3 ploughs in lordship. Then 4 men's ploughs, now 1.

Meadow, 24 acres; woodland, 500 pigs; then 1 mill, now 2. Then 2 cattle, 7 pigs, 37 sheep; now 8 cattle, 21 pigs, 6 asses, 130 sheep, 13 beehives.

Value then £8; when acquired 40s. Value now £7.

5 He also holds from him CURLING TYE (Green), which Grim held before 1066 as a manor, for 1 hide.

Then 2 villagers, now 4; always 9 smallholders. Then 4 slaves, now none. Always 2 ploughs in lordship; 1 men's plough.

Meadow, 22 acres; woodland, 40 pigs; then 1 mill, now none.

Value then and later 40s; now £4.

Godric also has ½ hide from Ralph, which he has by exchange as he states; but the Hundred does not know. Always ½ plough.

Value 10s.

Hundred of DUNMOW

6 Ralph holds (Little) DUNMOW in lordship which Aethelgyth, a free woman, held as a manor for 4½ hides. Always 3 ploughs in lordship. Then 7 men's ploughs, now 6.

Always 15 villagers; 1 priest. Then 12 smallholders, now 16;

Sēp . x . ſer . Silua . CL . porc . L . ac . p̄ti . m̄ . ɪ . moł . Tc̄ . ɪɪɪ . runc . xɪ . anim . xL . porc .
. xv . ou . xxɪɪɪ . cap . m̄ . xɪ . runc . xxɪ . an . xxx . porc . cɪɪɪɪ . ou . Lɪɪɪ . cap . vɪɪɪ .
uaſa apū . Tc̄ 7 p uał . vɪɪɪ . liƀ . m̄ . x . Huic t̄re addita ē . ɪ . hiđ . q̄m ten
. ɪ . liƀ hō . t . r . e . Sēp . ɪ . car . 7 . ɪ . uiłł . 7 . ɪ . borđ . 7 . ɪ . ſer . Silu . xxɪɪɪɪ . porc .
. x . ac . p̄ti . Vał . xx . ſoł . Et huic man . ađjac& adhuc . dim hiđ quā
tenuit . ɪ . ſoc anteceſſoris baignardi . 7 . adhuc ten& Tc̄ . ɪ . car . 7 . dim
in dn̄io . m̄ . ɪ . Sēp . ɪ . uiłł . 7 . ɪ . ſer . 7 . ſilu . xx . porc . ɪx . ac . p̄ti . Vał sēp
. xx . ſoł.

⌐ Wimbeis ten& . R . in dn̄io qđ tenuit Ailid t . r . e . p man . 7 . p . vɪɪɪ .
hiđ . Sēp . ɪɪɪ . car . in dn̄io . Tc̄ . xxɪ . car hom . m̄ . xv . Sēp . xxvɪ . uiłł . 7 . ɪ . pƀr
Tc̄ . xvɪɪɪɪ . borđ . m̄ . Lv . Tc̄ . vɪ . ſer . m̄ null . Tc̄ ſilu . ꝺ . porc . m̄ . cccc .
xL . ac . p̄ti . Tc̄ . ɪɪ . runc . 7 . ɪɪɪɪ . an . Lx . porc . cxx . ou . ɪɪɪɪ . uaſa apū .
m̄ . ɪɪ . runc . ɪɪɪɪ . anim . xxvɪɪɪ . porc . Lxxx . ou . ɪɪɪɪ . uaſa apū . Tc̄ uał
. xɪɪ . liƀ . m̄ . xx .

⌐ Hunđ de Wenfiſtreu . Boroolditunā ten& Modƀt de . R . qđ
tenuit Aluric liƀ hō . t . r . e . p Man . 7 . p . ɪ . hiđ . Sēp . ɪ . car . in dn̄io .
tc̄ . ɪɪɪ . borđ . m̄ . ɪɪɪɪ . Silu . xx . porc . Tc̄ . ɪɪ . runc . ɪ . anim . ɪ . porc . xv . ou .
m̄ . ɪɪ . runc . ɪ . anim . ɪɪ . porc . xxxɪɪɪ . ou . xxxɪɪɪɪ . cap . Vał xxx . ſoł .

⌐ Metcinges ten& Bernard . de . R . qđ ten . liƀa femina . p . Man . 7 . p . đ
hiđ . t . r . e . m̄ . ɪ . borđ . Silu . xɪɪ . porc . Tc̄ uał . x . ſoł . m̄ . ɪɪɪ .

always 10 slaves.
Woodland, 150 pigs; meadow, 50 acres; now 1 mill. Then 3
cobs, 11 cattle, 40 pigs, 15 sheep, 23 goats; now 11 cobs,
21 cattle, 30 pigs, 104 sheep, 53 goats, 8 beehives.
Value then and later £8; now [£] 10.
1 hide was added to this land, which 1 free man held before
1066. Always 1 plough;
1 villager; 1 smallholder; 1 slave.
Woodland, 24 pigs; meadow, 10 acres.
Value 20s.
A further ½ hide is attached to this manor, which 1 Freeman
of Baynard's predecessor held and still holds. Then 1½ ploughs in
lordship, now 1.
Always 1 villager; 1 slave.
Woodland, 20 pigs; meadow, 9 acres.
Value always 20s.

[Hundred of UTTLESFORD]
7 Ralph holds WIMBISH in lordship, which Aethelgyth held before
1066 as a manor, for 8 hides. Always 3 ploughs in lordship. Then
21 men's ploughs, now 15.
Always 26 villagers; 1 priest. Then 19 smallholders, now 55;
then 6 slaves, now none.
Woodland, then 500 pigs, now 400; meadow, 40 acres. Then 2
cobs, 4 cattle, 60 pigs, 120 sheep, 4 beehives; now 2 cobs,
4 cattle, 28 pigs, 80 sheep, 4 beehives.
Value then £12; now [£] 20.

Hundred of WINSTREE
8 Modbert holds BARN HALL from Ralph which Aelfric, a free man,
held before 1066 as a manor, for 1 hide. Always 1 plough in
lordship.
Then 3 smallholders, now 4.
Woodland, 20 pigs. Then 2 cobs, 1 (head of) cattle, 1 pig,
15 sheep; now 2 cobs, 1 (head of) cattle, 2 pigs, 33 sheep,
34 goats.
Value 30s.

[Hundred of LEXDEN]
9 Bernard holds MESSING from Ralph, which a free woman held as a
manor, for ½ hide before 1066.
Now 1 smallholder.
Woodland, 12 pigs.
Value then 10s; now 3[s].

⌐Hund de Clauelinga . In Magellana tenuit . ı . lıb hõ . t . r . e.
. xxx . ac . qd ten& Amelfrid de . R . Sep . ı . car . Tc . ual . v . fol . m . x,
⌐Hund de hidingforda . Pentelauuã tenuit lıba femina . t . r . e
p Man . 7 . p . ıııı . hıd . 7 . ııı . uirg . Sep . ııı . car in dñio . 7 . v . car

car hom . 7 . vııı . uilt . tc 7 p . ı . bord . m . vııı . Tc . vııı . fer . m null .
Silu . cc . porc . xxx . ac . pti . Sep . ı . mol . Tc . ıı . runc . xxıı . anim . xLvııı.
porc . x . ou . vııı . uafa apũ . m . ııı . runc . xxıııı . anim . xx . porc . Lxxx.
ou . vııı . uafa apũ . Et . xvııı . foc . de . ıı . hıd . 7 . xxx . ac . 7 hnt . v . car.
tc . ıııı . fer . m . ı . m . ıııı . bord . Silu . x . porc . x . ac . pti . Hoc totũ ual
t . r . e . x . lıb . m . xvı . De hoc manerio . ten& Galicer . xxx . ac . 7 ual
. x . fol in eod ptio.
⌐Hund de Witbrickefherna . Burneham ten& . R . in dñio
qd tenuit Aluuart lıb hõ . t . r . e . p . Man . 7 . p . ıııı . hıd . 7 . xıı . ac.
Sep . ı . uilt . tc . vı . bor . m . xıı . tc . ıııı . fer . m null . Sep . ıı . car in dñio
7 . ı . car . hom . Paft . ccc . ou . Tc . ıı . runc . ıııı . anim . xıı . porc.
. cc . ou . m . vı . runc . xııı . anim . xvı . porc . cccxxxvı . ou . Tc
ual . ıııı . lıb . m . c . fol . In Ead uilt . x . libi hões . t . r . e . hntes . vııı.
hıd . 7 . xxvııı . ac . qd ten& . R . in dñio . Tc . x . bord . m . xvı . Sep
. vıı . fer . 7 . vııı . car . m . ı . mol . Paft . bc . ou . Tc . 7 p ual . vıı . lıb.
m . vııı . lıb . hanc trã reclamat . R . baignard p efcangio
⌐Hund de Celmeresfort . Baduuen ten& Germund de . R.
qd tenuit Leuuin p Man . 7 . p . ıııı . hıd . Sep . ıı . uilt . 7 . ıı . bord . Tc
. ıx . fer . m . vıı . Sep . ıııı . car . in dñio . Tc . int hões . ı . car . m null.

Hundred of CLAVERING

10   In MANUDEN 1 free man held 30 acres before 1066. Amalfrid holds
it from Ralph. Always 1 plough.
Value then 5s; now 10[s].

Hundred of HINCKFORD

11   A free woman held PENTLOW before 1066 as a manor, for 4 hides
and 3 virgates. Always 3 ploughs in lordship; 5 men's ploughs;   70 a
8 villagers. Then and later 1 smallholder, now 8; then 8 slaves,
now none.
Woodland, 200 pigs; meadow, 30 acres; always 1 mill. Then 2
cobs, 22 cattle, 48 pigs, 10 sheep, 8 beehives; now 3 cobs,
24 cattle, 20 pigs, 80 sheep, 8 beehives.
18 Freemen with 2 hides and 30 acres have 5 ploughs.
Then 4 slaves, now 1; now 4 smallholders.
Woodland, 10 pigs; meadow, 10 acres.
Value of the whole of this before 1066 £10; now [£] 16.
Of this manor, Walchere holds 30 acres.
Value 10s in the same assessment.

Hundred of 'WIBERTSHERNE'

12   Ralph holds BURNHAM in lordship which Alfward, a free man,
held before 1066 as a manor, for 4 hides and 12 acres.
Always 1 villager. Then 6 smallholders, now 12; then 4 slaves,
now none. Always 2 ploughs in lordship; 1 men's plough.
Pasture, 300 sheep. Then 2 cobs, 4 cattle, 12 pigs, 200 sheep;
now 6 cobs, 13 cattle, 16 pigs, 336 sheep.
Value then £4; now 100s.
In the same village 10 free men who had 8 hides and 28 acres
before 1066. Ralph holds it in lordship.
Then 10 smallholders, now 16. Always 7 slaves; 8 ploughs.
Now 1 mill; pasture, 600 sheep.
Value then and later £7; now £8.
Ralph Baynard claims back this land by exchange.

Hundred of CHELMSFORD

13   Germund holds (Little) BADDOW from Ralph, which Leofwin held
as a manor, for 4 hides.
Always 2 villagers; 2 smallholders. Then 9 slaves, now 7.
Always 4 ploughs in lordship. Then among the men 1
plough, now none.

Silu . c . porc . i . ac . p̄ti . Sēp . i . mot . Tc̄ . vii . runc . xlvii . an̄ . cviii .

porc . lxxx . ou . m̄ . x . runc . liii . anim̄ . clxiii . ou . Tc̄ 7 poſt

ual . c . ſot . m̄ . vi . lib . 7 . v . libi hōes . tenuer̄ . ii . hid . 7 . xxxi . ac .

q̄ poſſent ire q̄ uellent . M̄ ten& Idē Germ . 7 . iiii . franci .

Sēp . iii . bord . 7 . i . ſer . tc̄ . ii . car . m̄ . i . Silu . xxvi . porc . xiii . ac . p̄ti .

Sēp ual . xx . ſot .

⌐ Haningefeldā ten& Berengeri de . R . qd̄ tenuit Normann̄ p . m̄ .

7 . p . iii . hid . Tc̄ . iii . uilt . m̄ nult . m̄ . ix . bord . Sēp . ii . ſer . tc̄ . ii . car in̄ dn̄io

m̄ . i . tc̄ . i . car hom . m̄ . d̄ . Silu . cc . porc . M̄ . iii . an̄ . xxiii . porc . xlvii . ou .

. iiii . cap . Tc̄ 7 p̄ ual . xl . x . ſot . m̄ . iiii . lib .

⌐ Hund de Tendringa . Adem ten& . Germund de . R . qd̄ tenuit

Ednod p Man̄ . 7 . p . v . hid . 7 . dim̄ . tc̄ . vii . uilt . m̄ . xvii . Sēp . iiii . bord .

7 . viii . ſer . 7 . iii . car . in dn̄io . 7 . iii . car . hom . Silu . xxxiii . porc .

. ii . ac . p̄ti . i . piſc . Paſt . c . ou . tc̄ . ii . runc . 7 . xiii . an̄ . l . porc . l . ou . m̄ .

. iii . runc . iiii . ac . an̄ . xxvii . porc . cxviii . ou . Tc̄ . 7 p̄ ual . vii . lib . m̄ . ix .

⌐ Rameſeiam ten& . Roḡ . qd̄ ten̄ . Aluric cāp . p Man̄ . 7 . p . vii . hid . 7 . xxxv .

ac . Sēp . xviii . uilt . Tc̄ . vi . bord . m̄ . ix . Sēp . vi . ſer . 7 . iii . car . in dn̄io .

Tc̄ . int hōes . vii . car . m̄ . v . Silu . lx . porc . viii . ac . p̄ti . m̄ . i . mot . i . ſat .

tc̄ ual . xii . lib . m̄ . xv . tc̄ . i . runc . 7 . xx . an̄ . xxii . porc . cxv .

ou . m̄ . ii . runc . xx . anim̄ . xl 7 ix . porc . ccc . ix . ou . viii . uaſa apū .

⌐ Micheleſtou ten& Bernard . de . R . qd̄ tenuit Alric p . Man̄ . 7 p

. ii . hid . 7 . dim̄ . Tc̄ . iii . bor . m̄ . i . Tc̄ . iii . ſer . m̄ nult . Sēp . ii . car . i dn̄io .

tc̄ int hōes . dim̄ . car . m̄ . n̄ . iiii . ac . p̄ti . Tc̄ . ii . runc . vi . an̄ . xxvii . porc .

. cl . ou . m̄ . xxv . porc . lxxxiii . ou . Tc̄ ual lxx . ſot . m̄ . iiii . lib .

Woodland, 100 pigs; meadow, 1 acre; always 1 mill. Then 7 cobs, 47 cattle, 108 pigs, 80 sheep; now 10 cobs, 53 cattle, 163 sheep.

Value then and later 100s; now £6.

5 free men held 2 hides and 31 acres; they could go whither they would. Now Germund also holds (it). 4 Frenchmen.

Always 3 smallholders; 1 slave. Then 2 ploughs, now 1.

Woodland, 26 pigs; meadow, 13 acres.

Value always 20s.   70 b

14 Berengar holds (East) HANNINGFIELD from Ralph, which Norman held as a manor, for 3 hides.

Then 3 villagers, now none; now 9 smallholders; always 2 slaves. Then 2 ploughs in lordship, now 1. Then 1 men's plough, now ½.

Woodland, 200 pigs. Now 3 cattle, 23 pigs, 47 sheep, 4 goats.

Value then and later ... s; now £4.

Hundred of TENDRING

15 Germund holds (Little) OAKLEY from Ralph, which Ednoth held as a manor, for 5½ hides.

Then 7 villagers, now 17. Always 4 smallholders; 8 slaves; 3 ploughs in lordship; 3 men's ploughs.

Woodland, 33 pigs; meadow, 2 acres; 1 fishery; pasture, 100 sheep. Then 2 cobs, 13 cattle, 50 pigs, 50 sheep; now 3 cobs, 4 cattle, 27 pigs, 118 sheep.

Value then and later £7; now [£] 9.

16 Roger holds RAMSEY, which Aelfric Kemp held as a manor, for 7 hides and 35 acres.

Always 18 villagers. Then 6 smallholders, now 9. Always 6 slaves; 3 ploughs in lordship. Then among the men 7 ploughs, now 5.

Woodland, 60 pigs; meadow, 8 acres; now 1 mill; 1 salt-house.

Value then £12; now [£] 15.

Then 1 cob, 20 cattle, 22 pigs, 115 sheep; now 2 cobs, 20 cattle, 49 pigs, 309 sheep, 8 beehives.

17 Bernard holds MICHAELSTOW from Ralph, which Alric held as a manor, for 2½ hides.

Then 3 smallholders, now 1; then 3 slaves, now none. Always 2 ploughs in lordship. Then among the men ½ plough, now none.

Meadow, 4 acres. Then 2 cobs, 6 cattle, 27 pigs, 150 sheep; now 25 pigs, 83 sheep.

Value then 70s; now £4.

7 . ii . ſoc̛ . ten& . R . in ſuo eſcang̅ . ſic̅ ſui hões dic̅t . ſed alij n̅ teſtant̛ .
niſi ipſi ſoli . de manerio q̇d uocat̅ Laleforda ꞉ tenentes . dim̅ hiđ .
7 . xxxv . ac̛ . Tq̇đ ten& Iđē . B . de . R . tc̅ . i . car̛ . m̅ . dim̅ . tc̅ . ual̅ .
. viii . ſol̅ . m̅ . x . 7 in Witelebroc . ten& Rog̅ . i . hiđ de . R . q̇đ ten̅
Aluric̛ . ꝓ . Man̅ . Sēp . i . bord . 7 . i . car̛ . 7 . i . ac̛ . p̅ti . val̅ . x . ſol̅ . 7 hec

t̅ra . n̅ jacuit in alijs t̅ris . hec . iii . maner̛ ual̅ . xx . lib̅ .

⌐Hund de Vdeleſfort . Wendenā ten& Amelfrid q̇đ tenuit . i . lib̅
hō . Aluuin̅ ſtille . ꝓ Man̅ . 7 . ꝓ . i . hiđ . 7 dim̅ . 7 . xxx . ac̛ . 7 . R . k̅t i eſcangio .
Sēp . v . uilt̅ . 7 . iii . bord . 7 . ii . ſer̛ . 7 . ii . car̛ . in dñio . 7 . i . car̛ . hom̅ . Silu . lxxx .
porc̛ . iii . ac̛ . p̅ti . Tc̅ . ual̅ . iiii . lib̅ . m̅ . v .

⌐Dim̅ Hund de Froſſeuùella ꞉ Henham ten& . R . i dñio q̇đ
tenuit Ailid ꝓ Man̅ . 7 . ꝓ . xiii . hiđ . 7 . đ . x . ac̛ . min̅ . Tc̅ 7 p̅ . xviii . uilt̅
m̅ . viii . Tc̅ 7 p̅ . v . bord . m̅ . xxxviii . tc̅ . 7 p̅ . viii . ſer̛ . m̅ nult̅ . Sēp
. iiii . car̛ . in dñio . 7 . viii . car̛ hom̅ . Silu . cc . porc̛ . xvi . ac̛ . p̅ti . Tc̅ . iiiͤ
runc̛ . viii . anim̅ . lxxx . por̛ . clx . ou̅ . xvi . uaſa ap̅ . m̅ . viii . runc̛ .
vii . anim̅ . c . porc̛ . lxxx . ou̅ . x . uaſa ap̅ . Tc̅ ual̅ . xii . lib̅ . m̅ . xx .

⌐Aſcendunā ten& . R . in dñio q̇d tenuit . Ailid . ꝓ Man̅ . 7 . ꝓ . ii . hiđ . Tc̅
xiiii . uilt̅ . m̅ . xx . Tc̅ . iii . bord . m̅ . ix . Tc̅ . ii . ſer̛ . m̅ . nult̅ . Sēp . ii . car̛
in dñio . 7 . iiii . car̛ . hom̅ . Silu . c . porc̛ . vi . ac̛ . p̅ti . i . ac̛ . uineæ . tc̅ .
. ii . runc̛ . v . an̅ . lx . porc̛ . cc . ou̅ . x . uaſa ap̅ . m̅ . i . runc̛ . vii . an̅ . lx . porc̛
lxv . ou̅ . iii . uaſa ap̅ . Tc̅ ual̅ . vi . lib̅ . m̅ . viii . 7 . ii . ſoc̛ tenentes . xv . ac̛
libæ . ꝛos accep̅ . R . in eſcang̅ . ual̅ . iii . ſol̅ .

Ralph holds 2 Freemen — in exchange so his men state; but others do not testify except for those alone from the manor which is called Lawford — who hold ½ hide and 35 acres, which Bernard also holds from Ralph.

Then 1 plough, now ½.

Value then 8s; now 10[s].

In *WITELEBROC* Roger holds 1 hide from Ralph, which Aelfric held as a manor.

Always 1 smallholder; 1 plough.

Meadow, 1 acre.

Value 10s.

This land did not lie in the other lands.

Value of these three manors £20.

71 a

Hundred of UTTLESFORD

18 Amalfrid holds WENDON (Lofts) which 1 free man, Alwin Still, held as a manor for 1½ hides and 30 acres. Ralph has it in exchange.

Always 5 villagers; 3 smallholders; 2 slaves; 2 ploughs in lordship; 1 men's plough.

Woodland, 80 pigs; meadow, 3 acres.

Value then £4; now [£] 5.

Half-Hundred of FRESHWELL

19 Ralph holds HENHAM in lordship, which Aethelgyth held as a manor, for 13½ hides less 10 acres.

Then and later 18 villagers, now 8; then and later 5 smallholders, now 38; then and later 8 slaves, now none. Always 4 ploughs in lordship; 8 men's ploughs.

Woodland, 200 pigs; meadow, 16 acres. Then 3 cobs, 8 cattle, 80 pigs, 160 sheep, 16 beehives; now 8 cobs, 7 cattle, 100 pigs, 80 sheep, 10 beehives.

Value then £12; now [£] 20.

20 Ralph holds ASHDON in lordship, which Aethelgyth held as a manor, for 2 hides.

Then 14 villagers, now 20; then 3 smallholders, now 9; then 2 slaves, now none. Always 2 ploughs in lordship; 4 men's ploughs.

Woodland, 100 pigs; meadow, 6 acres; 1 acre of vines. Then 2 cobs, 5 cattle, 60 pigs, 200 sheep, 10 beehives; now 1 cob, 7 cattle, 60 pigs, 65 sheep, 3 beehives.

Value then £6; now [£] 8.

2 Freemen who hold 15 acres freely. Ralph acquired them in exchange.

Value 3s.

Hund de Rochefort. In Pacheſham ten& Tedric pointel. dim

hiđ.7.xv.qđ tenuit.ı.liƀ hõ tc.ıı.borđ.m̃.v.Sẽp.ı.car.Paſt.ʟ.ou̓,

Sẽp ua᷈t᷈.xx.ſot᷈. hoc reclamat.ʀ.ꝑ eſcangio.

Hunđ de Tureſtapla Langheforđã tenuit Gola. 7 Agelmar

ꝓ Man̓.7.ꝓ.ııı.hiđ.7.dim̃.7 hanc dim̃ hiđ tenuit Agelmar ad censũ

de ſco paulo.ſ; ʀ.inde ẽ ſaiſit.7 Goisfriđ ten& totũ de.ʀ.Sẽp

ı.uill᷈.Tc.ıııı.bor.m̃.ıx.tc.ıııı.ſer.m̃.ııı.Tc in dñio.ııı.car.m̃.ıí.

71 b

Sĩlua.xx.porc̓.xxv.ac̓.p̃ti.Sẽp.ı.mot᷈.Tc.ııı.runc̓.v.anĩm.xxtıíí,

porc̓.xʟ.ou̓.m̃.ıı.runc̓.ıııı.anim.xʟ.porc̓.ʟxxx.ou̓.Tc ua᷈t᷈.c.ſot᷈

7 qñ rec ſimit᷈.m̃.ıııı.liƀ.Tc.ibi fuer̃.v.liƀi hões de.ı.hiđ.7.dim̃.m̃

.ıııı.hões.Te.ı.car̃.7.dim̃.m̃.ı.Te.ı.bor.m̃.ııı.tc.ı.ſer.m̃.n̄.tc.ua᷈t᷈.

.xxx.ſot᷈.m̃.xx.

Toleſhuntã ten& Bernarđ de.ʀ.qđ ten̓ Ailmar̓ ꝓ.Man̓.7.ꝓ.ııı.hiđ

7.vııı.ac̓.Tc.ıııı.uill᷈.m̃.vııı.Sẽp.v.borđ.Tc.ıııı.ſer.m̃.ı.Sẽp.ı.car̃

7.dim̃.in dñio.7.ıı.car̃ hom̓.Silu̓.cc.porc̓.Paſt.xx.ou̓.v.ſalinæ.

Tc.ıı.runc̓.vı.anim.xx.porc̓.c.ou̓.M̃.ıı.runc̓.v.an̓.xx.porc̓.

.c.ou̓.xxvııı.cap̃.Sẽp ua᷈t᷈.ʟx.ſot᷈. In Eađ uill᷈.vııı.liƀi hões.de.

.ı.hiđ.7.dim̃.7.xıııı.ac̓.Sẽp.ıı.borđ.7.ıı.car̃.va᷈t᷈.xx.ſot᷈.hanc

tram ht.ʀ.baignarđ.ꝓ eſcangio.

.XXXIIII.Terre RANulfi piperelli. Hunđ de ƀdeſtapla. In bura

ten& Serlo de.Ranulfo.ı.car̃.7.ı.ſer.qđ tenuit Aleſtan̓ liƀ homo.

Paſt.cxx.ou̓.Tc.ı.runc̓.c.ou̓.xıııı.porc̓.ıııı.uitul̃.m̃.ıı.runc̓

.c.ou̓.xıııı.porc̓.ıııı.uit᷈.Tc ua᷈t᷈.xx.ſot᷈.m̃.xʟ.

Hundred of ROCHFORD

21 In PAGLESHAM Theodoric Pointel holds ½ hide and 15 [acres],
which 1 free man held.
>   Then 2 smallholders, now 5. Always 1 plough.
>   Pasture, 50 sheep.
>   Value always 20s.
>   Ralph claims this back by exchange.

Hundred of THURSTABLE

22 Cola and Aelmer held LANGFORD as a manor, for 3½ hides. Aelmer
held this ½ hide from St. Paul's for the customary dues; but
Ralph is in possession of it and Geoffrey holds the whole from
Ralph.
>   Always 1 villager. Then 4 smallholders, now 9; then 4 slaves,
>   now 3. Then 3 ploughs in lordship, now 2.
>   Woodland, 20 pigs, meadow, 25 acres; always 1 mill. Then 3   71 b
>   cobs, 5 cattle, 24 pigs, 40 sheep; now 2 cobs, 4 cattle,
>   40 pigs, 80 sheep.
>   Value then 100s; when acquired, the same; now £4.
>   Then 5 free men with 1½ hides were there; now 4 men. Then
>   1½ ploughs, now 1.
>   Then 1 smallholder, now 3; then 1 slave, now none.
>   Value then 30s; now 20[s].

23 Bernard holds TOLLESHUNT from Ralph, which Aelmer held as a
manor, for 3 hides and 8 acres.
>   Then 4 villagers, now 8. Always 5 smallholders. Then 4 slaves,
>   · now 1. Always 1½ ploughs in lordship; 2 men's ploughs.
>   Woodland, 200 pigs; pasture, 20 sheep; 5 salt-houses. Then 2
>   cobs, 6 cattle, 20 pigs, 100 sheep; now 2 cobs, 5 cattle,
>   20 pigs, 100 sheep, 28 goats.
>   Value always 60s.
>   In the same village 8 free men with 1½ hides and 14 acres.
>   Always 2 smallholders; 2 ploughs.
>   Value 20s.
>   Ralph Baynard has this land by exchange.

34   **LANDS OF RANULF PEVEREL**

Hundred of BARSTABLE

1 In BOWERS (Gifford) Serlo holds from Ranulf 1 hide, 1 plough
and 1 slave which Alstan, a free man, held.
>   Pasture, 120 sheep. Then 1 cob, 100 sheep, 14 pigs, 4 calves;
>   now 2 cobs, 100 sheep, 14 pigs, 4 calves.
>   Value then 20s; now 40[s].

Phenge ten& Idē Serlo de.R.q̄d tenuit lib̄ hō p man.7 p.1.hid.q̄
t.r.Witti effect ē hō antecefforis Ranulfi piperelli.f; trā fuam
fibi non dedit.Quando ū rex dedit trā Ranulfo faifiuit illam cū

cū alia.In q̄ erat tē.1.car.m̄ nulla.Paſt.xxx.ou.Tē ual.xx.fol.
m̄.x. Ingā ten& Idē Serlo qd tenuit Alfid t.r.e.p.Man.7 p.1.hid.7
xx.ac.Sep.1.car.tē.111.bord.m̄.1111.Silu.xxx.porc.Tē ual.xx.fol
m̄.x.

Hund de Witham Hadfeldam ten&.R.in dn̄io.qd ten
Ailmar.t.r.e.p Man.7 p.ix.hid.7 Lxxxii.ac.Sep.v.car in dn̄io
Tē.xiii.car.hom.m̄.xi.Tē.xii.uilt.m̄.xiii.Tē.xii.bord.m̄ xxxviiī.
Tē.x.fer.m̄.vii.Silu.bcc.porc.L.ac.p̄ti.Tē.11.mot.m̄.1.Tē.vi.
runc.7.1111.pulli.7.vi.uac.7.viii.uit.cL.ou.c.porc.m̄r.v.runc.
.1111.pulli.v.uacæ.vii.uit.Lvii.ou.xxxix.porc.xx.cap.Tē
ual.xvi.lib̄.m̄.xx.7 hoc maneriū recep̄ tantū ualens ut modo.
De hoc manerio ten& Serlo.7 Ernulf.7 Ricard.111.hid.7.xx.
ac.7 ual.1111.lib̄.in eod p̄tio.7.1111.hid.tenent.v.milit.7.xv.
ac.de.R.qd tenuer̄.xiii.libi hōes.t.r.e.Sep.vii.car.xvi.bord.
.11.uilt.7.11.fer.7.1.mot.ual.1111.lib̄.

Blundeſhala.ten& Humfrid de.R.qd tenuit brictmar
t.r.e.p man.7 p.11.hid.7.dim.Sep.11.car.in dn̄io.Tē.1.car hōu
m̄.1.7.dim.Sep.11.uilt.Tē.111.bor.m̄.v.tē.vi.fer.m̄.1111.xviii.
ac.p̄ti.7.1.mot.7.1.foc.de.xv.ac.Tē.1.runc.1111.an.7.1111.uit.
.Lx.ou.xvi.porc.m̄.11.runc.1111.uac.7.1111.uit.Lxxx.ou.xxxvi.porc.
Sēp ual.1111.lib̄.

2 Serlo also holds VANGE from Ranulf, which a free man, who after 1066 was made the man of Ranulf Peverel's predecessor, held as a manor for 1 hide; but he did not give his land to him. However when the King gave land to Ranulf he took possession of it with the other (land). On it there was then 1 plough, now none.
    Pasture, 30 sheep.
Value then 20s; now 10[s].

3 Serlo also held INGRAVE, which Alfsi held before 1066 as a manor, for 1 hide and 20 acres. Always 1 plough.
    Then 3 smallholders, now 4.
    Woodland, 30 pigs.
Value then 20s; now 10[s].

Hundred of WITHAM

4 Ranulf holds HATFIELD (Peverel) in lordship, which Aelmer held before 1066 as a manor, for 9 hides and 82 acres. Always 5 ploughs in lordship. Then 13 men's ploughs, now 11.
    Then 12 villagers, now 13; then 12 smallholders, now 38; then 10 slaves, now 7.
    Woodland, 700 pigs; meadow, 50 acres; then 2 mills, now 1. Then 6 cobs, 4 foals, 6 cows, 8 calves, 150 sheep, 100 pigs; now 5 cobs, 4 foals, 5 cows, 7 calves, 57 sheep, 39 pigs, 20 goats.
Value then £16; now [£] 20.
    He acquired this manor at as much value as now.
    Of this manor, Serlo, Arnulf and Richard hold 3 hides and 20 acres.
Value £4 in the same assessment.
    5 men-at-arms hold 4 hides and 15 acres from Ranulf, which 13 free men held before 1066. Always 7 ploughs;
    16 smallholders; 2 villagers; 2 slaves.
    1 mill.
Value £4.

5 Humphrey holds BLUNT'S HALL from Ranulf, which Brictmer held before 1066 as a manor, for 2½ hides. Always 2 ploughs in lordship. Then 1 men's plough, now 1½.
    Always 2 villagers. Then 3 smallholders, now 5; then 6 slaves, now 4.
    Meadow, 18 acres; 1 mill. 1 Freeman with 15 acres. Then 1 cob, 4 cattle, 4 calves, 60 sheep, 16 pigs; now 2 cobs, 4 cows, 4 calves, 80 sheep, 36 pigs.
Value always £4.

⁊Terlingā ten& Ricard de.R.qd̄ tenuit Ailmar teinn reḡ.t.r.e.
p̄ Man.7 p̄.II.hid.7.dim.7.xxx.ac.Sēp.II.car.in dn̄io.7.III.car
hom̄.Tc̄.xi.uilt.m̄.v.m̄.xi.bord.Tc̄.v.ſer.m̄.null.Silū.cl.porc̄.

xx.ac.p̄ti.Paſt.c⸳ou.Tc̄.i.mol.m̄.II.7.II.dom in coleceſtra.uña
reddit.vi.d̄.7.alfa.xiiii.7.i.lib hō.de.v.ac.7 reddebat anteceſſori
Ranulfi.x.d̄.7.R.m̄ ſimil.Tc̄.xii.anim.clxxx.ou.l.cap.xl.porc̄.
m̄.II.runc.7⸳II.pult.viii.an̄.lxxv.ou.xvi.cap.xxxiiii.porc̄.Tc̄ ual
.viii.lib⸱7 qn̄ rec̄ ſimil.m̄.vi.lib.

⁊Fairſtedam ten& Turold qd̄ ten Brictmar.t.r.e.p̄.m̄.7 p̄.lv.ac.
Sēp.II.car in dn̄io.7.II.car hom̄.7.iiii.uilt.Tc̄.vii.bor.m̄.x.Tc̄.iiii.
ſer⸱m̄.iii.Silū.c.porc̄.xl.ac⸱p̄ti.Paſt de.iiii.d̄.m̄.i.mol.Tc̄.i.runc.
xiii.ou.vi.porc̄.m̄.II.runc.cxxiiii.ou.xxxii.porc̄.iiii.uac̄.c̄ uitul.
.iiii.uaſa ap̄.7.xv.ac.ibi jacebāt t.r.e.de qb₂ Saſuual deſaiſiuit
7 jacent ad feudū.G.de magna uilt.Tc̄ ual.iiii.lib.m̄.c.ſol.

⁊Hund de beuentreu. Hame ten& .R.in dn̄io qd tenuit Aleſtan̄
lib hō.t.r.e.p̄.man.7 p̄.viii.hid.7.xxx.ac.7 hoc maneriū dedit
Wilt rex.R.piper.7 Robto grenoni.Tc̄.v.car in dn̄io m̄.iiii.tc̄.
.viii.car hom̄.m̄.xii.Tc̄.xxxii.uilt.m̄ xlviii.Tc̄.xvi.bord.m̄
lxxx.i.min.Sēp.iii.ſer.Silū.c.porc̄.lx.ac.p̄ti.Tc̄.ix.mol.m̄.viii.
Tc̄.i.runc.i.uac̄.iii.porc̄.M.II.runc.II.pult.II.uac̄ cū uit.xx.por.
lx.ou.Tc̄ ual.xvi.lib.7 qn̄ recepunt.xii.lib.m̄ ual.xxiiii.lib.
7 de hoc manerio ht.R.grēno medietatē.

⁊Hund de Dōmauua. Cicchenai ten& Garin de.R.qd̄ tenuit
Siuuard.i.tegn̄ regis.ē.p̄ Man.7 p̄.II.hid.7.dim.Sēp.iii.car i dn̄io.
7.II.car hom̄.tc̄.II.uilt.m̄ null.Tc̄.vii.bor.m̄.i.p̄br.7.xiiii.
bord Silū.lx.porc̄.xx.ac.p̄ti.Tc̄.II.runc.iii.uac̄ c̄ uit.lx.oues
xx.porc̄.xxiiii.cap̄.m̄.iii.runc.vi.uac̄.vitul.c.ou.xxx.por.

.xxx.cap̄.Tc̄ ual.c.ſol.m̄.vii.lib.

6   Richard holds TERLING from Ranulf which Aelmer, a King's thane,
held before 1066 as a manor, for 2½ hides and 30 acres. Always
2 ploughs in lordship; 3 men's ploughs.
    Then 11 villagers, now 5; now 11 smallholders; then 5 slaves,
      now none.
    Woodland, 150 pigs; meadow, 20 acres; pasture, 100 sheep;   72 b
      then 1 mill, now 2. 2 houses in Colchester, one pays 6d, the
      other 14[d]. 1 free man with 5 acres paid Ranulf's
      predecessor 10d and now [pays] Ranulf the same. Then 12
      cattle, 180 sheep, 50 goats, 40 pigs; now 2 cobs, 2 foals,
      8 cattle, 75 sheep, 16 goats, 34 pigs.
Value then £8; when acquired, the same; now £6.

7   Thorold holds FAIRSTEAD, which Brictmer held before 1066 as a
manor, for 55 acres. Always 2 ploughs in lordship; 2 men's
ploughs;
    4 villagers. Then 7 smallholders, now 10; then 4 slaves, now 3.
    Woodland, 100 pigs; meadow, 40 acres; pasture at 4d; now 1
      mill. Then 1 cob, 13 sheep, 6 pigs; now 2 cobs, 124 sheep,
      32 pigs, 4 cows with calves, 3 beehives.
    15 acres lay there before 1066 of which Saswalo dispossessed
(him) and they lie in G(eoffrey) de Mandeville's Holding.
Value then £4; now 100s.

    Hundred of BECONTREE
8   Ranulf holds (West) HAM in lordship which Alstan, a free man,
held before 1066 as a manor, for 8 hides and 30 acres. King
William gave this manor to Ranulf Peverel and Robert Gernon.
Then 5 ploughs in lordship, now 4. Then 8 men's ploughs, now 12.
    Then 32 villagers, now 48; then 16 smallholders, now 80 less 1.
      Always 3 slaves.
    Woodland, 100 pigs; meadow, 60 acres; then 9 mills, now 8.
      Then 1 cob, 1 cow, 3 pigs; now 2 cobs, 2 foals, 2 cows with
      calves, 20 pigs, 60 sheep.
Value then £16; when acquired £12. Value now £24.
Robert Gernon has half of this manor.

    Hundred of DUNMOW
9   Warin holds CHICKNEY from Ranulf which Siward, 1 thane of King
Edward's, held as a manor for 2½ hides. Always 3 ploughs in
lordship; 2 men's ploughs.
    Then 2 villagers, now none; then 7 smallholders, now 1 priest
      and 14 smallholders.
    Woodland, 60 pigs; meadow, 20 acres. Then 2 cobs, 3 cows
      with calves, 60 sheep, 20 pigs, 24 goats; now 3 cobs, 6 cows
      [with] calves, 100 sheep, 30 pigs, 30 goats.   73 a
Value then 100s; now £7.

Willingehalam ten& Rauenot de . R . q̊d ten̊ . Siuuard . t . r . e . p̄ Man
7 p̊ . I . hið . 7 . I . uirg̊ . 7 . dim . Sep̄ . III . car̊ in dn̄io . Tc̄ . dim . car̊ hom̊ . m̊ . I.
Tc̄ . I . uiƚƚ . m̊ . III . Sep̄ . VI . borð . tc̄ . VI . ſer̊ . m̊ . IIII . Siƚu . cxx . porc̊ . XII . ac̊.
p̊ti . Tc̄ . III . runc̊ . XVI . anim̊ . xxx . porc̊ . m̊ . III . runc̊ . IIII . pulli . XVI.
anim̊ . c . ou . LXV . porc̊ . V . uaſa ap̊ . Tc̄ uaƚ . c . ſoƚ . 7 qn̄ rec̊ . VI . liɓ . m̊ . x.
huic tr̄æ addit̊ e̊ . I . ſoc̊ . q̊ue tenuit antec̊ . R . piperelli 7 . Adhuc ten&
. R . 7 Rauenot de illo . 7 adhuc addite ſt̄ huic tr̄æ . xxx . ac̊ . t . r . Wiƚƚ.
qs ten̊ liɓ hō t . r . e . vaƚ . x . ſoƚ.

Hund de Wibricteſherna   Odeham ten& . R . in dn̄io . q̊d
ten̊ Siuuard p̊ Man . 7 p̊ . V . hið . Sep̄ . IIII . uiƚƚ . Tc̄ . IX : borð . m̊ . VIII . Tc̄
. V . ſer̊ . m̊ . II . Sep̄ . II . car̊ . in dn̄io tc̄ . IIII . car̊ . hom̊ . m̊ . I . 7 . dim . III.
ac̊ . p̊ti . Siƚu . cc . porc̊ . Tc̄ . II . runc̊ . VI . uac̊ . IIII . uiƚ . LX . ou . xx . porc̊.
XLV . cap̊ . m̊ . III . runc̊ . II . puƚt . IIII . uac̊ . IIII . uiƚ . c̄xxxv . ou . XLVI.
porc̊ . c . cap̊ . Sep̄ uaƚ . c . ſoƚ.

Meldonam ten& . R . in dn̄io q̊d ten̊ . Siuuard . t . r . e . p̄ . Man . 7 . p̊.
. V . hið . 7 . dim . 7 . x . ac̊ . Tc̄ . XVI . uiƚƚ . m̊ . IX . m̊ . x . bor . Sep̄ . III . ſer̊.
7 . II . car̊ in dn̄io . tc̄ . x . hom̊ . m̊ . V . x . ac̊ . p̊ti . Siƚu . L . porc̊ . I . moƚ.
Tc̄ . II . runc̊ . m̊ ſimiƚt̄ . 7 m̊ . III . uac̊ . IIII . uiƚ . cxL . poues . xxix . porc̊.
Sep̄ uaƚ . XII . liɓ.

Haleſheiam ten& Serlo de . R . q̊d ten̊ . Idē . S . p̄ man̊ . 7 . p̊ . IIII.
hið . 7 . dim . Sep̄ . IIII . uiƚƚ . tc̄ . IIII . ſer̊ . m̊ . III . Tc̄ . II . car̊ . m̊ . I . Tc̄
. I . car̊ . hom̊ . m̊ . dim . Siƚu . LX . porc̊ . Tc̄ . II . runc̊ . II . uac̊ . II . uiƚ.
LX . ou . V . porc̊ . m̊ . II . runc̊ . IIII . uac̊ . c . ou . IX . porc̊ . Vaƚ . IIII . liɓ.

73 b

Haleſleiam ten& Godric de . R . q̊d tenuit Ailmar liɓ hō . t . r . e.
p̄ Man̊ . 7 . p̊ dim hið . 7 . xx . ac̊ . Sep̄ . I . uiƚƚ . Tc̄ . II . borð . m̊ . nuƚt . Sep̄ . I . car̊
in dn̄io . Siƚu . Lxxx . porc̊ . Vaƚ . xx . ſoƚ.

10 Ravenot holds WILLINGALE (Doe) from Ranulf, which Siward held before 1066 as a manor, for 1 hide and 1½ virgates. Always 3 ploughs in lordship. Then ½ men's plough, now 1.

Then 1 villager, now 3. Always 6 smallholders. Then 6 slaves, now 4.

Woodland, 120 pigs; meadow, 12 acres. Then 3 cobs, 16 cattle, 30 pigs; now 3 cobs, 4 foals, 16 cattle, 100 sheep, 65 pigs, 5 beehives.

Value then 100s; when acquired £6; now [£] 10.

To this land has been added 1 Freeman whom Ranulf Peverel's predecessor held and (whom) Ranulf still holds and Ravenot from him.

Also added to this land after 1066 were 30 acres which a free man held before 1066.

Value 10s.

Hundred of 'WIBERTSHERNE'

11 Ranulf holds WOODHAM (Mortimer) in lordship, which Siward held as a manor, for 5 hides.

Always 4 villagers. Then 9 smallholders, now 8; then 5 slaves, now 2. Always 2 ploughs in lordship. Then 4 men's ploughs, now 1½.

Meadow, 3 acres; woodland, 200 pigs. Then 2 cobs, 6 cows, 4 calves, 60 sheep, 20 pigs, 45 goats; now 3 cobs, 2 foals, 4 cows, 4 calves, 135 sheep, 46 pigs, 100 goats.

Value always 100s.

12 Ranulf holds MALDON in lordship, which Siward held before 1066 as a manor, for 5½ hides and 10 acres.

Then 16 villagers, now 9; now 10 smallholders. Always 3 slaves; 2 ploughs in lordship. Then 10 men's [ploughs], now 5.

Meadow, 10 acres; woodland, 50 pigs; 1 mill. Then 2 cobs, now the same; now 3 cows, 4 calves, 140 sheep, 29 pigs.

Value always £12.

13 Serlo holds HAZELEIGH from Ranulf, which Siward also held as a manor, for 4½ hides.

Always 4 villagers. Then 4 slaves, now 3. Then 2 ploughs, now 1. Then 1 men's plough, now ½.

Woodland, 60 pigs. Then 2 cobs, 2 cows, 2 calves, 60 sheep, 5 pigs; now 2 cobs, 4 cows, 100 sheep, 9 pigs.

Value £4.

14 Godric holds HAZELEIGH from Ranulf which Aelmer, a free man, **73 b** held before 1066 as a manor for ½ hide and 20 acres.

Always 1 villager. Then 2 smallholders, now none. Always 1 plough in lordship.

Woodland, 80 pigs.

Value 20s.

Hund de Wenfiftreu: Legrā ten& Turold de͛.R.q̃d ten.

.A.t̃.r̃.e.p̃ man.7.p̃.ı.hid̃.xɪɪ.ac̃.7.dim̃.mín.Sēp.ı.car̃.in dñio
m̃ dim̃.car̃ hom̃.Tc̃.ı.bord̃.m̃.ɪɪɪɪ.tc̃.ɪɪɪɪ.fer.m̃.ı.Silu.xvɪ.porc̃.
Tc̃.ı.runc̃.v.uac̃.v.uit.c.ou̇.m̃.ɪɪ.runc̃.ɪɪɪɪ.uac̃.v̇.uit.cɪɪɪ.
ou̇.Tc̃ uat.xxx:fot.m̃.xx.

Edburgetunā ten&.R.in dñio q̃d tenuit.ı.lib̃ ho͛.t͛.r͛.e.p̃ Man͛.
7.p̃.ı.hid̃.7.dim̃.7.ı.uirg̃.Sēp.ı.car̃.in dñio.7.dim̃.car̃.hom̃.
7.ɪɪɪɪ.bord̃.7.ı.fer.Silu:ʟx.porc̃.ɪɪɪɪ.ac̃.p̃ti.Tc̃ uat.ʟx.fot.m̃.ʟ.

Wighebgā ten& Algar de.R.q̃d ten͛.ı.lib̃ ho͛.t͛.r͛.e.p̃.Man͛.7.p̃
dim̃.hid̃.Sēp.ı.car̃.tc̃.ı.bor.m̃.ɪɪ.Vat.x.fot.

Hund de Wdelesfort. Deppedanā ten&.R.in dñio.q̃d ten͛.
Siuuard͛.p̃ Man͛.7.p̃:xvı.hid̃.7.dim̃.Sēp.vı.car̃.in dñio.7.
xɪ.car̃.hom̃.7.xxxvɪ.uitt.Tc̃ 7 p̃.ı.bord̃.m̃.xvɪɪ.sēp.xɪɪ.fer:
Silu.m̃.porc̃.xʟ.ac̃.p̃ti.Sēp.ı.mot.m̃.ɪɪ.arpenni uineæ
portantes.7 alij.ɪɪ.ñ portantes.Tc̃.vı.runc̃.xxvɪɪɪ.anim̃.
.cʟ.ou̇.ccʟ.porc̃.vı.uafa ap̃.m̃.vɪɪ.runc̃.ɪɪ.pulli.x.anim̃.
cʟxvɪɪɪ.ou̇.cx.porc̃.ɪɪɪ.uafa ap̃.Tc̃ 7 p̃ uat xxɪɪɪɪ.lib̃.m̃
xxx. De hoc manerio ten& Vitat de.R.xv.ac̃.7.uat.x.fot
in eod͛ p̃tio.

Ambdanā ten&.R.in dñio.q̃d ten͛.Siuuard͛ p̃ Man͛.7.p̃
.v.hid̃.Sēp.ɪɪɪ.car̃.in dñio.7.vı.car̃.hom̃.Tc̃ 7 p̃.xɪɪɪ.uitt

.m̃.xvɪɪɪɪ.Tc̃.ı.bord̃.Poft.ɪɪ.m̃.vɪɪ.Sēp.vı.fer.Tc̃ 7 p̃ filu.ccʟ.porc̃.m̃
.cc.xxx.ac̃.p̃ti.Tc̃.ɪɪ.runc̃.vı.ánim̃,xʟ.ou̇.xʟ.porc̃.v.uafa apu̇
m̃.ɪɪɪ.runc̃.ı.pult.xɪɪɪɪ.anim̃.ʟxvɪɪɪ.ou̇.xxx.porc̃.ı.uas̃.apu̇.Sēp
uat.xɪɪ.lib̃.f; R.inde habuit p.ɪɪɪ.annos.unoq̃q;.xvɪɪɪ.lib̃.hanc
uittā calumpniat̃ abbas de eli.7 hūnd teftat̃ qd jacuit ad ecctam

15 Thorold holds LAYER from Ranulf, which A. held before 1066 as a manor, for 1 hide less 12½ acres. Always 1 plough in lordship. Now ½ men's plough.

> Then 1 smallholder, now 4; then 4 slaves, now 1.
> Woodland, 16 pigs. Then 1 cob, 5 cows, 5 calves, 100 sheep; now 2 cobs, 4 cows, 5 calves, 103 sheep.

Value then 30s; now 20[s].

16 Ranulf holds ABBERTON in lordship, which 1 free man held before 1066 as a manor, for 1½ hides and 1 virgate. Always 1 plough in lordship; ½ men's plough.

> 4 smallholders; 1 slave.
> Woodland, 60 pigs; meadow, 4 acres.

Value then 60s; now 50[s].

17 Algar holds WIGBOROUGH from Ranulf, which 1 free man held before 1066 as a manor, for ½ hide. Always 1 plough.

> Then 1 smallholder, now 2.

Value 10s.

18 Ranulf holds DEBDEN in lordship, which Siward held as a manor, for 16½ hides. Always 6 ploughs in lordship; 11 men's ploughs;

> 36 villagers. Then and later 1 smallholder, now 17; always 12 slaves.
> Woodland, 1000 pigs; meadow, 40 acres; always 1 mill. Now 2 *arpents* of vines bearing (fruit) and another two not bearing (fruit). Then 6 cobs, 28 cattle, 150 sheep, 250 pigs, 6 beehives; now 7 cobs, 2 foals, 10 cattle, 168 sheep, 110 pigs, 3 beehives.

Value then and later £24; now [£] 30.
Of this manor, Vitalis holds 15 acres from Ranulf.
Value 10s in the same assessment.

19 Ranulf holds AMBERDEN (Hall) in lordship, which Siward held as a manor, for 5 hides. Always 3 ploughs in lordship; 6 men's ploughs.

> Then and later 13 villagers, now 19; then 1 smallholder, later 2, now 7; always 6 slaves.
> Woodland, then and later 250 pigs, now 200; meadow, 30 acres. Then 2 cobs, 6 cattle, 40 sheep, 40 pigs, 5 beehives; now 3 cobs, 1 foal, 14 cattle, 68 sheep, 30 pigs, 1 beehive.

74 a

Value always £12. But Ranulf has had from it £18 each (year) for three years.
The Abbot of Ely lays claim to this village and the Hundred testifies that it lay in (the lands of) the Church.

⌐Hund de Hidingforda. Stabingā ten&.R.in dñio qd̄ tenuit
Siuuard t.r.e. ℏ.man. 7 ℏ.iii. hid̄.7.xxx.ac̄.Tc̄.car̄.in dñio.7.qñ
rec̄.vi.m̄.v.Sep.xi.car̄.hom̄.Tc̄ 7 p̄ xviii.uilt.m̄.xix.Tc̄ 7 poſt.
xiiii.bor.m̄.xxxi.Tc̄ 7 p̄.xiii.fer̄.m̄.xi.Silu.cc.porc̄.xxiiii.ac̄
p̄ti.Tc̄.i.mot.7 qñ rec̄.i.7 dim̄.m̄.ii.m̄.ii.arpenni uineæ.7.d̄.
7.dimidi tantū portat.Tc̄.v.runc̄.v.uac̄.c.ou.l.porc̄.v.uaſa
apū.Tc̄ uat.x.lib.P̄.xii.m̄.xvi.lib.De ℏ Man̄.Vitat xxxv.ac̄.7.x.ſot uat.
⌐Henies.ten& Turold de.R.qd tenuit Vluuin lib hō t.r.e.   ⌐in eod.p̄tio.
ℏ man̄.7 ℏ.ii.hid̄.7.dim̄.7.xlv.ac̄.ſep.ii.car̄ in dñio.7.iii.car̄
hom̄.7.v.uilt.7.xi.bord̄.Tc̄ 7 p̄.ii.fer̄.m̄.nult.Silu.lxxx.porc̄.
xii.ac̄.p̄ti.ſep.i.mot.Tc̄.ii.runc̄.v.uac̄.cū uit.l.ou.xiiii.
porc̄.iii.uaſa apū.m̄.i.runc̄.ix.uac̄.c̄ uit.cxxxiiii.ou.xxxvi.
porc̄.7 huic manerio p̄tin& de Sudbia.xxii.d̄.de conſuetudine.
Tc̄.uat.xl.ſot.m̄.iiii.lib.
⌐Lamers ten& Turold de.R.qd tenuit Algar.t.r.e.ℏ.Man̄.
7 ℏ.iii.hid̄.7.dim̄.Sep.ii.car̄.in dñio.Tc̄ 7 p̄.ii.car̄.7 dim̄.hoū.
m̄.ii.Sep.iiii.uilt.m̄.viii.bord̄.Silu.lxx.porc̄.xiii.ac̄.p̄ti.
Tc̄.vi.uac̄.c̄ uit.liiii.ou.xi.porc̄.m̄.vii.runc̄.v.putt.x.uac̄.
viii.uit.xx.ou.liiii.porc̄.lx.cap̄.vi.uaſa ap̄.Tc̄ uat.iiii.lib

m̄.vi.In Lamers tenuit Aluuard.i.hid̄ 7 dim̄ ℏ man̄.t.r.e.m̄ ten&
Id̄ē.T.de Ranulfo.Sep.i.car̄ in dñio.7.i.car̄ hom̄.7.ii.uilt.Tc̄.iii.
bord̄.m̄.ix.Silu.xxx.porc̄.vii.ac̄.p̄ti.Tc̄ uat.xl.ſot.m̄.lx.
Hæe due t̄re erant ſic diuiſæ duob; fratrib; t.r.e.Poſt ea date ſ̄
Ranulfo ℏ.i.manerio ut dic̄t ſui hōc̄s.
⌐Hund de Witbric̄teſherna.Dunā ten&.R.in dñio qd̄
tenuit Siuuard ℏ.Man̄.7 ℏ.xiiii.hid̄.Tc̄.ii.uilt.m̄.iiii.Tc̄.iii.bor.
m̄.xv.Tc̄.xii.fer̄.m̄.vi.Sep.v.car̄ in dñio.Tc̄.ii.car̄ hom̄.m̄.iii.

Hundred of HINCKFORD

20 Ranulf holds STEBBING in lordship, which Siward held before 1066 as a manor, for 3 hides and 30 acres. Then ... ploughs in lordship; when acquired 6; now 5. Always 11 men's ploughs.

  Then and later 18 villagers, now 19; then and later 14 smallholders, now 31; then and later 13 slaves, now 11.

  Woodland, 200 pigs; meadow, 24 acres; then 1 mill, when acquired 1½, now 2; now 2½ *arpents* of vines and only the ½ bears (fruit).

  Then 5 cobs, 5 cows, 100 sheep, 50 pigs, 5 beehives.

Value then £10; later [£] 12; now £16.

Of this manor, Vitalis [holds] 35 acres.

Value 10s in the same assessment.

21 Thorold holds (Great) HENNY from Ranulf which Wulfwin, a free man, held before 1066 as a manor for 2½ hides and 45 acres.

Always 2 ploughs in lordship; 3 men's ploughs;

  5 villagers; 11 smallholders. Then and later 2 slaves, now none.

  Woodland, 80 pigs; meadow, 12 acres; always 1 mill. Then 2 cobs, 5 cows with calves, 50 sheep, 14 pigs, 3 beehives; now 1 cob, 9 cows with calves, 134 sheep, 36 pigs.

To this manor belongs 12d of the customary due from Sudbury.

Value then 40s; now £4.

22 Thorold holds LAMARSH from Ranulf, which Algar held before 1066 as a manor, for 3½ hides. Always 2 ploughs in lordship.

Then and later 2½ men's ploughs, now 2.

  Always 4 villagers. Now 8 smallholders.

  Woodland, 70 pigs; meadow, 13 acres. Then 6 cows with calves, 54 sheep, 11 pigs; now 7 cobs, 5 foals, 10 cows, 8 calves, 20 sheep, 54 pigs, 60 goats, 6 beehives.

Value then £4; now [£] 6.   74 b

  In LAMARSH Alfward held 1½ hides as a manor before 1066. Now Thorold also holds them from Ranulf. Always 1 plough in lordship; 1 men's plough;

  2 villagers. Then 3 smallholders, now 9.

  Woodland, 30 pigs; meadow, 7 acres.

Value then 40s; now 60[s].

  These two lands were divided thus between two brothers before 1066; later on they were given to Ranulf as 1 manor as his men state.

Hundred of 'WIBERTSHERNE'

23 Ranulf holds DOWN (Hall) in lordship, which Siward held as a manor, for 14 hides.

  Then 2 villagers, now 4; then 3 smallholders, now 15; then 12 slaves, now 6. Always 5 ploughs in lordship. Then 2 men's ploughs, now 3.

Silu̇.L.porċ.Past̀.L.ou̇.Tc̄ 7 p̊ uaɫ.x.liɓ.m̊.xiii.De hoc manerio
ten& Afcelin̊.i.hid̀.7.dim̊.de.R.7 uaɫ.xx.foɫ in eod̊ p̄tio.

⌐Lalinge ten&.R.in dn̄io qd̊ tenuit Brun.liɓ ho̊.t̊.r̊.e̊.p̊ Man̊.
7 p̊.ii.hid̀.7.dim̊.7.xxxv.ac̊.Sēp.ii.fer̊.7.ii.car̊.Silu̇.xx.porċ.
Past̀.L.ou̇.m̊.i.piſc̊.Tc̄ 7 p̊ uaɫ.iiii.liɓ.m̊.iii.liɓ.7.xv.foɫ.

⌐In Duna tenuer̊.viii.liɓi ho̅c̅s.v.hid̀.vi.ac̊ min̊.qd̊ ten&.R.
in dn̄io.Sēp.vi.bord̀.7.ii.car̊.7 dim̊.Tc̄ 7 p̊ uaɫ.Lx.foɫ.m̊.iiii.liɓ
7.x.foɫ.

⌐Stanefgata̅ ten& Rad fili̊.brien qd̊ tenuit Siuuard̊ p̊ Man̊.
7 p̊.viiij.hid̀.7.dim̊.t̊.r̊.e̊.Sēp.ii.uiɫɫ.Tc̄.xxii.bord̀.m̊.xviii.
Tc̄.viii.fer̊.m̊.iii.Tc̄.iiii.car̊ 7 dim̊ in dn̄io.m̊.iiii.Sēp.iii.
car̊ hom̊.Silu̇.Lx.porċ.Past̀.Lx.ou̇.Tc̄ 7 p̊ uaɫ.x.liɓ.m̊.viii.

⌐Hund̊ de Laſſendena Pereſteda̅ ten& Id̊e.R.qd̊ tenuit
Brictmar̊.t̊.r̊.e̊.p̊ man̊.7 p̊.i.hid̀.7.dim̊.Tc̄.v.bor̊.m̊.x.Tc̄.iiii.
fer̊.m̊.null̊.Sēp.ii.car̊.in dn̄io.Silu̇.c.porċ.viii.ac̊.p̄ti.Tc̄.ii.
runc̊.x.an̊.Lxxx.ou̇.xv.porċ.xx.cap̊.ii.uaſa apu̅.m̊.i.eq̊.

7.i.pull̊.Lx.ou̇.xx.porċ.ix.cap̊.ii.uaſa apū.Sēp uaɫ.iiii.liɓ.
7.i.liɓ ho̊ ſēp ten&.v.ac̊.7 fuit c̄omdat anteceſſori.R.ſ; c̄ tr̄a ſua
poſſ& ire q̊ uell&.7 m̊.h̊t.R.Tc̄.i.car̊.m̊.dim̊.Tc̄ uaɫ.xvi.foɫ
m̊.xii.

⌐Hund̊ de Angra.Plumtuna̅ ten& Rauenot de.R.qd̊
ten̊.Vluric̊.p̄br de heroldo p̊.xiiii.ac̊.libe.7 m̊ h̊t.R.id̊o qd̊
anteceſſor ej̊ fuit faifit ſ; n̄ p̄tinuit ad eu̅∴ fic comitat̊ teſtat̊.
Sēp.i.uiɫɫ.7.d̊.car̊.Silu̇.xx.porċ.i.ac̊.7.dim̊.p̄ti.ual.v.foɫ

Woodland, 50 pigs; pasture, 50 sheep.
Value then and later £10; now [£] 13.
Of this manor, Ascelin holds 1½ hides from Ranulf.
Value 20s in the same assessment.

24 Ranulf holds LAWLING in lordship which Brown, a free man, held
before 1066 as a manor for 2½ hides and 35 acres.
  Always 2 slaves; 2 ploughs.
  Woodland, 20 pigs; pasture, 50 sheep; now 1 fishery.
  Value then and later £4; now £3 15s.

25 In DOWN (Hall) 8 free men held 5 hides less 6 acres, which Ranulf
holds in lordship.
  Always 6 smallholders; 2½ ploughs.
  Value then and later 60s; now £4 10s.

26 Ralph son of Brian holds STANSGATE, which Siward held as a
manor, for 9½ hides before 1066.
  Always 2 villagers. Then 22 smallholders, now 18; then 8
    slaves, now 3. Then 4½ ploughs in lordship, now 4. Always
    3 men's ploughs.
  Woodland, 60 pigs; pasture, 60 sheep.
  Value then and later £10; now [£] 8.

Hundred of LEXDEN
27 Ranulf also holds PRESTED, which Brictmer held before 1066 as a
manor, for 1½ hides.
  Then 5 smallholders, now 10; then 4 slaves, now none. Always
    2 ploughs in lordship.
  Woodland, 100 pigs; meadow, 8 acres. Then 2 cobs, 10 cattle,
    80 sheep, 15 pigs, 20 goats, 2 beehives; now 1 mare and 1   75 a
    foal, 60 sheep, 20 pigs, 9 goats, 2 beehives.
  Value always £4.
  1 free man has always held 5 acres and was under the patronage
of Ranulf's predecessor, but he could go with his land whither he
would. Now Ranulf has it. Then 1 plough, now ½.
  Value then 16s, now 12[s].

Hundred of ONGAR
28 Ravenot holds PLUNKER'S (Green) from Ranulf, which Wulfric the
priest held from Harold freely, for 14 acres. Now Ranulf has it
because his predecessor was in possession of it; but it did not
belong to him, so the Hundred testifies.
  Always 1 villager; ½ plough.
  Woodland, 20 pigs; meadow, 1½ acres.
  Value 5s.

⁊Hunð de Celmeresfort . Springafeldā ten& . Roƀ . de . R.

qð tenuit Aleſtan ꝓ man̄ . 7 ꝓ . v . hið . 7 . xx . ac̄ . Tc̄ . vi . uiħ . m̄

. iiii . Tc̄ . iii . borð . m̄ . x . Tc̄ . viii . bor . m̄ . vi . Sēp . iii . car̄ . in dn̄io.

Tc̄ . 7 . ꝑ . iii . car̄ . hom̄ . m̄ . ii . Silu̅ . xxx . porc̄ . xxv . ac̄ . ꝑti . Sēp . i .

moƚ . Tc̄ . ii . runc̄ . xii . anim̄ . c . ou̅ . L . porc̄ . M . iiii . runc̄ . v . puƚƚ .

xxvi . au̅ . xl . ou̅ . xxv . porc̄ . xii . cap̄ . iƚ . aſini . i . uas ap̄ . Tc̄ . uaƚ . v .

liƀ . m̄ . vi . 7 . ii . liƀi h̅o̅es tenuer̅ . xiii . ac̄ . qð ħt . R . vaƚ . ii . ſoƚ.

⁊Radendunam ten& . Rað fiƚi brien qð tenuit . Siuuarð . ꝓ Man̄ .

7 ꝓ . i . hið . 7 . xxx . ac̄ . Sēp . i . bor . 7 . i . car̄ in dn̄io . Silu̅ . vi . porc̄ . Sēp

uaƚ . ꝣxv . ſoƚ . 7 abƀia de eli calumpniaƚ .

⁊Dimið Hunð de Melduna . In Melduna ten& . R . in dn̄io

dim̄ hið . 7 . xxiiii . ac̄ . qð tenuit Siuuarð . t . r . e . ꝓ . man̄ . Tc̄ . i . borð .

m̄ . iii . vaƚ . v . ſoƚ . 7 hec tr̄a apꝑtiata e in . xii . liƀ de melduna

⁊Hunð de Tendringa . Tendrinḡa ten& . R . in dn̄io

qð tenuit Olui liƀe ꝓ man̄ . 7 ꝓ dim̄ hið . 7 . xxx . ac̄ . 7 R . ħt in

eſcangio . Tc̄ . ii . ſer̄ . m̄ . i . Tc̄ . ii . car̄ . Poſt 7 m̄ . i . Silu̅ . xxx . porc̄ .

. ii . ac̄ . ꝑti . Tc̄ 7 ꝑ uaƚ . xx . ſoƚ . m̄ lx .

⁊Cice ten& Turolð de . R . qð tenuit Siuuarð ꝓ man̄ . 7 ꝓ . ii . hið . 7 . ð .

Tc̄ . 7 . ꝑ . ix . uiħ . m̄ . vi . Tc̄ . 7 ꝑ . xii . bor . m̄ . xi . Sēp . vii . ſer̄ . Tc̄ . 7 ꝑ . iiii .

Hundred of CHELMSFORD

29 Robert holds SPRINGFIELD from Ranulf, which Alstan held as a manor, for 5 hides and 20 acres.

Then 6 villagers, now 4; then 3 smallholders, now 10; then 8 smallholders, now 6. Always 3 ploughs in lordship. Then and later 3 men's ploughs, now 2.

Woodland, 30 pigs; meadow, 25 acres; always 1 mill. Then 2 cobs, 12 cattle, 100 sheep, 50 pigs; now 4 cobs, 5 foals, 26 cattle, 40 sheep, 25 pigs, 12 goats, 2 asses, 1 beehive.

Value then £5; now [£] 6.

2 free men held 13 acres, which Ranulf has.

Value 2s.

30 Ralph son of Brian holds RETTENDON, which Siward held as a manor, for 1 hide and 30 acres.

Always 1 smallholder; 1 plough in lordship.

Woodland, 6 pigs.

Value always 25s.

The Abbey of Ely lays claim to it.

Half-Hundred of MALDON

31 In MALDON Ranulf holds ½ hide and 24 acres in lordship, which Siward held before 1066 as a manor.

Then 1 smallholder, now 3.

Value 5s.

This land is assessed in the £12 from Maldon.

Hundred of TENDRING

32 Ranulf holds TENDRING in lordship, which Wulfwy held freely as a manor, for ½ hide and 30 acres. Ranulf has (it) in exchange.

Then 2 slaves, now 1. Then 2 ploughs, later and now 1.

Woodland, 30 pigs; meadow, 2 acres.   75 b

Value then and later 20s; now 60[s].

33 Thorold holds ST. OSYTH from Ranulf, which Siward held as a manor, for 2½ hides.

Then and later 9 villagers, now 6; then and later 12 smallholders, now 11; always 7 slaves. Then and later 4

car̅ in dn̅io . m̅ . III . Tc̅ . 7 p̅ . VII . car̅ hom̅ . m̅ . V . Silu̅ . ɒccc . porc̅ . IIII . ac̅.

p̅ti . Past̅ . cc . ou̅ . se̅p . I . mol̅ . Tc̅ . VI . runc̅ . L . anim̅ . ccc . ou̅ . XL . porc̅.

. VI . uasa apu̅ . M̅ . IIII . runc̅ . IIII . an̅ . Lxviii . ou̅ . xxxvii . porc̅ . xviii.

cap̅ . Tc̅ 7 p̅ ual̅ . IX : lib̅ . m̅ .VIII.

/ Fretinga ten& Ide̅ . T . de . R . qd̅ tenuit Ketel . ꝑ . man̅ . 7 ꝑ . II . hid̅.

Tc̅ . II . bor̅ . m̅ . III . Tc̅ . III . fer̅ . m̅ . II . Tc̅ . in dn̅io . II . car̅ . m̅ . I . Se̅p . I . car̅

hom̅ . Silu̅ . cL . porc̅ : IIII . ac̅ . p̅ti . Tc̅ . I . runc̅ . IIII . an̅ . IIII . uit̅ . c.

ou̅ . XL . porc̅ . M̅ . I . runc̅ . II . uac̅ . II . uit̅ . LXVI . ou̅ . XX . porc̅ . VI . uas

apu̅ . Tc̅ ual̅ . XL . fol̅ . m̅ . LX.

/ Hund̅ de Rochefort Legra̅ ten& . R . in dn̅io . qd̅ tenuit . I . lib̅

ho̅ . ꝑ man̅ . 7 ꝑ . I . hid̅ . Se̅p . II . uilt̅ . 7 . II . bor̅ . 7 . I . car̅ in dn̅io . 7 . dim̅

car̅ hom̅ . 7 . V . bor̅ . sup aq̅m . q̅ n̅ tenent tr̅a . Past̅ . c . ou̅ . Tc̅ . I . runc̅.

. V . uac̅ . V . uit̅ . c . ou̅ . m̅ . II . runc̅ . IIII . uac̅ . V . uit̅ . cIII . ou̅ . Tc̅

ual̅ . XL . fol̅ . m̅ . c.

/ Hund̅ de Tureftapla . Tolefhunta̅ ten& Humfrid̅ de . R.

qd̅ tenuit Siuuard̅ ꝑ man̅ . 7 ꝑ . IIII . hid̅ . 7 . dim̅ . 7 . xxx . ac̅ . Tc̅ . IX.

uilt̅ . m̅ . x . Tc̅ . IIII . bord̅ . m̅ . xIII . tc̅ . x . fer̅ . m̅ . VI . Se̅p . III . car̅ in

dn̅io . 7 . III . car̅ hom̅ . I . falina . V . ac̅ . p̅ti . Past̅ . xxx . ou̅ . Silu̅ . cL.

porc̅ . Tc̅ . III . runc̅ . xx . anim̅ LXXX . ou̅ . LX . porc̅ . m̅ . III . runc̅.

xx . an̅ . cLx . ou̅ . xxxvii . porc̅ . xviii . cap̅ . Se̅p ual̅ . c . fol̅.

In hoc manerio tenuer̅ . IIII . lib̅i ho̅es . dim̅ . hid̅ . 7 . V . ac̅ . f; Rad̅

baign̅ h̅t ea̅ 7 hugo de montfort̅.

/ Goldhangra̅ ten& Ricard̅ de . R . qd̅ te̅nuit Leuuin̅ 7 vluard̅

p̅br ꝑ man̅ . 7 . ꝑ . II . hid̅ . 7 dim̅ . 7 . xxv . ac̅ . Tc̅ . III . bor̅ . m̅ . xIIII . Se̅p

. II . fer̅ . Tc̅ . II . car̅ in dn̅io . m̅ . I . m̅ . I . car̅ hom̅ Silu̅ . Lxxx . porc̅ . Past̅.

. L . ou̅ . III . ac̅ . 7 dim̅ . p̅ti . Tc̅ . LI . ou̅ . VIII . porc̅ . m̅ . I . runc̅ . I . uac̅.

. III . ou̅ . III . porc̅ . Se̅p ual̅ . xL . fol̅ . In̅ Ead̅ . II . lib̅i ho̅es de . VII . ac̅ . 7 . d̅.

7 ual̅ . xx . d̅.

ploughs in lordship, now 3. Then and later 7 men's ploughs, now 5.

Woodland, 800 pigs; meadow, 4 acres, pasture, 200 sheep; always 1 mill. Then 6 cobs, 50 cattle, 300 sheep, 40 pigs, 6 beehives; now 4 cobs, 4 cattle, 68 sheep, 37 pigs, 18 goats.

Value then and later £9; now [£] 8.

34 Thorold also holds FRATING from Ranulf, which Ketel held as a manor, for 2 hides.

Then 2 smallholders, now 3; then 3 slaves, now 2. Then 2 ploughs in lordship, now 1. Always 1 men's plough.

Woodland, 150 pigs; meadow, 4 acres. Then 1 cob, 4 cattle, 4 calves, 100 sheep, 40 pigs; now 1 cob, 2 cows, 2 calves, 66 sheep, 20 pigs, 6 beehives.

Value then 40s; now 60[s].

Hundred of ROCHFORD

35 Ranulf holds LEIGH in lordship, which 1 free man held as a manor, for 1 hide.

Always 2 villagers; 2 smallholders; 1 plough in lordship; ½ men's plough; 5 smallholders above the water who do not hold land.

Pasture, 100 sheep. Then 1 cob, 5 cows, 5 calves, 100 sheep; now 2 cobs, 4 cows, 5 calves, 103 sheep.

Value then 40s; now 100[s].

Hundred of THURSTABLE

36 Humphrey holds TOLLESHUNT (D'Arcy) from Ranulf, which Siward held as a manor, for 4½ hides and 30 acres.

Then 9 villagers, now 10; then 4 smallholders, now 13; then 10 slaves, now 6. Always 3 ploughs in lordship; 3 men's ploughs.

1 salt-house; meadow, 5 acres; pasture, 30 sheep; woodland, 150 pigs. Then 3 cobs, 20 cattle, 80 sheep, 60 pigs; now 3 cobs, 20 cattle, 160 sheep, 37 pigs, 18 goats.

Value always 100s.

In this manor 4 free men held ½ hide and 5 acres. But Ralph Baynard has it, and Hugh de Montfort.

76 a

37 Richard holds GOLDHANGER from Ranulf, which Leofwin and Wulfward the priest held as a manor, for 2½ hides and 25 acres.

Then 3 smallholders, now 14; always 2 slaves. Then 2 ploughs in lordship, now 1. Now 1 men's plough.

Woodland, 80 pigs; pasture, 50 sheep; meadow, 3½ acres.

Then 51 sheep, 8 pigs; now 1 cob, 1 cow, 3 sheep, 3 pigs.

Value always 40s.

In the same (Goldhanger) 2 free men with 7½ acres.

Value 20d.

Canedfeldam ten& Albic in dnio . qd tenuit Vluuin . t . r . e . p . Man.

7 . p . ii . hid . Sep . ii . car in dnio . Tc . iiii . car hom . m . iii . Sep . x . uilt.

Tc . iiii . bor . m . ix . Sep . iiii . fer . Silu . clx . porc . li . ac . pti . i . mot.

Tc . vii . an . ii . runc . xx . porc . lxxx . ou . iii . uafa ap . m . viii . an.

. iii . runc . xxx . porc . c . ou . iii . uafa ap . Sep uat . vi . lib.

Vdechefhale ten& . A . in dnio qd tenuit Vluuin p . m . 7 . p

. i . hid . Sep . ii . car . in dnio . Tc . iii . car hom . m . i . Tc . xi . uilt . m . vi.

Tc . ii . bor . m . iiii . Sep . iiii . fer . Silu . c . porc . xlviii . ac . pti.

Tc . vi . an . ii . runc . xx . porc . lx . ou . iii . uafa ap . m . viii . an.

. ii . runc . xxx . porc . lxxx . ou . iii . uafa ap . Sep uat . lx . fot.

76 b

Huic tre addita e . i . uirg . 7 . viii . ac . qs ten . lib ho . t . r . e . m ten& . Rad

de . A . Sep . i . car . in dnio . Tc . i . bor . m . iii . Silu . xxx . porc . ix . ac . pti.

Tc . uat . xvi . fot . m . xxx.

Hund de Vdefesfort . Tunrefleam ten& Rad de . A . qd tenuit

Ailmar lib ho . t . r . e . p Man . 7 . p . v . hid . Tc . 7 p . ii . car . in dnio . m . iii.

Sep . iii . car hom . 7 . i . pbr . 7 . xi . uilt . 7 . v . bord . Tc 7 p filu . c . porc.

m . lxxx . xii . ac . pti . Tc . cxx . ou . xl . porc . lx . cap . viii . an . iii . runc.

. v . uafa ap . M . cxl . ou . lx . porc . Aliud fimilit . Tc 7 p uat vi . lb . m . vii.

Dim . Hund de Clauelinga . Vggheleam ten& . Rad de . A . qd

tenuit Vluuin p man . 7 . p . v . hid . Sep . iii . car . in dnio . 7 . iiii . car.

hom . Tc . x . uilt . Poft . 7 . m . vii . Tc . 7 p . i . bor . m . x . tc 7 p . vi . fer . m . ii.

Tc 7 p filu . cc . porc . m . clx . xxv . ac . pti . tc . v . an . l . porc . clx.

ou . ii . runc . l . cap . ii . uafa ap . m . iii . an . xxii . porc . lxxx . ou . iiii.

runc . xx . cap . ii . uafa ap . Tc uat . vi . lib . m . viii.

Hundred of DUNMOW

1 Aubrey holds (Great) CANFIELD in lordship, which Wulfwin held
as a manor, for 2 hides. Always 2 ploughs in lordship. Then 4
men's ploughs, now 3.
   Always 10 villagers. Then 4 smallholders, now 9; always 4
   slaves.
   Woodland, 160 pigs; meadow, 51 acres; 1 mill. Then 7 cattle,
   2 cobs, 20 pigs, 80 sheep, 3 beehives; now 8 cattle, 3 cobs,
   30 pigs, 100 sheep, 3 beehives.
Value always £6.

2 Aubrey holds UDECHESHALE in lordship, which Wulfwin held before
1066 as a manor, for 1 hide. Always 2 ploughs in lordship. Then
3 men's ploughs, now 1.
   Then 11 villagers, now 6; then 2 smallholders, now 4;
   always 4 slaves.
   Woodland, 100 pigs; meadow, 48 acres. Then 6 cattle, 2 cobs,
   20 pigs, 60 sheep, 3 beehives; now 8 cattle, 2 cobs, 30 pigs,
   80 sheep, 3 beehives.
Value always 60s.
   To this land has been added 1 virgate and 8 acres, which a free   76 b
man held before 1066. Now Ralph holds (it) from Aubrey.
Always 1 plough in lordship.
   Then 1 smallholder; now 3.
   Woodland, 30 pigs; meadow, 9 acres.
Value then 16s; now 30[s].

Hundred of UTTLESFORD

3 Ralph holds THUNDERLEY (Hall) from Aubrey which Aelmer, a free
man, held before 1066 as a manor for 5 hides. Then and later 2
ploughs in lordship; now 3. Always 3 men's ploughs;
   1 priest; 11 villagers; 5 smallholders.
   Woodland then and later, 100 pigs, now 80; meadow, 12 acres.
   Then 120 sheep, 40 pigs, 60 goats, 8 cattle, 3 cobs, 5
   beehives; now 140 sheep, 60 pigs, otherwise the same.
Value then and later £6; now [£] 7.

Half-Hundred of CLAVERING

4 Ralph holds UGLEY from Aubrey, which Wulfwin held as a manor,
for 5 hides. Always 3 ploughs in lordship; 4 men's ploughs.
   Then 10 villagers, later and now 7; then and later 1 smallholder,
   now 10; then and later 6 slaves, now 2.
   Woodland then and later, 200 pigs, now 160; meadow, 25 acres.
   Then 5 cattle, 50 pigs, 160 sheep, 2 cobs, 50 goats, 2
   beehives; now 3 cattle, 22 pigs, 80 sheep, 4 cobs, 20 goats,
   2 beehives.
Value then £6; now [£] 8.

Hund de Hidingforda . Haingheham ten& . A . in dñio . qd ten.

Vluuin ꝑ man . 7 ꝑ . II . hid . Sep . IIII . car . in dñio . 7 . VI . car . hom . 7 . XV

uitł . 7 . VII . bor . 7 . VIII . ſer . Silu . cc . porc . XXX . ac . p̃ti . Tc . I . moł . m̃ . ii.

m̃ . VI . arpenni . uineæ . Tc . XI . an . CXL . ou . LXXX . porc . IIII . runc.

M . CLX . ou . c . porc . I . runc . c . cap . 7 . XIII . ſoc . q n poſant recede

tenentes . I . hid . 7 . X . ac . Sep . V . car . Tc . XV . uitł . m̃ . XVIII . m̃ . XXII.

bor . Tc . VI . ſer . m̃ . II . hntes . III . car . Silu . LX . porc . XLIII . ac . p̃ti . Sep

. I . moł . Tc uał . XIII . lib . m̃ . XX . Huic manerio jacent . XV . burg

in ſudbia 7 appt in itł . XX . lib . De hoc manerio ten& . Rob blund

XXXV . ac . Garin . XXV . ac . Pincun . XV . ac . Godun . XV . ac . hntes

77 a

. V . car . 7 . uał . VII . lib in eod ptio.

Dim Hund de Thunreſtau . Belcamp ten& . A . in dñio qd

tenuit Vluuin . t . r . e . ꝑ Man . 7 . ꝑ . II . hid . 7 . dim . Sep . IIII . car hom.

7 . VII . car . hom . Tc . 7 p . XIII . uitł . m̃ . XV . Tc . 7 p . IX . bor . m̃ . XIIII.

Tc . 7 p . VI . ſer . m̃ . VIII . Silu . XX . porc . LX . ac . p̃ti . M . XI . arpenni uineæ.

. I . portat . Tc XXIIII . an . CLX . ou . LXXX . porc . II . runc . m̃ . XXVIII . an.

. cc . ou . c . porc . II . runc . Huic man adjacent . sep . VII . ſoc . de . I.

hid . 7 . dim . 7 . XV . ac . Sep . III . car . 7 . dim . m̃ . IIII . bor . X . ac . 7 . dim . p̃ti.

Tc . 7 p uał . XIIII . lib . m̃ . XVIII . De hoc man . ten& . Eniſant de . A.

dim . hid . 7 . XXX . ac . Witł peccatu . dim . hid . Suad . XXX . ac . 7 . vał

. IIII . lib . in eod . ptio.

Hund de Hidingaforda . Herſam ten& . Adelelmus de . A.

qd tenueſ . II . ſochemani de anteceſſore . Albici . ita qd non poſant

recede ſine licentia ej . sep . I . car . 7 . dim . Tc . V . bor . m̃ . X . Tc . ſilu.

XL . porc . m̃ . XXX . VII . ac . p̃ti . Vał . XX . ſot

Hundred of HINCKFORD

5 Aubrey holds (Castle) HEDINGHAM in lordship, which Wulfwin
held as a manor, for 2 hides. Always 4 ploughs in lordship; 6
men's ploughs;
15 villagers, 7 smallholders; 8 slaves.
Woodland, 200 pigs; meadow, 30 acres; then 1 mill, now none;
now 6 *arpents* of vines. Then 11 cattle, 140 sheep, 80 pigs,
4 cobs; now 160 sheep, 100 pigs, 1 cob, 100 goats.
13 Freeman who could not withdraw (and) who held 1 hide
and 10 acres. Always 7 ploughs.
Then 15 villagers, now 18; now 22 smallholders; then 6 slaves,
now 2; who have 3 ploughs.
Woodland, 60 pigs; meadow, 43 acres; always 1 mill.
Value then £13; now [£] 20.
To this manor are attached 15 burgesses in Sudbury; they are
assessed in the £20.
Of this manor, Robert Blunt holds 35 acres, Warin 25 acres,
Pinson 15 acres, Godwin 15 acres; who have 5 ploughs.   77 a
Value £7 in the same assessment.

Half-Hundred of 'THUNDERLOW'

6 Aubrey holds BELCHAMP (Walter) in lordship, which Wulfwin held
before 1066 as a manor, for 2½ hides. Always 4 men's ploughs;
7 men's ploughs.
Then and later 13 villagers, now 15; then and later 9 smallholders,
now 14; then and later 6 slaves, now 8.
Woodland, 20 pigs; meadow, 60 acres; now 11 *arpents* of vines,
1 bears (fruit). Then 24 cattle, 160 sheep, 80 pigs, 2 cobs;
now 28 cattle, 200 sheep, 100 pigs, 2 cobs.
To this manor have always been attached 7 Freemen with 1½
hides and 15 acres. Always 3½ ploughs.
Now 4 smallholders.
Meadow, 10½ acres.
Value then and later £14; now [£] 18.
Of this manor, Enisant holds from Aubrey ½ hide and 30 acres,
William Peche ½ hide, Suadus 30 acres.
Value £4 in this assessment.

Hundred of HINCKFORD

7 Aethelhelm holds HORSEHAM (Hall) from Aubrey, which 2 Freemen
held from Aubrey's predecessor on condition that they could not
withdraw without his permission. 45 acres. Always 1½ ploughs.
Then 5 smallholders, now 10.
Woodland then 40 pigs, now 30; meadow, 7 acres.
Value 20s.

⁊Hund de Lexendana . Coles ten& . A . in dñio qđ tenuit
Vluuin� . p̄ Man̄ . 7 . p̄ . v . hiđ . Sēp . uilł . 7 . xiii . bor . 7 . vi . ſeꝛ . Tc̄.
. iii . caꝛ . in dñio . m̄ . v . Tc̄ . inꞇ h̄oes . iii . caꝛ . m̄ . iiii . Silu̅ . cccc . poꝛc̄.
. xl . ac̄ . p̄ti . ii . moł . Tc̄ . xx . uac̄ . 7 xix . an̄ . cxx . ou̅ . lx . por . lx . cap̄.
. iii . runc̄ . m̄ . xlv . an̄ . clx . ou̅ . lxxx . poꝛc̄ . lxxx . cap̄ . iiii . runc̄ . 7
. vi . aſini . 7 . xx . equæ . 7 . iiii . ſoc̄ manſeꝛ in his . v . hiđ . 7 . x . bor.
7 . iiii . ſeꝛ . Tc̄ . 7 p̄ uał . x . liḃ . m̄ . xii . De hoc manerio ten& Dimidi
blanc̄ . i . hiđ . 7 . vii . bor . 7 . ii . caꝛ . in dñio . 7 . i . caꝛ . hom̄ . 7 . uał . xlv.
ſoł . in eod p̄tio.

⁊Hund de Tendringa   Ḃenetleiam ten& . A . in dñio qđ tenuit
Vluuin̄ p̄ . Man̄ . 7 . p̄ . iii . hiđ . Tc̄ 7 p̄ . vii . uilł . m̄ . vi . Tc̄ . v . boꝛ . m̄ . x . Sēp.
. iiii . ſeꝛ . Tc̄ . iiii . caꝛ . in dñio . m̄ . iii . Tc̄ inꞇ . v . caꝛ . m̄ . iiii . Silua . cl . poꝛc̄.
. vi . ac̄ . p̄ti . Paſt . cl . ou̅ . i . ſalina . Tc̄ . iii . runc̄ . c . ou̅ . xx . an̄ . xl . poꝛc̄.
m̄ . c . ou̅ . & . iii . runc̄ . xxvi . an̄ . xl . poꝛc̄ . Tc̄ . uał . vi . liḃ . m̄ . x.

⁊Druurecurt ten& . A . in dñio . qđ tenuit Vluuin̄ p̄ man̄ . 7 . p̄ . vi . hiđ.
Tc̄ . viii . uilł . m̄ . vi . Tc̄ . vi . boꝛ . m̄ . xii . Sēp . vi . ſeꝛ . 7 . iii . caꝛ . in dñio
7 . vi . caꝛ hom̄ . iii . ac̄ . p̄ti . Paſt . cc . ou̅ . Tc̄ . iii . runc̄ . xii . an̄ . cc . ou̅.
xl . por . 7 m̄ ſimiliꝛ Tc̄ uał . vi . liḃ . m̄ . xii.

⁊Fulepet ten& Eduuarđ de . A . qđ tenuit Vluuin̄ p̄ Man̄ . 7 . p̄ . ii.
hiđ . Sēp . xvii . uilł . Tc̄ . iii . bor . m̄ . i . Tc̄ . iii . ſeꝛ . m̄ null̄ . Tc̄ . in dñio
. ii . caꝛ . m̄ . i . Sēp . v . caꝛ . hom̄ . Silu̅ . xv . poꝛc̄ . x . ac̄ . p̄ti . ii . ſał . Tc̄ . xii.

Hundred of LEXDEN

8   Aubrey holds (Earls) COLNE in lordship, which Wulfwin held as a manor, for 5 hides.

    Always ... villagers; 13 smallholders; 6 slaves.

    Then 3 ploughs in lordship, now 5. Then among the men 3 ploughs, now 4.

    Woodland, 400 pigs; meadow, 40 acres; 2 mills. Then 20 cows, 19 cattle, 120 sheep, 60 pigs, 60 goats, 3 cobs; now 45 cattle, 160 sheep, 80 pigs, 80 goats, 4 cobs, 6 asses and 20 mares.

    4 Freemen dwelt on these 5 hides; 10 smallholders; 4 slaves.

  Value then and later £10; now [£] 12.

  Of this manor, Demiblanc holds 1 hide. 7 smallholders. 2 ploughs in lordship. 1 men's plough.

  Value 45s in the same assessment.

Hundred of TENDRING   77 b

9   Aubrey holds (Great) BENTLEY in lordship, which Wulfwin held as a manor, for 3 hides.

    Then and later 7 villagers, now 6; then 5 smallholders, now 10; always 4 slaves.

    Then 4 ploughs in lordship, now 3. Then among [the men] 5 ploughs, now 4.

    Woodland, 150 pigs; meadow, 6 acres; pasture, 150 sheep; 1 salt-house. Then 3 cobs, 100 sheep, 20 cattle, 40 pigs; now 100 sheep, 3 cobs, 26 cattle, 40 pigs.

  Value then £6; now [£] 10.

10   Aubrey holds DOVERCOURT in lordship, which Wulfwin held as a manor, for 6 hides.

    Then 8 villagers, now 6; then 6 smallholders, now 12.

      Always 6 slaves;

    3 ploughs in lordship; 6 men's ploughs.

    Meadow, 3 acres; pasture, 200 sheep. Then 3 cobs, 12 cattle, 200 sheep, 40 pigs; now the same.

  Value then £6; now [£] 12.

11   Edward holds BEAUMONT from Aubrey, which Wulfwin held as a manor, for 2 hides.

    Always 17 villagers. Then 3 smallholders, now 1; then 3 slaves, now none.

T   Then 2 ploughs in lordship, now 1. Always 5 men's ploughs.

    Woodland, 15 pigs; meadow, 10 acres; 2 salt-houses. Then 12

an̄ . CL . ou . xxx . porc̄ . II . runc̄ . M̄ . IIII . an̄ . c . ou . xxx . por . I . runc̄ .
. III . uaſa ap̄ . Tc̄ ual . c . ſol . m̄ . VIII . lib̄ . huic manerio ptin& . I . ſoc̄ .
q̇ n̄ pot̄at recede a t̄ra ſine licentia anteceſſoris Albici . tenens . II . hid
xv . ac̄ . min̄ . Tc̄ . II . uilt . m̄ . null . Tc̄ . II . bor . m̄ . III . Tc̄ . I . ſer . m̄ null . Sep . I . car
in dn̄io . Tc̄ . int̄ hōes . I . car̄ . m̄ . n̄ . Silu . L . porc̄ . II . ac̄ . p̄ti . Tc̄ ual . xx . ſol .
m̄ . xL .

⌐ Dimid̄ Hund̄ de Froſſeuuella . Bumeſted̄a ten& Adelelm̄ .
de . A . qd̄ tenuit Vluuin̄ . p . man̄ . 7 . p̄ . II . hid̄ . Sep̄ . VII . uilt . 7 . III . bor .
7 . IIII . ſer . Tc̄ . 7 . p̄ . II . car̄ . in dn̄io . m̄ . II . 7 . dim̄ . Tc̄ . 7 . p̄ . II . car̄ . hōu
m̄ . I . 7 . dim̄ . Silu . xx . porc̄ . v . ac̄ . p̄ti . Tc̄ . VII . anim̄ . VIII . porc̄ . I . runc̄ .
. v . ou . xv . cap̄ . III . uaſa ap̄u . m̄ . xII . an̄ . xL . porc̄ . v . runc̄ . Lxxx .
ou . xL . cap̄ . v . uaſa ap̄u . Tc̄ ual . v . lib̄ . m̄ . VIII .

78 a

⌐ Redeuuintram ten& Dim̄ blanc̄ . de . A . qd̄ tenuit Aluric̄ ſochem̄ .
p̄ Man̄ . 7 . p̄ dim hid̄ . 7 . xv . ac̄ . 7 pot̄at uende t̄ra ſ; ſoca 7 ſaca rema
nebat anteceſſori . Albici . Tc̄ . IIII . uilt . m̄ . II . Tc̄ . I . bor . m̄ . v . Tc̄ . I . ſer .
m̄ . II . Tc̄ . I . car̄ . in dn̄io . m̄ . II . Tc̄ . II . car̄ . hom̄ . m̄ . I . Silu . xxx . porc̄ . Ix .
ac̄ . p̄ti . Tc̄ ual . xx . ſol . m̄ . Lx .

⌐ In Stauintuna ten& Renold̄ de . A . xxx . ac̄ . qd̄ tenuit Aluuin̄ .
7 . Ordric̄ . tenuit . xv . ac̄ . 7 . iſti . II . fuer̄ in ſoca regis . ſ; eos dedit
Albico . Sep̄ . III . uilt . 7 . II . bor . 7 . I . car̄ . Silu . x . por . III . ac̄ . p̄ti . Tc̄
ual . xx . ſol . m̄ . xxx . In Ead̄ ten& qd̄a anglic̄ . de . A . xL . ac̄ .
qs tenuit Aluric̄ . ſoc̄ . potens uende t̄ra . ſ; ſoca 7 ſaca remanebat .
Sep̄ . II . bor . 7 . I . car̄ . ual . x . ſol .

cattle, 150 sheep, 30 pigs, 2 cobs; now 4 cattle, 100 sheep, 30 pigs, 1 cob, 3 beehives.
Value then 100s; now £8.

To this manor belongs 1 Freeman who could not withdraw from the land without the permission of Aubrey's predecessor (and) who holds 2 hides less 15 acres.

Then 2 villagers, now none; then 2 smallholders, now 3; then 1 slave, now none.

Always 1 plough in lordship. Then among the men 1 plough, now none.

Woodland, 50 pigs; meadow, 2 acres.
Value then 20s; now 40[s].

Half-Hundred of FRESHWELL

12 Aethelhelm holds (Helions) BUMPSTEAD from Aubrey, which Wulfwin held as a manor, for 2 hides.

Always 7 villagers; 3 smallholders; 4 slaves. Then and later 2 ploughs in lordship, now 2½. Then and later 2 men's ploughs, now 1½.

Woodland, 20 pigs; meadow, 5 acres. Then 7 cattle, 8 pigs, 1 cob, 5 sheep, 15 goats, 3 beehives; now 12 cattle, 40 pigs, 5 cobs, 80 sheep, 40 goats, 5 beehives.

Value then £5; now [£] 8.

13 Demiblanc holds RADWINTER from Aubrey, which Aelfric, a   78 a
Freeman, held as a manor, for ½ hide and 15 acres; he could sell his land but the full jurisdiction remained with Aubrey's predecessor.

Then 4 villagers, now 2; then 1 smallholder, now 5; then 1 slave, now 2. Then 1 plough in lordship, now 2. Then 2 men's ploughs, now 1.

Woodland, 30 pigs; meadow, 9 acres.
Value then 20s; now 60[s].

14 In STEVINGTON (End) Reginald holds 30 acres from Aubrey, which Alwin held; and Ordric held 15 acres. These two were in the King's jurisdiction but he gave them to Aubrey.

Always 3 villagers; 2 smallholders; 1 plough.

Woodland, 10 pigs; meadow, 3 acres.
Value then 20s; now 30[s].

In the same (Stevington End) an Englishman holds from Aubrey 40 acres which Aelfric, a Freeman, held; he could sell his land but the full jurisdiction remained.

Always 2 smallholders; 1 plough.
Value 10s.

TERRA Petri ualonienſis . Hund de Herlaua.

Sceringā ten& Petr̃ in dñio qđ tenuer̃.iii.libi hões.t.r.e
p man.7 p.v.hiđ.7.xxx.ač.Sep.v.car̃ in dñio.7.i.car̃.homin̄.
7.iii.uiłł.Tč.iii.bor.m̃.vi.Sep.viii.ſer.Silu.c.por.xxxii.
ač.p̃ti.Sep.i.mol.Tč.viii.uač.c̃ uił.7.i.runč.xxxv.ou.xvi.
porč.m̃.ii.runč.7.i.mul.7.i.aſin.lxxxiiii.ou.lvi.por.iii.uaſa
apū Tč 7 p uał.c.ſoł.m̃.vi.lib.

⌐ Lattunā ten& Turgis de.P.qđ tenuit lib hõ.t.r.e.p Man.

7.p.ii'.hiđ.7.dim̃.7.xxx.ač.Tč.ii.car̃ in dñio m̃.i.dim̃.car̃.homin̄.
Sep.i.uiłł.7.i.pbr̃.m̃.iiii.bor.Tč.iiii.ſer.m̃ null.Silu.ccc.l.porč.
xxxv.ač.p̃ti.Sep uał.lx.ſoł.

Perindunā ten&.Rog̃.de.P.qđ tenuit.i.lib hõ.t.r.e.p.man̄.7.p.
.iii.hiđ.Tč.ii.car̃.in dñio.m̃.i.7.dim̃.m̃ dim̃ car̃ hom̃.Tč.i.bor.
m̃.v.Sep.iii.ſer.Silu.c.porč.xlv.ač.inẽ p̃tũ 7 mareſc.Sep.i.mol
7.v.ač træ additæ ſt.q̃s ten lib hõ.t.r.e.Tč.viii.an̄.7.xli.ou.M
.xiiii.an̄.7.i.runč.7.lxxvi.ou.7.xxvi.porč.7.iii.uaſa ap̃.Tč 7 p
uał.xl.ſoł.m̃ lx.

⌐ In Walda ten&.Rađ.xxx.ač.đe.P.qđ tenuit lib hõ.t.r.e.p.c̃ð.
Sep.i.car̃.7.ii.ſer.7.i.bor.Silu.c.por.ii.ač.p̃ti.uał.xx.ſoł.

⌐ Hund de beuentreu.Leintunā ten& P.in dñio qđ tenuit Suen̄
ſuart.p Man̄.7.p.iii.hiđ.Sep.i.car̃.in dñio.7.i.car̃.hom̃.tč⸗.m̃.ii.

Hundred of HARLOW

1   Peter holds SHEERING in lordship, which 3 free men held before
1066 as a manor, for 5 hides and 30 acres. Always 5 ploughs in
lordship; 1 men's plough;
>   3 villagers. Then 3 smallholders, now 6; always 8 slaves.
>   Woodland, 100 pigs; meadow, 32 acres; always 1 mill. Then
>   8 cows with calves, 1 cob, 35 sheep, 16 pigs; now 2 cobs,
>   1 mule, 1 ass, 84 sheep, 56 pigs, 3 beehives.
Value then and later 100s; now £6.

2   Thorgils holds LATTON from Peter, which a free man held before
1066 as a manor, for 2½ hides and 30 acres. Then 2 ploughs in
lordship, now 1. ½ men's plough.
>   Always 1 villager; 1 priest. Now 4 smallholders; then 4 slaves,
>   now none.
>   Woodland, 350 pigs; meadow, 35 acres.
Value always 60s.

78 b

3   Roger holds (Little) PARNDON from Peter, which 1 free man held
before 1066 as a manor, for 3 hides. Then 2 ploughs in lordship,
now 1½. Now ½ men's plough.
>   Then 1 smallholder, now 5; always 3 slaves.
>   Woodland, 100 pigs; 45 acres of meadow and marsh; always 1
>   mill. 5 acres of land have been added, which a free man held
>   before 1066. Then 8 cattle and 41 sheep; now 14 cattle, 1
>   cob, 76 sheep, 26 pigs and 3 beehives.
Value then and later 40s; now 60[s].

4   In (NORTH)WEALD (BASSETT)Ralph holds 30 acres from Peter, which
a free man held before 1066 as a manor.
>   Always 1 plough; 2 slaves; 1 smallholder.
>   Woodland, 100 pigs; meadow, 2 acres.
Value 20s.

Hundred of BECONTREE

5   Peter holds LEYTON in lordship, which Swein Swart held as a
manor, for 3 hides. Always 1 plough in lordship. Then 1 men's
plough, now 2.

Tc̅ . vii . uitt . m̅ . x . Sep . ii . bor . Silu̅ . xxx . porc̅ . xxiiii . ac̅ . p̅ti . Tc̅ . i . mol
m̅ nutt . q̅ . t̅ . r . Witti . inde ablatus . e̅ . Tc̅ . ii . pisc̅ . m̅ nutt . m̅ . i . runc̅ .
7 . xi . porc̅ . Tc̅ uat . xx . sot . 7 q̅n rec̅ n̅ erat ibi p̅t sola tra̅ . 7 m̅ uat
xL . sot .

⌐ Hecham ten & . P . in d̅nio qd̅ tenuit haldan lib̅ ho̅ . t̅ . r̅ . e̅ .
.p . man . 7 .p . v . hid̅ . Sep . ii . car . in d̅nio . 7 . iiii . car . hom̅ . Tc̅ . viii .
uitt . m̅ . x . Tc̅ . ii . bor . m̅ . iii . Sep . iiii . ser . Silu̅ . ccc . porc̅ . xviii . ac̅ .
p̅ti . tc̅ . iii . pisc̅ . 7 . d̅ . m̅ nutt . Tc̅ . i . bou̅ . m̅ . xv . anim̅ . 7 . i . runc̅ .
7 . xxxvii . porc̅ . 7 . ii . uafa ap̅ . Tc̅ . uat . Lx . sot . m̅ . iiii . lib̅ . 7 . x . sot .
7 q̅n rec̅ hoc maneriu̅ n̅ inuenit p̅t unu̅ boue̅ . 7 una̅ ac̅ . feminata̅
7 . de his . v . hid̅ . qs fup̅ dixi : una̅ tenuer̅ . ii . libi ho̅es . t̅ . r̅ . e̅ .

quæ huic manerio ad̅dita e̅ t̅ . r̅ . Witti . 7 ualebat t̅ . r̅ . e̅ . x . sot . m̅
xx . 7 hoc ten & Witt de Petro ualoniensi .

⌐ Lochetuna̅ ten & . Rad̅ . de . P . qd̅ tenuit vluric̅ lib̅ ho̅ . t̅ . r̅ . e̅ . .p . m̅ . 7 .p . i . hid̅ .
7 . xxx . ac̅ . Sep . i . car in d̅nio . m̅ . v . bor . Silu̅ . Lxxx . porc̅ . vi . ac̅ . p̅ti . Tc̅ uat
x . sot . m̅ . xx .

⌐ Dim̅ Hund̅ de Thunreslau Belindune ten & Rad̅ fatat̅ . de . P .
qd̅ tenuit Aluric̅ lib̅ homo . t̅ . r̅ . e̅ . .p man . 7 . .p . iii . hid̅ . 7 . dim̅ . Sep . ii .
car . in d̅nio . 7 . i . car . hom̅ . Tc̅ . 7 p . iii . bor . m̅ . ix . Sep . iiii . ser . xxxiii .
ac̅ . p̅ti . Tc̅ . v . uac̅ . c̅ uit . 7 . xxx . porc̅ . m̅ . xxxiii . anim̅ . 7 . xxviii . porc̅ .
Tc̅ uat . xL . sot . m̅ . c .

⌐ Binefleam ten & . P . in d̅nio qd̅ tenuit Vluuin t̅ . r̅ . e̅ . .p . i . hid̅ . Sep
. i . car . in d̅nio . 7 . dim̅ . car . hom̅ . 7 xiii . bor . Tc̅ 7 p . ii . ser . m̅ . i . Silu̅ .
xx . porc̅ . iiii . ac̅ . p̅ti . Vat . xx . sot . hanc tram̅ . P . in uadimonio juffu
regis . ne tam̅ pd̅ & fua̅ confuetudine̅ . tefte ep̅o baiocenfi .

Then 7 villagers, now 10; always 2 smallholders.

Woodland, 30 pigs; meadow, 24 acres; then 1 mill, now none, it was taken away from there after 1066; then 2 fisheries, now none. Now 1 cob and 11 pigs.

Value then 20s; when acquired, there was nothing there except the land. Value now 40s.

6   Peter holds HIGHAM (Hill) in lordship which Haldane, a free man, held before 1066 as a manor, for 5 hides. Always 2 ploughs in lordship; 4 men's ploughs.

Then 8 villagers, now 10; then 2 smallholders, now 3; always 4 slaves.

Woodland, 300 pigs; meadow, 18 acres; then 3½ fisheries, now none. Then 1 ox; now 15 cattle, 1 cob, 37 pigs and 2 beehives.

Value then 60s; now £4 10s; when he acquired this manor he found nothing except 1 ox and 1 sown acre.

Of these 5 hides which I have mentioned above, 2 free men held 1 before 1066 which was added to this manor after 1066.   79 a
Value before 1066, 10s; now 20[s].

William holds this from Peter of Valognes.

7   Ralph holds LOUGHTON from Peter which Wulfric, a free man, held before 1066 as a manor, for 1 hide and 30 acres. Always 1 plough in lordship.

Now 5 smallholders.

Woodland, 80 pigs; meadow, 6 acres.

Value then 10s; now 20[s].

Half-Hundred of 'THUNDERLOW'

8   Ralph the Haunted holds BALLINGDON from Peter which Aelfric, a free man, held before 1066 as a manor for 3½ hides. Always 2 ploughs in lordship; 1 men's plough.

Then and later 3 smallholders, now 9; always 4 slaves.

Meadow, 33 acres. Then 5 cows with calves and 30 pigs; now 33 cattle and 28 pigs.

Value then 40s; now 100[s].

[Hundred of HINCKFORD]

9   Peter holds 'BINSLEY' in lordship, which Wulfwin held before 1066, for 1 hide. Always 1 plough in lordship; ½ men's plough.

13 smallholders. Then and later 2 slaves, now 1.

Woodland, 20 pigs; meadow, 4 acres.

Value 20s.

Peter (has) this land in pledge by the King's order, provided that he does not lose his customary due; (to which) the Bishop of Bayeux is witness.

Lochintunā ten& . P . in dn̄io q̄d tenuit Leofcild . ꝑ . man̊ . 7 ꝑ . I . hid̄ .
tc̄ . III . bor . m̂ . II . Tc̄ . II . ſer . m̂ nulł . Sep̄ . I . car . Silu . xxx . porc̊ . IIII ,
ac̊ . p̄ti . Sep̄ . I . mot Tc̄ ual̄ . Tc̄ ual̄ . xx . ſot 7 q̄n rec̊ . xxx . m̂
ual̄ . xx . ſot .

Taindenā ten& . P . in dn̄io . q̄d tenuit Hacun ꝑ man̊ . 7 ꝑ . III .
hid̄ . 7 . d̄ . 7 . LXXX . ac̊ . Tc̄ . VII . uiłt . m̂ . XII . tc̄ . III . bor . m̂ . IIII . Sep̄ .
. V . ſer . Silu . CCCC . porc̊ . XVI . ac̊ . p̄ti . I . mot . Tc̄ . II . uac̊ . 7 . III . runc̊ .
7 . LIIII . porc̊ . 7 . XLVII . ou . m̂ . II . runc̊ . 7 . LXXXXII . porc̊ . 7 CLVII . ou .
7 . XII . uaſa ap̄u . Tc̄ ual̄ . LX . ſot . m̂ . c . 7 . VII . libi hōes tenuer̊ . II . hid̄ .
7 . I . uirg̊ . 7 . dim . q̄d m̂ ten& Petr̊ . Sep̄ . II . ſer . 7 . I . bor . Tc̄ 7 p̊ . VI . car̊ .

m̂ . IIII . Silu . CXL . porc̊ . xx . ac̊ . p̄ti . Sep̄ ual̄ XLVI , ſot . 7 hoc eſt
ꝑ eſcangio ut ipſe . P . dic̊ . 7 . dim . hid̄ . 7 . XL . ac̊ . ten& Galt̄ . de . P . q̄d
tenuit Vluuin̊ . 7 petr̊ ht̄ in uadimonio ſic̄ ipſe dicit conceſſu reg̊
Tc̄ . I . uiłt . m̂ null̊ . m̂ . III . bor . To̊ . I . ſer . m̂ nulł . Tc̄ . II . car . Poſt 7 m̂ . I .
Silu . c . porc̊ . VII . ac̊ . p̄ti . tc̄ ual̄ . XVI . ſot . m̂ . xx .

Wallam ten& . Rad̄ . fatat̊ de . P . q̄d tenuer̊ . II . libi hōes . t̊ . r̊ . e̊ .
ꝑ . II . man̊ . 7 ꝑ . II . hid̄ . 7 . XL . ac̊ . 7 Petr̊ ht̄ in eſcangio . Tc̄ 7 p̊ . VII .
uiłt . m̂ . XIII . Tc̄ 7 p̊ . III . bor . m̂ . VIII . Tc̄ 7 p̊ . IX . ſer . m̂ . VII . Tc̄ . V . car̊
in dn̄io . Poſt . III . m̂ . II . Tc̄ 7 p̊ . II . car̊ . 7 dim hom̊ . m̂ . V . Silu . M̄ ð . porc̊
XL . ac̊ . p̄ti . Tc̄ . III . uac̊ . 7 . I . runc̊ . 7 . XXXV . porc̊ . 7 . V . ou . 7 . III . cap̊ .
m̂ . XVII . an̊ . 7 . I . runc̊ . 7 . XXVIII . porc̊ . 7 . LXX . ou . 7 . V . uaſa ap̄u .
Tc̄ ual̄ . VII . lib̄ . 7 q̄n rec̊ . VI . lib̄ . m̂ ual̄ . XII . lib̄ . 7 q̄da hō libe
tenuit XL . ac̊ . q̄e ht̄ . P . in eſcangio . Sep̄ . IIII . uiłt . m̂ . II . bor . Silu .
LX . porc̊ . V . ac̊ . p̄ti . Sep̄ . I . car . 7 ual̄ . xx . ſot .

10 Peter holds LOUGHTON in lordship, which Leofcild held as a manor, for 1 hide.
  Then 3 smallholders, now 2; then 2 slaves, now none. Always
    1 plough.
  Woodland, 30 pigs; meadow, 4 acres; always 1 mill.
  Value then 20s; when acquired 30[s]. Value now 20s.

[Hundred of ONGAR]
11 Peter holds THEYDON (Bois) in lordship, which Hakon held as a
  manor, for 3½ hides and 80 acres.
    Then 7 villagers, now 12; then 3 smallholders, now 4; always
    5 slaves.
    Woodland, 400 pigs; meadow, 16 acres; 1 mill. Then 2 cows,
    3 cobs, 54 pigs and 47 sheep; now 2 cobs, 92 pigs, 157 sheep
    and 12 beehives.
  Value then 60s; now 100[s].
    7 free men held 2 hides and 1½ virgates, which Peter now holds.
    Always 2 slaves; 1 smallholder. Then and later 6 ploughs,
    now 4.   79 b
    Woodland, 140 pigs; meadow, 20 acres.
  Value always 46s.
    This is by exchange, as Peter himself states.
    Walter holds from Peter ½ hide and 40 acres, which Wulfwin
  held. Peter holds (it) in pledge, so he states, by the King's grant.
    Then 1 villager, now none; now 3 smallholders; then 1 slave,
    now none. Then 2 ploughs, later and now 1.
    Woodland, 100 pigs; meadow, 7 acres.
  Value then 16s; now 20[s].

[Hundred of HARLOW]
12 Ralph the Haunted holds (NORTH) WEALD (BASSETT) from Peter,
  which 2 free men held before 1066 as 2 manors, for 2 hides and
  40 acres. Peter has (it) in exchange.
    Then and later 7 villagers, now 13; then and later 3 smallholders,
    now 8; then and later 9 slaves, now 7. Then 5 ploughs in
    lordship, later 3, now 2. Then and later 2½ men's ploughs,
    now 5.
    Woodland, 1500 pigs; meadow, 40 acres. Then 3 cows, 1 cob,
    35 pigs, 5 sheep and 3 goats; now 17 cattle, 1 cob, 28 pigs,
    70 sheep and 5 beehives.
  Value then £7; when acquired £6. Value now £12.
    A man held 40 acres freely, which Peter has in exchange.
    Always 4 villagers. Now 2 smallholders.
    Woodland, 60 pigs; meadow, 5 acres. Always 1 plough.
  Value 20s.

Ingam ten& . W . de . R . qd tenuit Oſlac . t . r . e . ʃSep . i . car p man'. 7. II. hid.
in dn̄io . 7 . i . car . hom . tc̄ . v . bor . m̄ . ix . tc̄ . ii . ſer . m̄ . nulł . Silua .
. c . porc . Tc̄ . xiiii . anim . lx . ou . lx . porc . m̄ . viii . an . c . ou . xx .
porc . iii . uaſa ap̄ . Tc̄ . uał . xl . ſoł . m̄ . xxx .

ᴦRameſdanā . ten& Humfrid de . R . qd tenuit Siric̄ libe ꝑ . ii . hid .

7 . xxx . ac̄ . Tc̄ . ii . car . in dn̄io . m̄ . i . 7 . dim̄ . m̄ . dim̄ . car . hom̄ . 7 . i . lib h̄o .
Sep . iii . ſer . 7 . i . bor Silu . c . porc . ii . ac̄ . p̄ti . Nichil inuenit . m̄ . iiii . an .
. ii . runc̄ . lviii . ou . xxi . porc̄ . Tc̄ uał . lx . ſoł . m̄ . xl .

ᴦHund de Herlaua . Ruindune . ten& . R . in dn̄io qd tenuit
Inguar lib h̄o . t . r . e . ꝑ Man̄ . 7 ꝑ . vi . hid . Sep . iii . car . in dn̄io . 7 . iiii . car . hom̄ .
tc̄ . xii . uiłł . m̄ . viii . Tc̄ . ii . bor . m̄ . xii . Tc̄ . viii . ſer . m̄ . iii . Silu . cxx . porc .
lx . ac̄ . p̄ti . Paſt . de . ii . ſoł . i . mol . Tc̄ . vi . an . lx . ou . xxx . porc . m̄ .
. x . anim̄ . lx . ou . xxx . porc . x . eq̄ . Tc̄ uał . vi . lib . m̄ . ix . huic mancrio
adjac& . i . ꝫiuuita herlaua . qd ten& Ricard de . R . ꝑ . i . hid . 7 . i . uirḡ .
Sep . i . car . Tc̄ . ii . uiłł . m̄ . i . Silu . l . porc . vii . ac̄ . p̄ti . Tc̄ . 7 ꝑ uał . xxv .
ſoł . m̄ . xxx . huic tr̄e addite ſt̄ . iiii . hid . tr̄æ . qs tenuer̄ . v . libi
h̄oes . t . r . e . Sep . iiii . car . tc̄ . iii . uiłł . m̄ . ii . Tc̄ . v . bor . m̄ . vii . Tc̄ . i . ſer
m̄ nulł . Silu . lx . porc . xxv . ac̄ . p̄ti . Sep uał . iiii . liꝫ .

ᴦPerendunā ten& Roḡ de . R . qd tenuit Alſi bolla lib h̄o . t . r . e .
ꝑ . man̄ . 7 ꝑ . ii . hid . Tc̄ . i . car . in dn̄io . m̄ . i . 7 . dim̄ . Tc̄ . i . uiłł . m̄ . v . bor .
Sep . i . ſer . Silu . cxl . por . xviii . ac̄ . p̄ti . Tc̄ . xii . an . m̄ . viii . xxxiiii .
porc . lxxx . ou . Tc̄ uał . xxx . ſoł . m̄ . xl .

Hundred of BARSTABLE

1 W. holds INGRAVE from Ranulf, which Oslac held before 1066 as
   a manor, for 2 hides. Always 1 plough in lordship; 1 men's plough.
       Then 5 smallholders, now 9; then 2 slaves, now none.
       Woodland, 100 pigs. Then 14 cattle, 60 sheep, 60 pigs; now
           8 cattle, 100 sheep, 20 pigs, 3 beehives.
   Value then 40s; now 30[s].

2 Humphrey holds RAMSDEN from Ranulf, which Siric held freely,
   for 2 hides and 30 acres. Then 2 ploughs in lordship, now 1½.   80 a
       Now ½ men's plough; 1 free man. Always 3 slaves; 1
           smallholder.
       Woodland, 100 pigs; meadow, 2 acres. He found nothing;
           now 4 cattle, 2 cobs, 58 sheep, 21 pigs.
   Value then 60s; now 40[s].

Hundred of HARLOW

3 Ranulf holds ROYDON in lordship which Ingvar, a free man, held
   before 1066 as a manor for 6 hides. Always 3 ploughs in lordship;
       4 men's ploughs. Then 12 villagers, now 8; then 2 smallholders,
           now 12; then 8 slaves, now 3.
       Woodland, 120 pigs; meadow, 60 acres; pasture at 2s; 1 mill.
           Then 6 cattle, 60 sheep, 30 pigs; now 10 cattle, 60 sheep,
           30 pigs, 10 horses.
   Value then £6; now [£] 9.
       To this manor is attached 1 outlier (called) HARLOW, which
   Richard holds from Ranulf for 1 hide and 1 virgate. Always 1
   plough.
       Then 2 villagers, now 1.
       Woodland, 50 pigs; meadow, 7 acres.
   Value then and later 25s; now 30[s].
       To this land have been added 4 hides of land which 5 free men
   held before 1066. Always 4 ploughs.
       Then 3 villagers, now 2; then 5 smallholders, now 7; then 1
           slave, now none.
       Woodland, 60 pigs; meadow, 25 acres.
   Value always £4.

4 Roger holds PARNDON from Ranulf which Alfsi Bowl, a free man,
   held before 1066 as a manor for 2 hides. Then 1 plough in
   lordship, now 1½.
       Then 1 villager; now 5 smallholders; always 1 slave.
       Woodland, 140 pigs; meadow, 18 acres. Then 12 cattle; now
           8 (cattle), 34 pigs, 80 sheep.
   Value then 30s; now 40[s].

Perendunā ten& Alured . de . R . qd tenuit Alueua liba femina
ᵽ Man 7 . ᵽ . dim̄ . hid̄ . Sēp . dim̄ . car̄ . 7 . ı . bor . Silu̅ . xxx . porc̄ .
. v . ac̄ . p̄ti . val . xı . fol.

In Perenduna ten& Roḡ de . R . xxxv . ac̄ . qs tenuit Ỻtin lib̄ hō
t . r . e . Sēp . dim̄ . car̄ . Silu̅ . xx . porc̄ . ıı . ac̄ . p̄ti . val . vı . fol.

Waldā ten& . Ricard̄ . de . R . qd tenuit Goduin lib̄ hō . t . r . e .
ᵽ . m̄ . 7 . ᵽ . dim̄ . hid̄ . 7 . xv . ac̄ . Sēp . ı . car̄ . in dn̄io . 7 . dim̄ . car̄ hom̄ .

80 b

Tc̄ . ı . uilt . m̄ . ıı . Sēp . ı . bord . Tc̄ . ıı . fer . m̄ . ı . Silu̅ . cc . porc̄ . ıı . ac̄ . p̄ti . Tc̄ . xx .
porc̄ . m̄ . ʟx . xvıı . ænim . ʟxv . ou̅ . 7 . ııı . runc̄ . Tc̄ ual . xx . fol . m̄ . xxx .

In Nafinga ten& . Odo de . R . ı . hid̄ . 7 . ı . uilt . 7 . ıııı . bor . 7 . ı . car̄ . 7 . ual .
xx . fol.

Hund de Waltham . Nafingā . 7 Epingā tenuer̄ . ıı . libi hōes . t . r . e .
ᵽ . Man̄ . 7 ᵽ . ıııı . hid̄ . 7 . dim̄ . xv . ac̄ . min̄ . Tc̄ . ııı . car̄ . in dn̄io . m̄ . ıı . Sēp .
. ııı . car̄ . hom̄ . Tc̄ . xı . uilt . m̄ . vıı . m̄ . ıx . bord . tc̄ . ııı . fer . m̄ nult . Silu̅ . c . por .
. ʟıııı . ac̄ . p̄ti . Paſt . de . xxxıı . d̄ . Tc̄ . ı . mot . m̄ . n̄ . Tc̄ . vıı . anim̄ . 7 xxx . porc̄ .
m̄ . ıı . an̄ . 7 . xvııı . por . hoc eſt in Nafinga . 7 In Eppinges . ıı . anim̄ .
7 . xxvı . ou̅ . 7 . vı . porc̄ . Sēp ualent . ıııı . lib̄ . Nafinga . ʟx . fol 7 Eppinḡ
xx . fol . 7 P̄t hoc addita ē huic tr̄e . ı . hid̄ . quā tenuit lib̄ hō . t . r . e .
7 adhuc ten& . Tc̄ . ı . car̄ . m̄ . dim̄ . Tc̄ . ıı . bor . m̄ . ııı . Silu̅ . xx . porc̄ .
xıı . ac̄ . p̄ti . Tc̄ ual . x . fol . m̄ . xx . 7 adhuc . ı . uirḡ tr̄æ . que addita ē
t . r . Witti . 7 ᵽtinebat in Waltham . t . r . e . quā inde tulit . R . fr̄ ilgeri .
ut hund̄ teſtat̄ . 7 ual . ııı . fol . Hoc totū ten& . R . in dn̄io .

5 Alfred holds PARNDON from Ranulf which Aelfeva, a free woman, held as a manor for ½ hide. Always ½ plough;
> 1 smallholder.
> Woodland, 30 pigs; meadow, 5 acres.
> Value 11s.

6 In PARNDON Roger holds 35 acres from Ranulf which Thurstan, a free man, held before 1066. Always ½ plough.
> Woodland, 20 pigs; meadow, 2 acres.
> Value 6s.

7 Richard holds (NORTH) WEALD (BASSETT) from Ranulf which Godwin, a free man, held before 1066 as a manor for ½ hide and 15 acres. Always 1 plough in lordship; ½ men's plough.
> Then 1 villager, now 2; always 1 smallholder.   80 b
>> Then 2 slaves, now 1.
> Woodland, 200 pigs; meadow, 2 acres. Then 20 pigs; now 60 pigs, 17 cattle, 65 sheep and 3 cobs.
> Value then 20s; now 30[s].

[Hundred of WALTHAM]
8 In NAZEING Odo holds 1 hide from Ranulf.
> 1 villager; 3 smallholders. 1 plough.
> Value 20s.

Hundred of WALTHAM
9 2 free men held NAZEING and EPPING before 1066 as a manor, for 4½ hides less 15 acres. Then 3 ploughs in lordship, now 2. Always 3 men's ploughs.
> Then 11 villagers, now 7; now 9 smallholders; then 3 slaves, now none.
> Woodland, 100 pigs; meadow, 54 acres; pasture at 32d; then 1 mill, now none. Then 7 cattle and 30 pigs; now 2 cattle and 18 pigs: this is in Nazeing. In Epping, 2 cattle, 26 sheep and 6 pigs.
> Value always £4: Nazeing 60s; Epping 20s.
> Besides this, 1 hide has been added to this land, which a free man held before 1066 and still holds. Then 1 plough, now ½.
> Then 2 smallholders, now 3.
> Woodland, 20 pigs; meadow, 12 acres.
> Value then 10s; now 20[s].
> A further 1 virgate of land, which was added after 1066 and belonged to Waltham [Holy Cross] before 1066, which Ranulf brother of Ilger took from there, as the Hundred testifies.
> Value 3s.
> Ranulf holds all this in lordship.

Hund de . Rochefort . Thorp . ten& Odo de . R . qd tenuit . t . r . c.

Inguar ꝓ Man . 7 . ꝑ . ii . hid . 7 . dim . Sep . iiii . uiłł . 7 . iiii . bor . 7 . iiii . fer.
7 . ii . car . in dnio . 7 . iii . car . hom . Silu . lx . porc . Past . c . ou . Tc . ii.
an . 7 . ii . runc . 7 . c . ou . 7 . xxx . porc . M . ii . anim . 7 . i . runc . 7 . c . ou.
7 . vii . porc . 7 . xviii . cap . 7 . iiii . uafa ap . Tc 7 p uał . iiii . lib . m . vi.

Hund de Hidingforda Bridebroc ten& . R . in dnio . qd ten.
. i . lib ho . t . r . e . ꝓ . man . 7 . ꝑ . ii . hid . Tc . iii . car . in dnio . Poft . ii.
m . iii . Sep . iii . car . hom . Tc 7 p . vii . uiłł . m . vi . Tc 7 . p . i . bor.
m . ix . Sep . iiii . fer . Silu . xvi . porc . xxii . ac . ꝑti . Tc . xv . animał

7 . l . porc . 7 . lxxx . ou . 7 . xiii ; 7 . xxv . cap . m . iiii . an . 7 . x . porc.
7 . lv . ou . 7 . ii . runc . Tc . 7 p uał . viii . lib . m . ix.

Babitna ten& . R . in dnio . qd tenuit Inguar . ꝓ . Man . 7 . ꝑ . ii . hid.
t . r . e . Sep . ii . car . in dnio . 7 . iiii . car . hom . 7 . vi . uiłł . m . vii . bor . Tc 7 p.
. ii . fer . m . iii . xxxi . ac . ꝑti . fep . i . mot . Tc 7 p uał . vii . lib . m . viii.
his . ii . manerijs . adjacent . fep . ii . foc . de . v . ac.

Geldham ten& Galt de . R . qd tenuit lib ho . t . r . e . ꝓ man . 7 . ꝑ . dim.
hid . Tc . i . car . Poft nulla . m . i . ix . ac . ꝑti . Tc . nich . M . ii . an . 7 . i . runc.
7 . xxx . ou . 7 . ii . porc . uał . xx . foł.

Hund de Witbrictefherna . Niuuelanda ten& . W . de . R . qd
tenuit Inguuar . t . r . e . ꝓ man . 7 . ꝑ . i . hid . 7 . dim . 7 . xxxv . ac . m . iiii.
bor . fep . i . fer . 7 . i . car . in dnio . Tc uał . xx . foł . Poft 7 . m . xxx . 7 . vii.
ac . 7 . dim . qs ten& . i . lib ho . 7 uał . vii . d.

Hundred of ROCHFORD

10 Odo holds THORPE(HALL) from Ranulf, which Ingvar held before 1066 as a manor, for 2½ hides.
> Always 4 villagers; 4 smallholders; 4 slaves; 2 ploughs in lordship; 3 men's ploughs.
> Woodland, 60 pigs; pasture, 100 sheep. Then 2 cattle, 2 cobs, 100 sheep and 30 pigs; now 2 cattle, 1 cob, 100 sheep, 7 pigs, 18 goats and 4 beehives.

Value then and later £4; now [£] 6.

Hundred of HINCKFORD

11 Ranulf holds BIRDBROOK in lordship, which 1 free man held before 1066 as a manor, for 2 hides. Then 3 ploughs in lordship, later 2, now 3. Always 3 men's ploughs.
> Then and later 7 villagers, now 6; then and later 1 smallholder, now 9; always 4 slaves.
> Woodland, 16 pigs; meadow, 22 acres. Then 15 cattle, 50 pigs,   81 a 80 sheep, 13 ... and 25 goats; now 4 cattle, 10 pigs, 55 sheep and 2 cobs.

Value then and later £8; now [£] 9.

12 Ranulf holds BAYTHORN (End) in lordship, which Ingvar held as a manor, for 2 hides before 1066. Always 2 ploughs in lordship; 4 men's ploughs;
> 6 villagers. Now 7 smallholders; then and later 2 slaves, now 3. Meadow, 31 acres; always 1 mill.

Value then and later £7; now [£] 8.
> 2 sokemen with 5 acres have always been attached to these 2 manors.

13 Walter holds YELDHAM from Ranulf, which a free man held before 1066 as a manor, for ½ hide. Then 1 plough, later none, now 1.
> Meadow, 9 acres. Then nothing; now 2 cattle, 1 cob, 30 sheep and 2 pigs.

Value 20s.

Hundred of 'WIBERTSHERNE'

14 W. holds ST. LAWRENCE from Ranulf, which Ingvar held before 1066 as a manor, for 1½ hides and 35 acres.
> Now 4 smallholders. Always 1 slave; 1 plough in lordship.

Value then 20s; later and now 30[s].
> 7½ acres which 1 free man holds. Value 7d.

⌐Bubingeordā.ten& Ricard̄ de.R.qđ tenueꞃ.ıı.liƀi hōes.t.r.e.
p.ı.hiđ.7.xxx.ac̄.Tc̄.ı.bor.m̄.ıı.Tc̄.ıııı.ſer.m̄.ıı.Tc̄.ıı.car̄.in dn̄io
p 7 m̄.ı.Silu.ʟxxx.porc̄.ıııı.ac̄.p̄ti.ſep.ı.uac̄.7.ııı.porc̄.7.cvıı.ou.
Tc̄ ual.xʟ.ſoł.m̄.ʟx.

⌐Hund de Celmeresfort Gingā ten&.R.in dn̄io.qđ tenuit
Inguuara.p Man̄.7.p.ıx.hiđ.Tc̄.xvııı.uiłł.m̄.xvı.tc̄.vııı.bor.
m̄.xx.tc̄.v.ſer.m̄.vıı.Tc̄.in dn̄io.ıı.car̄.m̄.ı.Tc̄.in̄ hōes.xıı.
car̄.M̄.ıx.Silu.ɔcc.porc̄.m̄.vıı.anim̄.7.ʟx.ou.Tc̄.ual.vııı.
liƀ.m̄.x.7.ı.liƀ hō.ten.xx.ac̄.7.ual.ııı.ſoł. In Eađ ten&
Wiłł.de boſc.ıı.hiđ.7.xxvı.ac̄.de.R.7 ꞓt in ſuo eſcangio.
qđ tenuit Alfega.7 Algar.t.r.e.m̄.ııı.bor.Tc̄.ıı.ſer.m̄.ı.

81 b

Tc̄.ıı.car̄.in dn̄io.m̄.ı.Silu.ʟx.porc̄.Paſt.c.ou.val.xʟ.ſoł.
⌐Cubrigeam ten& Wiłł.de.R.qđ tenuit Aluuin.p man̄.7.p dim̄.
hiđ.7.vı.ac̄.7.dim̄.7.dim̄.car poteſt eſſe.ı.ac̄.p̄ti.Silu.xx.porc̄.
val.x.ſoł.
⌐Gingā tenueꞃ.ıı.puellæ.liƀæ p ʟxxx.ac̄.m̄.R.in ſuo eſcangio.7.W.
de eo.Sep.ı.car̄.Val.xv.ſoł.
⌐Hund de Tendringa.In Derleiā tenuit Edric de Eſtorp.ı.man.
de.ıı.hiđ.7.dim̄.m̄ ten&.R.p.ı.hiđ.7.dim̄.7.Roꞡ de illo.Tc̄.ıı.
uiłł.m̄.ı.Tc̄.ı.ſer.m̄ nułł.Tc̄ 7 p.ı.car in dn̄io.m̄.dim̄.Tc̄.7.p.ı.car̄
hom̄.m̄ nułł.7.ııı.car̄ poſſꞇ eſſe.Silu.xx.porc̄.ıııı.ac̄.p̄ti Tc̄ 7 p
ual.xxx.ſoł.m̄.x.hanc trā ꞓt.R.p eſcangio.ꞓt &iā in ſoca
de Laleforda.xv.ac̄.7.ibi man&.ı.hō.q reddit.vıı.ſoł.7.vııı.đ.

[Hundred of ONGAR]

15 Richard holds BOBBINGWORTH from Ranulf, which 2 free men held before 1066, for 1 hide and 30 acres.

Then 1 smallholder, now 2; then 4 slaves, now 2. Then 2 ploughs in lordship, later and now 1.

Woodland, 80 pigs; meadow, 4 acres. Always 1 cow, 3 pigs and 107 sheep.

Value then 40s; now 60[s].

Hundred of CHELMSFORD

16 Ranulf holds MOUNTNESSING in lordship, which Ingvar held as a manor, for 9 hides.

Then 18 villagers, now 16; then 8 smallholders, now 20; then 5 slaves, now 7. Then 2 ploughs in lordship, now 1. Then among the men 12 ploughs, now 9.

Woodland, 700 pigs. Now 7 cattle and 60 sheep.

Value then £8; now [£] 10.

1 free man holds 20 acres. Value 3s.

17 In the same (Mountnessing) William of Bosc holds 2 hides and 26 acres from Ranulf, and he has (it) in exchange, which Alfheah and Algar held before 1066.

Now 3 smallholders; then 2 slaves, now 1. Then 2 ploughs in lordship, now 1.   81 b

Woodland, 60 pigs; pasture, 100 sheep.

Value 40s.

18· William holds COWBRIDGE from Ranulf, which Alwin held as a manor, for ½ hide and 6½ acres. ½ plough possible.

Meadow, 1 acre; woodland, 20 pigs.

Value 10s.

19 2 girls held FOUCHERS freely for 80 acres. Now Ranulf (holds it) in exchange, and W. from him. Always 1 plough.

Value 15s.

Hundred of TENDRING

20 In 'DERLEIGH' Edric of Easthorpe held 1 manor at 2½ hides. Now Ranulf holds (it) for 1½ hides, and Roger from him.

Then 2 villagers, now 1; then 1 slave, now none. Then and later 1 plough in lordship, now ½. Then and later 1 men's plough, now none. 3 ploughs possible.

Woodland, 20 pigs; meadow, 4 acres.

Value then and later 30s; now 10[s].

Ranulf has this land by exchange. He also has 15 acres in the jurisdiction of Lawford. 1 man dwells there, who pays 7s 8d.

TERRA Tihelli brittonis.   Hund de Vdelesforda.

Gerdelai . tenueř . ii . liƀi hões . t . r . e . ꝑ Man . 7 . ꝑ . i . hid . Sep . i . car
in dnĩo . 7 . ii . boƌ . m̃ . vii . Tc . ſilu . xl . porc . P 7 m̃ . xxx . x . ac.
ꝑti Tc . v . anim . xiiii . ou 7 . xxvi . porc . 7 . xxxii . cap . 7 . i . runc
7 . i . uas apũ . m̃ . iiii . añ . 7 . xiiii . porc . 7 . xxxviii . ou.
7 . iii . uaſa aꝑ . 7 . i . runc . Hoc ten& Serlo de . tihello
hanc třã reclamat Tiheſſ de dono regis . Tc . uaƚ . xvi.
ſoƚ . m̃ . xx.

82 a

⸋Hunƌ de Froſſeuuella . Steintunã . ten& Tiheſſ in dnĩo . qƌ
tenuit Oſlac liƀ hõ . t . r . e . ꝑ . man . 7 . ꝑ . xlii . ac . 7 . dim . Sep . ii . car.
in dnĩo . Tc ꝑ ꝑ . i . bor . m̃ . iii . Sep . iiii . ſer . v . ac . ꝑti . Tc . v . añ . 7 . v . porc.
7 . x . ou . 7 . ii . uaſa apũ . M . v . uac . 7 . i . runc . 7 . xxx . porc . 7 . l . ou . 7.
. i . uas . apũ . Tc . 7 ꝑ uaƚ . lx . ſoƚ . m̃ . c . ſoƚ . 7 . i . unciã auri.
⸋Redeuuintrã ten& Goderet de . T . qƌ . tenuit Lefſiu . t . r . e . ꝑ
man . 7 . ꝑ dim . hid . 7 . dim . uirg̃ . Sep . ii . car in dnĩo . 7 . i . car hom̃ . 7.
. iiii . uiƚƚi . Tc . v . bor . m̃ . vii . Silu . lx . porc . viii . ac . ꝑti . tc . vi . añ.
m̃ . iiii . 7 . xviii . porc . 7 m̃ ſimiƚ . tc xlix . ou . m̃ . xxxii . iiii . uaſa
apũ . tc xx . cap . m̃ nuƚƚ . Tc uaƚ . xx . ſoƚ . m̃ lx . hoc reclamat
Tiheſſ de dono regis.
⸋Bunſtedã . ten& . T . in dnĩo qƌ tenuit Leuuin cilt . t . r . e . ꝑ
man . 7 . ꝑ . iiii . hid . Sep . iiii . car in dnĩo . tc . iiii . car . hom̃ . m̃ . ii.
tc . ix . uiƚƚ . m̃ . vii . Sep . viii . bor . 7 . viii . ſer . Silu . c . porc . vii.
ac . ꝑti . Sep . vi . anim . tc . xxiiii . porc . m̃ . xl . tc . xl . ou . m̃ . M . cxv.
Tc . i . runc . m̃ . i . 7 . i . puƚƚ . tc . uaſa aꝑ . m̃ . iii . Tc uaƚ . vi . liƀ . m̃ . ix.
⸋Hunƌ de Hindingaforda . Bumeſtedã . ten& . T . in dnĩo
qƌ tenuit . liƀ hõ . t . r . e . ꝑ man ; 7 . ꝑ . i . uirg̃ . Sep . iii . car in dnĩo
7 . ii . car . hom̃ . 7 . v . uiƚƚ . 7 . xiii . bor . 7 . vi . ſer . Silu . xx . por.
xv . ac . ꝑti . Sep . i . moƚ . Tc 7 ꝑ uaƚ . lx . ſoƚ . m̃ . vi . liƀ.

Hundred of UTTLESFORD

1   2 free men held YARDLEY before 1066 as a manor, for 1 hide.
Always 1 plough in lordship.
    [Then] 2 smallholders, now 7.
    Woodland, then 40 pigs, later and now 30; meadow, 10 acres.
        Then 5 cattle, 14 sheep, 26 pigs, 32 goats, 1 cob and 1
        beehive; now 4 cattle, 14 pigs, 38 sheep, 3 beehives and
        1 cob.
    Serlo holds this from Tihel. Tihel claims this land as the
King's gift.
Value then 16s; now 20[s].

Hundred of FRESHWELL   82 a

2   Tihel holds STEVINGTON (End) in lordship which Oslac, a free man,
held before 1066 as a manor for 42½ acres. Always 2 ploughs in
lordship.
    Then [and] later 1 smallholder, now 3; always 4 slaves.
    Meadow, 5 acres. Then 5 cattle, 5 pigs, 10 sheep and 2 beehives;
        now 5 cows, 1 cob, 30 pigs, 50 sheep and 1 beehive.
Value then and later 60s; now 100s and 1 ounce of gold.

3   Guthred holds RADWINTER from Tihel, which Leofsi held before
1066 as a manor, for ½ hide and ½ virgate. Always 2 ploughs in
lordship; 1 men's plough;
    4 villagers. Then 5 smallholders, now 7.
    Woodland, 60 pigs; meadow, 8 acres. Then 6 cattle, now 4;
        18 pigs, now the same; then 49 sheep, now 32; 4 beehives;
        then 20 goats, now none.
Value then 20s; now 60[s].
Tihel claims this as the King's gift.

4   Tihel holds (Helions) BUMPSTEAD in lordship, which Young Leofwin
held before 1066 as a manor, for 4 hides. Always 4 ploughs in
lordship. Then 4 men's ploughs, now 2.
    Then 9 villagers, now 7. Always 8 smallholders; 8 slaves.
    Woodland, 100 pigs; meadow, 7 acres. Always 6 cattle. Then
        24 pigs, now 40; then 40 sheep, now 115; then 1 cob,
        now 1 (cob) and 1 foal; then ... beehives, now 3.
Value then £6; now [£] 9.

Hundred of HINCKFORD

5   Tihel holds (Steeple) BUMPSTEAD in lordship, which a free man
held before 1066 as a manor, for 1 hide and 1 virgate. Always 3
ploughs in lordship; 2 men's ploughs;
    5 villagers; 13 smallholders; 6 slaves.
    Woodland, 20 pigs; meadow, 15 acres; always 1 mill.
Value then and later 60s; now £6.

Sturmere ten& . T . in dn̄io qd̄ tenuit lib̄a femina t . r . e .
p̄ man . 7 p̄ . ɪ . hid . 7 . dim̄ . 7 . xv . ac̄ . Sep . ɪɪ . car̄ . in dn̄io . 7 . ɪ . car̄ .
hom̄ . 7 . ɪɪ . uiłł . ɪɪɪ . bor . Tc̄ . 7 . p̄ . ɪ . ser̄ . m̄ . ɪɪ . xvɪ . ac̄ . p̄ti . Tc̄ . uac̄ .
7 . ɪɪ . runc̄ . 7 . ʟx . porc̄ . 7 . ɪɪɪ . uasa apū . m̄ . ɪɪɪɪ . anim̄ . 7 . ɪ . runc̄ .

7 . ɪ . pułł . 7 . xʟɪɪɪɪ . porc̄ . 7 . ʟxxɪɪ . oū . 7 . ɪɪɪ . uasa apū . Tc̄ uał . xʟ . soł .
m̄ . ʟx .
S̨urmere ten& . T . in dn̄io qd̄ tenuit . lib̄ . hō . t . r . e . p̄ . m̄ . 7 . p̄ . ɪ . hid .
7 . dim̄ . Sep . ɪɪ . car̄ . in dn̄io . 7 . ɪ . uiłł . 7 . vɪ . ser̄ . xx . ac̄ . p̄ti . ɪ . moł .
Tc̄ . vɪ . an̄ . 7 . ɪ . runc̄ . 7 . xɪɪ . porc̄ . 7 . ʟx . oū . m̄ . xɪɪ . an̄ . 7 . xxx . porc̄ .
7 . c . oū . ɪɪ . min̄ . 7 . ɪ . runc̄ . 7 . ɪɪɪ . pułł . Tc̄ 7 p̄ . uał . xʟ . soł . m̄ . ʟx .
Tiliḃiam ten& . T . in dn̄io qd̄ tenuit lib̄ hō . t . r . e . p̄ man . 7 . p̄ . ɪ . hid .
7 . xxxvɪɪɪ . ac̄ . Sep . ɪɪɪ . car̄ . in dn̄io . 7 . ɪ . car̄ . hom̄ . 7 . v . uiłł . 7 . ɪ . borđ .
7 . vɪ . ser̄ . Siłu . xx . porc̄ . xvɪɪɪɪ . ac̄ . p̄ti . Tc̄ . xv . an̄ . 7 . xʟ . porc̄ . 7
ʟxxx . oū . 7 . vɪ . uasa ap̄ . m̄ . v . an̄ . 7 . ɪ . runc̄ . 7 . xxxvɪ . porc̄ . 7 . ʟxɪɪɪ .
oū . Tc̄ 7 p̄ uał . ʟx . soł . m̄ . c .

. xxxɪx . Terra Rogeri de Ramis . Hund de Hidingforda .

Raines ten& Roḡ in dn̄io . qd̄ tenuit Aluuin lib̄ hō . t . r . e .
p̄ manerio . 7 . p̄ . ɪ . hid . 7 . xx . ac̄ . Sep . ɪɪ . car̄ . in dn̄io . Tc̄ . 7 . p̄ . ɪɪɪɪ .
car̄ hom̄ . m̄ . ɪɪɪ . Tc̄ 7 p̄ . ɪx . uiłł . m̄ . vɪɪɪ . Sep . v . bord . tc̄ . 7 p̄ . ɪɪɪɪ .
ser̄ . m̄ . ɪɪɪ . Siłu . c . porc̄ . ɪ . moł . Tc̄ . vɪɪɪ . uac̄ . m̄ . ɪɪɪ . tc̄ .
. ɪ . runc̄ . m̄ nułł . Sep . c . oū . tc̄ . xxx . porc̄ . m̄ . xʟ . Sep uał . ɪɪɪɪ . lib̄ .
De hoc manerio ten& . Roḡ . de . R . xxx . ac̄ . 7 Wiḃga . xxx . ac̄ .
7 uał . xx . soł in eod p̄tio .

Raines ten& . R . in dn̄io . qd̄ tenuit Edric lib̄ hō . t . r . e . p̄ Man .
7 . p̄ . ɪ . hid . tc̄ . ɪɪ . car̄ . in dn̄io . P̄ 7 m̄ . ɪ . m̄ dim̄ . car̄ . hom̄ . 7 . ɪɪɪ . bor . tc̄ 7 p̄
. vɪ . ser̄ . m̄ . ɪɪɪ . Siłu . xʟ . porc̄ . xɪɪɪ . ac̄ . p̄ti . Sep uał . ʟx . soł .

6 Tihel holds STURMER in lordship, which a free woman held before
1066 as a manor, for 1½ hides and 15 acres. Always 2 ploughs in
lordship; 1 men's plough.
  2 villagers; 3 smallholders. Then and later 1 slave, now 2.
  Meadow, 16 acres. Then a cow, 2 cobs, 60 pigs and 3 beehives;
    now 4 cattle, 1 cob, 1 foal, 44 pigs, 72 sheep and 3 beehives. 82 b
Value then 40s; now 60[s].

7 Tihel holds STURMER in lordship, which a free man held before
1066 as a manor, for 1½ hides. Always 2 ploughs in lordship;
1 villager; 6 slaves.
  Meadow, 20 acres; 1 mill. Then 6 cattle, 1 cob, 12 pigs and 60
    sheep; now 12 cattle, 30 pigs, 100 sheep less 2, 1 cob and
    3 foals.
Value then and later 40s; now 60[s].

8 Tihel holds TILBURY (-JUXTA-CLARE) in lordship, which a free man
held before 1066 as a manor, for 1 hide and 38 acres. Always 3
ploughs in lordship; 1 men's plough;
  5 villagers; 1 smallholder; 6 slaves.
  Woodland, 20 pigs; meadow, 19 acres. Then 15 cattle, 40 pigs,
    80 sheep and 6 beehives; now 5 cattle, 1 cob, 36 pigs and
    63 sheep.
Value then and later 60s; now 100[s].

39   **LAND OF ROGER OF RAISMES**

  Hundred of HINCKFORD
1 Roger holds RAYNE in lordship which Alwin, a free man, held
  before 1066 as a manor for 1 hide and 20 acres. Always 2 ploughs
  in lordship. Then and later 4 men's ploughs, now 3.
    Then and later 9 villagers, now 8; always 5 smallholders.
    Then and later 4 slaves, now 3.
    Woodland, 100 pigs; meadow, 11 acres; 1 mill. Then 8 cows,
      now 3; then 1 cob, now none; always 100 sheep. Then 30
      pigs, now 40.
  Value always £4.
    Of this manor, Roger holds 30 acres from Roger, and Wiberga
  (holds) 30 acres.
  Value 20s in the same assessment.

2 Roger holds RAYNE in lordship which Edric, a free man, held   83 a
  before 1066 as a manor for 1 hide. Then 2 ploughs in lordship;
  later and now 1. Now ½ men's plough;
    3 smallholders. Then and later 6 slaves, now 3.
    Woodland, 40 pigs; meadow, 13 acres.
  Value always 60s.

⟨V⟩ Hedingham ten& Garengeᴙ de.R.qd̅ tenuit Goduin lib̅ hō̅.t̄.r̄.c̄.
p̰.man̄.⁊ p̰.dim̄.hid̄.Sēp.ɪɪ.caᴙ in dn̄io.⁊.ɪɪɪ.caᴙ.hom̄.⁊.vɪɪɪ.uilt̄.
Tc̄.⁊ p̄.ɪ.bor.m̂.ɪɪɪ.Tc̄.ɪɪɪɪ.ſeᴙ.Poſt ⁊ m̂.ɪɪ.Tc̄.⁊ p̄.filu̅.ꝺc.por.m̂.ꝺ.
xvɪɪɪ.ac̄.p̊ti.Huic manerio sēp adjacent.ɪɪ.ſoc̄.de.ɪɪɪ.ac̄.Tc̄ ⁊ p̄.ual̄
.ɪɪɪɪ.lib̄.m̂.c.ſol̄.

⟨V⟩ Hund̄ de Laſſendana . Metcinges ten& . R . in dn̄io qd̄ tenuit
Ormaᴙ lib̅ hō̅.t̄.r̄.c̄.p̰ man̄.⁊ p̰ dim̄.hid̄.Tc̄.vɪ.uilt̄.m̂.ɪɪɪ.Tc̄.xɪɪ.
bor.m̂.xvɪɪɪ.Tc̄.vɪ.ſeᴙ.m̂.ɪɪɪɪ.Sēp.ɪɪ.caᴙ in dn̄io.Tc̄.in̄t hōes.v.caᴙ
m̂.ɪɪɪ.Silu̅.xʟ.por.xx.ac̄.p̊ti.m̂.ɪ.mol̄.Sēp.ɪɪ.runc̄.⁊.ɪɪ.uac̄.
cu̅ uit̄.⁊.c.ou̅.tc̄.xxx.por.m̂.xx.Sēp.xxxv.cap̄.Sēp ual̄.c.ſol̄.
de hoc manerio ten& Anſchetilĺ de.R.xvɪ.ac̄.⁊.ual̄.v.ſolᴙ in eod̄
p̄tio.⁊.ɪɪɪ.ſoc̄ tenentes libᴙ.xvɪɪɪ.ac̄.p̄tinent huic manerio q̂s ten&
Gerold̄ de.R.⁊.Rog̅ dic̄ ſe eos habᴙ in eſcangio.Sēp.dim̄.caᴙ.Tc̄.⁊ p̄.
ual̄.x.ſolᴙ.m̂.ɪɪɪ.

⟨V⟩ Delham.ten&.R.in dn̄io.qd̄ tenuit Aluric̄.cap̄.p̰ man̄.⁊.p̰.
.ɪɪ.hid̄.⁊.dim̄.tc̄.vɪɪ.uilt̄.m̂.v.Sēp.xxɪɪɪɪ.bor.tc̄.ɪɪɪɪ.ſeᴙ.m̂.ɪɪɪ.
Tc̄.ɪɪ.caᴙ.in dn̄io.m̂.ɪɪɪ.tc̄.in̄t hōes.x.caᴙ.m̂.v.Silu̅.ccʟ.porc̄.
xʟ.ac̄.p̊ti.Tc̄.ɪ.mol̄.m̂.ɪɪ.Tc̄.ɪɪ.runc̄.m̂.x.Tc̄.v.uac̄.m̂.ɪɪɪ.
Tc̄.xʟ.ou̅.m̂.c.Tc̄.xxv.por.m̂.xxx.Sēp ual̄.xɪɪ.lib̄.
De hoc manerio ten& Gerold̄.xxx.ac̄.⁊.ual̄.x.ſolᴙ.in eod̄ p̄tio.
In bura h̅t.R.xxv.ac̄.Sēp.ɪɪɪ.bor.⁊.dim̄.caᴙ.Silu̅.xv.porc̄.

83 b
.ɪ.ac̄.p̊ti.Val̄.vɪɪ.ſolᴙ.

3 Warengar holds (Sible) HEDINGHAM from Roger which Godwin, a free man, held before 1066 as a manor for ½ hide. Always 2 ploughs in lordship; 3 men's ploughs;
  > 8 villagers. Then and later 1 smallholder, now 3; then 4 slaves, later and now 2.
  > Woodland, then and later 600 pigs, now 500; meadow, 18 acres.
  To this manor have always been attached 2 Freemen with 3 acres.
  Value then and later £4; now 100s.

Hundred of LEXDEN
4 Roger holds MESSING in lordship which Ordmer, a free man, held before 1066 as a manor for ½ hide.
  > Then 6 villagers, now 3; then 12 smallholders, now 18; then 6 slaves, now 3. Always 2 ploughs in lordship. Then among the men 6 ploughs, now 3.
  > Woodland, 40 pigs; meadow, 20 acres; now 1 mill. Always 2 cobs, 2 cows with calves, and 100 sheep. Then 30 pigs, now 20; always 35 goats.
  Value always 100s.
  Of this manor, Ansketel holds 16 acres from Roger.
  Value 5s in the same assessment.
  3 Freemen belong to this manor, who hold 18 acres freely (and) whom Gerald holds from Roger. Roger states he has them in exchange. Always ½ plough.
  Value then and later 10s; now 3[s].

5 Roger holds DEDHAM in lordship, which Aelfric Kemp held as a manor, for 2½ hides.
  > Then 7 villagers, now 5; always 24 smallholders. Then 4 slaves, now 3. Then 2 ploughs in lordship, now 3. Then among the men 10 ploughs, now 5.
  > Woodland, 250 pigs; meadow, 40 acres; then 1 mill, now 2. Then 2 cobs, now 10; then 5 cows, now 3; then 40 sheep, now 100; then 25 pigs, now 30.
  Value always £12.
  Of this manor, Gerald holds 30 acres. Value 10s in the same assessment.

6 In (Mount) BURES Roger has 25 acres.
  > Always 3 smallholders; ½ plough.
  > Woodland, 15 pigs; meadow, 1 acre.
  Value 7s.

83 b

⟨V⟩ Hunđ de Tendringa . Bradefeldā ten& . R . in dñio . qđ tenuit

Aluric̄ camp . ᵱ man̄ . 7 . ᵱ . ɪɪɪɪ . hiđ ⸱ 7 . dim̄ . Tc̄ . vɪɪ . uiłł . Poſt 7 . m̄ . ɪɪɪɪ

Sēp . x . bor . 7 . ɪɪ . ſer . 7 . ɪɪ . car̄ . in dñio . tc̄ . 7 p . vɪɪ . car̄ . hom̄ . m̄ . ɪɪɪ . Silu.

xxx . porc̄ . ɪ . ſał . Tc̄ . ɪɪɪɪ . uac̄ . c̄ uił . m̄ nułł . Sēp . c . oũ . Tc̄ . xx . porc̄ .

m̄ . xxxɪɪɪ . Tc̄ . 7 ᵱ uał . vɪɪ . liƀ . m̄ . Lx . ſoł . De hoc manerio ten&

queđā uxor ſui militis . Dimiđ . hiđ . 7 . uał . x . ſoł in eođ ᵱtio .

⟨V⟩ Erlegam ten& . R . in dñio qđ tenuit Bond̄ ᵱ . man̄ . 7 . ᵱ . ɪ . hiđ .

Sēp . ɪ . uiłł . Tc̄ . xɪ . bor . m̄ . x . tc̄ . ɪ . ſer̄ . m̄ . n̄ . Sēp . ɪɪ . car̄ . in dñio .

tc̄ . 7 p . ɪx . car̄ . hom̄ . m̄ . ɪ . Silu . xL . por . ɪɪɪɪ . ac̄ . 7 . dim̄ . ᵱti . Tc̄ . xL . oũ ,

m̄ . c . Tc̄ . ɪɪ . uac̄ . 7 . ɪɪɪ . runc̄ . m̄ nułł . Tc̄ . 7 . p uał . ɪɪɪɪ . liƀ . m̄ . xxx . ſoł .

De hoc manerio ten& Rađ de haſtinges . xxx . ac̄ . 7 uał . x . ſoł

in eođ . ᵱtio .

⟨V⟩ Maneſtunā ten& . R . in dñio qđ tenuit Alſelm t . r . e . ᵱ . man̄ .

7 . ᵱ . ɪ . hiđ . 7 . xxv . ac̄ . Sēp . ɪ . uiłł . Tc̄ . 7 . p̄ . ɪɪɪɪ . bor . m̄ . ɪɪɪ . Sēp . ɪ . ſer .

tc̄ . 7 p . ɪɪ . car̄ in dñio . m̄ . ɪ . tc̄ . inƒ hōes . ɪ . car̄ . m̄ nułł . Silu . xv . porc̄ .

. ɪ . ac̄ . 7 . dim̄ . ᵱti . Paſt . xv . oũ . m̄ . ɪ . ſał . Tc̄ . 7 p uał . ɪɪɪɪ . liƀ . m̄ . xx . ſoł .

⟨V⟩ Mitteſleam ten& uxor ~~Albici~~ ᴴᵉⁿʳⁱᶜⁱ· de . R . qđ tenuit Alric̄ ᵱ . man̄ .

7 . ᵱ . ɪ . hiđ . Sēp . ɪ . borđ . tc̄ . ɪɪ . car̄ . m̄ . nułł . Tc̄ uał . xx . ſoł . m̄ . ɪɪ . ſoł .

⟨Γ⟩ In Cliua ten& . R . in dñio . vɪɪɪ . liƀos hōes . de . xxx . ac̄ . 7 . ɪ . car̄ .

7 . uał . v . ſoł .

⟨Γ⟩ In herlegā ten& . R . i dñio . vɪ . liƀos hōes . de . ɪ . hiđ . 7 . ɪɪ . car̄ . 7 uał .

xL . ſoł . De hoc ten& . Rađ . x . ac̄ . 7 . Reſtołt . xL . ac̄ . 7 uał . xx .

ſoł in eođ ᵱtio . hoc eſt ᵱ eſcangio .

Hundred of TENDRING

7 Roger holds BRADFIELD in lordship, which Aelfric Kemp held as a manor, for 4½ hides.

> Then 7 villagers, later and now 4. Always 10 smallholders; 2 slaves; 2 ploughs in lordship. Then and later 7 men's ploughs, now 3.
>
> Woodland, 30 pigs; 1 salt-house. Then 4 cows with calves, now none; always 100 sheep. Then 20 pigs, now 33.

Value then and later £7; now 60s.

Of this manor, the wife of his man-at-arms holds ½ hide.

Value 10s in the same assessment.

8 Roger holds ARDLEIGH in lordship, which Bondi held as a manor, for 1 hide.

> Always 1 villager. Then 11 smallholders, now 10; then 1 slave, now none. Always 2 ploughs in lordship. Then and later 9 men's ploughs, now 1.
>
> Woodland, 40 pigs; meadow, 4½ acres. Then 40 sheep, now 100; then 2 cows and 3 cobs, now none.

Value then and later £4; now 30s.

Of this manor, Ralph of Hastings holds 30 acres.

Value 10s in the same assessment.

9 Roger holds JACQUES HALL in lordship, which Alfhelm held before 1066 as a manor, for 1 hide and 25 acres.

> Always 1 villager. Then and later 4 smallholders, now 3; always 1 slave. Then and later 2 ploughs in lordship, now 1. Then among the men 1 plough, now none.
>
> Woodland, 15 pigs; meadow, 1½ acres; pasture, 15 sheep; now 1 salt-house.

Value then and later £4; now 20s.

10 Henry's wife holds MISTLEY from Roger, which Alric held as a manor, for 1 hide.

> Always 1 smallholder. Then 2 ploughs, now none.

Value then 20s; now 2s.

11 In CLIFF Roger holds in lordship 8 free men with 30 acres. 1 plough.

Value 5s.

12 In ARDLEIGH Roger holds in lordship 6 free men with 1 hide. 2 ploughs.

Value 40s.

> Of this, Ralph holds 10 acres, Restald (holds) 40 acres.

Value 20s in the same assessment. This is by exchange.

TERRA Joħis filij Walerami . Nutleam ten& Joħs fili ernucū̄
de Joħe . qđ tenuit Harold . t . r . e . ꝑ . man . 7 . ꝑ . IIII . hiđ . 7 . xxx . ac .
tc̄ . v . car . in dn̄io . m̄ . III . tc̄ . IIII . car . hominū . m̄ . II . Tc̄ . VII . uiłł . m̄ . v .
Tc̄ . xIII ₍ bor . m̄ . xI . tc̄ . IIII . ſer . m̄ . nułł . Tc̄ . ſiłu . cccxxx . por . m̄ .
. ce . xxIIII . ac . ꝑti . Sēp . I . moł . Paſt . de . vI . đ . Tc̄ . I . runc . 7 . II . uac .
m̄ nichil . Tc̄ . uał . vII . lib . m̄ . vI .

⌐Hund de Hidingforda . Salinges ten& Turſtin de . Joħe .
qđ tenuit . I . lib ħo t . r . e . ꝑ maner . 7 . ꝑ . dim . hiđ . Tc̄ . II . car . in dn̄io .
Poſt nułł . m̄ . I . Tc̄ . I . car . 7 . dim . hom . Poſt nulla . m̄ . dim . Tc̄ . III . uiłł .
7 . I . pbr . Poſt . I . m̄ . II . uiłł . 7 . I . pbr . Tc̄ . 7 . ꝑ . III . bor . m̄ . v . Tc̄ . IIII . ſer .
P 7 . m̄ . III . Tc̄ . 7 ꝑ ſiłu . ccL . porc . m̄ . cc . x . ac . ꝑti . Vał . Lx . ſoł .

⌐Mapledeſtedam ten& Oſmund de Joħe . qđ . Grim lib ħo . t . r . e . ꝑ
man . 7 . ꝑ . dim . hiđ . Tc̄ . II . car . in dn̄io . Poſt nulla . m̄ . I . Tc̄ . II . bor .
Poſt . I . m̄ . v . 7 . I . pbr . Sēp . II . ſer . Tc̄ . ſiłu . Lx . por . Poſt 7 . m̄ . xvI .
. III . ac . ꝑti . Tc̄ . I . moł . quē m̄ ten& Wiłł de garenda . ꝑ uadimonio .
Tc̄ . nichil rec . m̄ . II . uac . 7 . xIIII . porc . 7 . LvII . ou . Tc̄ . uał . xL .
ſoł . Poſt 7 . m̄ . xxx .

⌐Heni . ten& Roḡ de . Joħe qđ tenuit lib ħo . t . r . e . ꝑ . maner .
7 . ꝑ . II . hiđ . 7 . dim . Tc̄ . II . car . in dn̄io . Poſt . I . m̄ . II . Sēp . I . car .
hom . tc̄ . 7 ꝑ . I . uiłł . m̄ nułł . Sēp . III . bor . 7 . II . ſer . Tc̄ . ſiłu . Lx . porc .

poſt . 7 . m̄ . xxx . xII . ac . ꝑti . Tc̄ . vI . anim . 7 . xv . porc . 7 . xI . ou . m̄ . v . runc .
7 . vIII . an . 7 . xxx . porc . 7 . LxvI . ou . 7 . xv . cap . huic manerio jac&
una conſuetudo . de . xxII . đ . 7 . ob . quæ ē de Sutbia . Tc̄ uał . xL . ſoł .
Poſt . 7 m̄ . L .
In Bura ten& hugo de . I . xv . ac . qs tenuit Toſti lib ħo . Sēp . dim .
car . 7 . II . uiłł . 7 . II . bor . Silu . IIII . porc . I . ac . ꝑti . vał . vI . ſoł . hec tra
ē in comitatu de Sudfolc .

Hundred of WITHAM

1 John son of Ernucion holds NOTLEY from John, which Harold held before 1066 as a manor, for 4 hides and 30 acres. Then 5 ploughs in lordship, now 3. Then 4 men's ploughs, now 2.

Then 7 villagers, now 5; then 13 smallholders, now 11; then 4 slaves, now none.

Woodland, then 330 pigs, now 200; meadow, 24 acres; always 1 mill. Pasture at 6d. Then 1 cob and 2 cows; now nothing.

Value then £7; now [£] 6.

Hundred of HINCKFORD

2 Thurstan holds (Great) SALING from John, which 1 free man held before 1066 as a manor, for ½ hide. Then 2 ploughs in lordship, later none, now 1. Then 1½ men's ploughs, later none, now ½.

Then 3 villagers and 1 priest, later 1, now 2 villagers and 1 priest; then and later 3 smallholders, now 5; then 4 slaves, later and now 3.

Woodland, then and later 250 pigs, now 200; meadow, 10 acres.

Value 60s.

3 Osmund holds (Little) MAPLESTEAD from John which Grim, a free man, [held] before 1066 as a manor for ½ hide. Then 2 ploughs in lordship, later none, now 1.

Then 2 smallholders, later 1, now 5 and 1 priest; always 2 slaves.

Woodland, then 60 pigs, later and now 16; meadow, 3 acres; then 1 mill, which William of Warenne now holds as a pledge.

Then he acquired nothing; now 2 cows, 14 pigs and 57 sheep.

Value then 40s; later and now 30[s].

4 Roger holds HENNY from John, which a free man held before 1066 as a manor, for 2½ hides. Then 2 ploughs in lordship, later 1, now 2. Always 1 men's plough.

Then and later 1 villager, now none. Always 3 smallholders; 2 slaves.

Woodland, then 60 pigs, later and now 30; meadow, 12 acres.   84 b

Then 6 cattle, 15 pigs and 11 sheep; now 5 cobs, 8 cattle, 30 pigs, 66 sheep and 15 goats.

To this manor belongs a customary due of 22½d which is from Sudbury.

Value then 40s; later and now 50[s].

5 In BURES Hugh holds from John 15 acres which Tosti, a free man, held. Always ½ plough;

2 villagers; 2 smallholders.

Woodland, 4 pigs; meadow, 1 acre.

Value 6s.

This land is in the County of Suffolk.

Hund de Angra   Fifhidam ten& Rog de Johe qd tenuit
Leuric.t.r.e.ꝑ man.7.ꝑ.i.hid.7.dim.7.xxx.ac.Tc.xii.uitt.m.vii.
tc.7.ꝑ.ii.bor.m.x.sep.iiii.ser.7.ii.car.in dnio.tc.7.ꝑ.iiii.car
hom.m.iii.Silu.cccc.porc.x.ac.ꝑti.m.i.mol.m.xi.uac.7.xi.
porc.7.lx.ou.7.i.uas aꝑ.Tc.7.ꝑ.uat.v.lib.m.vii.

Altam Fifhida ten& Ide de eod.qd tenuit Aleftan ꝑ man.7.ꝑ
xxx.ac.Sep.iii.bor.Tc.i.car.m nutt.Silu.xl.porc.vi.ac.ꝑti.Sep
uat.xx.fot.

Angra.ten& Ide de eod qd tenuit Leuric.ꝑ man.7.ꝑ.iii.uirg.
Sep.vi.bor.7.i.ser.7.i.car.in dnio.Silu.cc.porc.viii.ac.ꝑti.m.
xxx.porc.7.xl.ou.Tc.uat.xl.fot.7.qn rec.xx.fot.m uat.xl.fot.

Hund de Ceffeorda.Auileiam tenuit libe fuan t.r.e.ꝑ.man.
7.ꝑ.iii.hid.7.dim.m ten& Johs in dnio.ꝑ tantude.Tc.viii.uitt.m.vi.
tc.iii.bor.m.v.tc.iiii.ser.m.i.tc.ii.car.in dnio.m.i.tc.int hoes
.iii.car.m.ii.lx.ac.ꝑti.Tc 7 ꝑ uat.viii.lib.m.c.fot.7 qda lib ho
vlsi tenuit.dim.hid.qm poffet uende.f; uualeram ꝑat ihois addidit
eu huic manerio.Sep.i.uitt.7.i.bor.tc.dim.car.m nichil.Tc.uat

.x.fot.7.qn rec.fimilit.m uat.vii.fot.

Hundred of ONGAR

6 Roger holds FYFIELD from John, which Leofric held before 1066 as a manor, for 1½ hides and 30 acres.

Then 12 villagers, now 7; then and later 2 smallholders, now 10. Always 4 slaves; 2 ploughs in lordship. Then and later 4 men's ploughs, now 3.

Woodland, 400 pigs; meadow, 10 acres; now 1 mill. Now 11 cows, 11 pigs, 60 sheep and 1 beehive.

Value then and later £5; now [£] 7.

7 He also holds the other FYFIELD from the same (John), which Alstan held as a manor, for 30 acres.

Always 3 smallholders. Then 1 plough, now none.

Woodland, 40 pigs; meadow, 6 acres.

Value always 20s.

8 He also holds (High) ONGAR from the same (John), which Leofric held as a manor, for 3 virgates.

Always 6 smallholders; 1 slave; 1 plough in lordship.

Woodland, 200 pigs; meadow, 8 acres. Now 30 pigs and 40 sheep.

Value then 40s; when acquired, 20s. Value now 40s.

Hundred of CHAFFORD

9 Swein held AVELEY freely before 1066 as a manor, for 3½ hides. Now John holds (it) in lordship, for as much.

Then 8 villagers, now 6; then 3 smallholders, now 5; then 4 slaves, now 1. Then 2 ploughs in lordship, now 1. Then among the men 3 ploughs, now 2.

Meadow, 60 acres.

Value then and later £8; now 100s.

A free man, Wulfsi, held ½ hide which he could sell; but Waleran, John's father, added him to this manor.

Always 1 villager; 1 smallholder. Then ½ plough, now nothing.

Value then 10s; when acquired, the same. Value now 7s.   85 a

TERRA.Robti filij Corbutionis. Hund de bdeſtapla.Doddenhenc

ten& Girard de.R.qd tenuit Aluric libe.t.r.e.p man.7.p.1.hid.7.xvii.ac.

Sep.1.car.Silu.xx.por.Val.xx.ſol.

Hund de Witham Smalelant ten& Nigell de.R.qd tenuit comes

Algar.p man.7.p.ii.hid.Sep.1.car.7.1.bor.7.1.ſer.ix.ac.pti.m.ii.

partes piſcinæ.Tc.ii.anim.m.iiii.Tc.1.por.m.xxv.m.ii.pull.

tc.vi.ou.m.xxxv.Tc.vi.cap.m null Sep ual.xx.ſol.

Hund de beuentreu.Leintuna ten&.R.in dnio.qd tenuit

Harold.t.r.e.p man.7.p.iiii.hid.7.dim.Tc.ii.car.in dnio.m null.

Sep.1.car.hom.Tc.iii.uill.m.v.7.1.pbr.Tc.iiii.bor.m.vi.tc.iiii.ſer.

m null.Silu.ccc.porc.xl.ac.pti.Tc.vii.piſc.m null.Tc.1.mol.m.n.

7.adhuc poſst reſtaurari.ii.car.Tc.ual.iiii.lib.m.xx.ſol.

In Leintuna.ten&.R.iii.hid.qs tenebat.viii.ſoc.t.r.e.

tc.iiii.car.m null.m.vi.uill.7.1.bor.Silu.x.por.

xxx.ac.pti.Dim.piſc.tc.m.n.Tc ual.lx.ſol

m.xx.7 iſti ſoc reddebant.t.r.e.conſuet

ad hauelingas.maneriu reg.7.m reddt.

Hundred of BARSTABLE

1   Gerard holds DODDINGHURST from Robert, which Aelfric held
    freely before 1066 as a manor, for 1 hide and 17 acres. Always 1
    plough.
        Woodland, 20 pigs.
    Value 20s.

Hundred of WITHAM

2   Nigel holds SMALLANDS from Robert, which Earl Algar held as a
    manor, for 2 hides. Always 1 plough;
        1 smallholder; 1 slave.
        Meadow, 9 acres; now 2 parts of a fishery. Then 2 cattle, now
            4; then 1 pig, now 25; now 2 foals; then 6 sheep, now 35;
            then 6 goats, now none.
    Value always 20s.

Hundred of BECONTREE

3   Robert holds LEYTON in lordship, which Harold held before 1066
    as a manor, for 4½ hides. Then 2 ploughs in lordship, now none.
    Always 1 men's plough.
        Then 3 villagers, now 5 and 1 priest; then 4 smallholders, now 6;
            then 4 slaves, now none.
        Woodland, 300 pigs; meadow, 40 acres; then 7 fisheries, now
            none; then 1 mill, now none. A further 2 ploughs can be
            restored.
    Value then £4; now 20s.

4   In LEYTON Robert holds 3 hides, which 8 Freemen held before
    1066. Then 4 ploughs, now none.
        Now 6 villagers; 1 smallholder.
        Woodland, 10 pigs; meadow, 30 acres; then ½ fishery, now
            none.
    Value then 60s; now 20[s].
        These Freemen paid a customary due before 1066 to the King's
    manor of Havering (-atte-Bower); they pay it now.

⌐Lalinge . ten& . W . de . R . q̅d̅ tenuit
Leuin̅c lib̅ ho̅ . t̅ . r̅ . e̅ . p̅ . manerio

7 p̅ . IIII . hid̅ . 7 . dim̅ . te̅ . III . bor . m̅ . v . Se̅p . IIII . ſer̅ . 7 . II . car̅ . Paſtura
XL . ou̅ . Te̅ . II . runc̅ . m̅ . III . Te̅ . VII . an̅ . m̅ . IX . Te̅ . CVII . ou̅ . m̅ . CXXIIII .
Te̅ . VI . cap̅ . m̅ . nult̅ . Te̅ uat̅ . III . lib̅ . m̅ . IIII . ⌐Hund de Celme...fort.

⌐Haningefelda̅ ten& Ranulf̅ de . R . q̅d̅ tenuit Aleſtan̅ . lib̅ ho̅ . t̅ . r̅ . e̅
p̅ man̅ . 7 . p̅ . I . hid̅ . 7 . dim̅ . m̅ . I . bor . 7 . I . ſer̅ . 7 ſe̅p . I . car̅ . II . ac̅ . p̅ti . Silu̅
. XII . porc̅ . Se̅p uat̅ . XXX . ſot̅ .

⌐Waltham ten& . W . de . R . q̅d̅ . tenuit Vlsi̅ p̅ maner̅ . 7 . p̅ . I . hid̅ . 7 . XXX . ac̅ .
te̅ . I . uitt̅ . m̅ null̅ . te̅ . IX . bor . m̅ . XI . Se̅p . I . ſer̅ . 7 . I . car̅ . Silu̅ . XXX . por .
. VIII . ac̅ . p̅ti . Se̅p . I . mot̅ . Te̅ uat̅ . XXX . ſot̅ . m̅ . XL .

⌐In Ead̅ ten& Ranulf̅ . de . R . I . lib̅m ho̅em . de . XXX . ac̅ . que̅ inuaſit
. R . Se̅p . dim̅ . car̅ . vat̅ . IIII . ſot̅ .

⌐Bedeneſtedam ten& Nigell̅ de . R . q̅d̅ tenuit Stercher . p̅ man̅ .
7 . p̅ . III . hid̅ . 7 . dim̅ . Te̅ . II . uitt̅ . m̅ . null̅ . Se̅p . VII . bor . 7 . II . ſer̅ . 7 . I . car̅
in d̅n̅io . 7 . I . car̅ . hom̅ . Silu̅ . c . porc̅ . I . ac̅ . 7 . dim̅ . p̅ti . Te̅ . I . runc̅ . 7 . IIII .
uac̅ . cu̅ uit̅ . m̅ null̅ . Te̅ . XL . ou̅ . m̅ . XXX . te̅ . XVI . por . m̅ . VII . Te̅ uat̅ .
XL . ſot̅ . m̅ . L . 7 q̅d̅a lib̅ ho̅ tenuit dim̅ hid̅ . que̅ inuaſit . R . m̅ ten&
                    Godefrid de eo . te̅ . 7 . p̅ . dim̅ . car̅ . m̅ nult̅ . Silu̅ . x . porc̅ .
                    vat̅ . x . ſot̅ .

                    Hund de Tendringa . Fuletuna̅ ten&
                    Girard̅ de̅ . R . q̅d̅ tenuit Ednod lib̅ ho̅ . t̅ . r̅ . e̅
                    p̅ man̅ . 7 . p̅ . II . hid̅ . 7 . dim̅ . 7 . XX . ac̅ .
                    te̅ . I . uitt̅ . m̅ . IIII . Se̅p . II . bor . 7 . II . ſer̅ .
                    7 . II . car̅ . in d̅n̅io . te̅ . I . car̅ hom̅ .
                    m̅ . nult̅ . III . ac̅ . p̅ti . Paſt . LX . ou̅ .

Te̅ . IIII . anim̅ . m̅ . III . Te̅ . I . runc̅ . m̅ . null̅ . Te̅ . X . por . m̅ . XX . Te̅ . XL .
ou̅ . m̅ . XX . Te̅ . uat̅ . L . ſot̅ . 7 q̅n̅ rec̅ . XX . ſot̅ . m̅ uat̅ . L . ſot̅ .

5 W. holds LAWLING from Robert which Leofing, a free man, held
before 1066 as a manor for 4½ hides.   85 b
   Then 3 smallholders, now 5. Always 4 slaves; 2 ploughs.
   Pasture, 40 sheep. Then 2 cobs, now 3; then 7 cattle, now 9;
      then 107 sheep, now 124; then 6 goats, now none.
Value then £3; now [£] 4.

Hundred of CHELMSFORD

6 Ranulf holds HANNINGFIELD from Robert which Alstan, a free
man, held before 1066 as a manor for 1½ hides.
   Now 1 smallholder; 1 slave. Always 1 plough.
   Meadow, 2 acres; woodland, 12 pigs.
Value always 30s.

7 W. holds WALTHAM from Robert which Wulfsi held as manor, for
1 hide and 30 acres.
   Then 1 villager, now none; then 9 smallholders, now 11.
      Always 1 slave; 1 plough.
   Woodland, 30 pigs; meadow, 8 acres; always 1 mill.
Value then 30s; now 40[s].

8 In the same (Waltham) Ranulf holds from Robert 1 free man
with 30 acres whom Robert annexed. Always ½ plough.
Value 4s.

9 Nigel holds 'BENSTED' from Robert, which Starker held as a manor,
for 3½ hides.
   Then 2 villagers, now none. Always 7 smallholders; 2 slaves;
      1 plough in lordship; 1 men's plough.
   Woodland, 100 pigs; meadow, 1½ acres. Then 1 cob and 4 cows
      with calves, now none; then 40 sheep, now 30; then 16 pigs,
      now 7.
Value then 40s, now 50[s].
   A free man, whom Robert annexed, held ½ hide. Now Godfrey
holds (it) from him. Then and later ½ plough, now none.
   Woodland, 10 pigs.
Value 10s.

Hundred of TENDRING

10 Gerard holds FOULTON from Robert which Ednoth, a free man,
held before 1066 as a manor for 2½ hides and 20 acres.
   Then 1 villager, now 4. Always 2 smallholders; 2 slaves; 2
      ploughs in lordship. Then 1 men's plough, now none.
   Meadow, 3 acres; pasture, 60 sheep. Then 4 cattle, now 3;   86 a
      then 1 cob, now none; then 10 pigs, now 20; then 40 sheep,
      now 20.
Value then 50s; when acquired, 20s. Value now 50s.

Hund de . Rochefort . Pachefham ten& Idē . G . de . R . qđ tenuit
liƀ hō . p̃ . manerio . 7 . p̃ . dim . hiđ . 7 . xxx . ac̃ . Sēp . ii . bor . 7 . i . car̃ . in dñio
Tc̃ ual̃ . xl . fol̃ . m̃ . v.

Hund de Tureftapla . Tolefhuntā ten& Malger de . R . qđ
tenuit Sercar . p̃ mañ . 7 . p̃ . i . hiđ . Tc̃ . v . uilt̃ . m̃ . iiii . Tc̃ . i . bor . m̃ . vi.
Tc̃ . v . fer̃ . m̃ . ii . Tc̃ . 7 . p̃ . ii . car̃ . m̃ . i . in dñio . Tc̃ . 7 . p̃ . ii . car̃ . hom̃.
m̃ . i . Silũ . c . por̃ . i . ac̃ . p̃ti . Paft . lx . ou . Tc̃ . xv . an̄ . m̃ . ii . uac̃.
7 . i . uit̃ . Tc̃ . l . ou . m̃ . xxv . Tc̃ . i . runc̃ . m̃ null̃ . Tc̃ . ii . uafa ap̃ . m̃ . n̄.
Tc̃ . ual̃ . iiii . liƀ . Poft . iii . m̃ . xl . fol̃.
7 viii . liƀi hōes tenuer̃ . iiii . hiđ . 7 . ii . ac̃ . 7 . poffent ire q̃ uellent.
q̃s . Roƀ . inuafit . 7 . m̃ tenent . iiii . milites de . R . tc̃ . iiii . fer̃ . m̃ . ii.
fēp . ii . car̃ . filu . cxx . por̃ . Paft . lx . ou . i . fal̃ . Val̃ . l . fol̃.

TERRA Galteri diaconi . Hund de ƀdeftapla . In bura ten&
Galt̃ . ii . hiđ . de t̃ra Teddrici fris fui . 7 q̃dam miles ten& de eo . Sēp . i.
car̃ . 7 . i . bor̃ . 7 . i . fer̃ . 7 . xxx . ac̃ uaftatæ filuæ . Paft . lx . ou . huic manerio
addite ſt . xl . ac̃ . t̃ . regis Witti . q̃s tenuit liƀ hō . t̃ . r̃ . ē . 7 illas
habuit Tedric̃ . 7 . tc̃ ualebant . p̃dictæ hidæ . xl . fol̃ . 7 . m̃ . fimilit̃ . 7
xl . ac̃ . ual̃ . viii . fol̃ . 7 . iiii . đ . In dñio recepit Galt̃ . iiii . animal̃.

m̃ . fimilit̃ . Tc̃ . ii . runc̃ . m̃ . i . Tc̃ . c . ou . ii . min̄ . m̃ . lv . Tc̃ . x . . . . por̃c̃.
m̃ . xi.

Hund de Witbricteſherna . Purlai ten& Galt̃ in dñio qđ tenuit
Leuuin . t̃ . r̃ . e . p̃ mañ . 7 . p̃ . iii . hiđ . 7 . dim . Sēp . ii . uilt̃ . m̃ . i . bor . Tc̃.
. iii . fer̃ . m̃ . i . Tc̃ . ii . car̃ in dñio . m̃ . i . 7 . dim . Sēp . dim . car̃ . hom̃ . filũ.
. lx . por̃c̃ . Sēp . viii . anim̃ . Tc̃ . v . runc̃ . m̃ . iiii . Tc̃ . clii . ou . m̃ . lxxx.
tc̃ . lxii . por̃ . m̃ . xlvii . m̃ . xxiii . cap̃ . Sēp ual̃ . lx . fol̃.

Hundred of ROCHFORD

11 Gerard also holds PAGLESHAM from Robert, which a free man held
as a manor, for ½ hide and 30 acres.
    Always 1 smallholder; 1 plough in lordship.
    Value then 40s; now 5[s].

Hundred of THURSTABLE

12 Mauger holds TOLLESHUNT (Major) from Robert, which Starker
held as a manor, for 1 hide.
    Then 5 villagers, now 4; then 1 smallholder, now 6; then 5
    slaves, now 2. Then and later 2 ploughs in lordship, now 1.
    Then and later 2 men's ploughs, now 1.
    Woodland, 100 pigs; meadow, 1 acre; pasture, 60 sheep. Then
    15 cattle, now 2 cows and 1 calf; then 50 sheep, now 25;
    then 1 cob, now none; then 2 beehives, now none.
    Value then £4; later [£] 3; now 40s.
    8 free men, whom Robert annexed, held 4 hides and 2 acres
    and could go whither they would. Now 4 men-at-arms hold (them)
    from Robert.
    Then 4 slaves, now 2. Always 2 ploughs.
    Woodland, 120 pigs; pasture, 60 sheep; 1 salt-house.
    Value 50s.

42   LAND OF WALTER THE DEACON

Hundred of BARSTABLE

1 In BOWERS (Gifford) Walter holds 2 hides of his brother
Theodoric's land. A man-at-arms holds from him.
    Always 1 plough; 1 smallholder; 1 slave.
    Woodland, 30 acres, laid waste; pasture, 60 sheep.
    To this manor 40 acres were added after 1066, which a free
    man held before 1066. Theodoric had them.
    Value of the said hides, then 40s; now the same.
    Value of the 40 acres, 8s 4d.
    Walter acquired in lordship 4 cattle, now the same; then 2 cobs,   86 b
    now 1; then 100 sheep less 2, now 55; then 1 ... pigs, now 11.

Hundred of 'WIBERTSHERNE'

2 Walter holds PURLEIGH in lordship, which Leofwin held before
1066 as a manor, for 3½ hides.
    Always 2 villagers. Now 1 smallholder; then 3 slaves, now 1.
    Then 2 ploughs in lordship, now 1½. Always ½ men's plough.
    Woodland, 60 pigs. Always 8 cattle. Then 5 cobs, now 4; then
    152 sheep, now 80; then 62 pigs, now 47; now 23 goats.
    Value always 60s.

⁋Eiſtanes ten& Galt in dīnio. qđ. tenuit Dodinc. t̃. r̃. e̅. ꝑ. maner̃
7. ꝑ. ıı. hiđ. T̃c. vı. car̃. in dīnio. m̃. ıııı. T̃c. v. uiłł. 7. ı. pbr̃. M̃. ı. pbr̃
7. ııı. uiłł. T̃c. ıı. bor. m̃. xxv. T̃c. vıı. ſer̃. m̃. ı. T̃c. filu̅. ɒccc. por.
m̃. cccc. xxvı. ac̃. p̃ti. ı. mol̃. S̃ep. vı. uac̃. ıııı. uit̃ m̃. xv. añ. t̃c.
. ıı. runc̃. m̃. vı. T̃c. ʟxxx. ou̅. m̃. cxx. T̃c. ʟxxıııı. porc̃. m̃ ʟxıı.
T̃c. xxıııı. cap̃. m̃. xxxıııı. ıı. uaſa apū. T̃c uał. vıı. lib̃. m̃. vıııı.
⁋Purlai ten& Galt in dīnio. qđ tenuit Leuuin̄ cilt. ꝑ man̄. 7. ꝑ. v.
. hiđ. t̃. r̃. e̅. T̃c. x. uiłł. m̃. v. T̃c. ı. bor. m̃. vı. S̃ep. ıııı. ſer̃ 7. ııı. car̃.
in dīnio. 7. ıııı. car̃. hom̃. filu̅. c. porc̃. Paſt. c. ou̅. T̃c uał. vıı. lib̃. m̃.
uał. vı. lib̃.
⁋Fennā ten&. ı. miles de. G. qđ tenuit lib̃ ho̅. ꝑ man̄. 7. ꝑ. ıı. hiđ. ſep.
. ıı. bor. 7. ı. ſer̃. 7. ı. car̃. 7. uał. ʟ. ſoł. / H̃ de Laſſendena.
⁋Colun. ten&. ı. miles de. G. qđ tenuit Leuuin̄. ꝑ man̄. 7. ꝑ. đ.
hiđ. 7. xııı. ac̃. S̃ep. xıı. borđ. 7. ıı. ſer̃. 7. ıı. car̃. in dīnio. 7. ı. car̃.
hom̃. filu̅. c. porc̃. xııı. ac̃. p̃ti. S̃ep. ı. mol̃. T̃c. vı. anim̃. m̃. ıı.
t̃c. ıı. runc̃. m̃ nuł. t̃c. xıı. ou̅. m̃. xxıııı. T̃c. xvı. porc̃. m̃. xıııı.
m̃ xııı. cap̃. 7. ııı. uaſa. ap̃. S̃ep uał. xʟ. ſoł.

⁋Hunđ de Tendringa. Wicā ten& Galt in dīnio qđ tenuit
Edeua regina ꝑ man̄. 7. ꝑ. ıııı. hiđ. S̃ep. xıııı. uiłł. T̃c. xvııı. borđ. m̃
xxvııı. T̃c. ıııı. ſer̃. m̃. ııı. S̃ep. ıııı. car̃. in dīnio. T̃c. 7 ꝑ. xıı. car̃. hom̃.
m̃. vııı. Silu̅. c. porc̃. vııı. ac̃. p̃ti. T̃c. xıı. an̄. m̃. xıııı. S̃ep. ıı. runc̃.
T̃c. c. ou̅. m̃. ʟxxxıııı. T̃c. xʟ. porc̃. m̃ ʟxxı. T̃c. xxx. cap̃. m̃. xxxıııı.
t̃c. vıı. uaſa ap̃. m̃. x. T̃c. 7 ꝑ uał. vı. lib̃. 7. x. ſoł. m̃. vał. x. lib̃.
7 hanc t̃rā dedit. E. regina Walto poſt aduentū reg̃ Wiłłi.

[Hundred of DUNMOW]

3 Walter holds (Little) EASTON in lordship, which Doding held as a
   manor, for 2 hides. Then 6 ploughs in lordship, now 4.
   Then 5 villagers and 1 priest, now 1 priest and 3 villagers;
       then 2 smallholders, now 25; then 7 slaves, now 1.
   Woodland, then 800 pigs, now 400; meadow, 26 acres; 1 mill.
       Always 6 cows; 4 calves. Now 15 cattle; then 2 cobs, now 6;
       then 80 sheep, now 120; then 74 pigs, now 62; then 24 goats,
       now 34; 2 beehives.
   Value then £7; now [£] 8.

[Hundred of 'WIBERTSHERNE']

4 Walter holds PURLEIGH in lordship, which Young Leofwin held as
   a manor, for 5 hides before 1066.
   Then 10 villagers, now 5; then 1 smallholder, now 6. Always 4
       slaves; 3 ploughs in lordship; 4 men's ploughs.
   Woodland, 100 pigs; pasture, 100 sheep.
   Value then £7. Value now £6.

5 1 man-at-arms holds STOW MARIES from Walter, which a free man
   held as a manor, for 2 hides.
   Always 2 smallholders; 1 slave; 1 plough.
   Value 50s.

Hundred of LEXDEN

6 1 man-at-arms holds COLNE (Engaine) from Walter, which Leofwin
   held as a manor, for ½ hide and 13 acres.
   Always 12 smallholders; 2 slaves; 2 ploughs in lordship; 1 men's
       plough.
   Woodland, 100 pigs; meadow, 13 acres; always 1 mill. Then 6
       cattle, now 2; then 2 cobs, now none; then 12 sheep, now
       24; then 16 pigs, now 14; now 13 goats and 3 beehives.
   Value always 40s.

Hundred of TENDRING   87 a

7 Walter holds WIX in lordship, which Queen Edith held as a manor,
   for 4 hides.
   Always 14 villagers. Then 18 smallholders, now 28; then 4
       slaves, now 3. Always 4 ploughs in lordship. Then and later
       12 men's ploughs, now 8.
   Woodland, 100 pigs; meadow, 8 acres. Then 12 cattle, now 14;
       always 2 cobs. Then 100 sheep, now 84; then 40 pigs, now
       71; then 30 goats, now 34; then 7 beehives, now 10.
   Value then and later £6 10s. Value now £10.
   Queen Edith gave this land to Walter after King William's arrival.

Brumleiam ten& . I . miłes de Galło qđ ten . E . regina . p̄ maner̄
7 . p̄ . II . hiđ . xx . ac̄ . min̄ . Sēp . I . uiłł . tē . xvII . bor . m̄ . xv . Tē . IIII . ſer.
m̄ . III . Sēp . II . car̄ . in dn̄io . tē . int̄ h̄oes . vI . car̄ . m̄ . IIII . Silŭ . xL . porc̄.
. IIII . ac̄ . p̄ti . tē . Ix . anim̄ . m̄ . vII . tē . II . runc̄ . m̄ . IIII . Tē . c . oŭ . m̄ . cc.
tē . xII . por . m̄ . xxx . m̄ . II . uaſa apū . Tē uał . v . lib̄ . m̄ . IIII.

Hunđ đe Vdelesforda . Ceſtrefort . ten& . I . mił de Galło qđ tenuit
. E . regina . p̄ man̄ . 7 . p̄ . v . hiđ . Sēp . x . uiłł . tē . IIII . bor . m̄ . xvI . tē.
. IIII . ſer . m̄ . I . Sēp . II . car̄ . in dn̄io . 7 . III . car̄ . hom̄ . Silŭ . xx . porc̄ . vIII . ac̄.
p̄ti . Sēp . I . moł . Tē . II . anim̄ . m̄ . IIII . Tē . I . runc̄ . m̄ . nułł . Tē . xxxvI.
oŭ . m̄ . xLIII . tē . xvI . porc̄ . m̄ . xxxIIII . m̄ . xxIII . cap . Tē . uał . c.
ſoł . m̄ . vI . lib̄.

XLIII Terra Rogeri bigoti Hunđ de Hidingfort.

Hidingham ten& Garenger̄ de . R . p̄ . xxv . ac̄ . qs tenuer̄t
. xv . lib̄i h̄oes . t . r̄ . e . Sēp . v . car̄ . 7 . dim̄ . 7 . I . uiłł . 7 . II . ſer . Silŭ . Lxx . porc̄.
. xI . ac̄ . p̄ti . tē uał . xL . ſoł m̄ . IIII . lib̄ . In Eađ uilla tenuer̄ . III . lib̄i h̄oes
. t . r̄ . e . xLvIII . ac̄ . tr̄æ . 7 . dim̄ . M ten& Iđē . G . de . R . Sēp . II . car̄ in dn̄io
7 . II . car̄ hom̄ . 7 . v . uiłł . Tē . vI . ſer . m̄ . IIII . Tē . ſilŭ . cc . porc̄ . m̄ . cLx.
xxIIII . ac̄ . p̄ti . m̄ . I . moł . Tē uał . xL . ſoł . m̄ . Lx . De his xLvIII . ac̄.
ñ teſtat̄ Hunđ . R . qđ inde de parte regis eſſ& ſaiſit . Has . II . tr̄as
ten& . Garenger̄ . 7 Roḡ de Ramis cału̅pniat̄ eas . ſ; nec hunđ ei
teſtatur.

8 1 man-at-arms holds (Little) BROMLEY from Walter, which Queen
Edith held as a manor, for 2 hides less 20 acres.
 Always 1 villager. Then 17 smallholders, now 15; then 4 slaves,
  now 3. Always 2 ploughs in lordship. Then among the men
  6 ploughs, now 4.
 Woodland, 40 pigs; meadow, 4 acres. Then 9 cattle, now 7;
  then 2 cobs, now 4; then 100 sheep, now 200; then 12 pigs,
  now 30; now 2 beehives.
 Value then £5; now [£] 4.

Hundred of UTTLESFORD
9 1 man-at-arms holds (Little) CHESTERFORD from Walter, which
Queen Edith held as a manor, for 5 hides.
 Always 10 villagers. Then 4 smallholders, now 16; then 4 slaves,
  now 1. Always 2 ploughs in lordship; 3 men's ploughs.
 Woodland, 20 pigs; meadow, 8 acres; always 1 mill. Then 2
  cattle, now 4; then 1 cob, now none; then 36 sheep, now 43;
  then 16 pigs, now 34; now 23 goats.
 Value then 100s; now £6.

43   LAND OF ROGER BIGOT   87 b

Hundred of HINCKFORD
1 Warengar holds (Sible) HEDINGHAM from Roger for 25 acres, which
15 free men held before 1066. Always 5½ ploughs;
 1 villager; 2 slaves.
 Woodland, 70 pigs; meadow, 11 acres.
 Value then 40s; now £4.
  In the same village 3 free men held 48½ acres of land before
 1066. Now Warengar also holds (them) from Roger. Always 2
 ploughs in lordship; 2 men's ploughs;
 5 villagers. Then 6 slaves, now 4.
 Woodland, then 200 pigs, now 160; meadow, 24 acres; now
  1 mill.
 Value then 40s; now 60[s].
  Concerning these 48 acres, the Hundred does not testify for
 Roger that he was put in possession of them on the King's behalf.
  Warengar holds these 2 lands. Roger of Raismes claims them,
 but the Hundred does not testify for him either.

Pebeners. ten& Idē. G. de. R. q̄d tenuer̄. iii. libi hōes. t. r. e. sep. i. car
7. dim̄. 7. i. bord̄. filu̅. viii. porc̄. iii. ac̄. 7. dim̄. p̄ti. Tc̄ ual. xl. sol. m̄
. iiii. lib

Ouitunam ten&. R. in dn̄io. q̄d tenuit lib hō. t. r. e. p̄ man̄. 7 p. i. hid̄.
7. xxx. ac̄. sep. ii. car̄ in dn̄io. 7. ii. car̄. hom̄. Tc̄. iiii. uill. Post 7. m̄.
. iii. Tc̄. vi. bor. Post 7 m̄. v. sep. ii. ser̄. xxiiii. ac̄. p̄ti. Tc̄ ual. xl.
sol. m̄. iiii. lib.

Belcham ten& Rob̄ de uals de. R. q̄d ten̄. vi. libi hōes. t. r. e.
p. i. hid̄. 7. xxxviii. ac̄. 7. dim̄. Sep. iii. car̄. in dn̄io. tc̄. 7 p.
. i. car̄. hom̄. m̄. dim̄. Tc̄. iii. uill. Post 7. m̄. ii. Tc̄. 7 p. ix.
bor. m̄. xii. Tc̄. iiii. ser̄. Post 7. m̄. i. Silu̅. xxx. porc̄. xv.
ac̄. p̄ti. Tc̄ ual. lx. sol. m̄. c.

Heni. ten& Idē. R. de. R. q̄d tenuer̄. v. libi hōes

. t. r. e. p. i. hid̄. 7 dim̄. iiii. ac̄. min. Sep. iiii. car̄. in dn̄io. Tc̄. iiii.
uill. Post 7. m̄. i. Tc̄. 7. p. ii. bor. m̄. iii. Sep. ii. ser̄. tc̄. 7 p filu̅. xxx.
porc̄. m̄. xx. xviii. ac̄. p̄ti. Tc̄. 7 p ual. xl. sol. m̄. lxiiii.

Westunā ten& hugo de hofdenc q̄d tenuer̄. iiii. libi hōes. t. r. e.
q̄ fuer̄ de foca Algari. p. i. hid̄. 7. l. ac̄. Sep. v. car̄. in dn̄io. tc̄. 7. p.
. v. bor. m̄. x. tc̄. 7 p. ix. ser̄. m̄. iiii. Silu̅. vi. porc̄. xxiiii. ac̄. p̄ti. m̄.
. i. mol. Tc̄. 7 p ual. lx. sol. m̄. iiii. lib.

2   Warengar also holds PEBMARSH from Roger, which 3 free men held
    before 1066. Always 1½ ploughs;
        1 smallholder.
        Woodland, 8 pigs; meadow, 3½ acres.
    Value then 40s; now £4.

3   Roger holds OVINGTON in lordship, which a free man held before
    1066 as a manor, for 1 hide and 30 acres. Always 2 ploughs in
    lordship; 2 men's ploughs.
        Then 4 villagers, later and now 3; then 6 smallholders, later
            and now 5; always 2 slaves.
        Meadow, 24 acres.
    Value then 40s; now £4.

4   Robert of Vaux holds BELCHAMP (Otten) from Roger, which 6 free
    men held before 1066, for 1 hide and 38½ acres. Always 3
    ploughs in lordship. Then and later 1 men's plough, now ½.
        Then 3 villagers, later and now 2; then and later 9 smallholders,
            now 12; then 4 slaves, later and now 1.
        Woodland, 30 pigs; meadow, 15 acres.
    Value then 60s; now 100[s].

5   Robert also holds HENNY from Roger, which 5 free men held
    before 1066, for 1½ hides less 4 acres. Always 4 ploughs in lordship.   88 a
        Then 4 villagers, later and now 1; then and later 2 smallholders,
            now 3; always 2 slaves.
        Woodland, then and later 30 pigs, now 20; meadow, 18 acres.
    Value then and later 40s; now 64[s].

6   Hugh of Houdain holds WESTON (Hall) which 4 free men, who were
    of Algar's jurisdiction, held before 1066 for 1 hide and 50 acres.
    Always 5 ploughs in lordship.
        Then and later 5 smallholders, now 10; then and later 9 slaves,
            now 4.
        Woodland, 6 pigs; meadow, 24 acres; now 1 mill.
    Value then and later 60s; now £4.

TERRA Robti malet. Hund de hedingfort. Stanesteda.

ten& Hub de . Robto . qd tenuit Goduin lib hō . t . r . e . p man.

7 .p . ı . hid . sep . ıı . car . in dnio . Tc . 7 p . v . car . hom . m . ıııı . Tc . x . uilt.
Poſt . vııı . m̄ . ıııı . Sep . vıı . bor . tc . vıı . ſer . m̄ . vı . Tc . ſilu . ɔ . porc.
m̄ . cccc . x . ac . p̄ti . tc . ı . mot . m̄ . ıı . Huic manerio adjac& . ı . hid.
7 . dim . 7 . Lıı . ac . qs tenuer . ſochemani . t . r . e . tc . ıııı . car . m̄
. ıııı . 7 . dim . tc . 7 p . vı . bor . m̄ . xxıııı . tc . ıııı . ſer . m̄ . ı . Silua.
xxx . porc . xvı . ac . p̄ti . Tc xvı . an . v . runc . Lx . ou . L . cap . xL.
por . x . uaſa . apū . m̄ . x . an . L . ou . xxvı . cap . xL . porc . vııı . uaſa
apū . tc . uat . vı . lib . m̄ . ıx . 7 . ı . ſoc . q n̄ potat recede a tra
tenens . xx . ac . 7 . uat . ıı . ſot.

⌐ Goldingham ten& Ide hub . de . R . qd tenuit lib hō Goduin.
t . r . e . p man . 7 .p . ıı . hid . Tc . ıı̄ı̄ . car . in dnio . Poſt 7 . m̄ . ıı . Sep.

vı . uilt . 7 . v . bor . Tc . 7 p . vı . ſer . m̄ . ıı . Sep . xvı . ac . p̄ti . huic maner.
adjacebant . ıııı . ſoc . de . xvıı . ac . 7 . ı . ac . p̄ti . Tc . x . an . 7 . ıı . runc.
. L . ou . xL . caporc . m̄ . xıı . an . ı . runc . ccLx . ou . Lxv . por . v . uaſa apū
tc uat . Lx . ſot . m̄ . vı . lib . ⌐ Hund de Laſſendena.

⌐ Colun . ten& . R . in dnio . qd tenuit Aſſorin . p man . 7 .p . ı . hid . 7 . xxx . ac.
Sep . vıı . uilt . 7 . xv . bor . tc . ıııı . ſer . m̄ . ııı . 7 ſep . ııı . car . in dnio.
tc . int hōes . v . car . m̄ . ıııı . Silu . cccc . porc . ſep . ı . mot . xııı . ac p̄ti.
Tc . xıı . anim . ııı . runc . Lx . por . xL . cap . xx . ou . m̄ . vı . an . xx . porc.
. xxx . ou . ııı . uaſa ap . Sep . uat . vı . lib . 7 . tc . fuit . ı . ſoc . q libe tenuit
. ı . uirg . m̄ . ht . R . ſep . dim . car . Tc . uat . vııı . ſot . m̄ . vıı,

LAND OF ROBERT MALET

1 Hubert holds STANSTEAD (Hall) from Robert which Godwin, a free
man, held before 1066 as a manor for 1 hide. Always 2 ploughs
in lordship. Then and later 5 men's ploughs; now 4.
　　Then 10 villagers, later 8, now 4; always 7 smallholders. Then 7
　　　slaves, now 6.
　　Woodland, then 500 pigs, now 400; meadow, 10 acres; then 1
　　　mill, now 2.
　　To this manor are attached 1½ hides and 52 acres, which
Freemen held before 1066. Then 4 ploughs; now 3½.
　　Then and later 6 smallholders, now 24; then 4 slaves, now 1.
　　Woodland, 30 pigs; meadow, 16 acres. Then 16 cattle, 5 cobs,
　　　60 sheep, 50 goats, 40 pigs, 10 beehives; now 10 cattle, 50
　　　sheep, 26 goats, 40 pigs, 8 beehives.
Value then £6; now [£] 9.
　　1 Freeman, who could not withdraw from the land, who holds
20 acres.
Value 2s.

2 Hubert also holds GOLDINGHAM (Hall) from Robert which Godwin,
a free man, held before 1066 as a manor for 2 hides. Then 3
ploughs in lordship, later and now 2.
　　Always 6 villagers; 5 smallholders. Then and later 6 slaves,　　88 b
　　　now 2.
　　Meadow, always 16 acres.
　　To this manor were attached 4 Freemen with 17 acres and 1
acre of meadow.
　　Then 10 cattle, 2 cobs, 50 sheep, 40 pigs; now 12 cattle, 1 cob,
　　　260 sheep, 65 pigs, 5 beehives.
Value then 60s; now £6.

3 Robert holds (Wakes) COLNE in lordship, which Azorin held as a
manor, for 1 hide and 30 acres.
　　Always 7 villagers; 15 smallholders. Then 4 slaves, now 3.
　　　Always 3 ploughs in lordship. Then among the men 5
　　　ploughs, now 4.
　　Woodland, 400 pigs; always 1 mill. Meadow, 13 acres. Then 12
　　　cattle, 3 cobs, 60 pigs, 40 goats, 20 sheep; now 6 cattle,
　　　20 pigs, 30 sheep, 3 beehives.
Value always £6.
　　Then there was 1 Freeman who held 1 virgate freely. Now
Robert has (it). Always ½ plough.
Value then 8s; now 7[s].

Paruā colun ten& Galf de . R . qđ tenuit Goduin . p man . 7 p . I .
hiđ . 7 . I . uirḡ . Tc . vIII . bor . m̄ . xvII . tc . IIII . ſer . m̄ . I . Silu . xxx . porc .
. xI . ac . p̄ti . I . moł . Tc . uał . xL . ſoł . m̄ . Lx . 7 c in p̄tio de Staneſteda .
in . Ix . liƀ .

XLV Terra Wiłłi de Scohies . Mortunā ten& Wiłłs in dn̄io .
qđ tenuit Sexi . p manerio . 7 . p . I . hiđ . 7 . xx . ac . Tc . IIII . uiłł . m̄ .
. III . Sep . xvI . bor . Tc . vI . ſer . m̄ . IIII . tc . 7 . p . III . car . in dn̄io . m̄ . IL,
tc . 7 p . II . car . hom . m̄ . I . 7 . dim . Silu . cccc . porc . xx . ac . p̄ti .
Tc . runc . m̄ . IIII . tc . vIII . uac . 7 . vI . uiłł . m̄ . xI . an̄ . m̄ . xxxvI . ou .
Tc . Lx . por . m̄ . xIIII . tc . xxx . cap . m̄ . Lx . Tc uał . vIII . liƀ . m̄ . x .
7 . I . liƀ ho tenuit . xLIII . ac . 7 . dim . m̄ . W . inuaſit . 7 . n̄ p̄tinebat
iſti manerio qđ ten& Rad de . eo . S p . I . uiłł . 7 . II . bor . 7 . I . ſer .

89 a
7 . I . car . in dn̄io . 7 . dim . car . hom . Sep uał . xx . ſoł . ſ; hucuſq; habuit
xxx . ſoł .

TERRA Rogeri . Pictauenſis . Hund de Leſſendena . Burā ꞉XLVI꞉
tenuit Vlmer p man . 7 . p . I . hiđ . m̄ . R . p tantundē . Tc . vI . uiłł . 7 . qn̄
rec ſimiliꝉ . m̄ . v . Sep . Ix . bor . Tc . 7 . p . vI . ſer . m̄ . IIII . Tc . 7 . p . III . car . in dn̄io꞉
m̄ . II . Tc . 7 . p . III . car . hom . m̄ . I ꞉ 7 . dim . Silu . ccc . porc . xII . ac . p̄ti . ſep ꞉
. I . moł . 7 adhuc ſep ptinent . III . uiłł . 7 . II . bor . h̄ntes . I . car . Tc . II . runc .
xIIII . anim . Lxxx . ou . xxvIII . porc . xxvI . cap . m̄ . vII . anim . LIIII . ou .
. vI . por . Tc . 7 poſt uał . vII . liƀ . m̄ . xI . 7 . qn̄ rec ſimiliꝉ . 7 . vIII . liƀi hōes
tenueꝛ . dim . hiđ . 7 . xxx . ac . ſep . III . car . 7 . III . ac . p̄ti . Silu . xxx . porc .
hoc ap̄p̄tiatū c ſup̄ .

4 Walter holds COLNE (Engaine) from Robert, which Godwin held
as a manor, for 1 hide and 1 virgate.
Then 8 smallholders, now 17; then 4 slaves, now 1.
Woodland, 30 pigs; meadow, 11 acres; 1 mill.
Value then 40s; now 60[s].
It is in the £9 assessment of Stanstead (Hall).

45   LAND OF WILLIAM OF ÉCOUIS

Hundred of ONGAR

1 William holds MORETON in lordship, which Saxi held as a manor,
for 1 hide and 20 acres.
Then 4 villagers, now 3; always 16 smallholders. Then 6 slaves,
now 4. Then and later 3 ploughs in lordship, now 2. Then
and later 2 men's ploughs, now 1½.
Woodland, 400 pigs; meadow, 20 acres. Then ... cobs, now 4;
then 8 cows and 6 calves, now 11 cattle; now 36 sheep; then
60 pigs, now 14; then 30 goats, now 60.
Value then £8; now [£] 10.
1 free man held 43½ acres. Now William has annexed him. He
did not belong to this manor which Ralph holds from him.
Always 1 villager; 2 smallholders; 1 slave;   89 a
1 plough in lordship; ½ men's plough.
Value always 20s, but up to now he has had 30s.

46   LAND OF ROGER OF POITOU

Hundred of LEXDEN

1 Wulfmer held (Mount) BURES as a manor, for 1 hide. Now Roger
(holds it) for as much.
Then 6 villagers, when acquired the same, now 5; always 9
smallholders. Then and later 6 slaves, now 4. Then and later
3 ploughs in lordship, now 2. Then and later 3 men's ploughs,
now 1½.
Woodland, 300 pigs; meadow, 12 acres; always 1 mill.
A further 3 villagers and 2 smallholders have always belonged,
who have 1 plough.
Then 2 cobs, 14 cattle, 80 sheep, 28 pigs, 26 goats; now 7
cattle, 54 sheep, 6 pigs.
Value then £7; now [£] 11; when acquired, the same.
8 free men held ½ hide and 30 acres. Always 3 ploughs.
Meadow, 3 acres; woodland, 30 pigs.
This is assessed above.

Bercolt tenuit Leuuin Croc.ꝑ man.7.ꝑ.ɪ.hið.7.xxv.aꞓ.m̅.Roᵹ.
ſimiliꞇ.Tꞓ.vɪɪ.uiℓℓ.P̅ 7.m̅.v.Tꞓ.v.bor.7.qn̅ receꝑ.vɪɪ.m̅.v.Sep̅
.ɪɪ.ſer.Tꞓ.7.ꝑ.ɪɪ.car...dn̅io.m̅.ɪ.tꞓ.7.ꝑ.ɪɪ.car.hom.m̅.ɪ.Silu.ccc.porꞓ.
.vɪɪɪ.aꞓ.p̅ti.Sep̅.ɪ.moℓ.huic man ptin&.ɪ.biuuita quæ uocaꞇ.Bradefelda.
.ꝑ.dim.hið.7.xxx.aꞓ.Tꞓ.7.ꝑ.ɪ.car.m̅.nuℓℓ Tꞓ.reꞓ.R.in dn̅io.
.ɪ.runꞓ.7.xɪɪɪɪ.anim.7.xLvɪɪɪ.ou.7.c.ou.7.vɪ.porꞓ.xxxɪɪ.eap.
m̅.ɪɪɪɪ.anim.Lxxx.ou.xɪ.porꞓ.Tꞓ.uaℓ.vɪ.li℔.7.qn̅ recepit.vɪɪ.
m̅ uaℓ.Lx.ſoℓ.7.vɪɪ.li℔i hōes tenuer.dim hið.7.xɪ.aꞓ.7.dim.tꞓ.
7.ꝑ.ɪɪ.car.m̅.ɪ.ɪɪ.aꞓ.p̅ti.7.apptiatu̅ e̅ in ſup̅dictis li℔.

Hund de Tendringa.In Bradefelda tenuit Leuuin.dim.hið.
7.xv.aꞓ.tꞓ.ɪ.bor.7.ɪ.ſer.m̅.n̅.Tꞓ.7 ꝑ.ɪ.car.m̅.n̅.Tꞓ uaℓ.xL.ſoℓ.

7.qn̅ recepit.xxx.ſoℓ.m̅.uaℓ.v.ſoℓ.

.xLvɪɪ. **T**ERRA Hugonis de Gurnai. Hund de Hidingaforda.
Liſtuna̅ ten&.Goisfrid.talebot qð tenuit li℔ homo ꝑ man.7.ꝑ dim.hið.
7.xxx.aꞓ.Sep̅.ɪɪ.car.in dn̅io.7.ɪ.car.hom.Tꞓ.7.p̅.vɪ.bor.m̅.v.tꞓ.7 p̅.
.ɪɪɪ.ſer.m̅ nuℓℓ.xxx.aꞓ.p̅ti.dim.moℓ.Tꞓ.ɪɪɪ.uaꞓ.c̅ uiꞇ.xɪɪ.ou.
.vɪɪ.porꞓ.ꞹ.ɪɪɪ.uaꞓ.c̅ uiꞇ.xxɪɪ.ou.vɪɪɪ.uaſa ap̅.Sep̅ uaℓ.Lxvɪɪɪ.ſoℓ.

Hund de Tendringa.Erleiam tenuit Osbt̅.ꝑ.man.7.ꝑ.ɪɪ.hið.
7.dim.m̅.ten& Agnes.Tꞓ.xvɪ.uiℓℓ.Poſt 7.m̅.vɪɪ.tꞓ.ɪɪɪɪ.bor.
m̅ nuℓℓ.tꞓ.ɪɪɪɪ.ſer.m̅ nuℓℓ.Sep̅.ɪɪ.car.in dn̅io.Tꞓ.inꞇ hōes.vɪɪɪ.car.
7.qn̅ reꞓ.vɪ.m̅.ɪɪɪ.Silu.xL.porꞓ.ɪɪɪ.aꞓ.p̅ti.m̅.ɪɪ.moℓ.Tꞓ.xxx.
ou.v.porꞓ.m̅.xLɪɪɪɪ.ou.vɪɪɪ.porꞓ.vɪɪ.an.x.cap.ɪɪɪ.uaſa apu̅.
Tꞓ uaℓ.vɪ.li℔.Poſt 7.m̅.ɪɪɪɪ.

2   Leofwin Croc held (West) BERGHOLT as a manor, for 1 hide and
25 acres. Now Roger (holds it) for the same.

    Then 7 villagers, later and now 5; then 5 smallholders, when
      acquired 7, now 5; always 2 slaves. Then and later 2 ploughs
      [in] lordship, now 1. Then and later 2 men's ploughs, now 1.
    Woodland, 300 pigs; meadow, 8 acres; always 1 mill.

    To this manor belongs 1 outlier which is called BRADFIELD, for
½ hide and 30 acres. Then and later 1 plough, now none.

    Then Roger acquired in lordship 1 cob, 14 cattle, 48 sheep,
      100 sheep, 6 pigs, 32 goats; now 4 cattle, 80 sheep, 11 pigs.
Value then £6; when acquired [£]7. Value now 60s.

    7 free men held ½ hide and 11½ acres. Then and later 2 ploughs,
now 1.

    Meadow, 2 acres.

It is assessed in the above pounds.

Hundred of TENDRING

3   In BRADFIELD Leofwin held ½ hide and 15 acres.

    Then 1 smallholder and 1 slave, now none. Then and later 1
      plough, now none.

Value then 40s; when acquired 30s. Value now 5s.   89 b

47   LAND OF HUGH OF GOURNAI

Hundred of HINCKFORD

1   Geoffrey Talbot holds LISTON, which a free man held as a manor,
for ½ hide and 30 acres. Always 2 ploughs in lordship; 1 men's
plough.

    Then and later 6 smallholders, now 5; then and later 3 slaves,
      now none.

    Meadow, 30 acres; ½ mill. Then 3 cows with calves, 12 sheep,
      7 pigs; now 3 cows with calves, 22 sheep, 8 beehives.

Value always 68s.

Hundred of TENDRING

2   Osbert held ARDLEIGH as a manor, for 2½ hides. Now Agnes holds (it).

    Then 16 villagers, later and now 7; then 4 smallholders, now
      none; then 4 slaves, now none. Always 2 ploughs in lordship.

    Then among the men 8 ploughs, when acquired 6, now 3.

    Woodland, 40 pigs; meadow, 3 acres; now 2 mills. Then 30
      sheep, 5 pigs; now 44 sheep, 8 pigs, 7 cattle, 10 goats,
      3 beehives.

Value then £6; later and now [£] 4.

ᚹHund de Laſſendena. Forham ten& Goiſfrid de . Hugone.

qđ tenuit Eſbern ꝓ man . 7 . ꝓ . II . hiđ . Tc . x . uiłł . m̃ . VII . tc . v . bor.

m̃ . XI . Tc . v . ſer . m̃ . IIII . Sep . III . car . in dñio . Tc . v . car . hom . m̃ . III.

Silu . e . porc . XII . ac . p̃ti . Sep . I . moł . Tc . II . runc . 7 . III . uac . cũ

uiłł . LX . ou . XII . cap . VIII . porc . x . uaſa . ap . m̃ . II . runc . VIII . an.

LXXX . ou . XXV . cap . x . porc . VI . uaſa ap . 7 . III . libi h̃oes . tenent

. XIII . ac . Sep . dim . car . Sep . uał . VII . lib . 7 . x . ac . abſtulit

Roḡ Picłauenſis . de iſto manerio . ſic hunđ teſtať.

Tᴇʀʀᴀ Witłi Piperelli.

Torindunam ten& Drogo de Wiłło . qđ tenuit . Ailmar lib h̃o

t . r . e . ꝓ man . 7 . ꝓ . I . hiđ . 7 . dim . m̃ ſť . III . hiđ . 7 . dim . 7 . XXI . ac

Sep . II . car . in dñio . Tc . II . car . hom . m̃ . III . Tc . I . uiłł . m̃ . non.

Tc . IIII . bor . m̃ . XI . Tc . III . ſer . m̃ . II . Tc . I . uac . LX . ou . XI . por.

m̃ . v . uac . XV . porc . LX . ou . Tc . IIII . ſoc . 7 . modo ſimiliť tenentes

. II . hiđ . 7 . dim . 7 . XXI . ac . de ead tr̃a . 7 . inde ablate ſł . LVI . ac.

Sep ibi ẽ . ſilua . e . porc . Paſt . LX . ou . Tc uał . LX . ſoł . m̃ . c.

ᚹHund de Ceſſeurda . Turruc . ten& . W . in dñio . qđ ten.

Ailmar . t . r . e . ꝓ man . 7 . ꝓ . III . hiđ . 7 . XLII . ac . Tc . II . uiłł . m̃ . III.

tc . XI . bor . m̃ . XVIII . Sep . II . ſer . 7 . II . car . in dñio . tc . IIII . car . hou

. m̃ . v . Paſt . c . ou . ſep . I . piſc . Tc . II . uiłł . LVIII . ou . I . runc . m̃.

. v . uac . IIII . uiłł . LXXXV . ou . VIII . porc . Tc . uał . VI . lib . 7 qñ rec.

m̃ . XII . lib . 7 . unciã auri . In hoc manerio jacebant . IX . ſoc . t . r . e.

tenentes . III . hiđ . m̃ . ſť . v . ſoc . 7 . tenent . I . hiđ . 7 . dim . 7 . Giſłebť

h̃o ep̃i baiocenſis tenet . I . hiđ . 7 . dim . x . ac . min . 7 . hunđ neſc

qm̃ . XX . ac . &iam ten& Anſchetiłł . h̃o ep̃i . Londoniæ . que

jacebant in hoc manerio . t . r . e . 7 ſimiliť neſcit hunđ.

Hundred of LEXDEN

3 Geoffrey holds FORDHAM from Hugh, which Esbern held as a
manor, for 2 hides.
> Then 10 villagers, now 7; then 5 smallholders, now 11; then 5
> slaves, now 4. Always 3 ploughs in lordship. Then 5 men's
> ploughs, now 3.
> Woodland, 100 pigs; meadow, 12 acres; always 1 mill. Then 2
> cobs, 3 cows with calves, 60 sheep, 12 goats, 8 pigs, 10
> beehives; now 2 cobs, 8 cattle, 80 sheep, 25 goats, 10 pigs,
> 6 beehives.
> 3 free men hold 13 acres. Always ½ plough.
> Value always £7.
> Roger of Poitou took away 10 acres from this manor; so the
> Hundred testifies.

48   LAND OF WILLIAM PEVEREL   90 a

[Hundred of BARSTABLE]

1 Drogo holds (East) HORNDON from William which Aelmer, a free
man, held before 1066 as a manor for 1½ hides. Now there are 3½
hides and 21 acres. Always 2 ploughs in lordship. Then 2 men's
ploughs, now 3.
> Then 1 villager, now none; then 4 smallholders, now 11; then
> 3 slaves, now 2.
> Then 1 cow, 60 sheep, 11 pigs; now 5 cows, 15 pigs, 60 sheep.
> Then 4 Freemen and now the same, who hold 2½ hides and 21
> acres of this land. 56 acres have been taken away from it.
> There has always been woodland, 100 pigs. Pasture, 60 sheep.
> Value then 60s; now 100[s].

Hundred of CHAFFORD

2 William holds (Grays) THURROCK in lordship, which Aelmer held
before 1066 as a manor, for 3 hides and 42 acres.
> Then 2 villagers, now 3; then 11 smallholders, now 18. Always
> 2 slaves; 2 ploughs in lordship. Then 4 men's ploughs, now 5.
> Pasture, 100 sheep; always 1 fishery. Then 2 villagers, 58
> sheep, 1 cob; now 5 cows, 4 calves, 85 sheep, 8 pigs.
> Value then and when acquired £6; now £12 and an ounce of gold.
> 9 Freemen belonged in this manor before 1066, who held 3
> hides. Now there are 5 Freemen and they hold 1½ hides. Gilbert,
> a man of the Bishop of Bayeux, holds 1½ hides less 10 acres; the
> Hundred does not know how. Also Ansketel, a man of the Bishop
> of London, holds 20 acres which lay in (the lands of) this manor;
> likewise the Hundred does not know (how).

Terra Radulfi de Limeſeio . Brandunā ten& . Rad
in dnīo . qd̄ tenuit lib̄ hō . t . r . e . p man . 7 . p . ii . hid . 7 . dim̄ .
xv . ac . min . Sēp . ii . car . in dnīo . 7 . iii . car . hom . 7 . vii . uiłł

90 b

7 . vii . bor . 7 . iiii . ſer . Silu . x . porc . xxxii . ac . p̄ti . i . mołł . Tc̄ ual .
. iiii . lib̄ . P 7 m̄ . vi . Huic manerio addidit Harduin t . r . Wiłłi .
xx . ac . Sēp . dim . car . m̄ . i . bor . Tc̄ . ſilu . xx . por . m̄ . vi . App̄tiatū c̄ ſup̄ .

In Niuetuna . jae& . i . ſoc . hn̄s . dim . car . ſēp ; 7 . ual . iii . ſoł

Hund de Angra . Cinghe uuellā ten& . R . in dnīo qd̄ tenuit
Harold de Rege . E . p man . 7 . p . vii . hid . Sēp . xix . uiłł . 7 . ii . bor . 7
. ii . car . in dnīo . Tc̄ . xvi . car . hom . m̄ . xi . Silu . ḋccc . porc . xxxi .
ac . p̄ti . ſep . i . moł . Tc̄ uał . viii . lib̄ . m̄ . x . 7 . vi . libi . hōes . manſer
in . ii . hid . 7 . xv . ac . q̄s m̄ ħt . Rob̄ greno . ex dono regis ſic ipſe . dic̄ . 7
Tc̄ . habebant . iii . car . m̄ ii . Silu . xl . porc . viii . ac . p̄ti . Tc̄ . i . moł .
m̄ . nułł . Sēp uał . xl . ſoł . 7 . q̄dā lib̄ hō ten& 7 . tenuit . xxx . ac .
quē m̄ ħt pet̄r uicecomes . Tc̄ . i . car . m̄ . dim . Silu . xxx . porc . ii . ac .
p̄ti . vał . v . ſoł . De iſta t̄ra habuit . P . libatore c̄ ſuo feudo .

In ſup̄dicto manerio de Brumduna rec̄ . R . iii . anim . xv . ou .
xv . por . i . runc . m̄r . vi . anim̄ . xxiiii . ou . xviii . porc . i . runc .
7 In Cingheuuella . rec̄ . vi . an . 7 . xvii . ou . 7 . xi . porc . m̄ . x . an .
. lx . ou . xx . porc . Rad de Limeſeio . ten& . vi . ac . de ſoca reġ . ſ;
anteceſſor ej inuaſit .

[Hundred of HINCKFORD]

1 Ralph holds BRUNDON in lordship, which a free man held before
1066 as a manor, for 2½ hides less 15 acres. Always 2 ploughs in
lordship; 3 men's ploughs;
    7 villagers; 7 smallholders; 4 slaves.   90 b
    Woodland, 10 pigs; meadow, 32 acres; 1 mill.
    Value then £4; later and now [£] 6.
    To this manor Hardwin added 20 acres after 1066. Always ½
plough.
    Now 1 smallholder.
    Woodland, then 20 pigs, now 6.
    It is assessed above.

2 In *NIUETUNA* lies 1 Freeman who has always had ½ plough.
    Value 3s.

Hundred of ONGAR

3 Ralph holds CHIGWELL in lordship, which Harold held from King
Edward as a manor, for 7 hides.
    Always 19 villagers; 2 smallholders; 2 ploughs in lordship.
        Then 16 men's ploughs, now 11.
    Woodland, 800 pigs; meadow, 31 acres; always 1 mill.
    Value then £8; now [£] 10.
    6 free men dwelt on 2 hides and 15 acres, whom Robert
Gernon has by the King's gift, so he states.
        Then they had 3 ploughs, now 2.
    Woodland, 40 pigs; meadow, 8 acres; then 1 mill, now none.
    Value always 40s.
    A free man, whom Peter the Sheriff now has, holds and held
30 acres. Then 1 plough, now ½.
    Woodland, 30 pigs; meadow, 2 acres.
    Value 5s.
    Peter had delivery of this land with his own Holding.

[Hundred of HINCKFORD]

4 In the above-mentioned manor of BRUNDON Ralph acquired
        3 cattle, 15 sheep, 15 pigs, 1 cob; now 6 cattle, 24 sheep,
        18 pigs, 1 cob.

[Hundred of ONGAR]

5 In CHIGWELL he acquired
        6 cattle, 17 sheep and 11 pigs; now 10 cattle, 60 sheep, 20 pigs.

6 Ralph of Limésy holds 6 acres of the King's jurisdiction, but his
predecessor annexed it.

T̃RRA.Roƀti de todeneio.Hund de Vdelesfort.Ceſeuuic
tenuit.ı.liƀ hõ.t̃.r̃.e̓.p.m̃.7.p.ı.hid.7.dim̃.Sep.ı.car̃.ı̇ dñio.
7.ıı.car̃.hom.T̃c.7 p̃.ıııı.uiłł.m̃.ııı.m̃.ıı.bor.Sıłu.c.porc̃.ꭓıııı.ac̓.
p̃ti.Vał.xʟ.ſoł.

91 a

Terra Radulfi de Tedeneio.Hund de Herlaua.In
Oueſham ten& Roḡ de.R.dim̃ hid q̓m tenuit Etmar̃.Sẽp.ı.car̃.   .ʟı.
Sılu.xıı.porc̃.T̃c.uał.x.ſoł.m̃.xv.
⌐ Laghefarã ten&.Roḡ de.R.qd̃ tenuit Sexi̓ p man̓.7.p.ı.hid.
t̃c.ıııı.uiłł.m̃.ııı.m̃.vıı.bor.T̃c.ıııı.ſer̃.m̃.ııı.T̃c.ıı.car̃.in dñio
m̃.ı.Sılu.xxx.porc̃.xvı.ac̓.p̃ti.Sẽp.xııı.porc̃.7.ʟx.ou̓.7.ıııı.uac̓.
Sẽp uał.ʟxx.ſoł.

Terra Walt̃i de doai.Hund de Ceſſeurda.Vpmunſtre
ten& Walt̃ in dñio.qd̃ tenuit Suen̓ ſuart p man̓.7.p.vı.hid.7.d̃
7.xxx.ac̓.Sẽp.vııı.uiłł.t̃c.v.bor.m̃.vıı.Sẽp.ıııı.ſer̃.7.ıı.car̃
in dñio.T̃c.v.car̃.hom.m̃.ıııı.Sılu.cc.porc̃.vııı.ac̓.p̃ti.T̃c.ı̇.
pułł.m̃.ñ.M.ʟxxxv.ou̓.7.xxv.ou̓.T̃c.uał.vıı.liƀ.m̃.vııı.
7.x.ac̓.jacuer̃ in hoc manerio q̃s ten&.G̓.de magna uiłł.in ſuo
eſcangio ut dicit.
⌐ Reineham ten&.Gałt̃ in dñio.qd̃ tenuit Lefſtan̓ p̃poſit̓.t̃.r̃.e̓.
p man̓.7.p.vııı.hid.T̃c.ııı.car̃.in dñio.m̃.ıı.t̃c.vı.car̃.hom.
m̃.v.Sẽp.xıı.uiłł.T̃c.ıı.bor.m̃.ıx.T̃c.v.ſer̃.m̃.ıııı.cv.ou̓.
.xx.por.ı.runc̃.Sẽp.uał.x.liƀ.huic manerio addita eſt.dim̃.
hid.q̃m tenebant.ııı.liƀi hões̓.t̃.r̃.e̓.7.p.W.rex uenit Gałt̃   ★

50   LAND OF ROBERT OF TOSNY

Hundred of UTTLESFORD
1   1 free man held CHISWICK before 1066 as a manor, for 1½ hides.
Always 1 plough in lordship; 2 men's ploughs.
    Then and later 4 villagers, now 3; now 2 smallholders.
    Woodland, 100 pigs; meadow, 4 acres.
    Value 40s.

51   LAND OF RALPH OF TOSNY   91 a

Hundred of HARLOW
1   In HOUSHAM (Hall) Roger holds ½ hide from Ralph, which Edmer
held. Always 1 plough.
    Woodland, 12 pigs.
    Value then 10s; now 15[s].

[Hundred of ONGAR]
2   Roger holds LAVER from Ralph, which Saxi held as a manor, for 1
hide.
    Then 4 villagers, now 3; now 7 smallholders; then 4 slaves,
      now 3. Then 2 ploughs in lordship, now 1.
    Woodland, 30 pigs; meadow, 16 acres. Always 13 pigs, 60 sheep
      and 4 cows.
    Value always 70s.

52   LAND OF WALTER OF DOUAI

Hundred of CHAFFORD
1   Walter holds UPMINSTER in lordship, which Swein Swart held as a
manor, for 6½ hides and 30 acres.
    Always 8 villagers. Then 5 smallholders, now 7. Always 4 slaves;
      2 ploughs in lordship. Then 5 men's ploughs, now 4.
    Woodland, 200 pigs; meadow, 8 acres. Then 1 foal, now none;
      now 85 sheep and 25 sheep.
    Value then £7; now [£] 8.
    10 acres lay in (the lands of) this manor, which G(eoffrey) de
Mandeville holds in exchange, as he states.

2   Walter holds RAINHAM in lordship, which Leofstan the reeve held
before 1066 as a manor, for 8 hides. Then 3 ploughs in lordship,
now 2. Then 6 men's ploughs, now 5.
    Always 12 villagers. Then 2 smallholders, now 9; then 5 slaves,
      now 4.
    105 sheep, 20 pigs, 1 cob.
    Value always £10.
    To this manor has been added ½ hide, which 3 free men held
before 1066. [And after] King William came, Walter

eos addidit fuo manerio . cui . n̄ adjacebant . t . r . e . ut confulat
teftat . 7 . t̄c . habebant . 1 . car . m̄ . dim . 7 . qn rec . dim . val . xx . fol.

ꝟ Hund de Tendringe : Holandā ten Leftan ꝑ . vi . hid : 7 . d . Sep . xvɪɪ . uilt . T̄c . 7 p̊ . x . bor.
m̊ . xɪ ;

91 b

T̄c . 7 p̊ . v . fer . m̊ : ɪɪɪ , t̄c : 7 p̊ . ɪɪɪɪ . car in dnio . m̊ . ɪɪɪ . T̄c . 7 p̊ . xɪ . car hom̊ . m̊ . vɪɪɪ.
Silu . c : porc : xɪɪɪɪ . ac . p̊ti . Sep ual . xɪɪɪɪ . lib.

LIII . TERRA Mathei mauritanienfiS . Hund de Dōmauuā.

ꝟ Eftanes ten& . ꟿ . in dnio q̊d tenuit : Achi lib ho . t . r . e . ꝑ . man̊.
7 ꝑ . v . hid . T̄c . v . car . in dnio . 7 . qn rec . ɪɪɪɪ . m̊ . ɪɪɪ . t̄c . x . car . hom̊.
m̊ . vɪɪ . T̄c . xɪ . uilt . 7 . ɪ . p̄br . m̊ . xv . uilt . 7 . ɪ . p̄br . T̄c . x . bor . m̊.
. xvɪ . T̄c . x . fer . m̊ . ɪx . Silu . cc . porc . t̄c ꞉ m̊ . cl . lxvɪɪ . ac . p̊ti . Sep
. ɪ . mol . 7 . ɪ . runc . 7 . vɪɪɪ . an . . xxx . por . 7 . lx . ou . 7 . x . cap.
7 . ɪɪɪ . uafa ap . T̄c . ual . x . lib . 7 . qn ree fimilit . m̊ ual . xv . lib.

ꝟ Hund de Celmeresfort . Gingā ten& . ꟿ . q̊d tenuit Anfchill.
ꝑ . man̊ . 7 . ꝑ . v . hid . Sep . vɪɪ . uilt . 7 . vɪɪɪ : bor . 7 . ɪɪɪɪ . fer . 7 . ɪɪ . car.
in . dnio . 7 . ɪɪɪ . car . hom . Silu . ccc . porc . 7 . ɪ . runc . v . anim.
. xx . porc : xxx . ou . T̄c : ual . fol . m̊ . vɪ . lib.

LIIII Terra Comitiffe de Albamarla . Hund de Hidingfort.
Barleā . ten& . in dnio . q̊d tenuit Leuuin lib ho . t . r . e . ꝑ man̊.
7 . ꝑ . ɪɪ . hid . 7 . xxx . ac . T̄c . ɪɪɪ . car . in dnio . Poft 7 . m̊ . ɪɪ . Sep : v.
car . hom . 7 . x . uilt . 7 . v . bor . Silu . xxx . porc . xl . ac . p̊ti.
7 . vɪɪ . anim . 7 . xxv . ou . 7 . xxɪɪɪɪ . cap . xxvɪɪɪ . porc . ɪɪ . uafa
apu . T̄c . 7 p̊ ual . vɪɪɪ . lib . m̊ . xɪɪ.

91 a, b

added them to his manor, to which they were not attached
before 1066, as the County testifies. Then they had 1 plough,
now ½, when acquired ½.
Value 20s.

Hundred of TENDRING
3 Leofstan holds HOLLAND for 6½ hides.
Always 17 villagers. Then and later 10 smallholders, now 11;
then and later 5 slaves, now 3. Then and later 4 ploughs in   91 b
lordship, now 3. Then and later 11 men's ploughs, now 8.
Woodland, 100 pigs; meadow, 14 acres.
Value always £14.

53 LAND OF MATTHEW OF MORTAGNE

Hundred of DUNMOW
1 Matthew holds (Great) EASTON in lordship which Aki, a free man,
held before 1066 as a manor for 5 hides. Then 5 ploughs in
lordship, when acquired 4, now 3. Then 10 men's ploughs, now 7.
Then 11 villagers and 1 priest, now 15 villagers and 1 priest;
then 10 smallholders, now 16; then 10 slaves, now 9.
Woodland, then 200 pigs, now 150; meadow, 67 acres. Always
1 mill; 1 cob, 8 cattle, 30 pigs, 60 sheep, 10 goats and
3 beehives.
Value then £10; when acquired the same; value now £15.

Hundred of CHELMSFORD
2 Matthew holds MARGARETTING, which Askell held as a manor, for
5 hides.
Always 7 villagers; 8 smallholders; 4 slaves; 2 ploughs in
lordship; 3 men's ploughs.
Woodland, 300 pigs. 1 cob, 5 cattle, 20 pigs, 30 sheep.
Value then ... s; now £6.

54 LAND OF THE COUNTESS OF AUMÂLE

Hundred of HINCKFORD
1 She holds BORLEY in lordship which Leofwin, a free man, held
before 1066 as a manor for 2 hides and 30 acres. Then 3 ploughs
in lordship, later and now 2. Always 5 men's ploughs;
10 villagers; 5 smallholders.
Woodland, 30 pigs; meadow, 40 acres. 7 cattle, 25 sheep, 24
goats, 28 pigs, 2 beehives.
Value then and later £8; now [£] 12.

Hund de Tendringa. Sciddinchov.ten& in dnio qd
tenuit Aluric p maner. 7 .p. ii. hid. Sep. xv.bor.tc.iiii.fer.

92 a

poft 7 .modo. i.Tc.ii.car.in dnio p 7 .m.i.Tc.iiii.car.hom.Poft.
7.m.ii.Silu.xL.porc.vi.ac.pti.Tc.i.mot.7.i.pifc.m.n.paft.xL.
ou.Tc.iii.uac.iii.uilt.xL.ou.ii.runc.xxx.porc.m.i.runc.iii.an.
xLviii.ou.Sep.uat.Lx.fot.

TERRA Judith comitiffæ. Hund de beuentreu. Wilcu-
meftou tenuit Wallef comes t.r.e.p.man.7.p.x.hid.7.dim.
Sep.ii.car.in dnio.Tc.xv.car.hominu.m.xxii.Tc.xxv.uilt
m.xxxvi.Tc.i.bor.m.xxv.Sep.iiii.fer.Silu.ccc.porc.Lxxx.ac.
pti.Paft.de.viii.fot.Sep.i.mot.Tc.vi.pifcinæ.m.i.m.viii.
anim.i.runc.xxxv.por.Lx.ou.xx.cap.Tc uat.xv.lib.m.
xxviii.lib.7.ii.uncias auri.

.LV.

TERRA Frodonis.fris abbis. Redeuuintra ten&.F.in dnio
qd tenuit Orgar p man.7.p.i.hid.7.i.uirg.Sep.xv.uilt.7.vi.bor.
7.iii.7.iii.car.in dnio.7.vi.car.hom.Silu.c.porc.xxx.ac.pti.
Tc.x.anim.Lx.ou.L.porc.xxv.cap.i.uas ap.m.xviii.an
cxL.ou.xxxvii.porc.xxx.cap.iiii.uafa ap.Tc uat.viii.
lib.m.xv.De hoc manerio ten& Alger.de Frodone.xxx.ac.
7.uat.x.fot.in eod.ptio.

LVI.

92 b

.LVII. TERRA Saffelini. Hund de bdeftapla.
Stantmere. 7 Winthelle.qs tenet.S.tenuer.Alric.7.Vluuin.
p man.7.p.ii.hid.7.xxx.ac.Sep.ii.car.in dnio.7.ii.bou hom.
Silu.xL.porc.Tc.i.runc.7.vii.porc.7.xv.ou.m.i.runc.Lxx.ou.
xviii.por.xx.cap.Sep uat.L.fot.

Hundred of TENDRING
2 She holds OLD HALL in lordship, which Aelfric held as a manor,
for 2 hides.

> Always 15 smallholders. Then 4 slaves, later and now 1. Then 92 a
> 2 ploughs in lordship, later and now 1. Then 4 men's ploughs,
> later and now 2.
>
> Woodland, 40 pigs; meadow, 6 acres; then 1 mill and 1 fishery,
> now none; pasture, 40 sheep. Then 3 cows, 3 calves, 40
> sheep, 2 cobs, 30 pigs; now 1 cob, 3 cattle, 48 sheep.

Value always 60s.

55   LAND OF COUNTESS JUDITH

Hundred of BECONTREE
1 Earl Waltheof held WALTHAMSTOW before 1066 as a manor, for
10½ hides. Always 2 ploughs in lordship. Then 15 men's ploughs,
now 22.

> Then 25 villagers, now 36; then 1 smallholder, now 25; always
> 4 slaves.
>
> Woodland, 300 pigs; meadow, 80 acres; pasture at 8s; always 1
> mill. Then 6 fisheries, now 1. Now 8 cattle, 1 cob, 35 pigs,
> 60 sheep, 20 goats.

Value then £15; now £28 and 2 ounces of gold.

56   LAND OF FRODO THE ABBOT'S BROTHER

[Half-Hundred of FRESHWELL]
1 Frodo holds RADWINTER in lordship, which Ordgar held as a
manor, for 1 hide and 1 virgate.

> Always 15 villagers; 6 smallholders; 3 ...; 3 ploughs in lordship;
> 6 men's ploughs.
>
> Woodland, 100 pigs; meadow, 30 acres. Then 10 cattle, 60
> sheep, 50 pigs, 25 goats, 1 beehive; now 18 cattle, 140 sheep,
> 37 pigs, 30 goats, 4 beehives.

Value then £8; now [£] 15.
Of this manor, Algar holds 30 acres from Frodo.
Value 10s in the same assessment.

57   LAND OF SASSELIN   92 b

Hundred of BARSTABLE
1 Alric and Wulfwin held STANMER and CRAYS HILL, which Sasselin
holds as a manor, for 2 hides and 30 acres. Always 2 ploughs in
lordship; 2 men's oxen.

> Woodland, 40 pigs. Then 1 cob, 7 pigs and 15 sheep; now 1 cob,
> 70 sheep, 18 pigs, 20 goats.

Value always 50s.

⌐Hund de Witham . In Nutlea ten& . S . dim̓ ̣ hiđ . 7 . xxii . ac̓.
qđ tenuit Leuecilđ . t̓ . r̓ . e̓ . Tc̄ . i . car̓ . m̂ . dim̄ . tc̄ . i . an̓ . m̂ . iiii . 7 . xii.
ou̓ . vi . porc̓ . i . runc̄ . Val . x ̣ fol.

⌐Hund de Wenfiftreu Legrā ten& . S . qđ tenuer̓ . ii . libi hōes
t̓ . r̓ . e̓ . p̱ maner̓ . 7 . p̱ . viii . hiđ . Tc̄ . iiii . car̓ . in dn̄io . m̂ . ii . Sēp . ii . car̓.
hom̓ . 7 . i . uilt . 7 . xvii . bor . tc̄ . viii . fer . m̂ . iii . Tc̄ . filu̓ . c . porc̓ . m̂ . lx.
. vii . ac̓ . p̓ti . Tc̄ . xxiiii . anim̓ . cc . ou̓ . xxiii . porc̓ . iii . runc̓ . iiii.
uafa ap̓ . m̂ . vii . an̓ . cxxv . ou̓ . ix . porc̓ . iii . runc̓ . iiii . uafa apu̓.
Sēp . ual . vii . lib.

⌐Dim̂ Hund de Clauelinga . Pincepo ten& . S . qđ tenuit lib̓ hō
p̱ . man̓ . 7 . p̱ . i . hiđ . Sēp . i . car̓ . m̂ . iii . bor . 7 . i . fer̓ 7 . iiii . ac̓ . p̓ti . 7
xviii . ou̓ . 7 . xviii . porc̓ . Val . xx . fol.

⌐Hund de Ceffeurda . In Cikedic ten& . S . i . maner̓ . de . i . hiđ.
7 . dim̓ . 7 . xxx . ac̓ . qđ tenuit Orgar̓ lib̓ hō . t̓ . r̓ . e̓ . Tc̄ . i . car̓ . in dn̄io
m̂ . i . 7 . dim̓ . Sēp . ii . car̓ . hom̓ . Tc̄ . iii . uilt . m̂ . iiii . Sēp . vi . bor . Tc̄
. ii . fer̓ . m̂ . null̓ . Silu̓ . c . porc̓ . Paſt . lx . ou̓ . Tc̄ . l . ou̓ . xxiiii . por
. iiii . runc̓ . xii . anim̓ . m̂ . iiii . an̓ . xii . ou̓ . vi . por . i . runc̓ . Tc̄
ual . lx . fol . m̂ . iiii . lib̓ . 7 . i . foc̓ . fuit in hac tr̓a de . xv . ac̓ . q̓s potāt
uende . f; foca jacebat in Warleia . tr̓a sc̄i pauli . Sēp . dim̓ . car̓ . 7

93 a
ual . iii . fol.
Hund de Vdelesfort . Banhuntā ten& . S . p̱ maner̓ . qd . ten̓.
Aluric̓ lib̓ hō . t̓ . r̓ . e̓ . p̱ . man̓ . 7 . p̱ . ii . hiđ . Quando recep̄ . iiii . bor̓.
7 . m̂ . Sēp . i . car̓ . in dn̄io . m̂ . dim̓ . car̓ . hom̓ . x . ac̓ . p̓ti . Tc̄ . i.
an̓ . 7 . i . porc̓ . m̂ . xxx . ou̓ . ii . an̓ . i . runc̓ . Tc̄ . 7 p̱ ual . xl . fol . m̂ . lv.

Hundred of WITHAM

2 In NOTLEY, Sasselin holds ½ hide and 22 acres, which Leofcild held before 1066. Then 1 plough, now ½.
Then 1 (head of) cattle, now 4; 12 sheep, 6 pigs, 1 cob.
Value 10s.

Hundred of WINSTREE

3 Sasselin holds LAYER, which 2 free men held before 1066 as a manor, for 8 hides. Then 4 ploughs in lordship, now 2. Always 2 men's ploughs;
1 villager; 17 smallholders. Then 8 slaves, now 3.
Woodland, then 100 pigs, now 60; meadow, 7 acres. Then 24 cattle, 200 sheep, 23 pigs, 3 cobs, 4 beehives; now 7 cattle, 125 sheep, 9 pigs, 3 cobs, 4 beehives.
Value always £7.

Half-Hundred of CLAVERING

4 Sasselin holds PINCHPOOLS, which a free man held as a manor, for 1 hide. Always 1 plough.
Now 3 smallholders; 1 slave.
Meadow, 4 acres. 18 sheep and 18 pigs.
Value 20s.

Hundred of CHAFFORD

5 In CHILDERDITCH, Sasselin holds 1 manor of 1½ hides and 30 acres, which Ordgar, a free man, held before 1066. Then 1 plough in lordship, now 1½. Always 2 men's ploughs.
Then 3 villagers, now 4; always 6 smallholders. Then 2 slaves, now none.
Woodland, 100 pigs; pasture, 60 sheep. Then 50 sheep, 24 pigs, 4 cobs, 12 cattle; now 4 cattle, 12 sheep, 6 pigs, 1 cob.
Value then 60s; now £4.
1 Freeman was in this land with 15 acres, which he could sell, but the jurisdiction lay in St. Paul's land of (Little) Warley.
Always ½ plough.
Value 3s.   93 a

Hundred of UTTLESFORD

6 Sasselin holds BONHUNT as a manor which Aelfric, a free man, held before 1066 as a manor, for 2 hides.
When acquired and now, 4 smallholders. Always 1 plough in lordship. Now ½ men's plough.
Meadow, 10 acres. Then 1 (head of) cattle and 1 pig; now 30 sheep, 2 cattle, 1 cob.
Value then and later 40s; now 55[s].

Ṫra Gisleƀti filij Turoldi. Hund̄ de Vdelesfort. Wicam .I.VIII.

tenuit Sexi . t . R . e . liƀ hō . p̄ . man . 7 . p̄ . III . hid̄ . 7 . XIII . ac̄ . tc̄

7 . p̄ . VIII . uitt . m̄ . IX . Tc̄ . 7 p̄ . VIII . bor . m̄ . XI . Sēp . III . fer . 7 . II . car.

in dn̄io . 7 . III . car . hom . Tc̄ . 7 . p̄ . filu . c . por . m̄ . LX . X . ac̄ . p̄ti.

Sēp uat . VII . liƀ . Tc̄ . I . runc̄ . L . ou . XXX . por . XXXVI . cap . m̄ . I . runc̄.

XL . ou . XXX . cap . XXVI . porc̄ . II . an.

⌐Terra Witti Leuric . Scilcheham tenuit Anfgot liƀ hō

t . r . e . p̄ man . 7 . p̄ . VIII . hid̄ . Sēp . VI . uitt . Tc̄ . VIII . bor . m̄ . X . Sēp .LIX.

. III . fer . 7 . II . car . in dn̄io . 7 . III . car . hom . Paſt . c . ou . Sēp uat

. VI . liƀ.

⌐Ṫra Hugonis de ſc̄o q̄ntino . Horninduna tenuit Winge

t . r . e . p̄ man . 7 . p̄ . I . hid̄ . 7 . dim̄ . sēp . I . car . in dn̄io . Tc̄ . III . bor. .LX.

m̄ . IIII . Silu . X . porc̄ . VIII . pars piſcinæ . Sēp . I . runc̄ . I . an.

. XXX . ou . I . porc̄ . vat . XX . fot . De hac tr̄a abſtulit Goduin.

. II . manſiones.

⌐Hund̄ de Wenfiſtreu . Wigheƀga . tenuit Aluric̄ . liƀ hō

p̄ man . 7 . p̄ . II . hid̄ . Sēp . I . car . in dn̄io . tc̄ . I . bor . m̄ . II . tc̄ . II . fer.

m̄ . III . Tc̄ . I . mot . m̄ . n̄ . Sēp . I . runc̄ . 7 . VII . an . 7 . I . porc̄ . Tc̄.

. LV . ou . m̄ . XLV . Sēp uat . XXX . fot.

⌐Hund̄ de Laxendena . Parua bricceiam . tenuit Wluard

t . r . e . p̄ man . 7 . p̄ . dim̄ . hid̄ . 7 . XV . ac̄ . m̄ ten& Hugo de dono

reginæ . p̄ tantund̄ . filu . X . porc̄ . IIII . ac̄ . p̄ti . tc̄ . I . bor . 7 . I . fer.

7 . m̄ . fimit . Sēp . I . runc̄ . VII . anim̄ . XXV . por . LIII . ou . Tc̄ . 7 p̄

uat . XX . fot . m̄ . XVI.

58   LAND OF GILBERT SON OF THOROLD

Hundred of UTTLESFORD

1   Saxi, a free man, held WICKEN (Bonhunt) before 1066 as a manor, for 3 hides and 13 acres.

Then and later 8 villagers, now 9; then and later 8 smallholders, now 11. Always 3 slaves; 2 ploughs in lordship; 3 men's ploughs.

Woodland, then and later 100 pigs, now 60; meadow, 10 acres.

Value always £7.

Then 1 cob, 50 sheep, 30 pigs, 36 goats; now 1 cob, 40 sheep, 30 goats, 26 pigs, 2 cattle.

59   LAND OF WILLIAM LEOFRIC

[   ]

1   Ansgot, a free man, held *SCILCHEHAM* before 1066 as a manor, for 7 hides.

Always 6 villagers. Then 8 smallholders, now 10. Always 3 slaves; 2 ploughs in lordship; 3 men's ploughs.

Pasture, 100 sheep.

Value always £6.

60   LAND OF HUGH OF ST. QUENTIN

[Hundred of BARSTABLE]

1   Winge held HORNDON (-on-the-Hill) before 1066 as a manor, for 1½ hides. Always 1 plough in lordship.

Then 3 smallholders, now 4.

Woodland, 10 pigs; the eighth part of a fishery. Always 1 cob, 1 (head of) cattle, 30 sheep, 1 pig.

Value 20s.

From this land Godwin took away 2 places.

Hundred of WINSTREE

2   Aelfric, a free man, held WIGBOROUGH as a manor, for 2 hides.   93 b
Always 1 plough in lordship.

Then 1 smallholder, now 2; then 2 slaves, now 3.

Then 1 mill, now none. Always 1 cob, 7 cattle and 1 pig.

Then 55 sheep, now 45.

Value always 30s.

Hundred of LEXDEN

3   Wulfward held LITTLE BIRCH before 1066 as a manor, for ½ hide and 15 acres. Now Hugh holds it by the Queen's gift, for as much.

Woodland, 10 pigs; meadow, 4 acres.

Then 1 smallholder and 1 slave; now the same.

Always 1 cob, 7 cattle, 25 pigs, 53 sheep.

Value then and later 20s; now 16[s].

.LXI. TERRA Edmundi filij Algoti . Hor̄ninduna . tenueꝛ

.ıı . liƀi hōes . t̄ . r̄ . e . ꝓ man . 7 ; ꝑ . ıı . hid . 7 . dim . 7 . xv . ac . t̄c.

.ııı . car̄ . in dn̄io . m̄ . ıı . t̄c . ıı . car̄ . hom . m̄ . ı . Sēꝑ . ı . uilt . t̄c . xıııı.

bor . m̄ . xvı . T̄c . ııı . ſer̄ . m̄ . null . Paſt . ʟ . ou . ꭕıı . ac . ꝑti . T̄c . v.

anim . ı . runc̄ . xx . por . c . ʟ . ou . m̄ . xxxv . ou . Vaɫ . ʟ . ſoɫ.

In Ead uiɫɫ . e q̄da diacon̄ habens . xxx . ac . 7 . q̄rta parte eccliæ

7 . jac& ad elemofina regis.

⁊ Matcinge ten& . E . qd tenuit Almar̄ Holefeſt . t̄ . r̄ . e . 7 . ꝓ . ı.

hid . 7 . dim . 7 . ꝓ man . T̄c . ıı . car̄ . in dn̄io . m̄ . ı . t̄c . ııı . car̄ . 7 . d̄ı

hom . m̄ . ııı . T̄c . vıı . uiɫɫ . m̄ . ıx . m̄ . ıııı . bor . t̄c . ıııı . ſer̄ . m̄.

null . Silu . ʟ . porc̄ . vııı . ac̄ . ꝑti . T̄c . vıı . uac̄ . ı . porc̄ . c . ou . v . min;

xʟ . cap̄ . ı . runc̄ . vı . uaſa ap̄ . m̄ . ıııı . an̄ . ıx . por . xxıııı . ou.

.ıı . uaſa . apū . Sēꝑ uaɫ . c . ſoɫ.

⁊ T

TERRA . Rōgi Mareſcalchi . Hund de ƀdeſtapla. .LXII.

Nezendena ; tenuit Aluuard dore . t̄ . r̄ . e . ꝓ man . 7 . ꝓ . xʟ . ac.

m̄ ten& . R . T̄c . dim . car̄ . m̄ . nuɫɫ . Sēꝑ uaɫ . ıııı . ſoɫ . 7 . In Nutlea.

; v . ac̄ . qs tenuit . Cola liƀ hō . 7 . uaɫ . ıııı . ſoɫ.

Bertuna tenuit Vluuin̄ hapra . ꝓ man . 7 . ꝓ . dim . hid . m̄ . R.

t̄c . ı . car̄ . m̄ . dim . ı . ac̄ . ꝑti . t̄c . uaɫ . x . ſoɫ . m̄ . v.

⁊ Lohou tenuit Aluuin̄ . ꝓ man . 7 . ꝓ . xʟ . ac̄ . m̄ . R . Sēꝑ . dim . car̄.

ſilu . ııı . por . vaɫ . v ; ſoɫ.

61 LAND OF EDMUND SON OF ALGOT

Hundred of BARSTABLE

1 2 free men held HORNDON (-on-the-Hill) before 1066 as a manor, for 2½ hides and 15 acres. Then 3 ploughs in lordship, now 2. Then 2 men's ploughs, now 1.
   Always 1 villager. Then 14 smallholders, now 16; then 3 slaves, now none.
   Pasture, 50 sheep; meadow, 12 acres. Then 5 cattle, 1 cob, 20 pigs, 150 sheep; now 35 sheep.
   Value 50s.
   In the same village is a deacon who has 30 acres and ¼ of a church. He lies in the King's alms.

[Hundred of HARLOW]

2 Edmund holds MATCHING, which Aelmer Holdfast held before 1066 for 1½ hides, as a manor. Then 2 ploughs in lordship, now 1. Then 3½ men's ploughs, now 3.
   Then 7 villagers, now 9; now 4 smallholders; then 4 slaves, now none.
   Woodland, 50 pigs; meadow, 8 acres. Then 7 cows, 1 pig, 100 sheep less 5, 40 goats, 1 cob, 6 beehives; now 4 cattle, 9 pigs, 24 sheep, 2 beehives.
   Value always 100s.

94 a

62 LAND OF ROGER MARSHAL

Hundred of BARSTABLE

1 Alfward Dore held NEVENDON before 1066 as a manor, for 40 acres. Now Roger holds it. Then ½ plough, now none.
   Value always 4s.

[Hundred of WITHAM]

2 In NOTLEY, 5 acres which Cola, a free man, held.
   Value 4s.

[Hundred of LEXDEN]

3 Wulfwin Hapra held 'BYRTON' as a manor, for ½ hide. Now Roger (holds it). Then 1 plough, now ½.
   Meadow, 1 acre.
   Value then 10s, now 5[s].

4 Alwin held *LOHOU* as a manor, for 40 acres. Now Roger (holds it).
   Always ½ plough.
   Woodland, 3 pigs.
   Value 5s.

Terra Àdami Filij durandi malis oꝑib; Hund de Dōmauua.

Willinghehalā tenueꝝ . v . libi hōes . t . r̃ . e . ꝑ maneꝝ . 7 . ꝑ . dim̃.
hid . tc̄ . ii . car̃ . m̃ . i . m̃ . vi . bor . val . x . fol.

Hund de Hidingfort . Horſtedafort . tenuit Godric . lib hō
ꝑ . xv . ac̃ . t . r̃ . e . m̃ . ten& . A . Tc̄ 7 . p̃ . i . car̃ . m̃ . dim̃ . Sēp . v . bor.
Silu . xi . porc . iii . ac̃ . p̃ti . Tc̄ ual . x . fol . m̃ . xiii.

Tra Goſcelm̃i Loremarij . Hund de beueñtreu Ilefort

tenueꝝ . ii . libi hōes . t . r̃ . e . ꝑ man̄ . 7 . ꝑ . iii . hid . xxx . ac̃ . min̄ . tc̄
. ii . car̃ . iñ dñio . m̃ . i . tc̄ . car̃ . 7 . dim̃ . hom . m̃ . i . Tc̄ . vii . uill̃ . m̃ . iiii.

94 b

Tc̄ . iiii . bor . m̃ . vi . Tc̄ . i . feꝝ . m̃ . n̄ . Silu . xx . porc . xx . ac̃ . p̃ti.
m̃ . i . mol . 7 . i . piſc . Sēp . ual . iiii . lib.

.LXV. Tra Johis nepotis Walerami . Hund de Wdelesfort.

Alfenham teñ Meruena liba fem . t . r̃ . e . ꝑ man̄ . 7 . ꝑ . iiii . hid.
Sēp . ii . car̃ . in dñio . Tc̄ . 7 . p̃ . vii . car̃ . hom . m̃ . vi . Sēp . viii . uill̃.
Tc̄ . 7 p̃ . i . bor . m̃ . xii . Sēp . v . feꝝ . Tc̄ filu . m̃ ccc . por . 7 . qn̄ rec.
. m̃c . m̃ . m̃ . xii . ac̃ . p̃ti . fep . i . mol . 7 . ccxx . ou . 7 . viii . uac.
7 . lx . porc . 7 . i . runc . 7 . i . pull . Tc̄ . 7 p̃ ual . vi . lib . m̃ . viii.

.LXVI. Tra Willi diaconi . Hund de Wenfiſtreu . Peltendunā.

tenuit Turchill lib hō . t . r̃ . e . ꝑ man̄ . 7 . ꝑ . v . hid . Sēp . ii . car̃ . iñ
dñio . 7 . ii . car̃ . hom . Tc̄ . iiii . uill̃ . m̃ . iii . tc̄ . ix . bor . m̃ . x . Tc̄ . ii . feꝝ . m̃ . iiii.

94 a, b

63   LAND OF ADAM SON OF DURAND MALZOR

Hundred of DUNMOW

1   5 free men held WILLINGALE before 1066 as a manor, for ½ hide.
Then 2 ploughs, now 1.
   Now 6 smallholders.
   Value 10s.

Hundred of HINCKFORD

2   Godric, a free man, held STEBBINGFORD (House) for 15 acres before
1066. Now Adam holds it. Then and later 1 plough, now ½.
   Always 5 smallholders.
   Woodland, 11 pigs; meadow, 3 acres.
   Value then 10s; now 13[s].

64   LAND OF JOCELYN LORIMER

Hundred of BECONTREE

1   2 free men held ILFORD before 1066 as a manor, for 3 hides less
30 acres. Then 2 ploughs in lordship, now 1. Then 2½ men's
ploughs, now 1.
   Then 7 villagers, now 4; then 4 smallholders, now 6; then 1   94 b
     slave, now none.
   Woodland, 20 pigs; meadow, 20 acres; now 1 mill and 1 fishery.
   Value always £4.

65   LAND OF JOHN NEPHEW OF WALERAN

Hundred of UTTLESFORD

1   Merwen, a free woman, held ELSENHAM before 1066 as a manor,
for 4 hides. Always 2 ploughs in lordship. Then and later 7 men's
ploughs, now 6.
   Always 8 villagers. Then and later 1 smallholder, now 12;
     always 5 slaves.
   Woodland, then 1300 pigs, when acquired 1100, now 1000;
     meadow, 12 acres. Always 1 mill; 220 sheep, 8 cows, 60
     pigs, 1 cob and 1 foal.
   Value then and later £6; now [£] 8.

66   LAND OF WILLIAM THE DEACON

Hundred of WINSTREE

1   Thorkell, a free man, held PELDON before 1066 as a manor, for 5
hides. Always 2 ploughs in lordship; 2 men's ploughs.
   Then 4 villagers, now 3; then 9 smallholders, now 10; then 2
     slaves, now 4.

Silu̶.ʟx.porc̄.ɪ.ſaɭ.7.ɪ.ecclia.de.xxx.ac̄.Sēp.dim̄.caῤ.7.ɪ.ſoc̄.de xvɪɪ.
ac̄.De his.v.hid̄.tulit ħamo dapifer.ʟxxx.ac̄.de arabili tῤa.7.
.cc.ac̄.de mareſc.qd̄ totū adjacebaῤ huic manerio.t̄.ῤ.e̅.7 poſt
aduentū regis Wɪɪɪɪ.ſic ħund̄ teſtaῤ.7 ħanc occupationē pr̄epimus
in manu regis.Tc̄.ſup̄dictū manēriū cū hoc toto 7 qn̄ rec̄.uaɭ.vɪ.liɓ.
7.m̄.uaɭ.c.ſoɭ.7 qd̄ inde ablatū e̅ uaɭ.xx.ſoɭ.

ᚠ Hund̄ de hidngfort.Scaldefort tenuit Godere liɓ ħo̅.p̄ maħ.
7.p̄ dim̄.hid̄.t̄.ῤ.e̅.Tc̄.7 p̄.ɪ.caῤ.m̄.ɪ.7.dim̄.tc̄.ɪɪɪ.ſeῤ.m̄.ɪ.boῤ.

95 a

ſilu̶.xɪɪ.porc̄.vɪɪ.ac̄.p̄ti.Tc̄ uaɭ.xʟ.ſoɭ.m̄.ʟ.

ᚠ T̄ra Galῠi coci.Hund̄ de Hidingfort.Scaldefort tenuit   LXVII.
liɓ ħo̅.t̄.ῤ.e̅.p̄ maħ.7.p̄.dim̄.hid̄.tc̄.7 p̄.ɪ.caῤ.7.dim̄.m̄.ɪ.Sēp.ɪ.
uiɪɪ.7.ɪɪɪ.bor.tc̄.7 p̄.ɪɪ.ſeῤ.m̄.ɪ.Silu̶.vɪɪɪ.porc̄.xɪ.ac̄.p̄ti.Tc̄.ɪɪ.
runc̄.7.xɪɪ.anim̄.7.ʟx.porc̄.7.ʟɪɪɪ.ou̶.7.ɪɪɪ.cap̄.m̄.x.anim̄.7
.vɪɪɪ.porc̄.7.ʟɪɪɪ.ou̶.7.xx.cap̄.7.v.uaſa.ap̄.Tc̄ uaɭ.xʟ.ſoɭ.m̄.ʟ.
ᚠ In Aſſeuuella.tenuit Felaga.dim̄.hid̄.p̄ maħ.m̄.Galῠ.Tc̄.ɪɪɪ.
bor.m̄.vɪɪ.Tc̄.ɪ.caῤ.7.dim̄.m̄.ɪ.Silu̶.ʟx.por.xɪ.ac̄.p̄ti.tc̄.ɪ.uac̄.7.
.xxx.porc̄.7.v.ou̶.m̄.ɪɪɪɪ.an̄.7.vɪɪɪ.porc̄.7.ʟɪɪɪ.ou̶.Tc̄.uaɭ.xʟ.
ſoɭ.m̄.ʟx.

ᚠ Hund̄ de ɓdeſtapla   .ɪ̇XVIII.
ᚠ T̄RA Moduini   Wicfort tenuit Eduin grut liɓe.p̄ maneῤ
7.p̄.dim̄.hid̄.Sēp.ɪ.caῤ.7.ɪ.bor.ɪɪɪɪ.ac̄.p̄ti.Vaɭ.x.ſoɭ.

Woodland, 60 pigs; 1 salt-house; 1 church with 30 acres.
Always ½ plough; 1 sokeman with 17 acres.
From these 5 hides, Hamo the Steward took 80 acres of arable land and 200 acres of marsh, which were all attached to this manor before 1066 and after King William's arrival, as the Hundred testifies. We have received this appropriation (to be placed) in the King's hand.
Value of the said manor with all this, then and when acquired, £6.
Value now 100s. Value of what was taken from it, 20s.

Hundred of HINCKFORD
2   Godhere, a free man, held SHALFORD as a manor, for ½ hide before 1066. Then and later 1 plough, now 1½.
    Then 3 slaves; now 1 smallholder.
    Woodland, 12 pigs; meadow, 7 acres.   95 a
    Value then 40s; now 50[s].

67   LAND OF WALTER COOK

Hundred of HINCKFORD
1   A free man held SHALFORD before 1066 as a manor, for ½ hide.
    Then and later 1½ ploughs, now 1.
        Always 1 villager; 3 smallholders. Then and later 2 slaves, now 1.
        Woodland, 8 pigs; meadow, 11 acres. Then 2 cobs, 12 cattle, 60 pigs, 53 sheep and 3 goats; now 10 cattle, 8 pigs, 53 sheep, 20 goats and 5 beehives.
    Value then 40s; now 50[s].

2   In ASHWELL (Hall) Fellow held ½ hide as a manor. Now Walter (holds it).
        Then 3 smallholders, now 7. Then 1½ ploughs, now 1.
        Woodland, 60 pigs; meadow, 11 acres. Then 1 cow, 30 pigs and 5 sheep; now 4 cattle, 8 pigs and 53 sheep.
    Value then 40s; now 60[s].

68   LAND OF MODWIN

Hundred of BARSTABLE
1   Edwin Groat held WICKFORD freely as a manor, for ½ hide. Always 1 plough;
        1 smallholder.
        Meadow, 4 acres.
    Value 10s.

Hund de Witham .   In Witham . ten& . ꝏ . 1 . hiđ . q̇m
tenuit Harold . Sẽp . 1 . car . Tc . 1 . bor . m̃ . 11 . Silu . x11 . porc . tc . v111 . ac . p̃ti .
. m̃ . 1111 . 7 alias tulit . Goisfriđ baignard . Tc . 1111 . por . m̃ . v11 . Tc . xx .
oũ . m̃ . xl . Tc . 1111 . an . m̃ . x . m̃ . 11 . runc . val . xx . fol .

Hund de Witbricteſherna . Criccheſeiam tenuit Aluuard
t . r . e . p . man . 7 . p . 1 . hiđ . Tc . 11 . bor . m̃ . 1 . Sẽp . 1 . car . paſt . xl . oũ . m̃
lxxxv . oũ . Sẽp ual . xxx . fol .

Hund de Wenſiſtreu . Legrã tenuit liƀ hõ . t . r . e . p . man .

95 b

7 . p . 11 . hiđ . Sẽp . 11 . car . in dñio . tc . v . bor . m̃ . 1111 . Sẽp . 11 . feƌ . Silu .
. xx . porc . Tc . xxx11 . oũ . m̃ . c . Tc . 1 . uac . cũ uit . m̃ . x . anim . m̃
xl . cap . 7 . 11 . runc . Tc . v11 . por . m̃ . x . Sẽp ual . lx . fol .

Hund de Laſſendena Crepinges . tenuit Aluuard p . 1 . uirg
træ . m̃ ten& . moduin . Tc . 1 . car . m̃ . dim . 11 . ac . p̃ti . Silu . xl . porc .
val . x . fol . hoc tenuit . 1 . liƀ hõ .

In Dunilanda tenuit Laghemann . 1 . uirg . m̃ ten& Moduin . Sẽp
. 1 . bor . tc . 7 p . dim . car . m̃ null . Tc ual . x . fol . m̃ . v1 .

Hund de Tendringa . Tendringã tenuit Aluric p . xv .
ac . m̃ . Mođ . p . man . 7 p tant . Tc . 11 . feƌ . m̃ . 1 . Sẽp . 1 . car . val . xx . fol
Sẽp . 1 . runc . m̃ . 1111 . por . 7 . 1111 . cap . 7 . x . oũ . 7 . v1 . an . hoc ē in dñio .

Dereleiam tenuit Goduin pƀr . p . man . 7 p . 1 . hiđ . 7 . v . ac . M ten&
. ꝏ . Tc . 1 . car . m̃ . null . Tc ual . x . fol . m̃ . xxx . đ .

Hundred of WITHAM

2 In WITHAM Modwin holds 1 hide, which Harold held. Always 1 plough.
>   Then 1 smallholder, now 2.
>   Woodland, 12 pigs. Meadow, then 8 acres, now 4; Geoffrey Baynard took the others. Then 4 pigs, now 7; then 20 sheep, now 40; then 4 cattle, now 10; now 2 cobs.
>
>   Value 20s.

Hundred of 'WIBERTSHERNE'

3 Alfward held CREEKSEA before 1066 as a manor, for 1 hide.
>   Then 2 smallholders, now 1.
>   Always 1 plough. Pasture, 40 sheep. Now 85 sheep.
>
>   Value always 30s.

Hundred of WINSTREE

4 A free man held LAYER before 1066 as a manor, for 2 hides.   95 b
>   Always 2 ploughs in lordship.
>   Then 5 smallholders, now 4; always 2 slaves.
>   Woodland, 20 pigs. Then 32 sheep, now 100; then 1 cow with a calf, now 10 cattle; now 40 goats and 2 cobs; then 7 pigs, now 10.
>
>   Value always 60s.

Hundred of LEXDEN

5 Alfward held CREPPING for 1 virgate of land. Now Modwin holds it.
>   Then 1 plough, now ½.
>   Meadow, 2 acres; woodland, 40 pigs.
>
>   Value 10s.
>   1 free man held this.

6 In (East) DONYLAND Lawman held 1 virgate. Now Modwin holds it.
>   Always 1 smallholder. Then and later ½ plough, now none.
>   Value then 10s; now 6[s].

Hundred of TENDRING

7 Aelfric held TENDRING for 15 acres. Now Modwin (holds it) as a manor, for as much.
>   Then 2 slaves, now 1. Always 1 plough.
>
>   Value 20s.
>   Always 1 cob. Now 4 pigs, 4 goats, 10 sheep and 6 cattle.
>   This is in lordship.

8 Godwin the priest held 'DERLEIGH' as a manor, for 1 hide and 5 acres. Now Modwin holds it. Then 1 plough, now none.
>   Value then 10s; now 30d.

.LXIX.⊬TRRA Ilbodonis . Wicfort tenueꞃ . ii ; liƀi h̅o̅es ; t . ꞃ . e . ꝑ . xl . ac.
&.m̅ ten& Ilbodo ſimil . Se̅p . dim̅ . caꞃ . 7 . ii . liƀi h̅o̅es ; val . xl . đ,

⊬Hunđ de Hidingfórt . Liſtuna̅ ten& Ilbodo . qđ tenuit liƀ h̅o̅
t . ꞃ . e . ꝑ . man ; 7 . ꝑ . dim̅ . hiđ . 7 . i . uirg . Se̅p . ii . caꞃ . in đn̅io . 7 . i . caꞃ , hom̅,
7 . v . bor . 7 . iiii ; ſeꞃ . 7 . xxx . ac . ꝑti . 7 . dim̅ . mol . Se̅p . v . an̅ . 7 . i . tunc̅.
7 . xliii . ou . 7 . xv . porc̅ . 7 Val . lx . ſol . 7 vii . liƀos h̅o̅es ten&
Ilbodo . tenentes . dim̅ . hiđ . t . ꞃ . e . Tc̅ . 7 qn̅ rec̅ . ii . caꞃ . m̅ . dim̅ ; 7 ; iiii ;
; bor ; Tc̅ ual ; xx . ſol . m̅ . xv ; ſol . 7 . vi . đ;

96 a

Dunilandam tenueꞃ . iiii . liƀi h̅o̅es . ꝑ . i ; hiđ . 7 . dim̅ . 7 . viii . ac̅ . m̅ ten& . I.
tc̅ . ii . caꞃ . iuꞇ eos . m̅ . i . caꞃ . m̅ . iii . bor ; ii . ac̅ . ꝑti . tc̅ . ual . x . ſol . m̅ . vii.

⊬Tra Hgheƀni Hund de ƀdeſtapla . Nezendeña̅ tenuit Touꞝ.   ,LXX.
liƀ h̅o̅ . t . ꞃ . e . ꝑ . liiii . ac̅ . Tc̅ . i . caꞃ . m̅ . nuꝉꝉ . Tc̅ ual . x . ſol . m̅ . iii . ſoꝉ.
7 . iiii . đ.

⊬Dunilanđa̅ tenuit Moduin̅ . ꝑ dim̅ . hiđ . 7 . xii . ac̅ . m̅ ten& hagheƀꞇ
ꝑ tant̅ . Se̅p . ii . bor . Tc̅ . i . caꞃ . m̅ nuꝉꝉ . Tc̅ ual . xiiii . ſoꝉ . m̅ . x.
Raineham tenuit . i . pƀr liƀe ꝑ . dim̅ . hiđ . m̅ . ten& . hag̅ . tc̅ . dim̅.
caꞃ . m̅ . n̅ . Val . x . ſol.

95 b, 96 a

69   LAND OF ILBOD

Hundred of BARSTABLE

1   2 free men held WICKFORD before 1066, for 40 acres. Now Ilbod holds it for the same. Always ½ plough;
     2 free men.
Value 40d.

Hundred of HINCKFORD

2   Ilbod holds LISTON, which a free man held before 1066 as a manor, for ½ hide and 1 virgate. Always 2 ploughs in lordship; 1 men's plough;
     5 smallholders; 4 slaves.
     Meadow, 30 acres; ½ mill. Always 5 cattle, 1 cob, 43 sheep
        and 15 pigs.
Value 60s.
     Ilbod holds 7 free men who held ½ hide before 1066. Then and when acquired, 2 ploughs, now ½.
     4 smallholders.
Value then 20s; now 15s 6d.

[Hundred of LEXDEN]   96 a

3   4 free men held (East) DONYLAND for 1½ hides and 8 acres. Now Ilbod holds it. Then 2 ploughs among them, now 1 plough.
     Now 3 smallholders.
     Meadow, 2 acres.
Value then 10s; now 7[s].

70   LAND OF HAGEBERN

Hundred of BARSTABLE

1   Tovi, a free man, held NEVENDON before 1066, for 54 acres. Then 1 plough, now none.
Value then 10s; now 3s 4d.

[Hundred of LEXDEN]

2   Modwin held (East) DONYLAND for ½ hide and 12 acres. Now Hagebert holds it for as much.
     Always 2 smallholders. Then 1 plough, now none.
Value then 14s; now 10[s].

[Hundred of CHAFFORD]

3   1 priest held RAINHAM freely, for ½ hide. Now Hagebern holds it. Then ½ plough, now none.
Value 10s.

TRa Tedrici pointel. Tilibiam ten& Hunald de . Tedrico.

qd tenuit lib hō . t . r . e . p man . 7 . xlv . ac . Sep . dim . car . 7 . i . bor.

. 7 . iiii . ac . pti . Past . l . ou . Tc ual . vii . sol . m . viii.

Hund de Witbricteſherna . Fanbruge tenuit Godric

lib hō . t . r . e . p man . 7 . p . viii . hid . m . T . in dnio . Tc . xii . uilt

m . ii . m . x . bor . tc . x . ſer . m . v . Sep . ii . car . in dnio . tc . iiii . car.

hom . m . ii . Silu . cc . porc . hic fuer . ii . libi . hōes hntes . l . ac.

pt ſupdictas hid . Tc . ii . runc . x . anim . x . porc . cl . ou . m

. ii . runc . v . aſini . viii . anim . xx . por . cc . ou . Sep ual . vii . lib.

Tedric . ten& . i . hid . 7 . dim . p eſcangio de Cogheſhala qd tenuit

Tiſelin . Tc . ii . car . m nuℓt . Tc . iii . bor . m nuℓt . Silu . iii . por.

xii . ac . pti . Tc ual . xx . ſol . m . x .

96 b

Hund de . Rochefort . Suttunam ten& . T . in dnio . qd tenuit

lib hō . t . r . e . p man . 7 . p . ii . hid . 7 . xxx . ac . Sep . ii . car . in dnio . 7.

. vi . ſer . Tc . i . bor . m . ix . Silu . l . porc . Past . c . ou . iiii . ac . pti . huic

manerio jacebant . iii . libi hōes . un tenebat . d . hid . 7 poſat abire

fine licentia dni ipsi manſionis . 7 . ali tenebat . xxx . ac . qs ten&.

Grimboℓd | de . T . 7 tci . xxx . ac . qs ten& hunold . |7 poſant abire

In dnio . rec . T . ii . runc . 7 . vii . an . vi . por . c . ou . vi . uaſa apu.

m . ii . runc . vii . an . xxi . porc . cvi . ou . Tc int totū ual . iiii.

lib . m . vii . De hoc manerio ten& . Rob . de . T . dim . hid . 7.

. ii . bor . 7 . ii . car . 7 ual . x . ſol . in eod ptio . 7 huic manerio ad

jacebat . i . ſoc . q ñ poſat recede ;

1 Hunald holds TILBURY from Theodoric, which a free man held
   before 1066 as a manor, for 45 acres. Always ½ plough;
   1 smallholder.
   Meadow, 4 acres; pasture, 50 sheep.
   Value then 7s; now 8[s].

Hundred of 'WIBERTSHERNE'
2 Godric, a free man, held (North) FAMBRIDGE before 1066 as a
   manor, for 8 hides. Now Theodoric (holds it) in lordship.
   Then 12 villagers, now 2; now 10 smallholders; then 10 slaves,
      now 5. Always 2 ploughs in lordship. Then 4 men's ploughs,
      now 2.
   Woodland, 200 pigs.
   2 free men were here, who had 50 acres separate from the
   above-mentioned hides.
   Then 2 cobs, 10 cattle, 10 pigs, 150 sheep; now 2 cobs, 5 asses,
      8 cattle, 20 pigs, 200 sheep.
   Value always £7.

3 Theodoric holds 1½ hides, by exchange for Coggeshall, which
   Tesselin held. Then 2 ploughs, now none.
   Then 3 smallholders, now none.
   Woodland, 3 pigs; meadow, 12 acres.
   Value then 20s; now 10[s].

Hundred of ROCHFORD   96 b
4 Theodoric holds SUTTON in lordship, which a free man held before
   1066 as a manor, for 2 hides and 30 acres. Always 2 ploughs in
   lordship;
   6 slaves.
   Then 1 smallholder, now 9.
   Woodland, 50 pigs; pasture, 100 sheep; meadow, 4 acres.
   To this manor belonged 3 free men. One held ½ hide; he could
   go away without the permission of the lord of this place. The
   second held 30 acres which Grimbald holds from Theodoric,
   value 10s; the third (held) 30 acres which Hunold holds, value 10s;
   they could go away.
   In lordship Theodoric acquired 2 cobs, 7 cattle, 6 pigs, 100
      sheep, 6 beehives; now 2 cobs, 7 cattle, 21 pigs, 106 sheep.
   Value then in total £4; now [£] 7.
   Of this manor, Robert holds ½ hide from Theodoric.
   2 smallholders; 2 ploughs.
   Value 10s in the same assessment.
   To this manor was attached 1 Freeman, who could not
   withdraw.

.LXXII. TRA . Rogeri . dē ſalu& dñas . Hund de Witham Ruenhale
tenuit Vlſi lib hō ‚p . man ; 7 .‚p . xxx . ac . t . r . e . ſēp . ı . car . val . xx . ſot.

Hund de hidingfort . Felſtede . tenuit . vlſi ſub comite . Algaro.
‚p . man . 7 .‚p dim hid . 7 . xxx . ac . Sēp . ıı . car . in dñio . 7 . ııı . ſer.
ſilu . xx . porc . x . ac . p̄ti . Tē . ual . xxx . ſot . m̄ . xL.

Baduuen . tenuit Vlſi lib hō ‚p . man . 7 .‚p . ı . hid . 7 . dim . Tē . ı . bor
‚p 7 . m̄ . ııı . Sēp . ıııı . ſer . 7 . ıı . car . in dñio . Silu . xL . porc . vııı . ac . p̄ti.
Sēp . ual . xL . ſot.

.LXXIII. Tra Giſlebti ſilij . ſalomonis . Hund de . Hidingfort . In

97 a

Feleſteda tenuit lib hō . xxx . ac . quas ten& . G . ſēp . ı . car . val . xx . ſot.

TRA Willi ſilij conſtantini . Taindenā tenuit . Suen . ‚p . man.   ★   . LXXIIII.
7 .‚p . ıı . hid . t . r . e . 7 . xL . ac . m̄ ten& . W . ſimil . Tē . v . uilt . ‚p 7 . m̄ . ıııı.
tē . 7 . ‚p . vıı . bor . m̄ . x . tē . ıııı . ſer . m̄ nult . Sēp . ıı . car . in dñio . tē . int
hōes . ıııı . car . P 7 . m̄ . ııı . Silu . b . porc . xx . ac . p̄ti . ſēp . ı . mot . Tē . 7 ‚p
ual . Lx . ſot . m̄ . c.

Tra Anſgeri coci . Aluielea tenuit Godeman libæ ‚p . L . ac . Sēp   . LXXV.
dim . car . 7 In Stifort tenuit lib hō . xxv . ac . 7 . int iſtā trā 7 . ſup̄dictā
ē ſēp . dim . car . 7 . ual . x . ſot.

72   LAND OF ROGER GOD-SAVE-LADIES

Hundred of WITHAM

1   Wulfsi, a free man, held RIVENHALL as a manor, for 30 acres before 1066. Always 1 plough.
Value 20s.

Hundred of HINCKFORD

2   Wulfsi held FELSTED under Earl Algar as a manor, for ½ hide and 30 acres. Always 2 ploughs in lordship;
     3 slaves.
     Woodland, 20 pigs; meadow, 10 acres.
     Value then 30s; now 40[s].

[Hundred of CHELMSFORD]

3   Wulfsi, a free man, held (Great) BADDOW as a manor, for 1½ hides.
     Then 1 smallholder, later and now 3. Always 4 slaves; 2 ploughs
        in lordship.
     Woodland, 40 pigs; meadow, 8 acres.
     Value always 40s.

73   LAND OF GILBERT SON OF SOLOMON

Hundred of HINCKFORD

1   In FELSTED a free man held 30 acres, which Gilbert holds.   97 a
     Always 1 plough.
     Value 20s.

74   LAND OF WILLIAM SON OF CONSTANTINE

[Hundred of ONGAR]

1   Swein held THEYDON as a manor, for 2 hides and 40 acres before 1066. Now William holds it for the same.
     Then 5 villagers, later and now 4; then and later 7 smallholders,
        now 10; then 4 slaves, now none. Always 2 ploughs in
        lordship. Then among the men 4 ploughs, later and now 3.
     Woodland, 500 pigs; meadow, 20 acres; always 1 mill.
     Value then and later 60s; now 100[s].

75   LAND OF ANSGER COOK

[Hundred of CHAFFORD]

1   Godman held AVELEY freely, for 50 acres. Always ½ plough.

2   In STIFFORD a free man held 25 acres. There has always been ½ plough between this land and the above-mentioned (land).
     Value 10s.

Ꞇra Rotti filij Roſcelini. Hund de Vdelesfort. Haidenam.
tenuit Aluuin lib homo . t . r . e . p man . 7 . p . v . hid . 7 . xv . ac.
ſep . xviii . uitt . Tc . iii . bor . Poſt 7 . m . vii . ſep . v . ſer . 7 . iii . car . in
dnio . 7 . viii . car . hom . 7 . viii . ac . pti . Silu . viii . porc . ii . runc.
. cc . vi . ou . xl . porc . xiii . uaſa ap . m . i . runc . ccvi . ou . xx . por.
. x . uaſa ap . Tc 7 p uat . x . lib . m . xii . 7 qda anglic Goduin ten&
ſep . xii . ac . ſep . i . bor . 7 . Leuuin ſimilit . v . ac . 7 . uat . xii . d,

Ꞇra Radulfi Pinel . Hund de Tendringa . Brubeleiam.
7 Weſtnanetuna . tenuit . Brictmar . p man . 7 . p . iiii . hid . 7 . d.
7 fuer . ibi . ii . hallæ . m ten& . R . Sep . v . uitt tc . 7 . p . xxv . bor

97 b

m . xxiii . Tc . vi . ſer . m . ix . Tc . iii . car . in dnio . m . ii . Tc . 7 p.
. x . car . hom . m . vi . Silu . dc . porc . xvi . ac . pti Sep uat . vii . lib.
hanc tra deſeruiuit . R . erga . G . de magnauilla p hoc qd ipſe
. G . dixit ei . qtin rex ſibi dederat ſeRuitiu illi træ . ſ; p duas uices
dedit de ſuo cenſu miniſtris regis . qn rex miſit legatos ſuos in hanc
tra.

.LXXVIII. Ꞇra Rotti filij Gotti . Beleſtedam tenuer . iii . libi hoes p . man.
7 . p . i . hid . 7 . d . 7 . xl . ac , Sep . iii . bor . 7 . i . ſer . 7 . ii . car . in dnio . Silu,
. x . porc . xv . ac . pti . Tc . uat . xxx . ſot . m . l.

.LXXIX . Ꞇra Rainaldi baliſtarij . Phenbruge ten& . R . de rege.
p . man . 7 . p . iii . hid . 7 . dim . ſep . i . uitt . 7 . vii . bor . 7 . ii . car . in dnio.

76   LAND OF ROBERT SON OF ROZELIN

Hundred of UTTLESFORD
1   Alwin, a free man, held HEYDON before 1066 as a manor, for 5
hides and 15 acres.
Always 18 villagers. Then 3 smallholders, later and now 7.
Always 5 slaves; 3 ploughs in lordship; 8 men's ploughs.
Meadow, 8 acres; woodland, 8 pigs. [Then] 2 cobs, 206 sheep,
40 pigs, 13 beehives; now 1 cob, 206 sheep, 20 pigs, 10
beehives.
Value then and later £10; now [£] 12.
Godwin, an Englishman, has always held 12 acres.
Always 1 smallholder.
Leofwin likewise has always held 5 acres.
Value 12d.

77   LAND OF RALPH PINEL

Hundred of TENDRING
1   Brictmer held (Great) BROMLEY and *WESTNANETUNA* as a manor,
for 4½ hides. There were 2 halls there. Now Ralph holds (them).
Always 5 villagers. Then and later 25 smallholders, now 23;   97 b
then 6 slaves, now 9. Then 3 ploughs in lordship, now 2.
Then and later 10 men's ploughs, now 6.
Woodland, 600 pigs; meadow, 16 acres.
Value always £7.
Ralph gave service for this land to G(eoffrey) de Mandeville,
because the same G(eoffrey) stated to him how the King had given
him the service of that land; but on two occasions he gave of his
dues to the King's officers when the King sent his Commissioners
into this land.

78   LAND OF ROBERT SON OF GOBERT

[Hundred of CHELMSFORD]
1   3 free men held BELSTEAD (Hall) as a manor, for 1½ hides and 40
acres.
Always 3 smallholders; 1 slave; 2 ploughs in lordship.
Woodland, 10 pigs; meadow, 15 acres.
Value then 30s; now 50[s].

79   LAND OF REGINALD GUNNER

[Hundred of ROCHFORD]
1   Reginald holds (South) FAMBRIDGE from the King as a manor, for
3½ hides.
Always 1 villager; 7 smallholders; 2 ploughs in lordship;

7 . 11 . car̄ . hom̄ . Paſt̄ . c . ou . Sēp ual . c . ſot . ſed monachi de
eli calumpniat̄ & hundret eis teſtat̄ . & dimidiā hidā ſaiſiuit juxta
illam trā p̄ aduentū regis Witti que p̄ annum ual . xxx . ſot .

.LXXX . ⌐ Terra Gonduini   Hund de Tureſtapla . Toleſhuntam
tenuit Alric̄ . p̄ man̄ . 7 . p̄ . 1 . hid̄ . m̄ ten& . G . Sēp . 11 . bor . tē . 1111 . ſer .
m̄ . v . Tē . 1 . car̄ . m̄ . dim̄ . tē ual . xxx . ſot . 7 . qn̄ recepit ualebat
xx . ſot . m̄ ual . x . ſot

LXXXI ⌐ TERRA Ottonis aurifabri . Hund de hidingfort .

98 a
Gleſtingethorp . tenuit Comes Algar̄ . p̄ dim̄ . hid̄ . m̄ ten& Otto . ſimit .
Sēp . 111 . car̄ . in dn̄io . 7 . 111 . car̄ hom̄ . Tē . x111 . bor . m̄ . xv1 . Sēp . v1 . ſer .
Silu . Lx . porc̄ . xxv . ac̄ . p̄ti . Lxxx . ou . xxx11 . anim . Lxxxv111 . por .
7 . 111 . runc̄ . 7 . x11 . ſoc̄ fuer̄ . t . r . e . m̄ . ſt . x1 . manentes in hoc man̄ .
7 . tenent . dim̄ . hid̄ . 7 . xxx . ac̄ . Sēp . 1111 . bor . 7 . 1 . car̄ . 7 . 1 . ſer . Tē . ual .
. x . lib̄ . m̄ . x11 . 7 . qn̄ . R . dedit . xv .

⌐ Tra Giſlebti p̄bri . Hund de Hidincfort . Mildeltunā tenuer̄ .   .LXXXII .
. 1x . ſoc̄ . comitis Algari . p̄ . 1 . hid̄ . 7 . dim̄ . 7 . xxv111 . ac̄ . Sēp . 1 . car̄ . 7 . d̄ .
in dn̄io . 1111 . ac̄ . 7 . dim̄ . p̄ti . ual . xx . ſot . hanc trā reclamat ex dono
reginæ .

⌐ Hund de b̄deſtapla
⌐ Tra Grimi p̄poſiti . In bura ht . Grim̄ . 11 . hid̄ . In q̄b̄z erat . 1 . car̄ .   .LXXXIII .
7 . 11 . ſerui . t . r . e . m̄ ū ſt . 11 . car̄ . in dn̄io . 7 . dim̄ . car̄ . hom̄ . 111 . uitt .
. v1 . bor . 111 . ſer . Paſtura . c . ou . 7 de iſtis . 11 . ḥ hid̄ ē una de hominib̄z foriſfactis .

97 b, 98 a

2 men's ploughs.
Pasture, 100 sheep.
Value always 100s, but the monks of Ely lay claim to it and the
Hundred testifies for them. He took possession of ½ hide next to
that land after King William's arrival, which (land's) value is 30s
a year.

80   LAND OF GUNDWIN

Hundred of THURSTABLE
1 Alric held TOLLESHUNT as a manor, for 1 hide. Now Gundwin
holds it.
    Always 2 smallholders. Then 4 slaves, now 5. Then 1 plough,
      now ½.
Value then 30s. Value when acquired 20s. Value now 10s.

81   LAND OF OTTO THE GOLDSMITH

Hundred of HINCKFORD
1 Earl Algar held GESTINGTHORPE for ½ hide. Now Otto holds it for   98 a
the same. Always 3 ploughs in lordship; 3 men's ploughs.
    Then 13 smallholders, now 16; always 6 slaves.
    Woodland, 60 pigs; meadow, 25 acres. 80 sheep, 32 cattle, 88
      pigs and 3 cobs.
    12 Freemen were there before 1066; now there are 11
dwelling in this manor. They hold ½ hide and 30 acres.
    Always 4 smallholders; 1 plough; 1 slave.
Value then £10; now [£] 12; when the King gave it [£] 15.

82   LAND OF GILBERT THE PRIEST

Hundred of HINCKFORD
1 9 Freemen of Earl Algar held MIDDLETON for 1½ hides and 28
acres. Always 1½ ploughs in lordship.
    Meadow, 4½ acres.
Value 20s.
    He claims this land by the Queen's gift.

83   LAND OF GRIM THE REEVE

Hundred of BARSTABLE
1 In BOWERS (Gifford) Grim has 2 hides in which there were 1 plough
and 2 slaves before 1066, but now there are 2 ploughs in lordship
and ½ men's plough.
    3 villagers; 6 smallholders; 3 slaves.
    Pasture, 100 sheep; woodland, ½ hide and 10 acres, laid waste.
    One of these 2 hides is from men who committed offences

erga regē . quā poſt aduentū . reg addidit . G . ad ſuā aliā trā . p . R.
filiū Wimarc . uicecomite . ſic ipſe . G . dicit . 7 hoc totū ual . t . r . e.
xl . ſol . m . l . ⌠ In Celdeuuella tenuit Godman lib hō . xx . ac . 7 . foris
fact: non potuit emdare . Dedit aut . Grim regi p . eo: xxx . ſol.
7 . p licentiā hubti de portu ten& trā . 7 ual . xx . d.

⌐Tra Vlueue uxoris Phin . Hund de bdeſtapla In Pice
ſeia erant . t . r . e . iii . hid . qs ten& Vlueua . Tc . ii . car . in dīio . 7   . LXXXIIII.

7 . i . uiſt de dim . car . 7 . iiii . ſer . 7 . i . mol . Paſt . lx . ou . Dim . hid ſiluæ . m.
. ii . car . in dīio . iii . bor . v . ſer . Val . lx . ſol . M his hid . addite ſt aliæ . iii.
hid . 7 . xxx . ac . ſiluæ . in qbʒ manent . viii . libi hōes . c . ii . car . Paſt . cxxx . ou.
Int totū ual . lx . ſol . 7 . iſtæ . iii . hid . remanent regi.
⌐Hund de Wibricteſherna . Lacendunā tenuit . Phin . lib hō . t . r . e.
p . man . 7 . p . v . hid . 7 . xv . ac . m ten& . v . Tc . vi . uiſt . m . iii . bor.
Tc . iiii . ſer . m . v . Sep . iii . car . in dīio . vii . runc . xiii . an . xxxi . porc.
. ccxlv . ou . Sep ual . iiii . lib.

. LXXXV. ⌐In Hund de Ceffeurda . tenuit Eduuard fili Suani . dim . hid.
m ten& Edeua uxor ej . Tc . i . car . m . dim . Paſt . xxx . ou . ual . x . ſol.

. LXXXVI. ⌐Tra Turchilli ppoſiti Hund de Celmeresfort In Walfarā
ten& . T . i . hid . x . ac . min . Sep . iii . bor . 7 . i . ſer . 7 . i . car . in dīio . tc

98 a, b

against the King, which after the King's arrival Grim added to his
other land through Robert son of Wymarc, the Sheriff, so Grim
himself states.
Value of all this before 1066, 40s; now 50[s].

2   In CHADWELL Godman, a free man, held 20 acres. He committed
    an offence and could not pay compensation. But Grim gave 30s
    to the King on his behalf and holds the land by permission of
    Hubert of Port.
    Value 20d.

84   LAND OF WULFEVA WIFE OF FINN

Hundred of BARSTABLE
1   In PITSEA there were 3 hides before 1066, which Wulfeva holds.
    Then 2 ploughs in lordship; 1 villager with ½ plough; 4 slaves.   98 b
        1 mill; pasture, 60 sheep; woodland, ½ hide.
    Now 2 ploughs in lordship. 3 smallholders; 5 slaves.
    Value 60s.
        Now there have been added to these hides 3 other hides and
    30 acres of woodland in which dwell 8 free men with 2 ploughs.
        Pasture, 130 sheep.
    In total value 60s. These 3 hides still belong to the King.

Hundred of 'WIBERTSHERNE'
2   Finn, a free man, held LATCHINGDON before 1066 as a manor, for
    5 hides and 15 acres. Now Wulfeva holds it.
        Then 6 villagers; now 3 smallholders; then 4 slaves, now 5.
            Always 3 ploughs in lordship.
        7 cobs, 13 cattle, 31 pigs, 245 sheep.
    Value always £4.

85   [LAND OF EDWARD SON OF SWEIN]

In the Hundred of CHAFFORD
1   Edward son of Swein held ½ hide. Now Edeva his wife holds it.
    Then 1 plough, now ½.
        Pasture, 30 sheep.
    Value 10s.

86   LAND OF THORKELL THE REEVE

Hundred of CHELMSFORD
1   In WALTER (Hall) Thorkell holds 1 hide less 10 acres.
        Always 3 smallholders; 1 slave; 1 plough in lordship. Then

inf hões.dim̃.car̃.Silu̅.xl.porc̃.vi.ac̃.p̃ti.Tc̃ ual̃.xx.sol̃.m̃.xxx.

⌐ 7 q̇dā famul̃ regis ten&.viii.ac̃.7.ual̃.ii.sol̃.

.LXXXVII. ⌐ 7 q̇dā lib̃ hõ noē Stanard tenuit 7.ten& de rege.xxx.ac̃.7
ptinent ad Witheresfelda.Sep̃.iii.bor.Tc̃.i.car̃.m̃.dim̃.Silu̅.
.viii.porc̃.vii.ac̃.p̃ti.sep̃.i.mol̃.ual̃.viii.sol̃.

.LXXXVIII. ⌐ 7 Goduin diacon̄ tenuit 7.ten&.ix.ac̃.7.ual̃.xvi.d̃.
7.i.hõ Witti.filij grossæ ten&.ii.ac̃.de soca regis.7 reddit cõ
suetudinē reg̃.

Lib̃i homines regis. In Hundret de Laxendena h̃t rex.vii.lib̃os homines.7 hos p̃po .LXXXIX
sit hunḋ hab&.tenentes dim̃ hiḋ.7 ual̃.viii.sol̃.7.i.lib̃ homo tenuit.iii.ac̃.7.d̃.
7 in his ē pastā.c.ouib;7.t̃ra.ad.ii.boues.Tc̃ ual̃.x.sol̃.7 q̇ndo.Rob̃ de monte
begonis inuasit: ualebat.x.sol̃.m̃ nichil.
7.i.lib̃ hõ tenuit.xiii.ac̃.ibi ē sep̃.i.car̃.7 silu̅.xx.porc̃.7.i.ac̃.p̃ti.Tc̃ ual̃.x.sol̃.m̃ reddit
.xx.sol̃.7 Ricard̃ hõ hamonis inuasit istā t̃ram.7 h̃t hucusq̇ ej̃ spolia

⌐INVASIONES SVp̃ reg̃ in Exsessa. In Horninduna inuasit Goduin
gudhen.ii.mansiones.quæ s̃t de t̃ra quā hug̃ de s̃co quintino de rege tenet.
7 inde dedit uadem

                                                    .XC.

among the men ½ plough.
Woodland, 40 pigs; meadow, 6 acres.
Value then 20s; now 30[s].

2 A servant of the King holds 8 acres, value 2s.

87 [LAND OF STANHARD]

[Hundred of HINCKFORD]
1 A free man, Stanhard by name, held and holds from the King 30
acres. They belong to Wethersfield.
Always 3 smallholders. Then 1 plough, now ½.
Woodland, 8 pigs; meadow, 7 acres; always 1 mill.
Value 8s.

88 [LAND OF GODWIN THE DEACON]

1 Godwin the deacon held and holds 9 acres.
Value 16d.

2 1 man of William son of Gross holds 2 acres of the King's
jurisdiction and pays the King's customary due.

89 [LAND OF] THE KING'S FREE MEN 99 a

In the Hundred of LEXDEN
1 The King has 7 free men. The Hundred-reeve has these, who hold
½ hide.
Value 8s.

2 1 free man held 3½ acres. In these there is pasture for 100 sheep;
land for 2 oxen.
Value then 10s. Value when Robert of Montbegon annexed it, 10s;
now nothing.

3 1 free man held 13 acres. Always 1 plough there.
Woodland, 20 pigs; meadow, 1 acre.
Value then 10s; now it pays 20s.
Richard, a man of Hamo, annexed that land. He still has the booty
from it.

90 ANNEXATIONS IN THE KING'S DESPITE IN ESSEX
[GODWIN WOODHEN'S ANNEXATIONS]

[Hundred of BARSTABLE]
1 In HORNDON (-on-the-Hill) Godwin Woodhen annexed 2 places
which belong to the land which Hugh of St. Quintin holds from
the King. He has given a pledge for them.

In eadē uilla idē Goduin̾ . inuafit . III . uirgatas
terræ ſup regē de tr̄a cu͡jdā libi . hōis que remanet regi p judiciū
hundret 7 iterū dedit uadē . In danruna . XV . ac̄ tr̄e q̓s tenuit
uluuinus . & remanent regi ꝙetæ : ⌐ INvaſio tedrici . puintel

⌐ In thurrucca quā . t . r . e . ten̾ . XI . libi . hōes . I . h̄ ; 7 dimidia . 7 . XLII.
ac̄ . tr̄e . 7 . m̄ . III . car̄ . in dn̄io . tc̄ . m̄ . II . Past̄ . ad . XXX . o . Tc̄ uat̄ . XL . I s,
m̄ . XX . & hanc . tr̄a . inuaſit . t . pointel 7 ē in manu regis.

99 b

Hund de Wenfiſtreu . Legram tenuit . Vluric̾ lib̄ hō . t . r . e . ꝑ . man̾ . 7 . ꝑ . II . hid̄.
7 . hoc inuaſit . Idē . T . tc̄ . II . car̄ . m̄ . nulla . nec qn̄ rec̄ . m̄ . II . bor . Tc̄ ſilu . XL . por . m̄ XXX.
Tc̄ uat̄ . LX . ſot̄ . 7 qn̄ rec̄ . XL . m̄ . XX ⊹7 In burnham inuaſit . T . XV . ac̄ . 7 . dim̄.
7 . tm̄ erant in manu regis pquā hec placita fierent.
Hund de Rochefort . Stanbruge inuaſit . T . qd̄ . tenuit . lib̄ hō . t . r . e . ꝑ man̾ . 7 . ꝑ
. I . hid̄ . 7 . dim̄ . 7 . XX . ac̄ . 7 hoc man̄ tenent . III . milit̄ . de . T . Tc̄ . III . uitt̄ . m̄ . II.
Tc̄ . I . ſer̄ . m̄ . null̄ . Tc̄ . II . bor . m̄ . V . Sēp . I . car̄ . in dn̄io . Tc̄ . II . car̄ . hom̄ . m̄ . I . Tc̄ uat̄ . XL,
ſot̄ . m̄ . c . Pachefham inuaſit . T . qd̄ tenuer̄ . II . libi . hōes . ꝑ . dim̄ . hid̄ . 7 . XV . ac̄ . Sēp.
. I . car̄ . vat̄ . XX . ſot̄ . Hec . II . maneria tenuit . T . pointel ꝓ eſcangio de coghes -
hala . 7 m̄ st̄ in manu reḡ .

2   In the same village Godwin also annexed 3 virgates of land in the King's despite from the land of a free man, which still belong to the King by the judgement of the Hundred. Again he has given a pledge.

3   In DUNTON 15 acres of land which Wulfwin held and (which) still belong to the King undisputed.

THEODORIC POINTEL'S ANNEXATION(S)

4   In (Little) THURROCK, which 11 free men held before 1066 and (hold) now, 1½ hides and 42 acres of land. Then 3 ploughs in lordship, now 2.
     Pasture for 30 sheep.
     Value then 41s; now 20[s].
     Theodoric Pointel annexed this land. It is in the King's hand.

Hundred of WINSTREE   99 b
5   Wulfric, a free man, held LAYER before 1066 as a manor, for 2 hides. Theodoric also annexed this. Then 2 ploughs, now none, nor when acquired.
     Now 2 smallholders.
     Woodland, then 40 pigs, now 30.
     Value then 60s; when acquired 40[s]; now 20[s].

[Hundred of 'WIBERTSHERNE']
6   In BURNHAM Theodoric annexed 15½ acres. However, they were in the King's hand before these pleas were brought about.

Hundred of ROCHFORD
7   Theodoric annexed (Little) STAMBRIDGE, which a free man held before 1066 as a manor, for 1½ hides and 20 acres. 3 men-at-arms hold this manor from Theodoric.
     Then 3 villagers, now 2; then 1 slave, now none; then 2 smallholders, now 5. Always 1 plough in lordship. Then 2 men's ploughs, now 1.
     Value then 40s; now 100[s].

8   Theodoric annexed PAGLESHAM, which 2 free men held for ½ hide and 15 acres. Always 1 plough.
     Value 20s.
     Robert holds from him.
     Theodoric Pointel held these 2 manors by exchange for Coggeshall. Now they are in the King's hand.

7 In Midebroc inuaſit . xx . aꞔ . Sēp . i . uiɫɫ . 7 uaɫ
. iiii . ſoɫ . 7 ſoca jac& in ecclia ſcæ trinitatis de cantorbury . ut hunđ teſtatur .
hoc &iam tenuit . T . pointel ꝓ eſcangio , 7 ē in manu regis.

Ⅴ Inuaſio Ranulfi piperelli . In Terlinga inuaſit . R . v . liƀos . hōes . tenentes . iii .
hiđ . xv . aꞔ . min . t . r . e . de hoc manerio ten& . Roǥ . de . R . ii . hiđ . 7 . lxxx . aꞔ .
7 . Ranulf . xxx . aꞔ . Tꞔ . iii . car . 7 . dim . m̃ . vi . tꞔ . ii . uiɫɫ . m̃ . v . m̃ . v . bor . Silu .
. xx . porc . xxii . aꞔ . p̃ti . Tꞔ uaɫ lxxv . ſoɫ . m̃ . iiii . liƀ . 7 . xv . ſoɫ .
7 in . Widituna . inuaſit . R . xxx . aꞔ q̃s ten& in dñio . 7 uaɫ . v . ſoɫ
7 In Staneſgata . inuaſit . R . i . hiđ . 7 . xxx . aꞔ . qđ ten& . Rađ fili brien de eo . qđ
tenuer . ii . liƀi . hōes . t . r . e . Sēp . ii . bor . 7 . i . car . Paſt . xx . ou . Tꞔ uaɫ . xv . ſoɫ
m̃ . x . 7 in Henies xx . aꞔ . 7 . đ . q̃s tenuer . xii . liƀi hōes . t . r . e . m̃ ten& Turold .
7 uaɫ . iii . ſoɫ . 7 in Lamers . ii . aꞔ . liƀe træ 7 . uaɫ . iiii . đ

Ⅴ Inuaſio hugonis de monteforti in Exſeſſa.
Hugo de montſ . inuaſit . i . liƀm homine ſup regē . 7 . W . fili groſſæ . x . liƀos . hōes . hij
oms tenebant . iii . hiđ . 7 . ix . aꞔ . t . r . e . In qƀ� tꞔ . viii . car . 7 . dim . m̃ vii . 7 . dim .
Sēp . xiii . bor . 7 . v . ſer . Tꞔ . ii . moɫ . m̃ . i . Silu . clvii . porc . xxx . aꞔ . p̃ti . Sēp uaɫ . vi .
liƀ . 7 . ii . ſoɫ .

9   In *MIDEBROC* he annexed 20 acres.
     Always 1 villager.
     Value 4s.
     The jurisdiction lies in (the lands of) the Church of Holy Trinity, Canterbury, as the Hundred testifies.
     Theodoric Pointel also held this by exchange. It is in the King's hand.

RANULF PEVEREL'S ANNEXATION(S)

[Hundred of WITHAM]

10   In TERLING Ranulf annexed 5 free men who held 3 hides less 15 acres before 1066. Of this manor, Roger holds 2 hides and 80 acres from Ranulf and Ranulf (holds) 30 acres. Then 3½ ploughs, now 6.
     Then 2 villagers, now 5; now 5 smallholders.
     Woodland, 20 pigs; meadow, 22 acres.
     Value then 75s; now £4 15s.

[Hundred of UTTLESFORD]

11   In WIDDINGTON Ranulf annexed 30 acres, which he holds in lordship.
     Value 5s.

[Hundred of 'WIBERTSHERNE']

12   In STANSGATE Ranulf annexed 1 hide and 30 acres, which Ralph son of Brian holds from him (and) which 2 free men held before 1066.
     Always 2 smallholders; 1 plough.
     Pasture, 20 sheep.
     Value then 15s; now 10[s].

[Hundred of HINCKFORD]

13   In (Great) HENNY 20½ acres which 12 free men held before 1066. Now Thorold holds (them).
     Value 3s.

14   In LAMARSH 2 acres of free land. Value 4d.

HUGH DE MONTFORT'S ANNEXATION(S) IN ESSEX   100 a

15   Hugh de Montfort annexed 1 free man in the King's despite and William son of Gross (annexed) 10 free men. All these held 3 hides and 9 acres before 1066, in which there were then 8½ ploughs, now 7½.
     Always 13 smallholders; 5 slaves.
     Then 2 mills, now 1; woodland, 157 pigs; meadow, 30 acres.
     Value always £6 2s.

7 adhuc . iiii . libos h̄oes inuasit . de . ii . hid . 7 . xx . ac̄ . quæ ual xxx . sol .

7 . erant ibi . tc̄⁄ ii . car̄ . 7 . dim̄ . m̄ null . 7 in hund de Laxendena inuasit . iii . libos

. h̄oes . tenentes . i . hid . 7 . xxx . ac̄ . in q̇bꝫ erant . iii . car̄ . m̄ . ii . 7 . dim̄ . Tc̄ . i . bor̄ . m̄ . vi .

Silu . c . porc̄ . xii . ac̄ . p̄ti . Tc̄ ual . xxx . sol . m̄ . l . 7 . un ex his . tribꝫ jac& ad

feudū sc̄i petri de . Westmonstio ad feringas . 7 hoc ē testimonio hundreti . set

fuit libat hugoni . in̄ numero suoꝫ manerioꝫ ⁄ ut dicunt sui homines .

7 In Botingham . xv . ac̄ . træ . q̊s tenuit lib h̄o . 7 m̄ ten& . W . fili grossæ 7 ual

xxxii . đ

⌐ In Hund de Cesseorda ē . i . lib h̄o de . xl . ac̄ . q̇ ptinebat ad hauelingas . t̄ . r̄ . ē .

quē m̄ h̄t . Sc̄s Petr̄ . de uuestmonastio . q̇a sua sponte uenit ad abbiam . 7 n̄ reddit

consuetudinē ad hauelingas .

⌐ Inuasio . G . de magna uill . Mascebiam tenuit Alueua liba femina . t̄ . r̄ . ē . quā

m̄ ten& . Vluric̄ . ex dono regis . 7 . G . eam inuasit sup rege . in q̇ trā ē . i . hid . 7 sēp . i .

car̄ . 7 . i . ser̄ . 7 . viii . ac̄ . p̄ti . Tc̄ ual . x . sol . m̄ . xxx . 7 in Canefelda . viii . ac̄ . træ

q̊s . G . inuasit sup regē . 7 . Ricard̄ ten& . de . eo .

⌐ . Wigghepet tenuit . Boso lib h̄o . t̄ . r̄ . ē . p̄ . man̄ . 7 p̄ . ii . hid . 7 . dim̄ . tc̄ 7 p̄ . ii . car̄ .

in dn̄io . m̄ . i . 7 . dim̄ . tc̄ . iiii . car̄ . hom̄ . Post 7 . m̄ . vi . Tc̄ . 7 p̄ . vii . uill . m̄ . viii .

tc̄ . v . ser̄ . post 7 m̄ . vii . Silu . xxx . porc̄ . xxiiii . ac̄ . p̄ti . Sēp . i . mol tc̄ . 7 p̄

ual . c . sol . m̄ . vi . lib .

16 He annexed a further 4 free men with 2 hides and 20 acres.
Value 30s. Then there were 2½ ploughs, now none.

In the Hundred of LEXDEN
17 He annexed 3 free men who held 1 hide and 30 acres, in which
there were 3 ploughs, now 2½.
Then 1 smallholder, now 6.
Woodland, 100 pigs; meadow, 12 acres.
Value then 30s; now 50[s].
One of these three (free men) belongs to the Holding of St.
Peter's, Westminster, at Feering; this is with the witness of the
Hundred. But he was delivered to Hugh in the numeration of
his manors, as his men state.

18 In BOCKINGHAM 15 acres of land, which a free man held. William
son of Gross now holds (them). Value 32d.

[ANNEXATION OF ST. PETER'S, WESTMINSTER]

In the Hundred of CHAFFORD
19 There is 1 free man with 40 acres, who belonged to Havering
(-atte-Bower) before 1066, whom St. Peter's, Westminster, now
has because he came of his own accord to the Abbey; he does not
pay customary dues to Havering (-atte-Bower).

GEOFFREY DE MANDEVILLE'S ANNEXATION(S)

[Hundred of DUNMOW]
20 Aelfeva, a free woman, held MASHBURY before 1066, which Wulfric
now holds by the King's gift. G(eoffrey) annexed it in the King's
despite. In which land there is 1 hide. Always 1 plough;
1 slave.
Meadow, 8 acres.
Value then 10s; now 30[s].

21 In CANFIELD 8 acres of land which G(eoffrey) annexed in the King's
despite. Richard holds (them) from him.

[Hundred of UTTLESFORD]
22 Boso, a free man, held ROCKELL'S FARM before 1066 as a manor,
for 2½ hides. Then and later 2 ploughs in lordship, now 1½. Then
4 men's ploughs, later and now 6.
Then and later 7 villagers, now 8; then 5 slaves, later and now 7.
Woodland, 30 pigs; meadow, 24 acres; always 1 mill.
Value then and later 100s; now £6.

Wicgepet. tenuit . lib hō . t . r . e . p man . 7 p . iii . hid . tc . 7 p . ii . car . in dnio . m
. i . 7 . dim . m . i . car . hom . 7 . i . uilt . Sep . v . bor . tc . i . fer . m . null . Sep ual . xl .
fot . 7 In Wendena . ten . lib hō . vi . ac . 7 . dim . 7 . ual . ii . fol .

In pherneham ten . iiii . libi . hōes . t . r . e . iii . hid . 7 . iii . uirg . 7 m tenent . iiii
milit de . G . Tc . 7 p . viii . car . m . v . tc . 7 p . vi . uilt . m . iii . tc . 7 p . iiii . bor . m . xv .
tc . 7 p . vii . fer . m . iii . tc . 7 p . filu . lx . por . m . l . xiiii . ac . pti . Sep ual . vi . lib .

In Stanburna . dim . hid . ten . lib hō . t . r . e . tc . 7 p . ii . car . in dnio . m nult .
Sep . dim . car . hom . 7 . iii . bor . 7 . i . fer . xii . ac . pti . Tc . 7 p . ual . xl . fot . m . l .

In Wefuunic . vi . libi hōes . t . r . e . de . i . hid . 7 . xlvi . ac . tc . i . car . m . nult . tc . 7 p
. xv . fot . m . x .

In Archefdana tenuit Goduin fech . i . hid . viii . ac . min . modo e in manu reg
Tc . i . bor . 7 . i . car . m . nich . ii . ac . pti . Tc . ual . xx . fot . m . x . 7 ifta tra . tenuit . G .
de magna uilt . 7 . xv . ac . tenuit . Vlmar . ad feudu Anfgari fub . G . 7 . co
mitat non teftat .

⌐ Hugo de bnerijs . tenebat . xxxvii . ac . de rege . qd negauit 7 . poftea
fuit derationata ad opus reg . 7 . dedit uade . Sep . i . car . in dnio . 7 . i . bor . Silu .
xl . porc . iiii . ac . pti . tc . ual . x . fot . m . xx .

23 A free man held ROCKELL'S FARM before 1066 as a manor, for 3   100 b
hides. Then and later 2 ploughs in lordship, now 1½. Now 1
men's plough;
     1 villager. Always 5 smallholders. Then 1 slave, now none.
Value always 40s.

24 In WENDENS a free man holds 6½ acres. Value 2s.

[Half-Hundred of CLAVERING]
25 In FARNHAM 4 free men held 3 hides and 3 villagers before 1066.
Now 4 men-at-arms hold (them) from G(eoffrey). Then and later
8 ploughs, now 5.
     Then and later 6 villagers, now 3; then and later 4 smallholders,
       now 15; then and later 7 slaves, now 3.
     Woodland, then and later 60 pigs, now 50; meadow, 14 acres.
Value always £6.

[Hundred of HINCKFORD]
26 In STAMBOURNE a free man held ½ hide before 1066. Then and
later 2 ploughs in lordship, now none. Always ½ men's plough;
     3 smallholders; 1 slave.
     Meadow, 12 acres.
Value then and later 40s; now 50[s].

[Hundred of 'WIBERTSHERNE']
27 In *WESUUNIC* 6 free men before 1066 with 1 hide and 46 acres.
Then 1 plough, now none.
Value then and later 15s; now 10[s].

[Hundred of UTTLESFORD]
28 In ARKESDEN Godwin Sech held 1 hide less 8 acres. Now it is in
the King's hand.
     Then 1 smallholder and 1 plough; now nothing.
     Meadow, 2 acres.
Value then 20s; now 10[s].
     Geoffrey de Mandeville held that land. Wulfmer held 15 acres
in Asgar's Holding under Geoffrey; the County does not testify.

[HUGH OF BERNIÈRES'S ANNEXATION]

29 Hugh of Bernières used to hold 37 acres from the King, which he
denied; later on it was adjudged to the King's use and he gave a
pledge. Always 1 plough in lordship;
     1 smallholder.
     Woodland, 40 pigs; meadow, 4 acres.
Value then 10s; now 20[s].

⌐In Plesinchov . tenut lib hō . 1 . hiđ . tŕæ . q̃m humfrid aurei testiculi . inuasit
sup . regē . Sep . 1 . cař . in dñio . 7 . vii . bor . 7 . ii . seŕ . Silu . xxx . porč . vii . ač . p̃ti .
tē . 1 . mot . tē ual . xvi . sot . m̃ . xxiii .

⌐In Wighebga addidit Hamo dapifer . ii . soč . reḡ . q̃s inuasit sup rege . de .
xxx . ač . 7 ual . iiii . sot . 7 In Careseia . viii . ač . 7 ual . viii . đ . 7 in Stanburna . X

+ . xl . ač . q̃s ten . Alestan lib hō . 7 . xii . libi hões . t . r . e . 7 adhuc . hīt Sēp . ii . cař . 7 . iii . bor . 7 ual . xl . sot .

⌐In Hunđ de Odelesfort . occupauit . W . cardun . 1 . soč . de . viii . ač . 7 . jac̃t
ad Cishelle . de feudo . G . de magna uilt . 7 . ual . ii . sot .

101 a

⌐Dim̃ . Hunđ de . Clauelinga . Inuasio Suani . Bolitunā 7 . Bertunā . ten
Goduin lib hō . de Heroldo . t . r . e . p man . 7 . p . iiii . hiđ . 7 . dim̃ . m̃ tenđ Alured
de . eo . Sep . ii . cař . in dñio . 7 . v . car . hom . 7 . vii . uitt . 7 . xiii . bor . 7 . v . seŕ . Silu .
. xx . porč . ii . ač . p̃ti . Tē . 7 p ual . iiii . lib . m̃ . vi . hanc tŕā inuasit Rob fili
uuimarc t . r . Witti . 7 . adhuc tenđ . Suen .

[HUMPHREY GOLDENBOLLOCKS'S ANNEXATION]

[Hundred of DUNMOW]

30 In 'PLESINGHO' a free man held 1 hide of land, which Humphrey Goldenbollocks annexed in the King's despite. Always 1 plough in lordship;
> 7 smallholders; 2 slaves.
> Woodland, 30 pigs; meadow, 7 acres; then 1 mill.

Value then 16s; now 23[s].

[HAMO THE STEWARD'S ANNEXATION]

[Hundred of WINSTREE]

31 In (Little) WIGBOROUGH Hamo the Steward added 2 Freemen of the King's with 30 acres, whom he annexed in the King's despite. Value 4s.

[Hundred of 'WIBERTSHERNE']

32 In NORTHEY ISLAND 8 acres. Value 8d.

[Hundred of HINCKFORD]

33 In STAMBOURNE 40 acres, which Alstan, a free man, and 12 free men held before 1066 and still have. Always 2 ploughs;
> 3 smallholders.

Value 40s.

[WILLIAM CARDON'S ANNEXATION]

In the Hundred of UTTLESFORD

34 William Cardon appropriated 1 Freeman with 8 acres. He belongs to (Great) Chishill, of Geoffrey de Mandeville's Holding. Value 2s.

Half-Hundred of CLAVERING   101 a

SWEIN'S ANNEXATION

35 Godwin, a free man, held BOLLINGTON (Hall) and *BERTUNA* from Harold before 1066 as a manor, for 4½ hides. Now Alfred holds (them) from him. Always 2 ploughs in lordship; 5 men's ploughs;
> 7 villagers; 13 smallholders; 5 slaves.
> Woodland, 20 pigs; meadow, 2 acres.

Value then and later £4; now [£] 6.
> Robert son of Wymarc annexed this land after 1066. Swein still holds (it).

In Magghedana . Inuafit Albic de uer . i . hid . 7 . dim . 7 . xv . ac . qd ten .

. iii . libi hões . t . r . e . Tc . v . car . Poft 7 m̃ . iiii . Sẽp . vi . uitt . 7 . vi . bor . 7 . iii . fer .

Silu . xxx . porc . 7 . ix . ac . p̃ti . tc 7 p̃ uat . lx . fot . m̃ . iiii . lib .

7 In Smaltuna . xv . ac . tr̃æ . q̃s ten lib hõ . t . r . e . Tc . i . car . Poft . dim . m̃

nutt . 7 . uat . iii . fot . / In Mappefteda 7 In Pebeners . inuafit uxor albici . de uer . +

X . v . libos hões . de . i . ac . 7 . iiii . parte al ᵗ i . qd tenuit Tidbald fub ea . 7 uat . iii . fot .

/ . Rad . baignard inuafit in . henhã . dim . hid . 7 . x . ac . qd tenuer̃ . ii . libi

hões . t . r . e . Sẽp . i . car . uat . xii . fot . 7 In Celueftuna . i . hid . 7 . xliii . ac .

q̃s tenuer̃ . vi . libi . hões . t . r . e . Tc . 7 p̃ . iiii . car . m̃ . iii . xv . ac . p̃ti . uat . xl . fot .

/ In bolintuna tenuit . i . lib . hõ . xx . ac . t . r . e . 7 . adhuc ten & . f; celauit 7 idõ dedit uadē

7 uat . x . fot .

/ In Phernᵉham tenuit lib hõ . xxx . ac . m̃ ten & . Rad Latimar . f; celauit . 7

idõ dedit uad . 7 . uat . x . fot .

[AUBREY DE VERE'S ANNEXATIONS]

36 In MANUDEN Aubrey de Vere annexed 1½ hides and 15 acres, which 3 free men held before 1066. Then 5 ploughs, later and now 4.
    Always 6 villagers; 6 smallholders; 3 slaves.
    Woodland, 30 pigs; meadow, 9 acres.
Value then and later 60s; now £4.

[Hundred of HINCKFORD]
37 In SMALTON 15 acres of land, which a free man held before 1066. Then 1 plough, later ½, now none.
Value 3s.

[AUBREY DE VERE'S WIFE'S ANNEXATION]

38 In (Little) MAPLESTEAD and in PEBMARSH Aubrey de Vere's wife annexed 5 free men with 1 acre and the fourth part of another which Theobald held under her. Value 3s.

[RALPH BAYNARD'S ANNEXATIONS]

[Hundred of FRESHWELL]
39 Ralph Baynard annexed ½ hide and 10 acres in HENHAM, which 2 free men held before 1066. Always 1 plough. Value 12s.

[Hundred of HINCKFORD]
40 In COUPALS FARM 1 hide and 43 acres, which 6 free men held before 1066. Then and later 4 ploughs, now 3.
    Meadow, 15 acres.
Value 40s.

[1 FREE MAN'S ANNEXATION]

[Half-Hundred of CLAVERING]
41 In BOLLINGTON (Hall) 1 free man held 20 acres before 1066. He still holds (them), but he concealed (the fact) and so he has given a pledge. Value 3s.

[RALPH LATIMER'S ANNEXATION]

42 In FARNHAM a free man held 30 acres. Now Ralph Latimer holds (them), but he concealed (the fact) and so he has given a pledge. Value 10s.

⎰In Liffildeuuella . tenuit . ten& sep . ɪ . liƀ hō . xxx . aċ . 7 . ual . vɪ . fol . 7 . vɪɪɪ . đ.

⎰Inuafio Turoldi In Hanies tenueꝛ . ɪɪɪɪ . liƀi hōes . t̊ . ꞃ̊ . e̊ . xvɪɪɪ . aċ.

7 . adhuc tenent . Sep . dim̊ . caꝛ̊ int eos ⸗ 7 . ual . ɪɪɪ . fol.

In Lamers inuafit . Turold⁹ . xʟvɪɪ . aċ . q̊s tenueꝛ . vɪɪɪ . liƀi hōes . t̊ . ꞃ̊ . e̊ . 7 adhuc tenent. Sep . dim̊ . caꝛ̊ . 7 ual . v . fol.

⎰In vafio Walerami . In Heni . dim̊ . hid . 7 . x . aċ . 7 . & . dim̊ . qđ tenueꝛ . vɪɪ . liƀi hōes . t̊ . ꞃ̊ . e̊ . 7 hn̄t sep . ɪ . caꝛ . 7 . ɪɪɪɪ . aċ . p̊ti . 7 . ual . x . fol . hoc ten& Roḡ de . Ioħe . In halfteda ten̊ . Vluuin⁹ . x . aċ . q̊s inuafit Waleꝛ̊ . Sep . ɪ . caꝛ . t̄c . . ɪ . bor . m̊ . xʟ . t̄c . ɪɪɪ . feꞃ . m̊ . null⁹ . Silu . xvɪ . por . v . aċ . p̊ti . t̄c ual . xx . fol . m̊ . xxx.

⎰In branchetreu . xxx . aċ . tꞃæ tenueꝛ . ɪɪɪ . liƀi hōes . t̊ . ꞃ̊ . e̊ . 7 . ual . ɪɪɪ . fol . hanc tꞃā inuafit Ledmaꝛ⁹ de hamefteda . 7 . tenuit ad feudū Ricardi . 7 . R . n̄ ē inde fibi tutor.

⎰Invafio . Ricardi filij . Comitis Gifleƀti . Almar⁹ de ƀlea . Golftan. Aluric de Alreforda . Vluric de branduna . Ifti tenent . dim̊ hid . 7 . vɪ . aċ. 7 tenuerunt . t̊ . ꞃ̊ . e̊ . m̊ tenet eos . Goifmeꝛ⁹ . de . R . Sep . ɪ . caꝛ . 7 . ɪ . bor . 7 . v . aċ . Sep ual . xxvɪɪɪ . fol.

[1 FREE MAN'S ANNEXATION]

43 In *LIFFILDEUUELLA* 1 free man held (and) has always held 30 acres. Value 6s 8d.

THOROLD'S ANNEXATION(S)

[Hundred of HINCKFORD]

44 In (Great) HENNY 4 free men held 18 acres before 1066 and still hold (them). Always ½ plough among them. Value 3s.

45 In LAMARSH Thorold annexed 47 acres which 8 free men held   101 b before 1066 and still hold. Always ½ plough. Value 5s.

WALERAN'S ANNEXATION(S)

46 In HENNY ½ hide and 10½ acres, which 7 free men held before 1066. They have always had 1 plough.
    Meadow, 4 acres.
Value 10s.
    Roger holds this from John.

47 In HALSTEAD Wulfwin held 10 acres which Waleran annexed. Always 1 plough.
    Then 1 smallholder, now 40; then 3 slaves, now none.
    Woodland, 16 pigs; meadow, 5 acres.
Value then 20s; now 30[s].

[LEDMER OF HEMPSTEAD'S ANNEXATION]

48 In BRAINTREE 3 free men held 30 acres of land before 1066. Value 3s. Ledmer of Hempstead annexed this land and held it of Richard's Holding. Richard is not his protector for it.

ANNEXATION(S) OF RICHARD SON OF COUNT GILBERT

49 Aelmer of Borley, Goldstan, Aelfric of Alderford, Wulfric of Brundon. These men hold ½ hide and 6 acres and held (them) before 1066. Now Goismer holds them from Richard. Always 1 plough;
    1 smallholder.
    5 acres.
Value always 28s.

In Phincinghefelda ten& Ernald de .R . lxxx . ac . qd tenuit brictic . lib
hō . t . r . e . Sep . ii . car . in dnio . Tc . 7 p . i . uilt . m̄ . nult . Tc . 7 p . iii . bor . m̄ . viii .
Sep . iii . ser . Tc filu . xl . porc . m̄ . xxx . Tc . 7 p ual . xl . sot . m̄ . lx .
Ad Laceleam tenuit Grim . dim hid . q̄m ten& Ernald . Sep . ii . car . tc . 7 p
. iiii . bor . m̄ . viii . Tc . ii . ser . m̄ . null . tc 7 p silu . lxxx . por . m̄ . lx . x . ac .
p̄ti . tc . 7 p ual . xl . sot . m̄ . lx .
Ad Ersham tenuit brictmar lib hō . i . hid . t . r . e . m̄ ten& Wielard .
Tc . 7 p . i . car . m̄ . i . 7 . dim̄ . tc . ii . bor . Post 7 m̄ . vii . ix . ac . p̄ti . Tc ual . xxx . sot
post 7 m̄ . xl .

In Weninghou ten& Germund xxxvii . ac . 7 . dim̄ . qd .

102 a
qd tenuit Coleman lib hō . t . r . e . Sep . iii . car . in dnio . Tc . 7 . p . ii . car . hom . m̄ . iii .
. i . ser . Silu . iiii . porc . x . ac . p̄ti . tc . ual . lx . sot . m̄ . iiii . lib . 7 . x . sot .
In Geldeham ten& burnart . xl . ac . q̄s tenuit . Goduin lib hō . t . r . e . Sep . i . car .
7 . ii . bor . Silu . x . porc . v . ac . p̄ti . Tc ual . xx . sot . Post 7 m̄ . xxx .
In barlea ten& Anschetill . dim̄ . hid . 7 . xxiii . ac . qd ten . Grim . 7 . Godeua . libi
hōes . t . r . e . Tc . i . car . m̄ . i . 7 . dim̄ . Tc . 7 p . iii . bor . m̄ . v . ix . ac . p̄ti . Tc . ual . xx . sot
post . xxx . m̄ . xl .
In Topesfelda ten& . Rad . xv . ac . qd tenuit Alestan lib hō . t . r . e . Sep . i . car .
tc . 7 p . iiii . bor . m̄ . vii . tc . 7 p . iiii . ser . m̄ . null . Silu . xx . por . vi . ac . p̄ti . Tc .
7 p ual . xx . sot . m̄ . xxx .

50 In FINCHINGFIELD Arnold holds 80 acres from Richard which Brictric, a free man, held before 1066. Always 2 ploughs in lordship.

> Then and later 1 villager, now none; then and later 3 smallholders, now 8; always 3 slaves.
> Woodland, then 40 pigs, now 30.

Value then and later 40s; now 60[s].

[Hundred of DUNMOW]

51 At LASHLEY (Hall) Grim, a free man, held ½ hide which Arnold holds. Always 2 ploughs.

> Then and later 4 smallholders, now 8; then 2 slaves, now none.
> Woodland, then and later 80 pigs, now 60; meadow, 10 acres.

Value then and later 40s; now 60[s].

[Hundred of HINCKFORD]

52 At HORSEHAM (Hall) Brictmer, a free man, held 1 hide before 1066. Now Widelard holds (it). Then and later 1 plough, now 1½.

> Then 2 smallholders, later and now 7.
> Meadow, 9 acres.

Value then 30s; later and now 40[s].

53 In HOWE Germund holds 37½ acres which Colman, a free man, held before 1066. Always 3 ploughs in lordship. Then and later 2 men's ploughs, now 3.   102 a

> 1 slave.
> Woodland, 4 pigs; meadow, 10 acres.

Value 60s; now £4 10s.

54 In YELDHAM Bernard holds 40 acres which Godwin, a free man, held before 1066. Always 1 plough;

> 2 smallholders.
> Woodland, 10 pigs; meadow, 5 acres.

Value then 20s; later and now 30[s].

55 In BORLEY Ansketel holds ½ hide and 23 acres, which Grim and Godiva, free men, held before 1066. Then 1 plough, now 1½.

> Then and later 3 smallholders, now 5.
> Meadow, 9 acres.

Value then 20s; later 30[s]; now 40[s].

56 In TOPPESFIELD Ralph holds 1·5 acres which Alstan, a free man, held before 1066. Always 1 plough.

> Then and later 4 smallholders, now 7; then and later 4 slaves, now none.
> Woodland, 20 pigs; meadow, 6 acres.

Value then and later 20s; now 30[s].

In Topesfelda . ten& . G . xv . ac . q̄d tenuit . duua . Sēp . ı . car . in dñio . 7 . ı . car
hominū . 7 . ııı . uilt . 7 . ıı . bor . 7 . ıı . ſer . Silu . xxx . porc . vııı . ac . p̄ti . Tc̄
7 p̄ uat . ʟ . ſot . m̄ . ʟx .

In Nortuna ten& Maſcherell . ᴌv . ac . q̄d tenuit . briſtric lib hō . t . r . e .
tē . ı . car . in dñio . poſt . 7 . m̄ . ıı . Sēp . ı . car . hom . 7 . v . uilt . Tc̄ . 7 poſt
. v . bor . m̄ . vııı . Tc̄ . 7 p̄ . ııı . ſer . m̄ . ıı . Silu . xʟ . por . x . ac . p̄ti . Tc̄ uat . xʟ .
ſot . poſt 7 . m̄ . ʟx .

⌐ In bebenhers tenuit Leuecilt . lib hō . ııı . ac . 7 . adhuc ten& . 7 . Deroll
in Alfelmeſtuna . ıııı . ac . 7 . holt . lib hō . ı . ac . 7 In bumeſteda Leuuin
7 Lemar . v . ac . 7 In Salinges Algar . xx . ac . 7 In Oluituna . briſtolf
xxx . ac . Iſti oñs habebant . t . r . e . ııı . car . Tc̄ . 7 p̄ . ııı . bor . m̄ . vııı .
tē . 7 p̄ . ıı . ſer . m̄ null . Silu . xıı . por . vııı . ac . 7 . dim . p̄ti . Tc̄ 7 p̄
uat . xxx . ſot m̄ . xʟv . 7 . ıı . đ .

De iſtis ſup̄diĉtis hōibȝ habuit Wiſgar comdationē tantū .

In benediſc . inuaſit Wiſgar antec . R . xxx . ac . p̄qua rex uenit in hanc tr̄a .
7 poſt ea habuit Ingelric illā . 7 hunđ teſtat q̄d p̄tinebat ad feudū Ingelrici . ſ;
huc uſqȝ tenuit illā . R .

In bȳrdefelda . tenuit Felaga . ı . hid . 7 . xxx . ac . de comite . Algaro . 7 poſtq
rex uenit in hanc patriā inuaſit . R . iſtā terrā q̄m n̄ tenuit anteceſſor ej
ut hunđ teſtat . Sēp . ııı . uilt . m̄ . vıı . bor . tē . ııı . ſer . m̄ . ı . tē . ı . car . 7 . dim
in dñio . m̄ . ı . Sēp . ı . car . hom . Sjlu . c . por . xxvıı ac . p̄ti . m̄ . ı . mot . tē uat
. ıııı . lib . m̄ . ʟx . ſot .

In hocſenga tenuit Felaga dim . hid . m̄ ten& . Ric . ſic iſtā ſup̄diĉtā . 7 . Galt
de eo . Sēp . ıı . uilt . 7 . ı . car . Silu . ıı . porc . ıııı . ac . p̄ti . vat . xıı . ſot .

57 In TOPPESFIELD G. holds 15 acres, which Dove held. Always 1 plough in lordship; 1 men's plough;
> 3 villagers; 2 smallholders; 2 slaves.
> Woodland, 30 pigs; meadow, 8 acres.

Value then and later 50s; now 60[s].

58 In CORNISH HALL Mascerel holds 55 acres which Brictric, a free man, held before 1066. Then 1 plough in lordship, later and now 2. Always 1 men's plough;
> 5 villagers. Then and later 5 smallholders, now 8; then and later 3 slaves, now 2.
> Woodland, 40 pigs; meadow, 10 acres.

Value then 40s; later and now 60[s].

59 In PEBMARSH Leofcild, a free man, held 3 acres and still holds (them).

60 In ALPHAMSTONE Derwulf (holds) 3 acres and Hold, a free man, 1 acre.

61 In (Steeple) BUMPSTEAD Leofwin and Leofmer (hold) 5 acres.

62 In (Great) SALING Algar (holds) 20 acres.

63 In OVINGTON Brictwulf (holds) 30 acres.
> All these had 3 ploughs before 1066.
> Then and later 3 smallholders, now 8; then and later 2 slaves, now none.
> Woodland, 12 pigs; meadow, 8½ acres.

Value then and later 30s; now 45[s] 2d.
> Of the above-mentioned men Withgar had only the patronage.

64 In BENDYSH (Hall) Withgar, Richard's predecessor, annexed 30   102 b
acres after the King came to this land. Later on Engelric had it. The Hundred testifies that it belonged to Engelric's Holding, but up to now Richard has held it.

65 In (Great) BARDFIELD Fellow held 1 hide and 30 acres from Earl Algar. After the King came to this land, Richard annexed that land which his predecessor did not hold, as the Hundred testifies.
> Always 3 villagers. Now 7 smallholders; then 3 slaves, now 1.
> Then 1½ ploughs in lordship, now 1. Always 1 men's plough.
> Woodland, 100 pigs; meadow, 27 acres; now 1 mill.

Value then £4; now 60s.

66 In *HOCSENGA* Fellow held ½ hide. Now Richard holds (it) as (he holds) the above-mentioned land. Walter (holds) from him.
> Always 2 villagers; 1 plough.
> Woodland, 2 pigs; meadow, 4 acres.

Value 12s.

In Hafinghā tenuit lib̄ hō . 11 . ac̄ . 7 . dim̄ . in hund̄ de Laxedana . m̄ ten& . R.
7 . ibi ē m̄ . 1 . mol . reddens . xv . fol . 7 tn̄ erat cm̄dat antec̄ Ricardi.

In Hund̄ de Laxendena tenuit Luttin in Colun . xl . ac̄ . m̄ ten& . R.
7 in hac tr̄a antec̄ ej nullā habuit confuetudinē . n cōmdationē . Tc̄ . 1111 .
bor . m̄ . vi . Sēp . 1 . car̄ . Silu . xx . por . 1111 . ac̄ p̄ti . m̄ . 1 . mol . val . xx . fol.

In Crepinga . ten& Aluuard̄ . lx . ac̄ . 7 . 1111 . ac̄ . 7 . 1111 . ac̄ . 7 . dim̄ . libē . qd̄ . m̄
ten& . R . ficuti aliā . tc̄ . fub ipfo . 1111 . bor . m̄ . vi . Sēp . 1 . car̄ . Silu . xx . porc .
. 11 . ac̄ . p̄ti . val . xx . fol.

7 Aluui uenator tenuit libē . dim̄ hid̄ . 7 . xxvi . ac̄ . 7 . dim̄ . m̄ ten& . R.
in b̄colt fic aliā . tc̄ . 11 . bor . m̄ . vi . Sēp . 1 . car̄ . Silu . xv . por . 11 . ac̄ . p̄ti.
Tc̄ . dim̄ mol . m̄ n̄ . tc̄ ual . xx . fol . m̄ . xxxvi.

In Colun tenuit vluric libē . v . ac̄ . m̄ . R . fic alios . val . 11 . fol.

In Forhā tenuit Touillda . 111 . ac̄ . m̄ . R . fic alios . 7 ual . vii . d̄.

In b̄colt ten̄ . Goding . vi . ac̄ . m̄ . R . tc̄ . d̄ . car̄ . m̄ . 11 . bou . 1 . ac̄ . p̄ti . tc̄ ual . xxxii . d̄.
m̄ . v . fol.

103 a

In Halfteda tenuit lib̄ hō . t . r . c . 11 . ac̄ . 7 . dim̄ . 7 ual . xxx . d̄ . Iftos denarios
recepit Aluret p̄pofit . R . 7 inde dedit uadē.

In Herfham tenuit lib̄a femina . xxx . ac̄ . m̄ ten& Wielard de rege ut dic̄.
f; hund̄ non teftat . 7 . R . fili comitis . G . habuit feruitiū . Tc̄ . dim̄ . car̄ . m̄ . n̄ .
m̄ . 11 . bor . Val . x . fol.

In branchetreu . 111 . libi hōes . t . r . e . xxx . ac̄ . qs Letmar p̄pofit reclamauit ad
feudū . Ricardi . f; hōes illi n̄ teftant . 7 inde dedit uadē . 7 ual . 111 . fol.

67 In *HASINGHAM* a free man held 2½ acres in the Hundred of LEXDEN. Now Richard holds (them).
    Now 1 mill there, which pays 15s.
    However, he was under the patronage of Richard's predecessor.

In the Hundred of LEXDEN

68 Lutting held 40 acres in COLNE. Now Richard holds (them). In this land his predecessor had no customary due nor patronage.
    Then 4 smallholders, now 6. Always 1 plough.
    Woodland, 20 pigs; meadow, 4 acres; now 1 mill.
    Value 20s.

69 In CREPPING Alfward holds freely 60 acres and 4 acres and 4½ acres, which Richard now holds (on the same terms) as the other land.
    Then under him 4 smallholders, now 6. Always 1 plough.
    Woodland, 20 pigs; meadow, 2 acres.
    Value 20s.

70 Alfwy Hunter held ½ hide and 26½ acres freely. Now Richard holds (them), in (West) BERGHOLT, (on the same terms) as the other land.
    Then 2 smallholders, now 6. Always 1 plough.
    Woodland, 15 pigs; meadow, 2 acres; then ½ mill, now none.
    Value then 20s; now 36[s].

71 In COLNE Wulfric held 5 acres freely. Now Richard (holds them on the same terms) as the others. Value 2s.

72 In FORDHAM Tovild held 3 acres. Now Richard (holds them on the same terms) as the others. Value 7d.

73 In (West) BERGHOLT Goding held 6 acres. Now Richard (holds them). Then ½ plough, now 2 oxen. Meadow, 1 acre. Value then 32d; now 5s.

[Hundred of HINCKFORD]   103 a

74 In HALSTEAD a free man held 2½ acres before 1066. Value 30d. Alfred, Richard's reeve, has acquired those pence and has given a pledge for them.

75 In HORSEHAM (Hall) a free woman held 30 acres. Now Widelard holds (them) from the King, as he states; but the Hundred does not testify. Richard son of Count Gilbert has had the service. Then ½ plough, now none.
    Now 2 smallholders.
    Value 10s.

76 In BRAINTREE 3 free men (held) 30 acres before 1066, which Ledmer the reeve has claimed for Richard's Holding; but the latter's men do not testify. He has given a pledge for them. Value 3s.

In Ceauride.xxx.ac̄.q̄s teñ Vluric̄ lib̄ hō.t̄.r̄.e̊.m̄ ten& Garner̄ hō.Ricardi.
7 uocauit Ilbodonē ad tutorē.7 p̄ ea n̄ adduxit tutorē.7.ual̄.vιιι.ſol̄.
In Ead̄ uill̄ teñ.ιι.lib̄i hōes.dim̄.hid̄.t̄.r̄.e̊.hanc tr̄a inuaſit Ailmar̄ p̄poſit
.R.7 reuocauit eū ad tutorē.ſ; ipſe ſibi defuit.7.ex hoc dedit ille uadē.7
ual̄.xvι.ſol̄.

⌐Monachi de cantorb̄ia tenent in Lalinga.ι.hid̄.q̊m tenebant.ιιι.lib̄i hōes
 t̄.r̄.e̊.Sēp.ι.car̄.ual̄.xx.ſol̄.hec tr̄a addita ē illi manerio t̄.r.Witti.

⌐In Colun ten& Turb̄n.xxιι.ac̄.ſine dono reḡ 7.nulla̅ reddit conſuet̄.

⌐Henric̄ de Ferrerijs inuaſit.ι.lib̄m hominē.de.xvι.ac̄.in Stepla.
 7 ual̄.ιι.ſol̄.

⌐.W.Leuric inuaſit in Sciddeha̅.ι.lib̄m hom̄.de.vι.ac̄.ual̄.xιι.đ.   ★
⌐In bumeſteda inuaſit Rob̄ blund̄.x.ac̄.q̊s tenuit Edui lib̄ hō Sēp.ι.car̄.
 ual̄.xx.ſol̄.

103 b

⌐In Mildetuna Inuaſit.R.malet.xv.ac̄.q̄s teñ lib̄ hō.t̄.r̄.e̊.Sēp.dim̄
 car̄.ual̄.v.ſol̄.

[Hundred of DUNMOW]

' In CHAURETH 30 acres which Wulfric, a free man, held before 1066. Now Warner, a man of Richard's, holds (them). He called Ilbod as a protector. Later on he did not produce a protector. Value 8s.

In the same village 2 free men held ½ hide before 1066. Aelmer, Richard's reeve, annexed this land and called him as a protector but he failed him. Because of this he has given a pledge. Value 16s.

[ANNEXATION OF THE MONKS OF CANTERBURY]

[Hundred of 'WIBERTSHERNE']

) The monks of Canterbury hold 1 hide in LAWLING, which 3 free men used to hold before 1066. Always 1 plough. Value 20s.
   This land was added to the manor after 1066.

[THORBERN'S ANNEXATION]

[Hundred of LEXDEN]

) In COLNE Thorbern holds 22 acres without the King's gift. He has paid no customary due.

[HENRY OF FERRERS'S ANNEXATION]

[Hundred of 'WIBERTSHERNE']

Henry of Ferrers annexed 1 free man with 16 acres in STEEPLE. Value 2s.

[WILLIAM LEOFRIC'S ANNEXATION]

2 W(illiam) Leofric annexed 1 free man with 6 acres in SCIDDEHAM. Value 12d.

[ROBERT BLUNT'S ANNEXATION]

[Hundred of FRESHWELL]

In (Helions) BUMPSTEAD Robert Blunt annexed 10 acres which Edwy, a free man, held. Always 1 plough. Value 20s.

[ROBERT MALET'S ANNEXATION]

[Hundred of HINCKFORD]   103 b

In MIDDLETON R(obert) Malet annexed 15 acres, which a free man held before 1066. Always ½ plough. Value 5s.

Frodo fr̄ abbis tenuit u͡cuſq̴ ɪɪ . libos hōes . In Staumtuna q̃s Orgar̄ ante
ceſſor ej⁹ inuaſit . manentes in ſoca reḡ . 7 . ħnt . xx . aċ . Sēp . dim̄ . car̄ . 7
ual . ɪɪɪɪ . ſol.

In Ciſhella tenuit Leuuin⁹ . v . aċ . 7 m̄ ten& . Roḡ de otburuiłł.
i dō qd̄ anteceſſor ej⁹ fuit ſaiſit⁹.

In Hund̄ de Rochefort jacent . xv . aċ . de angra . qd̄ ten& Berengar⁹
hō comitis . E . tunc ual . xv . d̄ . m̄ . xx.

Hundret de colece**stra** . In eadē coleceſtra tenuit.
Godric⁹ . ɪ . lib hō tēpr̄ regis eaduuardi . ɪɪɪɪ . manſiones . tr̄æ.
7 unā ecclam . & . ɪɪɪɪ . hidas in Greneſteda . Quo mortuo filij ej.
terrā inquat dimiſerunt . partes . Quarū rex habet duas . in
quibus ptinent due dom̄⁹ in burgo . quæ sēp regi reddiderunt.
conſuetudinem . 7 adhuc reddt̄ . In duabus hidis . tc̄ . ɪɪ . car̄.
in dn̄io . 7 m̄ . Tc̄ . ɪɪɪ . uiłłi 7 m̄ . Tc̄ . ɪɪ . ſ . 7 m̄ . Tc̄ xxɪɪɪɪ . aċ p̄ti.
7 mareſc 7 m̄ . Tc̄ . ɪ . mol . m̄ . dim̄ . Tc̄ ual xʟ . ſol . 7 m̄ . Et
de duabɜ alijs partibɜ ħt comes euſtachi . ɪ . ħ . Et ioħs
fili⁹ Walerami . alterā . ħ . Et in q̃rta Comitis euaſtachij . ē.
tota eccła . 7 q̃rta pars molendini . 7 . q̃rta pars p̄ti . tc̄ . ɪ . car̄.
m̄ . nulla . 7 ualit ıt̄ totū . xxx . ſol . Et in q̃rta parte
ioħs fuit . ɪ . car̄ tēpr̄ . r̄ . æ . m̄ . nulla . Et quarta pars molendini.
q̃rta pars p̄ti . ; 7 ual ınt̄ totū . xxx . ſ . Et de his duabɜ partibɜ
nullā habet rex conſuetudinē.

Et burgenſes calumpniant̄ . v . hidas de lex ſendena
ad conſuetudinē . 7 Cootū ciuitatis . quæ jacuer̄t ad p̄dictā
tr̄ā quā tenebat Godric⁹.

[ANNEXATION OF FRODO THE ABBOT'S BROTHER]

[Hundred of FRESHWELL]

85 Frodo the Abbot's brother has held up to now 2 free men in
STEVINGTON (End), whom Ordgar his predecessor annexed (and)
who dwelt in the King's jurisdiction. They have 20 acres. Always
½ plough. Value 4s.

[ROGER OF AUBERVILLE'S ANNEXATION]

[Hundred of UTTLESFORD]

86 In CHISHILL Leofwin held 5 acres. Now Roger of Auberville holds
(them) because his predecessor was in possession.

[BERENGAR'S ANNEXATION]

In the Hundred of ROCHFORD

87 lie 15 acres of ONGAR, which Berengar, a man of Count Eustace's,
holds. Value then 15d; now 20[d].

B Hundred of COLCHESTER   104 a

1 In the same COLCHESTER before 1066, 1 free man, Godric, held 4
pieces of land and a church, and 4 hides in GREENSTEAD. On his
death his sons separated the land into four parts. The King has
two of these, in which belong two houses in the Borough which
have always paid a customary due to the King and still pay (it).
In 2 hides, then and now 2 ploughs in lordship.
Then and now 3 villagers; then and now 2 slaves.
Then and now meadow and marsh, 24 acres; then 1 mill, now ½.
Value then and now 40s.
From the two other parts Count Eustace has 1 hide and John
son of Waleran (has) the other hide. In Count Eustace's fourth,
a whole church, ¼ mill, and ¼ of the meadow. Then
1 plough, now none.
Value in total 30s.
In John's fourth was 1 plough before 1066, now none.
¼ mill and ¼ of the meadow.
Value in total 30s.
From these two parts the King has no customary due.

2 The burgesses claim 5 hides of LEXDEN, which belonged to the
said land which Godric used to hold, (to be liable) to the
customary due and the city's levy.

Ísti st̄ burgenſes regis . q̇ reddunt 9ſuetudinē

Coleman . habet . ı . domū de colecesTRA . ten̄ . 7 . v . ac̄ . tr̄æ.
& sēp . reddit regi conſuetudinē . Leuuin . ıı . dom̄ . 7 . xxv .
ac̄ . tr̄æ . Vluric̄ . ı . dom̄ . Eduin p̄r̄ . ı . dom̄ . 7 . xx . ac̄.
T̄chill . ı . đ . 7 nouē . ac̄ . Ulſtan̄ eudlac . ıııı . dom̄ . 7 xx .
ac̄ . Leuuin . ı . dom̄ . 7 . x . ac̄ . Manuuin . ıııı . dom̄ . 7 . xxx . ac̄.

104 b

Aluric̄ . ı . dom̄ . 7 . v . ac̄ . Herdedun̄ . x . đ . 7 dim̄ . xx . ac̄.
Alfeihc p̄r̄ . ı . dom̄ . 7 . xxv . ac̄ . Leuot . ı . dom̄ . 7 . xv . ac̄.
Vluric̄ . ı . dom̄ . 7 . vıı . ac̄ . Suertlinc̄ . ı . dom̄ . 7 . x . ac̄.
Aluuart . ı . dom̄ . 7 . ıı . ac̄ . Eduin̄ . ı . dom̄ . Goda . xııı . dom̄.
7 . xx . ac̄ . Sprot . ıı . đ . 7 . ııı . ac̄ . Edric̄ . ıııı . dom̄ . 7 . xv . ac̄.
Goduuin . ı . đ . 7 . xv . ac̄ . Goduuin uuachefet . 7 filij ej̄ . v . đ.
7 . xıı . ac̄ . Blanc̄ . vı . dom̄ . 7 . xx . ac̄ . Aluric̄ . ıı . dom̄.
7 . xıııı . ac̄ . Stanart . ıı . đ . 7 . dim̄ . 7 . x . ac̄ . Goduin̄ . ı . đ.
7 . ıx . ac̄ . Vluric̄ . ıı . đ . 7 . ı . ac̄ . Alsi . ı . đ . 7 . ıııı . ac̄ . 7 . dim̄.
Aluuardus . ıı . đ . 7 . xxııı . ac̄ . Manuuin . ıı . đ . 7 . vıı . ac̄.
Leffeffe . ı . đ . 7 . ıı . ac̄ 7 dim̄ . Leuuin . x . ac̄ . Vluuin . ı . đ.
7 . ıı . ac̄ . 7 dim̄ . Godinc̄ . ıı . đ . 7 . x . ac̄ . Goda . ı . đ . 7 . vıı . ac̄.
Vluuin . monitor . ı . đ . 7 . vıı . ac̄ . Alfgar . ı . đ .   Vluart.
. ıı . đ . 7 . ı . ac̄ . Aluuin̄ . ı . đ . 7 . x . ac̄ . Alfgar p̄r̄ . ı . đ . 7 . ı . ac̄.
Frent . ı . đ . 7 . ıı . ac̄ . Oſgot . ıı . đ . 7 . ı . ac̄ . Vluric̄ . ıı . đ.
Artur̄ . ı . đ . 7 . ıııı . ac̄ . Eduin̄ . ı . đ . 7 . ıııı . ac̄ . Saluare . ı . đ.
7 . vıı . ac̄ . Leflet . ııı . đ . 7 . xxv . ac̄ . 7 . ı . mot . Aluric̄ . ı . đ.
Goduuin . ı . đ . Sprot . ı . đ . 7 . ııı . ac̄ . Grimolf . ıı . đ . 7 . ıx . ac̄.
Sagar̄ . ı . đ . 7 . x . ac̄ . Aluric̄ . ı . đ . Aluuin . ııı . đ . 7 . ıx . ac̄.
Vluric̄ . ı . đ . 7 . vı . ac̄ . Sprot . ı . đ . 7 . ııı . ac̄ . Vluuart . ı . đ.
7 . vııı . ac̄ . Leuuin̄ . ı . đ . 7 . x . ac̄ . conſilio . Goduin̄ . ı . dom̄.
Golſtan̄ . ı . đ . 7 . v . ac̄ . Vluuin̄ . ı . đ 7 . ıııı . ac̄ . Vluuart.
ı . đ . 7 . ııı . ac̄ . Vluuin̄ . ıı . đ . 7 . vıı . ac̄ . Goduuin . ıı . dom̄.
7 . vı . ac̄ . conſilio . Alfsi . ıı . đ . Lefſtan̄ . ı . đ . 7 . ı . ac̄ . Godric̄ . ı . đ.

105 a

Alric̄ . ı . đ . Not . ı . đ . Brictuuin̄ . ı . đ . 7 . v . ac̄ . Lefflet . ı . đ.
Alric̄ . ı . đ . 7 . ıııı . ac̄ . 7 . dim̄ . Eduuin̄ . ı . đ . 7 . ıı . ac̄ . 7 dim̄.
Scadebutre . ı . đ . Manuuin . ıııı . ac̄ . Golduuin̄ . ı . đ . Vluric̄.
ı . đ . 7 . ıı . ac̄ . Oſiet . ı . đ . Eduuin̄ . ı . đ . 7 . x . ac̄ . Vluric̄ . ıı . đ.
7 . v . ac̄ . Aluuin . ıı . đ . Eduuin̄ . ı . đ . 7 . ııı . ac̄ . Vluuin̄ . ı . đ.
Blacſtan̄ . ıı . đ . Manſtan̄ . ıı . đ . 7 . x . ac̄ . Aluric̄ . ı . đ . 7 . ı . ac̄.
Leuuin̄ . ı . đ . Aluuin̄ . ıı . đ . 7 . xxıı . ac̄ . Leuuin̄ . ıı . đ . Edric̄.

3a These are the King's burgesses who pay the customary due:
Colman has 1 house in COLCHESTER; and he holds 5 acres of land
and has always paid the customary due to the King. Leofwin
(holds) 2 houses and 25 acres of land; Wulfric, 1 house; Edwin
the priest, 1 house and 20 acres; Thorkell, 1 house and nine acres;
Wulfstan Eadlac, 4 houses and 20 acres; Leofwin Crist, 1 house
and 10 acres; Manwin, 4 houses and 30 acres; Aelfric, 1 house   104 b
and 5 acres; Hardekin, 10½ houses (and) 20 acres; Alfheah the
priest, 1 house and 25 acres; Leofwold, 1 house and 15 acres;
Wulfric, 1 house and 7 acres; Swartling, 1 house and 10 acres;
Alfward, 1 house and 2 acres; Edwin, 1 house; Goda, 13 houses
and 20 acres; Sprot, 2 houses and 3 acres; Edric, 4 houses and 15
acres; Godwin, 1 house and 15 acres; Godwin Weakfeet and his
son, 5 houses and 12 acres; Blanc, 6 houses and 20 acres; Aelfric,
2 houses and 14 acres; Stanhard, 2½ houses and 10 acres; Godwin,
1 house and 9 acres; Wulfric, 2 houses and 1 acre; Alfsi, 1 house
and 3½ acres; Alfward, 2 houses and 23 acres; Manwin, 2 houses
and 7 acres; Leofsexe, 1 house and 2½ acres; Leofwin, 10 acres;
Wulfwin, 1 house and 2½ acres; Goding, 2 houses and 10 acres;
Goda, 1 house and 7 acres; Wulfwin the summoner, 1 house and
7 acres; Alfgar, 1 house; Wulfward, 2 houses and 1 acre; Alwin,
1 house and 10 acres; Alfgar the priest, 1 house and 1 acre;
Freond, 1 house and 2 acres; Osgot, 2 houses and 1 acre; Wulfric,
2 houses; Arthur, 1 house and 4 acres; Edwin, 1 house and 4 acres;
Saeware, 1 house and 7 acres; Leofled, 3 houses, 25 acres and 1
mill; Aelfric, 1 house; Godwin, 1 house; Sprot, 1 house and 3
acres; Grimwulf, 2 houses and 9 acres; Saegar, 1 house and 10
acres; Aelfric, 1 house; Alwin, 3 houses and 9 acres; Wulfric, 1
house and 6 acres; Sprot, 1 house and 3 acres; Wulfward, 1 house
and 8 acres; Leofwin, 1 house and 10 acres by agreement; Godwin,
1 house; Goldstan, 1 house and 5 acres; Wulfwin, 1 house and 4
acres; Wulfward, 1 house and 3 acres; Wulfwin, 2 houses and 7
acres; Godwin, 2 houses and 6 acres by agreement; Alfsi, 2 houses;
Leofstan, 1 house and 1 acre; Godric, 1 house; Alric, 1 house;   105 a
Not, 1 house; Brictwin, 1 house and 5 acres; Leofled, 1 house;
Alric, 1 house and 4½ acres; Edwin, 1 house and 2½ acres;
Shed-butter, 1 house; Manwin, 4 acres; Goldwin, 1 house; Wulfric,
1 house and 2 acres; Osgeat, 1 house; Edwin, 1 house and 10 acres;
Wulfric, 2 houses and 5 acres; Alwin, 2 houses; Edwin, 1 house
and 3 acres; Wulfwin, 1 house; Blackstan, 2 houses; Manstan, 2
houses and 10 acres; Aelfric, 1 house and 1 acre; Leofwin, 1
house; Alwin, 2 houses and 22 acres; Leofwin, 2 houses; Edric,

ı.đ.Leuuin̉.ı.đ.Vued.ı.đ.Vlsı̉.ı.đ.Goldric.ıı.đ.

7.xxıı.ac̄.Goda.xxıı.ac̄.Calebot.vıı.ac̄.Manſtan.ıı.đ.

7.ı.ac̄.Ulfeih.ı.đ.Manuuin̉.ı.đ.Winemer̉.ı.đ.Sacrim̉.

ııı.đ.7.ıııı.ac̄.Leuric̉.ı.đ.Vluuart.ı.đ.7.ıııı.ac̄.Vl

uuin̉.ı.đ.7.x.ac̄.Lefflet.ı.đ.7.xxv.ac̄.Godric̉.ı.đ.

Dereman̉.ı.đ.Tſtan̉.ı.đ.DuHel.ı.đ.7.dim̄.ac̄.Goddæ.ıı.đ.

Got cıtt.ı.đ.7.ı.ac̄.Stan.ı.đ.Oriet̉.ı.đ.Alfſtan̉.ı.đ.

Touı̉.ı.đ.Goldinc.ı.đ.Leuiet.ı.đ.7.ıı.ac̄.Blacſtan.ı.đ.

Manuuin̉.ı.đ.Aluuin̉.ı.đ.Lefſun̉.ıı.đ.Aluric̉.ı.đ.7.ıı.ac̄.

Brumman.ı.đ.Aluuin̉.ı.đ.Saulf.ıı.đ.7.dim̄.7.x.ac̄.

Leuuin̉.ııı.ac̄.Vluric̉.ı.đ.Alfſtan̉.ı.đ.Goduuin̉.ııı.ac̄.

Golduin̉.ı.đ.Goduuin̉.ı.đ.7.ı.ac̄.Wicga.ı.đ.Ledmar̉.ı.đ.

Vlſtan̉.ıı.đ.Godeſun̉.ı.đ.7.ııı.ac̄.Elebolt.ıı.đ.7.ı.ac̄.

Goduuin̉.ı.đ.Godeua.ı.đ.Lefſtan̉.ı.đ.Eduardus pr̄.ı.đ.

Hacon.ı.đ.Ailbrieſt.ı.đ.Tate.ı.đ.Sauuart.ı.đ.Berda.

ı.đ.7.v.ac̄.Vluuart.pr̄.ı.đ.7.ı.ac̄.Cullinc.ıı.đ.7.vıı.ac̄.

Aluuolt.ı.đ.Filieman.ı.đ.7.v.ac̄.Godeua.ı.đ.

105 b

Siuuardus.pr̄.ı.đ.7.ıııı.ac̄.Pic.ı.đ.Vluuin̉.ııı.đ.7.ıııı.ac̄.

Leueua.ı.đ.7.ıııı.ac̄.7.dim̄.Aluric̉.xv.ac̄.Aluuen.ıı.đ.

Vluric̉.ı.đ.7.ı.ac̄.7.dim̄.Witt.peccatū.ı.đ.Beſt.ı đ.Roſelı̉.

ı.đ.7.ıııı.ac̄.Leuuin̉.ı.đ.7.ıı.ac̄.Goda.ı.đ.Vluuin̉.ı.đ.

Leueſun̉.ı.đ.Golman̉.ı.đ.Pote.ıııı.ac̄.Godric̉.ı.đ.Siricus.

ı.đ.7.ıı.ac̄.Alric̉.ı.đ.7.ıı.ac̄.Liuidi.ı.đ.Brictric̉.ı.đ.

7.ıx.ac̄.7.dim̄.Lefſtan̉.ı.đ.Vudebil.ı.đ.Blacſtan.ı.đ.

Alflet.ı.đ.Vlueua.ı.đ.7.xx.ac̄.Goda.ı.đ.7.xx.ac̄.

Aſcere.ı.đ.7 xıx.ac̄.Godric̉.ı.đ.Brunloc.ı.đ.Alnod.ıı.đ.

7.ıııı.ac̄.Goduuin̉.ı.đ.7.x.ac̄.Leuuin̉.ı.đ.7.x.ac̄.

Aluric̉.pr̄.ııı.đ.7.ıı.ac̄.Rogerius.ı.đ.7.ıııı.ac̄.Godric̉.

ı.đ.Aluric.ı.đ.7.ıı.ac̄.Suertinc.ı.đ.7.x.ac̄.Godid.ıı.đ.

7.xıııı.ac̄.Brunuin̉.ı.đ.7.ııı.ac̄.Vluuin̉.ı.đ.Brungar̉.

ıı.đ.7.xvııı.ac̄.Sunegot.ı.đ.Siuuard̉.ı.đ.7.vı.ac̄.7.dim̄.

Vlſtan̉.xı.ac̄.Leffiuf.ıı.đ.7.vııı.ac̄.Sagrim.ı.đ.Vluuin̉.

ı.đ.Leuuin̉.ı.đ.Leuric̉.ı.đ.Godinc̉.ı.đ.7.ı.ac̄.Weſtan.

ıı.đ.7.xxx.ac̄.Ainolf.ı.đ.7.xv.ac̄.Tunric.ı.đ.

Alſtan.v.ac̄.Alffius.ı.đ.Goldere.ı.ac̄.Godſune.ı.ac̄.7.dim̄.

Vluuin̉.ı.đ.Aluric̄.ı.đ.Goduuin̉.ı.đ.Pecoc.ı.đ.Aluuin.ı.đ.

Brictric.ı.đ.Manuuin̉.ı.đ.Vluric.ı.đ.Godſune.7.dim̄.

7.vı.ac̄.Brunuin̉.ı.đ.Manuuin̉.ı.đ.Edric̉.ı.đ.Leueua.

1 house; Leofwin, 1 house; Wulfgith, 1 house; Wulfsi, 1 house;
Goldric, 2 houses and 22 acres; Goda, 22 acres; Calebot, 7 acres;
Manstan, 2 houses and 1 acre; Wulfheah, 1 house; Manwin, 1
house; Winemer, 1 house; Saegrim, 3 houses and 4 acres; Leofric,
1 house; Wulfward, 1 house and 4 acres; Wulfwin, 1 house and 10
acres; Leofled, 1 house and 25 acres; Godric, 1 house; Derman, 1
house; Thurstan, 1 house; Dublel, 1 house and ½ acre; Godday, 2
houses; Got Chill, 1 house and 1 acre; Stan, 1 house; Ordgeat, 1
house; Alfstan, 1 house; Tovi, 1 house; Golding, 1 house; Leofgeat,
1 house and 2 acres; Blackstan, 1 house; Manwin, 1 house; Alwin,
1 house; Leofson, 2 houses; Aelfric, 1 house and 2 acres; Bruman,
1 house; Alwin, 1 house; Saewulf, 2½ houses and 10 acres;
Leofwin, 3 acres; Wulfric, 1 house; Alfstan, 1 house; Godwin, 3
acres; Goldwin, 1 house; Godwin, 1 house and 1 acre; Wicga, 1
house; Ledmer, 1 house; Wulfstan, 2 houses; Godson, 1 house
and 3 acres; Aethelbald, 2 houses and 1 acre; Godwin, 1 house;
Godiva, 1 house; Leofstan, 1 house; Edward the priest, 1 house;
Hakon, 1 house; Aethelbrict, 1 house; Tate, 1 house; Saeward,
1 house; Beard, 1 house and 5 acres; Wulfward the priest, 1 house
and 1 acre; Culling, 2 houses and 7 acres; Alfwold, 1 house;
Filiman, 1 house and 5 acres; Godiva, 1 house; Siward the priest, 105 b
1 house and 4 acres; Pic, 1 house; Wulfwin, 3 houses and 4 acres;
Leofeva, 1 house and 4½ acres; Aelfric, 15 acres; Alwen, 2 houses;
Wulfric, 1 house and 1½ acres; William Peche, 1 house; Best, 1
house; Rosell, 1 house and 4 acres; Leofwin, 1 house and 2 acres;
Goda, 1 house; Wulfwin, 1 house; Leofson, 1 house; Goldman, 1
house; Pote, 4 acres; Godric, 1 house; Siric, 1 house and 2 acres;
Alric, 1 house and 2 acres; Lundi, 1 house; Brictric, 1 house and
9½ acres; Leofstan, 1 house; Woodbill, 1 house; Blackstan, 1
house; Aelfled, 1 house; Wulfeva, 1 house and 20 acres; Goda, 1
house and 20 acres; Aeschere, 1 house and 19 acres; Godric, 1
house; Brunloc, 1 house; Alnoth, 2 houses and 4 acres; Godwin,
1 house and 10 acres; Leofwin, 1 house and 10 acres; Aelfric the
priest, 3 houses and 2 acres; Roger, 1 house and 4 acres; Godric,
1 house; Aelfric, 1 house and 2 acres; Swarting, 1 house and 10
acres; Godith, 2 houses and 14 acres; Brunwin, 1 house and 3
acres; Wulfwin, 1 house; Brungar, 2 houses and 18 acres; Sunegod,
1 house; Siward, 1 house and 6½ acres; Wulfstan, 11 acres;
Leofswith, 2 houses and 8 acres; Saegrim, 1 house; Wulfwin, 1
house; Leofwin, 1 house; Leofric, 1 house; Goding, 1 house and
1 acre; Wigstan, 2 houses and 30 acres; Ainulf, 1 house and 15
acres; Tunric, 1 house; Alstan, 5 acres; Alfsi, 1 house; Godhere, 1
acre; Godson, 1½ acres; Wulfwin, 1 house; Aelfric, 1 house;
Godwin, 1 house; Peacock, 1 house; Alwin, 1 house; Brictric, 1
house; Manwin, 1 house; Wulfric, 1 house; Godson, 6½ acres;
Brunwin, 1 house; Manwin, 1 house; Edric, 1 house; Leofeva,

1 . đ . Ouuin . 1 . đ . Alſtan . 11 . đ . Aluolt . vi . ac̄ . 7 dim . Manuin.
1 . đ . 7 . v . ac̄ . aluuart . 1 . đ . 7 . xv . ac̄ . Lemerus . x . ac̄.
Abbas s̄c̄i Eadmundi . 11 . đ . 7 . xxx . ac̄ . Stanhert . 1 . dom.

106 a

Vluuin . 1 . đ . Sæuucle . 1 . đ . Leuret . 1 . đ . 7 vi . ac̄ . Alueua . x . ac̄.
Vlſtan . 1 . đ . 7 . xiii . ac̄ . Leuuin . 11 . đ . Leueua . 1 . đ . Aluric . 1 . đ.
Godric . 1 . đ . 7 . ix . ac̄ . Vlric . 1 . đ . 7 . iiii . ac̄ . Vluuin . 1 . đ
Aluuen . 1 . đ . Teſcho . 11 . đ . 7 . xx . ac̄ . træ . 7 debet conſuetudines
regi 7 numquā reddit . Vluricus . iii . ac̄ . Stotinc . 1 . đ . Herſtan .
. 1 . đ . Leuric . 1 . đ . 7 . xlii . ac̄ . Edric . 1 . đ . Dela . 1 . đ . Hunec . 11 . đ.
Manuuin . 11 . đ . Aluric . 11 . đ . Got hugo . vi . ac̄ . Leuuinus . 1 . đ.
7 . xxv . ac̄ . Dimidi . blanc . iiii . đ . Lefſune . 1 . ac̄ . Alueua.
1 . đ . Leueua . iii . ac̄ . Sueno . 1 . đ . Vlsi . 1 . đ . Alflet . 1 . đ . Rađ
pinel . iiii . đ . infra muros . 7 . v . ac̄ . 7 non reddidit . conſuetudinē
7 indedit uadē . Orlaf . iii . ac̄ . 7 . dim . Galt̄ . 11 . đ . Horrap . 1 . đ.
Aluuin . 1 . đ . Stamburc . 1 . đ . Vlſtan . 11 . đ . 7 . v . ac̄ . Chentinc.
1 . đ . Sprot . 1 . đ . 7 . v . ac̄ . Eduuin . 1 . đ . 7 . iii . ac̄ . Got flet.
xx . ac̄ . Manſune . x . ac̄ . Godinc . 1 . đ . 7 . v . ac̄ . Vlueua . v . ac̄.
Vluric . 1 . đ . 7 . 1 . ac̄ . 7 . dim . Lorchebret . 1 . đ . 7 . x . ac̄ . Goldere.
1 . đ . P̄t ſuam t̄ram habent . iſti burgenſes . li . ac̄ . p̄ti.
Amo Hamo dapifer . 1 . đ . 7 . 1 . curiā . 7 . 1 . hidā . træ . 7 . xv . burgenſes.
7 hoc tenuit ante ceſſor ſuus . Thurbn . tēp̄r . r . e . Et hoc totū
p̄t ſuam aulā reddebat conſuetudinē tēp̄r regis . e . 7 adhuc
reddt̄ burgenſes . de ſuis capitibus . Set de t̄ra ſua . & de hida quā
tenent de hamone n̄ c̄ reddita conſuetudo . In hida . 1 . car̄ . tc̄ ꞉ m̄
nulla . Tc̄ . vi . ac̄ . p̄ti . 7 . m̄ . & hoc totū uat . tēp̄r . r . e . iiii . lib̄.
7 . qđo ſimit . recep̄ . & m̄ . xl . ſot . ⫽ Manſune . 11 . đ . 7 . iiii . ac̄.
Goda . 1 . đ . ⫽ Eudo dapif . v . đ . 7 xl . ac̄ . træ . quas tenebant.

106 b

burgenſes tēp̄r . r . e . 7 reddebant . omnē conſuetudinē burgenſiū.
M ů n̄ reddt̄ 9ſuedinē . n de ſuis capitibus . Hoc totū c̄ quarte parte
æcclæ s̄c̄i petri ꞉ reddit xxx . ſot . ⫽ Huḡ . de monte forti . 1 . đ.
quam ten tēp̄r . e . Godric . ſuus ante ceſſor 7 reddebat tc̄ conſuetudinē regis . M n̄ reddit nec poſtea reddidit . ex quo Hugo habuit.

1 house; Owin, 1 house; Alstan, 2 houses; Alfwold, 6½ acres;
Manwin, 1 house and 5 acres; Alfward, 1 house and 15 acres;
Ledmer, 10 acres; the Abbot of St. Edmund's, 2 houses and 30
acres; Stanhard, 1 house; Wulfwin, 1 house; Seafowl, 1 house; 106 a
Leofred, 1 house and 6 acres; Aelfeva, 10 acres; Wulfstan, 1 house
and 13 acres; Leofwin 2 houses; Leofeva, 1 house; Aelfric, 1
house; Godric, 1 house and 9 acres; Wulfric, 1 house and 4 acres;
Wulfwin, 1 house; Alwen, 1 house; Tesco, 2 houses and 20 acres
of land, and he owes customary dues to the King and never pays;
Wulfric, 3 acres; Stoting, 1 house; Herstan, 1 house; Leofric, 1
house and 42 acres; Edric, 1 house; Dela, 1 house; Hunning, 2
houses; Manwin, 2 houses; Aelfric, 2 houses; Got Hugh, 6 acres;
Leofwin, 1 house and 25 acres; Demiblanc, 4 houses; Leofson, 1
acre; Aelfeva, 1 house; Leofeva, 3 acres; Swein, 1 house; Wulfsi,
1 house; Aelfled, 1 house; Ralph Pinel, 4 houses below the walls,
and 5 acres, and he has not paid the customary due and has given
in a pledge; Ordlaf, 3½ acres; Walter, 2 houses; Horrap, 1 house;
Alwin, 1 house; Stanburg, 1 house; Wulfstan, 2 houses and 5
acres; Kenting, 1 house; Sprot, 1 house and 5 acres; Edwin, 1
house and 3 acres; Got Fleet, 20 acres; Manson, 10 acres; Goding,
1 house and 5 acres; Wulfeva, 5 acres; Wulfric, 1 house and 1½
acres; Lorce Bret, 1 house and 10 acres; Goldhere, 1 house;
   Apart from their land, those burgesses have 51 acres of meadow.

b Hamo the Steward (has) 1 house, 1 court, 1 hide of land and 15
burgesses; his predecessor Thorbern held this before 1066. All
this, apart from his hall, paid the customary due before 1066; the
burgesses still pay (a tax assessed) on their heads, but a customary
due has not been paid from their land and from the hide which
they hold from Hamo. In the hide, 1 plough then, now none.
   Meadow, then and now 6 acres.
Value of all this before 1066 £4; when acquired, the same;
now 40s.

c Manson (has) 2 houses and 4 acres; Goda, 1 house.

d Eudo the Steward (has) 5 houses and 40 acres of land, which the
 burgesses used to hold before 1066. They paid all the customary 106 b
due of burgesses; but now they do not pay the customary due,
apart from (a tax assessed) on their heads. The whole of this,
with ¼ of St. Peter's Church pays 30s.

e Hugh de Montfort (has) 1 house, which Godric his predecessor
held before 1066. Then it used to pay the King's customary due;
now it does not pay, nor did it pay later on, since Hugh has had it.

Rǥ pictauienſis . I . đ . quam tenuit . alflet ſua ante ceſſor.

tēpr̄ . r . e . 7 reddebat conſuetudinē regis ; m̄ n̄ reddit nec reddit

ex quo Roǥ habuit . Euſtachi . comes XII . đ 7 unā quā occupauit

engelric . 7 reddebant conſuetudinē regis tēpr̄ . r . e . M̊ n̄ reddŧ

nec reddiderunt ex quo euſtachi habuit . 7 ualent . XII . ſoł.

Wiłł nepos eр̄i . II . đ . quam ten thurchiłł 7 reddit conſuetudinē

Otto . aurifab . III . đ . que jacent ad eſceldeforde quas tenebat.

Alueua . comitiſſa . 7 reddebant conſuetudinē regis . 7 . m̄ n̄ reddŧ ;

& hoc . ē . de tr̄a regina . Abbas de uueſtmonaſtio . IIII . đ

quas tēpr̄ . r . e . tenuit comes haroldus ad ferigens . & tē reddebant

conſuetudinem . m̄ n̄ reddŧ . Goisfridus de magna uilla . II . đ.

quas ten . Geni tēpr̄ . r . e . ad erligam . 7 reddebant conſuetudinē

m̄ non reddŧ . Sueno . I . đ . quā tenuit . Goda . tēpr̄ . r . e . ad elmeſteda.

7 tē reddebant conſuetudinē regis . m̄ reddŧ n caput hōis.

Wiłł de uuateuilla . I . đ . de ſue none quā ten . Rob uuimarc.

tēpr̄ . regis . e . 7 reddebat conſuetudinē . m̄ n̄ reddit . Turſtinus

uuiſcart . III . đ . de iohanne filio uualera 7 dim̄ hidā . trē . qđ

tēpr̄ . r . e . tenuer̄ duo burgenſes 7 reddebant conſuetudinē.

regis . m̄ n̄ reddŧ conſuedo . Illa dim̄ hida uał . tē x . ſoł . 7 . qdo.

receр̄ . VI . ſoł . m̄ . v . s . Ran piperełł . v . đ . quas tenuit . Ailmar

tēpr̄ . regis . e . ad terlingas . 7 reddebant conſuet . m̄ n̄ reddunt.

Quarū una extra muras . ē . Rad baignart . I . đ . quā tenet.

Ailmar . mclc . tēpr̄ . r . e . ad collenſum te . 7 reddebant conſuet . m̄ . n̄.

f Roger of Poitou (has) 1 house, which Aelfled his predecessor held before 1066. It used to pay the King's customary due; now it does not pay and has not paid since Roger has had it.

g Count Eustace (has) 12 houses and one which Engelric has annexed. They paid the King's customary due before 1066; now they do not pay, and have not paid since Eustace has had them. Value 12s.

h William the Bishop's nephew (has) 2 houses, which Thorkell held. He pays the customary due.

j Otto the Goldsmith (has) 3 houses which belong to Shalford, which Countess Aelfeva used to hold. They used to pay the King's customary due; now they do not pay. This is of the Queen's land.

k The Abbot of Westminster (has) 4 houses, which Earl Harold held before 1066 (belonging) to Feering. Then they used to pay the customary due; now they do not pay.

l Geoffrey de Mandeville (has) 2 houses, which Ginni held before 1066 (belonging) to Ardleigh. They used to pay the customary due; now they do not pay.

m Swein (has) 1 house, which Goda held before 1066 (belonging) to Elmstead. Then they used to pay the King's customary due; now they only pay (a tax assessed) on a man's head.

n William of Vatteville (holds) 1 house from Swein, which Robert Wymarc held before 1066. It used to pay the customary due; now it does not pay.

p Thurstan Wishart (holds) 3 houses from John son of Waleran, and ½ hide of land, which 2 burgesses held before 1066. They used to pay the King's customary due; now they do not pay the customary due.
   Value of the ½ hide, then 10s; when acquired, 6s; now 5s.   107 a

q Ranulf Peverel (has) 5 houses, which Aelmer held before 1066 (belonging) to Terling. They used to pay the customary due; now they do not pay. One of these is outside the walls.

r Ralph Baynard (has) 1 house, which Aelmer Milk held before 1066 (belonging) to Tolleshunt. They used to pay the customary due; now they do not.

Abbatiſſa de bchingis . iii . d . tēpr . r . e . & tc reddebat . conſuetudinē ;
m̄ . n̄ Albic . de uer . ii . d . 7 . iii . ac tr̄æ . qs tenuit . Vluuin . ſuus
ante ceſſor . tēpr . r . e . Tc reddebant conſuetudinem.
Dominium regis in coleceſtra . cii . ac tr̄æ . de qbȝ ſt . x . prati.
in quibȝ ſt . x . bord . Et . cc . 7 . xl . ac inter paſt . 7 fruĉteĉtam
& hoc totū jacet ad firmā regis . In cōmune burgenſum . iiii.
xx . ac tr̄æ ; & circa murum . viii . percæ . de q toto p annū habent
burgenſes . lx . ſot . ad feruicium regis ſi op fuerit . ſin autē :' in cōmune
diuidt ;
Eſt autē conſuetudo ut uno qq anno quinto decimo die
poſt paſcha reddant burgenſes regij duas marcas argenti
7 hoc ptinent ad firmā regis . Pt ea de una quaq domo.
p annum . vi . denarios quæ reddē poteſt ad uiĉtū ſolda -
riorum regis . vt . ad expeditionē tr̄æ t maris ; & hoc n̄ ē ad firmā.
Et hoc ſit ſi rex ſoldarios habuerit t expeditionē fecerit.
Et propt hos . vi . denarios tota ciuitas ex omnib; debitis reddebat
tēpr . r . e . xv . lib . 7 . v . ſot . 7 . iii . d in uno quoq anno ; De quibȝ
reddebant monetarij . iiii . lib . tēpr . regis . e . M reddit . iiii.
xx . lib . 7 . iiii . ſextarios mellis ut . xl . ſot . iiii . Et pter hoc
. c . ſot . uice comiti de gerſuma . Et . x . ſot . 7 . viii . d ad pbendarios

107 b

paſcendos . Et pter hoc reddunt burgenſes de coleceſtra & de mel -
duna . xx . lib . p moneta . 7 hoc conſtituit . Waleram . & aduocaȷt
regē adturtorē . qd condonauit illis . x . lib . & ten . Walchelin.
epc . querit ab illis . xl . lib.
In coleceſtra ē quedā ecĉle ſci Petri quā . tenuit . ii . pri . tēpr . r . e.
in elemaſina regis . cui adjacent . ii . h . terræ . in quibus erant . ii . car.
7 . m̄ . Tc . iii . b . m̄ . iiii . Tc . iii . s . m̄ . ii . Tc . xii . ac . pti . 7 m̄ . Tc . i . mot.
7 m̄ . Tc . ii . domus in burgo . 7 m̄ . Tc totū uat . xxx . ſot . m̄ . xlviii . ſot.
De hac elemoſina reclamat . Rob . f . rad . de hatingis . iii . partes.
7 eudo dapifer tenet quartā . & tēpr . r . e . reddebant conſue -
-tudinē . 7 . m̄ non reddit.

s The Abbess of Barking (had) 3 houses before 1066. Then it used to pay the customary due; now it does not.

t Aubrey de Vere (has) 2 houses and 3 acres of land, which Wulfwin his predecessor held before 1066. Then they used to pay the customary due.

4 The King's lordship in Colchester (is) 102 acres of land, of which 10 are of meadow, in which are 10 smallholders. Also 240 acres of pasture and scrubland. All this lies in the King's revenue.

5 In the burgesses' common property (are) 24 acres of land, and 8 perches round the wall, from the whole of which the burgesses have 60s a year for the King's service, if it should be needed, but if not, it is divided in common.

6 There is, moreover, a custom that every year, on the fifteenth day after Easter, the royal burgesses should pay 2 marks of silver. This belongs to the King's revenue.

Apart from this, from each house that can pay, 6d a year for the supplies of the King's mercenaries for a (military) expedition either on land or on sea; this does not belong to the (King's) revenue. This is to be whether the King has mercenaries or makes a (military) expedition. For these 6 pence, the whole city used to pay £15 5s 3d before 1066, in each year, out of all things owed (to it).

Of this (sum) the moneyers used to pay £4 before 1066; now it pays £80 and 4 sesters of honey or 40s 4[d].

Apart from this, 100s to the Sheriff in gifts; and 10s 8d for feeding the prebendaries. 107 b

Apart from this, the burgesses of Colchester and of Maldon pay £20 for the mint. Waleran arranged this. They summon the King as protector (to the fact) that he pardoned them £10. Bishop Walkelin holds (it); he demands £40 from them.

7 In Colchester is St. Peter's Church which 2 priests held before 1066 in the King's alms (and) to which are attached 2 hides of land, in which were, and (are) now, 2 ploughs.

Then 3 smallholders, now 4; then 3 slaves, now 2.

Meadow, then and now 12 acres; then and now 1 mill; then and now 2 houses in the Borough.

Total value then 30s; now 48s.

Of this alms, Robert son of Ralph of Hastings claims 3 parts, and Eudo the Steward holds the fourth. Before 1066 they used to pay the customary due; now it does not pay.

ESSEX HOLDINGS
ENTERED ELSEWHERE IN THE SURVEY
The Latin text of these entries is given in the county volumes concerned

In HUNTINGDONSHIRE

D   **DECLARATIONS OF THE SWORN MEN**   DB 208 a

EHu

7 They testify that the lands of Aelfric of Yelling and
Hemingford were St. Benedict's; and that they had been
granted to Aelfric for his life-time on the condition that
after his death they should revert to the church, and
BOXTED with them. However Aelfric was killed in the
battle at Hastings, and the Abbot recovered his lands,
until Aubrey de Vere dispossessed him.

In KENT

5   **LAND OF THE BISHOP OF ROCHESTER**   DB 8 d

EKt

(In WROTHAM Hundred)

104 Adam holds Chalk from the Bishop . . .

In Essex there is 1 hide which rightly belongs to this   9 a
manor. Godwin son of Dudeman held it; now Ranulf
Peverel holds it.

In NORFOLK

38   **LAND OF ROBERT OF VERLY**   LDB 262 a

ENf

The Hundred of (North) GREENOE

3 In (Field) Dalling G(odwin), the uncle of Ralph, held 11
Free men before 1066; 1c. of land. Now R(obert) of
Verly holds them, saying that he holds it by exchange for
RODING, in another county . . .

In this he vouches Robert Blunt as the deliverer.

In SUFFOLK

1
ESf 1

96 LAND OF THE KING, of which Peter of Valognes has LDB 286 b
charge.

SAMFORD Hundred and a Half.

Harold held Harkstead before 1066; as an outlier in
BRIGHTLINGSEA in the county of Essex; 5 acres of land.

Then 21 villagers, later and now 8; always 13
smallholders; then 4 slaves.

Always 2 ploughs in lordship; then 8 men's ploughs,
later 2, now 1;

Meadow, 4 acres. A church; always 1 cob; 3 cattle;
7 pigs; 12 sheep.

Value then and later £6 at face value, now £6 by weight
and 30s at face value.

It has 12½ furlongs in length and 12 in width; 30d
in tax.

ESf 2
32 **LAND OF GEOFFREY DE MANDEVILLE** LDB 411 b

7 In Ipswich 1 dwelling: it belongs to MOZE.

NOTES

ABBREVIATIONS used in the Notes:

AN ... Anglo-Norman.

Appx ... Appendix.

arr ... *arrondissement*.

Battle 1980 ... *Proceedings of the Battle Conference on Anglo-Norman Studies III, 1980*, ed. R. Allen Brown (Boydell Press, Woodbridge, Suffolk, 1981).

DB ... Domesday Book.

DBE ... H. C. Darby, *Domesday England* (Cambridge 1977).

DG ... H. C. Darby and G. R. Versey, *Domesday Gazetteer* (Cambridge 1975).

ECE ... C. R. Hart, *The Early Charters of Essex* (revised edn., Leicester University Press, 1971).

Ellis ... Sir H. Ellis, *A General Introduction to Domesday Book* (2 vols. 1833, reprinted 1971).

EPNS ... *The Place-Names of Essex*, ed. P. H. Reaney (*English Place-Name Society* xii, Cambridge 1935).

von Feilitzen 1945 ... O. von Feilitzen, 'Some unrecorded Old and Middle English personal names', *Namn och Bygd* xxxiii (1945), 69–98.

von Feilitzen 1968 ... idem, 'Some Old English uncompounded personal names and bynames', *Studia Neophilologica* xl (1968), 5–16.

von Feilitzen 1976 ... idem, 'The personal names and bynames of the Winton Domesday', *Winchester in the Early Middle Ages*, ed. M. Biddle (*Winchester Studies* i, Oxford 1976), 143–229.

Fellows Jensen ... G. Fellows Jensen, *Scandinavian Personal-Names in Lincolnshire and Yorkshire* (Copenhagen 1968).

Forssner ... T. Forssner, *Continental-Germanic Personal-Names in England in Old and Middle English Times* (Uppsala 1916).

Förstemann ... E. Förstemann, *Altdeutsches Namenbuch*, Band 1, *Personennamen* (2nd edn., Bonn 1900).

Gt ... Great.

Harmer, *AS Writs* ... F. E. Harmer, *Anglo-Saxon Writs* (Manchester University Press, 1952).

ICC ... The Cambridgeshire Inquiry, *Inquisitio Comitatus Cantabrigiensis*, quoted from the same edition as IE, below; on it see further, Cambridgeshire, Introduction.

IE, IEAL, IEBrev, IENV ... For these texts see Appx, The Ely Inquiry; references are to pages in *Inquisitio Comitatus Cantabrigiensis*, ed. N. E. S. A. Hamilton (1876); in the notes below, page numbers are not repeated when they are the same as for the preceding note within each LDB section.

Kökeritz ... H. Kökeritz, 'Notes on the pre-conquest personal names of Domesday Book', *Namn och Bygd* xxvi (1938), 25–41.

Latham ... R. E. Latham (ed.), *Revised Medieval Latin Word-List from British and Irish Sources* (*British Academy*, 1965).

LDB ... Little Domesday Book.

LibEl ... *Liber Eliensis*, ed. E. O. Blake (*Camden Society*, 3rd series, xcii, 1962).

Lt ... Little.

ME ... Middle English.

MLat ... Medieval Latin.

ModE ... Modern English.

MS ... Manuscript.

NED ... *A New English Dictionary* (Oxford 1888–1933).

NFr ... Norman French.

OBret ... Old Breton.

ODan ... Old Danish.

OE ... Old English.

OEB ... G. Tengvik, *Old English Bynames* (*Nomina Germanica* iv, Uppsala 1938).

OFr ... Old French.

OG ... Old German.

OIr ... Old Irish.

ON ... Old Norse.

ONFr ... Old Norman French.

OScand ... Old Scandinavian.

OSw ... Old Swedish.

OW ... Old Welsh.

OWScand ... Old West Scandinavian.

PNDB ... O. von Feilitzen, *The Pre-Conquest Personal Names of Domesday Book* (*Nomina Germanica* iii, Uppsala 1937).

Reaney ... P. H. Reaney, *A Dictionary of British Surnames* (2nd edn. by R. M. Wilson, 1977).
Redin ... M. Redin, *Studies on Uncompounded Personal Names in Old English* (Uppsala 1919).
Rom ... Romance.
Sawyer ... P. H. Sawyer, *Anglo-Saxon Charters, an Annotated List and Bibliography* (*Royal Historical Society*, 1968).
Seltén ... B. Seltén, *The Anglo-Saxon Heritage in Middle English Personal Names, Part II* (Lund 1979).
VCH ... *The Victoria History of the County of Essex*, i, edd. H. A. Doubleday, W. Page (1903), with Domesday section by J. H. Round.

The Editor is grateful to Mr. John McN. Dodgson for his advice on the more obscure place- and personal-names.

The text of the DB Survey for Essex is contained in Little Domesday Book (now preserved, with the larger volume, at the Public Record Office, London). The manuscript was written, by more than one scribe, on either side of leaves, or folios, of parchment (sheep-skin) measuring about 11 by 8 inches (28 by 20 cms). On each side, or page, is a single column, making two to each folio. The folios were numbered in the 17th century, and the two columns of each are here lettered a, b. Red ink was used to distinguish chapter and Hundred headings. Deletion was marked by putting a line (in the ink of the text) through incorrect words. The running title on the recto of folios was usually an abbreviated form of the name of the Landholder whom the chapter concerned; the running title on the verso was an abbreviation of the county name.

ESSEX. *EXSESSA*, *EXSAESSA*, abbreviated as *ESS̄*, *ĒSS* or *ESS*. At the top of the page, to the left of centre.

References to other DB counties are to the Chapter and Section of the editions in this series.

L	LANDHOLDERS. LDB does not give a heading to the list and does not list B (Colchester). Farley omits the Chapter-numbers 2–4, 19–21, 23–24, 29, 72, and 89–90, all of which are present, but faded, in the MS and facsimile. See also folios 9a and 17a for partial lists of landholders which were subsequently deleted.
L6	WESTMINSTER. Farley supplies the overline abbreviation for *er*, omitted in error in the MS.
L9	[BARK]ING. The three dots in Farley represent a mark in the MS, obscuring the first part of the place-name, but cf. Chapter 9, heading (folio 17b).
L15	CAEN. Farley misreads initial *k* in the MS name-form *kadomo* as a paragraph-mark followed by initial *c*.
L41	CORBUCION. Farley *corbucionis*, MS *corbutionis*.
L54	AUMÂLE. LDB *albamarla*; facsimile (in error) *albamarl*.
L64	JOCELYN. LDB *Goscelm(us)*, see 1,2 note.
L75	ANSGER. Farley *Ans̄*, MS *Ansḡ*.
L80	GUNDWIN. Facsimile (in error) *Gonduin*, omitting the final abbreviation-mark.
L89	FREE. Farley omits the otiose abbreviation-mark (standing for *er*) on the letter *b*, given in the MS.
1,1–4	HAROLD. Earl of Wessex (1053–), King 1066. For his landholding, see Ann Williams, 'Land and power in the eleventh-century: the estates of Harold Godwineson', *Battle 1980*, 171–187.
	RANULF BROTHER OF ILGER. See 37.
1,1	BENFLEET. Probably North Benfleet, see VCH 428, n.1.
	THEN. *T(un)c*, before 1066.
	NOW. *M(odo)*, in 1086.
	ALWAYS. *Se(m)p(er)*; before 1066 and still in 1086.
	THEN 3 SLAVES, NOW 3. There is perhaps a statistical error in LDB here, as this situation would have been better expressed as 'Always 3 slaves'.
	FREE MAN ... ONE OF THE VILLAGERS. He may have held the ½ hide mentioned in the next sentence and have suffered a loss of status when his land was given to the church.
	CHURCH OF ANOTHER MANOR. Probably St. Mary's Church mentioned in 6,1.
	49 ACRES. Farley and facsimile show the otiose abbreviation-mark over the letter *c* as in the MS.
1,2	PETER THE SHERIFF. See 36.

SWEIN AND BAYNARD. See *24* and *33*. The patronym 'Baynard' is used on its own here in relation to Ralph Baynard, being qualified by the title 'Sheriff'. Cf. 1,27 note.

THROUGH ... CATTLE PLAGUE. *p(er) mortem bestiaru(m)*. This occurred at some time between 1066 and 1086 and affected the number of ploughs through the death of the oxen which drew them.

4 ... The category of livestock has been omitted in LDB.

ILBOD. See *69*.

THEODORIC POINTEL. See *71*.

RANULF PEVEREL. See *34*.

VALUE 15s. The gap in Farley before *xv* represents an erasure in the MS.

WILLIAM SON OF GROSS. See 11,1 note.

RALPH BAYNARD. See *33*.

HAMO THE STEWARD. See *28*.

JOCELYN LORIMER. See *64*. LDB *Goscelm(us)* is in error for *Goscelin(us)*. ECE 44, note, identifies this hide with land at Terling said in the Ely land pleas of 1071 x 1075 to be held by one *Gotselm* but which formerly belonged to Ely; see *Inquisitio Comitatus Cantabrigiensis*, ed. N. E. S. A. Hamilton (1876), 193.

MONKS OF ... ELY. This hide is not mentioned in Chapter 10, but see IE 128.

1,3   PLOUGHS, NOW 31½. The ½ plough represents ½ a plough-team, 4 oxen.

ALL OF THE SHERIFFS. That is, it was a cumulative loss due to a disease which had continued since 1066, during which time there was a succession of Sheriffs in Essex.

SWEIN ... SHERIFFDOM. He had been replaced as Sheriff first by Ralph Baynard (*33*) and then by Peter of Valognes (*36*) before 1086.

GEOFFREY DE MANDEVILLE. See *30*.

COUNT EUSTACE. See *20*.

OSMUND OF ANJOU. LDB *angeuin(us)* from OFr *angeuin*, OEB 132.

ROBERT GERNON. See *32*.

HERTFORD, AMWELL, HODDESDON ... RALPH OF LIMESY. Ralph is recorded as holding 14½ hides at Amwell in 1086 (Hertfordshire 23,4), held by Earl Harold in 1066 and presumably including the outlier at Amwell mentioned here. The Hoddesdon and Hertford outliers are probably the woodland at Hailey belonging 'to 3 hides of Amwell' and the 24 acres of Hertford, respectively, which Ralph claimed from Geoffrey of Bec in 1086 (Hertfordshire 34,13 and 23,4 note). *Hodesduna* has been altered in the MS from *Hodestuna*.

LATER ON WE RECOVERED ½ HIDE. The use of the first person plural here reflects the compilation of the chapter on the King's lands by his own officials who had taken action to recover this ½ hide between 1066 and 1086, cf. 66,1. The ½ hide was at Ryes (see 28,6), and had been granted out again by the King in 1086.

RALPH OF MARCY. From Marcy (La Manche: arr. Avranches), OEB 97. See 28,6. Cf. also 20,6 for another annexation by him from Earl Harold's land.

1,4   HAVERING. VCH p. 429, n.6 takes *Haueringas* to be a plural Latin accusative form but it is in fact an OE plural nominative. Cf. 6,6 note on Feering.

ROBERT SON OF CORBUCION ... 3 HIDES. These were at Leyton (41,4), although 8 Freemen are recorded there. MS has an erasure after *M(odo)*, whence the gap in the facsimile, not shown by Farley.

HUGH DE MONTFORT ... FOURTH HIDE. At Leyton. See 27,3.

4½ HIDES. Presumably referring to those at Leyton in 41,3 although Havering is not mentioned there.

30 ACRES. Probably at Fyfield, see 40,7 note.

1,6   THEODORIC POINTEL. See *71*.

'STUDLY'. Lost, in Woodham Ferrers, EPNS 276.

ANOTHER VILLAGER. Farley *7.ali(us) uill(anus)* is in error for *7.i.ali(us) uill(anus)* of the MS.

1,9   EARL 'EDGAR'. In error for Earl Algar (he of 1,11 note), see Cambridgeshire 1,10; 15; 22 where he is correctly named. Cf. LibEl 166 where he is called *Elgarus*; the LDB error was probably caused by the misreading of a similar spelling. There may however have been some confusion with Earl Algar's son Earl Edwin (d.1071).

PICOT THE SHERIFF. Of Cambridgeshire in 1086.

1½ HIDES ... IN CAMBRIDGESHIRE. At Hinxton (Cambridgeshire 1,10; 22. EE1).

A MILL. Farley *7. mol(endinum)* is in error for *7.i.mol(endinum)* of the MS.

LATER. *P(ost)*; between 1066 and 1086.

1½ HIDES WHICH HARDWIN ... HOLDS. Probably at Babraham and Hinxton (Cambridgeshire 26,11; 14. EE1).

PAID SUIT. *reddebat soca(m)*, attended court or paid a fine in lieu.
PICOT HOLDS ½ HIDE. At Babraham (Cambridgeshire 1,15. EE1).

1,10 HORWULF. LDB *Horolf(us)*; OE *Heoruwulf*, PNDB 289.
TASCELIN THE PRIEST. See also 3,11.

1,11-12 EARL ALGAR. Of East Anglia 1051-52, 1053-57; of Mercia 1057-62. He was probably dead by 1066, see Harmer, *ASWrits*, 546-547. See also 1,9 note. For his wife Aelfeva, see B3j.
THE QUEEN. Probably Matilda, consort to William I, who appears to have been given the lands formerly belonging to Earl Algar, VCH 337. Cf. B3j.
OTTO THE GOLDSMITH. See *81*, and B3j.
AS DUES. *Ad censu(m)*; Otto was enjoying its revenue as a payment from the King.

1,11 LATER ON. *post ea*, with incorrect word division; so in MS.
RICHARD SON OF COUNT GILBERT. See *23*.
WALTER SON OF GILBERT. He was probably the same as Walter Cook, see *67* note.

1,13 LESS 15 ACRES. *min(us)* is written overline in the MS preceded by an insertion-sign in the form of a colon, repeated at the point of insertion in the text after *ac(re)*.
7 PIGS. In the MS *por(ci)* has been altered to *bor(darii)*. Farley is in error here and the correct reading is 'smallholders'.
COUNT ALAN. LDB *Alam(us)*, probably for *Alain(us)*. See *21*.
45 ACRES. See 23,28.

1,13a APART ... KING'S SERVICE. Perhaps referring to the general liability to help with the '3 burdens' of military service and the upkeep of bridges and fortifications.

1,14 'WIBERTSHERNE'. The Hundred rubric is in error for Barstable, being placed one entry too soon.
FISHERY. In the present edition *piscina* has in most counties been translated as 'fishpond' in distinction to *piscaria* 'fishery', but since in Essex only *piscina* occurs, it has been translated as 'fishery' throughout. Cf. DBE 279.

1,16 ULWINESCHERHAM. Unidentified; 'Wulfwine's *Cherham* or *Scherham*'. The primary place-name here is either OE *c(i)err* 'a turn, bend' or OE *scir* 'bright' with either OE *hām* 'estate' or *hamm* 'an enclosure'.

1,17 RANULF PEVEREL. He held 5½ hides and 10 acres in that part of Maldon which was in this Hundred, see 34,12. He also had another ½ hide and 24 acres in the Half-Hundred of Maldon, see 34,31.

1,17a BAYNARD. Probably Ralph Baynard (*33*).

1,18 GRIM THE REEVE. See *83*.
HAS ALWAYS HELD. Translating *ten& se(m)p(er)*.

1,19 LAYER. The boundary of Stanway partly overlaps with that of Layer de la Haye in Winstree Hundred.
LEXDEN. See also B2.
PETER. The Sheriff. Cf. 1,2.
RAYMOND GERALD. LDB *Reimund(us) girald(us)*, the second name probably being a patronym (OG *Gerald*, Forssner 103-104) although *filius* is omitted. Cf. 32,24 where it is stated that Raymond took away another villager in this Hundred.
ROGER OF POITOU. Cf. 32,24 where Roger is recorded in possession of the villager mentioned in preceding note. In 47,3 he is said to have appropriated another 10 acres in this Hundred.
32 PENNIES. That is two *ora* of 16 pence, see S. Harvey, 'Royal revenue and Domesday terminology', *Economic History Review* 2nd series xx (1967), 221-228.

1,20 3[s]. LDB omits *sol(idos)*.

1,21 HUNDRED OF CHAFFORD. In error for Chelmsford Hundred, in which Fingrith Hall lay, cf. EPNS 236. There is some scribal confusion between the two Hundreds in this and the following four entries. *cesfeworda* is a LDB error for *ceffeworda*.

1,22 FRIDEBERT. LDB *Frieb(er)t(us)*; either OG *Fridebert, Frithebert* or possibly OE *Frithubeorht*; see PNDB 254. Cf. *70* note *sub* Hagebern.
MARGARETTING. Identified by VCH 433, n.4.

1,23 THE QUEEN. Probably Matilda (as in 1,11-12 note).
SHERIFF OF SURREY. Named as Ranulf in Surrey 1c and 5,28.
[VALUE]. LDB omits *ual(uit)*.

1,24 16 HIDES ... 14. Engelric had taken 2 hides, see below.
BY WEIGHT. *ad pond(us)*, that is the coins were weighed (although apparently not assayed) rather than being accepted at face value. This was to counteract any payment in coins which had been clipped.

ENGELRIC ... OF IT. Cf. 20,51. Engelric was Count Eustace's predecessor.

ROBERT GERNON ... WOODLAND. Robert himself was probably the King's Forester in Essex, see VCH 347.

FREE. *lib(er)ae*, for *lib(er)e* and describing the intended tenure rather than the act of giving.

R(OBERT) BISHOP OF HEREFORD. Robert Losinga 1079-95.

IN WRITTLE ... 50s. Most of this information is repeated at 19,1.

1,25-27 PETER. The Sheriff.

1,25 SWEIN'S LAND. See 24,63 where however the King is said to have only 3s from customary dues.

RANULF PEVEREL. See 34,31 for his Maldon land in this Half-Hundred.

FOR 3s. *p(er).iii.sol(idos)*, that is 'to the value of 3s'.

BEFORE 1066 ... BY WEIGHT. Cf. 34,31 note.

1,26 HUNDRED OF TENDRING. *Tendring &* in Farley is in error for *Tenderingae* of MS.

HARKSTEAD. A Suffolk outlier of Brightlingsea, see ESf1.

P(ETER). Farley *p̂*, MS *P̂*.

4 CATTLE AND 5 PIGS. Apparently additional to the previous total. These figures do not tally with those for Harkstead in ESf1.

1,27 BAYNARD. Ralph Baynard (*33*), cf. 1,2 note. Here the context again allows the forename to be omitted.

WOODLAND. Farley *Silua*, MS *Silŭ*.

1 OUTLIER ... IT. Cf. 20,69.

ROGER OF RAISMES. See *39*.

CALLS ... DELIVERER. That is, to bear witness that he had delivered ownership, as Sheriff, on the King's behalf to Roger.

RICHARD SON OF COUNT GILBERT. He held Alresford (23,33) which came within the jurisdiction of Lawford.

WALERAN. The father of John (*40*).

HAGEBERT. Apparently OG *Hagabert, Hagibert* (Forssner 138) but cf. *70* note.

COUNT E(USTACE). Cf. 20,69 for his holding at Lawford.

BISHOP OF BAYEUX ... HIM. See 18,44 note.

RANULF ... 15 ACRES. See 37,20.

RALPH BAYNARD ... 35 ACRES. See 33,17.

ROGER ... LONDON. Probably he of 4,5.

1,28 SHELFORD. Cambridgeshire EE2.

THIS OUTLIER WAS. *Hec berewita erat*, altered from *Hec berewita e(st)*; so in MS. For *berewica*, OE *bere-wĩc*.

ROBERT GERNON. See *32*.

1,30 EDEVA. The Fair, some of whose land in Suffolk (1,61; 63-64; 67; 73) was later held by Earl Ralph and then by Godric the Steward. See also 21,2-5 note.

EARL RALPH. As 21,9 note.

2 HOLY TRINITY, CANTERBURY. That is Christ Church, Canterbury. The lands in this chapter were later subject to the Dean of Bocking, see VCH 340.

2,2 2 HIDES IN (WEST) MERSEA. Bocking Hall (in Winstree Hundred, EPNS 320-321), an estate in West Mersea granted with Bocking to Christ Church, Canterbury between 995 and 999 by AEthelric and Leofwynn (ECE, no. 30; Sawyer no. 1218).

2,4 HOLY TRINITY HOLDS. Repeated before 2,5-8.

LAWLING. For the annexation by the monks of 1 hide there, see 90,79.

2,6 ST. LAWRENCE. Formerly 'Newland', EPNS 224.

Folio 8a, foot. In the bottom margin (not shown by Farley, but in facsimile) is written *iii. v(irgate). iiii.7 d(imidia)..ii.' 7 d(imidia).xiiii.ii.iii.vii.* This is a list of the hidages in this chapter, the last figure being the sum of the hidages of 2,7-9 on folio 8b. Cf. notes on folios 20a,87a.

Folio 9a. A partial list of landholders (*3-8*) has been crossed through on this folio, the remainder of which is blank. A similar list occurs at folio 17a. These folios are the first leaves of quires 2 and 3 respectively of LDB and each list contains only those landholders whose Holdings form chapters in that particular quire which the list introduces. The presence of these lists in the MS reflects the fact that LDB was originally intended to be no more than a circuit return.

3,1 AELFTHRYTH. LDB *Alftred queda(m) femina*; PNDB 181.

3,2 BISHOP WILLIAM. Of London, 1051-75. See *4*, note.

COUNT EUSTACE ... 100 MANORS. See 20,4.

WOODLAND, 1000 [PIGS]. LDB omits *porci*.

3,5 ST. PAUL'S HELD. Literally 'St. Paul held'. Referring to St. Paul's Cathedral, London.

BRIAN. Farley *brieu*, MS *brien*.

FROM THE BISHOP. LDB *depo* is in error for *de ep(iscop)o*.

3,9 IN SOUTHMINSTER. The preposition *in* was added as an afterthought and is squeezed into the space before *Sudmunstrā*. Although the addition of *in* made the abbreviation-mark on the place-name incorrect, the scribe forgot to erase it.

BISHOP HOLDS IN LORDSHIP. The words *ep(is)c(opus) in d(omi)nio* are interlined in the MS and replace *xiiii.milites de ep(iscop)o* '14 men-at-arms from the Bishop', which is deleted; the plural verb *tenent* 'hold' is altered to the singular *tenet* by placing points above and below the letter *n*.

14 MEN. Probably the '14 men-at-arms' referred to in previous note.

KING CANUTE. 1016-35.

3,10 WERE 17 ACRES. LDB *fuere*, a short form for *fuerunt*. Also at 9,10 etc.

1 VIRGATE. ECE, no. 27, note, suggests that this is both the woodland in 32,5 and Glazenwood (EPNS 283).

3,11 TASCELIN THE PRIEST. See also 1,10.

AFTER HE CROSSED THE SEA. After 1066.

3,14 NOW ... The number in Farley is damaged but should read *ii*.

3,16 COLCHESTER. The Bishop's land is not referred to in *B*. The 14 houses and 4 acres may have been the land which in 1206 was referred to as a Soke, while the whole of 3,16 may be represented by the parish of St. Mary's-at-the-Walls; see VCH 424.

APART FROM THE LEVY. *p(re)t(er) Scotu(m)*. See B2 note.

4 It is suggested by VCH 339 that the lands in the present chapter represent those acquired by Bishop William (1051-75). Cf. the references in Hertfordshire (4,1;22) to lands bought by Bishop William.

4,1 CRANHAM. Formerly 'Bishop's Ockendon', EPNS 124-125.

4,2-3 TOTHAM. Rok Hall in Little Totham, VCH 440; Rook Hall, EPNS 312.

4,3 WILLIAM BOLD. LDB *Will(elmus) balt*; perhaps OFr *balt* rather than OE *beald* in this particular instance, OEB 340-341.

4,5 ROGER. Cf. 1,27 note.

TENDRING. New Hall in Tendring, VCH 440.

4,6 ANSKETEL. See 48,2 note.

4,10 HORNDON (-ON-THE-HILL). The estate of Cantis there, VCH 441, n.2 and 398-399.

4,16 HARLOW. Farley and MS *herlaua*; facsimile (in error) *herlauan*.

EDEVA. The Fair, who had also held Bishop's Stortford (Hertfordshire 4,22) from Bishop William of London. See 21,2-5 note.

4,18 BASSETTS. In Woodham Walter EPNS 232 (6"). The manorial name also survives in Bassett's Farm in Little Baddow, but that is in Chelmsford Hundred. The LDB spelling *Mildemet* is metathesized, as later forms of this (superseded) name show it to have meant 'middle meadowland', possibly because of its location between the water meadow along the R. Chelmer to the north and higher woodland to the south.

5 CANONS OF ST. PAUL'S. That is, of St. Paul's Cathedral, London.

5,1 LEE (CHAPEL). For this identification, see EPNS 163.

5,2-5 ST. PAUL'S HELD/HOLDS ... Literally, 'St. Paul held/holds'.

5,6 GODITH. Probably the woman called Gotild in 28,16.

A WRIT. *breue(m)*, apparently here referring to the written record of Godith's grant rather than to a writ of the King.

5,8 THURSTAN THE RED. LDB *Turstin(us) ruff(us)*; OEB 330-331.

THE OTHER NAVESTOCK. A different manor, but within the present parish.

5,10 HEYBRIDGE. Formerly 'Tidwoldington', EPNS 303-304.

½ HIDE. Recorded under Langford, see 33,22.

5,11 THE NAZE. LDB *AEduluesnasa(m)*, 'Eadwulf's or Ealdwulf's promontory', EPNS 354-355.

MARK OF SILVER. Later in the medieval period a 'mark' was an accounting term equal to 13s 4d. Here it is probably a term denoting weight.

6 ST. PETER'S WESTMINSTER. The abbey refounded by Edward the Confessor. See also 90,19 for an annexation by St. Peter's.

6,1 ST. PETER'S HAS. Literally, 'St. Peter has'.

ST. MARY'S CHURCH. Apparently a reference to a church at South Benfleet before 1066, rather than to St. Mary's Barking (9). See also 1,1 note.

WESTMINSTER. Farley *Westmonasterio*; MS *Westmonsterio*.

50 SHEEP ... PIGS. Farley omits an insertion mark in the form of a colon before *L* and after *mot*.

ST. MARTIN'S. See *12* note.

COUNTY. LDB *consulat(us)*.

6,4 ALSTAN STRIC. The byname may be a variant of the OE name *Stric(c)a* (Redin 79), here used as a patronym. The OWScand nickname *Strikr* 'boy', is also possible, see OEB 337.

6,6 BECONTREE. Farley *Beuentreu*, MS *Beuentrev*.

6,8 FEERING. See also 90,17. VCH, p. 444 and n.8 mistakes the OE nominative plural form *Pheringas* for a Latin accusative plural. Cf. 1,4 note on Havering and 9,7 note on Barking. See also 6,11 note.

2 HOUSES IN COLCHESTER. According to B3k the Abbot had 4 houses there belonging to Feering.

ROGER OF RAISMES. He held land adjacent at Messing, see 39,4.

MAUGER ... ARCHBISHOP. He held land at Orpington (Kent, 2,30) from the Archbishop of Canterbury.

HE IS ... KING'S HAND. Or 'it is'; *est* here could refer to either the ½ virgate or the free man.

6,9 ALRIC ... NAVAL BATTLE AGAINST KING WILLIAM. Alric was called Aethelric the Chamberlain in Harmer, *ASWrits*, no. 74 (Sawyer, No. 118). The location of the battle is not known.

FELL. Farley *cecidet*, MS *cecidit*.

WRIT. Harmer, *ASWrits*, p. 494, prints a spurious writ, claiming to be issued by King William I, confirming Kelvedon Hatch to Westminster Abbey. ECE, no. 82 note, suggests that it was fabricated to make good the lack of documentary evidence reported here.

6,10 [HUNDRED OF CHAFFORD]. LDB puts the Hundred heading one entry late, before 6,11.

6,11 EXCHANGE. Together with Feering (cf. 6,8), North Ockendon had been granted by King William between 1066 and 1075 to Westminster Abbey in exchange for Windsor, Berks., ECE, no. 73.

6,12 WENNINGTON. Farley *Wemtuna(m)*, MS *Wenituna(m)*.

ROBERT THE PERVERTED. LDB *Inuesiat(us)* may be derived from Latin *invertere*, 'to pervert'. OEB 348 refers to MLat *invasatus* 'invaded by a devil'. He was identical with Robert the Lascivious (*lasciuus*) in 32,28, see VCH 518, n.7.

6,13 *GEDDESDUNA*. Unidentified, OE *Gieddesdūne* 'at Gieddi's upland'. Between 1066 and 1075 it (*Gyddesdūne*) had been granted by King William to Deorman, ECE, no. 72.

6,15 TO BATTLE IN YORK(SHIRE) WITH HAROLD. A reference to the Battle of Stamford Bridge in 1066. Cf. 30,16 note.

7,1 HAROLD HELD WALTHAM (HOLY CROSS). Earl (later King) Harold, who greatly extended the landholding of the Canons of Waltham (*8*).

WOODLAND, 202 PIGS. So in MS but *ii.7.cc.* is probably a scribal error for *m̄.7.cc.*, that is 1200.

TRIBUTARIES. *Censarii, cens(it)ores*, chiefly in north-east Mercia, Yorkshire, Essex and Dorset, paid tribute in money, not work.

1 PLOUGH CAN BE RESTORED. The one plough in lordship lacking in 1086, see above.

HOLY CROSS. The Canons of Waltham (*8*).

RANULF BROTHER OF ILGER ... 30 ACRES. See 37,9 note.

A GATE. Aldgate in the City of London. In 1108 the Priory of Holy Trinity Aldgate was freed from its subjection to the Canons of Waltham. See W. Page, *London: its origin and early development* (London, 1929), 153-154 and *The cartulary of Holy Trinity Aldgate*, ed. G. A. J. Hodgett (*London Record Society* 7, 1971), nos. 1-11. (*Ex inf.* Dr. D. J. Keene).

BISHOP'S PREDECESSOR. Altered in MS from 'his predecessor', *suo antecessori*. Probably referring to Bishop Walchere, 1071-80.

8 CANONS OF WALTHAM. The college of secular canons, favoured by King Harold. The latter's heart is buried at Waltham.

8,3 WOODFORD. The gap in Farley after the place-name represents an erasure in the MS. WOODLAND ... NOW NONE. Added in the margin of the MS and here placed in the translation in its proper place.

8,4 1 PLOUGH ... RESTORED. That is, in lordship.

8,9 IN THIS MANOR. LDB *In ho manerio*, in error for *In hoc manerio*. 1 CARUCATE. LDB *.i.carř.fr̄ae*. Probably the land described at 32,29.

Folio 17a. A partial list of landholders (*9-18*) has been crossed through on this folio, the remainder of which is blank. See note to folio 9a.

9 ST. MARY'S BARKING. The Benedictine nunnery, founded in the mid-7th century and refounded in the mid-10th.

9,1 ST. MARY'S HOLDS. Literally, 'St. Mary holds'.

THOROLD OF ROCHESTER ... 30 ACRES. The 30 acres entered under the adjacent Chadwell in 18,11.

VILLAGERS' PLOUGHS. *car(uce) uill(an)is*, with dative of possession. An alternative to the more usual 'men's ploughs', *caruce hominum*.

9,2   RAVENGAR. LDB *Rauengari(us)*; OG *Hrabangar*, Forssner 212.

9,5   WOODHEN. LDB *cudhen* (here), *gudhen* (90,1). Unexplained OEB 390, but probably a byname **Wudhen* from OE *wude-henn* 'a female wood-cock'.

3 VIRGATES. See 90,2 where they are recorded as an annexation.

9,7   BARKING. VCH, p. 448 again mistakes the OE nominative plural form *Berchingas* for a Latin accusative plural. Cf. 6,8 note on Feering.

24 GOATS. So in MS, facsimile (in error) *xviiii*.

LONDON ... ½ CHURCH. A reference to All Hallows, Barking-by-the-Tower. The three dots in Farley at the foot of folio 17b represent an erasure (of *xiii*) in the MS.

ENGLISHMEN ... FRENCHMEN. The men of the Hundred jury, four French and four English.

JOCELYN LORIMER. He held land adjacent at Ilford (64,1).

9,8   WIGBOROUGH. The manor of Abbot's (formerly Abbess) Hall in Great Wigborough, EPNS 324.

3 HOUSES IN COLCHESTER. See B3s.

9,10   THERE WERE. *Fuere*; as in 3,10 note.

9,11   INGATESTONE. Owned by Barking Abbey until the Dissolution, EPNS 253–254.

9 CATTLE. LDB repeats *.ix.an(imales)* in error.

9,12   The gap before this entry in Farley represents a tear (repaired) in the MS. Cf. 10,1 note.

9,13   WILLIAM OF BOURSIGNY. Probably from Boursigny (Calvados); OEB 78.

10   ST. ETHELDREDA'S, ELY. Ely Abbey. For possessions alienated by 1086, not mentioned in this chapter, see 1,2. 18,36. 22,7. 25,3. 27,14. 30,27;41. 34,19. 79,1.

10,1   BROXTED. The same information is given in IE 125, IEBrev 172, IENV 175.

70 SHEEP ... MANOR. The gap in Farley at the two line-ends represents the reverse of the same tear referred to in 9,12 note.

9 ACRES ... £4. The last two lines on folio 18b are written in the MS over an erasure.

9 ACRES. See 25,12.

ALSO. Farley replaces the ampersand of the MS with the tironian *nota*.

10,2   RODING. See also IE 126. The information in 22,7–8 and IEAL 184 suggests that LDB is defective here as it appears that 22,7 was also alienated from Ely while the statistics in 10,2 include elements from both 22,7–8.

THIRD HIDE. See 22,8.

23 PIGS. LDB *xvviii*; IE *xviii*.

10,3   RETTENDON. See also IE 126, IEBrev 172, IENV 175.

3 PLOUGHS IN LORDSHIP. IEBrev lists 4.

SIWARD HOLDS. LDB *ten&* is an LDB error for *tenuit* 'held'.

1 HIDE AND 30 ACRES. See 34,30.

2 HIDES AND 30 ACRES; EUDO. See 25,20. Farley uses the same symbol for *q(ue)* in *q(ue) tenuit* as for *q(uia)* in *q(uia) antecessor*; in the MS and facsimile these symbols differ.

10,4   HADSTOCK. For this entry, see also IE 126. For the name represented by LDB *Cadenhou*, see EPNS 510–511.

10,5   LITTLEBURY. See also IE 126–127, IEBrev 172, IENV 175.

19 SMALLHOLDERS. IEBrev lists 16.

7 SLAVES. IEBrev lists 6.

CALLED STRETHALL. Farley *vocat(ur)*, MS *uocat(ur)*.

ALWIN LDB *Eluui(us)*; IE *Alwinus* (MSS B,C), *alfpinus* (MS A).

HUGH. IE 127, IEAL 182, Hugh of Bernières. Also in Cambridgeshire (27, etc).

HEYDON. According to IEAL 182 this was also appropriated by Hugh of Bernières. Farley *hamdena*, MS *haindena.*

ALWIN [HELD]. LDB omits *tenuit*.

WILLIAM CARDON. The byname is OFr *cardon* 'thistle'; OEB 368–369. The byname survives in Cardon's Hall in Chishall, VCH 356.

WRONGFULLY. *i(n)i(us)te(m)* Farley, in error for *i(n)i(us)te* of MS.

11   ST. EDMUND'S. Literally, 'St. Edmund'. The Abbey of Bury St. Edmunds, Suffolk.

11,1   WILLIAM SON OF GROSS. An undertenant of Hugh de Montfort (27,2. 90,15;18). See also 1,2 and 88,2.

11,3   FOR 4½ HIDES. So in MS, facsimile has '3½ hides'.

11,5   HUNDRED OF LEXDEN. LDB *Laxefelda*; this spelling would appear to be in error. The scribe of LDB has substituted the OE element *feld* for *denu* contained in Lexden, see EPNS 359,376.

11,7 (LITTLE) WALTHAM. The manor of Channels there, VCH 451, n.8.

Folio 20a, foot. Farley does not show the summary of hidages in Chapter 11 given in the bottom margin of the MS and facsimile. This reads *i.i.d(imidia) . iii. d(imidia) . iii. d(imidia) . iii. d(imidia).ii.v.* Cf. notes on folios 8a,87a.

12 ST. MARTIN'S, LONDON. St. Martin le Grand, founded by Engelric the predecessor of Count Eustace *(20)*.

12,1 OUTLIER. According to ECE, no. 84, dated 1068, this was at Mashbury.

13 ST. MARTIN'S, BATTLE. Battle Abbey, founded by King William on the battlefield of Hastings.

13,1 GOTI. See 28,1 note.

HUTTON. LDB *Atahov*, OE *æt* and *hōh*, 'at the hill', with later addition of *tūn* 'estate', EPNS 160.

FREE LAND. *lib(er)ae t(er)rae* (genitive singular). VCH 452, n.4, suggests it was free from geld.

13,2 HORSEHAM (HALL). Later in Freshwell Hundred, EPNS 509, VCH 452, n.5.

33 SHEEP. So in MS; facsimile '28'.

14 ST. VALÉRY'S. King William granted 12½ hides in Essex to the Abbey in 1068 (ECE, no. 85) to repay St. Valéry for having sent a favourable wind to enable him to cross the Channel before the Battle of Hastings.

14,1 MATCHING. VCH 452, n.8 identified this as Matching Barns in Hatfield Broad Oak but this was not confirmed by EPNS 43,45.

14,2 LINDSELL. The manor of Prior's Hall there, EPNS 487.

Folio 21a, lines 2-7. Farley omits to show an oblique gap caused by a (repaired) tear in the MS.

14,3 TAKELEY. The manor later called Warish Hall in Takeley, EPNS 535-536, whose name commemorates ownership by St. Valéry's.

14,5 WIDDINGTON. The manor of Prior's Hall there, EPNS 546.

20 SHEEP. LDB *.xx.ou(es)* is in error, probably for *.xx.bor(darii)*, '20 smallholders'.

14,6 ST. PETER'S CHAPEL. The estate was one of those near St. Peter's Chapel *(Ythancaestir c. 735)* on the site of the Roman fort of Othona (see EPNS 210–211). Identified by VCH 453,392 as the manor of East Hall in Bradwell.

14,7 HE ALSO HELD. LDB *teñ*, here for *tenuit*, governed as in 14,6 by 'Thorkell'.

15 HOLY TRINITY, CAEN. The Nunnery there, founded by Queen Matilda.

15,1 FELSTED. Granted to Holy Trinity in 1082 by King William and Queen Matilda, ECE, no. 92.

3 VIRGATES. Recorded at 72,2.

THE FOURTH. Recorded at 73,1.

16 ST. STEPHEN'S, CAEN. The Monastery there, founded by William the Conqueror.

16,1 PANFIELD. See ECE, no. 88, for King William's confirmation of Panfield to St. Stephen's between 1071 and 1077. It had been granted by Waleran son of Ranulf between 1069 and 1076, ECE, no. 86.

17 ST. OUEN'S. The Abbey at Rouen, dedicated to St. Audoenus.

17,1 ST. OUEN'S HELD. Literally, 'St. Ouen held'.

(WEST) MERSEA. The estate appears to have been granted to St. Ouen's by Edward the Confessor in 1046 (Sawyer, no. 1015; ECE, no. 63).

WALERAN TOOK IT AWAY. See B6 for Waleran's connection with Colchester.

17,2 KING'S MANOR AT LAYER. For the King's land there (said to be an outlier of Stanway manor) see 1,19.

FORFEITURES OF THE HUNDRED. The profits of jurisdiction in the Hundred court, see further Harmer, *ASWrits*, 73–85.

18 BISHOP OF BAYEUX. Odo, King William's half-brother. Although he was imprisoned from 1082-87, his lands were maintained as a unit.

18,1 THOROLD'S SON. As elsewhere in this chapter, this no doubt refers to Ralph son of Thorold of Rochester.

30 ACRES ... 1066. See 20,1.

18,2 WOODLAND, ½ HIDE. The measurement of woodland in hides, here, in 18,5 and in several entries in Chapter 24, is unusual in the DB Survey.

18,5 INGRAVE. The second part of the modern name preserves the name of the Domesday tenant, (Ralph) son of Thorold; EPNS 161.

WOODLAND. See 18,2 note.

3 HIDES. *v* deleted, *iii* interlined.

11 SMALLHOLDERS. Misplaced among the resources.

18,7 WHEATLEY. Later in Rochford Hundred, EPNS 195.

POINTEL. Probably Theodoric Pointel (71).
18,9 TEHER. A NFr form of OG *Theothere*, Forssner 228.
18,11 30 ACRES. At Mucking, see 9,1.
18,16 BARLING. The manor of Mucking Hall there, VCH 456, n.7.
18,17 2 OXEN. That is, ¼ plough-team.
18,18 23s. *xiii* with another *x* interlined.
18,19 POINTEL. As 18,7 note.
18,20 35 ACRES. *xxx* with *v* interlined.
18,21 AUBREY'S WIFE. That is, of Aubrey de Vere (35). Cf. 18,24.
      'NAPSTED'. Lost in Lt. Maplestead, EPNS 447. Cf. also 90,38 for Aubrey's wife's
      annexation at Lt. Maplestead.
18,21a TIHEL OF HELLÉAN. See 38, note.
18,23-24 Farley does not show two oblique tears (repaired) which affect the writing of these
      entries and 18,30-32 (on the reverse) in the MS.
18,23 BRADWELL QUAY. Formerly 'Hackfleet', EPNS 209–210.
18,24 AUBREY'S WIFE. As 18,21 note.
18,25 HERBERT'S NEPHEW. Or possibly his grandson (*nepos*). He was probably Hugh, who
      held Screveton (Nottinghamshire 7,6) from the Bishop.
18,26-27 MAUGER. As 6,8 note.
18,29 MANNING. LDB *Mannic(us)*; PNDB 324.
18,30-32 See 18,23–24 note.
18,30 RAINHAM. The manor of Southall there, VCH 458, n.3; South Hall, EPNS 128.
18,32 WILLIAM PEVEREL ... THURROCK. See 48,2.
18,33 CRANHAM. LDB *Craohv*; for the identification, see EPNS 124–125.
18,34 GILBERT ... 10 ACRES. See 48,2.
18,35 *LIMPWELLA*. Unidentified, a place named from a spring of some sort (OE *wella*). The first
      element looks like OE *(ge)limp*, 'an event, happening, accident'.
      BISHOP. LDB *comite*, 'Count', deleted.
18,36 ELY ABBEY. See IE 128, IEAL 188.
      2 MEN. IE, 'free men', *liberi homines*.
18,37 DANE. *dac(us)*; see OEB 135.
      BEREWIC. Unidentified, OE *bere-wīc*, 'outlier'.
      THOROLD. Perhaps in error for (Ralph) son of Thorold of Rochester.
18,38-43 R(ALPH); RALPH. Son of Thorold of Rochester.
18,39 ANAND THE DANE. ODan *Anund*, PNDB 161. For *dac(us)* see OEB 135.
      AS A MANOR. *iii* at first written, *m(anerio)* added overline as a correction.
18,40 SAEGAR. LDB *Segar(us)*; PNDB 352, s.n. *Saēgār*.
      PATCHING (HALL). VCH 459, n.9 misinterprets *Pacingas* as Latin accusative plural rather
      than as OE nominative plural.
18,41 This entry would appear to have been originally begun in LDB on the previous line, where
      the paragraph-mark and an initial *M* have been left in suspension.
18,42 THE OTHER MOULSHAM (HALL). Another manor, also within the area now called
      Moulsham Hall.
18,43 AETHELSTAN. LDB *Adstan(us)*; PNDB 188.
18,44 OTHER LAND. Possibly a reference to the ½ hide belonging to Lawford (in the same
      Hundred) mentioned in 1,27 as being held by Ralph son of Thorold under the Bishop
      of Bayeux.
19,1 [HUNDRED OF CHELMSFORD]. LDB omits the Hundred rubric.
      WRITTLE. See 1,24 for an almost duplicate entry.
      HAROLD'S HOLDING. Referring to Earl Harold; in 1,24 the same information is given
      in reference to 'the King's Holding'.
20   COUNT EUSTACE. Of Boulogne, brother-in-law of King Edward.
20,1 30 ACRES ... HOLDING. Entered under Vange (18,1), adjacent to Fobbing.
      ENGELRIC. Count Eustace's predecessor in many of his lands. The founder of St. Martin
      le Grand (12).
20,2 WARNER. The LDB form *Garner(us)* is an OFr form of OG *Warinhari*; Forssner 247–248.
20,3 THEN 2 PLOUGHS. In the MS, *ii* has been altered from *i*.
20,4 ORSETT. The manor of Loft Hall there, VCH 461, n.2.
      BISHOP OF LONDON. Bishop William, see 3,2.
20,4-5 100 MANORS. These are also mentioned in 3,2. They may refer to a total number of
      manors promised to Count Eustace by King William.
20,5 'GRAVESEND'. LDB *Grauesanda(m)*. Probably a detached part of Gravesend, Kent,

which lies on the opposite bank of the Thames to Barstable Hundred. Cf. the Chalk entry (EKt) for another connection between estates in Kent and Essex.

20,6 AELFRIC ... HOLDS. *Tenuit* 'held' altered to *Tenet* 'holds'.
30 ACRES. See 28,3. Cf. 1,3 note.

20,7 ALWAYS ... 1 PLOUGH. *Se(m)p(er)* in this instance means 'then and now', since a different figure is given for 'when acquired'.
HIRED MAN. Translating *mercennari(us)*.

20,8 QUEEN EDITH. The consort of Edward the Confessor and daughter of Earl Godwin of Wessex.
300 AND A HALF. That is, 350; unless *dim̄* has been entered in error through confusion with the line below.
COLCHESTER. See B3g for Count Eustace's houses there.
RICHARD OF SACKVILLE ... ½ MILL. See 25,1 note. He probably took his name from Sacquenville (Eure: arr. Evreux), OEB 111–112.

20,12 IWAIN. LDB *Iunain(us)* here, *Iunan(us)* 20,50. The first *n* in both spellings is in error for *u*. *Iwain* is OBret or OW.

20,13 ADELULF. Of Marck, see 20,15 note.
LATTON. The manor of Mark Hall there (EPNS 44), named from the byname of the 1086 subtenant. Cf. 20,15 note.
ERNULF. Probably OE *Earnwulf*, but possibly ODan *Arnulf*; PNDB 244.
AT A CHURCH. Translating *ad una(m) eccl(es)iam*. A possible alternative is '(belonging) to a church'.

20,14 BRICTMER. LDB *Brictnar(us)*.
;½ HIDE. *7 dim(idia) hid(a)* in Farley is in error for *p(ro) dim(idia) hid(a)* of MS.

20,15 ADELULF OF MARCK. From Marck (Pas-de-Calais), OEB 98. His first name is OG, Forssner 10. For his family and estates, see VCH 344.
DUNMOW. The manor of Marks there (EPNS 477), named from the family of the 1086 subtenant. Cf. 20,13 note.

20,17 THERE. LDB *.i.bi.* in error for *ibi*.

20,18 'PLESINGHO'. Lost, in Willingale Doe, EPNS 500–501. See also 90,30.

20,19 7 HIDES. NOW. Farley omits to show a gap, caused by an erasure, in the MS between *hid(is)* and *M(odo)*.
½ HIDE. See 28,9 note.

20,21 THEN 38 SHEEP. 'Then' *(tunc)* is interlined.

20,22;24 ADELULF. As 20,13 note.

20,27 (STEEPLE) BUMPSTEAD. The manor of Garnons there, VCH 464, n.6; EPNS 420, s.n. Garland's Farm.
CATTLE. Farley adds an otiose abbreviation-mark above *n* of *anim(ales)*, not in MS.

20,28 VCH 464, n.9, identifies this as Belchamp St. Ethelbert in Ovington (see EPNS 448, s.n. Allbrights), but this is not supported by EPNS 408–409 or by DG 131.
WHICH ... HELD. Deleted thus in MS.

20,29 ADELULF. As 20,13 note.
HOLDS. Deleted thus in MS.

20,30 20 ... LESS 1. LDB omits the category of livestock. Probably pigs or sheep.

20,32 VILLAGERS, NOW 3. *ii* altered to *iii* in MS.
14 SMALLHOLDERS. *xiiii*, the *x* has been altered from *i* in the MS.
ENGELRIC ... MANORS. Presumably those of Finchingfield (20,30) and Smeetham Hall (20,32).

20,34 ST. MARTIN'S. See *12* note.
VALUE ... 100s. Deleted thus in MS.

20,36- BLANCHED. Both the adjectives *candidus* and *blancus* are used here to describe pounds of
37 pennies which have been assayed.

20,36 COLCHESTER. As 20,8 note.

20,37 AELFRIC ... BOXTED. See EHu.
2 COBS. MS *iii* with last minim erased; facsimile *iii*.

20,39 COLCHESTER. As 20,8 note.

20,40 EDRIC. Called Edric of Easthorpe in 37,20 from his holding here.

20,41 COLNE. VCH 466, n.2 identifies this as Colne Engaine but this is not supported by EPNS 379 or by DG 134.
AELFRIC BIG. The byname *biga* is probably identical with ME *bigge* 'of large, bulky size', OEB 290–292.

20,42 GODRIC OF COLCHESTER. See B1-2.
20,43 AS MUCH. LDB has an otiose abbreviation-mark above *u* of *tantunde(m)*.
ACQUIRED 7, NOW 5. Farley does not show the gap in the text in MS, caused by an erasure between *vii* and *m(odo)*.
VALUE ALWAYS 5s. Corrected thus in MS.
20,44 AELFRIC'S FATHER HELD. There is a deletion of about two letters in the MS after *teñ*; *ten&* has probably been altered to *teñ* standing here for *ten(uit)*.
(AS) OF ENGELRIC'S HOLDING. Translating *de feudo ingelrici*, meaning that it had *formerly* been held by Engelric.
20,46 ONGAR. For an annexation there by a man of Count Eustace's, see 90,87.
20,49 (HIM). Alternatively '(them)', referring to the 10 acres.
20,50 IWAIN. See 20,12 note.
20,51 ENGELRIC ... 1066. See 1,24.
20,54 ADELULF. As 20,13 note.
20,56 UNDER THEM. That is, under Lambert before 1066 and under Engelric after 1066.
WHO ... DEFENDER. *unde reuocat ea(m)* [Farley error for *eu(m)* of MS] *ad defensore(m)*.
AS. LDB *u* is in error for *ut*.
20,57 TOLLESHUNT. VCH 468, n.6 identifies this as the manor of Tolleshunt Guines in Tollesbury. EPNS 305, s.n. Guines Court, does not quote the LDB form however.
THORBERN. Cf. *70* note *sub* Hagebern.
20,57-58 ADELULF. As 20,13 note.
20,60 ST. MARTIN'S. See *12* note.
20,61 'BLATCHAMS'. Lost, in Great Totham; EPNS 310-311.
VALUE 10s. LDB has omitted *Tunc* before *Val(uit)*.
20,62 AMALFRID. The LDB form *Alm̄frid(us)* is corrupt. The name is OG, Forssner 26.
FREE MAN. LDB repeats *lib(er)* in error.
20,63 ST. OSYTH. LDB *Cita(m)* is in error for *Cica(m)*. The place-name commemorates St. Osyth who is said to have founded a nunnery at *Cicc* in the 7th century, see EPNS 347-348. The present holding is identified by VCH 469, n.5, as the manor of Earl's Hall in St. Osyth.
BURNA. Unidentified, OE *burna* '(place at) the stream'.
30 ACRES. In the MS there is a deletion (?of *quas*) after *.xxx.ac(re)*.
20,64 TENDRING. The manor of Old Hall there, VCH 469, n.9.
AS MUCH. LDB *tantude(m)* is in error for *tantu(n)de(m)*.
20,65 HATO. OG *Hado, Hatto*, see Förstemann PN 790, s.n. *Hatho*.
20,67 ST. PAUL'S, LONDON. See *5*.
20,68-69 ADELULF. As 20,13 note.
20,69 LAWFORD. The manor of Dale Hall there, VCH 470, n.5. Cf. in 1,27 the reference to an outlier of 4 hides annexed by Engelric and held by Count Eustace.
THEM. Referring to the 3 Freemen.
20,70 TENDRING. VCH 470, n.7; as 20,64 note.
20,71 (AS) OF ENGELRIC'S HOLDING. See 20,44 note.
APPROPRIATED AFTER 1066. *t(empore) r(egis) Will(elm)i* has been altered, by deletion in MS, from *t(empore) r(egis) e(dwardi)*.
THESE 8 ACRES. Presumably those belonging to the 2 Freemen who had not been appropriated by Engelric.
HE PAID. The Freeman.
20,72 SIRED. Corrected from Siward; *Siuuard(us), -uuard(us)* underlined for deletion, -*red(us)* interlined.
3 PLOUGHS IN LORDSHIP. Farley does not show a gap caused by an erasure in MS between *car(uce)* and *in*. There are also deletions and alterations in the following line in MS.
20,74 200 SHEEP; 88 SHEEP. Thus in MS. The second lot of sheep may be in error for goats however.
20,75-76 BRICTWULF. According to ECE, no. 83, a writ of King William dated between 1066 and 1087, Brictwulf's lands were td be held by the Abbey of Bury St. Edmunds. This writ does not appear to have taken effect by the time of Domesday.
20,77 ENGELRIC. See 90,64 where Engelric is said to have also held an annexation of 30 acres at Bendysh (Hall).
20,79 ADELULF. As 20,13 note.
Folio 35 is a half-sheet in the MS, containing the whole of Chapter 21.
21 COUNT ALAN. Of Brittany, son-in-law of King William. His name is OBret *Alan*.
21,2-5 EDEVA. Probably Edeva the Fair, one of Count Alan's predecessors, see Cambridgeshire (Chapter 14) and Hertfordshire (Chapter 16). See also 1,30 note; 4,16 note; and 21,11-12.

21,3 AMONG MEADOW AND MARSH. Translating *int(er) p(ra)tu(m)* 7 *maresc*.
21,4 FINCHINGFIELD. The manor of Spain's Hall there (EPNS 427).
21,9 EARL R(ALPH). Of East Anglia. Called Ralph 'Wader' in Cambridgeshire 19,4. With
Earl Waltheof (see 55,1 note) and Earl Roger of Hereford, he rebelled against King William
in 1075 and ended his life in exile. The byname 'Wader', DB *Waders*, may be a place-name,
see OEB 119.
THIS LAND. *han* is a LDB error for *hanc*.
21,10 EMANUEL (WOOD). Between 1089 and 1093 this was granted by Count Alan to the Abbey
of Bury St. Edmunds, ECE, no. 104.
21,11-12 EDEVA. As 21,2-5 note.
21,12 HERVEY. *Herueu(us)* is a LDB error for *Herue(us)*.
22 WILLIAM OF WARENNE. Later created Earl of Surrey by King William II.
22,1 *UPHAM*. Unidentified, OE *up-hām*, or *up-hamm*, 'upper estate' or 'upper enclosure'.
22,3 HOLDFAST. Probably identical with Aelmer Holdfast, see 61,2 note.
22,4 ALWIN GOTTON. The rest of his land had lain in Herts. On his byname, probably deriving
from a lost place in that county, see Hertfordshire 10,6 note.
22,5 DOVE. LDB *Duua*. Either OE **dūfe* or ON *dúfa* 'a dove'; PNDB 227, Redin 116.
(GREAT) EASTON. The manor of Blamsters there, according to VCH 474, n.3.
22,6 MEN HELD. LDB *tenuit* has been corrected to *tenuerunt*, but rather untidily.
THEN 1 PRIEST. In the MS the *p* of *p(res)b(ite)r* has been altered from *b*.
VILLAGERS. In LDB the number of villagers 'then' has been altered from 7 to 9 and that
'now' from 9 to 7.
22,7 VATTEVILLE. Either the place in Eure or that in Seine-Inf., OEB 120. Cf. Robert in 23,41.
ABBOT OF ELY. See 10,2 note. Cf. IEAL 184.
22,8 NOW ... 3½ HIDES. See following note.
HIDE ... ADDED TO THIS MANOR. See 10,2 and IE 126, IEAL 184.
22,9 WULFBERT. LDB *Guib(er)t(us)* is probably in error for *Gulb(er)t(us)* a Rom form for OG
Wulfbert, PNDB 418; cf. Forssner 259. See also 22,12 note.
DUNMOW. The manor of Southall there, VCH 474, n.8.
22,10 SIMOND. OG *Sigemund*, with Rom *o < u*; cf. Forssner 225.
22,11 HALSTEAD. The manor of Hipworth Hall there, VCH 475, n.2.
22,12 (STEEPLE) BUMPSTEAD. The manor of Moyns there, VCH 475, n.4.
WULFBERT. LDB *Gulb(er)t(us)*, see 22,9 note.
22,13 HUNT'S HALL. Formerly 'Pooley', EPNS 450.
GLADIOU. It is uncertain whether the person named was a man or a woman. If a woman,
the form *Gladiou* might be from **Glædgeofa* a variant of OE **Glædgifu*. If a man, the final
element of the name has been obscured but could possibly have been originally *-uin* from
-wine, and thus the full name might be **Glædwine* (PNDB 261-262).
SLAVES, NOW 5. *null(us)*, 'none', deleted before '5'. Thus in MS, but not shown in
facsimile.
[THEN]. LDB omits *Tunc*.
22,14-15 WULFBERT LDB *Wlb(er)t(us)*. See 22,9 note.
22,14 VALUE ... S. LDB omits the numeral.
22,16 GODRIC SKIPPER. LDB *scipri*, probably an Anglicized form of OWScand *skipari* 'sailor';
OEB 267.
22,18 GODRIC POINC. OEB 328-329 derives the byname from OFr *poign(e)* 'fist'; since his first
name is OE, this would appear to be an Englishman with a French byname and the French
word might be a translation of an English byname such as *Hand* or *Fyst*.
22,19 WENDENS (AMBO). Little Wendon therein, VCH 476.
22,20 CHARDWELL. Formerly 'Ainsworth' see EPNS 517, VCH 476, n.2.
THEN 4. *T(un)c* has been altered in MS from *7c̄*.
THEN ... LDB omits the numeral.
22,21 (GREAT) CHISHILL. The manor of Tewes or Lisles there, VCH 476, n.4.
22,22 PAGLESHAM. The manors of East Hall and South Hall there, VCH 476, n.6.
SLAVES, NOW 3. In the MS *iii* was originally written at the end of the same line as *m(odo)*,
but was then erased and transferred to the following line.
22,23 [VALUE]. LDB omits *valuit*.
EXCHANGE IN NORMANDY. That is, in exchange for land in Normandy.
22,24 SAME EXCHANGE. That mentioned in 22,23.
OF THE KING'S JURISDICTION. Translating *e(st) de socna regis*.
23 RICHARD, SON OF COUNT GILBERT. In Kent Ch. 11 (col. 14b) he is also called Richard
of Tonbridge, while in Suffolk Ch. 76 (col. 448a) he appears to have been known as Richard

of Clare, which names referred to his important residences in these two counties. For his annexations in Essex, see 90,49–78. For the origin and distribution of his Holding, see R. Mortimer, 'The beginnings of the Honour of Clare', *Battle 1980*, 119–141.

23,1 MEADOW. LDB *ap(ra)ti* is in error for *p(ra)ti*.

23,2-3 WITHGAR. Richard's predecessor in most of his East Anglian estates, see Mortimer, 'Honour of Clare', 128–129.

23,2 16 PLOUGHS ... RESTORED. That is, the difference in number between the former 34 men's ploughs and the present 18.
AS ... FRENCH AND ENGLISH SAY. A reference to the Hundred jury. Farley *dīc* is in error for *dicī* of MS and facsimile.
WARNER. Probably he of 90,77.

23,4 W(ILLIAM) PECHE. See 35,6 note.
LEDMER THE PRIEST. Head of the collegiate church at Clare, Suffolk, founded *c.* 1045 by Aelfric the father of Richard's predecessor Withgar, see VCH 348.

23,5 ELINANT. The name is OG, Forssner 66–67.

23,6 2 PLOUGHS ... RESTORED. That is, to the lordship.

23,7 (GREAT) YELDHAM. For Richard's annexation at Yeldham, see 90,54.
GOISMER. Probably he of 90,49. The name is OG *Gausmar*, Forssner 127.

23,9 FINCHINGFIELD. For Richard's annexation here, also held from him by Arnold, see 90,50.

23,10 'BINSLEY'. Lost, in Bulmer; EPNS 418. See 35,6 note.
WIDELARD. LDB *Wielardus* is a NFr form of OG *Widelardus*, Forssner 253–254. Probably he of 23,42 and 90,52;75.

23,11 ALDERFORD. Cf. Aelfric of Alderford, associated with an annexation by Richard in 90,49.
12 [PIGS]. LDB omits *porc(i)*.

23,13 4 SMALLHOLDERS. In the MS, *iiii* has been altered from *iii*.
3 SLAVES. This is a Farley error of *iii* for the *iiii* of MS.

23,14 BULMER. Later the manor of Butler's Hall there, VCH 479, n.1.
MASCEREL. LDB *Mascerel* here, *Mascherell(us)* 90,58. Apparently an OFr byname from the verb *mascher*, 'to mix, chew up, grind, mash'; perhaps related to ModE *mash-roll*, *mash-rule*, 'a paddle or staff used by a brewer for stirring and mixing his mash', NED.

23,15 HOWE. In Finchingfield. LDB *Weninchou*; identified by VCH 479 n.2 and DG, although EPNS 427 is less certain. For Richard's annexation here, held from him by Germund, see 90,53.

23,16 BURES. An Essex hamlet of Bures St. Mary (Suffolk), see EPNS 420, VCH 408,479 n.4. Cf. 23,29 and 40,5.

23,18-19 PEBMARSH; ALPHAMSTONE. For Richard's annexations here, see 90,59–60.

23,19 5 ACRES. MS *xv* altered by deletion to *v*; facsimile *xv*.

23,21 (STEEPLE) BUMPSTEAD. See 90,61 for Richard's annexation here.

23,23 COUPALS FARM. Formerly Chelveston, EPNS 462.

23,24 TWINSTEAD. LDB *Tumesteda* is in error for *Tuinesteda*. Cf. *Bumesteda*, 3 lines above, which may have caused the error.

23,25 CHENEBOLTUNA. Unidentified, OE *Cynebeald-tūn*, 'Cynebeald's estate'.

23,26 HALSTEAD. For Richard's annexation there, see 90,74.

23,27 SUDBURY. In Suffolk (1,97).
THE WHOLE. That is, 23,16-27.

23,28 COLSEGE. LDB *Colsege*; possibly a corrupt form of *Colswegen* < ON *Kol(l)sveinn*, PNDB 218.
VALUE THEN 40s. The tironian *nota* in LDB after *T(un)c* is otiose.
45 ACRES. See 1,13.

23,29 BURES. As 23,16 note; see VCH 480, n.4.

23,30 [HUNDRED OF ONGAR]. LDB omits the Hundred rubric in error.
('MORRELL') RODING. A detached part of Ongar Hundred, now lost, in White Roding (EPNS 494-495). Identified by VCH 480, n.5.

23,31 (LITTLE) BENTLEY. LDB *Menetleam* is a sport form; one would have expected *Benetleam*, see EPNS 328.

23,32 (LITTLE) BROMLEY. The manor of Braham Hall there, VCH 480, n.7.
R(OGER). Cf. 23,31.

23,33 HE ALSO HOLDS. *Ide(m)* is taken here to refer to Algar; alternatively it could perhaps refer to R(oger) of 23,32.
KING'S JURISDICTION ... LAWFORD. Cf. 1,27.

23,34 COLNE. According to VCH 481, n.1, this was probably Berwick Hall in White Colne. For Richard's annexations there, see 90,68;71.

WHO HOLD. *tenentes* at the foot of folio 40b is deleted thus in MS.

23,35 FORDHAM. For Richard's annexation there, see 90,72. Farley *Sordeha(m)* is in error for *fordeha(m)* of MS.

23,36 (WEST) BERGHOLT. For Richard's annexations there, see 90,70;73.

23,37 *WITESUUORDA*. Unidentified, perhaps OE *Wihtesweorð*, 'Wiht's enclosure'.

COULD NOT. LDB *potat* is in error for *poterat*.

23,38 WALTER TIREL. LDB *Walt̃ tirelde.R* standing for *Walt(erus) tirel de. R(icardo)* with an erroneous repetition of the abbreviation-mark above *t* and a wrong word-division of *tirel* and *de*. For the byname Tirel, perhaps from OF *tirer* 'to draw', see OEB 226, Reaney 350. Walter was the son-in-law of Richard and the slayer of King William Rufus in 1100; A. L. Poole, *From Domesday Book to Magna Carta* (Oxford, 1951), 113-114.

FINN THE DANE. On him, see Mortimer, 'Honour of Clare', 128-129. For his wife, see *84*.

23,39 [MEN'S] PLOUGHS. LDB omits *hominum*.

23,41 VATTEVILLE. As 22,7 note.

[MEN'S] PLOUGHS. As 23,39 note.

23,42 BARDFIELD. Possibly Bardfield Saling, cf. VCH 481, n.8.

WIDELARD. See 23,10 note.

24 SWEIN OF ESSEX. Sheriff of Essex at a date between 1066 and 1086 in succession to his father Robert son of Wymarc and before Ralph Baynard (*33*); see VCH 345-346. For Swein's newly-built castle, see 24,17. For an annexation by him, see 90,35.

24,1 ROBERT. Son of Wymarc, formerly Sheriff of Essex, see preceding note.

24,1-3 WOODLAND ... HIDES. See 18,2 note.

24,4 ALWEN. LDB *Aluuen*; see PNDB 160-161 s.n. *Al-wynn*, a late OE form ot *AElfwynn* or of *AEthelwynn*.

ROBERT SON OF WYMARC. See 24,1 note.

1 HIDE THERE. LDB has *.i.bi* in error for *ibi*.

24,5 HORNDON (-ON-THE-HILL). The manor of Wythefeld there, VCH 482, n.14; Wyfields, EPNS 157.

24,7 AS A MANOR ... 15 ACRES. The order of the Latin is 'for 1 hide as a manor and 15 acres'.

24,8 GODITH, A FREE MAN. Here, as on other occasions, the DB Inquiry uses the term *liber homo* to describe status irrespective of gender. LDB *God&* stands for *Godet* from OE *Godgyth*, PNDB 264.

Folio 43a A line of writing has been erased in the MS above the present first line.

24,10 2 SMALLHOLDERS. MS *ii*, so in Farley but the ink has blotted on the second minim.

24,11 BEFORE 1066. Farley *t̃. r. E.*, interpreting an unusually-large *e* in MS as a capital. Its irregularity was in fact caused by its having been altered from *V*, probably the first two strokes of initial *W* of *Will(elm)i*.

24,13 NOW 1;1. Farley has substituted the tironian *nota* for the ampersand of MS.

24,14-15 WHEATLEY. In Rayleigh, EPNS 195. Swein gave land at Wheatley to St. Paul's before his death *c*. 1087, see ECE, no. 99.

24,16 3 COBS AND 1 COB. So in MS.

24,17 CASTLE. For a brief description and plan of Rayleigh Castle, see VCH 299-300.

24,18 WHO ... HAD. LDB *hntes*, omitting the abbreviation-mark from *h*.

24,20 HIS FATHER. Robert son of Wymarc.

NOW 2 COBS. In the MS a letter (?*c*) has been erased before *runc(ini)*.

24,22 PRITTLEWELL. The manor of Prior's Hall there, VCH 485, n.3.

PASTURE, 12 PIGS. *Past(ura)* here is an error in LDB for *Silua*.

GRAPINEL. Apparently a byname derived from OFr *grapon*, 'grapnel; grappling hook'.

24,23 SHOEBURY. Probably the manor of South Shoebury, see VCH 485, n.8.

24,24 THEN 3 COBS. *iii* in Farley is an error for *iiii* of MS.

24,26 160 SHEEP ... 23 SHEEP. So in MS.

24,27 WICARD. DB *Wiard(us)* from OG *Wichard*, Forssner 252-253. Cf. 24,56 note.

(GREAT) STAMBRIDGE. The manor of Barton Hall there, VCH 486, n.3.

24,28 SHOEBURY. Probably the manor of North Shoebury, cf. VCH 485, n.8.

24,30-32 ASCELIN. OFr *Ascelin*, from OG *Azelin*; Forssner 38-39.

24,30 50 PIGS. *.&.L.* is a Farley error for *.x.l.* of MS, the number of pigs should thus be 40.

24,35 ALFITH. LDB *Aluid*; probably from OE *AElfgyth*, cf. PNDB 174.

24,36-39 ROBERT. As 24,1 note.

24,41a SAID HUNDRED. That of Rochford, see rubric before 24,17.

24,43 Cf. 24,55, another entry concerning a holding here, with several identical statistics, suggesting the division of an earlier unit into equal parts.

ASHELDHAM. LDB *Hainctuna(m)*. Identified by VCH, 392-393. See also EPNS 208; and below 24,55.

THEN NOTHING. That is, no livestock.
NOW 3 CATTLE. *iiii* altered by erasure to *iii* in the MS.
24,46 HALLINGBURY. LDB *Halingebiam*, omitting the abbreviation-mark on *b*.
24,48 NOW 5 CATTLE. The first letter of *anim(ales)* has been altered, ?from *v*, in the MS.
24,49 [MEN'S] PLOUGHS. LDB omits *hominum*.
24,51 ABBERTON. The manor of Badcocks there, VCH 489, n.1.
24,53 1 PLOUGH ... RESTORED. This statement perhaps suggests that the figures for the lordship ploughs (then and later 4, now 5) have been reversed in error; or alternatively, that they have been misconstrued.
24,54 ROBERT. As 24,1 note.
24,55 See 24,43 note.
ASHELDHAM. LDB *Haintuna(m)*. See 24,43 note.
24,56 WICARD. LDB *Wicard(us)*, from the same name as in 24,27 note.
24,57 R(OBERT). As 24,1 note.
NAYLAND. The Essex part of the estate of Nayland (Suffolk), now represented by Gt. and Lt. Horkesley, VCH 408, 489, n.11.
4 [PLOUGHS]. LDB omits *caruce*.
24,59 FREE MEN. The facsimile adds an otiose abbreviation-mark to the ascender of *b* in *hominib(us)*.
WERE NO SMALLHOLDERS. Literally, 'was no smallholder', *null(us) bordari(us) erat*.
24,61 WARLEY. The manor of Franks in Great Warley, VCH 490, n.8; EPNS 134.
17 PIGS. Farley omits the abbreviation-mark above *c* of *porc(i)*.
VALUE THEN £4. Farley does not show the gap in the MS, caused by a repair, between *ual(uit)* and *.iiii*. See also 24,66 note.
24,62 KENNINGTONS. In Aveley, EPNS 122. According to VCH 490, n.10, it was later known as the manor of Bretts.
WULFSTAN. LDB *Vstan(us)* is probably a palaeographical error for *Vlstan(us)*, due to confusion between *l* and caroline minuscule *s*.
24,63 ROBERT. As 24,1 note.
MALDON. Probably the manor of Southouse and Sayers there, VCH 491, n.1.
THE KING ... DUES. See 1,25 note.
HE AIDS. That is, Gunner aids.
HORSE ... SHIP. This obligation is not mentioned in the other entries concerning Maldon. A ship levy was imposed in 1008 at the rate of one ship per 310 hides. For the 1008 levy and earlier references to ships owed to the King, see Harmer, *ASWrits*, 266–267.
24,64 ELMSTEAD. For a house in Colchester belonging to Elmstead, see B3m.
24,65-66 ROBERT. As 24,1 note.
24,65 ODARD. The Rom form of OG *Authart*; Forssner 194.
LESS 10 ACRES. *x* has been altered from *7* in the MS.
ACQUIRED NOTHING. That is, no livestock.
24,66 4 SMALLHOLDERS THERE. Farley does not show the gap in the MS between *s(un)t* and *.iiii.* caused by the reverse of the repair at 24,61.
25 EUDO THE STEWARD. The King's Steward, called Eudo son of Hubert in Cambridgeshire 25 and Hertfordshire 31.
25,1 RICHARD. Of Sackville, cf. 20,8 (Rivenhall) whence the ½ mill was acquired; VCH 379.
25,2 75 [SHEEP]. LDB omits *oues*.
LEOFSI. LDB *Lefsi(us)*. VCH 492, note 3, suggests that this is a bad spelling for *Lisois(us)*, that is Lisois of Moutiers, who is mentioned in 25,5.
25,3 See also IE 130, IEAL 187; and below 30,41.
('MORRELL') RODING. Tentatively identified by VCH 492, n.4. See above 23,30 note.
SAEMER. Also at 30,41.
45 ACRES. See 28,8 note.
NOW £6. IE (?in error), £5.
25,4 1 COB ... LDB may have omitted some livestock here.
WORTH THAT MUCH. Presumably £6.
25,5 LISOIS. Of Moutiers (probably Moutiers-Hubert, Calvados; OEB 102). He was also mentioned in connection with manors of Eudo in Bedfordshire (21,13) and Cambridgeshire (25,9). See also 25,2 note.
WAS OUTLAWED. LDB *utllagauit*.
250 [SHEEP]. LDB omits *oues*.
WRINGEHALA. Unidentified, perhaps OE *Wringehale*, 'at the nook of land at the place with a bend', cf. A. H. Smith, *English Place-Name Elements*, ii, EPNSoc 26, Cambridge 1956, s.v. *wrēo, *wrio*.

25,6 WULFRIC CAVE. LDB *cassa* is a scribal error for *caffa*, cf. *cauuā* 30,28. The byname is from OE *cāf*, 'quick, bold', OEB 343. Leofwin Cave occurs in Bucks. 57,8.

25,9 *LANDUNA*. Unidentified, OE **lang-dūne* 'at the long upland'.

25,10 *ACLETA*. Unidentified, OE *āc-hliðe*, 'at the oak-hillside'.
1½ [HIDES]. LDB omits *hidis*.

25,11 Duplicated at 25,25 but there said to be in lordship.
PIROT. LDB *Pirot* is almost certainly a palaeographical error for *Picot*, as in Cambridgeshire (25,1-2; see note there) and Bedfordshire (21,14-15. 24,18;24). Picot was Sheriff of Cambridge.

25,12 RICHARD. ECE, no. 91, note, identifies him as Richard son of Count Gilbert (*23*).
9 ACRES. See also 10,1 and IE 128-129, IEAL 187.

25,15 TAKELEY. The manor of Colchester Hall there, VCH 494, n.3.

25,19 (ABBESS) RODING. For the identification, see VCH 492, n.4.

25,20 CHURCH OF ELY. See also 10,3 and IE 126, IEAL 187.

25,23 ... COBS. LDB omits the numeral.

25,24 AELFRIC WAND. The byname is from OE *wand* 'mole', OEB 367.

25,25 EUDO ... LORDSHIP; FOR 3½ HIDES. Deleted thus in MS. Farley omits a large marginal cross which occurs in the MS at this point and which may be a contemporary indication of the duplication of text with that of 25,11 above. Cf. 30,50 note.

25,26 AELFRIC WAND. LDB *uuants* is an AN form of the byname discussed in 25,24 note.

26 ROGER OF AUBERVILLE. He possibly came from Auberville-la-Renaut (Seine Inf: arr. Le Hâvre); OEB 104-105.

26,1 ONE OF THESE MANORS. *unu(m) maneriu(m) ex istis*; LDB treats each of the 2 free men's property as a separate manor here, although at the beginning of the entry it refers to only one manor.

26,2 THEN ... [PLOUGHS]. LDB omits *caruce* and the numeral.
WHO HAVE 1 PLOUGH. *h(abe)ntes .i. car(ucam)* is probably to be taken to refer to all the population rather than just the 3 slaves.

26,5 CHISHILL. Probably the manor of 'Lisles' in Gt. Chishill, VCH 496, n.11. For Roger's annexation there, see 90,86.

27 HUGH DE MONTFORT. He came from Montfort-sur-Risle (Eure: arr. Bernai); OEB 100-101. See 90,15-18 for his annexations.

27,1 RAMSDEN. This entry is said by VCH 497, n.1, to refer to Downham, adjacent to Ramsden Bellhouse and Crays.

27,2 KELVEDON. The manor there later known as Felix Hall, VCH 497, n.2.

27,3 HAVERING (-ATTE-BOWER). See 1,4.

27,7 VALUE OF THE WHOLE OF THE ABOVE. That is, of 27,1-7.

27,8 *HALESDUNA*. Unidentified, OE *Haegelesdūn*, 'Hægel's upland'; see EPNS 215, s.n. Hazeleigh.

27,9 'STUDLY'. As 1,6 note.
WHICH ... HELD. *tenuit* is a Farley error for *tenent* of MS.
[THEN] 1½ PLOUGHS. LDB omits *Tunc*.

27,12 'WIBERTSHERNE'. Farley *Witbrictesherna* is in error for *Wibrictesherna* of the MS.
ST. PETER'S CHAPEL. This entry is said by VCH 499, n.1, to refer to the manor of Battails in Bradwell-on-Sea; EPNS 211, s.n. Buckles Grove.

27,14 See also IE 129, IEAL 186.
'BENSTED'. Bensted Green (lost) in Sandon, see EPNS 266-267. Cf. VCH 389-390.
GUTHMUND. LDB *Gudmund(us)*, IE *Godmundus*. He was the brother of Abbot Wulfric of Ely, through whom, in order to make a good marriage, he obtained leases on several estates in East Anglia (including 'Bensted') belonging to the monks. After 1066 Hugh de Montfort took possession of Guthmund's holding, including the Ely lands. See LibEl 166-167, 424-425. Cf. 27,2;4-5;11;13.

27,15 QUEEN EDITH. As 20,8 note.

27,16 48 GOATS. LDB *cap(re)* may be in error for *oues*, 'sheep' here, since the following category is also goats.

27,17 HAGER. OG *Hager, Hagero*; Förstemann 717. Farley has modernised the word-division from *posthagra* of the MS.
DELIVERER. Someone with the authority or right to transfer possession.

27,18 HUMPHREY HOLDS TOLLESHUNT (D'ARCY). He is probably the Humphrey of 34,36.

28 HAMO THE STEWARD. For his annexations, see 90,31-33.

28,1 *ATELEIA*. Unidentified, OE *ātan-lēage*, 'at the clearing where oats are grown'.
GOTI. Probably he of 13,1, in the same Hundred.

28,3 30 ACRES. See 20,6.
28,5 (GREAT) BRAXTED. Westhall there, VCH 500, n.13; EPNS 284, s.n. West Hall Wood.
28,6 HARLOW. *herlaua* altered from *heru-* in the MS.
RALPH of Marcy. See 1,3 note.
RYES. In Hatfield Broad Oak, EPNS 41. See 1,3 note.
28,8 RODING. The manor of Marks Hall in Margaret Roding, EPNS 494, see VCH 501, n.4.
45 ACRES. The difference between the 1½ hides of before 1066 and the 1 hide and 15
acres of 1086. Perhaps the same as the 45 acres mentioned in 25,3 ('Morrell' Roding).
28,9 (LITTLE) WIGBOROUGH. See 90,31 for Hamo's annexation here.
BERNARD ... BAYNARD'S HOLDING. This hide of woodland may be the woodland for
200 pigs recorded in 33,23 (Tolleshunt, held in 1086 by Bernard from Ralph Baynard).
ENGELRIC ... HOLDS. Probably the ½ hide mentioned in 20,19 (Langenhoe).
28,11 STAMBOURNE. See 90,33 for Hamo's annexation here. LDB *Scanburne* is in error for *St-*.
28,12 NORTHEY ISLAND. For the identification, see VCH 502, n.5. This is the traditional site
of the Battle of Maldon in 991. See 90,32 for Hamo's annexation here.
28,13-14 GOTILD. From OG *Gothild*, PNDB 264-265, Forssner 120. See 28,16 note.
28,14 NAVESTOCK. For the identification, see VCH 502, n.7.
28,16 GOTILD. Probably the person (called Godith in 5,6) who gave ½ hide at Norton
Mandeville to St. Paul's after 1066. See also 28,13-14 note.
28,17-18 THORBERT. Cf. *70* note *sub* Hagebern.
29 HENRY OF FERRERS. From Ferrières-Saint-Hilaire (Eure: arr. Bernay): OEB 88.
29,2 60 PIGS. Farley omits to show a gap in the text, caused by an erasure in the MS between
Lx and *.porc(i)*.
29,3 STEEPLE. For Henry's annexation there, see 90,81.
29,5 BUTTSBURY. Formerly one of the Essex names in *Ginge, Inge*, EPNS 242-244 and
258-259.
30 GEOFFREY DE MANDEVILLE. Ancestor of the de Mandevilles, Earls of Essex. The place
from which he was named has not been positively identified, see OEB 96. For Geoffrey's
annexations, see 90,20-28.
30,1 (MARKS) TEY. The modern name preserves that of the family descended from Adam *de
Merck*, undertenants of the de Mandeville family; EPNS 400.
30,2 ASGAR. The Constable, Geoffrey de Mandeville's predecessor in a number of counties.
On him, see Harmer, *ASWrits*, 560-561 (s.n. Esgar, the staller); Ellis ii 43.
HE ... MAN. Leofday had been under the jurisdiction of Asgar but did not hold this land
from him. Nevertheless Geoffrey de Mandeville had taken it, as Asgar's successor in many
other places. Cf. following note.
30,3 BARKING ABBEY. Leofhild had been under Asgar's jurisdiction but only held Abbess
Roding as leasehold. Nevertheless, as in the previous note, Geoffrey de Mandeville had
seized it.
30,4 THOROLD. Geoffrey de Mandeville's steward, see ECE, no. 93.
OCKENDON. According to VCH 505, this is South Ockendon.
EXCHANGE. See also 52,1 note.
30,5 20 BEEHIVES. Farley omits to show a gap in the text, caused by the erasure in the MS of
two letters (*ac*), between *xx.* and *uasa*.
WALTER (HOLDS) 30 ACRES ... HUBERT 30 ACRES. This sentence repeats information
already given above, 30 acres being equal to 1 virgate.
30,10 PLOUGHS IN LORDSHIP. Farley *car(uce) . hom d(omi)nio* stands for *car(uce) . hoin
d(omi)nio* of the MS, where a correction has been made from 'men's ploughs' to 'ploughs in
lordship' but incompletely since *ho* should have been erased.
30,11 LESS 5 ACRES. Farley omits to show a gap in the text, caused by an erasure in the MS,
before *.v*.
RICHARD GARNET. LDB *gernet*, from OFr *gernat, grenat* 'garnet', OEB 369.
30,13 MASHBURY. See 90,20 for Geoffrey's annexation here.
30,16 GUARDS. LDB *huscarlo* (Latin dative singular). The term *huscarl* in Domesday Book
probably denoted a trained soldier. In Cambridgeshire (14,64) it is however also used as a
byname.
SCALPI. LDB *Scalpin(us)*; ON *Skálpi*, here with the Latin and OFr suffix *-in(us)* (PNDB
365 and § 148) but in Suffolk (16,35. 36,1-2;8;15) the same man is simply called
Scalpi(us), Scalp(us), Scapi(us). The latter form also occurs at 32,40 below.
YORK(SHIRE). LDB *ebroica*. The reference is probably to the northern rebellion against
King William in 1069-70, see Ann Williams (article cited in 1,1-4 note), 178-179.
J. H. Round (VCH 507) quoted the erroneous facsimile spelling *ehroica* and identified it

as Evreux. Although LDB *ebroica* is similar to later spellings for Evreux (*Ebricae* 1212, *Ebroyce* 1258) given by OEB 87, it is less likely to be that place here, on historical grounds, than York(shire). Also, the LDB form is comparable to the French form *Euroic* for York, referred to in Wace's *Brut*, see A. H. Smith, *The Place-Names of the East Riding of Yorkshire and York* (EPNSoc xiv, Cambridge 1937), 276, n.2. Cf. 6,15 (*Eurewic*).

30,18 MOZE. See also ESf 2.
WHEN ... LONDON. LDB *q(ua)n(do) remansit Londoniae*. It is unclear to whom this phrase refers, to King William or to Geoffrey.

30,19 RAINALM. LDB *Renelm(us)* from *Rainalm* the Rom form of OG *Raginhelm*, Forssner 210. Cf. 30,39 note.

30,20 ARDLEIGH. The manor of Martells Hall there, VCH 508, n.3. For 2 houses in Colchester belonging to Ardleigh, see B31.

30,21 12 HIDES. According to VCH 374, these were at East Tilbury.
(WEST) TILBURY. See 24,3.

30,22 (BLACK) NOTLEY. Identified by VCH 508.
CLAIMS ... THEM. That is, in relation to his ownership of them.

30,24 MARTEL. Here (as in 30,31–32;35;43) 'Martel' may refer to Geoffrey Martel of 30,3.
(LITTLE) HALLINGBURY. The manor of Monkbury there, VCH 508, n.11; Monksbury, EPNS 36.

30,25 MATCHING. The manor of Stock Hall there, VCH 509, n.2.

30,27 See also IE 127, IEAL 186.
(HIGH) EASTER. Identified by VCH 509. Pleshey Castle later stood on part of this land.
GUTBERT. Probably OG *Gutbert* (Förstemann PN 661) but possibly from OE *Cuthbeorht* with NFr *G* for *C*-.

30,28-30 HUGH OF BERNIÈRES. Named from one of the places called Bernières (-d'Ailly; -le Patry; -sur la Mer) in Calvados, see OEB 72. For an annexation by him, see 90,29.

30,28 WULFRIC CAVE. See 25,6 note.

30,30 (BERNERS) RODING. The modern name preserves that of the Domesday undertenant; EPNS 492. See 30,28-30 note.
THESE 3 MANORS. Those in 30,28–30.

30,31 BIGODS. Formerly called Alfriston, EPNS 475–476.

30,32 (LITTLE) DUNMOW. Probably the manor of South Hall there, VCH 510, n.7.

30,33 3 CATTLE ... SHEEP. Presumably 'now', but perhaps 'then and now'.

30,35 (WHITE) RODING. The manor of Maskelsbury there, VCH 511, n.1; EPNS 495, s.n. Mascallsbury.

30,36 DUNMOW. Possibly Shingle Hall in Gt. Dunmow, VCH 511, n.2.

30,38 (LITTLE) CANFIELD. The manor of Langthorns there, VCH 511, n.6. See 90,21 for Geoffrey's annexation of 8 acres at Canfield, also held of him by Richard.

30,39 RAINALM. LDB *Rainalm(us)*; as 30,19 note.

30,41 See also IE 129, IEAL 186.
1 FREE MAN. Named by IE as Saemer (*Samarus*). See also 25,3.
35 ACRES. IE, 30; IEAL, 34.
('MORRELL') RODING. See 25,3.

30,42 ASGAR. LDB *angari* is in error for *ansgari*.

30,43 (WHITE) RODING. Identified by VCH 512.
LEOFITH. LDB *Leuid*; from OE *Lēofgȳth*, PNDB 312.

30,44 Cf. 30,50 which repeats much of this information, with minor differences.
STOW MARIES. The second element of the modern name is from the medieval family name *de Marisco*, 'of the marsh', possibly referring to the same feature as the 'fen' in the name of the place in LDB *Fenne*. See EPNS 228–229.
FRIDEBERN. LDB *Frieb(er)n(us)*; OG *Fridebern, Frithu- Frethubern*; see PNDB 253–254. Cf. 70 note *sub* Hagebern.

30,45 6½ HIDES. LDB repeats 'hides', adding it above *.vi.* in order to avoid confusion with the preceding numerals describing Freemen.
11 CATTLE. The number of cattle may in fact be 12, but the MS has been erased and blotted here.

30,46 WILLIAM CARDON. See 10,5 note.
(GREAT) CHISHILL. The manor of Cardons there, VCH 512, n.5. See also 90,34.

30,49 ANSGAR'S ... LDB has probably omitted *tenuit pro* after *Angari*.

30,50 Farley omits to show a marginal cross which occurs in the MS, probably indicating the partial duplication of text between this entry and 30,44. Cf. 25,25 note.

30,51 *WENESUUIC*. Unidentified; the second element is OE *wic*, 'an industrial or trading settlement' with the genitive singular of either the OE personal-name *Wine* or of *wenn* 'a wen, blister; tumulus, hill'. Cf. 90,27 (*Wesuunic*), which may be a corrupt form of the same name.

THEY ALSO HOLD. That is, Godfrey and Evrard.

31 THE COUNT OF EU. From Eu (Seine Inf: arr. Dieppe), OEB 105.

31,1 (WEST) THURROCK. Identified by VCH 388.

32 ROBERT GERNON. The byname is from OFr *grenon* 'moustache', OEB 314-315.

32,3 WITHAM. Identified as Powers Hall therein, VCH 514, n.2.

32,5 RIVENHALL. Identified as the manor of Archers there, VCH 514, n.5.
WOODLAND. See 3,10 note.

32,7 CHINGFORD. Identified as the manor of Earl's Chingford, VCH 514, n.6.

32,8 (WEST) HAM. Identified by VCH 515, n.2. Cf. 34,8 which duplicates parts of this entry.
KING WILLIAM [GAVE]. LDB omits *dedit* but cf. 34,8.
MEADOW 60 ACRES. In the MS *lx.ac(re)* has been altered, ?from *lx.v.*
RANULF PEVEREL ... MANOR. See 34,8.

32,9 (EAST) HAM. Identified by VCH 515.

32,11 W. CORBUN. Perhaps from Corbon (Calvados), OEB 83-84, 127.

32,14 *LEGA*. Unidentified, OE *lege*, '(place at) the woodland clearing'.
GOTRE. From ON *Gautarr*, ODan, OSw *Gøtar*, PNDB 258. Cf. 32,45 note.

32,15 VIRLEY. LDB *Salcota(m)*; by 1291 the surname of the 1086 tenant Robert of Verly had been added to make *Salcote Verly*, but the modern form consists only of the affix. See EPNS 323.

32,17 TAKELEY. The manor of Bassingborns there, VCH 516, n.4.
CATTLE, NOW 3. In the MS *iii* has been altered from *ii*.
1 SMALLHOLDER. LDB *.i.b.* for *.i.bordarius*.

32,18 WENDENS (AMBO). Identified by VCH 516 as Great Wendon therein.

32,21 FARNHAM. The manor of Hertisho-bury there, VCH 517, n.2; EPNS 550, s.n. Hassobury.

32,23 (GREAT) MAPLESTEAD. Identified by VCH 517.

32,24 RAYMOND GERALD ... ROGER OF POITOU. See 1,19 notes.

32,25 WHICH THE HUNDRED-REEVE HAS. LDB *q(ua)s h(abe)t custos hundret*. At 89,1 the same man is described as *prepositus hundredi*.

32,26 ROBERT. Of Verly, see VCH 389.
(LITTLE) BIRCH. Identified by VCH 389.

32,27 STAPLEFORD (ABBOTTS). The manor of Batayles there, VCH 518, n.5; EPNS 79, s.n. Battles Hall.
AMONG THEM. It is unclear whether *int(er) eos* refers to the 5 free men or to the smallholders.

32,28 RAINHAM. Possibly the manor of Berwick there, VCH 518, n.6.
ROBERT THE LASCIVIOUS. LDB *Lasciuus*; OEB 348. The same as Robert the Perverted, see 6,12 note.

32,29 (SOUTH) WEALD. The manor of Caldecots there, VCH 518, n.8; EPNS 138, s.n. Calcott Hall. Cf. 8,9.
HUBERT OF PORT. Although his main holding was at Mapledurwell (Hampshire 24,1), he appears to have had jurisdiction over a group of men in Essex (cf. 83,2 below) and Suffolk (16,34). He took his name from Port-en-Bessin (Calvados: arr. Bayeux), OEB 108.

32,32 CHIGNALL. The manor of Chignall Zoyn in Chignall St. James, VCH 519, n.2.

32,33 CORP. Farley *Cōrp*, MS *Córp*. Redin 28, unexplained. The significance of the mark above *o* is not apparent and the form appears to be scribally corrupt; it might possibly be for *Cōsp*, an abbreviated form for OG *Gosbert* (Forssner 124, Förstemann PN 615), or, in insular minuscule, might be from *Cofsi* (< ON *Kofsi*, PNDB 306).

32,34 SELVA. LDB *Selua*; probably from ODan *Sylvi*, PNDB 382.
THEN 10 CATTLE. In the MS, *x* has been altered from *v*.

32,34-35 BORDA. LDB *borda*, from OE *Brorda*, PNDB 208. The LDB spelling was not given a capital initial and was perhaps confused with *bord(arius)* 'smallholder'.

32,36 AZO. LDB *Asso*. Cf. PNDB 170-171 s.n. *Azur*, and below, 44,3 note on AZORIN.
CULVERT'S FARM. Identified by VCH 519, n.8. LDB *Richeham*. See EPNS 238-239.

32,37 TOLLESHUNT (D'ARCY). Identified EPNS 307. See also below, 32,45.

32,38 AELFRIC KEMP. The byname is either OE *cempa* 'warrior' or a derivative of OWScand *kampr* 'moustache'. He also occurs in Cambridgeshire (21,2-3. 25,1-3).

32,38a TENDRING. The manor of Gernons there, VCH 520, n.3; EPNS 352, s.n. Grove Farm.

32,40 WILLIAM. Called William de Alno in Suffolk (36,1;15). It is uncertain to which place his byname refers, see OEB 67-68.

A MANOR IN SUFFOLK. William held several manors after Scalpi in Suffolk (Chapter 36, *passim*) but it is not possible to identify any with the one here referred to.

32,43 ARKESDEN. The manor of Mynchens there, VCH 521, n.2.

32,45 TOLLESHUNT (D'ARCY). The manors of Gernons and Verli there, VCH 521, n.5. See also 32,37.

GOTRE. LDB *Gotra*. The same name as is discussed 32,14 note.

33 RALPH BAYNARD. He had been Sheriff of Essex between Swein (*24*) and Peter of Valognes (*36*) at a date between 1066 and 1086. For his annexations, see 90,39–40. Castle Baynard in London was named after him.

33,1 PART OF THE CUSTOMARY DUE. Translating *s(un)t de sua consuetudine*, where *sua* refers to King William, who however is not mentioned in the present translation's rendering of *t(empore)* . *r(egis)* . *Will(elm)i* as 'after 1066'.

[BEE]HIVES. LDB omits *apium*.

33,2 3 ACRES. Probably of meadow, although LDB omits *prati*.

33,4 POINTEL. Probably to be identified as Theodoric Pointel (*71*).

WOODHAM (WALTER). Identified by VCH 522.

33,5 CURLING TYE (GREEN). Identified by EPNS 232. Cf. VCH 522, n.5.

33,6 (LITTLE) DUNMOW. Identified by VCH 522.

33,6-7 AETHELGYTH. Also Ralph's predecessor at 33,19–20. She was the widow of Thurstan son of Wine, whose will had included bequests of several of the estates later held in DB by Ralph Baynard, see ECE, no. 59 (Sawyer, no. 1531). See also 33,11 note.

33,11 A FREE WOMAN. Perhaps Aethelgyth (see 33,6-7 note), to whom Pentlow was bequeathed by her husband Thurstan.

MEN'S PLOUGHS. LDB repeats *car(uce)* in error, where the text starts a new page.

33,13 (LITTLE) BADDOW. Identified by VCH 524.

33,14 (EAST) HANNINGFIELD. The manor of Claydons there, VCH 524, n.3.

VALUE ... S. LDB *.xl.x.*, altered from *.xl.*, perhaps in error for *lxx*.

33,15 (LITTLE) OAKLEY. Identified by VCH 524. LDB *Adem* is in error for *Aclem*.

13 CATTLE. *xiii* has been altered in the MS from *viii*.

33,16 THEN 1 COB ... BEEHIVES. The livestock has been placed, unusually, after the value.

33,17 WHO HOLD ... 35 ACRES. That is, the 2 Freemen.

WHICH BERNARD. LDB *Tqd*, where the scribe has anticipated the *t* of *t(un)c* six words later, and has not erased it.

WITELEBROC. Unidentified; OE *hwītlēa-brōc*, 'brook at the place called the white wood or clearing'.

IN THE OTHER LANDS. *Witelebroc* had been held as a separate manor before 1066 but appears to have been counted as part of Michaelstow in 1086.

THESE THREE MANORS £20. Presumably Ramsey (£15), Michaelstow (£4 + 10s) and *Witelebroc* (10s).

33,18 WENDON (LOFTS). Identified by VCH 525, n.3.

ALWIN STILL. The byname is OE *stille* 'still, quiet', OEB 355.

33,19 HENHAM. For Ralph's annexation here, see 90,39. Henham was later in Uttlesford Hundred (EPNS 528). The Hundred rubric in LDB immediately before Henham may have been inserted one entry too soon (since Ashdon was later in Freshwell Hundred); however, both Henham and Ashwell were held by Ralph in lordship in 1086 and had been held by Aethelgyth in 1066 and thus there may have been a tenurial reason for regarding Henham as in Freshwell Hundred, where it has been left in the present translation.

33,19-20 AETHELGYTH. See 33,6-7 note.

33,20 1 ACRE OF VINES. The usual Domesday measure for vineyards is *arpent*.

33,21 [ACRES]. LDB omits *acre*.

33,22 ½ HIDE ... ST. PAUL'S. See 5,10.

33,23 TOLLESHUNT. This manor adjoined Tolleshunt D'Arcy, see VCH 532, n.6. Cf. 34,36.

AELMER. Called Aelmer Milk in B3r, which mentions a house in Colchester belonging to Tolleshunt.

WOODLAND. See 28,9 note.

34 RANULF PEVEREL. His lands later became part of the Honour of Peverel of London, having a distinct history from the Peverel lands in Chapter 48, see VCH 346. For Ranulf's annexations, see 90,10–14.

34,1 VALUE THEN. The facsimile omits the abbreviation-mark from *T(un)c*.

34,2 HE TOOK POSSESSION. Referring to Ranulf.

IT. Referring to the free man's land.

WITH THE OTHER. LDB repeats *cum* where the text begins a new page.

34,3 INGRAVE. Identified EPNS 161.
34,6 TERLING. See also 90,10 for Ranulf's annexations there.
2 HOUSES IN COLCHESTER. 5 are recorded in B3q.
34,7 15 ACRES ... SASWALO ... HOLDING. The personal name is Rom *Saxwalo*, Forssner 223.
He was an undertenant of Geoffrey de Mandeville in Berkshire (38,1-2) and Oxfordshire
(39,1-2) but neither he nor the 15 acres are mentioned in Chapter 30 describing Geoffrey's
Essex lands.
34,8 (WEST) HAM. See 32,8 note.
WHEN ACQUIRED. *q(ua)n(do) recep(er)unt*, 'when they (i.e. Ranulf Peverel and Robert
Gernon) acquired it'.
ROBERT GERNON ... MANOR. See 32,8.
34,9 WARIN. LDB *Garin(us)*; an OFr form of OG *Warin*, Forssner 246-247.
SIWARD. Probably he who was Ranulf Peverel's predecessor in other places in this Chapter
and also in Suffolk where (34,1-2) he was called Siward of Maldon from his tenure of
34,12 below.
[WITH] CALVES. LDB omits *c(um)* before *vitul(is)*, perhaps indicating misassociation
with *c(entum)* following.
34,10 RAVENOT. An Anglo-French or NFr diminutive from ON *Hrafn* and the OFr suffix *-ot*.
Also at 34,28.
WILLINGALE (DOE). Identified by VCH 528, n.1.
34,11 WOODHAM (MORTIMER). Identified by VCH 528.
100 GOATS. This is a Farley error for '5 goats'; MS *.v. cap(re)*.
34,12 MALDON. Called Little Maldon by VCH 528.
MEN'S [PLOUGHS]. LDB omits *caruce*.
SHEEP. Farley *poues*, MS *por*- altered to *pou*-; the *p* was meant to be erased in the MS but
was not.
34,13-14 HAZELEIGH. Respectively, the manors of Great and Little Hazeleigh, VCH 528, nn.4-5.
34,15 A. Perhaps, but not necessarily, an abbreviation for *Ailmar(us)* of 34,14.
34,16 ABBERTON. Ranulf Peverel subsequently granted it to St. Paul's, ECE, no. 96.
34,19 13 VILLAGERS, NOW 19. IE adds, 'and 1 Freeman', *sochemann(us)*.
ABBOT OF ELY. See IE 129, IEAL 189.
34,20 ... PLOUGHS. LDB omits the numeral.
VITALIS [HOLDS]. Probably he of 34,18.
34,21 (GREAT) HENNY. Identified by VCH 529. See 90,13 for Ranulf's annexation here, and
90,44 for Thorold's.
SUDBURY. Suffolk (1,97), to the north of Gt. Henny.
34,22 LAMARSH. See 90,14 for Ranulf's annexation here, and 90,45 for Thorold's.
TWO BROTHERS. Presumably Algar and Alfward.
34,24 LAWLING. The manor of Peverells there, VCH 530, n.5.
34,26 STANSGATE. See 90,12 for Ranulf Peverel's annexation here.
34,27 HAS IT. Alternatively, 'has him'.
34,28 RAVENOT. As 34,10 note.
PLUNKER'S (GREEN). For this identification, see EPNS 153.
½ PLOUGH. In the MS *.7. d(imidia) . car(uca)* has been altered from *.7.i.car(uca)*.
34,29 SPRINGFIELD. The manor of Springfield Hall, VCH 531, n.3.
SMALLHOLDERS. LDB repeats the *bordarius* category of population. Possibly the second
group is in error for *serui*, 'slaves'.
34,30 ABBEY OF ELY. See 10,3 and IE 126.
34,31 £12 FROM MALDON. This does not tally with the values given in 1,25.
34,33 ST. OSYTH. The manor of St. Clere's Hall there, VCH 531, n.8; EPNS 350, s.n. St. Clairs
Hall.
50 CATTLE. An unusually high number of cattle.
34,35 SMALLHOLDERS ABOVE THE WATER. They were probably fishermen dwelling on the
shore of the Thames Estuary here. In the MS *sup(er)* has been altered from *sub*!
34,36 TOLLESHUNT (D'ARCY). Identified by VCH 532, n.5.
RALPH BAYNARD. Cf. 33,23.
HUGH DE MONTFORT. Cf. 27,18.
35 AUBREY DE VERE. Named from Ver (La Manche: arr. Coutances) or Ver (Calvados),
see OEB 118. For his annexations, see 90,36-37.
35,1 (GREAT) CANFIELD. Identified by VCH 532.
WULFWIN. He was also Aubrey's predecessor in Cambridgeshire (29,1 note etc.).
35,2 *UDECHESHALE*. Unidentified, OE **Udeceshale*, 'at Udec's nook of land'; **Udec* may be a

diminutive of the recorded personal-name *Uda* (cf. *Udel* in Uttlesford, EPNS 516) but could be from a place-name *Wuda-hecc* 'Woodhatch', if the LDB spelling *ch* here represents [tʃ].

35,5 (CASTLE) HEDINGHAM. Identified by VCH 533. For Aubrey's annexation of 15 acres at Smalton here, see 90,37.

WHO ... PLOUGHS. *h(abe)ntes* probably refers to all the village population listed here, rather than to the slaves. The clause is another way of expressing the number of 'men's ploughs'. A similar construction is used below in relation to the ploughs belonging to Robert Blunt, etc.

SUDBURY. Suffolk (1,97).

ROBERT BLUNT. A landholder in Suffolk (*66*) and Middlesex (*17*), etc. See also 90,83. The byname is from OFr *blund, blond*, 'blonde, fair', OEB 294. In Wiltshire (*60*) he has the Latin byname *flavus* (OEB 313), 'yellow, blonde'; in Northamptonshire (*33*) the Latin byname *albus* 'white' (OEB 293); and in Norfolk (LDB folios 140,243) the OFr byname *blanchart* 'whitish' (OEB 293).

PINSON. LDB *Pincūn*, for *Pinc(io)un* from OFr *pinçon* 'finch', a nickname; see Reaney 274 s.n. Pinchen, Pinson.

GODWIN. LDB *Godun*.

35,6 HALF-HUNDRED OF 'THUNDERLOW'. This unit occurs only here and before 36,8. It was later subsumed into Hinkford Hundred. The meeting-place was in Bulmer parish, see EPNS 418. The inclusion of 'Binsley' in it (VCH 405–406) is not so in LDB, see 23,10 and 36,9.

BELCHAMP (WALTER). Identified by VCH 534.

4 MEN'S PLOUGHS. The first instance of LDB *car(uce) hom(inum)* is here in error for *car(uce) in dominio*.

ARPENT. The normal unit of extent for vineyards in the Domesday Survey, of unknown extent.

WILLIAM PECHE. LDB *peccatu(m)*, equivalent to OFr *peche* 'sin', OEB 353.

SUADUS. Perhaps a nickname from Latin *suadus* 'persuasive', but possibly it is OE *swaeth* 'bandage, wrapping' used as a byname, see von Feilitzen 1968, 14–15 in relation to *Osferth Swade beard*.

35,7 PREDECESSOR. LDB *antecessore*, with an otiose abbreviation-mark above *c*.

35,8 (EARLS) COLNE. The modern form commemorates the rank, as Earls of Oxford, of the DB tenant's descendants; EPNS 381.

... VILLAGERS. LDB omits the numeral.

DEMIBLANC ... 1 HIDE. The manor of Ingledethorp in White Colne; VCH 534, n.11, EPNS 384. White Colne was named from Demiblanc's byname 'half-white' (*dimidius blancus*), possibly referring to the colour of his hair. He also occurs in Colchester (B3a), where also cf. Blanc. J. H. Round (VCH 534, n.11) related the name Demiblanc to 'the name of a certain coin in Old French' but the source of his statement is unknown and the word has not been found in any dictionary.

35,9 (GREAT) BENTLEY. Identified by VCH 535, n.1.

AMONG [THE MEN]. LDB omits *homines*.

35,11 BEAUMONT. LDB *Fulepet*. The first OE name 'foul hollow' is the direct opposite of the later (by 1175–80) OFr one 'fair hill', EPNS 327–328.

35,12 (HELIONS) BUMPSTEAD. The manor of Bumpstead Hall there, VCH 535, n.8.

35,14 STEVINGTON (END). Identified by VCH 536, n.2, as the manor of Waltons in Ashdon.

36 PETER OF VALOGNES. The Sheriff of Essex and Hertfordshire in 1086, see VCH 349. He was named from Valognes (La Manche), OEB 117.

36,3 (LITTLE) PARNDON. Identified by VCH 536.

36,4 (NORTH) WEALD (BASSETT). For this identification, see VCH 397.

36,6 HIGHAM (HILL). In Walthamstow, EPNS 106–107.

I HAVE MENTIONED ABOVE. *sup(er)i(us) dixi*, a rare use of the first person in the Domesday texts. The subject of the verb may have been the Sheriff of Essex, whose Holding this was, rather than the compiler of LDB.

WILLIAM ... VALOGNES. *hoc*, if it agrees with any other word here, ought grammatically, to refer to the whole manor (*manerium*), rather than to just the 1 hide (*hida*), but it should probably be taken here as standing on its own and meaning 'that just described', i.e. the 1 hide.

36,8 HALF-HUNDRED OF 'THUNDERLOW'. See 35,6 note.

RALPH THE HAUNTED. LDB *fatat(us)*, unexplained OEB 389, but see Latham 186 s.v. *fatatus* 'haunted' *c*. 1212.

36,9 'BINSLEY'. See 23,10 note. VCH 405–406 puts it in 'Thunderlow' Half-Hundred but above at 23,10 it appears to be in Hinckford Hundred. Hundred-rubrics appear to have been omitted in this part of the present Chapter.

36,10 VALUE THEN. LDB repeats *T(un)c ual(uit)*.
36,11 THEYDON (BOIS). Identified by VCH 537, n.11.
36,12 RALPH THE HAUNTED. As 36,8 note.
       (NORTH) WEALD (BASSETT). As 36,4 note.
37   RANULF BROTHER OF ILGER. Ranulf appears consistently in the DB Survey as 'the brother of Ilger', although in IE (149) he is called 'the son of Ilger'. Ilger is from OG *Hilger*, see OEB 187.
37,1   INGRAVE. Identified by VCH 161.
37,2   FOUND NOTHING. No livestock, when acquired.
37,3   INGVAR. Ranulf brother of Ilger also took possessibn of Everton (Huntingdonshire 24,1) which had previously been held by Ingvar. The name *Ingvar* is ON (PNDB 298) and hence the spelling 'Ingward' used in the Hunts. translation is incorrect and should be altered to 'Ingvar'.
37,4-6 PARNDON. Probably Great Parndon, VCH 539.
37,4   ALFSI BOWL. LDB *bolla*, from the OE for 'bowl, cup'; OEB 294-295.
37,7   (NORTH) WEALD (BASSETT). As 36,4 note.
37,9   1 VIRGATE ... FROM THERE. The 30 acres mentioned in 7,1 as being held by Ranulf brother of Ilger.
37,11 13 ... LDB .*7.xiii;* Probably the missing category is 'cobs', *runcini*.
37,12 THESE 2 MANORS. Referring to 37,11-12.
37,13 THEN NOTHING. That is, no livestock before 1066.
37,14 ST. LAWRENCE. As 2,6 note. Identified as East Newland by VCH 540, n.5.
37,17 The text demands a new section here, although LDB has not supplied a paragraph mark.
       AND ... EXCHANGE. Perhaps the subject of this clause is Ranulf brother of Ilger, not William of Bosc; cf. 37,19.
37,19 FOUCHERS. Called *Gynge Puelle* in 1373, from the tenants before 1066, EPNS 159. Not Mountnessing as VCH 541.
       FREELY. LDB *lib(er)ae* is probably for *libere*, being influenced by the previous word *puellae*. The alternative translation, 'free girls', is less likely since it should have been written in the order *liberae puellae*.
       EXCHANGE. Cf. 37,16 note.
37,20 'DERLEIGH'. Lost, in Little Bromley; EPNS 333. Not, as VCH 541, Ardleigh.
       EDRIC OF EASTHORPE. He of 20,40.
       LAWFORD. Adjoining Little Bromley. See 1,27.
38   TIHEL THE BRETON. The forename is Breton *Tihellus*. In 18,21a he is called 'of Helléan' (Morbihan: arr. Pontivy; OEB 91), which byname has been fossilized in Helions Bumpstead, held by Tihel (38,4).
38,1   [THEN]. LDB has *7* in error for *T(un)c*.
38,2   STEVINGTON (END). As 35,14 note (VCH 541, n.9). Farley *Steintuna(m)* is in error for *Steuituna(m)* of the MS.
       THEN [AND] LATER. *T(un)c p(ro) p(ost)* is a Farley error for *T(un)c 7 p(ost)* of the MS.
       SMALLHOLDER, NOW 3. In the MS *iii* has been altered from *ii*.
38,3   GUTHRED. LDB *Goderet*; ON *Guthrǫdr* PNDB 279-280, Fellows Jensen 111.
38,4   (HELIONS) BUMPSTEAD. The manor of Helions there, VCH 541, n.11. See *38* note.
       ... BEEHIVES. LDB omits the numeral.
38,5   MANOR, FOR 1 HIDE. The semi-colon in Farley is a misreading of the MS where a full point after *man(erio)* has been misassociated with an insertion-mark below the line in the form of a comma. The insertion-mark is repeated in the MS, but not in Farley, before the interlineation of *7 p(ro) .i. hid(a)*.
38,6   44 PIGS. In the MS, *porc(i)* has been altered from *ou-*.
38,7   LDB omits the paragraph-mark before this entry.
39   ROGER OF RAISMES. LDB *de Ramis*; from Raismes (Nord), OEB 109.
39,1-2 RAYNE. The manor of Old Hall there, VCH 542, n.7.
39,1   MEADOW, 11 ACRES. The LDB interlineation reads *c 7 .xi. ac(re) p(ra)ti*. The *c* is most probably a repetition of the number of pigs, already given. '111 acres of meadow' is a very unlikely alternative.
       OF THIS MANOR. The paragraph-mark here does not distinguish a separate manor.
       WIBERGA. OG, Forssner 252.
39,3   WARENGAR. OG *Weringer*, Forssner 246. The LDB form has OFr *G*- for *W*-. Warengar also held lands in Sible Hedingham from Roger Bigot which Roger of Raismes claimed, see 43,1.

(SIBLE) HEDINGHAM. The manor of Greys there, VCH 543, n.2.

SLAVES, LATER AND NOW 2. In the MS *ii* has been altered from *i*.

39,7 WIFE. Cf. 39,10 note.

39,8 ARDLEIGH. The manor of Picotts there, VCH 543, n.6.

RALPH OF HASTINGS. Presumably named from Hastings, Sussex, although he is not identifiable in the DB Survey of that county. See also B7 note.

39,9 JACQUES HALL. Formerly 'Manston', EPNS 329.

ALFHELM. LDB *Alselm(us)* is in error for *Alfelm(us)*.

4 SMALLHOLDERS, NOW 3. In the MS *iii* has been altered from *ii*.

39,10 HENRY'S WIFE. 'Henry's' *Henrici* has been substituted for 'Aubrey's' *Alb(er)ici*. Possibly the 'wife of a man-at-arms' in 39,7.

39,11 CLIFF. In Mistley, EPNS 344.

40 JOHN SON OF WALERAN. For his father's annexations, see 90,46–47.

40,1 ERNUCION. Perhaps an extended form of OG *Ernust*, see OEB 181.

NOTLEY. Perhaps Black Notley, VCH 544.

40,2 THURSTAN. Probably Thurstan Wishart of B3p, who held 3 houses and ½ hide of land in Colchester from John son of Waleran.

(GREAT) SALING. Identified by VCH 544.

40,3 (LITTLE) MAPLESTEAD. Identified by VCH 544.

[HELD]. LDB omits *tenuit*.

AS A PLEDGE. Translating *p(ro) uadimonio*.

NOTHING. That is, no livestock.

40,4 HENNY. Roger also held from John an annexation here, see 90,46.

SUDBURY. Suffolk (1,97).

40,5 BURES. See 23,16 note.

40,7-8 HE ALSO HOLDS. That is, Roger of 40,6.

40,7 THE OTHER FYFIELD. A different manor, but within the present parish. VCH 545, n.5, suggests that this is the 30 acres mentioned under Havering-atte-Bower in 1,4.

40,8 (HIGH) ONGAR. Identified by VCH 545.

41 ROBERT SON OF CORBUCION. His patronym is perhaps OFr *Corbucion*, from Vulgar Latin *Corbutio*, an extended form of Latin *corvus*, 'raven'; OEB 178–179.

41,3 4½ HIDES. See 1,4 note.

Folio 85a, foot. Farley imitates the irregular shape of the bottom corner of the leaf in the MS here and on the reverse (85b).

41,4 8 FREEMEN HELD. In the MS *uiii* has apparently been altered by elongating the second minim below the line; since the verb *tenebat* is wrongly in the singular here, the scribe may have at first misread *uiii soc(hemanni)* in his exemplar as *unus soc(hemannus)*, before altering it to *uiii* but forgetting to correct the verb to *tenebant*.

FREEMEN ... HAVERING (-ATTE-BOWER). See 1,4 and note.

41,6 HUNDRED OF CHELMSFORD. Farley indicates an erasure in the MS by means of three dots, *Celme ... fort*; MS reads *Celme[.]sfort*, with only one letter erased.

41,9 'BENSTED'. As 27,14 note.

Folio 85b, foot. See note on folio 85a, foot.

41,11 VALUE ... NOW 5[s]. Farley omits to show a gap in the text, caused by an erasure in the MS, between *m(odo)*. and .*v*.

41,12 TOLLESHUNT (MAJOR). The modern form of the place-name commemorates Mauger, the DB undertenant; EPNS 307.

42 WALTER THE DEACON. The head of his Holding was at Little Easton (42,3), see VCH 349.

42,1 1 ... PIGS. Farley .*x....porc(i)* indicates a gall-stain in the MS obscuring the text here.

42,2 PURLEIGH. With 42,4 below, the manors of Frerne and Jakelets in Purleigh, VCH 548, n.3.

LEOFWIN. Probably Young Leofwin of 42,4 (see VCH 351). Cf. 42,6 note.

42,3 (LITTLE) EASTON. Identified by VCH 548.

42,4 PURLEIGH. As 42,2 note.

YOUNG LEOFWIN. See 42,2;6 notes.

42,5 STOW MARIES. See 30,44 note.

42,6 COLNE (ENGAINE). The manor of Overhall there, VCH 548, n.6.

LEOFWIN. Probably Young Leofwin of 42,4 (see VCH 351). Cf. 42,2 note.

42,7-9 QUEEN EDITH. As 20,8 note.

42,8 (LITTLE) BROMLEY. Identified by VCH 548.

42,9 (LITTLE) CHESTERFORD. Identified by VCH 549.

Folio 87a, foot. Farley omits to show a summary (?of hidages) which occurs in the bottom margin of the MS. It reads: .*v.ii.iiii.ii.* 7 *d(imidia)* .*iii.iii.* 7 *d(imidia)ii.v*. It does not fit the hidages of Chapter 42, however. Cf. notes on folios 8a,20a.

43   ROGER BIGOT. The ancestor of the Bigots, Earls of Norfolk. His byname was OFr and meant 'bigot', OEB 342.

43,1-2 WARENGAR. See 39,3 note.

43,1   (SIBLE) HEDINGHAM. Identified by VCH 549.
THESE 48 ACRES. LDB has '48' in error for '48½' here.
THESE 2 LANDS. The 25 acres and the 48½ acres.

43,4   VAUX. Unidentified; OEB 117.
BELCHAMP (OTTEN). The manor of Vaux there, named from the 1086 subtenant, VCH 549, n.6.

43,5   HENNY. Probably Little Henny, VCH 549, n.7.

43,6   HUGH OF HOUDAIN. Probably from Houdain (Pas-de-Calais: arr. Béthune), but cf. also Houdeng-au-Bosc (Seine-Inf.) and Houdain (Nord); OEB 92-93.

44   ROBERT MALET. His Holding, mainly in Suffolk, was later known as the Honour of Eye. His byname was OFr *malet*, a diminutive of *mal* 'evil', OEB 350-351. For his annexation of 15 acres at Middleton, see 90,84.

44,1   HUBERT. Called Hubert of Montchesny in Suffolk (57); VCH 550, n.4.

44,2   40 PIGS. LDB *caporč*, where the scribe began to write *cap(ri)*, 'goats', but changed to *porc(i)* without erasing either *ca* or the abbreviation-mark above *p*.

44,3   (WAKES) COLNE. Identified by VCH 550, n.10; EPNS 383.
AZORIN. LDB *Assorin(us)*. PNDB 170-171 s.n. ODan, OSw *Azur*. Cf. 32,36 note on Azo.

44,4   WALTER. In Suffolk (6,5;7) he is named as Walter of Caen.
COLNE (ENGAINE). LDB *Parua colun*. For this identification, see EPNS 379-380.

45   WILLIAM OF ÉCOUIS. From Écouis (Eure); OEB 114.

45,1   MORETON. According to ECE, no. 75, William of Écouis had granted the estate to St. Stephen's, Caen, between 1066 and 1077. It was later confirmed to St. Stephen's by King Henry II.
THEN ... COBS. LDB omits the numeral.
HOLDS FROM HIM. That is, from William.

46   ROGER OF POITOU. A younger son of Roger of Montgomery, Earl of Shrewsbury. He appears to have forfeited lands in Lancashire, Derbyshire, Nottinghamshire and Norfolk by 1086, possibly for supporting King William's rebellious son, Robert of Normandy.

46,1   WHO HAVE 1 PLOUGH. In the MS the *h* of *h(abe)ntes* has been altered from 7.
VALUE THEN. LDB *7 post*, 'and later' deleted after *T(un)c*.

46,2   LEOFWIN CROC. The byname is ON *krókr*, 'hook'; OEB 179. See also Reaney, s.n. Crook.
[IN] LORDSHIP. Farley indicates a blot in the MS by the use of three dots; however, the implication of loss of text is not warranted since *in* is clearly visible in the MS.
48 SHEEP, 100 SHEEP. Thus in MS.
ABOVE POUNDS. In the 60s (= £3), above.

46,3   LEOFWIN. Perhaps he of 46,2.

47   HUGH OF GOURNAI. From Gournai-en-Brai (Seine-Inf.: arr. Neufchâtel); OEB 90-91.

47,1   GEOFFREY TALBOT. The byname may be OFr *talebot*, 'pillager', but see further OEB 225 and Reaney 315. Cf. Calebot in B3a.

47,3   10 ACRES. Roger of Poitou held adjacent at both Mount Bures and West Bergholt. Cf. 1,19 note for another annexation by him in this Hundred.

48   WILLIAM PEVEREL. His lands later became part of the Honour of Peverel of Nottingham, see VCH 346; cf. *34* note.

48,1   (EAST) HORNDON. The manor of Abbots there (later held by Waltham Abbey), VCH 399.

48,2   (GRAYS) THURROCK. Identified by VCH 388.
THEN 11 SMALLHOLDERS. In the MS *xi* has been altered from *vi*.
2 VILLAGERS, 58 SHEEP. Thus in MS. LDB *uill'* is probably for *uit(uli)*, 'calves'.
GILBERT ... 10 ACRES. At Stifford, see 18,34.
ANSKETEL ... MANOR. Ansketel was the Bishop of London's tenant at Little Thurrock (4,6).

49   RALPH OF LIMÉSY. From Limésy (Seine-Inf.: arr. Rouen); OEB 95.

49,1   BRUNDON. In Suffolk since 1835, see EPNS 407, n.1. See also 49,4.
HARDWIN. On him, see VCH 553, n.7, and Suffolk (21,16).

49,2   *NIUETUNA*. Unidentified, OE *nīwe-tūn*, 'the new estate'.

49,3   CHIGWELL. The manor of Chigwell Hall there, VCH 553, n.10. See also 49.5.
PETER THE SHERIFF. See *36*.
HAD DELIVERY. Literally, 'had the deliverer', *habuit ... lib(er)atore(m)*.

49,4   This entry belongs with 49,1.

49,5   This entry belongs with 49,3.

49,6 6 ACRES. Unlocated, perhaps in Ongar Hundred.
50 ROBERT OF TOSNY. Named from Tosny (Eure), see OEB 116.
51 RALPH OF TOSNY. As *50* note.
51,2 LAVER. Perhaps Magdalen Laver, VCH 554, n.6.
SAXI. Probably the Guard (*huscarl*) of this name who was Ralph of Tosny's predecessor at Westmill, Hertfordshire 22,2.
52 WALTER OF DOUAI. From Douai (Nord); OEB 87.
52,1 UPMINSTER. The manor of Gaines there, VCH 554, n.9.
85 SHEEP AND 25 SHEEP. Thus in MS.
10 ACRES ... EXCHANGE. Perhaps part of the exchange mentioned in relation to the adjacent Ockendon in 30,4.
52,2 [AND AFTER]. Farley shows 7 . *p(ost)* as deleted and there is a line through it in the MS but it is uncertain whether this is more than a smudge since the text makes more sense here without a deletion.
53 MATTHEW OF MORTAGNE. From Mortagne (La Manche); OEB 101.
53,1 (GREAT) EASTON. Identified by VCH 555.
30 PIGS. Farley .*xxx* is in error for *cxx* (120) of the MS, where the text is affected by an ink smudge.
53,2 MARGARETTING. Identified by VCH 555, n.4.
VALUE THEN ... S. LDB omits the numeral.
54 COUNTESS OF AUMÂLE. King William's half-sister, Ellis i, 366–367.
54,2 OLD HALL. LDB *Sciddinchov*; formerly Sheddon or Sharing Hall in Mistley, EPNS 344. VCH 555, n.7 identifies as Manningtree, adjacent to Mistley.
55 COUNTESS JUDITH. Niece of King William and widow of Earl Waltheof (see following).
55,1 EARL WALTHEOF. Of Huntingdon and Northumbria, executed for treason in 1076 . (having joined two of his fellow Earls in rebellion, one of them Earl Ralph of 21,9 note).
56 FRODO THE ABBOT'S BROTHER. Brother of Abbot Baldwin of Bury St. Edmund's. See also 90,85.
ORDGAR. Frodo's predecessor, who had made the annexation recorded in 90,85.
56,1 3 ... LDB omits the category, probably *servi*, 'slaves'.
57 SASSELIN. A diminutive of OG *Saxo*; Forssner 223.
57,1 STANMER. In Ramsden Bellhouse, EPNS 168.
CRAY'S HILL. LDB *Winthelle*. In Ramsden Crays, EPNS 168–169.
2 MEN'S OXEN. That is, ¼ plough belonging to the men.
57,3 LAYER. Probably Layer Breton, VCH 556, n.7.
57,5 (LITTLE) WARLEY. See 3,11.
59,1 *SCILCHEHAM*. The same place as *Sciddeham* (90,82) where William annexed a free man. The name may be related to that of Sheddon or Sharing Hall, the former name of Old Hall (54,2) in Tendring Hundred, EPNS 344. The spelling is here scribally corrupt.
60 HUGH OF ST. QUENTIN. Probably from Saint-Quentin (La Manche: arr. Avranches); OEB 113.
60,1 WINGE. Probably from ODan, OSw *vinge* 'wing', PNDB 416, Redin 128.
GODWIN. Called Godwin Woodhen in 90,1 which records the same annexation.
60,3 THE QUEEN'S GIFT. Cf. the same phrase in 82,1 where Matilda is meant.
61 EDMUND SON OF ALGOT. The patronym is either ODan, OSw *Algot, Algut* or OG *Adalgot, Alfgot, Altgot*; OEB 170. He also held a mill from the Bishop of London in Stepney, Middlesex (3,10).
61,2 AELMER HOLDFAST. The byname is probably OE **Holdfæst* 'hold fast', OEB 221–222. Probably the same man as Holdfast in 22,3 who also held land in Harlow Half-Hundred before 1066.
Folio 94a, line 2. LDB began the *T* of *TERRA* and the paragraph-mark in the heading to Chapter 62 two lines too early and abandoned them, wishing to leave space between chapters.
62,1 ALFWARD DORE. The byname is probably OE *dora* 'humble-bee', but see further OEB 361–362.
62,3 WULFWIN HAPRA. OEB 347 suggests a byname derived from OE *(ge)haep* 'fit' with an AN suffix. A name such as OE **Haepp, *Haeppa* is also possible (cf. OG *Heppo*, etc., Förstemann 748; see Reaney s.v. *Happe*). Alternatively, *Hapra* might be a misreading of *Hafra*, an Anglicized form of OScand *Hafri*, a byname derived from ON *hafr* 'he-goat', see *Hafr, Hafri* in Fellows Jensen, 121.
'BYRTON'. Lost, in Stanway; EPNS 399.
62,4 *LOHOU*. Unidentified, probably OE **Lōh-hōe*; the second element is *hōh* 'a promontory, hill', and the first *lōg, lōh*, 'place', perhaps also 'hollow, camp, lair'.

63   ADAM SON OF DURAND MALZOR. The Latin byname *malis operibus* 'associated with bad works or evil deeds' corresponds to OFr *malesouvres*; OEB 349.

66   WILLIAM THE DEACON. Probably the same as William the Bishop's nephew in B3h, see note there.

66,1   WE HAVE RECEIVED ... HAND. Another instance of the use of the first person in LDB, here in the plural and reporting the work of the Domesday Commissioners. Cf. 1,3.

66,2   HUNDRED OF HINCKFORD. LDB *hidngfort* is in error for *hidingfort*.

67   WALTER COOK. The ½ hide at Shalford described in 67,1 is probably that mentioned in 1,11 as being held by Walter son of Gilbert, which suggests that these two Walters were identical. See also 90,66 note.

67,2   FELLOW. He of 90,65-66.

68   MODWIN. According to PNDB 328 this name is OG *Modwin* rather than an unrecorded OE **Mōdwine*; however, he appears to have been the former tenant in 70,2, which entry, like 68,6, relates to East Donyland, and this may lend weight to the OE derivation of his name.

68,1   EDWIN GROAT. The byname is from OE *grūt*, 'groats, coarse meal', OEB 376-377.

68,5   ALFWARD. Probably he of 90,69.

68,8   'DERLEIGH'. As 37,20 note.

69   ILBOD. The name is probably OG *Hildebodo, Hilbod*; Forssner 162.

69,2   LISTON. Either the manor of Over Hall or that of Netherhall there, VCH 561, n.7. VALUE THEN. In the MS the *T* of *T(un)c* appears to have been altered from *S* (?of *Semper*).

70   HAGEBERN. Here LDB has *Hgheb(er)ni*, below in 70,2 *hagheb(er)t(us)*. OG **Hagabern*; Forssner 138. Cf. also Hagebert in 1,27. There is persistent confusion in post-Conquest records between similar endings in the names Osbern (ON *Asbiorn*) and Osbert (OG *Osbert*). Cf. also in Domesday Essex the pairs of names Fridebern/Fridebert and Thorbern/Thorbert which may also have been confused; see references in Index of Persons.

70,2   MODWIN. See 68 note.
        HAGEBERT. See 70 note.

71   THEODORIC POINTEL. His byname is OFr *pointel*, 'point, sharp instrument', OEB 328-329. At 18,7;19 and 33,4 he is referred to by his byname alone. For his annexations, see 90,4-9.

71,3   COGGESHALL. See 90,7-8 for 2 manors obtained by Theodoric by a similar exchange. WHICH TESSELIN HELD. Referring to the 1½ hides.

72,2   ½ HIDE AND 30 ACRES. The 3 virgates recorded at 15,1.

72,3   (GREAT) BADDOW. Identified by VCH 562.

73,1   30 ACRES. Also mentioned in 15,1.

74   CONSTANTINE. Farley *constantini* is in error for *costantini* of the MS.

76,1   ALWIN. Probably Alwin Stickhare, Robert son of Rozelin's predecessor at Stepney, Middlesex (16,1).
        [THEN]. LDB omits *Tunc*.

77,1   (GREAT) BROMLEY. Identified by VCH 563.
        WESTNANETUNA. Unidentified; probably OE **Westmannatune*, 'at the estate of the men who live to the west', cf. Westmancote, Worcs., DEPN 508.
        SERVICE. LDB *seRuitiu(m)*, with *R* altered from *p*. The initial misreading was probably due to the similarity of *r* and *p* in insular minuscule.

79,1   MONKS OF ELY ... THEM. In the Ely land pleas of 1071 x 1075, Reginald *milis* is stated to hold 6½ hides in (South) Fambridge rightfully belonging to Ely; see *Inquisitio Comitatus Cantabrigiensis*, ed. N. E. S. A. Hamilton (1876), 193. See also IE 128.

80   GUNDWIN. Perhaps the same as Gundwin the Chamberlain (Suffolk *58*) and Gundwin the keeper of the granaries (Wiltshire 68,29). The name is OG *Gund(e)win*; Forssner 135.

81   OTTO THE GOLDSMITH. The craftsman who constructed the bejewelled tomb of King William at Caen, VCH 350-351. See also B3j note and 1,11-12.

81,1   GESTINGTHORPE. The manor of Overhall there, VCH 564, n.8.

82,1   THE QUEEN'S GIFT. Probably Matilda, see 1,11-12 note.

83   GRIM THE REEVE. See also 1,18.

83,1   ONE ... KING. 1 hide had been forfeited to the King for felony and Grim had been in a position, as Reeve, to acquire it for himself. Cf. 83,2.

83,2   HUBERT OF PORT. See 32,29 note.

84   WULFEVA WIFE OF FINN. Wife of Finn the Dane (23,38;43), see VCH 348-349. Her lands were granted to Eudo the Steward by King William II in 1099 or 1100, ECE, no. 124.

84,1   LORDSHIP; 1 VILLAGER. LDB repeats *7* where the text goes from recto to verso of the folio.

THESE HIDES. In the MS *hid(is)* has been altered from *his*. The scribe had here repeated the previous word by mistake.

88,2 THE KING'S CUSTOMARY DUE. Alternatively, 'the customary due to the King'.

89,1 HUNDRED-REEVE. See 32,25 note.

89,3 RICHARD. Probably he at 28,12;17-18.
HAMO. The Steward (*28*).

90 ANNEXATIONS. This Chapter records instances of unlawful occupation of lands in Essex, brought to light by the Domesday Survey. The entries fall into groups associated with particular institutions and individuals almost all of which are named as Landholders or undertenants in preceding Chapters.

90,1-4 These entries are by a different scribe to the one who wrote most of the rest of the county. He also wrote *B*, below.

90,1 WOODHEN. See 9,5 note.
2 PLACES. See 60,1.

90,2 3 VIRGATES. See 9,5.

90,3 DUNTON. This place is adjacent to Horndon-on-the-Hill.

90,4-9 THEODORIC POINTEL. See *71*.

90,4 (LITTLE) THURROCK. Identified by DG.
VALUE THEN 41s. LDB *.xl.i s(olidos)*.; it is not absolutely certain however that the stroke before *s(olidos)* should be taken as the number *i*, rather than an anticipation of *s* of *s(olidos)*. 40s would be more to be expected as a value than 41s.

90,6 BEFORE THESE PLEAS. LDB *p(rius)qua(m) hec placita fierent*; that is, before the Domesday Survey.

90,7 (LITTLE) STAMBRIDGE. Identified by VCH 566, n.18.

90,8 ROBERT ... HIM. Interlined, preceded by an insertion-mark in the form of a colon. In the MS this mark is repeated after *sol(idos)* but is not shown by Farley.
EXCHANGE ... COGGESHALL. See 71,3 for another 1½ hides obtained by Theodoric by a similar exchange.

90,9 *MIDEBROC*. Unidentified; either OE **Midelbrōc* 'marsh-meadow in the middle' or OE **Myðe-* or **Myðan-brōc* 'marsh-meadow at a confluence'.
HOLY TRINITY, CANTERBURY. See *2*.

90,10-14 RANULF PEVEREL. See *34*.

90,10 3 HIDES LESS 15 ACRES. That is, 2 hides and 105 acres. This had apparently become 2 hides and 110 acres by 1086 (2 hides and 80 acres + 30 acres), unless there is an error of computation here. Ranulf also held another 2 hides and 90 acres (2½ hides and 30 acres) there, see 34,6.

90,12 STANSGATE. See 34,26 for other land here held by Ralph son of Brian from Ranulf.

90,13 (GREAT) HENNY. Identified by VCH 567. See 34,21 for other land here held by Thorold from Ranulf. Cf. 90,44.

90,14 LAMARSH. See 34,22 for land as in preceding note. Cf. 90,45.
FREE LAND. Taking *lib(er)e* of LDB to stand for *lib(er)ae*, agreeing with *t(er)rae*.

90,15-18 HUGH DE MONTFORT. See *27*.

90,15 WILLIAM SON OF GROSS. Hugh's tenant at Kelvedon in 27,2 above.

90,17 HUNDRED OF LEXDEN. Hugh held Markshall (27,13) in this Hundred, adjacent to Feering.
FEERING. 6,8 above.

90,19 ST. PETER'S, WESTMINSTER. See *6*.
HAVERING-ATTE-BOWER. The King's manor, see 1,4.

90,20-28 GEOFFREY DE MANDEVILLE. See *30*.

90,20 MASHBURY. See 30,13 for Geoffrey's other land here.

90,21 CANFIELD. Richard held land from Geoffrey at Little Canfield (30,38).

90,22-23 ROCKELL'S FARM. Formerly '*Wyggepet*', EPNS 526-527.

90,25 FARNHAM. The manor of Earlsbury there, VCH 568, n.10; EPNS 550-551.

90,26 STAMBOURNE. The manor of Moone Hall there, VCH 568, n.11.

90,27 *WESUUNIC*. Perhaps the same place as that called *Wenesuuic* in 30,51, although the 6 free men are not necessarily the same in both entries, there being a different amount of land and a different 1066 value. However, it may be a different place and a different name; perhaps OE **Wesu-wīc* 'farm, etc. at a wet place', from *wese* 'soaked' and *wīc*, or OE **Wēsung-wīc* 'factory where soaking (e.g. of flax, dyeing, etc.) is carried on', from *wēsung* the gerund of OE *wēsan* 'to soak' and *wīc*.

90,28 GODWIN SECH. The byname is probably from OE *saec* 'sack', rather than OFr *sec* 'dry, withered'; cf. OEB 333-334 and Alwin Sack, Bedfordshire 4,5.

90,29 HUGH OF BERNIÈRES. See 30,28-30.
90,30 'PLESINGHO'. As 20,18 note.
  HELD. LDB *tenut* is in error for *tenuit*.
  HUMPHREY GOLDENBOLLOCKS. LDB *humfrid(us) aurei testiculi*; OEB 285. Perhaps a
  nickname for a man who had sired many children.
90,31-33 HAMO THE STEWARD. See *28*.
90,31 (LITTLE) WIGBOROUGH. Identified by VCH 569, n.3. For Hamo's land here see 28,9.
90,32 NORTHEY ISLAND. As 28,12 note.
90,33 STAMBOURNE. See 28,11 for Hamo's land here.
  40 ACRES ... 40s. Interlined in the MS.
90,34 WILLIAM CARDON. LDB *Cardun*, see 10,5 note.
  (GREAT) CHISHILL. Held by William from Geoffrey de Mandeville (30,46).
90,35 SWEIN. See *24*.
  BERTUNA. Unidentified, OE *bere-tūn*, 'outlier'.
  ROBERT SON OF WYMARC. See 24,1 note.
90,36-37 AUBREY DE VERE. See *35*.
90,37 SMALTON. In Castle Hedingham (cf. 35,5); EPNS 440.
90,38 AUBREY DE VERE'S WIFE. See also 18,21;24.
90,38 (LITTLE) MAPLESTEAD. Identified by VCH 569. Aubrey's wife held 'Napsted' here
  from Odo of Bayeux (18,21).
  5 FREE MEN ... 3s. Interlined in the MS.
90,39-40 RALPH BAYNARD. See *33*.
90,39 HENHAM. For Ralph Baynard's land here (13½ hides less 10 acres) see 33,19. Ralph's two
  holdings here would amount to 14 hides.
90,40 COUPALS FARM. As 23,23 note.
  After this entry the MS has a gap of about two lines. This gap is introduced in the facsimile
  by a paragraph-mark, not shown by Farley since in the MS it has been erased.
90,41 3s. *x* corrected to *iii*; so in MS.
90,42 RALPH LATIMER. He is named in ICC as Ely Abbey's tenant at Hardwick in 1086
  (Cambridgeshire 5,37 note), and may be identical with the Ralph who held Albury
  (Hertfordshire 4,11; adjacent to Farnham) from the Bishop of London in 1086.
90,43 *LIFFILDEUUELLA*. OE *Leofhildewella*, 'Leofhild's spring'. Unidentified, but possibly
  associated with Levit's Corner in Pebmarsh, see EPNS 447.
Folio 101a, foot. Farley's tapering of the right-hand margin in the last three lines of this page
  reflects a repair in the MS, also affecting the left-hand margin at the foot of folio 101b.
90,44-45 THOROLD. Ranulf Peverel's undertenant at Great Henny and Lamarsh, 34,21-22.
  Cf. also 90,13-14.
90,46-47 WALERAN. Father of John (*40*).
90,46 10½ ACRES. LDB repeats 'and', using both the tironian *nota* and the ampersand.
  JOHN. Son of Waleran, see *40*. For his land at HENNY held from him by Roger, see 40,4.
90,47 HELD. LDB *ten'*, probably for *ten(uit)*.
  NOW 40. LDB *xl* is almost certainly an error.
90,48 LEDMER OF HEMPSTEAD ... RICHARD. Ledmer is called Ledmer the reeve in 90,76
  which refers to the same annexation. He was the reeve of Richard son of Count Gilbert,
  who held Hempstead (23,41) in 1086.
  BRAINTREE. Probably Sandpit Leet, VCH 570, n.19.
90,49-78 RICHARD SON OF COUNT GILBERT. See *23*.
90,49 AELMER OF BORLEY. Cf. 90,55.
  AELFRIÇ OF ALDERFORD. Richard held 36 acres at Alderford (23,11).
  GOISMER. See 23,7 note.
  5 ACRES. Probably of meadow, if LDB has omitted *prati*.
90,50-51 ARNOLD. Probably he of 23,3;8-9.
90,50 FINCHINGFIELD. See 23,9 for 38 acres here, held by Arnold from Richard.
90,52 HORSEHAM (HALL). See also 90,75.
  WIDELARD. Probably he of 23,10;42 and 90,75.
90,53 HOWE. See 23,15 note.
  GERMUND. Richard's tenant in 23,15.
  WHICH COLMAN. LDB repeats *q(uo)d* where the text begins a new folio.
Folio 101b, foot. See note to folio 101a.
90,54 YELDHAM. Richard held Great Yeldham (23,7).
90,55 BORLEY. Cf. Aelmer of Borley in 90,49.

FREE MEN. Although Godiva was a woman, she could still technically be termed a *liber homo* in relation to her status.

90,56-57 TOPPESFIELD. Probably the manor of Scoteneys there, VCH 571, n.11; EPNS 464, s.n. Scotney's Farm.

90,58 CORNISH HALL. Formerly 'Norton', EPNS 426-427.

MASCEREL. See 23,14 note.

90,59-60 PEBMARSH; ALPHAMSTONE. See 23,18-19 for Richard's lands here.

90,61 (STEEPLE) BUMPSTEAD. See 23,21 for Richard's land here.

90,63 ALL THESE. The men named in 90,59-63. *oñs* is a LDB error for *oms̄, om(ne)s*.

THE ABOVE MEN. Either those in 90,59-63 or all the pre-1066 free men in 90,49-63.

WITHGAR. The predecessor of Richard son of Count Gilbert, see 90,64.

90,64 ENGELRIC. See 20,77 where he is said to have held 4½ hides at Bendysh (Hall) before Count Eustace.

90,65 (GREAT) BARDFIELD. Identified by VCH 572. For Richard's land there, see 23,39.

90,65-66 FELLOW. He of 67,2.

90,66 *HOCSENGA*. This is a Farley error for *hoosenga* of the MS. Unidentified, perhaps OE *hōsinge* 'place having to do with an association or company of people', from OE *hōs* (Beowulf 924).

WALTER. Possibly Walter Cook (67) who succeeded Fellow at Ashwell (67,2).

90,67 *HASINGHAM*. Unidentified, OE *Hasing-hām* or *Hasing-hamm*, 'Hasu's estate or Hasu's enclosure', cf. DEPN 224, s.n. Hassingham, Norfolk.

90,68 LUTTING. LDB *Luttin(us)*; PNDB 322.

COLNE. For Richard's holding there, see 23,34.

90,69 ALFWARD HOLDS. LDB *ten&* is in error for *tenuit*. Alfward is probably the pre-1066 tenant named in 68,5.

90,69-70 THE OTHER LAND. That in 90,68.

90,70 (WEST) BERGHOLT. For Richard's holding there, see 23,36.

90,71-72 THE OTHERS. LDB *alios*, probably agreeing with *locos* 'places' (understood); those in 90,69-70.

90,71 COLNE. As 90,68 note.

90,72 FORDHAM. For Richard's holding there, see 23,35.

TOVILD. LDB *Touillda*; ON *Tófa-Hildr*, 'Hildr the daughter of Tófi', PNDB 384.

90,73 (WEST) BERGHOLT. As 90,70 note.

2 OXEN. That is, ¼ plough.

90,74 HALSTEAD. For Richard's holding there, see 23,26.

90,75 HORSEHAM (HALL); WIDELARD. See also 90,52.

90,76 BRAINTREE ... LEDMER. See 90,48 note.

90,77 WARNER. Probably he of 23,2. He had given the tithes of this land to the Abbey of Bec by 1086, see ECE, no. 78.

ILBOD. See 69.

90,79 MONKS OF CANTERBURY. See 2.

LAWLING. For the monks' manor there, see 2,4.

90,80 THORBERN WITHOUT ... GIFT. The King had not granted them to him.

90,81 HENRY OF FERRERS. See 29.

STEEPLE. For Henry's holding there, see 29,3.

90,82 WILLIAM LEOFRIC. See 59.

SCIDDEHAM. The same place as *Scilcheham* in 59,1.

VALUE 12d. Farley omits to show a gap in the text, caused by an erasure in the MS, between *val(et)* and *.xii.d(enarios)*. The text erased is *ii.sol(idi)*.

90,83 ROBERT BLUNT. See 35,5 note.

90,84 ROBERT MALET. See 44.

90,85 FRODO THE ABBOT'S BROTHER. See 56.

STEVINGTON (END). LDB *Staumtuna* is in error for *Stauintuna*.

90,86 ROGER OF AUBERVILLE. See 26.

CHISHILL. For Roger's holding there, see 26,5.

90,87 ONGAR. For Count Eustace's holding here (in Ongar Hundred), see 20,46. The 15 acres were presumably a detached part of the manor of Ongar, perhaps for sheep-rearing.

B   This section is written by the same scribe as 90,1-4.

B1-2 GODRIC. Probably Godric of Colchester (20,42).

B1   4 PIECES OF LAND. LDB *.iiii.mansiones.t(er)rae*.

VALUE ... 30s. LDB *ualit* is in error for *ualet*.

B2   LEXDEN. See also 1,19.

CITY'S LEVY. LDB *Cootu(m) ciuitatis* is almost certainly a misreading of *scotu(m) ciuitatis*, cf. 3,16. VCH 574, note 15, emends to *compotum civitatis*, 'account of the city'.

B3a WULFSTAN EADLAC. LDB *eudlac*, OEB 217 takes the byname to be a side-form of OE *Ēadlāc*, resting on a derivation from an archaic form **eud-* which is unlikely at this date; a palaeographical confusion of *ea/eu* is more probable.

LEOFWIN CRIST. OEB 308 interprets the byname as OWScand **krist* 'cheep, peep', possibly applying to someone with a squeaky voice.

HARDEKIN. Farley *Herdedun(us)* is in error for *Herdechin(us)* of the MS, from OG **Hardekin* (PNDB 286).

LEOFWOLD. LDB *Leuot*, from OE *Lēofwald* (PNDB 316).

GODWIN WEAKFEET. LDB *uuachefet*, probably an original OE byname **Wācfēt*, 'weak feet'; OEB 339–340.

BLANC. LDB *Blanc(us)*. Cf. Demiblanc 35,8 etc.

LEOFSEXE. LDB *Leffesse* standing for *Lefsesse* from OE *Lēofsexe*, an Anglo-Scandinavian hybrid of OE *Lēof* and OScand *Saxi* (PNDB 352).

FREOND. LDB *Frent*, see von Feilitzen 1945, 80.

SAEWARE. LDB *Saluare*, from OE (feminine) *Sǣwaru* (PNDB 353).

BY AGREEMENT. LDB *consilio*, perhaps meaning here 'by mutual estimation'.

NOT. From OE *hnott*, 'bald-headed', see von Feilitzen 1945, 83.

SHED-BUTTER. LDB *Scadebutre*, an OE nickname from *butere* 'butter' and *sceadan* 'to separate, divide, give off' etc. Cf. ME *Sparebutter* in P. H. Reaney, *The Origin of English Surnames* (1967), 288.

WULFGITH. LDB *Vued*, from OE (feminine) *Wulfgyth*, cf. PNDB 420,280.

CALEBOT. This may be in error for OFr *Talebot* (see Geoffrey Talbot, 47,1 note), but may be a hitherto unrecorded OG name **Galabod, *Calabod* (cf. Förstemann 590–591).

DUBLEL. LDB *DuHel* is very probably an error for *Dublel*, an OFr byname meaning 'the double, the twin' (OEB 375).

GODDAY. LDB *Goddæ*; this may be an OE byname from *gōd* + *dǣge* meaning 'good maidservant' or one from *gōd-dæg* 'good day' (someone who gives a cheery greeting), Reaney 150 s.n. *Goodday*. Alternatively an OE masculine personal-name **Gōd-dæg* is also possible.

GOT CHILL. LDB *Got cill'*. Got is from ON *Gautr*, ODan *Gøt*, see von Feilitzen 1976, 160; *cill'* is from OE *cielle* 'chill', as a byname meaning 'the cold one' (cf. OEB 300). There were three Colchester burgesses with the forename *Got*, each distinguished by a byname; the other two were Got Hugh and Got Fleet, below.

ORDGEAT. LDB *Oriet(ur)* probably in error for *Oriet(us)*. See von Feilitzen 1945, 86.

AETHELBALD. LDB *Elebolt*; OE *AEthelbeald, Ethelbald, -bold*, cf. Seltén 25.

AETHELBRICT. LDB *Ailbriest*; OE *AEthelbriht, -beorht* (PNDB 182).

TATE. Either OE *Tat(a)*, masculine, or *Taete*, feminine; Redin 54,114.

BEARD. LDB *Berda*, from the OE personal-name *Bearda* (von Feilitzen 1945, 74 and 1976, 208; cf. Reaney, s.n. *Beard*).

FILIMAN. LDB *Filieman*; OG *Filiman*, a rather rare personal-name (Förstemann 505).

PIC. From *pīc* 'point', Redin 22. Cf. also OEB 326–327, where one possible significance of the corresponding byname given is of 'a man armed with a pick-axe', another being to describe 'a tall, thin person'.

BEST. Probably an OE nickname from either *bæst* 'bast, inner bark of a tree' or *bēost* 'beestings'; but possibly an early instance of the ME surname *Best(e)* from OFr *beste* 'beast', see Reaney s.n. *Best* and von Feilitzen 1968, 7.

ROSELL. From OFr *rossel*, 'red-faced, ruddy', see von Feilitzen 1976, 215; Reaney, s.n. *Russel*.

POTE. An OE personal-name and byname **Pota*, related to the verb OE *potian*, ME *pote* 'to push, poke, thrust' and the ME, ModE noun *pote* 'a poker, a plough-staff', see NED.

LUNDI. LDB *Liuidi*, probably from the OScand personal-name and byname *Lundi* (well-attested, e.g. Fellows Jensen 191).

WOODBILL. LDB *Vudebil*, an original byname from OE *wudubill* 'hatchet'; Kökeritz NOB 26, p. 36, von Feilitzen 1945, 92. The etymology suggested PNDB 417 is incorrect.

AESCHERE. An OE personal-name *AEschere*, see von Feilitzen 1945, 72 and 73 n.1.

SUNEGOD. LDB *Sunegot*; OG, see Forssner 226.

LEOFSWITH. LDB *Leffiuf*, OE (feminine) *Lēofswith*.

WIGSTAN. LDB *Westan*; OE *Wīgstān*, PNDB 413.

AINULF. LDB *Ainolf*; OG *Aginulf*, Forssner 15.

TUNRIC. OE *Tūnrīc*, so far recorded only here, von Feilitzen 1945, 90.

B

PEACOCK. LDB *Pecoc*, von Feilitzen 1945, 86.
6½ ACRES. .*7.dim'.7.vi.ac(ras)*. LDB .*7.dim'* may be in error for .*i. dom'*, '1 house'.
SEAFOWL. LDB *Saeuuele*; OE (Anglo-Scandinavian) *Saefugel*; OEB 162, Reaney s.n. *Saffel* (a ME surname in East Anglia and Essex).
TESCO. LDB *Tescho*; OG *Thieziko, Tizeko*, Förstemann 1417.
HERSTAN. OE *Herestān*, which occurs in D. Whitelock, *Anglo-Saxon Wills* (Cambridge, 1930), 3 (p. 14, 1.4), Sawyer 1539, of ?*c*. 950.
DELA. OE *Dela*, Redin 75, s.n. *Dealla*.
HUNNING. LDB *Hunec*; OE *Hunning*, PNDB 296.
GOT HUGH. LDB *Got hugo*, for the forename, see Got Chill, above. The byname here is a patronym from OG *Hugo* (Forssner 157–158) or OScand *Hughi*. Reaney, s.n. *Hugh*, overlooks this instance.
DEMIBLANC. See 35,8 note and cf. Blanc, above.
RALPH PINEL. See 77.
HORRAP. In its present form this resembles no known personal-name. It may possibly be a misreading of OE *Hofw(e)ard* (PNDB 291); alternatively a compound byname whose final element is OE *rāp* 'rope' might be suggested.
STANBURG. LDB *Stamburc*; OE (feminine) *Stanburg* (from ON *Steinbiǫrg*), PNDB 371, n.4.
GOT FLEET. LDB *Got flet*; for the forename, see Got Chill, above. The byname here probably represents the ON adjective *fljotr*, ME *flete* 'fleet, swift'; cf. OE *flēotig* 'swift', see Reaney, s.n. *Fleet*.
MANSON. LDB *Mansune*; probably OE **Mansuna*, PNDB 325.
LORCE BRET. LDB *Lorchebret*, 'Lorce the Breton'. For the byname, see OEB 133 (*Brito*), 130 (*Bryt*); Reaney, s.n. *Bret*. The forename is probably OBret, cognate with OIr *lorc* 'fierce', rather than OScand *Lurkr* (PNDB 322).

B3b HAMO THE STEWARD. LDB *Amo Hamo*, where the scribe has misspelt the name Hamo and has then written it correctly but has not erased his error.
COURT. Translating *curia*. The meaning is probably that of a group of houses built around a courtyard.
HELD THIS. LDB *tenūit* has an otiose abbreviation-mark above *u*.
A TAX ... HEADS. Translating *de suis capitibus*. Cf. *caput ho(min)is* in B3m. The burgesses paid a tax levied on individuals, rather than on households.
HAS NOT BEEN PAID. LDB *c̄ reddita* is in error for *e(st) reddita*.
B3c The paragraph-mark indicates this to be a separate section, although no value is given.
B3d THE CUSTOMARY DUE. LDB *(con)suedine(m)* is in error for *(con)suetudine(m)*.
ST. PETER'S CHURCH. See B7.
B3e BEFORE 1066. LDB *tēp̄.r.e.* is in error for *tēp̄.r.e.*, that is *te(m)p(ore) . r(egis).e(dwardi)*.
B3g COUNT EUSTACE. See 20,8 for a burgess of Colchester belonging to the Count's holding at Rivenhall; 20,36 for a house in Colchester belonging to his manor of Tey; and 20,39 for 2 houses belonging to his manor of Great Birch.
ENGELRIC. He had held the Count's manor of Great Birch (20,39) at a date between 1066 and 1086.
B3h WILLIAM THE BISHOP'S NEPHEW. Identical with William the deacon, see *66* note. VCH 418 suggests that he was the nephew of Bishop William of London, 1051–75, a suggestion supported by ECE, no. 94.
WHICH. *quam* (accusative singular) in error for *quas* (accusative plural), referring to '2 houses'.
B3j OTTO THE GOLDSMITH ... SHALFORD ... AELFEVA. Aelfeva was the wife of Earl Algar who held Shalford before 1066. Otto the Goldsmith (*81*) was in possession of it in 1086, see 1,11. In Cambridgeshire (1,18) he also held part of Litlington at a revenue in 1086 which Earl Algar had held.
THE QUEEN'S LAND. Probably Queen Matilda's, see 1,11–12 note.
B3k ABBOT OF WESTMINSTER; FEERING. See 6,8 where only 2 houses are recorded.
B3l GINNI. LDB *Geni(us)*; ODan *Ginni*, PNDB 261.
ARDLEIGH. For Geoffrey de Mandeville's holding there, see 30,20.
B3m ELMSTEAD. For Swein's holding there, see 24,64.
A TAX ... HEAD. See B3b note.
B3p THURSTAN WISHART. LDB *Turstinus uuiscart*; the byname is a patronym from ONFr *Wischard, Guisc(h)ard, -art*, see Reaney, s.n. *Wishart*. Probably he of 40,2.
THE CUSTOMARY DUE. LDB *consuedo* is in error for *consuetudinem*.
B3q TERLING. For Ranulf's holding there, also previously held by Aelmer, see 34,6. That entry records only 2 houses in Colchester however.

B3r TOLLESHUNT. For Ralph's holding there, see 33,23. The LDB form *collensum te* is corrupt.

THEY USED TO PAY. LDB *reddebant*, in error for *reddebat*, 'it used to pay'. Cf. B3s note.

B3s 3 HOUSES. Recorded under Barking Abbey's manor of Wigborough (9,8).

IT USED TO PAY. LDB *reddebat*, in error for *reddebant*, 'they used to pay'. Cf. B3r note.

B4 SCRUBLAND. Translating *fructecta*.

B6 THIS BELONGS. LDB *hoc p(er)tinent* is in error for *hoc p(er)tinet*. The custom in this sentence is being contrasted to that in the next which is *not* part of the King's revenue: *hoc n(on) e(st) ad firma(m)*.

THIS ... EXPEDITION. The King still had mercenaries to support while not actually on campaign.

FOR THESE 6 PENCE. Translating *propt(er) hos .vi. denarios*, but note that *propt(er)* is probably in error for *pret(er)* 'apart from', cf. following sentences beginning *p(re)ter hoc*.

NOW IT PAYS. If *reddit* is not in error for *reddunt*, then the subject of this clause is the mint.

£80. Expressed as *.iiii.xx. lib(ras)*.

SESTERS OF HONEY. A sester was usually 4, but sometimes 5 to 6, gallons, see R. E. Zupko, *A dictionary of English weights and measures from Anglo-Saxon times to the nineteenth century* (Univ. of Wisconsin Press, 1968), 155.

PREBENDARIES. A similar charge was put on the Boroughs of Norwich and Thetford (Norfolk 1,61;70).

WALERAN ... THIS. Waleran was the father of John (40) and is mentioned in 17,1 as having taken 1 house in Colchester away from St. Ouen's Abbey's land at West Mersea. He had apparently administered Colchester for the King at some time between 1066 and 1086 and may perhaps have done the same with Norwich (Norfolk, 1,63).

AS PROTECTOR. LDB *adturtore(m)* is in error for *ad tutore(m)*.

BISHOP WALKELIN. Of Winchester, 1070–98.

B7 ST. PETER'S CHURCH. See also B3d. LDB *eccl(esi)e* is in error for *eccl(esi)a*.

KING'S ALMS. Farley *elemasina* corrects the MS reading *clemasina*.

RALPH OF HASTINGS. LDB *hatingis* is in error for *hastingis*, cf. *hastinges*, folio 83b, (39,8). Ralph held 30 acres at Ardleigh, adjoining Colchester.

THE FOURTH. LDB has an otiose abbreviation-mark on *quarta(m)*, Farley places it above the *u*, the MS has it above the first *a*.

EKt Cf. note on 'Gravesend' at 20,5.

ESf 1 HARKSTEAD. See also 1,26.

The Hundreds and Half-Hundreds

Most of the twenty-one DB Hundreds and Half-Hundreds survived without much change into the 19th century. Some are termed alternately 'Hundred' or 'Half-Hundred' in DB and later medieval records and there appears to have been little actual difference in status between the two terms in the post-Conquest period — a small Hundred might occasionally be called a Half-Hundred, that was all. The tiny 'Thunderlow' Half-Hundred, in the north of the county, was later subsumed into Hinckford Hundred. 'Wibertsherne' Hundred was known as Dengie Hundred from the late 12th century onwards. The Royal Liberty of Havering-atte-Bower was created in 1465 out of the eastern part of Becontree Hundred.

Maldon appears from DB to have been in 1086 partly in its own (urban) Half-Hundred and partly in 'Wibertsherne' Hundred. Epping appears to have been partly in the Half-Hundred of Harlow and partly in that of Waltham.

There are a few changes in the Hundredal ascription of places between DB and later records. Gt. Coggeshall was placed in the DB Hundred of Witham, but was later in Lexden Hundred. Henham was placed in Freshwell Hundred but was later in that of Uttlesford. Horseham Hall was put in Hinckford Hundred but was later in Freshwell Hundred. Wheatley was put in Barstable Hundred but was later in that of Rochford.

The Hundredal units usually occur within chapters in more or less the order given in VCH, 409. This (excluding 'Thunderlow' Half-Hundred, which occurs only twice) is as follows: Barstable, Witham, Harlow, Waltham, Becontree, Dunmow, 'Wibertsherne', Winstree, Uttlesford, Clavering, Hinckford, 'Wibertsherne' (again), Lexden, Ongar, Chafford, Chelmsford, Maldon, Tendring, Uttlesford (again), Freshwell, Rochford, and Thurstable. This order does not represent any one geographical progression as it crosses and re-crosses the county several times.

The County Boundary
The county has its origin in the Kingdom of the East Saxons. Its inland boundary is mainly marked by major rivers — the Stour in the north, the Thames in the south and the Lea and the Stort in the west. There is however a small area in the north-west, adjacent to Hertfordshire and Cambridgeshire, which does not follow a watercourse and may have been fixed relatively late in the Anglo-Saxon period. Both along the Stour and the Thames there is evidence of some cross-river tenurial association with estates in Suffolk (Bures St. Mary and Nayland) and Kent (Chalk and Gravesend) before 1086.

The parish of Ballingdon cum Brundon was transferred to the Borough of Sudbury, Suffolk in 1832 and 1835 (EPNS 407, n.). Gt. and Lt. Chishill and Heydon were transferred to Cambridgeshire in 1895 (EPNS 520,529).

APPENDIX

THE ELY INQUIRY
Inquisitio Eliensis (IE)

The Ely Inquiry, usually referred to as IE, is a collection of material relating to holdings of Ely Abbey in Cambridgeshire, Essex, Hertfordshire, Huntingdonshire, Norfolk and Suffolk whose source appears to have been drafts (now lost) of the returns for three different circuits of the DB Survey. It was put together, for the benefit of Ely Abbey, very soon after 1086, but survives only in three manuscripts written in the second half of the 12th century — British Library, Cotton Tiberius A.vi, folios 38–70 (MS A); Trinity College Cambridge 0.2.41, pages 161–274 (MS B) and 0.2.1, folios 177v–213 (MS C) — of these, B and C are derived from a common source, while A is a copy of B. Although B is now thought to be the most reliable of the three manuscripts, IE was reproduced in record type in 1816 by Sir Henry Ellis from A (see DB4, 495–528). N. E. S. A. Hamilton also used A as the base text for his edition of IE in 1876 (*Inquisitio Comitatus Cantabrigiensis*, 97–168), but also gave variant readings from B and C in footnotes.[1]

For Essex, IE (Hamilton 125–130; and summaries at 122) supplies details of the Ely Abbey lordship holdings in the county (cf. above, Chapter *10*) and of other pieces of land claimed by the Abbey. The information given in IE is identical in type to that in DB Essex, differing only in a few small details. Hamilton also edited some other documents, subsidiary to IE, which are dependent upon, or relevant to, the DB Survey. The *Inquisitio Eliensis* Breviate (IE Brev; Hamilton 168–173) gives summaries of the numbers of ploughs and people in each of the Abbey's holdings, and the *Nomina Villarum* (IENV; Hamilton 174–175) lists the number of ploughs held by the villagers therein. These are followed by lists of holdings alienated from the Abbey's possession (IEAL; Hamilton 175–189) and an account of an inquiry into the Abbey's losses held between 1071 and 1075 (Hamilton 192–195). In the present volume, quotations from IE and its related documents have only been given where information occurs which is different or extra to that in LDB.

For further comments on IE, see R. Welldon Finn, 'The Inquisitio Eliensis reconsidered', *English Historical Review* lxxv (1960), 385–409. For the Ely Abbey claims, see E. Miller, 'The Ely land pleas in the reign of William I', *English Historical Review* lxii (1947), 438–456 and *Liber Eliensis*, ed. E. O. Blake, 426–432. See also the Introduction to the Cambridgeshire volume for a sample of text from IE.

---

1. Note that in the Cambridgeshire volume, Introduction, The Ely Inquiry, it is wrongly stated that Ellis and Hamilton edited IE from MS C and that Hamilton collated it to MSS A and B. The true situation is as stated in the present Appendix.

INDEX OF PERSONS

Familiar modern spellings are given where they exist. Unfamiliar names are usually given in an approximate late 11th century form, avoiding variants that were already obsolescent or pedantic. Spellings that mislead the modern eye are avoided where possible. Two, however, cannot be avoided; they are combined in the name 'Leofgeat', pronounced 'Leffyet', or 'Levyet'. The definite article is used before bynames where there is a probability that they described the individual, rather than one of his ancestors. While an attempt has been made to differentiate individuals with the same name, there remain several individuals who cannot be so differentiated. Readers are therefore advised that a group of references given under a single name (e.g. Aelmer) do not necessarily refer to the same individual; where the same name occurs more than once in a single entry (e.g. in B3a) and could refer to different individuals, the number of occurrences of the name is shown in brackets after the entry reference. *The chapter-numbers of listed landholders are printed in italics, as are the names of persons referred to in the text, but not named there, who have been identified in footnotes.*

Gobert, see Robert	
Goda	B3a(×6),m
Godbold	24,19;45;57
Godday	B3a
Godfrey	24,40. 30,51. 41,9
Godhere	4,17. 66,2
Goding	23,36. 28,4. 90,73. B3a(×3)
Godith	5,6. 24,8. 30,26. B3a
Godiva	90,55. B3a(×2)
Godman	24,54. 75,1. 83,2
Godmund	20,62
Godric of Colchester	20,42
Godric (of Colchester)	B1-2
Godric Poinc	22,18
Godric Skipper	22,16
Godric the Steward	1,30
Godric	4,12. 14,1. 18,9;41. 20,73. 24,12;16;25;29;43; 46;59-61. 32,33. 33,5. 34,14. 63,2. 71,2. B3a(×6),e
God-save-ladies, see Roger	
Godson	B3a(×3)
Godwin Sech	90,28
Godwin son of Dudeman	EKt
Godwin the deacon	*88*. 30,11
Godwin the priest	68,8
Godwin the uncle of Ralph	ENf
Godwin Weakfeet	B3a
Godwin Weakfeet's son	B3a
Godwin Woodhen	9,5. 90,1-3
Godwin (Woodhen)	60,1
Godwin	4,8;10. 20,23. 24,10. 25,2;5;22. 32,24;36. 35,5. 37,7. 39,3. 44,1-2;4. 76,1. 90,35;54. B3a(×10)
Goismer	23,7. 90,49
Goldenbollocks, see Humphrey	
Goldhere	B3a(×2)
Golding	B3a
Goldman	B3a
Goldric	B3a
Goldstan	1,8. 90,49. B3a
Goldwin	B3a(×2)
Got Chill	B3a
Got Fleet	B3a
Got Hugh	B3a
Goti	13,1. 28,1;9;11
Gotild	28,13-14;16
Gotre	32,14;45
Grapinel	24,22
Grim the reeve	*83*. 1,18
Grim	25,17. 35,5. 40,3. 90,51;55
Grimbald	71,4
Grimkel	32,42-43
Grimwulf	B3a
Groat, see Edwin	
Gross, see William	
Gundwin	*80*
Gunner	24,63;67
Gutbert	30,27
Guthmund	20,62. 27,2;4-5;11;13-14
another Guthmund	28,5
Guthred	38,3
Guy	20,30-31;72-73

Thorkell	14,3-7. 18,38. 24,9;58. 26,2. 30,5. 66,1. B3a,h
Thorold of Rochester	9,1. 18,36;43-44
Thorold (of Rochester)	20,1
Thorold (of Rochester), see Ralph	
Thorold	4,7. 18,37. 24,6-7. 30,4. 34,7;15;21-22;33-34. 90,13;44-45
Thorold, see Gilbert	
Thurstan the Red	5,8
Thurstan Wishart	B3p
Thurstan (Wishart)	40,2
Thurstan	37,6. B3a
Tidbald	3,2
Tihel of Helléan, the Breton	38. 18,21a
Tirel, see Walter	
Toli	30,17
Topi	32,34
Tosti	6,7. 40,5
Toti	23,1
Tovi	70,1. B3a
Tovild	90,72
Tunric	B3a
Ulf	20,12
Vitalis	23,3. 28,9. 34,18;20
W.	24,8;21. 30,16. 37,1;14;19. 41,5;7
W. Corbun	32,11
Wader, see Earl Ralph	
Bishop Walchere of Durham	7,1
Walchere	33,3;11
Waleran father of John	40,9
Waleran (father of John)	90,46-47
Waleran	1,27. 17,1. B6
Waleran, see John nephew of, John son of	
Bishop Walkelin (of Winchester)	B6
Walter Cook, son of Gilbert	*67*. 1,11
Walter (of Caen)	44,4
Walter of Douai	*52*
Walter son of Gilbert, see Walter Cook	
Walter the deacon	*42*. 1,27
Walter the deacon, see Theodoric	
Walter Tirel	23,38
Walter	4,8. 22,8. 24,2;14;28;46. 30,5;7-9;22-23. 32,38a. 36,11. 37,13. 90,66. B3a
Earl Waltheof	55,1
Wand, see Aelfric	
Warengar	39,3. 43,1-2
Warin	34,9. 35,5
Warin, see Gilbert	
Warner	20,2. 23,2. 24,21;43;47. 90,77
Weakfeet, see Godwin	
Wiberga	39,1
Wicard	24,27;56
Wicga	B3a
Widelard	23,10;42. 90,52;75
Wigstan	B3a
Bishop William (of London)	3,2;7-9;11-13. See also B3h note
William Bold	4,3
William Cardon	10,5. 20,71. 30,46. 90,34
William (de Alno)	32,40
William Leofric	*59*. 90,82
William of Bosc	37,17
William of Boursigny	9,13
William of Écouis	*45*

CHURCHES AND CLERGY

Barking (St. Mary's)	*9*. 30,3
Abbess	9,14. B3s
Battle (St. Martin's)	*13*
Bayeux, Bishop	*18*. 1,27. 4,9-10. 9,1. 20,1. 36,9. 48,2
[Bury] St. Edmund's	*11*
Abbot	11,1;7. B3a
Caen (Holy Trinity)	*15*
(St. Stephen's)	*16*
Canterbury (Holy Trinity)	*2*. 90,9
monks	90,79
Colchester (St. Peter's)	B3d;7
Durham, Bishop	*7*. See also Walchere
Ely (St. Etheldreda's)	*10*. 18,36. 22,8. 25,12;20. 34,30. EHu
Abbot	10,3;5. 18,36. 22,7. 25,3. 30,27;41. 34,19. EHu.
	See also Frodo
monks	1,2. 27,14. 79,1
Hereford, Bishop	*19*. See also Robert
London, Bishop	*3-4*. 20,4. 48,2. See also William
(St. Martin's)	*12*. 6,1. 20,34;60
(St. Paul's)	3,5;11. 20,67. 33,22. 57,5
canons	*5*
Rochester, Bishop	EKt
[Rouen] (St. Ouen's)	*17*
St. Mary's, ?	1,1 note. 6,1
St. Valéry	*14*
Waltham (Holy Cross)	7,1
canons	*8*
Westminster (St. Peter's)	*6*. 90,17;19
Abbot	6,7;10. B3k
Winchester, Bishop	See Walkelin
deacons	Godwin, Walter, William
free priest	Edwin
priests	Aelfric, Aelfgar, Aelfheah, Edward, Edwin, Gilbert,
	Godwin, Ledmer, Leofstan, Saewin, Siward,
	Tascelin, Thorkell, Wulfric, Wulfward

SECULAR TITLES AND OCCUPATIONAL NAMES

Burgess (*burgensis*) ... of Colchester B2;3a,b,d,p;5-6. Of Maldon B6. **Chamberlain** (*camerarius*) ... William. **[Constable** (*stalre*, but not used in the text of DB Essex)] ... Asgar. **Cook** (*cocus*) ... Ansger, Walter. **Count** (*comes*) ... Alan, of Eu, Eustace, Gilbert; (*consul*) ... Eustace. **Countess** (*comitissa*) ... Aelfeva, of Aumâle, Judith. **Earl** (*comes*) ... Algar, 'Edgar', Harold, Waltheof. **Forester of the King's woodland** (*foristarius de silva regis*) ... 1,24. **Goldsmith** (*aurifaber*) ... Otto. **Gunner** (*balistarius*) ... Reginald. **Hundred-reeve** (*custos hundredi, prepositus hundredi*) ... 32,25. 89,1. **Hunter** (*venator*) ... Alfwy. **King's free men** (*liberi homines regis*) ... *89*. **King's servant** (*famulus regis*) ... 1,16a. **King Edward's reeve** (*prepositus regis Edwardi*) ... Edwold, and 1,3. **[King] Harold's reeve** (*prepositus Haroldi*) ... 1,4;24. **Latimer** (*latimarus*) ... Ralph. **Lorimer** (*loremarius*) ... Jocelyn. **Marshal** (*marescalcus*) ... Roger. **Queen** (*regina*) ... Edith, Matilda. **Reeve** (*prepositus*) ... Aelmer, Alfred, Grim, Ledmer. **Sheriff** (*vicecomes*) ... Baynard, Peter of Valognes, Picot, Robert son of Wymarc, Swein. **Sheriff of Surrey** (*vicecomes de Surreia*) ... Ranulf. **Steward** (*dapifer*) ... Godric, Hamo, and 29,5. **Summoner** (*monitor*) ... Wulfwin. **Young** (*cild, cilt*) ... Aelfric, Leofwin.

INDEX OF PLACES

The name of each place is followed by (i) the abbreviated name of its Hundred and its location on the Map in this volume; (ii) its National Grid reference; (iii) chapter and section references in LDB. Bracketed chapter and section references denote mention in sections dealing with a different place. Unless otherwise stated, the identifications of EPNS and the spellings of the Ordnance Survey are followed for places in England; of OEB for places abroad. Inverted commas indicate lost places with known modern spelling; unidentifiable places are given in LDB spelling, in italic print. Places whose names have changed since 1086 are entered under their present name. The National Grid reference system is explained on all Ordnance Survey maps, and in the Automobile Association Handbooks; the figures reading from left to right are given before those reading from bottom to top of the map. All places which have been given grid references in the present index are in the 100 km grid square lettered TL, apart from those marked with a (*) which are in square TQ, and those marked with a (†) which are in square TM. Places with bracketed Grid references do not appear on 1 inch or 1:50,000 maps. Where LDB does not differentiate between what are now two distinct settlements (e.g. Great and Little Bardfield), both sets of Grid references are given. The Essex Hundreds and Half-Hundreds are Barstable (Ba), Becontree (Be), Chafford (Cha), Chelmsford (Che), Clavering (Cl), Dunmow (D), Freshwell (F), Harlow (Ha), Hinckford (Hi), Lexden (L), Maldon (M), Ongar (O), Rochford (R), Tendring (Te), 'Thunderlow' (Tl), Thurstable (Ts), Uttlesford (U), Waltham (Wa), 'Wibertsherne' (Wb), Winstree (Wn), Witham (Wt); the places in each Hundred are listed after the index, immediately before the Map. Ballingdon cum Brundon has been in Suffolk since 1832 and 1835. [Great and Little] Chishill and Heydon have been in Cambridgeshire since 1895.

	Map	Grid	Text
Abberton	Wn 2	99 19	20,20. 24,51. 34,16
Acleta	—	—	25,10
Alderford	Hi 42	(76 33)	23,11
Alderford, see Aelfric			
Alderton Hall	O 20	(*42 96)	8,7
Aldham	L 14	91 25	18,24
Alphamstone	Hi 34	87 35	11,4. 23,19. 90,60
Alresford	Te 30	†06 20	4,4. 18,44. 20,65. 23,33
Amberden Hall	U 29	55 30	34,19
Amwell (Herts)	—	37 12	1,3
Ardleigh	Te 10	†05 29	30,20. 32,40. 39,8;12. 47,2. B31
Arkesden	U 20	48 34	25,26. 26,3-4. 32,43. 90,28
Ashdon	F 4	58 41	33,20
Asheldham	Wb 18	97 01	24,43;55
Ashen	Hi 11	74 42	23,12
Ashingdon	R 7	*86 93	24,38
Ashwell Hall	Hi 48	70 30	67,2
Ateleia	—	—	28,1
Aveley	Cha 10	*56 80	18,27. 40,9. 75,1
Great Baddow	Che 20	72 04	15,2. 72,3
Little Baddow	Che 16	77 07	20,52. 33,13
Ballingdon (Suffolk)	Tl 2	86 40	36,8
[Great and Little] Bardfield	F 12	{67 30 {65 30	20,79. 23,39;42. 90,65
Barking	Be 11	*44 83	9,7. (9,5)
Barling	R 15	*93 89	5,12. 18,16
Barn Hall	Wn 5	92 14	33,8
Barnston	D 13	64 19	30,29
Barrow Hall	R 18	*92 88	23,43
Barstable Hall	Ba 18	(*70 89)	18,4
Basildon	Ba 19	*71 89	24,7-8
Bassetts	Wb 1	79 08	4,18

	Map	Grid	Text
Baythorn End	Hi 10	72 42	37,12
Beaumont	Te 24	†17 24	35,11
Beckney	R 1	*84 95	18,15
Belchamp [Otten, St. Paul, and Walter]	Hi 13	{ 80 41 79 42 82 40	5,3. 20,26;28. 43,4
Belchamp Walter	Tl 1	82 40	35,6
Belstead Hall	Che 9	72 10	22,18. 78,1
Bendysh Hall	F 7	60 39	20,77. 90,64
[North and South] Benfleet	Ba 14	{ *76 90 *77 86	1,1;14. 6,1. 24,13
'Bensted'	Che 23	(74 03)	27,14. 41,9
Bentfield Bury	Cl 9	49 26	32,19
Great Bentley	Te 28	†10 21	35,9
Little Bentley	Te 22	†12 24	21,9. 23,31
Benton Hall	Wt 15	82 13	11,1
Berden	Cl 2	46 29	24,54
Berewic	—	—	18,37
West Bergholt	L 11	95 28	23,36. 46,2. 90,70;73
Bertuna	—	—	90,35
Bigods	D 9	62 24	30,31
'Binsley'	Hi 25	(84 38)	23,10. 36,9
Great Birch	L 27	94 19	20,39
Little Birch	L 23	94 20	32,26. 60,3
Birchanger	U 32	50 22	1,10. 14,4. 30,48
Birch Hall	Te 26	†21 22	20,67
Birdbrook	Hi 17	70 41	37,11
'Blatchams'	Ts 4	(86 10)	20,61
Blunt's Hall	Wt 10	80 14	20,10. 34,5
Bobbingworth	O 7	53 05	37,15
Bocking	Hi 55	75 23	2,2
Bockingham	L 21	93 21	90,18
Bollington Hall	Cl 5	50 27	32,20. 90,35;41
Bonhunt	U 23	51 33	57,6
Boreham	Che 14	75 09	20,56. 22,17. 24,58
Borley	Hi 9	84 43	54,1. 90,55
Borley, see Aelmer			
Bowers Gifford	Ba 25	*75 87	6,3. 34,1. 42,1. 83,1
Boxted	L 4	99 33	20,37. 25,17. EHu
Boyton Hall	Hi 35	(71 33)	23,28. (23,29)
Bradfield	Te 9	†14 30	39,7. 46,2-3
Bradwell Quay	Wb 6	99 07	18,23
Braintree	Hi 59	75 23	90,48;76
Great Braxted	Wt 13	85 15	25,1
Little Braxted	Wt 12	83 14	4,14. 28,5
Brightlingsea	Te 33	†07 18	1,26. ESf1
Great Bromley	Te 20	†08 26	77,1
Little Bromley	Te 18	†09 27	23,32. 42,8
Broomfield	Che 8	70 10	30,9
Broxted	D 5	57 26	10,1. 25,12
Brundon (Suffolk)	Hi 15	86 42	49,1;4
Brundon, see Wulfric			
Bulmer	Hi 21	84 40	23,14
Bulphan	Ba 26	*63 85	9,2
Helions Bumpstead	F 5	65 41	35,12. 38,4. 90,83
Steeple Bumpstead	Hi 16	67 41	20,27. 21,5. 22,12. 23,21. 38,5. 90,61
Bures	Hi 40	90 34	23,16;29. 40,5
Mount Bures	L 2	90 32	39,6. 46,1
Burna	Te	—	20,63
Burnham	Wb 28	*94 96	33,12. 90,6

	Map	Grid	Text
Harkstead (Suff.)	H	†18 34	ESf1. (1,26)
Harlow	Ha 8	47 11	11,2. 20,14. 25,2. (37,3)
Hasingham	—	—	90,67
Hassenbrook Hall	Ba 29	(*68 83)	18,10. 24,6
Hastings (Sussex)	—	—	EHu
Hatfield Broad Oak	Ha 4	54 16	1,3. (28,6)
Hatfield Peverel	Wt 16	78 11	18,13. 34,4
Havering-atte-Bower	Be 2	*51 93	1,4. (27,3. 41,4. 90,19)
Hawkwell	R 9	*86 91	24,40. 25,11;25
Hazeleigh	Wb 12	83 03	34,13-14
Castle Hedingham	Hi 33	78 35	35,5
Sible Hedingham	Hi 36	77 34	39,3. 43,1
Hemingford (Hunts.)	—	—	EHu
Hempstead	F 9	63 37	23,41
Hempstead, see Ledmer			
Henham	F 13	54 28	33,19. 90,39
[Great and Little] Henny	Hi 26	{86 37 {86 38	34,21. 40,4. 43,5. 90,13;44;46
Hertford (Herts.)	—	32 12	1,3
Heybridge	Ts 7	85 07	5,10
Heydon (Cambs.)	U 4	43 39	10,5. 76,1
Higham Hill	Be 4	*35 90	36,6
Hockley	R 5	*82 93	9,13. 24,19;33
Hocsenga	—	—	90,66
Hoddesdon (Herts.)	—	37 08	1,3
[Great and Little] Holland	Te 36	{†21 19 {†20 16	20,68. 52,3
[East and West] Horndon	Ba 16	{*63 89 {*62 88	18,12. 24,1. 48,1
Horndon-on-the-Hill	Ba 28	*66 83	4,10. 20,2. 24,5. 60,1. 61,1. 90,1-2
Horseham Hall	Hi 6	66 43	13,2. 35,7. 90,52;75
Housham Hall	Ha 9	50 11	22,3. 51,1
Howbridge	Wt 14	(81 13)	4,15. 32,4
Howe	Hi 41	69 33	23,15. 90,53
Hunt's Hall	Hi 46	84 32	22,13
Hutton	Ba 3	*63 94	13,1
Ilford	Be 8	*44 86	64,1
Iltney Farm	Wb 10	88 04	20,16. 24,42
Ingatestone	Che 25	*65 99	9,11
Ingrave	Ba 7	*62 92	18,5. 34,3. 37,1
Ipswich (Suff.)	I	†15 44	ESf2
Jacques Hall	Te 4	†15 31	39,9
Kelvedon	Wt 5	85 18	6,5. 27,2
Kelvedon Hatch	O 18	*56 98	6,9. 18,25. 28,15
Kenningtons	Cha 8	*56 81	22,14. 24,62
Laindon	Ba 17	*68 89	3,1. 4,13
Lamarsh	Hi 31	88 36	34,22. 90,14;45
Lambourne	O 22	47 96	20,48
Landuna	—	—	25,9
Langdon	Ba 27	*67 86	24,2
Langenhoe	Wn 4	†01 17	20,19
Langford	Ts 6	83 09	33,2;22
Langham	L 5	†03 33	23,38
Lashley Hall	D 7	64 26	90,51
Latchingdon	Wb 21	88 00	1,6-7. 2,5. 27,5. 84,2
Latton	Ha 12	(46 10)	11,3. 20,13. 36,2
[High, Little, and Magdalen] Laver	O 3	{52 08 {54 09 {51 08	20,45;47. 51,2

	Map	Grid	Text
Lawford	Te 2	†08 31	1,27. 20,69. (23,33. 33,17. 37,20)
Lawling	Wb 17	90 01	2,4. 25,6. 34,24. 41,5. 90,79
Lawn Hall	Che 2	65 17	18,38
Layer [Breton, de la Haye, and Marney]	Wn 1	{94 18 / 96 19 / 92 17	1,19. 3,6-7. 20,21. 27,10. 34,15. 57,3. 68,4. 90,5. (17,2)
Lee Chapel	Ba 21	*69 88	5,1
Elmdon Lee	U 12	48 38	20,75
Lega	–	–	32,14
Leigh	R 22	*84 86	34,35
[Great and Little] Leighs	Che 3	{73 17 / 71 16	25,21. 30,16
Lexden	L 16	97 25	1,19. B2
Leyton	Be 7	*37 86	6,7. 27,3. 32,10. 36,5. 41,3-4
Liffildeuuella	–	–	90,43
Limpwella	–	–	18,35
Lindsell	D 4	64 27	14,2. 25,4
Liston	Hi 5	85 44	47,1. 69,2
Littlebury	U 8	51 39	10,5
Littlethorpe	R 20	(*91 87)	24,25
Lohou	–	–	62,4
London	–	–	(7,1. 9,7. 30,18. 31,1)
Loughton	Be 1	*42 96	8,4-5. 32,11. 36,7;10. (1,4)
Maldon	M	85 07	1,25. 24,63. 34,31. (B6)
Maldon	Wb M	85 07	1,17. 20,34. 34,12. See also Siward.
Manuden	Cl 8	49 26	32,16;22. 33,10. 90,36
Great Maplestead	Hi 38	80 34	32,23
Little Maplestead	Hi 39	82 33	40,3. 90,38
Margaretting	Che 26	66 00	1,22. 53,2
Markshall	L 12	84 25	27,13
Mashbury	D 17	65 11	12,1 note. 30,13. 90,20
Matching	Ha 7	52 12	14,1. 30,25. 32,6. 61,2
East Mersea	Wn 10	†05 14	24,49
West Mersea	Wn 9	†10 31	2,2. 17,1
Messing	L 28	89 18	33,9. 39,4
Michaelstow	Te 6	(†21 31)	33,17
Middleton	Hi 27	87 39	23,20. 82,1. 90,84
Midebroc	–	–	90,9
Milton	R 26	(*87 85)	2,7
Mistley	Te 3	†01 31	39,10
Moreton	O 5	53 07	45,1
Moulsham Hall	Che 1	72 18	18,41-42
Moulsham Lodge	Che 19	71 05	6,14
Mountnessing	Che 33	*64 96	37,16-17
Moze	Te 21	†20 26	30,18. ESf2
Mucking	Ba 33	*68 81	9,1;4
Mundon	Wb 16	87 02	25,5
'Napsted'	Hi 45	(81 32)	18,21
Navestock	O 17	*54 98	5,7-8. 28,14
Nayland	L 1	97 34	24,57
The Naze	Te 25	†23 23 etc.	5,11
Nazeing	Wa 1	41 06	8,2. 37,8-9
Nevendon	Ba 12	*73 91	62,1. 70,1
Newland Hall	Che 6	63 09	20,51
Newnham Hall	F 2	58 42	20,78
Newport	U 21	52 34	1,28
Newton Hall	D 10	61 22	30,28

	Map	Grid	Text
Niuetuna	—	—	49,2
Northey Island	Wb 4	87 06	28,12. 90,32
Norton Mandeville	O 9	58 04	5,6. 28,16
Cold Norton	Wb 23	*85 99	33,3
[Black and White] Notley	Wt 3	⎰76 20 ⎱78 18	20,6. 24,45. 28,3. 30,22. 40,1. 57,2. 62,2
Great Oakley	Te 16	†20 28	32,38
Little Oakley	Te 17	†21 28	33,15
[North and South] Ockendon	Cha 6	⎰*58 84 ⎱*60 83	1,21-21a. 6,10-11. 30,4
Old Hall	Te 1	(†10 32)	54,2
[Chipping and High] Ongar	O 11	⎰55 03 ⎱56 03	20,46. 40,8. (90,87)
Orsett	Ba 32	*64 81	3,2. 20,4
Osea Island	Ts 9	91 06	28,18
Ovington	Hi 12	76 42	43,3. 90,63
Paglesham	R 8	*92 93	6,15. 22,22. 33,21. 41,11. 90,8
Panfield	Hi 53	73 25	16,1. 23,6
[Great and Little] Parndon	Ha 11	⎰43 08 ⎱44 11	9,6. 20,12. 36,3. 37,4-6
Paslow Hall	O 12	57 03	8,6
Patching Hall	Che 11	69 08	18,40. 30,8. 32,35
Pebmarsh	Hi 43	85 33	23,18. 43,2. 90,38;59
Peldon	Wn 3	98 16	24,50. 66,1
Pentlow	Hi 1	81 46	33,11
Peyton Hall	Cl 3	48 28	22,10
Pinchpools	Cl 4	49 27	57,4
Pitsea	Ba 24	*73 87	84,1
Pledgdon Hall	Cl 7	55 27	25,16. 30,49
'Plesingho'	D 18	(59 08)	20,18. 90,30
Plumberow	R 6	*83 93	22,23. 24,31
Plunker's Green	O 19	(*58 97)	34,28
Prested	L 26	88 19	34,27
Prittlewell	R 23	*87 86	24,22
Pudsey Hall	R 3	*88 95	24,32;34;36-37
Purleigh	Wb 15	84 02	20,17. 27,4;6-7. 32,12. 42,2;4
Quendon	U 27	51 31	25,23
Quicksbury Farm	Ha 5	49 14	22,4
Radwinter	F 8	60 37	25,24. 35,13. 38,3. 56,1
Rainham	Cha 7	*52 82	18,30. 32,28. 52,2. 70,3
Ramsden [Bellhouse and Crays]	Ba 4	⎰*71 94 ⎱*70 93	3,3. 4,12. 18,6. 27,1. 32,1-2. 37,2
Ramsey	Te 12	†18 29	33,16
Rayleigh	R 11	*80 90	24,17-18
Rayne	Hi 58	73 22	3,8. 27,11. 28,4. 39,1-2
Rettendon	Che 29	*76 98	10,3. 25,20. 34,30
Rickling	U 26	49 31	1,29
Ridgewell	Hi 18	73 40	20,23
Ridley Hall	Wt 8	75 15	30,23
Rivenhall	Wt 4	82 17	20,8-9. 24,44. 32,5. 72,1
Rochford	R 12	*87 90	24,26
Rockell's Farm	U 15	46 36	90,22-23
Abbess Roding	O 2	57 11	25,19. 30,3
Beauchamp Roding	O 4	57 09	21,8
'Morrell' Roding	O 1	(56 15)	23,30. 25,3. (30,41)
[Aythorpe, Berners, High, Leaden, Margaret, and White] Roding	D 14	⎧58 15 60 09 60 17 59 13 59 12 56 13	1,8. 10,2. 22,7-8. 26,2. 28,8. 30,30;35;39-40; 43. ENf

	Map	Grid	Text
Rothend	F 6	(59 39)	21,11
Roydon	Ha 10	40 10	37,3
Runwell	Che 35	*75 94	5,9. 20,53-54
Ryes	Ha 3	52 16	28,6
St. Lawrence	Wb 11	96 04	2,6. 37,14
St. Osyth	Te 37	†12 15	3,14. 20,63. 34,33
St. Peter's Chapel	Wb 5	†03 08	14,6. 27,12
Great Saling	Hi 52	70 25	40,2. 90,62
Great Sampford	F 10	64 35	1,30
Little Sampford	F 11	65 33	23,40
Sampson's Farm	Wn 7	99 15	18,20
Sciddeham, Scilcheham	—	—	59,1. 90,82
Shalford	Hi 50	72 29	1,11. 66,2. 67,1 (B3j)
Sheering	Ha 6	50 13	36,1
Shelford (Cambs.)	—	45 51	(1,28)
Shelley	O 8	55 05	30,2
Shellow Bowells	D 20	60 07	1,5. 25,13. 30,33-34;41
Shenfield	Ba 2	*60 95	20,3
[North and South] Shoebury	R 25	{*92 86 (*93 84)	18,17. 24,23;28
Shopland	R 17	*89 88	20,80
Shortgrove	U 18	52 35	20,22;24. 32,42
Slampseys	Wt 2	73 19	3,4
Smallands	Wt 17	(81 10)	41,2
Smalton	Hi 37	(78 34)	90,37
Smeetham Hall	Hi 14	84 41	20,32
Southchurch	R 24	*90 86	2,8
Southminster	Wb 24	*96 99	3,9
Springfield	Che 12	71 08	32,33. 34,29
Stambourne	Hi 22	72 38	28,11. 90,26;33
Great Stambridge	R 13	*89 90	18,14. 24,27
Little Stambridge	R 10	*88 91	2,9. 90,7
Stanford Rivers	O 13	53 00	20,43-44
Stanmer	Ba 5	(*72 93)	57,1
Stansgate	Wb 7	93 05	34,26. 90,12
Stanstead Hall	Hi 51	82 28	44,1. (44,4)
Stansted Mountfitchet	U 31	51 24	32,16
Stanway	L 18	93 24	1,19
Stapleford Abbotts	O 23	*50 95	11,6. 32,27
Stapleford Tawney	O 16	*50 99	24,59
Stebbing	Hi 54	66 24	29,2. 34,20
Stebbingford House	Hi 57	67 22	63,2
Steeple	Wb 13	93 03	1,15. 25,7. 29,3. 90,81
Stevington End	F 3	59 42	21,12. 35,14. 38,2. 90,85
Stifford	Cha 11	*60 80	9,10. 18,32;34. 75,2
Stisted	Hi 56	79 24	2,3
Stow Maries	Wb 22	*83 99	30,44;50. 42,5
Strethall	U 7	48 39	10,5
'Studly'	Che 31	(81 00)	1,6. 27,9
Sturmer	Hi 7	69 43	38,6-7
Sudbury (Suff.)	—	87 41	23,27. (34,21. 35,5. 40,4)
Sutton	R 14	*88 89	24,30;35;39. 71,4
Takeley	U 33	55 21	14,3. 25,15. 32,17
Tendring	Te 23	†14 24	4,5. 20,64;70. 32,38a. 34,32. 68,7
Terling	Wt 9	77 14	1,2 note. 34,6. 90,10. B3q
[Great and Little] Tey	L 13	{89 25 89 23	20,36

	Map	Grid	Text
Marks Tey	L 17	91 23	30,1
Thaxted	D 1	61 31	23,2
Theydon [Bois, Garnon, and Mount]	O 15	{*44 99 / *47 99 / *49 99	24,60. 25,18. 36,11. / 74,1
Thorpehall	R 27	(*91 85)	37,10
Thorrington	Te 31	†09 19	18,43
Thunderley Hall	U 16	55 36	35,3
Thundersley	Ba 22	*78 88	24,16
[Grays and West] Thurrock	Cha 12	{*61 77 / *59 77	18,28-29;31. 31,1. 48,2. / (18,34)
Little Thurrock	Ba 34	*62 77	4,6. 90,4
Tilbury-juxta-Clare	Hi 19	75 40	38,8
[East and West] Tilbury	Ba 36	{*68 77 / *66 77	22,2. 24,3. 71,1. / (30,21)
Tillingham	Wb 14	99 03	5,5
Tilty	D 6	59 26	29,1
Tollesbury	Ts 5	95 10	9,14. 20,62
Tolleshunt [D'Arcy, Knights, and Major]	Ts 1	{92 11 / 92 14 / 90 11	18,45. 20,57;59-60. / 24,66. 27,18. 32,37;45. / 33,23. 34,36. 41,12. / 80,1. B3r
Toppesfield	Hi 28	73 37	20,33. 28,11. 90,56-57
[Great and Little] Totham	Ts 2	{86 13 / 88 11	4,2-3. 24,67. 27,16. / 28,17
Twinstead	Hi 30	86 36	23,24
Udecheshale	—	—	35,2
Ugley	Cl 6	51 28	35,4
Uleham's Farm	Wb 25	*87 98	4,17. 20,35
Ulting	Wt 18	80 08	33,1
Uluuinescherham	—	—	1,16
Upham	—	—	22,1
Upminster	Cha 4	*56 87	8,10. 18,26. 52,1
Vange	Ba 23	*72 87	18,1. 34,2
Virley	Wn 8	94 13	32,15
Great Wakering	R 21	*94 87	24,21
Little Wakering	R 19	*93 88	24,29
Saffron Walden	U 13	53 38	30,45
Wallbury	Ha 2	49 17	23,1
Walter Hall	Che 10	73 10	8,11. 18,39. 86,1
Waltham Holy Cross	Wa 4	38 00	7,1. (32,7. 37,9)
[Great and Little] Waltham	Che 4	{69 13 / 71 12	11,7. 20,55. 30,5-6. / 41,7-8
Walthamstow	Be 5	*37 89	55,1
Wanstead	Be 6	*40 88	3,5
[Great and Little] Warley	Cha 2	{*59 88 / *60 90	3,11. 9,9. 24,61. / (57,5)
North Weald Bassett	Ha 13	49 05	36,4;12. 37,7
South Weald	Cha 1	*57 93	8,9. 32,29
Weeley	Te 29	†15 21	25,22
Well Farm	Ba 11	(*67 91)	4,7
Wendens Ambo, Wendon Lofts	U 11	{51 36 / 46 38	22,19. 32,18. 33,18. / 90,24
Wenesuuic	—	—	30,51
Wennington	Cha 9	*53 80	6,12
Weston Hall	Hi 2	83 45	20,29. 43,6
Westnanetuna	—	—	77,1
Wesuunic	—	—	90,27
Wethersfield	Hi 47	71 31	1,13. 87,1. (23,28)
Wheatley	Ba 15	*79 90	18,7. 24,14-15
Great Whitmans	Wb 20	83 00	32,13

	Map	Grid	Text
Wicken Bonhunt	U 22	49 33	58,1
Wickford	Ba 6	*74 93	18,7-9. 24,9-12. 68,1. 69,1
Wickham Bishops	Ts 3	83 12	3,13
Wickham St. Paul's	Hi 29	82 37	5,4. 23,8
Widdington	U 28	53 31	14,5. 32,41. 90,11
[Great and Little] Wigborough	Wn 6	{96 15 {98 14	9,8. 28,9. 34,17. 60,2. 90,31
Willingale [Doe and Spain]	D 19	{59 07 {(58 06)	21,2. 24,47. 34,10. 63,1
Wimbish	U 17	58 36	33,7
Witelebroc	–	–	33,17
Witesuuorda	–	–	23,37
Witham	Wt 11	81 14	1,2. 20,11. 32,3. 68,2
Wivenhoe	L 25	†03 21	32,25
Wix	Te 15	†16 28	27,15. 42,7
Woodford	Be 3	*40 92	8,3
Woodham Ferrers	Che 30	*79 99	29,4
Woodham Mortimer	Wb 9	81 04	34,11
Woodham Walter	Wb 3	80 06	33,4
Woolston Hall	O 21	*44 95	1,20
Wormingford	L 3	93 32	32,24
Wrabness	Te 5	†17 31	11,8
Wringehala	–	–	(25,5)
Writtle	Che 17	67 06	1,24. 19,1. (20,51)
Yardley	U 25	59 32	38,1
[Great and Little] Yeldham	Hi 23	{75 38 {77 39	20,25. 21,6. 23,7. 37,13. 90,54
Yelling (Hunts.)	–	–	EHu
York(shire)	–	–	(6,15. 30,16)

Places not named
1,13a. 1,16a. 1,17a. 1,18. 1,31. 9,5. 12,1. 17,2. 18,21a. 30,21. 85,1. 86,2. 88,1. 88,2. 89,1. 89,2. 90,15. 90,16. 90,17. 90,19. 90,29. 90,49. 90,87. EKt.

Unnamed in Suffolk: (32,40)

Places not in Essex
Names starred are in the Index of Churches and Clergy. Apart from the SURREY entry, the rest are in the Indices of Persons and Places.

Elsewhere in Britain
CAMBRIDGESHIRE ... Ely*. Picot the Sheriff. Shelford. Co. DURHAM ... Durham*. HAMPSHIRE ... Winchester*. HEREFORDSHIRE ... Hereford*. HERTFORDSHIRE ... Amwell. Hertford. Hoddesdon. HUNTINGDONSHIRE ... Hemingford. Yelling. KENT ... Canterbury*. Chalk. Rochester, see Thorold. LONDON* ... see also Places Index. MIDDLESEX ... Westminster*. NORFOLK ... Field Dalling. SUFFOLK ... Bury St. Edmund's*. Harkstead. Ipswich. Sudbury. See also Unnamed Places. SURREY ... Sheriff, see Secular Titles. SUSSEX ... Battle*. Hastings, and see Ralph. YORKSHIRE. UNIDENTIFIED ... Gotton, see Alwin.

Outside Britain
More precise details as to location are given in the General Notes.
Alno ... William. Anjou ... Osmund. Auberville ... Roger. Aumâle ... Countess. Bayeux*. Bernières ... Hugh. Bosc ... William. Boursigny ... William. Brittany ... see Lorce Bret, Tihel the Breton. Caen* ... Walter. Corbon (?) ... W. Corbun. Denmark ... see Anand, Finn, and Odin the Danes. Douai ... Walter. Écouis ... William. Eu ... Count. Ferrers ... Henry. Gournai ... Hugh. Helléan ... Tihel. Houdain ... Hugh. Limésy ... Ralph. Mandeville ... Geoffrey. Marck ... Adelulf. Marcy ... Ralph. Montbegon ... Robert. Montfort ... Hugh. Mortagne ... Matthew.

Outside Britain (cont'd.)

Moutiers ... Lisois. Oilly ... Robert. Poitou ... Roger. Port ... Hubert. Raismes ... Roger. Rouen*. Sackville ... Richard. St. Quentin ... Hugh. St. Valéry*. Scales ... Hardwin. Sommery ... Robert. 'Spain' (Épaignes) ... Hervey. Tosny ... Ralph, Robert. Valognes ... Peter. Vatteville ... Robert, William. Vaux ... Robert. Vere ... Aubrey. Verly ... Hugh, Robert. Wader (?) ... Ralph. Warenne ... William.

MAPS AND MAP KEYS

The County Boundary is marked by thick lines, dotted for the modern boundary; Hundred boundaries by thin lines, broken where uncertain.

An open circle denotes a place in another county but referred to in this text, or in the Notes.

The letters of National Grid 10-kilometre squares are shown on the map border. Each four-figure square covers one square kilometre (5/8ths of a square mile).

Unidentified Places Not Mapped

Acleta
Ateleia
Berewic
Bertuna
Burna
Cheneboltuna
Geddesduna
Halesduna
Hasingham
Hocsenga
Landuna
Lega
Liffildeuuella
Limpwella

Lohou
Midebroc
Niuetuna
Sciddeham, Scilcheham
Udecheshale
Uluuinescherham
Upham
Wenesuuic
Wesuunic
Westnanetuna
Witelebroc
Witesuuorda
Wringehala

Barstable (Ba)

18 Barstable Hall
19 Basildon
14 North and South Benfleet
25 Bowers Gifford
26 Bulphan
 8 Great Burstead
10 Little Burstead
35 Chadwell
30 Corringham
 9 Crays Hill
 1 Doddinghurst
20 Dunton
13 Fanton Hall
31 Fobbing
37 'Gravesend'
29 Hassenbrook Hall
16 East and West Horndon
28 Horndon-on-the-Hill
 3 Hutton
 7 Ingrave
17 Laindon
27 Langdon
21 Lee Chapel
33 Mucking
12 Nevendon
32 Orsett
24 Pitsea
 4 Ramsden Bellhouse
   and Crays

 2 Shenfield
 5 Stanmer
22 Thundersley
34 Little Thurrock
36 East and West Tilbury
23 Vange
11 Well Farm
15 Wheatley
 6 Wickford

Becontree (Be)

11 Barking
10 East Ham
 9 West Ham
 2 Havering-atte-Bower
 4 Higham Hill
 8 Ilford
 7 Leyton
 1 Loughton
 5 Walthamstow
 6 Wanstead
 3 Woodford

Chafford (Cha)

10 Aveley
 3 Childerditch
 5 Cranham
 8 Kenningtons
 6 North and South
   Ockendon

 7 Rainham
11 Stifford
12 Grays and West Thurrock
 4 Upminster
 2 Great and Little Warley
 1 South Weald
 9 Wennington

Chelmsford (Che)

20 Great Baddow
16 Little Baddow
 9 Belstead Hall
23 'Bensted'
14 Boreham
 8 Broomfield
32 Buttsbury
 5 Chatham
18 Chelmsford
 7 Chignall
34 Cowbridge
15 Culvert's Farm
13 Cuton Hall
21 Danbury
22 Fingrith Hall
36 Fouchers
27 Fristling
24 Fryerning
28 East, South and West
   Hanningfield

Chelmsford (Che) *cont'd.*
25 Ingatestone
2 Lawn Hall
3 Great and Little Leighs
26 Margaretting
1 Moulsham Hall
19 Moulsham Lodge
33 Mountnessing
6 Newland Hall
11 Patching Hall
29 Rettendon
35 Runwell
12 Springfield
31 'Studly'
10 Walter Hall
4 Great and Little Waltham
30 Woodham Ferrers
17 Writtle

Clavering (Cl)
9 Bentfield Bury
2 Berden
5 Bollington Hall
1 Clavering
10 Farnham
8 Manuden
3 Peyton Hall
4 Pinchpools
7 Pledgdon Hall
6 Ugley

Dunmow (D)
13 Barnston
9 Bigods
5 Broxted
12 Great and Little Canfield
3 Chaureth
2 Chickney
11 Great and Little Dunmow
16 Good Easter
15 High Easter
8 Great and Little Easton
7 Lashley Hall
4 Lindsell
17 Mashbury
10 Newton Hall
18 'Plesingho'
14 Aythorpe Roding
Berners Roding
High Roding
Leaden Roding
Margaret Roding
White Roding
20 Shellow Bowells

1 Thaxted
6 Tilty
19 Willingale Doe and Spain

Freshwell (F)
4 Ashdon
12 Great and Little Bardfield
7 Bendysh Hall
5 Helions Bumpstead
1 Hadstock
9 Hempstead
13 Henham
2 Newnham Hall
8 Radwinter
6 Rothend
10 Great Sampford
11 Little Sampford
3 Stevington End

Harlow (Ha)
14 Epping
1 Great and Little
Hallingbury
8 Harlow
4 Hatfield Broad Oak
9 Housham Hall
12 Latton
7 Matching
11 Great and Little Parndon
5 Quicksbury Farm
10 Roydon
3 Ryes
6 Sheering
2 Wallbury
13 North Weald Bassett

Ongar (O)
20 Alderton Hall
7 Bobbingworth
24 Chigwell
14 Debden Green
6 Fyfield
10 Greensted
18 Kelvedon Hatch
22 Lambourne
3 High, Little and
Magdalen Laver
5 Moreton
17 Navestock
9 Norton Mandeville
11 Chipping and High Ongar
12 Paslow Hall
19 Plunker's Green
2 Abbess Roding

4 Beauchamp Roding
1 'Morrell Roding'
8 Shelley
13 Stanford Rivers
23 Stapleford Abbotts
16 Stapleford Tawney
15 Theydon Bois, Garnon
and Mount
21 Woolston Hall

Uttlesford (U)
29 Amberden Hall
20 Arkesden
32 Birchanger
23 Bonhunt
19 Chardwell
1 Great Chesterford
2 Little Chesterford
9 Great and Little Chishill
14 Chiswick
10 Chrishall
5 Crawleybury
24 Debden
6 Elmdon
30 Elsenham
3 Emanuel Wood
4 Heydon
12 Elmdon Lee
8 Littlebury
21 Newport
27 Quendon
26 Rickling
15 Rockell's Farm
18 Shortgrove
31 Stansted Mountfitchet
7 Strethall
33 Takeley
16 Thunderley Hall
13 Saffron Walden
11 Wendens Ambo and
Wendon Lofts
22 Wicken Bonhunt
28 Widdington
17 Wimbish
25 Yardley

Waltham (Wa)
3 Chingford
2 Epping
1 Nazeing
4 Waltham Holy Cross

In Other Counties
In Kent
G Gravesend

Colchester
C Colchester
1 Greenstead

Hinckford (Hi)
42 Alderford
34 Alphamstone
11 Ashen
48 Ashwell Hall
10 Baythorn End
13 Belchamp Otten, St. Paul
   and Walter
25 'Binsley'
17 Birdbrook
55 Bocking
9 Borley
35 Boyton Hall
59 Braintree
15 Brundon
21 Bulmer
16 Steeple Bumpstead
40 Bures
8 Claret Hall
32 Cornish Hall
3 Coupals Farm
60 Felsted
44 Finchingfield
4 Foxearth
24 Gestingthorpe
20 Goldingham Hall
49 Halstead
33 Castle Hedingham
36 Sible Hedingham
26 Great and Little Henny
6 Horseham Hall
41 Howe
46 Hunt's Hall
31 Lamarsh
5 Liston
38 Great Maplestead
39 Little Maplestead
27 Middleton
45 'Napsted'
12 Ovington
53 Panfield
43 Pebmarsh
1 Pentlow
58 Rayne
18 Ridgewell
52 Great Saling
50 Shalford
37 Smalton
14 Smeetham Hall
22 Stambourne

51 Stanstead Hall
54 Stebbing
57 Stebbingford House
56 Stisted
7 Sturmer
19 Tilbury-juxta-Clare
28 Toppesfield
30 Twinstead
2 Weston Hall
47 Wethersfield
29 Wickham St. Paul's
23 Great and Little Yeldham

Lexden (L)
14 Aldham
11 West Bergholt
27 Great Birch
23 Little Birch
21 Bockingham
4 Boxted
2 Mount Bures
15 'Byrton'
8 Earls, Wakes and White
   Colne
7 Colne Engaine
19 Copford
9 Crepping
6 Dedham
24 East Donyland
20 Easthorpe
22 Feering
10 Fordham
5 Langham
16 Lexden
12 Markshall
28 Messing
1 Nayland
26 Prested
18 Stanway
13 Great and Little Tey
17 Marks Tey
25 Wivenhoe
3 Wormingford

Maldon (M)
M Maldon

Rochford (R)
7 Ashingdon
15 Barling
18 Barrow Hall
1 Beckney
4 Canewdon
16 Eastwood

2 South Fambridge
9 Hawkwell
5 Hockley
22 Leigh
20 Littlethorpe
26 Milton
8 Paglesham
6 Plumberow
23 Prittlewell
3 Pudsey Hall
11 Rayleigh
12 Rochford
25 North and South Shoebury
17 Shopland
24 Southchurch
13 Great Stambridge
10 Little Stambridge
14 Sutton
27 Thorpehall
21 Great Wakering
19 Little Wakering

Tendring (Te)
30 Alresford
10 Ardleigh
24 Beaumont
28 Great Bentley
22 Little Bentley
26 Birch Hall
9 Bradfield
33 Brightlingsea
20 Great Bromley
18 Little Bromley
35 Great and Little Clacton
8 Cliff
14 'Derleigh'
11 Dickley
7 Dovercourt
19 Elmstead
13 Foulton
27 Frating
32 Frinton
34 Frowick Hall
36 Great and Little Holland
4 Jacques Hall
2 Lawford
6 Michaelstow
3 Mistley
21 Moze
25 The Naze
16 Great Oakley
17 Little Oakley
1 Old Hall
12 Ramsey

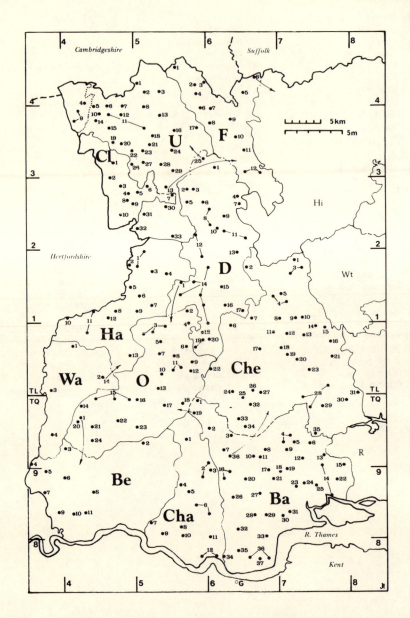

ESSEX HUNDREDS AND HALF-HUNDREDS (WEST)

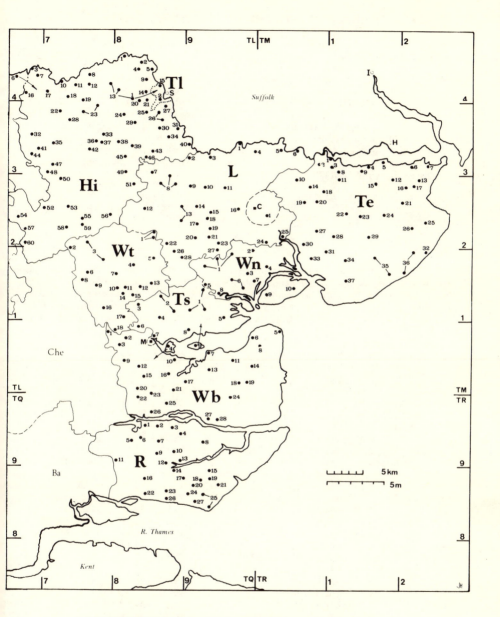

ESSEX HUNDREDS AND HALF-HUNDREDS (EAST)

SYSTEMS OF REFERENCE TO THE TWO VOLUMES OF DOMESDAY BOOK

The manuscript of the larger volume (here referred to as DB) is divided into numbered chapters, and the chapters into sections, usually marked by large initials and red ink. Farley did not number the sections and later historians, using his edition, have referred to the text of DB by folio numbers, which cannot be closer than an entire page or column. Moreover, several different ways of referring to the same column have been devised. In 1816 Ellis used three separate systems in his indices: (i) on pages i–cvii, 435–518, 537–570; (ii) on pages 1–144; (iii) on pages 145–433 and 519–535. Other systems have since come into use, notably that used by Vinogradoff, here followed. The present edition numbers the sections, the normal practicable form of close reference; but since all discussion of DB for two hundred years has been obliged to refer to folio or column, a comparative table will help to locate references given. The five columns below give Vinogradoff's notation, Ellis's three systems, and that used by Welldon Finn and others. Maitland, Stenton, Darby, and others have usually followed Ellis (i).

Vinogradoff	Ellis (i)	Ellis (ii)	Ellis (iii)	Finn
152a	152	152a	152	152ai
152b	152	152a	152.2	152a2
152c	152b	152b	152b	152bi
152d	152b	152b	152b2	152b2

The manuscript of Little Domesday Book (here referred to as LDB), in which the text of the Essex survey is preserved, has one column per page but is again divided into numbered chapters and the chapters into sections, usually distinguished by paragraph-marks. Modern users of LDB have referred to its text by folio number, e.g. 152(a) 152b. Farley's edition presents both *recto* and *verso* of a folio on one printed page. In Essex, the relation between the column notation and the chapters and sections is:

1a	Landholders	26a,b	18,45 — 20, 7	53a,b	27, 3 — 27,13	81a,b	37,11 — 38, 1		
b	1, 1 — 1, 2	27a,b	20, 7 — 20,19	54a,b	27,13 — 28, 2	82a,b	38, 2 — 39, 1		
2a,b	1, 2 — 1, 4	28a,b	20,19 — 20,27	55a,b	28, 3 — 28,12	83a,b	39, 2 — 39,12		
3a,b	1, 4 — 1,11	29a,b	20,28 — 20,37	56a,b	28,13 — 29, 2	84a,b	40, 1 — 40, 9		
4a,b	1,12 — 1,19	30a,b	20,37 — 20,46	57a,b	29, 2 — 30, 4	85a,b	40, 9 — 41,10		
5a,b	1,19 — 1,25	31a,b	20,46 — 20,56	58a,b	30, 4 — 30,13	86a,b	41,10 — 42, 6		
6a,b	1,25 — 1,27	32a,b	20,56 — 20,67	59a,b	30,14 — 30,22	87a,b	42, 7 — 43, 5		
7a,b	1,28 — 1,31	33a,b	20,67 — 20,75	60a,b	30,22 — 30,30	88a,b	43, 5 — 45, 1		
8a,b	2, 1 — 2, 9	34a,b	20,75 — 20,80	61a,b	30,30 — 30,40	89a,b	45, 1 — 47, 3		
9a	Landholders	35a,b	21, 1 — 21,12	62a,b	30,40 — 30,49	90a,b	48, 1 — 50, 1		
b	3, 1 — 3, 5	36a,b	22, 1 — 22, 9	63a,b	30,49 — 32, 5	91a,b	51, 1 — 54, 2		
10a,b	3, 6 — 3,13	37a,b	22,10 — 22,18	64a,b	32, 6 — 32,14	92a,b	54, 2 — 57, 5		
11a,b	3,13 — 4, 9	38a,b	22,19 — 23, 3	65a,b	32,14 — 32,23	93a,b	57, 5 — 61, 2		
12a,b	4, 9 — 5, 3	39a,b	23, 3 — 23,16	66a,b	32,23 — 32,30	94a,b	61, 2 — 66, 2		
13a,b	5, 3 — 5,12	40a,b	23,16 — 23,34	67a,b	32,30 — 32,40	95a,b	66, 2 — 69, 2		
14a,b	5,12 — 6, 9	41a,b	23,34 — 23,43	68a,b	32,40 — 33, 2	96a,b	69, 3 — 73, 1		
15a,b	6, 9 — 8, 1	42a,b	24, 1 — 24,10	69a,b	33, 2 — 33,11	97a,b	73, 1 — 81, 1		
16a,b	8, 1 — 8,11	43a,b	24,10 — 24,20	70a,b	33,11 — 33,17	98a,b	81, 1 — 88, 2		
17a	Landholders	44a,b	24,20 — 24,28	71a,b	33,17 — 34, 2	99a,b	89, 1 — 90,14		
b	9, 1 — 9, 7	45a,b	24,28 — 24,42	72a,b	34, 2 — 34, 9	100a,b	90,15 — 90,34		
18a,b	9, 7 — 10, 1	46a,b	24,42 — 24,53	73a,b	34, 9 — 34,19	101a,b	90,35 — 90,53		
19a,b	10, 2 — 11, 3	47a,b	24,53 — 24,61	74a,b	34,19 — 34,27	102a,b	90,53 — 90,73		
20a,b	11, 3 — 14, 2	48a,b	24,61 — 24,67	75a,b	34,27 — 34,36	103a,b	90,74 — 90,87		
21a,b	14, 2 — 15, 2	49a,b	25, 1 — 25,10	76a,b	34,36 — 35, 5	104a,b	B1 — B3a		
22a,b	15, 2 — 18, 5	50a,b	25,10 — 25,19	77a,b	35, 5 — 35,12	105a,b	B3a		
23a,b	18, 5 — 18,19	51a,b	25,19 — 25,26	78a,b	35,13 — 36, 6	106a,b	B3a — B3p		
24a,b	18,20 — 18,34	52a,b	26, 1 — 27, 3	79a,b	36, 6 — 37, 2	107a,b	B3p — B7		
25a,b	18,34 — 18,45			80a,b	37, 2 — 37,11				

TECHNICAL TERMS

Most of the words expressing measurements have to be translitterated. Translation may not, however, dodge other problems by the use of obsolete or made-up words which do not exist in modern English. The translations here used are given below in italics. They cannot be exact; they aim at the nearest modern equivalent.

ANTECESSOR. Person whom a tenant had followed in the rightful possession of his holding; also the previous holder of an office. *p r e d e c e s s o r*

BORDARIUS. Cultivator of inferior status, usually with a little land. *s m a l l h o l d e r*

CARUCA. A plough, with the oxen which pulled it, usually reckoned as 8. *p l o u g h*

CARUCATA. See 8,9 note. *c a r u c a t e*

CENSARIUS. See 7,1 note. *t r i b u t a r y*

COMMENDATUS (adj.). Relating to the situation in which a free man gave up rights over his land to someone who could guarantee his protection. *u n d e r   t h e   p a t r o n a g e   o f*

CONSUETUDO. A fixed rent or service payable at regular intervals. *c u s t o m a r y   d u e*

DOMINIUM. The mastery or dominion of a lord (*dominus*); including ploughs, land, men, villages, etc., reserved for the lord's use; often concentrated in a home farm or demesne. *l o r d s h i p*

FEUDUM. Continental variant, not used in England before 1066, of *feuum* (the Latin form of Old English *feoh*, cattle, money, possessions in general); either a landholder's holding, or land held under the terms of a specific grant. *H o l d i n g*

FIRMA. Old English *feorm*, provisions due to the King or lord; a fixed sum paid in place of these and of other miscellaneous dues. *r e v e n u e*

HIDA. A unit of land measurement, reckoned in DB at 120 fiscal acres; 4 *virgates*; see Sussex, Appendix. *h i d e*

HUNDREDUM and DIMIDIUM HUNDREDUM. Administrative districts within a shire, each of whose assemblies of notables and village representatives usually met once a month. *h u n d r e d* and *h a l f - h u n d r e d*

MANERIUM. A territorial and jurisdictional holding. *m a n o r*

PREPOSITUS. Old English *gerefa*, a local official of the King or lord. *r e e v e*

SOCA. 'Soke', from Old English *socn*, seeking, comparable with Latin *quaestio*. Jurisdiction, with the right to receive fines and other dues from those who paid suit to the court of the district in which such *soca* was exercised; jurisdiction included the right to settle a dispute or *saca*, from Old English *sāc*, and sometimes the terms *soca* and *saca* are used in combination to show that the jurisdiction is of the fullest sort. *j u r i s d i c t i o n* and (payment of) *s u i t*

SOCHEMANNUS. '*Soke man*', liable to attend the court of a *soca* and serve its lords; before 1066 often with more land and higher status than villagers; bracketed in the Commissioners' brief with the *liber homo* (free man); see Bedfordshire, Appendix. *F r e e m a n*

TEIGNUS. Person of superior status; originally one of the King's military companions, later often in his service in an administrative capacity. *t h a n e*

T.R.E. *tempore regis Edwardi*, in King Edward's time. *b e f o r e   1 0 6 6*

VILLA. Translating Old English *tūn*, estate, town, village. The later distinction between a small *village* and a large *town* was not yet in use in 1066. *v i l l a g e* or *t o w n*

VILLANUS. Member of a *villa*, usually with more land than a *bordarius*. *v i l l a g e r*

VIRGATA. A quarter of a hide; 30 fiscal acres in DB. *v i r g a t e*